History of The United States

Volume 1   Beginnings to 1877

The Authors

Lorna C. Mason is a professional editor and writer. Born in Colorado and raised in Kansas, she has spent most of her adult life in California. Mrs. Mason holds a M.A. in history from the University of California, Berkeley, and has taught history at both the secondary and junior college levels in California. She is the author of several social studies textbooks, both basal and supplementary. Mrs. Mason is the editor and publisher of *Voice of the Plains,* commentaries of rancher John Cogswell.

William Jay Jacobs is Coordinator of History and Social Sciences in the Darien, Connecticut, Public Schools. Dr. Jacobs is the author of numerous books of history and biography and has taught at Rutgers, Columbia, and Harvard universities.

Robert P. Ludlum served as President of Anne Arundel Community College, Maryland, and as Dean of the College of Arts and Sciences at Adelphi University. He also taught political science and history at Hofstra University and at Texas A&M University.

★ ★ ★ ★ ★ ★ ★ ★ ★ ★ ★ ★ ★ ★ ★ ★ ★ ★ ★ ★

History of The United States

Volume 1   Beginnings to 1877

Lorna C. Mason

William Jay Jacobs

Robert P. Ludlum

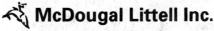
McDougal Littell Inc.
A Houghton Mifflin Company
Evanston, Illinois   Boston Dallas Phoenix

Special Curriculum Advisers

Larry Bybee
Secondary Social Studies Supervisor
Northside Independent School District
San Antonio, Texas

David Depew
Social Studies Consultant
Ector Independent School District
Odessa, Texas

Douglas E. Miller
Social Studies Department Chair
Fremont Union High School
Sunnyvale, California

Gail Riley
Social Studies Consultant
Hurst-Euless-Bedford School District
Bedford, Texas

Special Multicultural Adviser

Bartley L. McSwine
Coordinator of Secondary Education
Chicago State University

Consultants and Teacher Reviewers

George Allan
Ehret High School
Marrero, Louisiana

Robert Barnshaw
Washington Township
High School
Sewell, New Jersey

Jayne Beatty
Blue Springs High School
Blue Springs, Missouri

Emmie P. Beck
East Naples Middle School
Naples, Florida

Wanda J. Calloway
Lakeland High School
Lakeland, Florida

Ralph Clement
Bullard High School
Fresno, California

Jean Evans
Chamberlain High School
Tampa, Florida

I. Lisa Faulkner
Dominion Middle School
Columbus, Ohio

Ray Foley
Salesianum School
Wilmington, Delaware

Bernell Helm
Elyria City Schools
Elyria, Ohio

Eliseo C. Hernandez
Bowie Junior High
Odessa, Texas

Lannah Hughes
Green Run High School
Virginia Beach, Virginia

William Jones
Jacksonville Senior High School
Jacksonville, Arkansas

Ann Kashiwa
Mariner High School
Everett, Washington

Irene Kelley
St. Andrews Middle School
Columbia, South Carolina

Kevin Kelly
Lake Braddock High School
Burke, Virginia

Paul Kinzer
Lapeer East Senior High School
Lapeer, Michigan

Bill Koscher
Ludlow High School
Ludlow, Massachusetts

Charlotte Krause
Estrella Junior High School
Phoenix, Arizona

Katherine Lai
San Francisco USD
San Francisco, California

James Mathers
Washington Irving Junior High
School
Colorado Springs, Colorado

Janice Mays-Holder
Maxson Middle School
Plainfield, New Jersey

Ann Nunn
Higgens High School
Marrero, Louisiana

Clint Peterson
Bridgeport Schools
Bridgeport, Connecticut

Ed Smith
Classical High School
Providence, Rhode Island

Richard Terry
Linton High School
Schenectady, New York

Victor Tocwish
Chicago Public Schools
Chicago, Illinois

Robert Van Amburgh
City School District of Albany
Albany, New York

Marilyn Washington
Jordan High School
Los Angeles, California

John Wolff
Hopewell Valley School District
Central High School
Pennington, New Jersey

Karen Woodrey
Vail Middle School
Middletown, Ohio

Cover: Old North Bridge, Concord and Min-uteman statue, Concord, Massachusetts

Frontispiece: San Xavier del Bac Mission, Tucson, Arizona

Acknowledgments for permission to reprint copyrighted materials appear on page 718.

Student's Edition ISBN: 0–395–68861–2
Teacher's Edition–Nat ISBN: 0–395–68862–0

3456789–VH–97 96 95

★ CONTENTS ★

Marco Polo at the court of the emperor of China

John White returns to Roanoke Island

The fort at Jamestown

The British surrender at Yorktown, 1781

First Lady Abigail Adams in the unfinished White House

A *Californio* inspects his ranch

**Confederate troops fire on
Fort Sumter, 1861**

Classroom scene, Tuskegee Institute

SKILL REVIEW

Gaining Skill

Critical Thinking Skills

SPECIAL FEATURES

The Geographic Perspective

Historians' Corner

Cultural Literacy

Special Maps

CHARTS AND GRAPHS

MAPS

Dear Student:

If you are like most people your age, you are primarily concerned with the present and with the future. That is as it should be. Then why study the past?

One of the most important reasons to study the past is to learn more about who we are as individuals and what we are as a nation. When you study history, you find out that invisible threads link you to people, events, and ideas in the past. Why do you live where you live? What is your native language? How is your life different from that of your grandparents—and of their grandparents? What ideas have people suffered and died for in the past? Are these ideas important today?

In this history of the American people, we begin with the Native Americans and conclude with the Civil War and its aftermath. We show how the territory and people of the United States reflect an Indian, British, African, French, and Spanish heritage. We try to show the drama of the past, the agonies as well as the joys. We try to show the consequences of decisions made, and of decisions not made. Most of all, we try to make the past meaningful to you as you prepare yourself for life in the twenty-first century.

You will learn much this year. You will learn new words and new ideas. In these pages you will meet all kinds of people: heroes, villains, and just plain folk. You will be asked to think and to remember. In all of this, however, remember to use your imagination. Imagination can turn the words and pictures in this book into your own exciting video of the past.

The Authors

The Goals of This Book

History of the United States (Volume 1) was designed with three goals in mind:

1. To provide coverage of American history from earliest times through the present, with emphasis on events through the Civil War and Reconstruction.

2. To identify the major themes in American history and explain their importance at each stage in the development of the nation.

3. To convey a sense of the breadth of experiences and influences that have shaped the United States.

Comprehensive Coverage

The structure of this book reflects the first of those three goals. The book is divided into six units. Units One and Two set the stage by describing the Native American cultures that existed before Columbus's arrival as well as the European movements and events that led to an era of discovery and colonization of the Americas. Units Three through Five recount the birth of the United States, the creation of the Constitution, and the young nation's economic and geographic expansion. The last unit examines the causes, course, and effects of the Civil War and Reconstruction, and includes a final chapter summarizing American history from Reconstruction to the present day.

Themes in American History

To accomplish the second of the book's goals, the authors have identified seven Themes in American History. They are as follows:

Global Interactions From its earliest days as a colonial outpost, the United States has been a part of events in the rest of the world. The outside world has influenced the United States in its people, its ideals, and its form of government. As it grew, this nation played an increasingly important role abroad.

Constitutional Government Ours is a government of limited powers. These powers are derived from the consent of the governed and are divided among the branches of government. Over time, the size and power of the federal government have substantially increased.

Expanding Democracy Over the course of American history, as the concept of liberty has expanded, so too have the rights enjoyed by Americans. Groups that once suffered unfair treatment eventually received equal protection under the laws. These gains, however, came about only after much struggle, controversy, and hardship.

Economic Development Despite periods of stagnation and the continuing problem of poverty, the United States has had enormous economic success. One result was the building of the world's most powerful economy. Another was the belief in this nation as a land of opportunity for all.

Pluralistic Society Millions of people from nations around the world have come to live in the United States. That these many cultures have coexisted in a stable, democratic society is one of the United States' greatest triumphs. Yet racial and ethnic intolerance have posed roadblocks to the achievement of full equality.

American Culture The American people's diverse heritage, plus the legal guarantees of free expression, has produced a rich and dynamic culture.

Geography America has benefited greatly from its natural resources. Chief among these is the land itself. Natural abundance speeded industrial growth, encouraged immigration, and in many other ways contributed to American prosperity.

These themes reappear throughout the book. They are reviewed following Chapter 22, the last chapter. There, an essay and a timeline listing specific events highlight each theme's progression through American history.

Breadth of Influences

The third of the book's goals is to convey a sense of the breadth of American history. A history of the United States must include Presidents and senators, battles and treaties, laws and court decisions. To give a complete picture of this nation, however, it must do more. It must explain the many effects of geography and the importance of economic factors. It must show how Americans lived—what their homes were like, what they did for recreation, and how religion influenced their lives. It must demonstrate that public policy in a free society emerges from open discussion and compromise, and that controversy is a part of the democratic process.

Finally, it must pull all these facts together into one story. The people and events described in this book were separated by as many as thousands of miles and hundreds of years. Yet all played a part in building the nation of which you are a citizen today. What does it mean to be an American in the 1990s? The answer to that question lies not only in the present and future, but also in the past.

How This Book Helps You Learn

This book has been designed to make learning about American history easier and more enjoyable. Its many features are described below.

Units, Chapters, and Sections

History of the United States (Volume 1) is divided into 6 units and 22 chapters. Each unit, which contains three or more chapters, covers a specific period of time and deals with an important development in American history. The first page of each unit lists the chapters in the unit as well as the Themes in American History which are contained in that unit.

Each chapter opens with a picture reflecting the period of American history described in that chapter. Next to the chapter title is a list of Key Events—some of the important events in that chapter. These events are repeated at the end of each chapter in a timeline such as the one below.

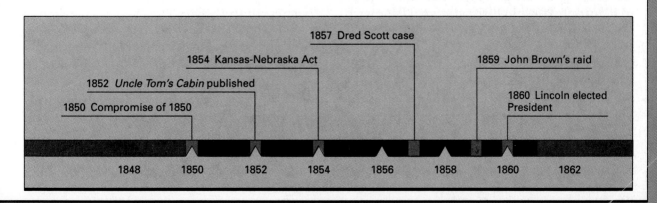

1857 Dred Scott case

1854 Kansas-Nebraska Act

1859 John Brown's raid

1852 *Uncle Tom's Cabin* published

1860 Lincoln elected President

1850 Compromise of 1850

1848   1850   1852   1854   1856   1858   1860   1862

Each chapter is divided into three or four sections. At the beginning of a section, in a box like the one below, you will find a list of Key Terms found in the section. Key Terms, which appear in the narrative in blue, are either vocabulary words or important terms in American history. They are all defined in the text when they are first introduced. You will also find the Main Idea—a brief preview of the focus of the section—and two or three Objectives. The Objectives are questions covering the material in the section; you should keep these questions in mind as you read.

At the end of each section is a Section Review. You will be asked to review the Key Terms in the section as well as important people and places. There will be questions covering the section Objectives, including a Critical Thinking question that asks you to analyze what you have learned.

At the end of each chapter are a summary of the chapter and the chapter timeline, followed by a Chapter Review. The Chapter Review includes a variety of exercises, including a map exercise, a skill review, citizenship and critical thinking questions, and writing assignments.

2 Changes on the Borderlands

★ Section Focus

Key Terms *vaquero* ■ *empresario* ■ Santa Fe Trail

Main Idea With Mexican independence from Spain, the northern provinces of Texas, New Mexico, and California experienced rapid change.

Objectives As you read, look for answers to these questions:
1. What new policies toward the northern provinces did the Mexican government put into effect?
2. What steps did Moses Austin and Stephen Austin take to establish a colony in Texas?
3. How did Anglo-Americans change Texas, New Mexico, and California?

Pictures

The illustrations in this book have been carefully chosen to broaden your understanding of people, places, and events. Illustrations include paintings, drawings, and photographs.

Maps and Charts

Numerous maps and charts appear throughout the book. Maps are an essential part of any history book, for they show where the events being described took place. Charts are a useful tool because they squeeze a lot of information into a small space.

Special Features

A number of special features have been woven into the text of *History of the United States (Volume 1).*

■ **Gaining Skill**, which appears in every chapter but the last one, helps you review and practice a variety of study skills. These skills make it possible for you to learn more effectively and efficiently. This feature reviews such skills as building vocabulary; reading graphs, charts, and maps; understanding primary and secondary sources; using the library; writing an outline; and taking tests.

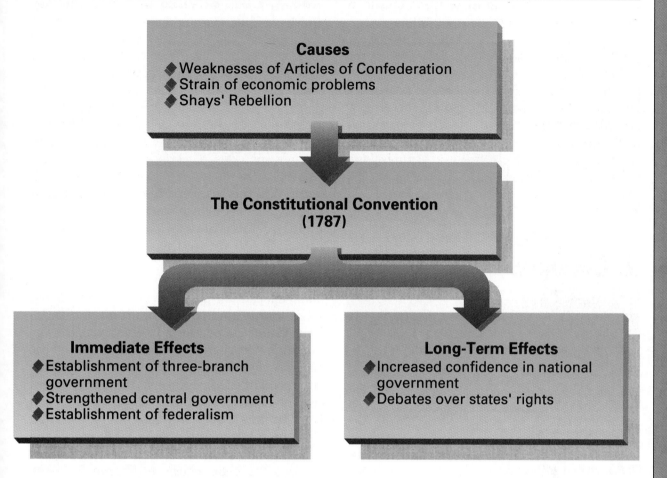

Causes
- ◆ Weaknesses of Articles of Confederation
- ◆ Strain of economic problems
- ◆ Shays' Rebellion

The Constitutional Convention (1787)

Immediate Effects
- ◆ Establishment of three-branch government
- ◆ Strengthened central government
- ◆ Establishment of federalism

Long-Term Effects
- ◆ Increased confidence in national government
- ◆ Debates over states' rights

■ **Cause and Effect** shows the causes and the effects of an important development in American history. An example is shown above.

■ **The Geographic Perspective**, located in each unit, explains in detail how geography influenced an event covered in that unit.

■ **American Mosaic: A Multicultural Perspective**, located at the end of each unit, profiles significant individuals from a variety of backgrounds.

■ **Historians' Corner**, also located at the end of each unit, compares and contrasts historians' views of issues in American history.

■ **Special Maps** present the continental United States as it appeared at three points in its history: 1790, 1900, and 1990. These maps convey the diversity of this nation and hint at the incredible changes the United States has undergone over the course of its history.

■ **Cultural Literacy** shows how our language has been influenced by historical events.

■ **Our Presidents** gives for each American President a portrait and an outline of his life and accomplishments in office.

■ **Historical Documents** provides extended excerpts of important documents in American history.

■ **Social History: Famous Firsts** lists new developments taking place in American society during a given period.

■ **Biography**, located in every chapter, presents biographies of important figures in American history. An example follows.

BIOGRAPHY

JUANA INÉS DE LA CRUZ (1651–1695) is considered one of the greatest poets of colonial Mexico. An exceptionally bright child, she begged her parents to disguise her as a boy so that she could attend the University of Mexico, but they refused. At age eighteen she joined a convent, where she assembled a large library and devoted herself to studying and writing. Twenty-five years later, having written many poems and plays that were published in Spain, she sold all her books and gave the money to the poor. She died in 1695 from an epidemic while nursing her fellow nuns.

Primary Sources

History of the United States (Volume 1) is rich in primary sources. As mentioned above, condensed Historical Documents appear throughout the text. Within the narrative itself, you will find firsthand accounts of the people and events of American history. They give you a true sense of history in the making. Some of these accounts, as well as statements by the makers of American history, have themselves become part of our nation's heritage. These are shown in special boxes like the one below.

> **"W**e shout for joy that we live to record this righteous decree."
> —*Frederick Douglass on the Emancipation Proclamation, 1863*

Finally, the two central documents in our history, the Declaration of Independence and the United States Constitution, are presented in full within the text.

Civics Handbook

This special 34-page survey examines the basic rights and responsibilities of citizenship in our democracy. It gives you the opportunity to review your knowledge of the nation's symbols and patriotic quotations. Key principles of representative government are presented, including detailed information on the three branches of government and the relationship among local, state, and federal powers. In addition, the section examines the roles of the individual and the government in the United States economy, and concludes with ideas for careers.

American Literature

To underscore the importance of literature in describing and enriching American history, selections of American Literature appear at the end of the book. There is one excerpt from a literary work for each chapter, along with introductory notes about the author.

Reference Section and Atlas

At the end of the book, a large Reference Section provides a variety of learning tools: a gazetteer, a Critical Thinking Skill Review, lists of the Presidents and the states, atlas maps, a list of important dates in American history, a glossary defining Key Terms, and an index.

Developing Geographic Literacy

Geography and American History

In this book you will learn about American history, about the people and events that shaped this country. To truly understand this history, however, you need to know where these events took place and where people lived and traveled. That understanding involves geography, the study of the physical environment and people's relationship with it.

To use geography to explore history you need geographic literacy: the ability to locate places, read maps, and identify geographic themes. You will also find that the knowledge of United States geography will make American history come alive. This section gives you the chance to review your geographic skills and your knowledge of American geography.

LOCATING PLACES

How do geographers describe a place? They would mention weather, landscape, plants and animals, and other *physical* characteristics. Or they might include distinctive *human* characteristics such as language, religion, food, and architecture.

Another way to describe a place is to identify its location. To pinpoint a place's location, geographers use a special method called the **grid system**. If you look at most of the maps in this book, you will see a system of intersecting lines that form a grid. The lines usually are numbered at the edge of the map. These imaginary lines on the earth's surface let you locate any place on earth accurately. Each place has an "address" on the grid, stated in degrees and minutes of latitude and longitude. (A degree, like an hour, contains 60 minutes. A full circle has 360 degrees.) This address is always the same, regardless of the kind of map used.

LATITUDE

The lines of **latitude** are parallel circles that run horizontally around the earth. They are also called **parallels**. A place can be located in terms of its distance from the equator (0 degrees) in degrees of north (N) or south (S) latitude.

LONGITUDE

On a globe, the lines of **longitude** run the length of the earth between the North and South poles. They are also referred to as **meridians**. The **prime meridian,** which

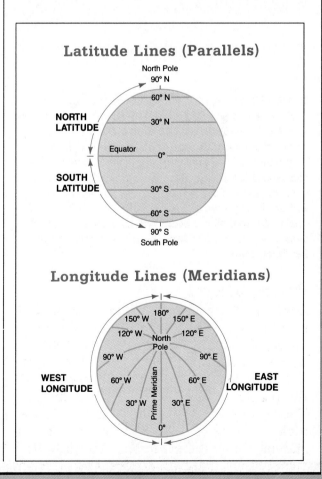

Latitude Lines (Parallels)

North Pole
90° N
60° N
30° N
NORTH LATITUDE
Equator 0°
SOUTH LATITUDE
30° S
60° S
90° S
South Pole

Longitude Lines (Meridians)

180°
150° W   150° E
120° W   North Pole   120° E
90° W   90° E
WEST LONGITUDE   60° W   Prime Meridian   60° E   EAST LONGITUDE
30° W   30° E
0°

passes through Greenwich, England, is at 0 degrees. From this meridian, locations are stated in degrees of east (E) or west (W) longitude. The dividing line that is on the opposite side of the earth is the 180 degree meridian. That meridian runs through the Pacific Ocean.

COORDINATES

Each place on earth, then, has a grid address made up of these two **coordinates**: degrees of N or S latitude and E or W longitude. With this address, you can locate a place on any map. Even without a map, you can learn some things about a place just by knowing its coordinates.

The grid system is used to divide the earth into halves, or **hemispheres**. (*Hemisphere* means "half a sphere.") The north-south dividing line is the equator. A place's latitude—N or S—tells you whether it is in the Northern or Southern Hemisphere. Similarly, the longitude E or W can tell you whether a place is in the Eastern or Western Hemisphere. The prime meridian and the 180 degree meridian form the imaginary boundary between the east-west halves of the earth.

For practice, use the world map in the Atlas at the back of the book to find the nations in which these grid locations lie: 40°N, 116°E; 34°N, 118°W; 34°S, 151°E; 1°S, 37°E. Which of these points is closest to the equator? Farthest from the equator? Which are in the Eastern Hemisphere?

MAP PROJECTIONS

A map is flat, like the page you are reading. The world, though, is round like a globe. These two facts pose a problem that mapmakers try to solve—how to show a round surface on a flat map. The solution is to make compromises in the way a map is drawn. The different approaches result in what are called **map projections**. Like the grid system, projections are mapmaking devices that help people get a better picture of what the earth is like.

Every map projection shows some features accurately and distorts others. Some show land areas and distances in correct proportions. Some show the shapes of continents accurately. Others show directions well. Maps usually are most accurate in the center and more distorted at the edges. Generally, the larger the area a map shows, the more distortions it will have.

Map projections often are named after the geographer or cartographer who invented them. A name can also give you information about what dimensions are most accurate in the projection or about how it was made. Each map in this book is labeled with the name of the projection it uses. You will find, among others, Lambert equal-area projections, the Albers conical equal-area projection, and the Robinson projection.

To read and interpret a map, you need to know something about the projection used in making it. The illustrations on the facing page show examples of four of the most commonly used projections. Use the information in the captions to compare them. If possible, also compare them with a globe.

One good way to compare projections is to look at how the lines of latitude and longitude appear. Try to imagine how the projection was made. For example, look at the Mercator projection. You can see that the lattitutde-longitude grid forms perfect squares. Since you know that the meridians (lines of longitude) curve to meet at the poles, you can assume that the sizes of areas in the north and south "edges" of this map must be distorted.

The conical projection (shown on the map on page G7) is accurate at middle latitudes. Because of this, it is often used to depict the United States, which lies mainly in the middle latitudes.

BUILDING MAP SKILLS

Learning the grid system and understanding projections are two basic steps in learning to read maps. You will find that this ability is a

Map Projections

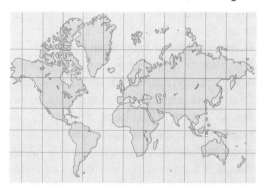

Mercator Projection. This projection shows direction accurately, but it distorts size, especially away from the equator. Landmasses near the North and South poles appear to be much larger than they really are. Sailors favor the Mercator projection because determining direction is the most important part of plotting a ship's course.

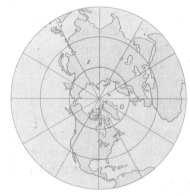

Polar Projection (equidistant). This projection is drawn from above either the North Pole or the South Pole. Size and shape are fairly true near the center of the map but become distorted the farther a landmass is from the pole. However, the distance from the pole to any point on the map is accurate. For this reason and because many of the shortest flying routes go over the pole, airplane pilots prefer this projection.

Robinson Projection. This projection shows accurately how the continents compare with each other in size. Because the oceans are not interrupted, their relative sizes are also shown clearly. There is some distortion of shape, however, near the edges of the map.

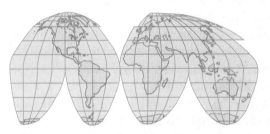

Goode's Interrupted Projection (equal-area). This projection cuts the world into sections. As a result, it shows sizes and shapes of continents better than other projections. Distances across water areas, however, are generally inaccurate.

useful skill both in and out of school. You need to read maps in studying geography, history, and some of the sciences. In everyday life you need to get information from street maps, highway maps, weather maps, and maps illustrating news stories on television and in magazines and newspapers. Airline pilots, ship captains, surveyors, builders, soldiers, and explorers are only a few of the people who must get accurate information from maps in order to do their jobs.

Before trying to read any map, you need to ask a few questions: What kind of map is it? What is its purpose? What special symbols and features does it use?

KINDS OF MAPS

Except for very specialized subjects, most maps can be classified broadly as either "physical" or "political." As its name suggests, a **physical map** emphasizes natural landforms and geographical features. It may use special colors and shadings to indicate elevation (height above sea level), precipitation, types of soil, types of plant life, or other physical features of the area shown. Dark and light shading may sometimes be used to show **relief**, the ruggedness of hills and mountains in an area.

A **political map** focuses on political divisions such as state and national borders. Because it shows fewer physical details, it can include more towns, cities, roads, and other human features. On this type of map, color is commonly used to show political boundaries or territorial possessions.

To compare physical and political maps of the same area, look at the two United States maps on pages 666–669 of the Atlas at the back of the book. Which one would you consult to find the capital of Arizona? Which one would you look at to learn more about the terrain of northern California?

SPECIAL-PURPOSE MAPS

In addition to showing physical or political characteristics, some maps have an additional special purpose. Often the title tells you what the map's purpose is or what specialized information it presents.

A book like this one commonly includes many **historical maps.** Such maps show a place as it appeared at a certain time in history. The map on the facing page is a historical map. Historical maps may show the territories of ancient kingdoms, changes in political boundaries, routes followed by explorers and pioneers, or similar information.

The map on page 228, for example, shows the routes that settlers took to cross the Appalachian Mountains in the late 1700s. The map on page 500 uses color to indicate the division of the country during the Civil War. Some historical maps, like the one on pages 670-671 of the Atlas, trace changes in territory over a period of time.

Other special-purpose maps give specific information about places or regions. Such maps may show religions, languages, population density, rainfall, crops, or similar

data. Be sure to read the title of map first to discover whether it is presenting specialized information.

MAP FEATURES AND SYMBOLS

No matter what their subject matter, maps use certain standard features and symbols to give as much information as possible in a small space. The **key,** or legend, tells you what symbols are used and what each one represents. For example, a dot usually represents a city; different sizes of dots may be used for city populations. A star symbol commonly means that a city is a state or national capital. On a road map, an airplane symbol points out the airport. In some maps in this book, an explosion symbol shows the site of a battle.

The key also gives you the meaning of colors and patterns used on the map. Textbook maps commonly use brighter colors for the areas that show the main subject of the map. The rest of the territory may be in a neutral color.

It is important to be sure of a map's direction, or **orientation.** Traditionally, north is at the top of a map, with east on the right and west on the left. This is not always true, however, particularly with certain types of map projections. Always check the directional symbol known as a **compass rose**. Its "N" arrow points to the North Pole.

Scale indicates how the size and distance on the map compare with reality. That is, one inch on a map may represent 60 miles (or about 100 kilometers) of real territory. With the map scale, you can find approximate distances and areas on the map. A map that includes a lot of territory—such as a world map—is said to be "large-scale." One that shows a fairly small area, such as a city street map, is "small-scale."

LOCATOR AND INSET MAPS

Two other features that sometimes appear on maps are locator maps and inset maps. In this book, **locator maps** are used to give you a larger context for a map. That is, they

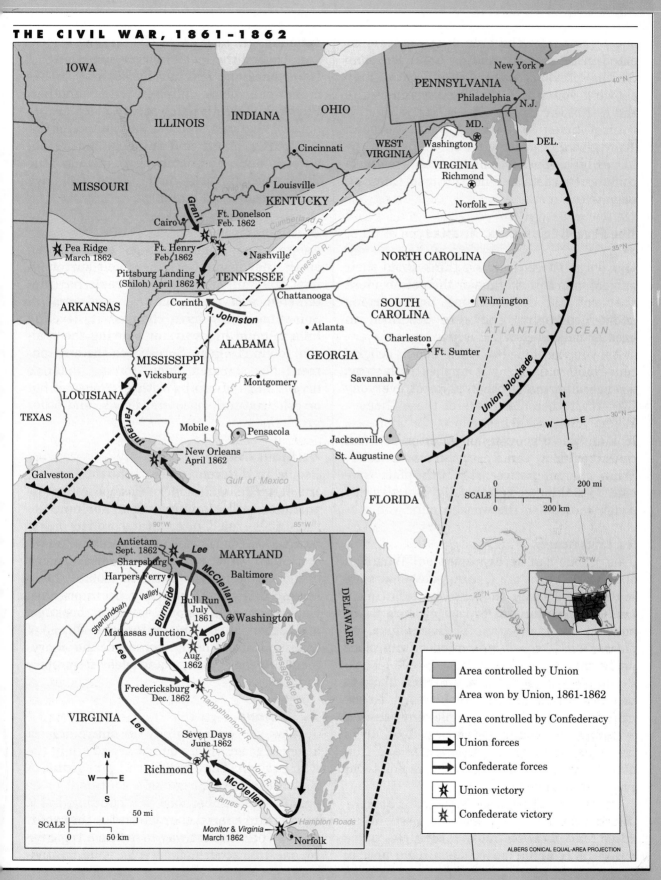

THE CIVIL WAR, 1861–1862

IOWA

ILLINOIS

INDIANA

OHIO

NEW YORK

PENNSYLVANIA

Philadelphia

N.J.

MD.

DEL.

MISSOURI

Cincinnati

WEST VIRGINIA

Washington

VIRGINIA

Richmond

Louisville

KENTUCKY

Grant

Cairo

Ft. Donelson
Feb. 1862

Norfolk

Cumberland R.

Pea Ridge
March 1862

Ft. Henry
Feb. 1862

Nashville

Tennessee R.

NORTH CAROLINA

ARKANSAS

Pittsburg Landing
(Shiloh) April 1862

TENNESSEE

Corinth

A. Johnston

Chattanooga

SOUTH CAROLINA

Wilmington

ATLANTIC OCEAN

Atlanta

ALABAMA

GEORGIA

Charleston

Ft. Sumter

MISSISSIPPI

Vicksburg

Montgomery

Savannah

Union blockade

LOUISIANA

Farragut

TEXAS

Mobile

Pensacola

Jacksonville

St. Augustine

Galveston

New Orleans
April 1862

Gulf of Mexico

FLORIDA

N
W   E
S

0   200 mi
SCALE
0   200 km

Inset Map

Antietam
Sept. 1862

Lee

MARYLAND

Sharpsburg

McClellan

Baltimore

Harpers Ferry

Valley

Burnside

Bull Run
July 1861

Washington

DELAWARE

Shenandoah

Manassas Junction

Pope

Aug. 1862

Chesapeake Bay

Fredericksburg
Dec. 1862

Rappahannock R.

VIRGINIA

Lee

Seven Days
June 1862

York R.

Richmond

McClellan

James R.

N
W   E
S

0   50 mi
SCALE
0   50 km

Monitor & Virginia
March 1862

Hampton Roads

Norfolk

Legend

Area controlled by Union

Area won by Union, 1861–1862

Area controlled by Confederacy

→ Union forces

→ Confederate forces

✦ Union victory

✦ Confederate victory

ALBERS CONICAL EQUAL-AREA PROJECTION

show you where the area of the map is located in relation to a larger area. The map on the previous page has a locator map showing you where that area is relative to the rest of the United States.

Inset maps have the opposite purpose. They give a close-up view of one part of the larger map—perhaps a city or an area with complicated detail. Find the inset map on page G5.

THE FIVE GEOGRAPHIC THEMES

One way that geographers think about their subject is in terms of major themes, or ideas that run through teaching and learning about geography. They are described in greater detail below.

As you continue to learn about geography—and to see how it applies to history, science, and many other parts of everyday life—try to become aware of these themes. When you visit a new place, for instance, look at it as a geographer might see it. Ask questions: How can I describe this location? What characteristics make this place special? "Thinking geographically" can give you a new outlook on the world around you.

1. LOCATION
This theme can be expressed as "Where in the world are we?" You have already learned one way to answer this question—the coordinates of latitude and longitude on the grid system. These can give you the accurate, *absolute* location of any place on earth.

In ordinary speech, you are more likely to describe location in a different way. To the question, "Where is it?" people often answer in terms of something else: next door, down the hall, east of Austin, south of the Mason-Dixon line. Phrases like this point out *relative* location.

2. PLACE
Place and *location* mean about the same thing in ordinary speech but have special meanings in geography. The idea of "place" goes beyond the idea of where something is. It includes the special characteristics that make one place different from another. Physical characteristics of any place are its natural features, such as landscape, physical setting, plants and animals, and weather. Human characteristics include the things people have made, from language and philosophy to buildings.

3. INTERACTIONS
As soon as human beings appeared on earth, they began to change their surroundings. For millions of years, people have interacted with their natural environment. Sometimes they have changed it, leveling hills to build highways or plowing the prairies to plant wheat. Sometimes the environment has changed them, forcing them to invent ways of coping with extremes of hot or cold, natural disasters, floods, and other problems.

4. MOVEMENT
People in different places interact through travel, trade, and modern methods of transportation and communication. For much of the 1800s, the United States relied on its natural defenses of two great oceans to protect itself from potential enemies. Today, even if Americans wished to isolate themselves, this would probably be impossible. Computers, television, satellite hookups, and other almost instantaneous forms of communication have increased the movement of people, things, and ideas from place to place.

5. REGIONS
Just as you cannot study an entire subject at once, geographers do not try to study the whole world. They break it into **regions.** A region can be as large as a continent or as small as a neighborhood or a building, but it has certain shared characteristics that set it apart. The simplest way to define a region is by one characteristic, such as political divi-

sion, type of climate, language spoken, or belief in one religion. Other regions are defined by more complicated sets of features.

REGIONS OF THE UNITED STATES

The map called "Land Regions of the United States" (below) is based on one method for defining regions—physical similarities in landscape and landforms.

Five of the regions shown on the map are highlands. Here the typical landforms are mountain chains, hills, and rugged plateaus.

The highland region in the eastern United States is the Appalachian Mountains and their foothills. (These foothills are sometimes called the piedmont.) A small highland region, the Ozark Highlands, is located to the west of the Appalachians. The western United States contains three different highland regions. The Rocky Mountains are part of a chain of high rugged mountains that begins in Alaska and runs the length of North and South America. Another mountain region is made up of several ranges that run parallel to the Pacific coastline of the United States. Between the coastal and Rockies mountains is a dry region of high plateaus, great rivers, and broad valleys, or basins. It is sometimes called the "High Plateaus and Basins."

The United States also contains two large lowland areas—the Coastal Plains and the Central Plains. They are generally low, flat areas well suited to agriculture. These regions have been very important in American history. The first settlements in the East and Southeast were made on the broad Coastal Plains. Cities and harbors here became centers for trade and population. The Central Plains, once forests and grasslands, became America's agricultural heartland, one of the world's richest farming regions.

These geographic regions have been the setting for thousands of years of American history. As you learn about events in American history, refer back to this map to get a better idea of the geographical setting in

LAND REGIONS OF THE UNITED STATES

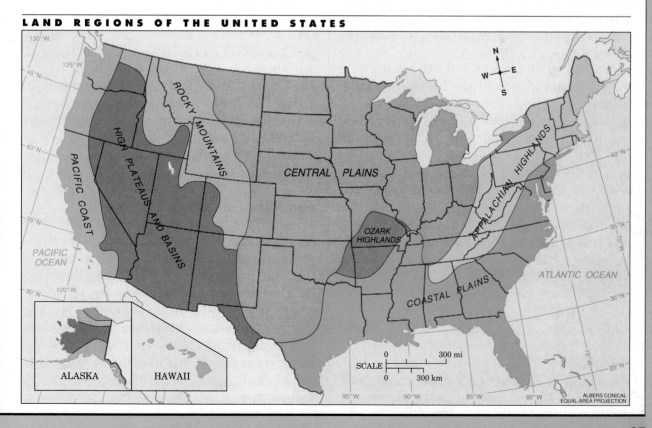

which they took place. This will make your study of American history a richer, more rewarding experience.

TEST YOUR GEOGRAPHIC LITERACY

Answer these questions to check your understanding of geography in history.

1. Lines of longitude measure (a) location north or south of the equator, (b) distance from the North Pole, (c) distance east or west of the prime meridian.

2. "Parallels" is another term for (a) lines of latitude, (b) meridians, (c) lines of longitude.

3. The continents of North and South America are located in the (a) Northern Hemisphere, (b) Eastern Hemisphere, (c) Western Hemisphere.

4. Of the following places, which one is nearest the prime meridian? (a) 42°N, 13°E (b) 37°N, 137°W (c) 4°N, 74°W

5. Generally, the most accurate portion of a map is the (a) area near the equator, (b) center of the map, (c) northern half of the map.

6. A map that shows shaded mountain ranges, deserts, and woodlands of Canada is a (a) historical map, (b) physical map, (c) political map.

7. To find what a dotted red line means on a map, you would look at the (a) key, (b) title, (c) grid.

8. A map on which one inch stands for 1,000 miles is (a) special purpose, (b) large-scale, (c) small-scale.

9. The "N" arrow on a map's compass rose points to the (a) top of the map, (b) North Pole, (c) prime meridian.

10. "Galveston is on the Gulf of Mexico, south of Houston." This statement describes (a) grid coordinates, (b) location, (c) place.

11. Which of the following is *not* one of the United States' highland regions? (a) Appalachians (b) Ozarks (c) Central Plains

12. The largest geographical region in the United States is the (a) Coastal Plains, (b) Rocky Mountains, (c) Central Plains.

13. The map on this page is a (a) political map, (b) historical map, (c) both a and b.

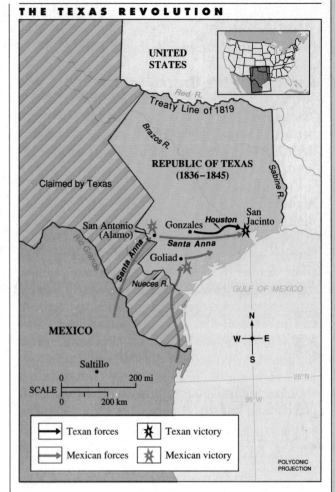

THE TEXAS REVOLUTION

14. On the map above, the movement of Texan and Mexican forces is shown by (a) explosion symbols, (b) arrows, (c) dots.

15. Which geographic theme is *not* illustrated by the map on this page? (a) location (b) movement (c) interaction.

FOR MORE PRACTICE

A. Choose a place you know well. List three physical and three human characteristics that make it different from other places.

B. Find the grid coordinates for the place where you live. Then use a globe or atlas to find the "opposite" addresses in the eastern and southern hemispheres. (For example, if you live at 38°N, 122°W, find what places are located at 38°S, 122°W, at 38°N, 122°E, and so on.)

UNIT ONE

America's Beginnings

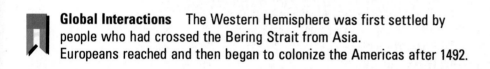

THEMES IN AMERICAN HISTORY

Global Interactions   The Western Hemisphere was first settled by people who had crossed the Bering Strait from Asia. Europeans reached and then began to colonize the Americas after 1492.

Geography   Huge advances in geographic knowledge resulted from voyages of exploration to the Americas.

Economic Development   The lure of wealth drew explorers and settlers to the Americas.

Pluralistic Society   People from several different nations came to the Americas, some searching for profits or freedom, others as slaves.

American Culture   Early American culture included both Indian and Spanish influences.

The first Americans migrated to the Western Hemisphere from Asia. This copper profile of a human head, which comes from the Caddoan culture of present-day Oklahoma, is more than 500 years old.

CHAPTER

1 The First Americans
(Beginnings–1500)

KEY EVENTS

c. 10,000 B.C.	Paleo-Indians enter the Americas
c. 3000 B.C.	Woodland Indians engage in long-distance trading
c. 1000 B.C.	Olmec culture develops
c. 500 B.C.	Hopewell culture established
c. 300	Teotihuacán built
c. 1325	Aztecs settle at Tenochtitlán
c. 1500	Inca empire at height

1 Peopling the Americas

> ### ★ Section Focus
>
> **Key Terms** anthropologist ■ archeologist ■ artifact ■ pre-Columbian ■ migration ■ Paleo-Indian ■ hunter-gatherer ■ domestication
>
> **Main Idea** People first arrived in the Americas many thousands of years ago. Over time they developed new ways of life, such as farming.
>
> **Objectives** As you read, look for answers to these questions:
> 1. How did the peopling of the Americas take place?
> 2. What was the cultural significance of the rise of agriculture?

An early scholar who thought seriously about the origin of the Native Americans was Thomas Jefferson. The man who would be the third President had a deep interest in all things far and near, past and present. Where, he asked two centuries ago, did America's native people come from? Jefferson suggested that the eastern inhabitants of Asia may have passed into America across the Bering Strait. The proof, he said, would be found in the study of languages. But no one 200 years ago, or even 100 years ago, had the evidence to prove Jefferson right or wrong. Today scientists have proof. Studies of languages, of blood types, of teeth, of bones, even of climate, all point to the answer. Jefferson was right.

STUDYING THE NATIVE AMERICANS
In 1492, when Christopher Columbus first met the inhabitants of the Caribbean island

of San Salvador, he did not wonder about their origin. He thought he knew. Believing he had reached the Indies, the fabled spice islands of Asia, Columbus called the people whom he met *Indians*.

Today our knowledge about Indians comes from **anthropologists** and **archeologists**. Anthropologists study human culture and development, both ancient and modern. Archeologists study **artifacts**—items made by humans—to learn about the past. They often work closely with other experts such as art historians, botanists, and geologists. Through their efforts a history of **pre-Columbian** (before Columbus) America is emerging.

THE PALEO-INDIANS
During the last Ice Age massive glaciers locked up so much water that ocean levels dropped. When that happened the Bering

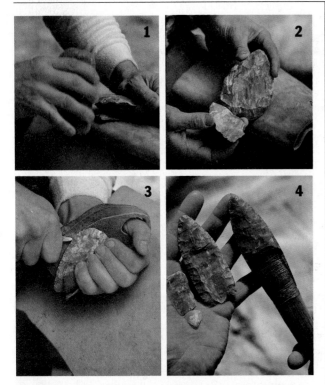

An artisan shows how Paleo-Indians made spear points 10,000 years ago. Using stone and bone tools, skilled workers created the points from chunks of flint. They made a groove in the point so it could be tied to a shaft. **TECHNOLOGY** Judging from the size of the finished points, what animals might have been hunted with them?

Strait between Asia and North America became dry land. The land was, in effect, a bridge connecting the two continents. The opening of this new land bridge encouraged migration—the movement of people from one region to another.

Scientists give the name Paleo-Indians to the people who migrated across the land bridge from Asia to America. (*Paleo* comes from a Greek word meaning "old.") It is hard to say precisely when the Paleo-Indians arrived here from Asia. Some came as early as 20,000 or even 40,000 years ago. Most, however, moved into North America about 12,000 years ago.

The waves of immigrants were not all the same. They spoke different languages and varied in their physical appearance. In general, however, they shared certain traits. Their hair was black and straight. They had little facial or body hair. Their skin color ranged from yellowish brown to light copper.

As the Paleo-Indians moved south, they found a lush land that supported much game. The Paleo-Indians survived primarily by hunting large game—such as woolly mammoths—that gathered at water holes or springs. These animals provided them with food and with skins for clothing. The Paleo-Indians used tools and weapons made of stone and bone. Because some of these artifacts have been found in grave sites, scholars think that the Paleo-Indians probably believed in an afterlife.

HUNTING AND GATHERING

As the climate warmed up, North America became drier. About the same time, the huge game animals became extinct. No one knows why for certain. Perhaps the Indians killed them all off. Maybe the climate changed so quickly that the large animals could not adapt.

Whatever happened, the Indians had to change their way of life to survive. Instead of depending on the meat of the giant mam-

BIOGRAPHY

LUCY M. LEWIS (1900?–   ) is a Native American potter from New Mexico. Lewis follows a pottery-making tradition that is over 1,000 years old. She is one of the few Acoma Indians who still dig their own clay, work it by hand, and fire it using dried cow dung for fuel. Here she coils clay to make a pot. The Acoma believe that creating pottery is a spiritual process. A renowned artist, Lewis says, "I mix my clay with me."

By studying artifacts, scientists have been able to reconstruct ancient settlements. This model shows what a Paleo-Indian settlement in the American Southwest might have looked like. **TECHNOLOGY** Name some of the items in the picture that the Indians created themselves by hand. What kinds of materials did they use? Where did the materials probably come from?

moth, they had to learn to hunt smaller animals like deer. Their tools thus changed from huge throwing spears to small spears, and finally to the bow and arrow.

In the new environment, the Indians changed their food-gathering patterns. They no longer depended only on hunting. Some came to depend on shellfish. Others became skilled at weaving nets to catch fish. People began to dig for edible roots and to gather berries, fruits, nuts, and grass seeds. Among their artifacts are digging sticks, baskets, fish hooks, and stone mortars for grinding seeds. Such people who depend for food on the wild plants and animals of their environment are called hunter-gatherers.

THE RISE OF AGRICULTURE

Hunter-gatherers learned from observation. A woman collecting grass seeds, for instance, would have seen that seeds sprout in moist and fertile soil. From that recognition it was but one step to sowing seeds.

Peoples the world over chose to take that step. About 10,000 years ago agriculture began in the river valleys of Asia with the domestication of both plants and animals. (Domestication is breeding plants or animals to meet specific human needs, such as food and transportation.) The domestication of wild grasses led to wheat and barley. The first domesticated livestock were sheep and goats. By 5,000 years ago people had begun to cultivate rice in southern China. At about the same time, people in central Mexico began to sow the seeds of wild corn.

The cobs of this wild corn were tiny, about the size of a strawberry. In time, Indian farmers developed a corn cob like the one today. The domesticated corn had a closed husk that prevented birds from eating the kernels. Dried, the corn would last months and even years. The domestication of corn thus meant a more stable food supply. From central Mexico the cultivation of corn spread south to Peru and north to what is now the United States.

In time the Indians would domesticate more than 100 plants. In Mexico people learned to cultivate pumpkins, peppers, beans, and tomatoes. Farmers in Peru raised gourds, lima beans, and potatoes. Other domestic plants once unique to the Western Hemisphere include pineapples, bananas, peanuts, tobacco, and cacao (chocolate beans).

The development of farming brought revolutionary changes in the way people lived. Agricultural peoples, unlike hunter-gatherers, did not have to move constantly in search of food. Thus they could stay in one place, building permanent settlements. They also had more leisure time, since farming allowed people to build up stocks of food.

With more leisure time, individuals could develop special skills and talents. As a result, arts and crafts flourished. As societies became more complex—larger, wealthier, more densely populated—systems of government became more complex as well.

2 Ancient Indian Cultures

Section Focus

Key Terms civilization ■ Mesoamerica ■ Olmec ■ glyphic writing ■ Maya ■ Aztec ■ tribute ■ empire ■ Inca ■ Hohokam ■ Anasazi ■ Hopewell culture ■ Mississippian culture

Main Idea Highly advanced societies developed in Middle America and Peru. Indian cultures of North America included the agricultural peoples of the Southwest and the mound builders of the Eastern Woodlands.

Objectives As you read, look for answers to these questions:
1. How did great civilizations develop in Middle America and Peru?
2. What ways of life did the Hohokam and Anasazi introduce to the Southwest?
3. What kinds of societies did Indians of the Eastern Woodlands develop?

The development of agriculture made it possible for some societies of Middle America and Peru to develop distinct and highly developed cultures, known as civilizations. That is, they had complex political, social, religious, and economic institutions. These civilizations also produced massive public works, which are witness to their mathematical knowledge, their organizational skill, and their religious devotion.

MESOAMERICAN CIVILIZATION
The first civilization in the Western Hemisphere arose in Mesoamerica, or Middle America. The "waist" of the Western Hemisphere, this tropical region extends from central Mexico in the north to the Isthmus of Panama in the south. (This isthmus, or narrow strip of land, separates North and South America.) It was in Mesoamerica that corn was first domesticated.

The mysterious Olmec culture produced colossal stone sculptures. This helmeted head, which may represent one of the Olmec rulers, is from a site in southern Mexico. **HISTORY** About how many years ago did the Olmec culture develop?

The "mother culture" of Mesoamerica was that of the Olmecs. The Olmec culture developed on the Gulf of Mexico near the present city of Veracruz. It was an unlikely place for a culture to bloom. This was a rain forest, humid and swampy. Yet, in this area about 1000 B.C. the Olmecs introduced traditions and skills that would influence Middle America for centuries.

The Olmecs built, not cities, but large religious centers that featured earthen temple mounds. They were the first in this hemisphere to devise glyphic writing—the use of symbols and images to express words and ideas. They may also have been the first to develop a calendar system. The Olmecs traded by land and sea with other parts of the hemisphere. In this way their culture spread.

Among those who learned from the Olmecs were the Mayas, a people living in the tropical rain forest of what is now Guatemala. They too had ceremonial centers. These centers were home to the priests and nobles who controlled the surrounding countryside. The power of these leaders probably came from their knowledge of astronomy and the calendar. Maya astronomers were the first in the world to invent a symbol for zero. The Maya calendar was one of the most accurate ever developed.

Maya culture declined in the Guatemala lowlands starting about A.D. 900. It continued for several centuries more, however, at sites in the Yucatán Peninsula.

Olmec culture also influenced people living in the Valley of Mexico, the site of present-day Mexico City. By A.D. 300 they had built the city of Teotihuacán (tay–oh–tee–wah–KAHN). This was a ceremonial center, but it was also a true city, with neighborhoods for both artisans and merchants. Rising above the city was a pyramid twenty stories high, now called the Pyramid of the Sun. Ranking at the top of the city's 250,000 people were the priest-rulers. They lived in magnificent stone-and-plaster houses decorated with murals and stone carvings.

One temple within Teotihuacán was dedicated to the god Quetzalcóatl (ket–sahl–KWAHT–uhl), symbolized by a feathered serpent. Quetzalcóatl was considered the carrier of civilization and the defender of good against evil. To keep such gods happy, the people of Teotihuacán made sacrifices of birds, animals, flowers, and even humans.

THE AZTECS

No amount of sacrifice, however, could protect the city when waves of war-loving barbarians began swooping out of the north about A.D. 650. They burned and plundered Teotihuacán. In time the invaders adopted much of the culture of the conquered. In the new society, however, warriors replaced priests as rulers. A time of almost constant warfare began.

The last of the barbarian waves from the north was that of the Aztecs, who moved into the Valley of Mexico sometime before 1300. Then in 1325 they settled at Tenochtitlán (tay–nahch–tee–TLAHN), a snake-infested island in Lake Texcoco (tay–SKOH–koh). A practical people, they ate the snakes. Then they began to conquer neighboring city-states. The conquered peoples were forced to pay tribute—offerings of goods and produce—to the Aztecs. With tribute flowing in, the Aztecs did not have to work for food. They were free to expand their army and conquer even more peoples. In this way, most of central Mexico became part of the Aztec empire. (An empire is a number of peoples or lands controlled by one nation or ruler.)

Tenochtitlán became a marvel of the Western Hemisphere with its gardens, canals, pyramid temples, and great markets. In 1500 no place in Europe could rival in beauty and size this island city of 300,000 people.

The most important god of the Aztecs was the war god Huitzilopochtli (wee–tsee–loh–POHTCH–tlee). This god, Aztecs believed, had a craving for human hearts. The Aztecs believed that as long as they kept their god happy he would reward them with military

victories. One purpose of war, therefore, was to collect captives who could be sacrificed to the god. It is said that more than 20,000 people were sacrificed when the temple to Huitzilopochtli was dedicated in 1490.

THE INCA EMPIRE

Along the west coast of South America there arose another great civilization. Much of that area was either desert or mountains. Yet there, in what is now Ecuador and Peru, people developed highly efficient farming communities. To make the best use of their land, they farmed on hillside terraces. Large canals carried water from the mountains to fields in the dry coastal valleys. The people also domesticated the llama and the guinea pig. They excelled at metal-working, creating beautiful objects from tin, copper, silver, and gold. Using both cotton and wool, they were among the finest weavers in the world.

With time, Peruvian political, social, and religious life became more complex. Powerful city-states developed. The rulers were a class of nobles and priests. One of these city-states was that of the Incas, whose capital was Cuzco. Cuzco, with an altitude of over 11,000 feet, is the oldest continually inhabited city in the Americas.

During the 1400s, Tenochtitlán, the Aztec capital, was larger than any European city. The Aztecs used canals and causeways for transportation. GEOGRAPHY Why does the map show flames in the mountains above the city?

In 1438 the Incas began to conquer neighboring states. By 1532 the empire stretched for 2,000 miles, occupying the land between the Pacific Ocean and the Andes Mountains. In area it was larger than Texas and Louisiana combined. Great stone roads knit the empire together. Armies as large as 30,000 enforced Inca authority. Probably about 6 million people lived in the Inca Empire.

THE HOHOKAM AND ANASAZI

People learn from each other, and always have. Scholars have traced ways in which the Mesoamerican culture influenced peoples to the north. One influence was agriculture. The desert people of the Southwest began raising corn and squash 4,000 years ago. Later they learned to grow beans. Over time, they developed distinct farming cultures that depended on what American Indians called the Three Sisters—corn, squash, and beans.

The Hohokam people may have migrated north from Mexico about 300 B.C. to settle in what is now central Arizona. To get water to their crops, they dug lengthy canals using only sticks as tools. The major canals in this system were more than 30 miles long.

The Incas built stone-walled farming terraces (left) to use their mountainous land more efficiently. Many of these finely engineered fields are still in use. Below, Peruvian Indians, descendants of the Incas, travel with their llamas along a surviving stretch of the Inca highway. CULTURE How do Inca building projects provide evidence of a complex, developed society?

The Hohokam culture broke up in the 1400s, perhaps because wars in Mexico cut off their trade and contact. The Hohokam people then became more like their neighbors. They survived through hunting, gathering, and a little farming.

During the same centuries, the Anasazi people of the Colorado Plateau also developed a culture based on agriculture. The ghost towns of the Anasazi remain in the canyons they once lived in. Their apartment-like dwellings clustered around one or more *kivas*. These were large round chambers, partly underground, that the men used for religious ceremonies and as workshops.

The Anasazi were good farmers. Learning from the Hohokam, they built small dams and irrigation ditches to catch water. They farmed on terraces to prevent erosion. To supplement their crops, they hunted game and gathered wild plants, seeds, and nuts.

The Anasazi were also traders. Roads 30 feet wide radiated out from Pueblo Bonito in Chaco Canyon. A thousand years ago people traveled these roads carrying wood from the mountains, pottery, cloth, baskets, and turquoise. Pieces of the turquoise would end up in the markets of faraway Mexico.

By 1300, however, the Anasazi were abandoning their villages. No one knows exactly why. From the study of tree rings, scientists do know that a terrible, 25-year drought began in 1275. The drought might have been too much for these desert farmers to survive.

Whatever the cause, the Anasazi moved to other sites in the Southwest, including the Rio Grande Valley of New Mexico. Their descendants—the Pueblo Indians—live there still.

ANCIENT WOODLAND CULTURES

Trade, and then agriculture, were the basis of complex cultures that emerged in the Eastern Woodlands. This is the region between the

The Anasazi of Mesa Verde in present-day Colorado built the spectacular Cliff Palace in this canyon's sandstone walls. The settlement, seen here in winter, contains more than 200 rooms and 23 kivas. GEOGRAPHY What advantages might cliff-dwellings have had?

Mississippi River and the Atlantic Coast. As early as 3000 B.C. the Woodland Indians were traveling long distances to trade useful stones, copper tools, and carved beads. The later Crystal River culture along Florida's Gulf Coast, for example, traded with both the Olmecs of Mexico and the peoples of the Great Lakes.

It is possible that the Crystal River people were the first people north of Mexico to build pyramid mounds. Woodland traders returned home from Florida with more than beautiful shells. They also carried new ideas—including the idea of building a mound.

Elaborate burial mounds became the most distinctive feature of the Hopewell culture, situated in the Ohio Valley. This culture, which emerged about 500 B.C., would last for about 1,200 years.

The religion of the Hopewell culture focused on death rituals. The people buried their leaders in huge mounds located in ceremonial centers. With the dead, they buried all the wealth that the deceased would need in the next world.

Hopewell nobles must have dressed in splendid fashion. In one burial site alone, archeologists found thousands of pearl beads, necklaces of grizzly-bear teeth, and copper ornaments. The Hopewell artists made beautiful objects of mica and carved stone as well as copper. Many of their objects represented animals and birds.

The Hopewell people began cultivating corn about A.D. 450. With the beginning of agriculture, some say, their trading activities declined. As a result, their communities became more isolated from each other. About 300 years later the Hopewell people took to the hills, where they built large earthworks for defense. Obviously there was unrest in the land, perhaps an invading people. These earthworks are the last evidence of the Hopewell culture.

THE MISSISSIPPIAN CULTURE

About A.D. 900 another mound culture emerged in the Southeast and Mississippi

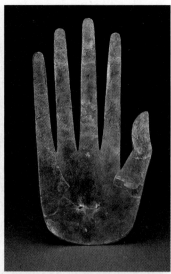

Hopewell artisans created beautiful objects for use as grave offerings. The mica cutout of a hand and the copper falcon come from southern Ohio. The wooden catlike figure was found in Florida. CULTURE Why might the Hopewell have admired the falcon?

Valley. This is known as the Mississippian culture. This culture had clear ties with Mexico.

The Mississippian people built their communities on the river flood plains. Such locations were good for farming because floods constantly renewed the fertility of the soil. Their towns featured large flat-topped mounds on which were built temples, meeting houses, and the homes of chiefs and priests. Common symbols in their art were the falcon and the jaguar. Both of these animals had long been honored in Mesoamerica.

The jewel of the Mississippian culture was

The largest Mississippian burial mounds may have taken a century or longer to reach their maximum size. This painting from 1850 shows a cross section of a mound in Louisiana.
RELIGION Why might the Indians have held religious ceremonies on top of the mounds?

Cahokia, in western Illinois. In its heyday, Cahokia boasted 30,000 residents and more than 1,000 mounds. The tallest mound at Cahokia rises ten stories from a sixteen-acre base. Near the mound, archeologists have discovered a circular pattern of posts. The shadows cast by the posts may have served as a kind of calendar. By keeping track of the sun's position, priests could tell farmers when to sow crops.

The Mississippian culture was fading by the 1500s, when Spanish explorers first arrived. The explorers, however, caught a glimpse of the society's splendor. A member of a Spanish expedition described a temple along the Savannah River in Georgia. Said the chronicler, the "ceiling . . . from the walls upward, was adorned like the roof outside with designs of shells interspersed with strands of pearls. Among the decorations were great headdresses of different colors of feathers. . . . It was an agreeable sight to behold."

Later Indians of the region could not say who built the mounds. Yet there seems little doubt that the tribes of the Southeast are descendants of the mound builders. These include the Cherokee, Creek, and Choctaw.

SECTION REVIEW

1. KEY TERMS civilization, Mesoamerica, Olmec, glyphic writing, Maya, Aztec, tribute, empire, Inca, Hohokam, Anasazi, Hopewell culture, Mississippian culture

2. PLACES Valley of Mexico, Tenochtitlán, Cuzco, Cahokia

3. COMPREHENSION Why are the Olmecs called the "mother culture" of Mesoamerica?

4. COMPREHENSION What did the Hohokam and Anasazi cultures have in common?

5. CRITICAL THINKING Why, as in the case of the Hopewell, might trading decline with the beginning of agriculture?

Gaining Skill: Using Historical Evidence

Historians try to build a true understanding of what happened and how people lived in the past. To do this, they examine many kinds of historical materials. Historians then evaluate each piece of evidence to decide whether it provides accurate information.

There are two types of historical information. **Primary sources** are materials written or made at the time they tell about. **Secondary sources** are descriptions or interpretations of the past, made by people not directly involved in the events described.

Primary sources can take a number of forms. *Written materials* include first-hand accounts of events by participants and witnesses. Government documents, church records, bills of sale, and ships' cargo lists can also provide valuable information. *Oral accounts* are spoken reports of historical incidents made by eyewitnesses of those incidents. *Pictures*—paintings, drawings, and photographs—can show how places looked and how people lived. Finally, *physical remains* provide important clues to the past. Physical remains include ancient buildings, artifacts, and even the bones of long-dead animals and human beings.

The picture below was painted by a Maya artist about 1,000 years ago. It shows life in a Maya seacoast village of that time. Study the picture and then answer the questions on a separate sheet of paper.

PRACTICING YOUR SKILL

1. Why would this painting be considered a primary source?

2. Do you think the picture provides accurate information about how the Maya people lived?

3. What kinds of sea animals were the Maya familiar with?

4. What can you tell about Maya houses from the picture?

5. What method of cooking is shown?

6. What methods of transportation are shown in the picture?

3 North America in 1500

Section Focus

Key Terms   social class ■ slash-and-burn farming ■ ecology ■ shaman ■ technology

Main Idea   A variety of Indian groups lived in North America. Each made use of the land and its resources and stressed a spiritual relationship with the environment.

Objectives   As you read, look for answers to these questions:
1. What differences were there among the peoples of North America? What similarities?
2. What spiritual views of the earth did most Indians share?

The first European explorers and settlers in the Americas left vivid accounts of the Indians they met. Yet these accounts have tended to "freeze" the Indians in time and place. The Europeans assumed that the Indians had always lived in the same place and in the same way. However, that is not true. Like peoples the world over, Indian groups moved from one territory to another. As they did, they changed their way of life when it was necessary to do so.

A Variety of Cultures

The Cheyenne, for instance, are usually thought of as Plains Indians who hunted buffalo. Originally, however, they were farmers in southern Minnesota. Once they migrated to the Plains, the Cheyenne continued a life that included both farming and hunting-gathering. Then, when the Spanish brought horses to the Plains in the mid-1500s, the Cheyenne abandoned farming to rely on hunting.

Indian societies had many different ways of life. Some devoted themselves to warfare. Others were peaceful, fighting only if necessary. In some societies all members were considered equal. Other societies were organized into social classes. A social class is a group of people who share the same status or degree of wealth in a society. Some societies emphasized the importance of individual feats of valor or of possessions to increase status. Others discouraged individualism and personal status-seeking.

Chiefs headed most Indian societies. The chief, either male or female depending on tradition, had only as much authority as the group was willing to give. Important decisions were made in consultation with other village leaders.

Living from the Land

Wherever they lived, Indians regulated their lives by the seasons. In each season they ate what was most abundant.

Indians of the Far West continued to rely on hunting and gathering for their food. They relied on an abundance of waterfowl, fish, game, nuts, edible roots, and berries. Even the Indians who practiced agriculture still hunted and gathered. In 1500 these included most of the Plains Indians, the desert farmers of the Southwest, and the Eastern Woodland Indians.

The Eastern Woodland Indians, for example, raised at least half of their food. For the Woodland Indians, growing crops was just one seasonal activity—and an activity for the women at that. While the women were tending the crops, the men were out hunting. The hunt provided meat as well as variety to their diet. The hunt also was necessary to provide the skins that would become fur robes, moccasins, and clothing.

After the fall harvest festivals, the Woodland Indians broke up into small family bands that would then establish winter hunting and gathering camps. In the spring they would reconvene for spring planting.

ARCTIC OCEAN

Bering Strait

INUIT

ALEUT

TLINGIT

NORTHWEST COAST

FAR NORTH

INUIT

INUIT

Hudson Bay

INUIT

CREE

KWAKIUTL

BLACKFEET

CHINOOK

PLATEAU

NEZ PERCE

CROW

CAYUSE

MODOC

SHOSHONE

MANDAN

SIOUX

CHIPPEWA

ALGONQUIN

OTTAWA

HURON

MOHAWK

SENECA

ONONDAGA

ONEIDA

CAYUGA

POMO

GREAT BASIN

GREAT PLAINS

SAUK

FOX

IROQUOIS

WAMPANOAG

PEQUOT

CALIFORNIA

CHEYENNE

ARAPAHO

ILLINOIS

MIAMI

DELAWARE

NAVAHO

MOHAVE

HOPI

ZUÑI

EASTERN WOODLANDS

SHAWNEE

POWHATAN

SOUTHWEST

APACHE

WICHITA

CHEROKEE

CHICKASAW

TUSCARORA

COMANCHE

SOUTHEAST

CREEK

CHOCTAW

SEMINOLE

MEXICO AND MIDDLE AMERICA

Gulf of Mexico

TAINO

ATLANTIC OCEAN

AZTEC EMPIRE

MAYA EMPIRE

CARIBBEAN

PACIFIC OCEAN

Caribbean Sea

N

W E

S

ARAWAK

CARIB

AMAZON

INCA EMPIRE

ANDES

| PLATEAU | Culture area |
| CAYUSE | Indian nation |

0   1,000 mi

SCALE

0   1,000 km

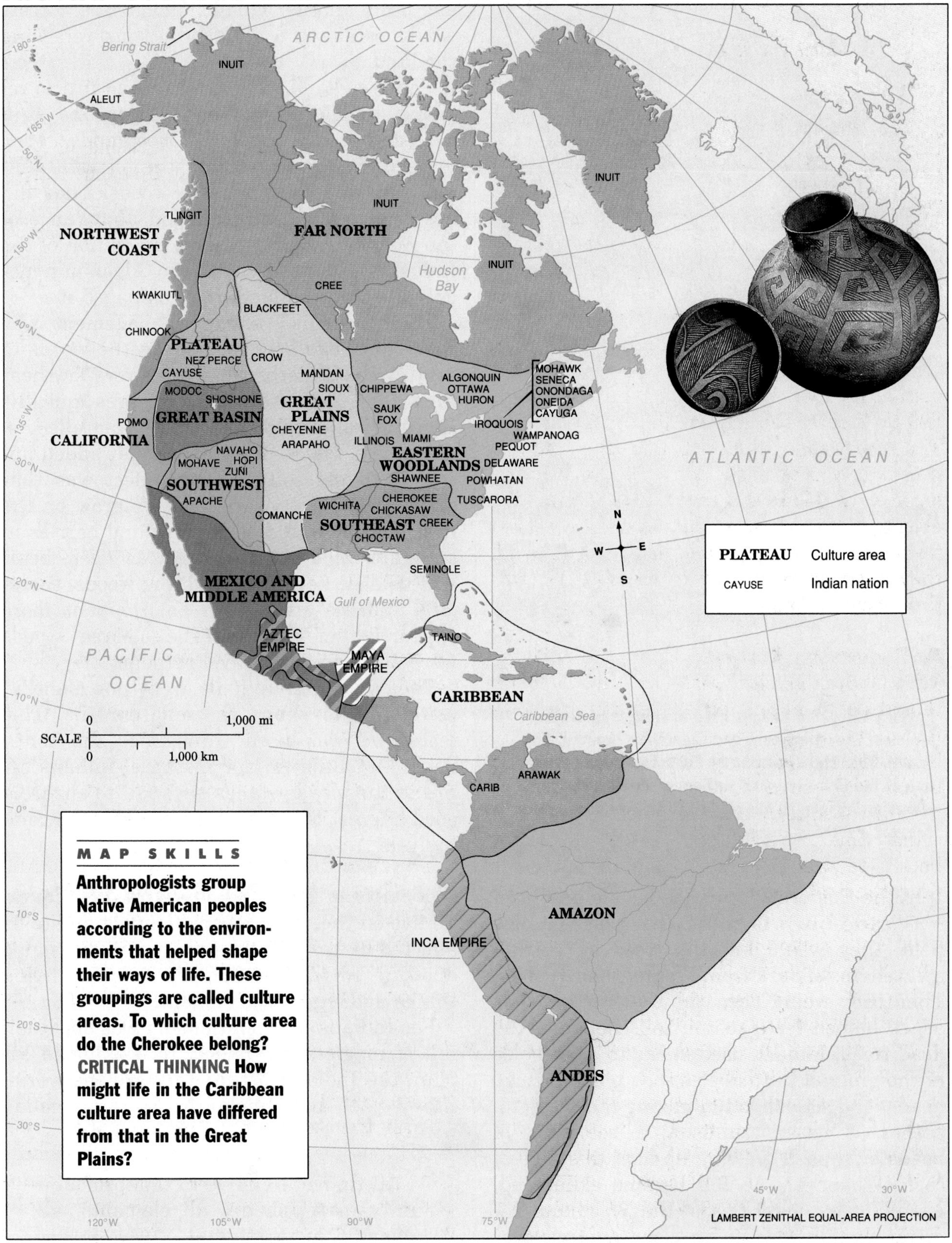

MAP SKILLS

Anthropologists group Native American peoples according to the environments that helped shape their ways of life. These groupings are called culture areas. To which culture area do the Cherokee belong?
CRITICAL THINKING How might life in the Caribbean culture area have differed from that in the Great Plains?

LAMBERT ZENITHAL EQUAL-AREA PROJECTION

Eastern Woodland Indians lived in villages of several families. They grew corn and vegetables, hunted, and fished. This 1585 painting by Englishman John White, one of the first European settlers in North America, shows an Algonquin village. **CULTURE** How does White suggest a thriving community?

In the Eastern Woodlands people practiced slash-and-burn farming. To prepare a new field, they would kill the trees by cutting away strips of bark from around their trunks. Then they would burn the underbrush. The ashes helped fertilize the soil. Between the dead trees, Indians used sticks to poke holes in the ground. In the holes they planted corn, beans, and squash, often mixing the seeds together. It was not unusual to see vines of beans or squash growing up next to stalks of corn. Whenever the soil became exhausted, usually after eight years, the Woodland Indians would move on to clear another plot

and build another village. Meanwhile, forests would retake the old fields, thus renewing the land.

The Woodland Indians also used fire to reshape the forests. When Europeans first looked on the Eastern Woodlands, they praised the "good ground," the plentiful animal life, and the park-like woods. They did not realize that the look and abundance of the woodlands were actually a creation of the Indians. Groups such as the Algonquin not only lived on the land; they managed it.

Their principal tool of management was fire. They regularly set fires in the woods to destroy the underbrush. These were low-heat fires that swept through an area quickly, sparing well-established trees. One effect of these fires was to make ashes that added nutrients to the soil. Another effect was that grass and berries were likely to grow on the fire-cleared ground. The grass and berries in turn attracted animals such as deer, bear, and wild turkeys. By firing the woods, therefore, Indians created an environment more supportive of wildlife. The cleared woods were also easier to travel through.

The Woodland Indians were not alone in using fire to shape the environment. This technique was used throughout the continent. In California, for instance, Indians set fire to the meadowlands each fall to ensure a good harvest of cereal-grass seed for the coming year.

A Spiritual Relationship with the Earth

To live on the earth means to affect and to be affected by it. Scientists today give the name ecology to the relationship between living things and their environment.

For Indians this relationship was spiritual, full of magic and wonder. In seeking to explain the Indians' attitude toward the world, Kiowa poet and scholar N. Scott Momaday wrote:

All things are alive in this profound unity in which are all elements, all animals, all things. . . . My father remembered that, as a boy, he had watched . . . the old man Koi-khan-hole, "Dragonfly," stand in the first light, his arms outstretched and his painted face fixed on the east, and pray the sun out of ground. His voice, for he prayed aloud, struck at the great, misty silence of the Plains morning, entered into it, carried through it to the rising sun. His words made one of the sun and earth, one of himself and the boy who watched, one of the boy and generations to come.

Indians believed, in other words, that all things were part of a larger whole. They also believed that each life form had certain powers. Establishing the right relationship with an animal or plant, stone or star, storm or cloud meant a person could share its spirit or essence. As a result, even hunting was not just an economic activity. It was also a spiritual activity. To an Indian, success in the hunt not only reflected individual strength. It also meant that a creature had given up its life. The hunter acknowledged that gift and thanked the creature's spirit.

> "**A**ll things are alive in this profound unity in which are all elements, all animals, all things. . . ."
>
> —*Kiowa poet and scholar*
> *N. Scott Momaday*

Because Indians had strong spiritual beliefs, religious leaders called shamans wielded great influence. Shamans were said to be able to communicate with the spirit world. They used their knowledge of curative plants to heal disease. They also drove evil spirits—the cause of sickness, according to Indians—from the bodies of sufferers.

CONFLICT OVER LAND USE

The coming of the Europeans to North America would change the land and its people. The

Woodland Indian women from the Mandan tribe bring firewood to a village on the Missouri River. Plains indians moved from their lodges on river bluffs to tree-protected lodges inland during winter. **GEOGRAPHY** Why might Indians have preferred a riverside location in good weather?

This painting by American artist George Catlin shows an Indian shaman. The shaman's fierce costume inspired awe in believers. **CULTURE** How might a European's impression of a shaman have differed from an Indian's impression?

Europeans brought deadly new diseases that killed many Indians. The Europeans brought with them new inventions such as the plow and the gun. These and the European attitude toward land use destroyed the hunting-gathering environment on which Indians depended.

Indian communities were generally neighborly to the first white settlers. The English settlers on the Atlantic Coast, however, did not understand the Indians' use of the woods. For the English, a solidly agricultural people, the best use of land was to improve it by farming. Rather than getting meat and skins through hunting, they raised cattle, sheep, and pigs in enclosed corrals or pastures.

Differences over the meaning of land ownership became a principal source of conflict between the white and Indian cultures. To a white person, land ownership meant controlling what happened to the land. To the Indians, land ownership meant having access to the things on the land during different seasons of the year. No one could own the land itself; a person could only have rights to its produce.

Disagreements between Native Americans and white settlers over land use eventually led to war. The settlers' use of the land threatened the Indian way of life, the very basis of their culture. In the end, the whites won because of their superior numbers and superior technology.

Technology—the use of science to make and to invent things—was the Europeans' ultimate weapon against the Indians. From the beginning of contact the Indians had eagerly traded for such things as steel knives, guns, and iron kettles. They did not, however, learn to produce these items themselves. In time they might have done so. If European technology had changed but slowly, the contact between cultures might have produced strong and independent Indian nations.

By the end of the 1800s, though, the white invaders were using the telegraph for communication, the railroad for transportation, and the steel plow for cutting the prairies. The Indians could not withstand a technology that allowed thousands of people to invade and destroy their hunting grounds. Thus the

Indians have lived in these dwellings in Taos, New Mexico, for more than 1,000 years. The name *Taos*, like so many other place names in the United States, is derived from an Indian word. **HISTORY** What can we learn about a society from the place names it uses?

fast-expanding technology of white people smashed the last resistance of the Indians.

The legacy of the Indians remains, however. It remains in the names of our states, our rivers, our towns. It remains among Indians today who seek to transmit their language, their knowledge, and their world view to their children. It remains in the words of Indians, past and present, who urge people to re-establish a bond with the earth. The words of Chief Seattle in 1854 did not die with him. In addressing the President he said, "Whatever befalls the earth befalls the sons of the earth. Man did not weave the web of life, he is merely a strand in it. Whatever he does to the web, he does to himself."

SECTION REVIEW

1. KEY TERMS social class, slash-and-burn farming, ecology, shaman, technology

2. COMPREHENSION Why were European accounts of Indians sometimes misleading?

3. COMPREHENSION What was the view of Indians regarding ownership of the land?

4. COMPREHENSION What signs of Native American influence remain in the United States today?

5. CRITICAL THINKING Name one advantage of the Indian view of land ownership and one advantage of the European view.

CHAPTER 1 SUMMARY AND TIMELINE

1. The first humans migrated to the Americas thousands of years ago over a land bridge that connected Alaska with Asia. These people, called Paleo-Indians, made tools and weapons out of stone and bone and lived by hunting large game animals. As these game animals became extinct, the Paleo-Indians developed new ways of getting food. They began to hunt smaller game and to gather plant foods that grew wild.

About 5,000 years ago, the Paleo-Indians learned how to farm. This led to the development of village life and the growth of more complex cultures.

2. A wide variety of cultures developed in the Americas over thousands of years. Highly advanced civilizations, including those of the Olmecs, Mayas, Aztecs, and Incas, arose in Mesoamerica and Peru. Indian cultures of the Southwest were influenced by contact with Mesoamerican civilizations. In the Eastern Woodlands, people of the Hopewell and Mississippian cultures developed complex societies based on trade.

3. North American Indians made use of the land and its resources to survive. In general, Indian societies regulated their lives by the seasons and believed that there was a strong spiritual relationship among all living things. Cultural differences between Native Americans and white settlers led eventually to war.

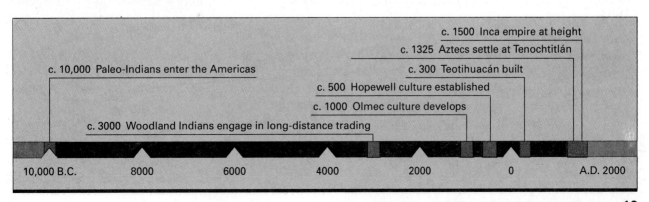

c. 1500 Inca empire at height
c. 1325 Aztecs settle at Tenochtitlán
c. 10,000 Paleo-Indians enter the Americas
c. 300 Teotihuacán built
c. 500 Hopewell culture established
c. 1000 Olmec culture develops
c. 3000 Woodland Indians engage in long-distance trading

| 10,000 B.C. | 8000 | 6000 | 4000 | 2000 | 0 | A.D. 2000 |

Chapter 1 REVIEW

PLACES TO LOCATE

Match the letters on the map with the places listed below. Write your answers on a separate sheet of paper.

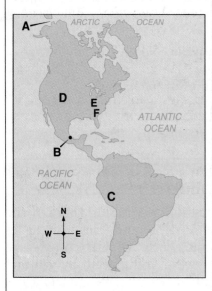

1. Mississippian culture
2. Inca civilization
3. Ice Age land bridge
4. Hopewell culture
5. Anasazi culture
6. Olmec culture

KEY TERMS

Match each of the following terms with its correct definition.

archeologist
artifact
civilization
domestication
ecology
empire
hunter-gatherer
shaman
slash-and-burn farming
tribute

1. Item made by human workmanship.
2. Breeding of animals and plants to meet human needs.
3. Forced payment to a conqueror.
4. Highly developed culture.
5. Relationship between living things and their environment.
6. Indian religious leader.
7. Person who depends on wild animals and plants for food.
8. Method used by Indians to prepare fields for cultivation.
9. Person who studies artifacts to learn about the past.
10. A number of peoples or lands controlled by one ruler or nation.

REVIEWING THE FACTS

1. Where did the first people in the Americas come from? When did they arrive?
2. What change forced the Paleo-Indians to become hunter-gatherers?
3. How and when did agriculture develop in the Americas? How did it change the Indians' way of life?
4. What was the "mother culture" of Mesoamerica?
5. What other civilizations developed in Mesoamerica and in South America?
6. What cultures north of Mexico were influenced by Mesoamerican cultures?
7. What were the distinctive features of the Hopewell and Mississippian cultures?
8. Describe the Indians' view of their relationship with the natural environment.
9. What changes did the Europeans introduce that affected Indians' ways of life?
10. Why did the Europeans defeat the Indians in the battle for control of the Western Hemisphere?

CITIZENSHIP

1. Which members of Maya society had the most power? Why?
2. What determined the amount of authority most Indian chiefs held?
3. How might the role of the individual in Indian society of the 1500s differ from the role of an individual in today's society? Explain your answer.

PRACTICING YOUR SKILL

Read the passage below and answer the questions that follow:

One of the most remarkable aspects of these vanished cultures to us is the lack of any certain evidence of contact between them and the rest of the world; the Incas and their predecessors in the Andes even developed in total isolation from the Aztecs in Mexico and the Maya in the Yucatán.

1. Is the passage from a primary or a secondary source?
2. What does the writer say about contact between Mesoamerican cultures?
3. On what does the writer base this conclusion?
4. Give an example of a primary source which, if discovered, would challenge the writer's conclusion.

CRITICAL THINKING SKILLS

1. ENVIRONMENT Chief Seattle said, "Whatever befalls the earth befalls the sons of the earth. Man did not weave the web of life, he is merely a strand in it." What did he mean? What evidence of his statement do we see today?

2. INFERRING Why does the discovery of artifacts in the graves of Paleo-Indians lead anthropologists to infer that these early Americans believed in an afterlife?

3. RELATING PAST TO PRESENT In this chapter you read about the spread of agriculture in the Western Hemisphere. What are some examples of the spread of knowledge and customs in the world today?

4. PARAPHRASING Reread the paragraphs under the heading "Ancient Woodland Cultures" (pages 10–11). Then tell in your own words the main ideas in those paragraphs.

PROJECTS AND ACTIVITIES

1. CREATING ARTWORK Find pictures or examples of Indian artwork. Use these as a guide to create your own pottery, beadwork, masks, or drawings using Indian themes.

2. WRITING A REPORT Write two paragraphs that describe the conflict between Indians and English settlers over land use. Write the first from the point of view of an Indian chief, the second from the point of view of an English settler.

3. CREATING A POSTER Create a poster that reflects Indian attitudes toward the environment.

WRITING ABOUT TOPICS IN AMERICAN HISTORY

1. CONNECTING WITH LITERATURE A selection from *Great River* by Paul Horgan appears on pages 630–631. Read it and answer the questions. Then write a short essay comparing the role of religion in Pueblo society to its role in the society in which you live.

2. APPLYING THEMES: GLOBAL INTERACTIONS Interactions between peoples sometimes benefit both sides. In the case of the Indians and the Europeans, however, this did not happen. Why?

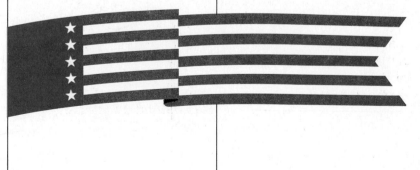

This world map of the 1200s, with Jerusalem at its center, symbolized religion's place in European society. In the 1400s Europe entered an era of new ideas and exploration.

2 Europeans Reach Outward (500–1500)

KEY EVENTS

500	Middle Ages begin
1000	Vikings reach North America
1271	Marco Polo starts his voyage across Asia
1300s	Renaissance begins
1438	Gutenberg invents the printing press
1492	Columbus reaches America
1498	Da Gama finds water route to Asia

1 An Awakening Europe

Section Focus

Key Terms   medieval ■ Middle Ages ■ feudalism ■ vassal ■ serf ■ Moor ■ Holy Land ■ Crusades ■ nationalism ■ Renaissance

Main Idea   Changes in society and pressures from the outside world moved Europe into a new age of exploration and discovery.

Objectives   As you read, look for answers to these questions:
1.   What was European society in the Middle Ages like?
2.   What were the effects of the Crusades?
3.   How did the Renaissance change life in Europe?

A knight there was, and he a worthy man,
Who, from the moment that he first began
To ride about the world, loved chivalry,
Truth, honor, freedom, and all
   courtesy.

Over 600 years ago the English poet Geoffrey Chaucer thus described one member of his society. In his poem *The Canterbury Tales,* Chaucer gives us portraits of 29 pilgrims traveling together to the holy shrine at Canterbury, England. Among the pilgrims are nuns, priests, monks, a merchant, a clerk, a lawyer, a weaver, a dyer, a sailor, a physician, a housewife, a plowman, and a miller. The group forms a cross-section of medieval society in the 1300s. The term *medieval* refers to the Middle Ages, the thousand-year period between A.D. 500 and 1500. The period

begins with the downfall of Rome's classical civilization and ends with the beginning of the modern era.

LIFE A THOUSAND YEARS AGO

The collapse of Rome about A.D. 500 caused the breakdown of order throughout Europe. Tribal chieftains fought over pieces of the once mighty empire. Out of the chaos came the system known as feudalism. In the feudal system, people vowed loyalty to a strong local lord in exchange for land and the lord's protection.

In medieval times there were no nations as we have today. Instead, kings and queens divided their lands among the lords. The lord promised to be loyal to the king or queen. By this promise the lord became a vassal. In turn, the lords had their own vassals. These were the less powerful nobles called knights. At the bottom were the common people. They worked the land for the nobles in exchange for military protection.

In A.D. 1000 most common people were serfs. Serfs were like slaves, except that they could not be bought or sold. Instead they were bound to the manor. The manor was the village and surrounding fields and woods. Serfs were forced to work the fields of the manor and could not leave without the permission of the landlord. The manor was self-sufficient; that is, it produced its own food, tools, and other necessities. There was little trade or contact between the manor and the outside world.

The serfs lived in small cottages in the manor village. The roofs were thatch—straw or twigs bound together tightly. The floor was packed earth. The only furniture might have been a wooden table and stools. People slept on straw mattresses. They cooked food over open fires and ate from dishes made of wood or baked clay. The manor house of the lord was larger and likely made of stone, but it was probably not much more comfortable than a serf's cottage.

THE DEVELOPMENT OF TRADE AND TOWNS

After A.D. 1000, life in Europe began to change. Improvements in farming led to prosperity and a boom in population. These developments, in turn, led to higher demand for goods. Trade increased to meet this demand. Towns arose at the major trading centers—at crossroads or places with good harbors. By the 1100s towns were sprouting up all over Europe.

Life in a medieval town differed greatly from life on a manor. Unlike serfs, townspeople had freedom to travel and make their own laws. Instead of serving a lord, people in towns worked as merchants, moneychangers, and artisans—skilled workers. Artisans practiced a variety of trades, from shoemaking and weaving to baking and metalwork.

Artisans and other townspeople did not fit the old categories of peasants and nobles. These merchants and tradespeople formed a new social class—the "middle class." This meant that they had more money and education than most serfs and ordinary laborers but less than most nobles. The pilgrims in Chaucer's *Canterbury Tales* include members of this new middle class.

THE IMPORTANCE OF RELIGION

Chaucer's *Canterbury Tales* tells us something else about Europe in the Middle Ages. Most people were faithful members of the Roman Catholic Church. People devoted much time to worship, to the celebration of holy days, and to pilgrimages to holy places. In fact, religion was so important that the Middle Ages are often called the Age of Faith.

The great wealth and power of the Church placed it at the center of medieval life. Few tasks, whether kingly or lowly, were done without the approval of the Church. All education took place within the Church. The Church also inspired an outpouring of music, art, literature, and architecture. The artistic glory of the Middle Ages was the Gothic cathedral, whose spires soared toward the heavens.

THREATS FROM ABROAD

War or the threat of war was a constant feature of medieval life. European kingdoms continually fought each other for power and territory. They also faced invasions by warriors from other lands.

This seal of the city of Bergen, Norway, shows a Viking vessel. HISTORY What hardships might Vikings have faced traveling long distances in these boats?

A halo of flame surrounds Mohammed's head in this painting of the founder of Islam. The prophet wears a veil because Islam disapproves of portraits showing the face of a holy person. **RELIGION** What other traditions influenced Islamic teachings?

From the north came the Vikings—ancestors of today's Norwegians, Swedes, and Danes. The Vikings sailed skillfully in open boats powered by sails and oars. Viking raids terrorized settlements along the coasts of western Europe. The Vikings also sailed into the Atlantic Ocean and settled on Iceland and Greenland. From Greenland, in about A.D. 1000, Viking adventurers explored the coast of North America, which they called *Vinland.*

The Vikings remained in Vinland for several years. Then, for unknown reasons, they left their settlements and returned home. Few Europeans even heard about the Viking voyages to North America. Even if they had, it is not clear that they would have cared. Most Europeans a thousand years ago were more concerned with earning a place in heaven than finding a new place on earth.

Another threat to Europe came from the south, where the armies of a new religion fought to spread their faith. Early in the seventh century, an Arab merchant named Mohammed had rejected the many gods most Arabs then believed in. Instead he began to preach that there was but one God, and that he, Mohammed, was God's messenger. Mohammed's teachings had roots in Hebrew, Christian, and Arab traditions. He gained many followers, known as Muslims. Muslim is the Arabic word for *one who submits* (to God). Their religion became known as Islam—Arabic for *submission.*

Propelled by a sense of unity and religious strength, Muslims launched holy wars against their neighbors and converted them to Islam. The pace of Islamic expansion was breathtaking. A mere hundred years after Mohammed's death in 632, Muslims known as Moors had conquered North Africa and the part of western Europe that is now Spain.

THE CRUSADES

Muslim armies also captured the Holy Land—the area of the Middle East where Jesus Christ had lived. Christians often made the long trip to the Holy Land for religious reasons. For Islam, which shares some beliefs with Christianity, the area was also holy.

For centuries after the Muslim conquest, Christians continued to visit the Holy Land. Around 1070, however, Muslims began to limit Christian pilgrims' access to the Holy Land. In 1095 the Pope, head of the Roman Catholic Church, called on Christians to make war on the Muslims and recapture the Holy Land. Europeans responded with enthusiasm. Filled with religious spirit and the desire for conquest, they marched east to fight the Muslims.

These military expeditions against the Muslims were called Crusades. Four separate Crusades spanned slightly over a century. The Crusades failed, and the Holy Land remained under Muslim control. Still, contact between Europe and the East changed history in important ways.

European Crusaders often took months to prepare for the long trip to the Holy Land. The different flags and crests on this ship showed that several noble families sponsored this voyage. TECHNOLOGY How was the vessel powered? What shows that the Crusaders are going off to war?

The Crusades drew thousands of Europeans to the lands east of the Mediterranean Sea. There they became familiar with foods, medicines, and other goods that were very rare and expensive in Europe. Some came from as far away as China. From China Europeans discovered silk and new dyes, as well as the ceramic dishes they called "china." Spices such as pepper, nutmeg, cloves, cinnamon, and ginger were among the most sought-after goods from the East. Europeans were used to bland food, and spices added delicious flavor. Most importantly, at a time before refrigeration, spices helped keep food from spoiling.

TRADER MARCO POLO

After they returned home, Crusaders continued to buy eastern goods. They got them from Italian merchants who had traded in the East for some time. These merchants exchanged European leather, tin, and woolen cloth for Asian spices, silks, and jewels.

The most famous of Italy's merchants was Marco Polo. When he was only seventeen, Marco Polo's father and uncle took him on an overland journey to China. Marco Polo lived and traveled in Asia for 24 years, from 1271 to 1295.

After his return home, Marco Polo told his adventures to a writer. Their book described the treasures Marco Polo had seen: splendid carpets, precious stones, and fine weapons. At the time, few Europeans believed Marco Polo. Imagine a black stone (coal) that burned! Imagine a parade of 5,000 elephants, each draped in cloth of silk and gold!

THE DECLINE OF FEUDALISM

The growth of trade and the rise of towns during the Middle Ages had an important result: they weakened the feudal system. Many serfs ran away from the manors to live in the towns. To keep laborers on the land, lords began to contract with them. As a result, hired labor began to replace serf labor. Manors also became less self-sufficient as lords relied more and more on trade with townspeople. As a result, the nobility began to lose power. At the same time, the townspeople became more influential.

As feudal lords lost their power, strong monarchs—kings and queens with great authority—emerged in Europe. Rulers in

England, France, and Portugal built especially strong governments. Under the feudal system, power had been shared among many lords. Now power began to concentrate at the center of these governments—the monarch's court. This type of government is called centralized government.

The newly powerful monarchs won the support of townspeople because they could raise large armies to enforce order. As countries became more unified, people could safely travel and trade flourished. For the first time in history, Europeans experienced a feeling of nationalism—love for and loyalty to one's country. European monarchs, with their subjects' support, sought to strengthen their countries by gaining influence in other parts of the world.

A New Spirit of Curiosity

As the medieval world expanded, a spirit of curiosity arose. Scholars eagerly read the writings from ancient Greece and Rome. Thinkers spoke in praise of human achievements. Leon Battista Alberti, an Italian writer, architect, and mathematician, declared, "Men can do all things if they will." Artists began drawing plants, animals, and people as they really looked. With support from wealthy businessmen, artists such as Leonardo da Vinci and Michelangelo Buonarroti created beautiful works of art. Also, contacts with Islamic culture in Spain brought Europeans greater knowledge of science, philosophy, and medicine.

This period of scientific curiosity, return to classical learning, and praise of humanity

Marco Polo, born in the trading center of Venice, astounded Europe with his tales of Asia. He not only visited the Chinese court, below, but toured Southeast Asia and India as well.
CULTURAL PLURALISM Why were most Europeans of the time unfamiliar with Asian cultures?

This painting, *The School of Athens,* by Renaissance artist Raphael, recalls the grandeur of classical Greece. The diagram (inset) shows how lines within the painting give the impression of depth and distance. CULTURE What other images in the painting give it a sense of depth?

came to be called the Renaissance (reh–nuh–SAHNS). Renaissance is a French term meaning "rebirth." The start of the Renaissance in northern Italy in the 1300s marked the beginnings of the modern age.

The growth of knowledge was fed by a new invention, the printing press. Around 1438 Johannes Gutenberg, a German goldsmith, invented a press that used movable metal type. No longer was it necessary to copy a book by hand. No longer was a book a rare treasure available only to a few. With the printing press, books could be made more quickly and cheaply. As books became available, new ideas and information spread quickly. One of the most popular new books was *The Travels of Marco Polo.* By now Europeans were interested in faraway places. They were ready to believe Marco Polo's tales.

SECTION REVIEW

1. KEY TERMS medieval, Middle Ages, feudalism, vassal, serf, Moor, Holy Land, Crusades, nationalism, Renaissance

2. PEOPLE AND PLACES Chaucer, Mohammed, Johannes Gutenberg, Marco Polo, Vikings, Vinland

3. COMPREHENSION Describe how the Crusades affected trade between Europe and Asia.

4. COMPREHENSION What factors led to the end of feudalism? What changes resulted from the rise of centralized government?

5. CRITICAL THINKING In what ways was the Renaissance an age of discovery? Why might some periods of history be full of discovery and not other periods?

2 The Search for New Sea Routes

Section Focus

Key Terms joint-stock company ■ capital ■ monopoly ■ profits ■ navigator ■ caravel

Main Idea The growth of trade led to a new economic system in Europe. Competition for trade routes increased knowledge of world geography.

Objectives As you read, look for answers to these questions:
1. Why did Europeans seek new sea routes to Asia?
2. What discoveries made voyages of exploration possible?

Imagine the boot shape in the Mediterranean Sea that is Italy. Then imagine boot straps high up on each side of the boot. The easternmost boot strap marks the location of Venice. The westernmost boot strap marks the location of Genoa. In the 1400s these two cities were among the richest and most powerful cities in Europe, for the Mediterranean Sea was the "crossroads" of the western world.

NEW FORMS OF FINANCE

Both Genoa and Venice were self-governing cities, or city-states. Both had grown from fishing villages into sea powers and trading states. Since the 1300s both cities had traded with Asian lands. They became gateways through which rare goods—spices, dyes, African wool, gold, and silks—reached the far corners of Europe.

Italian merchants needed large amounts of money to finance the growing trade. This need led to a revolution in how business was done. Venetian and Genoese bankers devised a new form of business arrangement: the joint-stock company. The joint-stock company made it possible to accumulate a large amount of capital, or money for investment, because a number of people pooled their

Genoese bankers, shown counting coins at left, were among the first in Europe. The walled city of Genoa, shown at right, had previously relied on the industries of fishing and trade for its great wealth. **ECONOMICS** How had Genoa become an important trading center? Why might a trading center have been a center of banking as well?

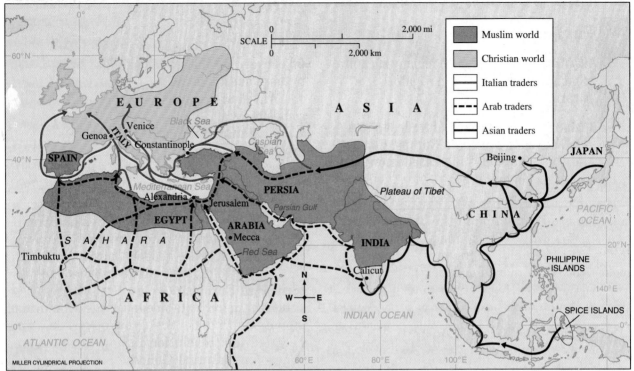

MAP SKILLS By the 1400s the Italian trading cities controlled trade in the Mediterranean Sea. What traders dominated trade in the Muslim world? What Asian countries supplied trade goods to Europe? **CRITICAL THINKING** Why was the Mediterranean crucial to world trade during the Middle Ages?

funds. By the mid-1400s, Genoa's Bank of St. George had branches throughout Europe.

RIVALRY OVER TRADE

Unlike Marco Polo, most Italian merchants did not actually go to Asia themselves. Instead they bought goods from Muslim traders who traveled to China, India, and other distant lands.

The Italians had persuaded Muslim traders to do business only with them. This gave the Italians a **monopoly** on the Asian trade. A monopoly is complete control over a product or service.

Other European countries envied the Italian cities. The Italians sold Asian goods for much more than they paid. As a result they made huge **profits**—money left after costs are paid. Merchants in other parts of Europe had no chance to share in the trade routes monopolized by the Italians. If, however, they

could discover another way to reach Asia, they too might become wealthy and powerful.

PORTUGUESE DISCOVERIES

Portugal led the search for new routes to Asia. The Portuguese king was one of the monarchs whose power had grown with the decline of feudalism. Early in the 1400s Prince Henry, the king's third son, began to challenge the unknown ocean that lapped Portugal's coastline. At the time, many people believed that the sea boiled at the equator, and so would the blood of any man who dared cross it. The ocean, they also thought, teemed with ferocious sea monsters.

Prince Henry wanted to find out more about the ocean for several reasons:

(1) He hoped to find an all-water route to the trading centers of Asia. This would break Italy's monopoly on trade with the East. It could help Portugal get rich.

(2) A powerful navy would help him defeat Muslim forces in North Africa.

(3) He wished to spread Christianity beyond Europe's borders.

(4) As a child of the Renaissance, he also wanted to learn more about the ocean and the lands that lay beyond it.

Henry began sending ships south from Portugal down the coast of Africa. Prince Henry did not actually sail with the Portuguese expeditions himself. Because he sponsored them, however, he became known as Henry the Navigator. A navigator is someone who knows the science of sailing ships.

To his seaside castle Henry invited geographers, astronomers, mapmakers, and sailors. These scientists reviewed each expedition's reports. Then they drew charts that allowed each expedition to go a little farther than the one before. No Europeans realized at the time just how huge the African continent is. It took courage to continue sailing south along what seemed like a never-ending coast.

Sailors were aided by improvements in navigation. Since the 1100s, sailors had known how to use compasses. These devices, invented by the Chinese, told sailors in which direction their ship was heading. But sailors also needed to know their location at sea. Henry's scientists helped develop the art of celestial navigation—navigating by the stars. They also rediscovered the astrolabe (AS–truh–layb), a navigational instrument known to the ancient Greeks. With these new tools to guide them, captains dared to sail into unknown waters.

Henry's shipbuilders also designed a double-rigged ship, the caravel. With triangular sails it could sail into the wind, and with square sails it could sail with the wind at its back. Such a ship gave sailors confidence. They knew they could get home again no matter how the winds blew.

PORTUGAL AND AFRICA

Portuguese ships continued to explore southward along the West African coast. Sailors learned about vast and rich kingdoms in

By the 1400s, the Kingdom of Benin had a rich artistic tradition that included wood and ivory sculpture as well as bronzework. CULTURE How does this carving show that the artist was familiar with the Portuguese?

West Africa. For centuries these kingdoms, such as Songhai (SONG–hy), Benin (beh–NEEN), Kongo, and Mali, had been trading with Muslims in North Africa (map, page 32). The centers of trade were Timbuktu and Gao, cities in the Mali kingdom on the Niger River. In Timbuktu, Africans exchanged bronzework from Benin and gold and cotton from Mali for salt, cloth, and copper from the north. Timbuktu also boasted a university where African Muslims studied subjects such as mathematics and religion.

The Portuguese found that people on the west coast of Africa were willing to trade with them. At first the Portuguese traded mostly for gold and ivory. By the early 1440s, however, they began to trade for slaves.

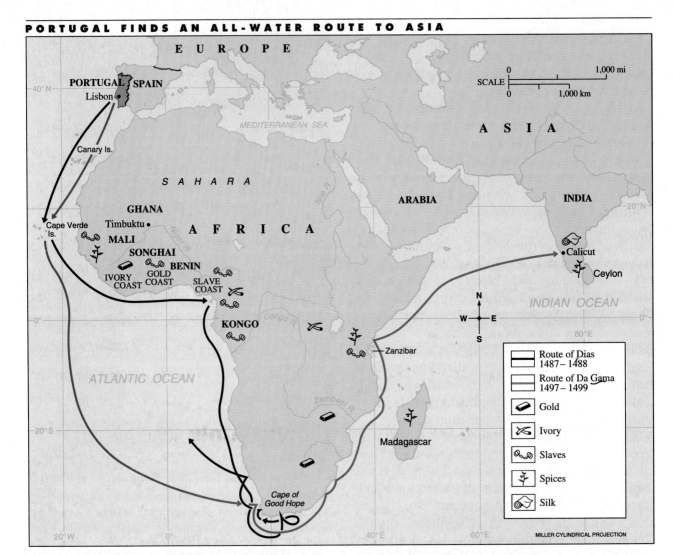

MAP SKILLS Portugal's route to the East bypassed Arab and Italian traders. **CRITICAL THINKING** How might Portugal's location have contributed to its discovery of this route?

Certain African peoples made slaves of prisoners of war. They used these slaves themselves and also sold them to Arabs who took them to be sold in Asia. Portuguese expeditions trading with the kingdom of Benin bought pepper, cotton cloth, ivory, and African slaves, and took them back to Europe. The Portuguese hoped that the sale of these slaves in Europe would help pay the cost of their voyages. They also wanted to use slaves as cheap labor on Portuguese farms. By the time of Prince Henry's death in 1460, almost 1,000 slaves were brought to Portugal each year. Other European nations soon followed Portugal into the slave trade.

A WATER ROUTE TO ASIA

Henry died before the first Portuguese sailing expedition crossed the equator in 1473. Then, in 1487, Bartolomeu Dias (DEE–ahs) sailed around the tip of Africa. The new king of Portugal hoped that Dias had found a route to India. So he named the tip of Africa the Cape of Good Hope.

In 1498 another Portuguese explorer, Vasco da Gama (DUH GAM–uh), fulfilled the king's hope. Da Gama followed Dias's route around the Cape of Good Hope and then continued north along the eastern coast of Africa. Then, turning east, he sailed across the Indian Ocean until he reached India.

Finally, the Portuguese had found an all-water route to Asia! The prediction of immense profits from the Asia trade proved true. Da Gama sailed home with a shipload of spices, silks, and jewels worth 6 times what the voyage had cost.

Transporting goods by water cost less than long overland voyages using caravans of pack animals. Italian merchants bought their goods from traders who traveled by land. Therefore, Portuguese merchants could sell goods from the East more cheaply than the Italians could. Portugal quickly became the leader in the rich Eastern trade. In the early 1500s Lisbon, Portugal's capital, became the richest port in Europe. Soon, however, Spain and other European nations would challenge Portugal's lead.

SECTION REVIEW

1. KEY TERMS joint-stock company, capital, monopoly, profits, navigator, caravel

2. PEOPLE AND PLACES Venice, Portugal, Henry the Navigator, Bartolomeu Dias, Vasco da Gama, Cape of Good Hope, Lisbon

3. COMPREHENSION What false ideas about geography did people have in 1400? How did Prince Henry try to learn more about geography?

4. COMPREHENSION Why did Portugal engage in the slave trade?

5. CRITICAL THINKING How might the Italian cities' monopoly on overland trade have hurt their interests in the long run?

3 The Achievement of Christopher Columbus

Section Focus

Key Term *Reconquista*

Main Idea Spain's desire to gain wealth and to spread the Catholic religion led it to support a voyage of exploration by Christopher Columbus.

Objectives As you read, look for answers to these questions:
1. What changes were going on in Europe at the time of Columbus's birth?
2. What did Columbus learn that prepared him for his momentous voyage?
3. Why did Ferdinand and Isabella decide to finance Columbus's voyage?

Christopher Columbus grew up in the Italian city-state of Genoa. Although his father and grandfather were wool weavers, Columbus was drawn to the city's busy waterfront. At age 14 he began going on trading voyages. One such voyage would change his destiny. Columbus was 25 when his ship was sunk by a hostile fleet off the coast of Portugal. He survived by holding on to an oar and swimming to shore. Once there, Columbus made his way to Lisbon, where his brother worked as a mapmaker. In Lisbon he would acquire the knowledge that would lead him west across the Atlantic.

COLUMBUS'S EDUCATION
Columbus learned mapmaking from his brother and taught himself to read and write Spanish. He also learned Latin, the language of most books at the time. Among the books he read were the works of Ptolemy, a mathematician and geographer from ancient Greece. Columbus also read *The Travels of Marco Polo*. Marco Polo's tales of the wealth

The voyages of Columbus linked Europe and the Americas and changed the world forever. This portrait of Columbus is one of the many that exist, but the great explorer looks different in each one. **TECHNOLOGY** What inventions helped Columbus make his revolutionary voyage?

Columbus also learned the practical skills of deep-sea navigation. He sailed south with a Portuguese fleet to Guinea on Africa's Gold Coast. During the voyage Columbus gained experience in sailing a caravel. Columbus also noticed that the winter winds off North Africa blew from the east. That observation would help ensure his future success.

COLUMBUS'S VISION

Within ten years of his soggy arrival on the Portuguese coast, Columbus formed the idea that became his life's passion: Why not sail *west* around the world to reach the Indies? (The Indies was the term used to describe the lands of the Far East.) At one time, many people believed that the earth was flat. By the 1400s, however, most educated Europeans knew that the earth was round. It made sense that by heading west, a ship would eventually circle the globe and arrive in the east. But as far as Europeans knew, no one had tried such a voyage before. The Viking voyages had been forgotten.

The globes and geographic calculations showed, however, that the ocean was too vast to cross. Columbus took heart from Biblical teachings, which stated that God made the world six parts land and one part water. From this, Columbus decided that the ocean was not nearly as wide as people supposed. The riches of the Indies lay, he said, not too far west across the ocean.

In 1484 Columbus approached the king of Portugal with his idea. The king's scientists found his math faulty. More importantly, the Portuguese were making good progress exploring the African coast and were not to be distracted. Neither was Columbus. He believed that God intended him to make great discoveries in order to spread Christianity. As one writer put it, he "had developed in his heart the unshakable conviction that he would find what he said he would find, as if he had it locked away in a trunk somewhere."

Columbus took his son Diego and went to neighboring Spain. There he talked with King Ferdinand and Queen Isabella about his

and wonders of Asia sparked Columbus's imagination. Columbus was particularly excited by his description of Japan, which was based only on hearsay and rumor. "Many of the apartments" Marco Polo wrote, "have small tables of pure gold of considerable thickness." He also claimed that the entire roof of the sovereign's palace was covered with a plating of gold.

Columbus had landed in the best place in the world to learn ocean navigation. Yet Portugal's navigational knowledge was considered a state secret. By marrying the daughter of a Portuguese sea captain, however, Columbus received the equivalent of a top-secret security clearance. He pored over his father-in-law's charts and maps. In this way, Columbus learned of the advances Portugal had made in exploration.

ideas. The monarchs were interested in the proposed voyage. They saw that it might bring Spain both gold and a jump on Portugal, its rival. Isabella, a fervently religious Catholic, also believed it was the duty of the Spanish to spread Christianity to other parts of the world.

The time, however, was not yet right. Ferdinand and Isabella were fighting to expel the Moors (North African Muslims) from the city of Granada, their last stronghold in Spain. The struggle to win back Spain was known as the *Reconquista* (ray–kahn–KEES–tah)—Spanish for "reconquest." The *Reconquista* had occupied Ferdinand and Isabella's ancestors for 800 years, and they were set on completing the job.

In 1492, after six years of waiting, Columbus was about to give up on Spain and offer his services to France. At last, however, Ferdinand and Isabella's armies took Granada and defeated the Moors. The monarchs had achieved their dream of an entirely Christian Spain. The king and queen were now ready to consider Columbus's dream. Isabella summoned Columbus and began negotiations.

Columbus proved a hard bargainer. This weaver's son insisted on being promoted to the nobility and given a coat of arms. He demanded the right to rule any lands he conquered. He asked for 10 percent of all wealth from those lands, and the grand title of Admiral of the Ocean Sea. After three months, the king and queen agreed to these demands. "You are going at our command," the monarchs told Columbus, "to discover and subdue the islands and continent in the ocean. It is only just and reasonable that since you expose yourself to danger to serve us, you should be rewarded for it."

> **"West; nothing to the north, nothing to the south."**
>
> —*Columbus to his crew*

With confidence and energy Columbus assembled his expedition at the Spanish port of Palos. At dawn on Friday, August 3, 1492, three ships—the *Niña* (NEE–nyah), *Pinta,* and *Santa María*—left the harbor on a southwest course. Columbus wanted to reach the latitudes where, he remembered, the winds blew toward the west. In the Canary Islands to the west of Morocco, he restocked his ships with wood, water, and meat. Then he gave his crew the course: "West; nothing to the north, nothing to the south." The great voyage had begun.

COLUMBUS'S DISCOVERY

Columbus and his crew of about 90 sailors, many of them teenagers, had a long and difficult voyage. Conditions were rough. Cooking was done on the ship's decks. Only a few officers had bunks. Nor did the low pay they received—about $10 per month—make the sailors any happier.

As the voyage went on, the crew grew nervous. Many began to fear they would never see Spain again. Columbus began to keep a false record. It showed the ships' daily progress to be less than it really was. Columbus kept the true distance from Spain to himself. Even this trick was not enough to calm the sailors. On October 10, after ten weeks at sea, the crew requested that Columbus turn back. Columbus convinced them to sail west for three more days. Just after midnight on October 12, the lookout on the *Pinta* sighted land.

BIOGRAPHY

ISABELLA OF CASTILE (1451–1504), strong-principled and visionary, at seventeen negotiated her marriage to Ferdinand of Aragon. With this union and the expulsion of the Moors, Isabella saw a united Spain. Her sponsorship of Columbus launched the Spanish empire.

N.C. Wyeth, an American illustrator of the early 1900s, drew this picture of Columbus and his crew as they might have appeared when they first landed on American soil. **NATIONAL IDENTITY** How does the story of Columbus's voyage reflect values Americans cherish?

No one is sure exactly where Columbus landed. It may have been Samana Cay, a tiny island in the Bahamas. Columbus named the island San Salvador. Here, Columbus saw no golden palaces or people wearing fine silks and jewels. Instead Columbus observed simple grass houses and people with few clothes at all.

Believing in error that the golden-roofed palaces of Japan glittered nearby, Columbus zigzagged through the Caribbean Sea in search of the lands Marco Polo had glowingly described. Columbus found no evidence of great cities. He did, however, find the islands and their inhabitants impressive in other ways. "The lands are all very beautiful," he reported. There were beautiful trees and birds "of a thousand sorts." The earth held "many mines of metals and there was a population of incalculable number. The people have no other weapons than the stems of reeds. . . . They are incurably timid. . . . They believe very firmly that I, with these ships and crews, came from the sky."

Columbus finally found enough gold on the island of Hispaniola (his–puhn–YO–luh) to convince himself that he indeed had reached Asia. He did not realize that he had landed at the edge of the continents of North America and South America. Indeed, he did not suspect that these continents even existed. In January 1493 he sailed homeward with hopeful reports for King Ferdinand and Queen Isabella.

Columbus was still determined to claim Asia's riches for Spain. He persuaded Ferdinand and Isabella to sponsor another voyage late in 1493. Twice more in later years, Columbus led Spanish fleets across the Atlantic Ocean. On these journeys he landed at islands in the Caribbean Sea. Although Columbus never saw North America, he sailed along the coasts of South and Central America. With each trip, Europeans gained more knowledge of the newly found lands.

SECTION REVIEW

1. KEY TERM *Reconquista*

2. PEOPLE AND PLACES Genoa, Christopher Columbus, King Ferdinand, Queen Isabella, Guinea, Gold Coast, Palos, Hispaniola

3. COMPREHENSION On what ideas did Christopher Columbus base his plans for reaching Asia?

4. COMPREHENSION Why did Spain decide to support Columbus's voyage?

5. CRITICAL THINKING What Renaissance ideas probably influenced Columbus? Explain your answer.

In building their pictures of the past, historians constantly ask the question *Why?* For example, when studying the European exploration of the Americas, historians might ask: *Why did some Europeans want to undertake such dangerous voyages?* or *Why did Spain lead in the colonization of the Americas?* or *What did the Europeans do once they had arrived in the Americas?* By asking such questions, historians are using **cause-and-effect reasoning**. This skill is essential to the study of history.

A cause is something that produces an event or development. An effect is the development produced by the cause. For example, because Italy had a monopoly on overland trade with the East, Portugal searched for alternative routes by water. This cause-and-effect relationship can be shown in the following diagram.

Italy monopolizes overland trade (Cause)	→	Portugal searches for sea route to Asia (Effect)

When reading history books, remember to look for language clues that indicate cause-and-effect relationships. The list that follows gives some examples of these words and phrases.

as a result	for this reason
because	led to
brought about	produced
caused	therefore
followed from	thus

Sometimes one effect may itself become the cause of another effect. This kind of cause-and-effect relationship is shown in the following diagram.

Cause	→	Effect / Cause	→	Effect

Such relationships may become clear only after many years have passed. Therefore, historians interested in causes and effects may have to study the periods long before and long after an event. Often they discover that several causes, or **multiple** causes, combined to produce a single effect. Similarly, a single cause may produce more than one effect. Multiple cause-and-effect relationships are shown in the next diagram.

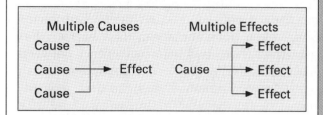

Multiple Causes
Cause ┐
Cause → Effect
Cause ┘

Multiple Effects
Cause → Effect, Effect, Effect

PRACTICING YOUR SKILL

Each statement below contains a cause and an effect. On a separate sheet of paper, make each statement into a cause-and-effect diagram by writing the cause on the left and the effect on the right, with an arrow connecting them. Remember, the cause may not be stated first in the sentence.

1. Contact with the East during the Crusades increased Europeans' demand for eastern goods.

2. The growth of trade along with the rise of towns and cities weakened the European feudal system.

3. Powerful monarchs won the support of townspeople because they could raise large armies to protect towns.

4. Renewed interest in classical civilization and contact with foreign lands helped produce the Renaissance in Europe.

5. Explorers could travel across the Atlantic Ocean because of improved navigational instruments.

4 In the Wake of Columbus

The first voyage of Christopher Columbus was remarkable in part because of all the changes it caused. For centuries Europeans had looked upon the ocean as a barrier. For centuries there had been no contact between Europe and the Western Hemisphere. With one voyage, Columbus changed that. The Atlantic Ocean became a "bridge" instead of a barrier.

Across this bridge Europeans transferred their culture to the Americas. Because Spain had sponsored Columbus, much of the Western Hemisphere would become Spanish in language and Catholic in religion. The mark of Spain on North and South America would be permanent.

THE COLUMBIAN EXCHANGE

Spanish settlers took not only their language and religion to the new lands but also their plants and animals. The first ships carried wheat and fruit trees. Later voyages brought domesticated animals such as horses, cattle, sheep, goats, and pigs. Thus, Europeans enlarged the food supply of the land they called "the New World." Besides plants and animals, Europeans also unknowingly carried diseases that killed millions of Indians. This transfer of plants, animals, and diseases from one hemisphere to another has been called the **Columbian exchange**, after Christopher Columbus.

On their return voyages Europeans carried back food plants that were unique to the Western Hemisphere. The foodstuffs of the Americas had been carefully developed by In-dian farmers. They eventually changed diets around the world and helped feed a rapidly growing world population. The poor of Europe were the first to accept the strange food plants from across the seas. In the 1600s the availability of corn ended the recurring famines in northern Italy. The use of potatoes, too, spread wherever there was a threat of famine. By the 1700s potatoes had become a staple food for Irish peasants.

Foods from the Americas would also become staples in the African diet. These included corn, manioc (a starchy root), peanuts, and sweet potatoes. In Asia, too, people made chili peppers, peanuts, and tomatoes part of their everyday meals. Other products grown first by Indians include chocolate, tobacco, and rubber.

The Columbian exchange had a devastating impact on the Indians. Indians had had no contact with diseases that were common in Europe. These included chicken pox, measles, smallpox, and flu. As a result, Indians had no immunity to these diseases. What was an ordinary case of flu to a European meant certain death for an Indian. These diseases spread to Indians who had never met a European. Death rates among Indians from European diseases climbed to 90 percent. Altogether, the Indian population of North America would drop from about 11 million in 1500 to about half a million by 1900.

A Kiowa Indian folk story from the 1800s captures some of the horror of the new diseases. The hero of the story is named Sayn-

Causes

◆ Renaissance spirit of curiosity
◆ Search for new trade routes
◆ Desire for adventure, glory, and riches
◆ Search for converts to Christianity

European Exploration (1400 – 1600)

Effects

◆ Europeans reach the Americas
◆ European settlement of the Americas
◆ Expanded knowledge of world geography
◆ Development of trade and growth of the middle class
◆ Conflict with American Indians

CHART SKILLS

Voyages of exploration dramatically changed the course of world history. **CRITICAL THINKING** Explain why European global exploration took place when it did, and not at some other period in history.

day. Off across the prairie, Saynday saw a dark spot coming toward him from the east, moving very slowly. After a while, Saynday saw that it was a man on a horse.

"Who are you?" the stranger asked.
"I'm Saynday. . . . Who are you?"
"I'm Smallpox. . . . I come from far away, across the eastern ocean. I am one with the white men—they are my people as the Kiowas are yours. Sometimes I travel ahead of them, and sometimes I lurk behind. But I am always their companion and you will find me in their camps and in their houses."

When Saynday asked Smallpox what he did, the horseman, who was dressed in black and spotted with red dust, had an answer. "I bring death. My breath causes children to wither like young plants in spring snow. . . . No people who have looked on me will ever be the same."

COLUMBUS AS COLONIZER

Today Columbus is honored for having had the courage, the skill, and the broad vision necessary to have made his daring voyage. Despite errors in navigation, he succeeded in reaching the Americas and returning home. Like other Europeans of his day, however, Columbus displayed narrow religious and racial views. He believed the Indians to be a simple people who would make good servants and who would benefit from Christianity, for he believed them to have no religion.

Columbus, in short, believed that Europeans were superior to Indians. This prejudice had terrible results. As the first ruler of Hispaniola, Columbus set the policies that killed or enslaved untold numbers of Indians.

On his first voyage Columbus had kidnapped several Taino Indians to take to Spain. He had already decided that the Indians "should make good servants" for they were "meek and without knowledge of evil." On his return to Hispaniola, Columbus sailed with 17 ships filled with about 1,200 men.

These men wished to settle in the lands Columbus had discovered. These settlers were known as colonists—people who leave their own country to settle and govern in another land.

COLUMBUS'S DOWNFALL

On his second voyage, Columbus carried instructions from Ferdinand and Isabella. They said that he should "treat the Indians very well and affectionately without causing them any annoyance whatever. . . ." Furthermore, Columbus was to "mete out severe punishment" to anyone who did mistreat the Indians.

Instead, Columbus rounded up enough Indians to fill twelve ships and sent them to Spain to be sold as slaves. He said that they were cannibals. He also suggested to the monarchs that shipments of slaves would pay for the cattle and other provisions the Spanish colonists needed.

The Taino Indians of Hispaniola finally revolted against mistreatment by the Spanish. Columbus's men then attacked them with crossbows, guns, and ferocious dogs.

At first Columbus had tricked the monarchs into thinking that the Indians he sent back as slaves were cannibals or prisoners of war. He went too far, however, when he gave colonists returning to Spain gifts of Indian slaves. "By what authority does the Admiral give my vassals to anyone?" demanded an angry Isabella. She ordered the Indians to be returned to their homeland as free people. As for Columbus, it was the end of his rule. His Crown-appointed successor sent him home in chains. Although later freed, Columbus was never again allowed to set foot on Hispaniola.

DEBATE OVER INDIAN SLAVERY

Despite Queen Isabella's concern, and particularly after her death in 1504, Spanish colonists continued to enslave the Indians. They did so as part of the encomienda system. By this system the Crown granted land to loyal colonists and also gave them Indians as laborers for a specific number of days each year. In exchange for encomiendas, the colonists promised to convert the Indians to Christianity, protect them, and look after their needs.

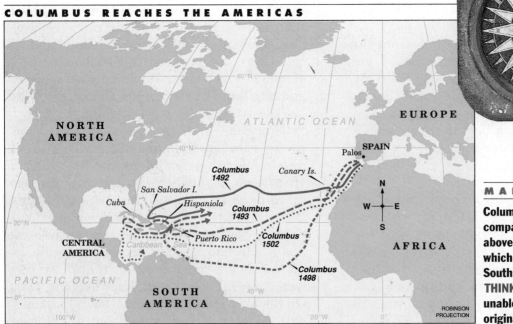

COLUMBUS REACHES THE AMERICAS

MAP SKILLS

Columbus relied on a compass, such as the one above, for navigation. On which voyage did he reach South America? CRITICAL THINKING Why was he unable to reach Asia as originally planned?

In reality, the colonists often mistreated the Indians. The Europeans saw the native peoples of the Americas as their inferiors. Many did not even believe Indians were human beings. The encomienda system bound the Indians for life to the colonists who owned the land that had once been theirs.

> ## "We came here to serve God, and also to get rich."
>
> —*Spanish adventurer*

Christianizing the Indians was a powerful motive for the colonists. So was gold. The Spaniard Bernal Diáz said it best: "We came here to serve God, and also to get rich."

LAS CASAS AND THE INDIANS

But how can you serve God and enslave the Indians? A young priest giving a sermon on Hispaniola in 1511 posed this question. Most colonists, including a landowner named Bartolomé de Las Casas, were shocked at his daring. Las Casas too had an encomienda, with slaves who worked in the mines and fields. Then in 1514 Las Casas had a deep spiritual change. Reading his Bible, and perhaps remembering the young friar's sermon, he decided "that everything done to the Indians thus far was unjust and tyrannical." He freed his Indians and became a friar himself. For the next 50 years Las Casas fought against those who abused the Indians.

The debate over the Indians centered on several issues. First, what was the nature of the Indians? Las Casas saw them as "simple people without evil." Others saw them as "naturally lazy and vicious . . . cowardly, and in general a lying, shiftless people." Second, what was the best way to Christianize them? For Las Casas, the answer was clear—peaceful persuasion. His opponents argued it would be easier to conquer the Indians and then spread the faith. Third, were the Indians naturally meant to be slaves? Las Casas answered with a ringing no. "Mankind is one," he said, "and all men are alike in that which concerns their creation. . . ."

The views of Las Casas helped convince the Pope to forbid Indian slavery. The encomienda system was replaced by a similar but more closely regulated system of forced labor. These changes did not take place until after the Spanish had conquered the Caribbean and much of the American mainland.

AFRICAN SLAVES IN THE WEST INDIES

In their fight against the Moors, Spain's nobles had developed certain values. First, they glorified warfare. Second, they looked down on manual work. Members of the lower order of the nobility—the hidalgos—would rather starve than till fields. Thus, they depended on slaves to provide the labor.

Spanish colonists in the West Indies needed large numbers of laborers for their farms, mines, and mills. After they had wiped out

---

BIOGRAPHY

BARTOLOMÉ DE LAS CASAS (1474–1566) came to Spanish America when he was 28 years old and was probably the first priest to be ordained there. Known as the "Apostle of the Indies" because of his efforts to help the Indians, he wrote a book which describes how cruelly the Spanish slaveowners treated the Indians.

the Indians with cruel treatment and disease, the colonists had to look elsewhere for laborers. They turned first to white slaves from Spain and then to Christian black slaves.

The demand for cheap labor continued to grow, however, because of the growing demand for sugar. Sugar cane was one of the sure roads to wealth for a colonial landowner. Growing and refining sugar cane, however, required a great amount of manual labor. For the sake of its sugar plantations, Spain agreed to allow direct trade in African slaves. As a result, there were 100,000 African slave laborers in the West Indies by 1540.

King Affonso of the Kongo, shown here receiving European ambassadors, tried unsuccessfully to stop the slave trade. Rulers in Benin and the Gold Coast also resisted at first. ETHICS Why might African traders have participated in selling fellow Africans into slavery?

The slave trade was conducted by African middlemen who delivered the slaves to ports on Africa's coasts. There they traded the slaves for cloth, iron, guns, and alcohol. The trade enriched some members of African coastal states. In contrast, the societies of the African interior, where most of the slaves came from, were weakened.

> "**O**ur country is becoming completely depopulated."
>
> —*King Affonso*

In 1526 King Affonso, ruler of the Kongo kingdom at the mouth of the Congo River, wrote the king of Portugal to protest the slave trade:

> Everyday these [slave] merchants take our people—sons of farmers as well as sons of nobles . . . to be sold as slaves. So great is this corruption and evil that our country is becoming completely depopulated.

Affonso was a Catholic who had been educated in Portugal. Still, his appeal to the Portuguese king was in vain. In the 1500s, 900,000 African slaves were shipped to the Americas. In the seventeenth century the number peaked at 3,750,000. All in all about 10 million Africans were forced into slavery in the Americas.

COLUMBUS'S PLACE IN HISTORY

In spite of his efforts, Columbus never reached Asia. Nor did he bring back the riches he and Spain's rulers had hoped for. The king and queen grew tired of supporting him. After his fourth voyage, they refused Columbus's requests for further funds. European geographers began to realize that Columbus had found not Asia, but unexplored lands. Columbus, however, insisted until his death that the islands he had explored were part of Asia.

In 1506 Columbus died, disappointed that he had not brought great riches to Spain. "I came to you at the age of 28," he wrote Ferdinand and Isabella, "and now I have not a hair on me that is not white, and my body is infirm and exhausted. All that was left to me and my brothers has been taken away and sold, even to the cloak that I wore, without hearing or trial, to my great dishonor."

Today, however, Columbus is honored as one of history's greatest explorers. The knowledge gained from his voyages erased the Latin words *terra incognita*—"unknown land"—from half the globe. Although he never knew it, Columbus opened the way for European settlement of the Americas. His achievement would forever change the course of world history.

SECTION REVIEW

1. KEY TERMS Columbian exchange, colonist, encomienda system, hidalgo

2. PEOPLE Bartolomé de Las Casas, King Affonso

3. COMPREHENSION How did the arrival of Europeans affect life in the Western Hemisphere?

4. COMPREHENSION What was the effect of the slave trade on Africa? On the Western Hemisphere?

5. CRITICAL THINKING How were the voyages of exploration similar to today's exploration of space? How were they different? Give specific examples.

CHAPTER 2 SUMMARY AND TIMELINE

1. During medieval times, Europeans knew little about the rest of the world. The Crusades increased contact between Europe and Asia. The Renaissance brought to Europe a new spirit of curiosity that led to explorations in many areas. The growth of trade led to the decline of feudalism and to the rise of powerful monarchs.

2. Newly powerful European nations searched for overseas trade routes. Portugal made advances in navigation. It also began the slave trade with Africa.

3. Fifteenth-century Europe brimmed with energy and new ideas. Columbus, inspired by this spirit of curiosity, set out to reach Asia by sailing westward from Europe in 1492.

4. Columbus's voyages changed the course of world history. The peoples of the Eastern and Western hemispheres exchanged plants, animals, and diseases in the years following Columbus's first voyage. Spaniards ruled their American colonies with an iron hand, killing and enslaving untold numbers of Indians. A severe labor shortage among sugar-growers in the Americas led to an increase in the slave trade and the enslavement of millions of Africans.

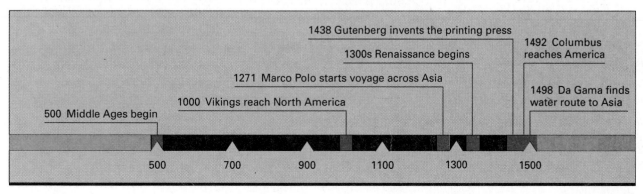

1438 Gutenberg invents the printing press

1300s Renaissance begins

1492 Columbus reaches America

1271 Marco Polo starts voyage across Asia

1498 Da Gama finds water route to Asia

1000 Vikings reach North America

500 Middle Ages begin

500   700   900   1100   1300   1500

PLACES TO LOCATE

Match the letters on the map with the places listed below. Then explain the importance of each place.

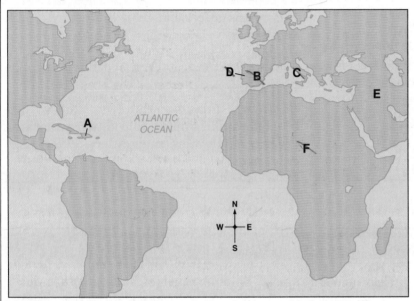

1. Hispaniola
2. Spain
3. Italy
4. Portugal
5. Asia
6. Africa

KEY TERMS

Use the following terms to complete the sentences.

**Columbian exchange
encomienda system
Middle Ages
monopoly
Renaissance**

1. During the _____ Europeans rediscovered classical learning.
2. Under the _____ Indians were enslaved and their lands taken.
3. Because of their _____ on trade with Asia, merchants could charge high prices.
4. Much of society lived under the feudal system during the _____.
5. The _____ resulted in new food crops for Europe.

PEOPLE TO IDENTIFY

Match each of the following people with the correct description.

**Johannes Gutenberg
Henry the Navigator
Queen Isabella
Bartolomé de Las Casas
Mohammed**

1. Spanish colonist who became a friar and fought against enslavement of Indians.
2. Spanish monarch who sponsored Columbus's voyage to the Americas.
3. Prince of Portugal who sponsored voyages around the west coast of Africa.
4. Arabian merchant who founded the Islamic religion.
5. German goldsmith who invented the printing press.

REVIEWING THE FACTS

1. What factors prevented Europe from expanding outward during the Middle Ages?
2. Why do the Vikings rarely get credit for "discovering" America?
3. What factors were responsible for the rise of the middle class in Europe?
4. Why did Europeans seek new trade routes to Asia?
5. What factors influenced Columbus's decision to seek a westward route to Asia?
6. Why did the Spanish monarchs decide to finance Columbus's voyage?
7. What were some of the practical effects of Columbus's arrival in the Western Hemisphere?
8. Why was Columbus unaware that he had landed in North America?
9. Why were African slaves brought to the Americas?
10. What were the effects for American Indians of contact with Europeans?

PRACTICING YOUR SKILL

Copy the chart below onto a separate sheet of paper. Then complete the chart by filling in the missing causes and effects.

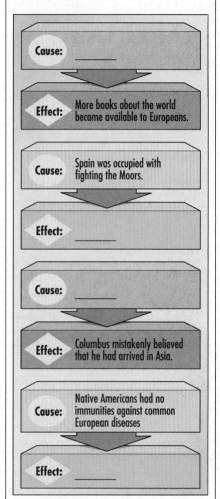

Cause: _____

Effect: More books about the world became available to Europeans.

Cause: Spain was occupied with fighting the Moors.

Effect: _____

Cause: _____

Effect: Columbus mistakenly believed that he had arrived in Asia.

Cause: Native Americans had no immunities against common European diseases

Effect: _____

CITIZENSHIP

1. Describe the system of government that existed in Europe during the Middle Ages.
2. How did this type of government change with the growth of trade and towns?
3. Describe the role of the Church during the Middle Ages. What is the relationship between church and society today?

CRITICAL THINKING SKILLS

1. RELATING PAST TO PRESENT In what ways was life in medieval Europe different from life in America today? In what ways was it similar?

2. FORMING A HYPOTHESIS Why did the Portuguese guard their navigational knowledge as a state secret?

3. RECOGNIZING BIAS What might account for the very different opinions of the Indians given by Las Casas and his opponents?

4. RELATING PAST TO PRESENT European navigators in the 1500s challenged legends and the unknown by sailing into unexplored waters to the west. What unexplored areas remain in today's world? How, in your view, should humans approach those areas?

PROJECTS AND ACTIVITIES

1. GIVING AN ORAL REPORT Find out more about one of the ways in which religion influenced the historic events you have read about in this chapter. Topics include: the *Reconquista,* the Crusades, efforts to Christianize the Indians, and the actions of Bartolomé de Las Casas. Tell the class what you have learned.

2. LABELING INFORMATION ON A MAP On an outline map of the world, label all the areas that were known to Europeans in 1500. Then list some of the trading goods each area contained that interested Europeans.

3. WRITING A PLAY Write a script for a short play taking place on the *Santa María,* as it crosses the ocean during Columbus's first voyage to the Americas.

WRITING ABOUT TOPICS IN AMERICAN HISTORY

1. CONNECTING WITH LITERATURE A selection from *History of the Indies* by Bartolomé de Las Casas appears on pages 631–632. Read it and answer the questions. Then answer the following question: What kind of thinking did the scientific advisers display in their arguments?

2. APPLYING THEMES: GEOGRAPHY Why might the scientific advisers to the Spanish monarchs have assumed that only a very small part of the earth was land?

On the heels of the Spanish explorers came the conquistadors, heavily armed soldiers who conquered much of the Western Hemisphere for Spain.

3 Spain Builds an Empire (1492–1700)

1 On to the Pacific

★ Section Focus

Key Terms Line of Demarcation ■ strait ■ convert ■ circumnavigate

Main Idea Explorers gradually learned that Columbus's new lands were another continent, not part of Asia.

Objectives As you read, look for answers to these questions:
1. Why did Spain claim most of the Americas?
2. How did explorers prove that the Americas were not Asia?

What happens when two people want the same thing? They may fight over it. One may give in to the other. Or, they may divide it. Nations are no different.

DIVIDING THE WORLD

Columbus's first voyage to the Americas triggered an intense dispute between Spain and Portugal over the new lands. Portugal now controlled the African coast, where it traded for slaves and gold (page 31). Portugal wanted a free rein to continue exploring the South Atlantic. Spain insisted, however, that it had the right to the lands Columbus had discovered.

Both Spain and Portugal turned to the Pope for a solution to their dispute. At the time, the Pope claimed the right to place non-Christian lands under the protection of Christian rulers.

In 1493 the Pope established the Line of Demarcation—an imaginary line around the earth, running north and south. The Line of Demarcation divided the world in half. Portugal could claim all non-Christian lands on one side of the line. Spain could claim such lands on the other side.

Spain and Portugal thought they were dividing Asia. No one knew at the time that the Line of Demarcation gave Spain the rights to most of two continents, North and South America. (See map, page 50.) Only years of exploration would reveal that fact.

EARLY EXPLORERS: VESPUCCI AND CABRAL

Amerigo Vespucci (ves–POOT–chee) was an Italian merchant and navigator who worked in Spain as an outfitter of ships. An outfitter made sure that a ship had the equipment and supplies needed for each voyage. As an outfitter, Vespucci helped prepare Columbus's ships.

Later, Vespucci went to sea himself. He served as a navigator for several expeditions to South America between 1499 and 1504. Unlike Columbus, Vespucci realized he had reached a new continent. In fact, he took all the credit for finding a new continent. "I have found a continent more densely populated and abounding in animals than our Europe,

Asia, and Africa. We may rightly call this continent the New World," Vespucci wrote. Impressed by these words, a German mapmaker named the new continent America after Amerigo Vespucci.

> "We may rightly call this continent the New World."
>
> —*Amerigo Vespucci*

For the next half-century, the name America was given only to South America. Maps of the time showed North America to be a vast peninsula connected to Asia.

While Spain was busily searching for new lands, one sailor from Portugal found them by accident. Pedro Cabral set out from Portugal with a small fleet in 1500. He planned to reach India by following Da Gama's route around Africa (page 32), but storms blew his fleet far to the west. Cabral found himself on the shores of Brazil, on the eastern edge of South America. According to the Line of Demarcation, Brazil lay within Portuguese control. Cabral claimed the region for Portugal. However, Portugal paid little attention to Brazil at first.

BALBOA CROSSES TO THE PACIFIC

Vasco Núñez de Balboa was one of the Spanish adventurers who had headed for the Americas. As a colonist on Hispaniola, he preferred swordplay to farming. Eager to find new adventures, he joined an expedition to set up a new settlement. The new colony was Darién, on the Atlantic side of the Isthmus of Panama.

In Darién, Balboa heard Indian reports of another ocean. Near that sea, the stories went, was a land (Peru) rich in gold. At last, thought Balboa, was an opportunity to make a fortune!

To find the sea, Balboa organized a large expedition in 1513. Moving southward, the group hacked their way through the jungle.

The jungle was alive with poisonous snakes and stinging mosquitoes. Indians, suspicious of the newcomers, threatened the Spaniards' lives. At last Balboa reached the crest of the mountains that form the spine of the Isthmus of Panama. Before him stretched the Pacific Ocean (or as Balboa named it, the "South Sea"). Four days later he walked into the ocean surf, touched it with his sword, and claimed the ocean for Spain.

Balboa failed in his dream of reaching Peru. The jealous and evil-tempered governor of Darién accused him of treason. Balboa was beheaded in the town square in 1519. The man who performed the execution was a new arrival, Francisco Pizarro (pih–ZAHR–oh). It was he who would conquer Peru more than a decade later.

During his lifetime, Amerigo Vespucci was celebrated as a great explorer and "discoverer." After his death his fame faded—but not before two continents were named for him. HISTORY Why did Vespucci call the Americas "the New World"?

One of the sailors on Magellan's voyage, Antonio Pigafetta, drew this picture of two other crew members trying out a native outrigger canoe near the Isle of Larrons (Guam). **GEOGRAPHY** What problems did Magellan face crossing the Pacific?

MAGELLAN'S REMARKABLE VOYAGE

In 1498 Vasco da Gama had sailed around Africa to reach India. Thereafter Portuguese trading ships made the voyage regularly to India and the Spice Islands beyond. A captain on one of these ships was Ferdinand Magellan.

Balboa's report of another ocean excited Magellan. Perhaps Columbus was right. Perhaps one could reach the Indies by sailing west. If so, the journey might be shorter than sailing east around Africa. First, though, it would be necessary to find a water passage through or around the Americas. Magellan thought he would find it by sailing south. After all, that was the way the Portuguese had rounded Africa.

The king of Portugal had doubts about Magellan, however, and told Magellan that he was free to offer his services elsewhere. Magellan next went to Spain. Impressed by Magellan's proposal, the king of Spain agreed to sponsor him.

In September 1519 Magellan set out from Spain with 5 ships and about 240 men. The ships crossed the rough Atlantic and then turned south along the coast of South America. As they continued south, the weather grew stormier and more bitter. So did tempers. Magellan executed one mutinous captain.

The expedition spent the winter on the coast near the tip of South America, repairing their boats. In the spring they set out again. Despite terrible storms and winds, Magellan found what he was looking for—a **strait** (narrow passage of water) between the two oceans. He knew it was a strait, not a river, because the water remained salty. This is the waterway now called the Strait of Magellan.

Before heading into the strait, Magellan sent men out to gather food for the long voyage ahead. When he thought they had prepared enough dried fish and smoked game, the ships lifted anchor and headed into the strait. Four days later they emerged into Balboa's South Sea. The ocean seemed so calm that Magellan renamed it the Pacific, meaning "peaceful."

CIRCLING THE GLOBE

For the next four and a half months, Magellan and his crew sailed across the Pacific. The ocean was far wider than Magellan had ever imagined. The voyage seemed endless. The fresh food lasted only a month. Hunger, thirst, and disease tortured the sailors.

One member of the crew, Antonio Pigafetta, had the job of writing an account of the

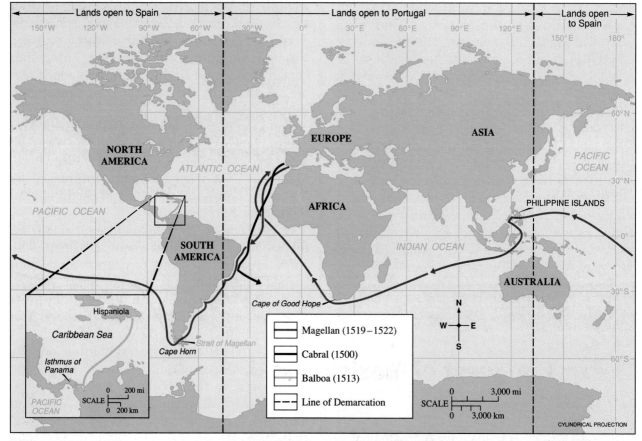

MAP SKILLS Cabral and Magellan desired sea routes to Asia, while Balboa's search, shown in the inset map, was for gold. What continents did the Spanish and Portuguese visit in the early 1500s? What land mass did Balboa have to cross to reach the Pacific Ocean? **CRITICAL THINKING** Explain why people in Brazil speak Portuguese today while those in the rest of South America speak Spanish.

expedition for the king. Of those terrible days on the Pacific, Pigafetta wrote:

> We ate biscuit, which was no longer biscuit, but powder of biscuits swarming with worms. . . . We drank yellow water that had been putrid for many days. We also ate some oxhides . . . ; often we ate sawdust from boards. Rats were sold for [gold], and even then we could not get them.

Nearly dead, the sailors at last reached the islands they named the Philippines. There, fresh food and fresh water helped them begin to regain their health.

In the Philippines, Magellan was pleased to **convert** a chief to the Catholic faith. (To convert is to change someone's beliefs, especially religious beliefs.) In his zeal to befriend the chief, Magellan became involved in a local war. He decided to take on the friendly chief's enemy. Magellan wanted to show how powerful the Spanish were and thereby demonstrate the power of their God. It was a costly mistake. In a beach assault, Magellan's forces were met by a hail of bamboo spears, and he was killed.

Despite the death of their leader, the expedition continued. The crew headed south to the Spice Islands, where they picked up a cargo of cloves and other spices.

Only one ship completed the journey. This was the *Victoria*, whose captain was Juan Sebastián del Cano. Del Cano sailed across the

Indian Ocean, around southern Africa, and then northward in the Atlantic. Three years after leaving Spain, the *Victoria* and its crew of eighteen Europeans and four Indians arrived home. These sailors were the first to circumnavigate—sail around—the earth. The spices on board more than paid for the cost of the expedition. In honor of the feat, the king of Spain allowed del Cano to add to his coat of arms a globe with the words, in Latin, "You were the first to encircle me."

The knowledge gained by the expedition was priceless. Here was the first real proof that the world was round. Furthermore, Europeans now knew that the Americas were not part of Asia. The mapmakers went back to their drawing boards.

SECTION REVIEW

1. KEY TERMS Line of Demarcation, strait, convert, circumnavigate

2. PEOPLE AND PLACES Amerigo Vespucci, Vasco Núñez de Balboa, Isthmus of Panama, Ferdinand Magellan, Strait of Magellan, Juan Sebastián del Cano

3. COMPREHENSION What was Balboa's main accomplishment?

4. COMPREHENSION Why was Magellan's voyage important?

5. CRITICAL THINKING What qualities make a good explorer? Did Magellan have those qualities? Explain.

2 The Conquest of Mexico and Peru

Section Focus

Key Terms conquistador ■ missionary ■ ally

Main Idea From the islands of the Caribbean, the Spanish began exploring the American mainland. Eventually they conquered Mexico and Peru.

Objectives As you read, look for answers to these questions:
1. Why did Spain explore the American mainland?
2. How did Spain conquer Mexico and Peru?

The restless, ambitious young men of Spain moved to Spain's Caribbean colonies by the hundreds. Like Balboa, most quickly became bored with the farming life. They dreamed of finding gold and glory for themselves. They dreamed of being conquistadors (kahn–KEES–tuh–dorz)—conquerors.

The conquistadors fought not only for gold and glory but also for God. Spain was deeply committed to Christianity and to the Roman Catholic Church. For eight centuries Spanish soldiers had fought to bring all of Spain under Christian control (page 35). Now they hoped to convert non-Christian peoples in the Americas to the Roman Catholic faith. Every

Spanish expedition contained missionaries, people sent abroad to do religious work. Most were friars, religious "brothers" who had vowed to live a life of poverty and service to others.

THE INVASION OF MEXICO

The story of the conquest of Mexico is a rich tale, full of intrigue and passion, drama and tragedy. It begins with Hernán Cortés (kor–TEZ), one of Spain's ambitious young men. Tired of studying law, Cortés sailed from Spain to Hispaniola in 1504. There he became a rich and respected colonist. Still, he dreamed of being a conquistador.

This painting depicts the arrival of Cortés and his men at Veracruz in 1519. Within two years the mighty empire of the Aztecs fell to Spanish rule. **TECHNOLOGY** What items in the picture suggest the power of the conquistadors?

In 1518 an expedition returned to Cuba with gold taken from the Indians on Yucatán. (The Yucatán Peninsula of Mexico is where the Maya civilization had last flowered.) Cortés organized an expedition to explore the mainland. In 1519 he left for Yucatán with 11 ships, 448 soldiers, 100 sailors, 2 priests, 16 horses, and 2 greyhounds.

Cortés landed on the coast of Yucatán. There he was challenged by a Maya army of 12,000. The Mayas probably would have overwhelmed the Spanish had not Cortés sent his small cavalry onto the field. In a scene out of the Middle Ages, armored men holding huge, metal-tipped lances galloped on armored horses toward the Indians. The Indians had never seen horses. Assuming the men on horseback to be monsters, they fled in terror. Cortés thus started off his conquest with both a technological and a psychological edge.

The defeated Indians offered gifts to the conquerors, including cotton cloth, gold ornaments, and female slaves. Among the slaves was Malinche (mah–LEEN–chay). Malinche was born an Aztec but was sold as a child to the Mayas. The Spanish christened her Marina. Because she knew more than one Indian language, Marina became a valuable interpreter. Her loyalty to Cortés would help him conquer the Aztecs.

From Yucatán the Spanish sailed west then north along the coast. The land seemed so abundant in resources that Cortés decided to make a permanent settlement. This was the port city of Veracruz.

MONTEZUMA'S REACTION

Meanwhile, swift runners carried news of Cortés to Montezuma (mahn–tuh–ZOO–muh), ruler of the Aztecs. Montezuma lived in the Aztec capital of Tenochtitlán. He was a mild and gentle man who did not quite know how to deal with the intruders.

One reason for his indecision was the legend of Quetzalcóatl (ket–sahl–ko–AHT–uhl). Centuries before, it was said, a white, bearded man had ruled Mexico in the name of Quetzalcóatl, the god of civilization. He had left Mexico, saying he would return from the east in the year Reed 1. According to the Aztec calendar, Cortés had landed in Reed 1, which occurred every 52 years. Montezuma asked himself: Had these men been sent by Quetzalcóatl?

Just in case, Montezuma had messengers greet the strangers at Veracruz. They were to bear gifts made of gold, feathers, gems, and shells. Montezuma told his messengers:

> Come forward, my valiant Jaguar Knights. . . . It is said that our lord has returned to this land. Go to meet him. Go to hear him. Listen well to what he tells you; listen and remember.

Cortés received the gifts and gave others in return. He let it be known he wanted even more gold. Then Cortés showed off his cavalry and the power of his cannon.

The terrified messengers returned to Montezuma. They told him of a weapon that could crack open a mountain and shatter a tree into splinters. "Their trappings and arms are all made of iron. . . . Their deer carry them on their backs wherever they wish to go. These deer, our lord, are as tall as the roof of a house."

Montezuma decided that Quetzalcóatl had sent Cortés to reclaim the throne of Mexico. He tried to bribe Cortés into staying away.

An Aztec artist drew the meeting between Cortés and Montezuma (bottom). The Aztecs gave the Spaniards gifts, including the knife shown below. HISTORY What might have impressed the artist most about the Spaniards?

Montezuma's messengers returned to Veracruz carrying dazzling gifts for the Spanish. Among the gifts were two plates as large as wagon wheels, one of gold and one of silver.

THE MARCH TO TENOCHTITLÁN

Such gifts, however, only made Cortés more eager than ever to conquer the Aztecs. He knew that many of his men were ready to turn back. Among them were the sailors, who preferred sailing to fighting. "And so, to make them all follow him whether they liked it or not, he resolved to destroy his ships," wrote his secretary, Francisco López de Gómara (GO–mah–rah).

In August 1519 Cortés set out for Tenochtitlán. Along the way he wooed those Indians who resented Aztec rule. They became his partners in a common cause, or allies.

Several months after leaving Veracruz, Cortés approached the magnificent city of Tenochtitlán, with its canals, gardens, markets, and temples. One of the conquistadors recalled:

> Gazing on such wonderful sights we did not know what to say or whether what appeared before us was real; for on the one hand there were great cities and in the lake ever so many more . . . and we—we did not number even 400 soldiers!

Montezuma's messengers again appeared. The Spanish must turn back, they told Cortés. Still, Cortés pushed ahead. Montezuma had enough warriors to stop Cortés, but he never used them. Always in the back of his mind was the idea that the Spanish had been sent by Quetzalcóatl.

When Cortés entered the heart of Tenochtitlán, Montezuma came to greet him. Montezuma housed the Spanish in his palace and showered them with gifts. Recalling the legend of Quetzalcóatl, Montezuma told Cortés:

> We have always expected and believed that some day men would come from [foreign] parts to subject and rule us, and I think you are the ones. . . . And so, my lord captain, you may be sure that we shall obey you, if you are not deceiving or tricking us, and that we shall share what we have with you.

Within a week Cortés took Montezuma hostage and ordered that his treasury be opened. It took the Spanish three days to divide up the immense treasure.

LA NOCHE TRISTE

Cortés had planned to rule Mexico with Montezuma as a puppet emperor (that is, a ruler in name only). This plan fell apart. Horrified

BIOGRAPHY

HERNÁN CORTÉS (1485–1547) was a great conquistador. Born in a small town in Spain, Cortés gladly accepted his family's offer to send him to Hispaniola. There he grew bored—"I came to get gold, not to till the soil like a peasant," he complained. In 1511 Cortés helped conquer Cuba and then spent seven prosperous years on that island. Hearing of gold on the Mexican peninsula of Yucatán, Cortés led an expedition there in 1519 and crushed the native Aztecs. Thereafter Cortés gradually lost power and influence. He died a forgotten man in Spain.

by the Aztec practice of human sacrifice, some Spanish soldiers tried to stop it. The Aztec priests then led an uprising against the Spanish. When Montezuma tried to restore order, an angry Aztec mob stoned him to death. Then the Spanish, carrying their new wealth, tried to sneak out of the city at night. They were found. Fierce fighting broke out in what the Spaniards later called *La Noche Triste* (LAH NO–cheh TREES–teh), or "The Night of Sorrow."

Several hundred Spaniards and 4,000 of their Indian allies died. "Among our men," wrote Gómara, "those who were most [loaded down] with clothing, gold, and jewels were the first to die, and those were saved who carried the least and forged ahead fearlessly. So those who died, died rich, and their gold killed them."

THE AZTECS ARE DEFEATED

The survivors of *La Noche Triste* retreated to join their Indian allies in the nearby mountains. There Cortés rebuilt his forces. He also built boats that could attack Tenochtitlán from the water. In May 1521 Cortés launched a full-scale attack on the Aztec capital. Cortés had help from an unexpected source: smallpox. It entered Mexico with the arrival of additional Spaniards. The deadly disease spread rapidly, greatly weakening Aztec resistance to the invaders.

> ## "Our inheritance, our city, is lost and dead."
>
> *—Aztec poem on the destruction of Tenochtitlán*

Cortés set out to destroy Tenochtitlán house by house, because he knew no other way to smash Aztec power. For more than three months the battle raged fiercely. Finally, with the city in ruins, Aztec power crumbled.

Cortés himself wept to see the destruction of what he called the most beautiful city in the world. An Aztec poet lamented:

> Broken spears lie in the roads;
> We have torn out hair in our grief.
> The houses are roofless now, and their
>   walls are red with blood. . . .
>
> We have pounded our hands in
>   despair
> Against the adobe walls, for our inheritance, our city, is lost and dead.

A NEW SOCIETY IN MEXICO

Mexico was now part of what the Spanish called New Spain. On the rubble of Tenochtitlán, the Spanish built Mexico City. A cathedral replaced the great Aztec temple the Spanish had destroyed.

One result of the conquest of Mexico was the mixing of Spanish and Indian culture. Few Spanish women were willing or able to settle in the new colony. Also, the Indian population was ravaged by diseases brought from Europe. Historians estimate that Mexico's population shrank from 25 million in 1500 to less than 2 million in 1600. Each population thus came to depend on the other. The two cultures, the Spanish and the Indian, merged to produce a new society, that of present-day Mexico.

THE CONQUEST OF PERU

The great wealth that Cortés found in Mexico revived Spanish interest in Peru. Francisco Pizarro received the king's permission to explore and conquer Peru. He returned to Panama and began to assemble supplies and soldiers for the undertaking.

In early 1531 Pizarro and his 180 men set sail. Pizarro first set up a base on the northern coast of Peru. Then the small force crossed into the mountains to make contact with Atahualpa (aht–uh–WAHL–puh), the Inca ruler. They reached him at the hot springs near Cajamarca (kah–hah–MAR–kuh), a town located about 9,000 feet above sea level.

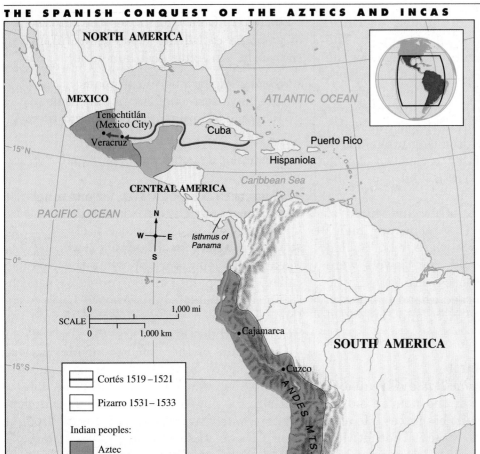

MAP SKILLS

The Spanish conquistadors invaded Mexico and South America. Which Indian empire did they invade first? On what continent was the Inca empire? **CRITICAL THINKING** What advantages over the Indians did Cortés and Pizarro share?

Pizarro invited Atahualpa to visit him in the town. Thinking the tiny force of Spaniards could pose no threat, Atahualpa did so. With him went 6,000 servants, nobles, and warriors.

In the town square Atahualpa listened politely as Pizarro's priest spoke to him through an interpreter. The priest handed Atahualpa a prayer book and tried to persuade him to become a Christian. Atahualpa was not interested. The Incas believed in a sun god and considered their ruler to be the sun god's child.

Angrily, Atahualpa threw the prayer book to the ground. Pizarro then dropped his handkerchief, the signal for an assault. Spanish soldiers then attacked the Incas. Trapped within the town walls, the Incas could not easily flee.

Pizarro took Atahualpa prisoner. To gain his freedom, Atahualpa promised rooms full of gold and silver objects as ransom. Pizarro waited until the treasure had been collected. Then he had Atahualpa strangled.

The conquistadors proceeded to take control of all of Peru. To do so, they took advantage of the Incas' superb road system. These roads extended 2,250 miles from the Inca city of Quito (KEE–toh) south to what is now central Chile. The roads allowed the conquistadors to establish their authority quickly. Pizarro, serving as governor of Peru, exercised that authority from Lima, the new capital he founded in 1535.

Pizarro turned out to be one of the most greedy of the conquistadors. His harsh treatment of the Indians led to many revolts and endless fighting. There was much jealousy and plotting among the Spanish themselves. Pizarro died as violently as he had lived. In 1541 he was killed by his own countrymen in a power struggle.

SECTION REVIEW

1. KEY TERMS conquistador, missionary, ally

2. PEOPLE AND PLACES Mexico, Hernán Cortés, Yucatán, Malinche, Montezuma, Tenochtitlán, New Spain, Francisco Pizarro, Peru, Atahualpa

3. COMPREHENSION Explain the goals of the conquistadors.

4. COMPREHENSION Why did Montezuma not know how to treat the Spanish?

5. CRITICAL THINKING How were a few hundred soldiers able to topple the great empires of Mexico and Peru?

3 The Lure of North America

Section Focus

Key Term adobe

Main Idea Spanish explorers made expeditions to North America in search of the same kind of riches that had been found in Mexico and Peru.

Objectives As you read, look for the answers to these questions:
1. What was the result of the early explorations of North America?
2. What areas in North America did the Spanish explore? What did they learn?

In Mexico and Peru the Spanish found more gold, silver, and gems than they had ever believed possible. They filled their ships with the beautifully made objects that had once belonged to the Inca and Aztec rulers. Then they enslaved the Indians to mine even more gold and silver.

The riches they had found whetted their appetite for more. It seemed quite possible that other places, as yet unknown, would also be as rich. Thus the Spanish turned their attention north of Mexico.

EXPLORING THE GULF COAST

The first Spaniard to explore the Gulf Coast—the coast of the Gulf of Mexico—was Juan Ponce de León (PON–say DAY lay–OHN). Early in his career he had conquered and then governed Puerto Rico. There he heard tales of a northern land with a "fountain of youth." The waters from this fountain, it was said, could make old people young again. In 1513 he set out to search for this fountain. In doing so, Ponce de León discovered the land he named Florida—"flower-covered." On his way back to Puerto Rico he landed on Mexico's Yucatán Peninsula.

In 1521, hearing the news of gold in Mexico, Ponce de León returned to Florida. With 200 men he landed on Florida's west coast. An Indian attack overwhelmed the landing party. The Spanish were forced to retreat to

A brisk tailwind filled the sails of the Spanish ships heading southward along the Florida coast. Yet the ships were making no progress. Some force more powerful than the wind was driving them back up the coast.

THE GULF STREAM

The commander of the three ships was the Spanish explorer Juan Ponce de León. In the spring of 1513, he had landed on the coast of Florida near present-day St. Augustine. Attempting to go south, however, Ponce de León discovered something else: the powerful ocean current we call the Gulf Stream.

The Gulf Stream is a strong "river" of warm tropical water that flows north along the Atlantic Coast of North America. A warm current of water in the cooler Atlantic Ocean, it averages about 95 miles wide and a mile deep.

GREAT CIRCULAR CURRENTS

As you can see from the map, the Gulf Stream is but one part of a great circular pattern of ocean currents in the North Atlantic Ocean. Notice, too, that in the Northern Hemisphere the currents move in a clockwise pattern. In the Southern Hemisphere they move counterclockwise. This effect, caused by the earth's rotation, is called the Coriolis force.

The Coriolis force affects all motion on the earth's surface,

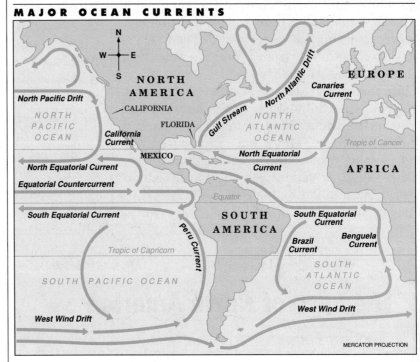

MAJOR OCEAN CURRENTS

MERCATOR PROJECTION

winds as well as ocean currents. The prevailing winds—which blow over wide areas of the earth—follow a circular pattern that is similar to that of the ocean currents. The prevailing winds add energy to the overall system of ocean currents. As in the case of the Gulf Stream, however, the direction of the current may not be related to the local winds.

CURRENTS AND SAILING ROUTES

Soon after Ponce de León's discovery, the Gulf Stream became an important part of the sailing route across the Atlantic. Sea captains avoided it on the westward journey from Spain. However, on their return from Mexico and the

Caribbean, they let the Gulf Stream carry them north to about Cape Hatteras, North Carolina. Then they launched their ships eastward.

Spain, realizing the importance of the Gulf Stream to navigation, fiercely defended its claim to Florida. To control the Florida coastline and to protect Spanish shipping, Spain established the fort of St. Augustine in 1565.

CRITICAL THINKING QUESTIONS

1. Would it be easier to sail north from Mexico's Atlantic coast or Pacific coast? Explain.
2. More than two centuries passed between the Spanish exploration of California in 1542 and Spanish settlement in 1769. Give one reason why.

Ponce de León and his men explored Florida while searching for the mythic "fountain of youth." Though they claimed the peninsula for Spain, he considered the trip unsuccessful. **HISTORY** How were Ponce de León's goals different from those of other explorers?

their ships. In the battle, Ponce de León received an arrow wound from which he shortly died.

Two years later Francisco Garay (gah–RAH–ee) led an expedition to the mouth of the Rio Grande. An earlier explorer had reported that it would be a good place to settle. When Garay reached the river, however, he decided that the site was not right for a city. Instead he headed south to Mexico.

The next expedition to the Gulf Coast was led by Pánfilo de Narváez (nahr–VAH–ays). He had helped conquer Cuba and had also fought alongside Cortés. In 1527, with a force of 400, Narváez set out from Spain to build a city in Florida.

Storms blew the ships off course, and the expedition found itself at Tampa Bay, on Florida's west coast. There, in April 1528, Narváez divided his group. The ships were to

continue on to the Rio Grande. The soldiers, with Narváez at their head, would reach the same place by land. Narváez had no idea just how far he really was from his goal.

The Narváez group headed inland and wandered about for months in a vain effort to find riches. Illness, Indian attacks, and lack of food beset his men. A year after he had landed, Narváez's goal was no longer riches but survival. He decided the only possible way to return to Mexico was by sea. Yet his ships were gone. (For a year the ships sailed up and down the Gulf Coast looking for Narváez, and then gave up.) He had no tools to build new ships.

Desperate, the Spanish decided to make do with what was available. Lacking axes, they cut trees with swords. They made nails out of stirrups. They used vines for ropes. They sewed together their shirts for sails. They killed horses and used the hides for waterskins. They then built five boats and the survivors, about 245 men, set off for Mexico.

The flimsy boats were not seaworthy enough. Narváez was drowned at sea somewhere west of the Mississippi Delta. Two boats with roughly 80 men beached near present-day Galveston, Texas, in November 1528. By the following spring, only 15 were still alive. The survivors spent the next six years as slaves of different Indian tribes. Finally four of these men planned an escape.

CABEZA DE VACA

The four survivors included Álvar Núñez Cabeza de Vaca (kah–BAY–zuh DAY VAH–kah) and Estevanico (es–tay–vahn–EE–ko). Cabeza de Vaca had been treasurer of the expedition. Estevanico was a slave of African and Arab descent. In 1535 Cabeza de Vaca and his companions began an eighteen-month walk to freedom. During their travels they walked unharmed through warlike tribes because they acted as medicine men, or healers.

Leaving the Texas coast, the survivors headed in a northwest direction. From the coastal plain they passed over the Edwards Plateau. Then they crossed the Rio Grande near the site of present-day El Paso. From there the travelers headed southwest on the long Indian trail that led to Mexico. Finally they reached a Spanish outpost. Welcomed as heroes, the four survivors were soon in Mexico City telling their tale.

Spanish officials were most interested in one question: Were there riches in the north? They had not seen riches, Cabeza de Vaca said, but the Indians had told of rich cities in the north. Cabeza de Vaca also reported that the mountains seemed to have ores of gold, iron, and copper.

Even the hint of riches was enough to inspire the Spanish. The report of rich cities revived memories of a medieval legend, that of the golden Seven Cities of Cíbola (SEE–bo–luh). In the years 1539–1542 three expeditions headed north. Each hoped to find Cíbola. Francisco Vásquez de Coronado would explore the interior. From Florida, Hernando de Soto would explore the South-east. Juan Cabrillo (kah–BREE–yo) would explore the California coast by sea.

THE CORONADO EXPEDITION

Before exploring the interior, Coronado wanted more information. In the spring of 1539 he sent a small scouting party on the trail north. The head of this group was a friar, Marcos de Niza (NEE–zuh). People called him Fray Marcos. His guide was Estevanico. Resuming the old role of healer, Estevanico was decked out with bells on his wrists and ankles. In his hand he rattled a "magic" gourd he had been given on his earlier journey.

Fray Marcos sent Estevanico on ahead. The two men communicated by sending Indian runners with messages. Near the border of present-day Arizona and New Mexico, Estevanico approached a Zuñi Indian town. He was certain it was Cíbola. From a distance the multi-storied pueblo looked grand. It was

Searching for gold, Coronado led his party through the present-day southwestern United States. Frederic Remington's painting of the expedition shows missionary priests traveling with Coronado. RELIGION What was the priests' main purpose?

1519	Alonso Álvarez de Piñeda maps the Texas coast for Spain.
1528	Fray Suárez, first Catholic bishop in present-day United States, arrives in Florida (April 14).
1533	Fortún Jiménez discovers and names (lower) California, believing it to be an island.
1539	Hernando de Soto leads armed conflict between American Indians and whites, in Alabama.
1565	Billiards brought to America by Spaniards who settle St. Augustine, Florida.
1609	Spanish settlers found Santa Fe, oldest U.S. capital.
1682	First Spanish missions built in Texas, near El Paso.

made of **adobe** (uh–DOH–bee)—sun-dried clay bricks. The Indians plastered the bricks with a yellow soil full of shiny particles of mica. In a certain light the adobe walls sparkled like gold.

Estevanico sent his gourd-rattle into the town as a goodwill gesture, but the gesture backfired. The gourd-rattle had once belonged to Zuñi enemies. The Zuñi killed Estevanico.

Fray Marcos viewed the Zuñi pueblo from afar and then scurried back to Mexico City. He reported that Cíbola was even larger than Mexico City.

By February of 1540 Coronado was ready to head north. His expedition eagerly moved out of the town of Compostela, on the west coast of Mexico. It included 300 soldiers, most of them Spanish cavalry. The youngest was seventeen, but most were in their early twenties. Hundreds of Mexican Indians, many with wives and children, went along as servants. Among their duties was tending the animals. These included 5,000 sheep, 500

head of cattle, 600 pack mules, and 552 horses.

Fray Marcos guided Coronado to what he claimed was Cíbola. Coronado was bitterly disappointed to find it only a mud-brick village. Tired and hungry, the Spanish drove the Zuñi from their town and feasted on the corn, beans, and turkeys they found there.

From this base, Coronado sent out exploration parties. At the head of one of these parties, García López de Cárdenas (KAHR–day–nahs) discovered the Grand Canyon.

EXPLORING QUIVIRA

Coronado moved on to spend the winter of 1540–1541 at a site on the Rio Grande. There he first met the Plains Indian the Spanish called the Turk. The Turk, full of fancy talk, told about a place called Quivira (kee–VEER–uh). In Quivira, said the Turk, the Spanish could find as much gold, silver, and jewels as they desired. Other Indians said the Turk was lying, but the Spanish wanted to believe him.

The bulk of the expedition followed the Turk out onto the Great Plains. The Plains were like a sea. There were no landmarks by which to set one's course. One soldier had the job of counting the steps taken each day so the group could plot their course. "In all that wilderness, they were appalled at how little mark so great a throng of men and women and beast made upon the grasses of the plain," wrote the historian Paul Horgan. "They left no trail, for the grass in the wind waved over their path like the sea over a galleon's wake."

At last they reached Quivira, located in what is now central Kansas. Coronado finally realized that the Turk was leading him on a wild goose chase. He killed the Turk and headed back toward the Rio Grande. Perhaps, he reasoned, the golden cities lay in another direction.

Before Coronado could find out, he was seriously injured when thrown from his horse. Disheartened and empty-handed, he led the expedition back to Mexico.

THE DE SOTO EXPEDITION

Hernando de Soto had no better luck than Coronado. He had landed at Tampa Bay in 1539 with a force of 600 fighting men. In his pursuit of gold, De Soto wandered through the Southeast for three years. He pushed as far north as present-day Tennessee and as far west as Arkansas. He was the first European to see the Mississippi River.

The De Soto expedition plundered Indian settlements for food, and enslaved Indians. De Soto was determined, ruthless, and cruel. To get rid of him, the Indians told him stories of riches to be found someplace far away.

In 1542 De Soto died of a fever along the lower Mississippi River. To prevent the Indians from learning of his death, De Soto's followers buried him in the river. Then they made rafts and floated down the river to the Gulf. Half of the expedition reached Mexico.

CABRILLO ON THE CALIFORNIA COAST

To learn about North America's west coast, Juan Rodríguez Cabrillo set sail in 1542. This old conquistador had been with Cortés when he conquered Tenochtitlán.

As Cabrillo's expedition sailed north along the California coast, he discovered San Diego Bay. Then Cabrillo died from a fall. The expedition sailed without him as far as Oregon and then returned to Mexico. Like Coronado and De Soto, Cabrillo found no gold.

The three expeditions, however, had greatly increased Spanish knowledge of North American geography. In the years to come, Spain would use this knowledge to build new settlements in North America.

SETTLING NEW MEXICO AND TEXAS

In 1598 Juan de Oñate (oh–NYAH–tay) led another expedition northward from Mexico. Unlike Coronado, he stayed on the eastern side of the Sierra Madre. The expedition followed a low mountain pass that led to El Paso del Norte, a ford on the Rio Grande. From El Paso, Oñate headed north up the Rio Grande. There he took over an Indian town, renaming it San Juan.

MAP SKILLS Spain sent many expeditions to explore the Americas. Who was first to cross the Rio Grande? **CRITICAL THINKING** Why did so many expeditions begin in the Caribbean region?

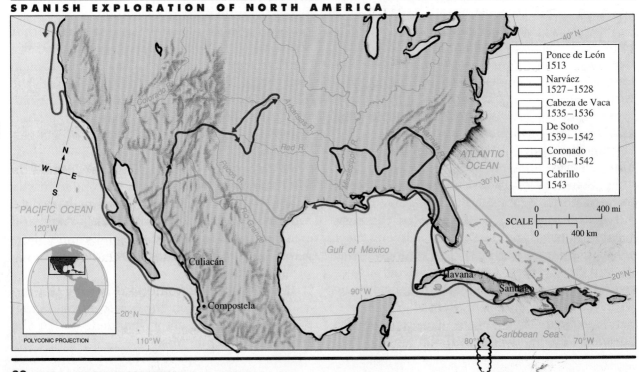

SPANISH EXPLORATION OF NORTH AMERICA

Ponce de León 1513
Narváez 1527–1528
Cabeza de Vaca 1535–1536
De Soto 1539–1542
Coronado 1540–1542
Cabrillo 1543

SCALE
0 400 mi
0 400 km

PACIFIC OCEAN
ATLANTIC OCEAN
Gulf of Mexico
Caribbean Sea
Culiacán
Compostela
Havana
Santiago
Colorado R.
Kansas R.
Red R.
Pecos R.
Rio Grande
Mississippi R.
POLYCONIC PROJECTION

Year	Explorer	Goal	Accomplishment
1492	Columbus	To reach Asia	Reached the West Indies; brought knowledge of Americas to Europe
1513	Balboa	To find gold and a sea	Crossed Panama and claimed the Pacific Ocean for Spain
1513	Ponce de León	To find a "fountain of youth"	Explored Florida
1519 - 1521	Cortés	To conquer Mexico and find gold	Defeated the Aztecs and seized gold
1519 - 1522	Magellan	To reach the Indies by sailing west	Expedition was first to circumnavigate the globe
1531 - 1533	Pizarro	To conquer Peru and find gold	Defeated the Incas and seized gold
1539 - 1542	De Soto	To find the golden Seven Cities of Cibola	Explored the Southeast but found no gold
1540 - 1542	Coronado	To find the golden Seven Cities of Cibola	Explored Texas and the Great Plains but found no gold

CHART SKILLS The Spanish had several reasons for exploration. Which explorers hoped to find gold? Which succeeded? **CRITICAL THINKING** In your opinion, which explorer was the most successful? Why?

The lure of Quivira remained. From San Juan, Oñate followed Coronado's route out into the Great Plains. He explored the Texas Panhandle, Oklahoma, and Kansas. Yet he found no more than Coronado.

In 1609 the Spanish colonists of San Juan founded a new town, Santa Fe. From Santa Fe the friars spread out to convert the Indians. For 70 years the colonists planted their fruit trees and tended their sheep.

Then in 1680 the northern pueblos rebelled. The Indians drove the Spanish from New Mexico. (Thirteen years later the Spanish would re-establish their authority.)

Ousted from New Mexico, the Spanish turned their attention to Texas. In 1684 a military party led by Juan Dominguez de Mendoza set out from El Paso to explore Texas. He was excited by what he found. Texas was "the richest land in all New Spain. . . ." Mendoza wrote. "Rich" no longer meant gold. "Rich" meant an abundance of natural resources—wild fruits, wild game, grasses, minerals. Mendoza set off to ask permission to settle Texas. Texas became a separate province of New Spain.

SECTION REVIEW

1. KEY TERM adobe

2. PEOPLE Juan Ponce de León, Cabeza de Vaca, Francisco Vásquez de Coronado, Hernando de Soto, Juan Rodríguez Cabrillo, Juan de Oñate

3. COMPREHENSION Why was Cabeza de Vaca's report of his journey so important?

4. COMPREHENSION What regions of North America were explored in the 1530s and 1540s?

5. CRITICAL THINKING How did the Spaniards' desire for gold blind them to other kinds of riches?

A good vocabulary makes it easier to learn American history or any other subject. If you can grasp the meaning of unusual words, you will finish your reading more quickly, and it will stay with you longer.

Your vocabulary will grow larger naturally if you read a wide range of books. You should also make an effort to learn and use the new words you come across. Here is one method for adding words to your vocabulary:

- As you read, be aware of words you do not understand. Pay close attention to the words that are somewhat familiar but that you cannot define exactly. These words are easiest to learn.
- Make a list of the words you want to learn and on what page you found them. When you have finished reading, make an index card for each word on your list.
- Look up each word in a dictionary. On the front of the index card, write down the pronunciation of the word. (It is easier to use and remember words that you know how to say.) On the back of the card, write down the word's meaning.
- Study your index cards from time to time until you have mastered the words. If possible, work them into your daily writing assignments so that you become comfortable using them.

CONTEXT CLUES

When you lack the time or the opportunity to look up an unfamiliar word in the dictionary, you can often figure out its meaning from the *context*—the setting in which it appears. Search the context for clues that help you understand the word. For example, on page 68 of Chapter 3, under the subheading "Trade and the Empire," you will find these sentences:

> The wealth of the Americas was shipped to Spain in galleons. Galleons collected their cargo at various Caribbean ports and sailed to Havana, Cuba.

Notice the word *galleon.* There are clues in the passage to its meaning. The first sentence tells you that a galleon was a ship. The second sentence tells you that it carried cargo and that it ran on wind power.

EXAMPLES

An example can explain an unfamiliar word by showing what kinds of things the word refers to. On page 63, for example, the following sentence appears:

> "Rich" meant an abundance of natural resources—wild fruits, wild game, grasses, minerals.

If the term *natural resources* is unfamiliar, you can figure out its meaning from the examples given. All of the items listed are found in nature and used for various purposes by humans. Therefore, that is what the term *natural resources* means.

SYNONYMS

Sometimes an unfamiliar word will be restated or defined. If you know the meaning of the second word, you can figure out the meaning of the unknown word. On page 68, under the subheading "Trade and the Empire," you will see this sentence:

> Upon reaching Spain, the galleons would unload their cargoes of precious metals (gold and silver). . . .

The term *precious metals* refers to gold and silver.

PRACTICING YOUR SKILL

1. What words are easiest to learn?
2. Why is it helpful to learn how to pronounce a new word?
3. Reread a section of this book that you have studied recently. Make a list of at least five unfamiliar words. Try using context clues, examples, and synonyms to figure out the meaning of each word. Then look up the words in a dictionary to see how well you have done.

4 Life in New Spain

Section Focus

Key Terms   viceroyalty ■ El Camino Real
■ hacienda ■ tenant ■ self-sufficient
■ Creole ■ mestizo ■ clergy
■ mercantilism ■ export ■ import

Main Idea   Spain's government, religion, and culture spread throughout its American empire.

Objectives   As you read, look for answers to these questions:
1. How did Spain organize and govern its empire?
2. What role did the Catholic Church play in the empire?
3. What ideas lay behind Spain's economic system?

They called them the "singing wheels." To a Spanish colonist in far-off Texas or New Mexico, it was a heavenly sound. It was the sound of mail bringing news of family and friends. It was the sound of new goods, perhaps a fine mirror or a good knife. The screeching made by the wooden cartwheels sent shivers up your back, and it could be heard for miles. An oxcart on a dusty road, a treasure-laden galleon—both are symbols of how Spain knit together its huge American empire.

SPAIN'S AMERICAN EMPIRE

By 1700 Spain's empire in the Americas included the northern and western parts of South America, all of Middle America, and the southern region of North America. The Spanish were able to conquer and settle such vast territory for three reasons.

(1) The Spanish were good mariners. Their skill at navigation made it possible to maintain regular contact between Spain and the Americas.

(2) The Spanish had a long tradition of fighting and conquering. This tradition had been shaped during the time of the *Reconquista* (page 35).

(3) The Spanish had experience in settling new territories. During the *Reconquista* they had learned how to convert people to Christianity. They had also learned how to extend the Crown's power to new lands. In these tasks, Spain was more experienced than any other European country.

NEW SPAIN

The empire was divided into large parts. Each part, called a **viceroyalty** (VYS–roy–uhl–tee), was ruled by a viceroy. The viceroy was named by the king. As the king's representative, the viceroy had royal powers.

Each viceroyalty was divided into provinces. The governor of each province reported to the viceroy. The governor in turn had power over the alcaldes (al–KAHL–deez). The alcalde was the top official in each community. He enforced the laws. The people had no say in forming the laws or choosing the officials who governed them.

By 1700 the Viceroyalty of New Spain included part of South America, Middle America, Mexico, the Caribbean, Florida, Texas, New Mexico, and California. The hub of New Spain was Mexico City. There lived the viceroy of New Spain.

TOWNS AND ROADS

From the first days of their conquest of Mexico, the Spanish had built towns and outposts ever outward from Mexico City. Each town followed a certain pattern. The streets were laid out on a square pattern called a grid. In the center of the grid was a plaza, or town square. Dominating the plaza was a cathedral or church.

The plaza was the focus of social activity. People gathered there to stroll or meet friends. On church holidays there were celebrations called fiestas. During fiestas the

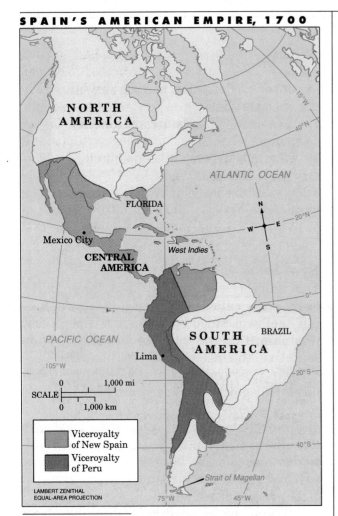

NORTH AMERICA

ATLANTIC OCEAN

FLORIDA

Mexico City

CENTRAL AMERICA

West Indies

PACIFIC OCEAN

SOUTH AMERICA

BRAZIL

Lima

105°W

0   1,000 mi

SCALE

0   1,000 km

Viceroyalty of New Spain

Viceroyalty of Peru

LAMBERT ZENITHAL EQUAL-AREA PROJECTION

Strait of Magellan

75°W   45°W

MAP SKILLS

Spain's huge American empire was divided into two viceroyalties. Which viceroyalty was farther south? Which one included areas of what is now the United States? CRITICAL THINKING What cultural results of the Spanish empire are observable in modern times?

people gathered in the plaza to parade, eat, dance, and listen to music.

Like spokes of a wheel, roads linked Mexico City to the most remote parts of the empire. One road followed Oñate's route from Chihuahua through El Paso to Santa Fe. Another road went to San Antonio and on to the missions in east Texas. Once a year a baggage train of carts and mules made the 1,500-mile journey to these far-flung outposts. Each major road in the empire was called **El Camino Real** (EL kah–MEE–no ray–AHL)—The King's Highway.

LARGE ESTATES

The Spanish divided the land into huge estates. In the 1500s these estates were organized as encomiendas (page 40). In the 1600s, however, the encomiendas were replaced with **haciendas**. The hacienda was a large estate like the encomienda. Unlike the encomienda, the hacienda did not bind the Indians to the land as slaves. Instead, Indians were free to leave the land. Those who chose to stay became **tenants**. That is, they lived on and worked land they did not own, keeping some of the produce for themselves and giving some to the landowner.

Hacienda was also the name given to the owner's house, which was built around a courtyard. In the courtyard was a well. All the rooms of the hacienda opened onto the courtyard. There, in nice weather, children played and women did their work. Neighboring families might gather in the courtyard for parties. A connecting courtyard might house the domestic animals. In the hacienda one was never far away from bleating goats and sheep or cackling chickens.

The hacienda was largely **self-sufficient**. That meant it made most of the things it needed. For instance, the hacienda raised and milled its own grain. From sheep and goats, residents of the hacienda spun wool and wove it into cloth. The women did the spinning. Men were likely to do the weaving.

SOCIAL CLASSES

In time, five social classes emerged in New Spain. At the very top, holding the most important jobs in the Church and the government, were Spaniards born in Spain. Below them were the **Creoles** (KREE–olz). Creoles were people of Spanish ancestry who had been born in New Spain. Most of the landowners, merchants, and businessmen were Creoles.

Below the Creoles came the **mestizos** (mes–TEE–soz). They made up the largest class in New Spain. Mestizos were of mixed Spanish and Indian ancestry. They became parish priests, laborers, artisans, and hacienda tenants. They were much poorer than the two classes at the top of society.

The bottom two groups in New Spain were the Indians and the African slaves. Most of the African slaves in Mexico worked on large farms along the coast.

THE FRONTIER MISSIONS

Wherever the Spanish went, the Church followed. In colonial New Spain there were two kinds of clergy, or religious officials. These were the priests and the friars. The priests set up parishes and ministered to the people of the parish. On the frontier the missionary friars worked to convert the Indians and to teach them Spanish ways.

The first northern missions were in New Mexico. Most missions in Texas were built in the early 1700s. In 1716 Father Francisco Hidalgo, with 12 friars, 25 soldiers, several families, and 1,000 head of livestock, set out for east Texas. He founded missions near the Neches River.

The east Texas missions were far from other Spanish settlements. Indian groups such as Apache and Comanche freely raided wagon trains from Mexico. In 1718, the governor chose the site of what is now San Antonio for a new mission and a presidio, or fort. Soldiers stationed at the presidio would protect the mission and the wagon trains.

In the 1700s the Spanish also built missions in Florida and California. Father Eusebio Kino (KEE–no) founded new missions in Baja (Lower) California. Father Junípero Serra (SAYR–rah) built a string of missions in the new province of Alta (Upper) California.

THE MISSION SETTLEMENT

The typical mission settlement consisted of several parts. The mission church was usually a simple building of stone or adobe. Its paintings and decorations combined Spanish and Indian art. The music, too, reflected both cultures.

Most mission settlements had a presidio of stone or adobe. It held quarters for the officers, barracks for the soldiers, and store-rooms.

Each mission settlement also had a town and fields. Mexican settlers and Indians lived in the town. Both men and women labored in the mission fields and tended the animals. Some of the villagers were blacksmiths or carpenters or weavers. They were important, for the frontier settlements had to make their own tools and clothing.

Once a mission was well established, the missionaries were supposed to turn it over to parish priests and move on. Sometimes this

BIOGRAPHY

JUANA INÉS DE LA CRUZ (1651–1695) is considered one of the greatest poets of colonial Mexico. An exceptionally bright child, she begged her parents to disguise her as a boy so that she could attend the University of Mexico, but they refused. At age eighteen she joined a convent, where she assembled a large library and devoted herself to studying and writing. Twenty-five years later, having written many poems and plays that were published in Spain, she sold all her books and gave the money to the poor. She died in 1695 from an epidemic while nursing her fellow nuns.

THE EXPANDING SPANISH FRONTIER

CALIFORNIA

Colorado R.

Santa Fe

NEW
MEXICO

ARIZONA

30°N

120°W

TEXAS

San Antonio

St. Augustine

FLORIDA

ATLANTIC OCEAN

70°W

30°N

Mississippi R.

PACIFIC
OCEAN

110°W

20°N

Gulf of Mexico

500 mi

500 km

20°N

Mexico City

N
W—E
S

80°W

By 1550
By 1600
By 1785
Mission

10°N

100°W   90°W

POLYCONIC
PROJECTION

MAP SKILLS

As Spanish missionaries moved northward to spread their faith, Spanish settlers followed. When was California settled? On what coast of North America was St. Augustine founded? **CRITICAL THINKING** What factors might have prevented Spanish settlement from moving farther north?

did not happen. Particularly in California the missions were run more like encomiendas. The Indians were treated like slaves. If they ran away, the soldiers tracked them down and brought them back. A French visitor to California in 1786 criticized a system in which the Indian was "too much a child, too much a slave, too little a man."

TRADE AND THE EMPIRE

The wealth of the Americas was shipped to Spain in galleons. Galleons collected their cargo at various Caribbean ports and sailed to Havana, Cuba. There they formed a convoy—a group of ships traveling together for protection. Ships were safer in a convoy because they could help each other deal with pirates and other emergencies. From Havana, convoys caught the Gulf Stream as it swept around the tip of Florida into the Atlantic. The northern coast of South America, with its busy ports and trade routes, was known as

the Spanish Main. The name then, as now, evoked an image of great wealth.

Upon reaching Spain, the galleons would unload their cargoes of precious metals (gold and silver), tropical woods, hides, and other products. On the return trip to New Spain they carried elegant fabrics, guns, furniture, and items of iron and steel.

This transatlantic trade was part of a new economic system called mercantilism. Two key ideas lay behind mercantilism:

(1) *The purpose of colonies was to benefit the parent country.* Spain established a state monopoly over all trade with the colonies. This meant that products of the Americas could be shipped only to Spain. Spain even told the colonies what goods to produce. Also, the colonies were supposed to buy whatever they needed from Spain alone. No other country could trade with the Americas.

(2) *A country could become more wealthy and powerful by building up its supply of pre-*

cious metals. Spain did this in two ways. First, Spain made sure that its exports (goods shipped abroad) were larger than its imports (goods brought in from abroad). Because Spain was selling more to other nations than it was buying from them, it became richer. Second, Spain took vast amounts of gold and silver from the Americas and added them to its treasury.

Indeed, American gold and silver made Spain the richest nation in Europe in the 1500s. Spain spent much of its new wealth on wars. It was unable, however, to force its will on the rest of Europe. In the meantime, other nations learned from Spain how to build an empire. They would challenge Spain's claim to all of North America.

CHAPTER 3 SUMMARY AND TIMELINE

1. An agreement among Spain, Portugal, and the Pope in 1493 gave Spain most of the Western Hemisphere. At first it was thought that the Americas were part of Asia. However, explorations by Vespucci, Balboa, and Magellan gave Europeans a clearer picture of world geography. Europeans realized that the Americas were separate from Asia.

2. In the early 1500s, Spanish conquistadors defeated Indian peoples on the American mainland. Cortés conquered the Aztecs of Mexico. Later, Pizarro conquered the Incas of Peru. Vast quantities of treasure flowed back to Spain.

3. Hoping that North America contained riches similar to those in Mexico and Peru, Spanish explorers searched parts of North America in the 1500s. They traveled through the Gulf Coast, Great Plains, and Southwest but found none of the treasure they sought.

4. Spain built an empire, called New Spain, out of its American territories. Missions, towns, and forts were built by the Spanish. Many Indians were put to work farming. Using mercantilist policies, Spain forced its colonies to trade only with Spain. It also took huge amounts of precious metals out of New Spain.

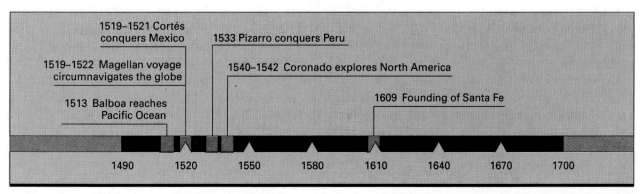

1519–1521 Cortés conquers Mexico

1533 Pizarro conquers Peru

1519–1522 Magellan voyage circumnavigates the globe

1540–1542 Coronado explores North America

1513 Balboa reaches Pacific Ocean

1609 Founding of Santa Fe

1490   1520   1550   1580   1610   1640   1670   1700

Chapter 3 REVIEW

PLACES TO LOCATE

Match each of the letters on the map with the places that are listed below.

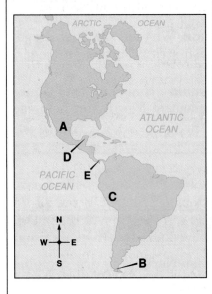

1. Isthmus of Panama
2. Mexico
3. Peru
4. Strait of Magellan
5. Yucatán

KEY TERMS

Define the terms in each of the following pairs.

1. convert; missionary
2. mercantilism; imports
3. clergy; conquistador
4. Creole; mestizo

PEOPLE TO IDENTIFY

Match each of the following people with the correct description.

Atahualpa
Vasco Núñez de Balboa
Francisco Vásquez de Coronado
Hernán Cortés
Ferdinand Magellan
Montezuma
Francisco Pizarro

1. Inca leader at the time of the Spanish conquest.
2. Leader of the first expedition to circumnavigate the earth.
3. Conquistador who defeated the Aztecs.
4. Explorer who crossed the Isthmus of Panama to find the Pacific Ocean.
5. Aztec leader at the time of the Spanish conquest.
6. Explorer who journeyed from Mexico to the Great Plains.
7. Conquistador who defeated the Incas.

REVIEWING THE FACTS

1. What role did the Pope play in establishing European claims over North and South America?

2. What was the purpose of Magellan's voyage around the world? What happened to Magellan on that voyage?
3. What were the goals of the conquistadors?
4. How did the Spanish defeat the Aztecs?
5. How did the Spanish defeat the Incas?
6. Why did the conquest of Mexico and Peru encourage Spanish exploration of North America?
7. Why did the Spanish view the expeditions into North America as failures?
8. List three reasons for Spain's success in conquering and settling North and South America.
9. What was the aim behind the building of missions on the frontier?
10. Describe the economic relationship between Spain and its American colonies.

CITIZENSHIP

1. When it built its American empire, Spain was an absolute monarchy—a nation in which the ruler holds complete power. How did the government structure of New Spain reflect this fact?
2. What *political* reason might Spain have had for trying to convert Indians to Christianity?

PRACTICING YOUR SKILL

Use your skill in learning vocabulary to match the following words from this chapter with their definitions.

cavalry (page 52)
cloves (page 50)
hack (page 48)
interpreter (page 52)
ransom (page 56)
rickety (page 59)

1. Person who translates messages
2. Kind of spice
3. Likely to fall apart
4. Soldiers on horseback
5. Payment demanded in return for release of a hostage
6. To chop roughly with a blade

CRITICAL THINKING SKILLS

1. DRAWING CONCLUSIONS
Spain and Portugal, competing for ownership of the Americas, turned to the Pope to find a solution. What does this tell you about the position of the Pope (and the Catholic Church) at the end of the 1400s?

2. WEIGHING BOTH SIDES OF AN ISSUE Why did some Indians become allies of Cortés in his battle against the Aztecs? Why might it have been a bad idea for them to do this?

3. MAKING COMPARISONS
Compare the expeditions led by Coronado, De Soto, and Cabrillo.

4. FORMING A HYPOTHESIS
Why did the Spanish build roads to connect Mexico City with the outlying parts of New Spain?

PROJECTS AND ACTIVITIES

1. WRITING A PLAY With a group of students, write a play dramatizing the struggle between the Spanish and the Aztecs for control of Mexico. The play might focus on one part of the conflict, such as Cortés's attempt to gain Indian allies or Montezuma's confusion over whether the Spaniards were really gods. Perform the play in class.

2. MAKING A TIMELINE Construct a timeline showing the different land expeditions and sea voyages discussed in this chapter.

3. MAKING A LIST Imagine that you are about to head north from Mexico on an overland expedition into the present-day United States. Make a list of the things you will need to be successful.

4. WRITING A LETTER Find out more about the Spanish missions in the 1600s. Then imagine that you are living in one of the frontier missions. Write a letter to a family member describing daily life at the mission. Include a diagram of the mission in your letter.

WRITING ABOUT TOPICS IN AMERICAN HISTORY

1. CONNECTING WITH LITERATURE A selection from *Estebanico* by Helen Rand Parish appears on pages 632–633. Read it and answer the questions. Then answer the following question: How did the expeditions north of Mexico lead to a more permanent Spanish presence in that area?

2. APPLYING THEMES: GEOGRAPHY How did Spain's economic policies determine which natural resources it valued in the Americas? What other kinds of resources might a nation value today?

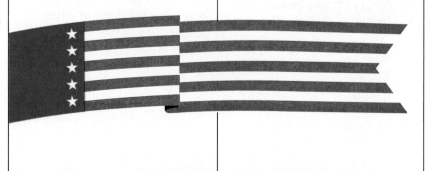

Queen Elizabeth I, England's beloved "Good Queen Bess,"
helped make England a potent rival of Spain in the struggle for
world power—including control of the new world.

CHAPTER

4 Challenges to Spanish Power (1492–1610)

KEY EVENTS

1497	Cabot sails to North America
1517	Reformation begins
1564	French establish Fort Caroline
1585	Colony started at Roanoke Island
1588	Spanish Armada defeated
1603	Champlain explores North America

1 Search for a Northwest Passage

★ Section Focus ★

Key Terms Grand Banks ■ Northwest Passage

Main Idea European explorers, searching for a water route to Asia, made important discoveries in North America.

Objectives As you read, look for answers to these questions:
1. What was the outcome of John Cabot's voyage across the Atlantic?
2. What voyages of exploration did France support? What was their goal?
3. What areas of North America were explored by Henry Hudson?

If Columbus had not reached America when he did, the honor might have gone to John Cabot (Giovanni Caboto). Like Columbus, Cabot was born in Genoa. In age they were just a few years apart. Like Columbus, Cabot learned seamanship in the Mediterranean and dreamed of sailing west to Asia. While Columbus ended up in Spain, Cabot ended up in England looking for support. After news of Columbus's voyage reached England, the king of England quickly approved Cabot's plan to search for unknown lands.

THE VOYAGE OF JOHN CABOT

In 1497 Cabot set out from England with a crew of eighteen. Because Cabot sailed farther north than Columbus, the distance across the sea was less. (Compare maps, pages 40 and 74).

Cabot crossed the Atlantic Ocean in two months and reached the northeastern coast of North America. His map and journals are lost, but he probably landed at Newfoundland. There he sighted plentiful forests and found the ocean teeming with fish. The English could catch fish simply by lowering baskets into the water and drawing them up. This rich fishing area was the Grand Banks.

Although disappointed to find no wealthy cities, Cabot was sure that he had reached Asia. He claimed the region for England and then headed back to Europe. In 1498 Cabot once again set sail across the Atlantic, hoping this time to reach Japan. It is not clear what happened on this voyage. Some say he did not return; others say his failure to reach Japan caused him to drop out of sight and memory.

Cabot's voyage, however, revealed another kind of wealth—the wealth in the Grand Banks. In their sturdy boats fishermen from England, France, and Holland crossed the Atlantic each spring to the Grand Banks. They returned with their holds full of cod and

NORTHERN EUROPEAN EXPLORATION OF NORTH AMERICA

Exploration sponsored by:
England
Netherlands
France
N
W
E
S
Hudson, 1610
Cartier, 1534-1536
Hudson Bay
Newfoundland
St. Lawrence R.
Cabot, 1497
Quebec
Champlain, 1603-1616
L. Superior
Hudson R.
L. Huron
L. Michigan
L. Ontario
L. Erie
Hudson, 1609
Verrazano, 1524
Roanoke
Mississippi R.
Fort Caroline
St. Augustine
ATLANTIC OCEAN
Gulf of Mexico
Drake, 1577-1580
PACIFIC OCEAN
Caribbean Sea
SCALE
0
800 mi
0
800 km
60°N
50°N
40°N
30°N
20°N
50°W
60°W
70°W
80°W
90°W
100°W
110°W
120°W
LAMBERT AZIMUTHAL EQUAL-AREA PROJECTION

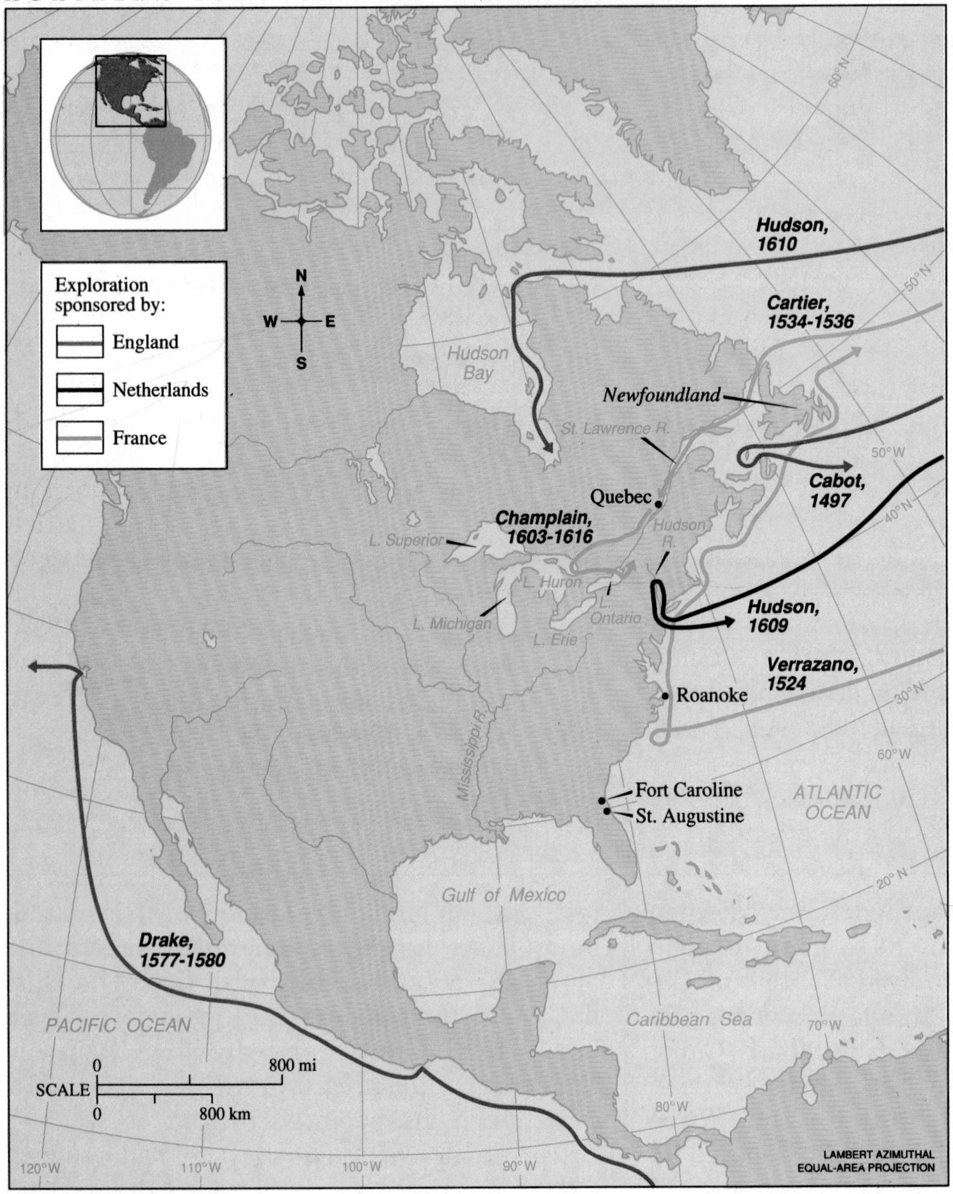

MAP SKILLS

After Columbus, European monarchs sent other expeditions to explore the Americas. Which Frenchmen explored the area around the St. Lawrence River? For which two nations did Henry Hudson sail? CRITICAL THINKING Why did Cartier and Hudson follow river routes inland from the coast?

mackerel. The fish fed the hungry of Europe, and the profits paid for more ships.

French Explorations of North America

By the early 1500s, Europeans had come to realize that the land across the Atlantic Ocean was not part of Asia. Europeans still wanted a quick and easy way to reach Asia. Explorers set out to find a water route around the Americas. Such a route, called the **Northwest Passage**, was the goal of several daring voyages of exploration.

One of the first explorers to seek a Northwest Passage was Giovanni da Verrazano (ver–uh–ZAH–no). Although Verrazano was Italian, his most important voyage was made for France.

In 1524 Verrazano sailed westward from France to look for a Northwest Passage to Asia. He followed the coast of North America from present-day North Carolina as far north as Newfoundland, Canada. Verrazano realized that the land he explored was not the same region that Columbus had discovered.

However, Verrazano found no passage through the land. Disappointed, he returned to France.

About ten years later, Jacques Cartier (kahr–TYAY), another explorer for France, sailed to America. In 1535 Cartier reached the St. Lawrence River in present-day Canada. Hoping this waterway might cut through the continent, Cartier followed the St. Lawrence for hundreds of miles. Finally he came to a large Indian village where the city of Montreal now stands. There rapids prevented Cartier's ships from going farther upstream, and Cartier had to abandon his pursuit of a Northwest Passage. Cartier's exploration, however, was the basis of French claims to lands drained by the St. Lawrence River.

Half a century later, France resumed the attempt to find a shortcut to Asia. In 1603 Samuel de Champlain (sham–PLAYN), a French sea captain, explored the Atlantic Coast from the mouth of the St. Lawrence River to the southern part of present-day Massachusetts. In 1608, at a site on the St. Lawrence River, Champlain founded a fur-trading post that he named Quebec. It was the first permanent French settlement in North America.

Champlain later traveled farther inland. He located Lake Champlain in present-day New York and explored the upper Great Lakes. Champlain learned, and taught others, much about the Indians and the geography of the region. His discoveries laid the foundation for French colonization in North America. Still, Champlain was disappointed not to find a shortcut to Asia.

THE VOYAGES OF HENRY HUDSON

Holland and England shared France's interest in a Northwest Passage. In 1609 Dutch merchants hired an English explorer named Henry Hudson to find a route to China. Sailing in a small ship named the *Half Moon,* Hudson followed a westward course across the Atlantic until he reached North America. Hudson came upon the river that now bears his name, the Hudson. He followed this river inland into present-day New York, opening the way for Dutch colonists to settle the region later.

Disappointed that the Hudson River was not a Northwest Passage, Hudson returned to Europe. In 1610, however, he made another trip to North America. This time he was sailing under the banner of his own country, England. In the small ship *Discovery,* Hudson and his crew headed to the northeast coast of present-day Canada. After fighting their way through an ice-blocked strait, they discovered a great body of clear water, today called Hudson Bay.

All summer, Hudson sailed these waters in search of a Northwest Passage to Asia. When winter came, he and his crew had to camp on the frozen shores of the bay. By spring, only a small amount of food was left. The crew had suffered so many hardships that most of the

Henry Hudson brought his son with him on his voyages to North America. In 1611 the crew rebelled after a bitter, icebound winter. They set their captain adrift in Hudson Bay, where Hudson and his son perished. GEOGRAPHY What search led Hudson to Canada?

men could take no more. They forced Hudson, his young son, and a few loyal sailors into a small boat. Then they set it adrift. Hudson was never heard from again. Only a few members of his crew managed to make their way back to England.

Hudson and other bold explorers did not find the waterway to Asia that they were seeking. However, they did do something even more important. They turned the attention of Europe away from Asia to the Americas. Europeans no longer looked at the Americas as a barrier blocking their way to Asia. They became interested in this new land for its own sake. Rising European interest in the Americas led to a new question: Who would control these new lands?

2 The Religious Challenge

Section Focus

Key Terms Reformation ■ Protestant

Main Idea Religious disputes during the 1500s gave rise to challenges to Spain's authority both in Europe and in the Americas.

Objectives As you read, look for answers to these questions:
1. How and why did a split in Christianity take place?
2. What effect did the religious disputes have on European history? On events in the Americas?

In 1493 the Pope had granted most of the Americas to Spain. Why, therefore, did England, France, and Holland make their own claims to parts of North America? One reason was that they too wanted wealth such as Spain had found in the Americas. Another reason was that in the 1500s half of Europe no longer recognized the Pope's authority.

THE REFORMATION

The development of printing in the 1400s brought about an important change. For the first time, ordinary people could afford to own a copy of the Bible. As a result, many people began to question the authority of the Roman Catholic Church. The Bible, they believed, described a simple religious faith, but the Church had grown rich, powerful, and corrupt. Critics also charged that the Church owned too much land and required too much money for support.

In 1517 a German priest named Martin Luther nailed to a church door his protests against corruption in the Church. Thus began the Reformation, the revolt against the Catholic Church. Those who revolted were called Protestants because of their *protests* against Catholic teachings.

**MARTIN LUTHER
(1483–1546) was a German priest whose teachings led to the Protestant Reformation. Luther attacked corruption in the Catholic Church and challenged the Pope's authority. When Luther refused to give up his beliefs, the Pope banished him from the Catholic Church. Luther later translated the Bible into German.**

Protestantism, the faith of the Protestants, spread rapidly, particularly in northern Europe. Soon Europe was bitterly divided between Protestants, who did not recognize the Pope's authority, and Catholics, who did.

The Spanish monarchs saw themselves as defenders of the Catholic Church against Protestants. They used the wealth of the Americas to finance campaigns against the Protestants. Religious wars and turmoil swept through Holland, France, and Germany during the 1500s. The religious passions of Europe also spilled over to the Americas.

A Protestant Colony in Florida

In the 1530s, while exploring the St. Lawrence River for France, Jacques Cartier had tried to start a colony near present-day Quebec. The attempt failed. For a time the French abandoned the idea of a colony in America.

The idea of a colony revived, however, as a result of religious strife in France. The French king was Catholic, but a growing number of French people had become Protestants. These Protestants were known as Huguenots (HYOO–guh–nahts). Among the Huguenots was the Admiral of France, Gaspard de Coligny (kol–een–YEE).

Coligny convinced royal officials to establish a Huguenot colony in the Americas. The colony would have served several purposes. Huguenots saw it as a refuge, a place where they could live free from persecution. Catholics liked the idea of getting the Huguenots out of France. The king of France also relished the thought of his flag flying on American shores and challenging Spanish claims in the Americas.

In 1564 a group of French colonists led by René de Laudonnière established Fort Caroline near present-day Jacksonville, Florida. The group included Huguenots as well as young noblemen bent on finding gold and adventure. None of them knew how to hunt, fish, or farm. After they wore out their welcome with the native Timucua Indians, who had fed them, they had nothing to eat. To survive, they ground up fish bones into a powder and made bread of it. They waited in despair for new supplies from France.

The Spanish Respond

In late August 1565 the longed-for help from France arrived. The little fort swarmed with activity. Then a week later "a huge hulk" approached the French ships anchored offshore. It was a Spanish warship. The commander, Pedro Menéndez de Avilés, called out: "Gentlemen, whence does this fleet come?"

"From France," was the answer.

This drawing shows the layout of the French Huguenot settlement of Fort Caroline on the east coast of Florida. **GEOGRAPHY** How did the colonists modify the landscape in order to help protect their fort?

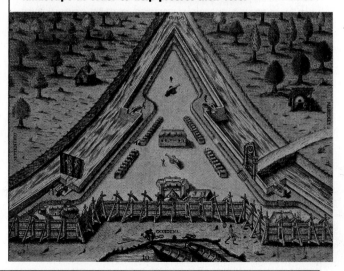

The Spanish built their first fort at St. Augustine in 1565. The fort that stands there today, Castillo de San Marcos, was begun in 1672 and now serves as a museum. **CULTURE** What is the value of restoring and maintaining historical sites?

"What are you doing here?" Menéndez asked.

"Bringing soldiers and supplies for a fort which the king of France has in this country, and for many others which he soon will have."

"Are you Catholics or Lutherans [Protestants]?"

"Lutherans," they answered.

Then Menéndez replied, "I . . . have come to this country to hang and behead all Lutherans whom I shall find by land or sea, according to instructions from my king. . . ."

The French quickly moved out to sea. After a short pursuit Menéndez gave up the chase. Returning to the coast, he sailed south a short distance and built a Spanish fort at St. Augustine. The fort took shape around an immense barnlike structure that was the dwelling of an Indian chief. Today St. Augustine is the oldest permanent European settlement existing in the United States.

The French had hoped to destroy the Spanish fleet and thereby cut off Menéndez. However, a tempest, the worst the Indians could remember, roared out of the south. The French fleet was scattered. For Menéndez the storm meant opportunity. With 500 men he marched overland through marsh and forest and driving rain to attack Fort Caroline. He destroyed the fort, killing 142 men, but sparing about 50 women and children.

The massacre was not over. When the storm blew itself out, several French ships had been wrecked on the sandbars. The fate of the shipwrecked survivors was grim. Except for a few carpenters whom he needed, Menéndez massacred the French. The reason, he made clear, was not that they were French, but that they were Protestant.

SECTION REVIEW

1. KEY TERMS Reformation, Protestant

2. PEOPLE AND PLACES Martin Luther, Fort Caroline, St. Augustine

3. COMPREHENSION What was Spain's attitude toward the Reformation?

4. COMPREHENSION What different purposes were served by the founding of Fort Caroline?

5. CRITICAL THINKING What lessons can you draw from the failure of Fort Caroline regarding the requirements for a successful colony?

When studying history, it is useful to compare statistics (numerical facts). Graphs present statistics in a way that is easy to understand. They help you grasp the meaning of statistics without being overwhelmed by them.

The most commonly used types of graphs are the line graph and the bar graph. On a **line graph,** such as the one shown below, information is plotted by dots, which are then connected by a line. A **bar graph** shows information in bars or columns. (See page 338 for an example of a bar graph.)

To read a bar or line graph, you need to understand its parts:

- The *title* tells you the topic and purpose of the graph.
- The *horizontal axis* runs along the bottom of the graph. Often it shows the time period—days, months, or years. Look for the label that explains the purpose of the axis.
- The *vertical axis* runs up one side of the graph. It often shows statistical informa-tion, such as quantities or prices. Like the horizontal axis, the vertical axis has a label that explains its purpose.

Another kind of graph used in this book is a **circle graph.** (See page 87 for an example of a circle graph.) A circle graph is often called a **pie graph** because it is cut into sections like a pie. Each "slice" represents a percentage of the whole.

PRACTICING YOUR SKILL

1. What is the title of the graph on this page?
2. (a) What does the horizontal axis show? (b) What does the vertical axis show?
3. What is the maximum value of imports that can be represented on this graph?
4. (a) What was the value of Spain's imports of gold and silver during the period 1546–1550? (b) What was the value during the period 1586–1590?
5. Give a one-sentence summary of the information presented in the graph.

IMPORTS OF GOLD AND SILVER FROM NEW SPAIN AND PERU

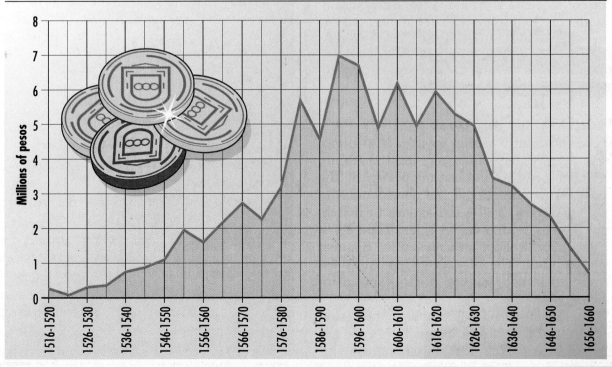

3 The English Challenge at Sea

Section Focus

Key Terms sea dog ■ armada ■ privateer

Main Idea Spain and England, divided by issues of religion and power, clashed during the 1500s. Their confrontation would affect the future of the Americas.

Objectives As you read, look for answers to these questions:
1. How did Protestantism come to England?
2. How and why did England raid Spanish shipping?
3. What was the outcome of Spain's attempt to conquer England?

The Reformation came to England in an unusual way. In the late 1520s and early 1530s King Henry VIII wanted a divorce from his wife, the daughter of Spanish monarchs Ferdinand and Isabella, because she had provided no male heir to the throne. The Pope adamantly opposed granting the divorce. Therefore, Henry broke from the Catholic Church. In its place he set up the Church of England as the state religion. Although independent of the Pope and considered Protestant, the Church of England kept the traditional Catholic practices.

After Henry's death in 1547, the Spanish plotted to restore England to Catholicism. Yet under the strong-willed, capable leadership of Queen Elizabeth I, England began to grow more powerful. Elizabeth vowed to keep England Protestant. She also hoped to grab a share of the wealth of the Americas.

DRAKE AND THE SEA DOGS

The transatlantic fishing voyages that began with John Cabot's discovery of the Grand Banks helped England become powerful. The fishing trips encouraged the development of fast, seaworthy craft—and sailors to match. Such speedy craft were also just right for a pirate on the lookout for a straggling Spanish treasure ship. The big, slow Spanish ships were easy targets for sea dogs—captains of English pirate ships.

The most famous of the sea dogs was Francis Drake. Drake felt a bitter hatred for the Spaniards. In 1567 his ship had been attacked by Spanish sailors pretending to be friendly. For many years afterward, Drake sought revenge by raiding Spanish vessels and Spanish towns. The Spanish feared him and called him "the Dragon." Spain's King Philip II offered a huge reward to anyone who could kill him.

Following a dispute with the Pope, King Henry VIII of England broke with the Catholic Church and brought Protestantism to England. Tensions between England and Catholic Spain increased as a result. **RELIGION** Why did Spain oppose the Reformation in England?

In 1581 Queen Elizabeth I made Francis Drake a knight for his daring campaigns against Spain. Drake had plundered silver and gold from Spanish colonies. He had also circumnavigated the world in his ship, the *Golden Hind*. ECONOMICS How did the English people benefit from Drake's attacks on the Spanish?

Drake's most famous accomplishment was to sail through the Strait of Magellan in 1578 and up the coast of Peru. The Spanish had never been attacked in their "Spanish lake," as they proudly called the Pacific Ocean. Drake, however, stole so much Spanish treasure that his ship, the *Golden Hind,* rode low in the water from its load of gold, silver, and gems.

To evade Spanish warships, Drake sailed north. He touched briefly on the California coast, and then sailed west across the Pacific. Drake became the first Englishman to circumnavigate the world.

For years Queen Elizabeth had looked the other way while English sea dogs attacked Spanish ships. With Spanish loot flowing into her treasury, Elizabeth did not need to tax her own people. When Drake returned to England, she knighted him for his achievement. She had received half the treasure. Furthermore, Drake had wounded Spanish pride and carried the English flag into new waters.

THE SPANISH ARMADA

For King Philip of Spain, the knighting of Drake was the last straw. He decided that the time had come to teach the English a lesson. He assembled an armada—a giant fleet—to invade England and restore Catholicism to that nation. Some people called it the "Invincible Armada" because they believed it could not lose. Even brave Englishmen like

Drake were worried. "There was never any force so strong as there is now . . . making ready against your Majesty," he warned Queen Elizabeth.

The armada of 130 ships sailed forth in the summer of 1588. It carried 8,000 sailors, 19,000 soldiers, and several hundred priests to reconvert the English to Catholicism. The Spanish commander was inexperienced and, worse, seasick. His ships were big and bulky. Waiting for them were England's small navy and numbers of privateers—privately operated armed ships. Old sea hands like Sir Francis Drake were junior admirals.

"There was never any force so strong as there is now . . . making ready against your Majesty."

—*Sir Francis Drake, describing the Spanish Armada*

The English had fewer ships, but these were better than the Spanish ones. The Spanish had built big ships in order to carry heavy cannons. The English, however, had found a way to make small cannons that were just as powerful as the larger Spanish ones. As a result, the English were able to build ships that were lighter, faster, and more deadly.

The two fleets first met in the English Channel. The English ships darted back and forth around the Spanish, firing and then sailing out of reach of the Spanish guns. The armada next headed for a French harbor, where it was supposed to pick up more soldiers for the invasion of England. However, the troops were not ready to board. The English sent burning ships into the harbor, setting many Spanish ships aflame.

Crippled by English attacks, the Spanish decided to head for home. Then a terrible storm hit. The storm, known as the "Protestant wind," delivered a knock-out punch to the weakened armada. Having lost half its

This painting by an unknown artist shows the ships of the Spanish Armada in battle against England in 1588. The Spanish attempt to invade England was a total failure. HISTORY How did the defeat of the armada affect events in the Americas?

ships to battle or storm, the Spanish fleet made an inglorious return to Spain.

The failure of the Spanish Armada meant that England would remain Protestant. Spain's pride had also been dealt a serious blow. The world now knew that Spain, for all its wealth and might, was not all-powerful. Other nations became braver about seeking commerce and empire in North America.

SECTION REVIEW

1. KEY TERMS sea dog, armada, privateer

2. PEOPLE AND PLACES Elizabeth I, Philip II, Francis Drake, English Channel

3. COMPREHENSION Why did Henry VIII break with the Catholic Church?

4. COMPREHENSION Why did Queen Elizabeth make Francis Drake a knight?

5. CRITICAL THINKING In what way was the battle between England and Spain in 1588 a religious as well as a political contest?

4 The First English Colony

★ ★

Section Focus

Key Term Roanoke Island

Main Idea The first English efforts to establish a colony in North America failed. This failure taught the English valuable lessons for the future.

Objectives As you read, look for answers to these questions:
1. Why did the English decide to establish colonies?
2. What problems did the first English colony face?
3. What lessons did the English learn about building colonies?

★ ★ ★ ★

For more than a century the English had been content to sail, to fish, and to rob in the new world, but not to settle. Why? One reason is that it was easier for the English to steal from the Spanish than to build their own settlements. Another reason is that people in England did not yet feel the need for settlements. In fact, the word *colony* did not even enter the English language until about 1550.

VISIONS OF A "WESTERN PLANTING"

Not until the 1580s did Richard Hakluyt, a seafaring geographer, propose that the English establish a colony or, in his words, a "planting." Hakluyt urged the English people to abandon their "sluggish security" and achieve what other nations had already accomplished.

A "western planting" would have many advantages for England, said Hakluyt.

(1) It would provide a place to send petty criminals.

(2) It would allow England to build overseas bases.

(3) It would provide a market for English exports of manufactured goods and at the same time serve as a source of raw materials for England.

(4) It would plant the Protestant faith in the Americas and keep the Spanish from "flowing over all the face . . . of America."

Hakluyt did not mention that such a colony should be able to feed itself. The English would have to learn that by experience.

THE FOUNDING OF ROANOKE

Sir Walter Raleigh, a soldier of sharp and witty mind favored by Queen Elizabeth, was the first Englishman to establish a colony across the seas. Raleigh claimed for England the Atlantic coast between the 34th and 45th parallels, roughly the area from present-day North Carolina to Maine. Raleigh named this region *Virginia* for England's Virgin Queen.

Under Raleigh's sponsorship, England's first colony was begun in 1585 at Roanoke Island off the coast of North Carolina. It lasted but a year. The survivors, starving because the Indians had stopped giving them food, begged passage home on a relief ship.

A SECOND ATTEMPT AT ROANOKE

The original settlement on Roanoke had been little more than a military post. When it failed, John White, a talented artist, convinced Sir Walter Raleigh to try a new approach. White's idea was to attract settlers who would bring their families with them and invest some of their own money in the colony. Each settler would receive 500 acres of land and some voice in the government of the colony.

In the spring of 1587, White set sail with his daughter, his son-in-law, and about 120 other men, women, and children. When the group reached Roanoke, they quickly started repairing the cottages left by the earlier settlers. It was clear to White, however, that he would have to get more supplies to maintain the colony through the winter.

John White founded a colony at Roanoke Island in 1587. By the time he returned in 1590, all the colonists had vanished, leaving behind only a puzzling message. **GEOGRAPHY** Why was Roanoke Island a poor site for a colony?

White was reluctant to leave Roanoke. He now had a newborn granddaughter as well—Virginia Dare, the first English child born in America. The other Roanoke colonists, however, believed that White should make the trip back to England for supplies. He finally agreed and departed late in the summer of 1587.

White was not able to return to Roanoke until 1590. A relief ship was supposed to have gone to Roanoke in 1588, but every seaworthy ship and sailor was needed to defend England against the Spanish Armada. When White finally did reach Roanoke, he was shocked at what he found. Not a soul remained at the settlement. The only clues were the letters *CRO* carved on a tree and the word *CROATOAN* on a doorpost. White assumed that the settlers had gone to a neighboring island where friendly Croatoan Indians lived. Storms, however, kept him from reaching the Croatoans and forced his return to England. To this day, no one knows for sure what really happened to the "lost colonists" of Roanoke Island.

LEARNING FROM EARLY EXPERIMENTS

John White lacked the funds to make another voyage to North America. Sir Walter Raleigh lacked interest. The Roanoke colony had been a great financial loss for Raleigh rather than a source of profit. Yet in a broader sense, the English did gain from the experience. Their failure at Roanoke taught them some useful lessons about founding colonies.

Roanoke Island had been chosen as the site of the first English colony largely for geographic reasons. The island was far enough south to have a relatively warm climate. Thus the Roanoke settlers would not have to face the bitter cold that had driven French settlers out of Newfoundland in the 1540s. It was hoped, too, that the climate would prove suitable for crops that could not be grown in England.

Though the weather was indeed mild, the colonists had overlooked a serious drawback of the island. Roanoke lacked a protected harbor where ships could safely anchor. The shallow coastal waters and shifting tides put ships in danger of running aground.

Choosing a poor location for their colony was not the only mistake the English made. Perhaps the most important reason for Roanoke's failure was the lack of people, funds, and supplies. Raleigh and his backers had underestimated the problems of building a settlement so far from Europe. Each time England sent colonists to Roanoke, first in 1585 and then in 1587, only about 100 people stayed. They were ill-prepared for the dangers they would have to face, such as enemy attacks, violent storms, and food shortages. The English soon realized that if American colonies were to thrive, better planning was necessary.

SECTION REVIEW

1. KEY TERM Roanoke Island

2. PEOPLE AND PLACES Richard Hakluyt, Walter Raleigh, Virginia, John White

3. COMPREHENSION What arguments did Richard Hakluyt use in favor of establishing overseas colonies?

4. COMPREHENSION Why did the first English settlement at Roanoke Island fail?

5. CRITICAL THINKING Why did the English make so many mistakes in the establishment of Roanoke?

CHAPTER 4 SUMMARY AND TIMELINE

1. Though their search for a Northwest Passage proved a failure, European explorers made discoveries in the Americas. John Cabot claimed land in eastern North America for England in 1497. France sponsored voyages by Verrazano, Cartier, and Champlain. Henry Hudson explored parts of present-day New York and Canada in the early 1600s.

2. Religious conflict in Europe spilled over into the Americas. The Reformation in Europe split Christianity into two groups, Catholics and Protestants. Spain saw itself as a defender of Catholicism against Protestantism. Spain prevented France from establishing a Protestant colony in Florida.

3. England and Spain clashed over issues of religion and power during the 1500s. English pirates raided Spanish treasure ships returning from the Americas. In 1588 the Spanish Armada tried but failed to conquer England and return it to Catholicism. The defeat of the Spanish Armada encouraged other European nations to challenge Spain's position in the Americas.

4. England made its first attempt to build an American colony when Sir Walter Raleigh began a settlement on Roanoke Island in 1585. It failed. A second settlement at Roanoke also failed. England learned valuable lessons from these experiences.

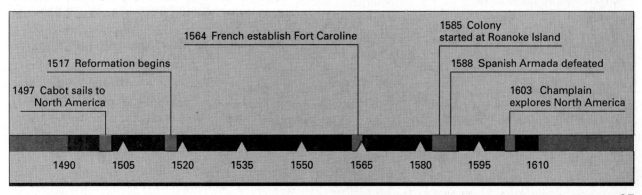

1497 Cabot sails to North America

1517 Reformation begins

1564 French establish Fort Caroline

1585 Colony started at Roanoke Island

1588 Spanish Armada defeated

1603 Champlain explores North America

1490 1505 1520 1535 1550 1565 1580 1595 1610

Chapter 4 REVIEW

PLACES TO LOCATE

Match each of the letters on the map with the places that are listed below.

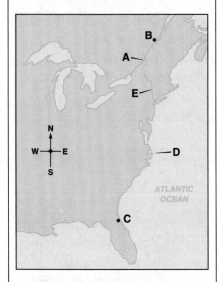

1. Hudson River
2. Quebec
3. Roanoke Island
4. St. Augustine
5. St. Lawrence River

KEY TERMS

Use the following terms to complete the sentences.

armada
Grand Banks
Northwest Passage
Protestant
Reformation
Roanoke Island
sea dog

1. A ___ was someone who revolted against the Catholic Church.

2. John Cabot found the ___, a rich fishing area off of North America.
3. A ___ was an English pirate who attacked Spanish shipping.
4. The first English colony in the Americas, at ___, failed.
5. In 1588 Spain sent a vast fleet called the ___ to conquer England.
6. The ___ was the rebellion, led by Martin Luther, against the Catholic Church.
7. European explorers sailed to the Americas looking for ___, a route to Asia.

PEOPLE TO IDENTIFY

Identify the following people and tell why each one was important.

John Cabot
Jacques Cartier
Samuel de Champlain
Elizabeth I
Francis Drake
Martin Luther
Philip II

REVIEWING THE FACTS

1. What was the major accomplishment of John Cabot's voyage to the Americas? What had he hoped to accomplish?
2. What goal did Henry Hudson seek in his explorations of the Americas?
3. How did the development of printing help cause the Reformation?

4. How did Spain react to the rise of Protestantism?
5. Why did Spain destroy the French settlement of Fort Caroline?
6. How did the Reformation come to England?
7. What actions of Francis Drake angered Spain? What was Queen Elizabeth's attitude toward Drake?
8. What happened to the Spanish Armada?
9. What happened to the first colony at Roanoke Island?
10. What lessons did the English learn from their failure at Roanoke?

CITIZENSHIP

1. The invention of the printing press helped make people more suspicious of Church authority. Might it also have made people more suspicious of government? Explain.
2. One reason England and France sought to build colonies in the Americas was to find a place for "undesirables." For England, this meant criminals; for France, Huguenots. Do you approve of this practice? Explain.
3. What reasons might have led English people to leave home and settle in Roanoke? Would those reasons have been different for families than for single persons? Explain.

PRACTICING YOUR SKILL

The circle graph below shows what happened to the ships of the Spanish Armada. Use it to answer the questions that follow.

Sank near England (7)

Sank on return voyage (59)

Survived (64)

1. How many ships were in the armada at the start?

2. How many ships remained when the armada arrived back in Spain?

3. When did the armada lose more ships, in battles with England or on the return trip to Spain?

4. Using information presented in the graph, make a general statement about the fate of the Spanish Armada.

CRITICAL THINKING SKILLS

1. LINKING PAST AND PRESENT European explorers of the 1500s made new discoveries by sailing into unexplored waters. What unexplored areas remain to be challenged in today's world?

2. MAKING COMPARISONS Compare Martin Luther's and Henry VIII's reasons for breaking with the Catholic Church.

3. CULTURAL CONFLICT What might explain why the Indians gave food to the first Roanoke colonists and then stopped giving them food?

4. FORMING A HYPOTHESIS What might the carving of the word *CROATOAN* at the site of the Roanoke colony tell about the fate of the colonists?

PROJECTS AND ACTIVITIES

1. MAKING A MAP Choose one of the following explorers—Cabot, Verrazano, Cartier, Champlain, or Hudson—and draw a map of his expedition to North America. (You may use the map on page 74 as a guide.) Use reference books to find out more about his expedition. On your map, use arrows to show the journeys. Explain the arrows in a map key. Use dates to show the progress of each exploration. Label all other necessary information on the map and give the map a title.

2. WRITING LETTERS Write two letters: one that Martin Luther might have written the Pope to explain his reasons for leaving the Catholic Church, and one the Pope might have written in response.

3. CREATING AN ADVERTISEMENT Imagine that you are trying to recruit people to settle in Roanoke. Write and illustrate an advertisement to persuade people to sail to America.

4. PRESENTING A PLAY Prepare a class play about the "lost colony" at Roanoke. Base the play on historical facts, but use your imagination to fill in unknown details. Write dialogue for the characters. Prepare scenery and costumes. With classmates, present the play for other classes.

WRITING ABOUT TOPICS IN AMERICAN HISTORY

1. CONNECTING WITH LITERATURE A selection from *Roanoke: A Novel of the Lost Colony* by Sonia Levitin appears on pages 634–635. Read it and answer the questions. Then answer the following question: Why was the issue of how to deal with the Indians so important for the Roanoke colonists?

2. APPLYING THEMES: GLOBAL INTERACTIONS England's defeat of the Spanish Armada changed the course of history in the Americas as well as in Europe. How might American history have been different if the Spanish Armada had succeeded?

UNIT 1: American Mosaic

★ A Multicultural Perspective ★

"American Mosaic" examines the ways people from a variety of traditions have enriched American history. These pages profile some of the diverse players who participated in the events discussed in each unit of this book.

This first Mosaic describes world leaders who, even before Columbus set sail, sent forth adventurers to explore unknown parts of the world. It also introduces a rich Native American cultural heritage—a heritage that was to be greatly affected by the arrival of people from Europe and Africa.

Almost 500 years before Columbus's voyage, in the year 1014, **Freydis** commanded a Viking expedition to the northern coast of North America. (Shown left is a tapestry from a Viking queen's ship.) Cruel and treacherous, Freydis was a noblewoman whose brother, Leif Ericson, had led the first known Viking voyage to America. Those Vikings had landed in a place they called Vinland, probably in Canada. Freydis traveled there too, along with another boat. Believing the people on this boat to be her rivals, Freydis led a bloody massacre of them. This tragic voyage to America was to be the last known one the Vikings made.

The Age of Exploration was not limited to Europe. In the early 1300s, the Mali Empire (map, right) stretched across West Africa. Its emperor, **Abu Bakiri II,** dreamed of reaching lands beyond his continent. He sent 200 ships off with the orders that they not return until they reached the end of the ocean. Only one came back, telling of others lost at sea. Bakiri decided to lead the next expedition himself. He never returned—nor did any of his ships. Some historians believe that one or more of these African ships may have made it to South America.

The Spanish called her Doña Marina, but she was born **Malinche** to a noble Aztec family. Sold as a slave to the Maya of Tabasco, Malinche learned to speak their language. When Cortés and his men rode into Tabasco, conquering the Maya there, they found in Malinche a valuable translator and a loyal helper. She saved Cortés as he led his men toward the Aztec capital. The empire's ruler, Montezuma, planned to kill the Spanish before they reached his city. Malinche heard of this plan and warned Cortés. Malinche later met Montezuma when she translated his words for Cortés (left).

The last emperor of the Aztecs, **Cuauhtemoc** (shown left surrounded by his subjects), led his people against the Spanish with bravery and determination. The nephew of Montezuma, Cuauhtemoc was only in his early twenties when he took over an empire almost entirely under Spanish control. Though his capital, Tenochtitlán, was under siege and had almost no food or water left, he refused to surrender. The Aztecs fought bravely until their city was a smoking ruin. Brought before Cortés, Cuauhtemoc touched the Spanish leader's dagger and asked for death. Cortés imprisoned him instead. In captivity Cuauhtemoc was tortured. Later, after hearing rumors that Cuauhtemoc was urging rebellion, Cortés had the former emperor hanged. Today, Cuauhtemoc is considered a national hero of Mexico.

Before English colonists arrived in America, Iroquois tribes had come together to form a con-

federation. The leader of this movement, **Hiawatha,** was born around 1525. (His wampum belt is shown above.) As a young man, Hiawatha became convinced of the importance of uniting the Cayuga, Mohawk, Oneida, Seneca, and Onondaga to ensure peace in the region that is now upper New York State. Skilled as a diplomat and speaker, Hiawatha convinced the five tribes to form the League of the Iroquois. Their chiefs pledged not to make war on each other.

Many scholars believe that one of the pilots of Christopher Columbus's first voyage, Pedro Alonzo Niño, was a black sailor.

One early leader in colonial Brazil was **Zambi,** a man described as "a Negro of singular courage, great presence of mind, and unusual devotion." He needed those virtues because his colony, Palmares, was under constant attack from the Portuguese. Portugal controlled Brazil, and Portuguese colonists brought thousands of African slaves there

(right). Many of them escaped to the jungle, and it was some of those runaways who founded Palmares. About 20,000 people lived within the settlement's great walls and followed the laws and customs of Africa. Attacked by the Portuguese army 25 times, Palmares was undefeated for 69 years. Finally, in 1697 the Portuguese succeeded in destroying the settlement. After their defeat, it is said, the soldiers of Palmares hurled themselves from a cliff rather than surrender.

HISTORIANS' CORNER

A New Look at Columbus's Voyages

From their earliest years in school, American students usually learn to think of Columbus's voyages and the European settlement of the Americas as heroic, exciting steps forward. Today, however, some historians consider this viewpoint too one-sided and Europe-centered. They are concerned with the effects—good and bad—of these events on other peoples.

Alfred W. Crosby

Of the three human groups chiefly involved in the linkages between the two worlds—Europeans and Euro-Americans, Africans and Afro-Americans, and Amerindians—the first has benefited most, by the obvious standard, population size. According to the demographer Kingsley Davis, about 50 million Europeans migrated to the New World between 1750 and 1930, and the populations of the lands to which most of them went increased 14 times, while that of the rest of the world increased by 2.5 times. In the same 180 years the number of Caucasians on earth increased 5.4 times, Asians only 2.3 times, and black Africans and Afro-Americans less than 2 times. . . .

Columbus's legacy to black Africans and their descendants is mixed. An estimated 10 million Africans crossed the Atlantic to the Americas, where they worked and died as chattel. . . . The slave trade transformed West African society . . . enriching some peoples and creating powerful states, and decimating others and de-stroying them as political and cultural entities. . . .

The total number of people lost to Africa was probably fewer than were added because of the cultivation of Amerindian crops brought to Africa by the slavers. The number of Afro-Americans in 1950 was . . . approximately one-fifth of all the blacks on the planet.

Columbus was the advanced scout of catastrophe for Amerindians. There were a few happy [results]—the flowering of equestrian cultures in the American grasslands, for instance—but on balance, the coming of whites and blacks brought disease, followed by intimidation, eviction . . . and obliteration of many peoples and ways of life. . . .

The most spectacular killer of Amerindians was smallpox. . . . Smallpox . . . spread to Mexico on the heels of Cortés, swept through Central America, and preceded Pizarro into the realms of the Incas. Witnesses estimated the losses at one-fourth, one-third, or even one-half of the infected populations. . . . Readers who are still skeptical about the killing poten-tial of new infections should turn to accounts of the Black Death in the Old World or to a consideration of the potentialities of AIDS in the 1980s. Imagine the consequences if AIDS were not a venereal but instead a breath-borne disease like smallpox.

From Alfred W. Crosby, *The Columbian Voyages, The Columbian Exchange, and Their Historians.* Copyright © 1987. Reprinted by permission of the American Historical Association.

Critical Thinking

1. What kind of evidence does the author present to show that Columbus's discoveries had uneven benefits for different groups of people?

2. According to the author, what factor offset the destruction that slavery brought to African countries and peoples?

3. What kinds of events does the author feel are missing from the American history textbooks that most students use today?

UNIT TWO

Colonial Settlement

CHAPTERS IN THIS UNIT

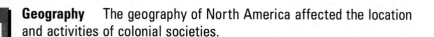

THEMES IN AMERICAN HISTORY

 Geography   The geography of North America affected the location and activities of colonial societies.

 Expanding Democracy   English colonists took important steps toward self-government during the 1600s.

Economic Development   The colonial economic systems filled the needs of European governments.

Pluralistic Society   The search for religious freedom led to the development of many different religious groups in colonial society.

 Global Interactions   Rivalry for North American colonies pitted Europe's most powerful nations against one another.

*E*nglish settlers moved by the thousands to North America during the 1600s. White wooden churches testify to the importance of religion in colonial life.

5 English Colonies Founded in North America (1607–1732)

1 Success at Jamestown

 Section Focus

Key Terms mercenary ■ investor ■ share of stock ■ charter ■ headright ■ indentured servant ■ House of Burgesses

Main Idea Despite many difficulties, England established its first permanent colony in the Americas in 1607 at Jamestown.

Objectives As you read, look for answers to these questions:
1. How did the English pay for the establishment of colonies?
2. What happened to the English settlement at Jamestown?

"Good Queen Bess," as Elizabeth I was called, still ruled England in 1600. During her long reign England had become richer (thanks partly to stolen Spanish treasure) and more powerful. Francis Drake was no longer alive, but the memory of his exploits was fresh. People continued to talk of Hakluyt's idea that England, too, should establish colonies in faraway places.

JOHN SMITH IN A CHANGING WORLD
For one young man the times were just too exciting to stay on the family farm. In 1600 John Smith was about twenty years old. Several years earlier he had finished his education and had gone off to France as a mercenary—a professional soldier hired by a foreign country. He had done well soldiering but was now back in England. Still refusing to farm, Smith craved knowledge of the world instead. He became a friend of the explorer Henry Hudson and read everything

John Smith helped create a successful English colony at Jamestown. **NATIONAL IDENTITY** How does this portrait suggest that Smith was a strong leader?

Lacking financial support from the Crown, English merchants formed joint-stock companies to pay for the building of colonies in North America. Investors in the companies shared the costs and profits of trading with the new colonies. ECONOMICS How did Richard Hakluyt encourage investment in American colonies?

Hakluyt had published. This included several volumes of the letters and records of all those who had explored the Americas.

Then a restless Smith returned to being a mercenary. This time he was captured by the Turks and sold into slavery. He worked as a slave several years before he killed his Turkish slaveowner in anger and escaped by horseback into Russia. When he finally made his way back to England, he learned that Queen Elizabeth had died in 1603. The new English monarch was her cousin, King James of Scotland.

Unlike the English Protestants, King James felt no hostility toward Spain. In a move highly unpopular with the English, James made peace with Spain. As a result, English privateers no longer had license to raid the Spanish Main. On the other hand, Spain released its claim to all of North America. With peace secured, England turned seriously to the idea of establishing colonies. Waiting in the wings was John Smith.

MERCHANT SUPPORT FOR COLONIES

The most enthusiastic support for new colonies came from the merchants. Merchants who had read Hakluyt's reports believed that the Americas offered valuable trade opportu-

nities. According to Hakluyt, the Americas were bursting with resources:

> [Explorers] found there gold, silver, copper, lead, and pearls in abundance; precious stones, as turquoises and emeralds; spices . . . as pepper, cinnamon, cloves; white and red cotton; . . . all kinds of beasts; . . . all kinds of fowls for food and feathers; . . . excellent vines in many places for wines; the soil apt to bear olives for oil; all kinds of fruits, as oranges, almonds, . . . figs, plums; . . . all kind of [fragrant] trees and date trees, cypresses, cedars . . . and exceeding quantity of all kind of precious furs . . . oil to make soap, and . . . fish.

The most serious problem facing the would-be colonizers was how to pay for a colony. The English had learned from Raleigh's experience in Roanoke that financing a colony was too costly for one person. The Spanish colonies had been financed by the monarchs, but English monarchs lacked such funds. To raise money, therefore, the English turned to joint-stock companies, the form of business organization started by the Genoese (page 29). The joint-stock companies were backed by **investors**, people who put money into a project in order to earn profits. Each investor received **shares of stock**—shares of ownership—in the company. Thus the investors jointly accepted the risks of a new enterprise. They would split any profits they made and divide any losses they suffered.

A group of London merchants organized the Virginia Company of London. Plymouth merchants organized a similar company, the Virginia Company of Plymouth. In 1606 King James granted each company a **charter** to set up outposts in North America. (A charter is a written contract giving certain rights to a person or group.) The Virginia Company of London received the right to settle the southern part of England's claim. The Virginia Company of Plymouth would settle the north-

ern part. The charters also granted each company a monopoly on trade in its colony.

THE FOUNDING OF JAMESTOWN

The London investors immediately began organizing an expedition. They bought three ships and hired captains. They were delighted when John Smith assumed responsibility for buying supplies. By now Smith was famous as both an adventurer and experienced soldier.

In 1606 the three ships set sail. On board were more than 100 men and boys, all volunteers. On the long sea voyage the men became bored and quarrelsome. Smith, who could be very haughty, so angered the captains that they decided to hang him when they reached land. Later they changed their

In 1607 Jamestown was settled as England's first permanent American colony. Its three walls made the fort easier to defend than a fort with four walls. HISTORY How was the fort protected?

minds, however, partly because the ex-soldier Smith was armed to the teeth.

Near the end of April 1607, the little ships entered the calmer waters of a great bay. Smith would later name it Chesapeake Bay. There, near the mouth of the James River, they decided to plant their outpost. They called it Jamestown in honor of King James.

TERRIBLE HARDSHIPS

From the start, the Jamestown settlers endured hardships. The site of the settlement was swampy and filled with mosquitoes. Many colonists fell sick from drinking the river water. As one colonist recalled, "There were never Englishmen left in a foreign country in such misery as we were in this newly discovered Virginia."

> "There were never Englishmen left in a foreign country in such misery as we were in this newly discovered Virginia."
>
> —*Jamestown settler*

The settlers also feared the nearby Powhatan Indians, who were well-organized and powerful. To make matters worse, Jamestown's settlers were greedy adventurers, not hardy pioneers. They were more interested in hunting for gold than in building shelters or growing food. By autumn of the first year, food supplies were low and two-thirds of the Jamestown settlers had died.

The struggling settlement would have failed had John Smith not taken control. Smith had settlers build defenses to make sure the colony could protect itself. He solved the food shortage by persuading the Powhatan Indians to trade corn to the colonists. To ensure that all settlers would work for the colony's survival, he set a new rule: "He that will not work neither shall he eat."

Smith's leadership was short-lived, however. Badly hurt in a gunpowder explosion, he returned to England in 1609. In the same year 800 more settlers, including family groups, arrived. But the worst was yet to come. That winter the Indians stopped trading food, and the settlers were too scared to leave the fort. It was a "starving time"—a time of eating rats and mice, a time of disease and death. Only 60 of the 838 settlers survived.

JAMESTOWN BEGINS TO PROSPER

The Roanoke colony had collapsed from lack of overseas support. In contrast, the Virginia Company kept sending new supplies and new settlers to Jamestown. The marriage of colonist John Rolfe to Pocahontas, daughter of Chief Powhatan, led to peace between the colony and the Indians. Gradually the colonists learned from the Indians how to grow corn, catch fish, and capture wild fowl.

Rolfe's greatest contribution to the colony, however, was learning how to grow high-quality tobacco. Tobacco, a plant native to the Western Hemisphere, quickly became very popular in England. In vain, King James complained. Smoking, said James, was a "vile and stinking" habit.

Rolfe's success with tobacco brought prosperity almost overnight. The statistics tell the tale:

Year	Pounds of Tobacco Sold
1616	2,500
1617	18,800
1618	49,700
1619	45,800
1620	119,000

The success of tobacco changed Jamestown in many ways. The Virginia Company considered the colonists to be employees. The colonists, however, did not want to grow tobacco that would benefit only the company. The tobacco harvest from an acre of land was worth ten times what a colonist was paid each year. Colonists wanted a larger share of the profits. The company responded by let-

POCAHONTAS (1595?–1617) helped maintain peace between the Jamestown settlers and the Indians. The daughter of a Powhatan chief, Pocahontas married the colonist John Rolfe in 1614. Two years later they went to England to raise money for the struggling Jamestown colony. There she developed smallpox and died. John Smith claimed that Pocahontas once saved his life when he had been captured by the Powhatan. Although not all historians believe Smith's story, they do agree that Pocahontas's marriage to Rolfe brought a time of peaceful relations between colonists and Indians.

ting settlers own land. When the land (and its produce) became their own, settlers worked longer and harder.

To attract new settlers, the company offered a 50-acre headright, or land grant, for each man, woman, or child who could pay his or her way to the colony. The population of Virginia rose from 600 in 1619 to 3,000 in 1621.

Still, more workers were needed. Those people who could not afford passage to America were encouraged to become indentured servants. Indentured servants sold their labor in exchange for passage to the colony. After laboring in the colony for an agreed-upon time, usually four to seven years, the indentured servants were free to take up a trade of their own.

Not all indentured servants came from England. In 1619 a Dutch ship brought about twenty Africans to Jamestown, where they became indentured servants. They were the first African settlers in the English colonies.

CHANGES IN GOVERNMENT

The colonists had long squirmed under the strict rule of the company governor. To provide for some local government, the Virginia Company decided that elected representatives (burgesses) of the settlers would meet at least once a year in a colonial assembly. This House of Burgesses, created in 1619, would make laws for the colony. The company, however, could veto those laws. The House of Burgesses was the first representative assembly in the colonies.

In 1622 a sudden Indian attack killed over 300 colonists and wrecked the colony's prosperity. The Virginia Company went bankrupt. In 1624, therefore, the Crown took over Virginia and began ruling it directly. In spite of the king's dislike of representative government, the House of Burgesses continued to meet. Over time it won back its power to make laws.

SECTION REVIEW

1. KEY TERMS mercenary, investor, share of stock, charter, headright, indentured servant, House of Burgesses

2. PEOPLE AND PLACES John Smith, Jamestown, John Rolfe

3. COMPREHENSION Why were joint-stock companies better able than individual persons to finance colonies?

4. COMPREHENSION What problems did Jamestown face at first?

5. CRITICAL THINKING Explain how individual initiative helped ensure the survival of the Jamestown colony.

2 The Pilgrims at Plymouth

Section Focus

Key Terms   Separatist ■ Mayflower Compact

Main Idea   Started in 1620 by a small group of English settlers, the Plymouth colony survived its difficult first year.

Objectives   As you read, look for answers to these questions:
1. Who settled at Plymouth and why?
2. Why did the Plymouth settlers establish their own rules for the colony?

In 1614 John Smith, the colonist who had done so much to save Jamestown, returned to North America as an explorer and mapmaker. Smith studied the region north of Virginia, an area he later called New England. He hoped to set up a settlement there. His attempts were foiled, however, first by a storm and then by pirates.

The people who did realize Smith's dream of a settlement in New England were a group of English folk eager to establish their own community. These were the Separatists, also known as Pilgrims.

THE VOYAGE OF THE PILGRIMS

In 1609, two years after settlers set out for Jamestown, the Separatists had moved to the city of Leiden in Holland. Unwilling to worship within the Church of England, they had been persecuted by King James. They fled to Holland because it was the most religiously tolerant society in Europe.

The Separatists lived and worshipped in Leiden for a few years, but they were not happy in their new home. Having been farmers in England, they had trouble finding work in the city. Also, their children began speak-

The 90-foot ship *Mayflower,* originally built to transport wine, carried a group of Separatists to Massachusetts in 1620. This 1882 painting shows the *Mayflower* covered with ice from its journey. **RELIGION** Why had the Separatists left England for Holland in 1607?

The Mayflower Compact (1620)

In 1620, shortly before they landed at Plymouth, 41 of the colonists aboard the Mayflower *drew up the Mayflower Compact. Under this written agreement, the colonists provided for self-government under majority rule of the male voters.*

We, whose names are underwritten, . . . having undertaken for the glory of God, and advancement of the Christian faith, and the honor of our King and country, a voyage to plant the first colony in the northern parts of Virginia, do by these presents, solemnly and mutually in the presence of God and one another, covenant and combine ourselves together into a civil body politic, for our better ordering and preservation, and furtherance of the ends aforesaid; And by virtue hereof do enact, constitute, and frame such just and equal laws, ordinances, acts, constitutions, and offices from time to time as shall be thought most [proper] and convenient for the general good of the colony unto which we promise all due submission and obedience. In witness whereof we have hereunto subscribed our names at Cape Cod the eleventh of November, in the year of our sovereign lord King James of England . . . anno domini 1620.

From B. P. Poore, ed., *The Federal and State Constitutions,* Part I, p. 931.

ANALYZING HISTORICAL DOCUMENTS

1. Explain in your own words what a colonist was agreeing to when he signed the Mayflower Compact.
2. Why was such a compact seen as necessary?
3. What is the document's historical significance?

---

ing Dutch instead of English. The Separatists again considered moving. They finally decided to ask the Virginia Company if they could settle in America "as a distinct body by themselves."

Thus it was that on a cold, raw November day in 1620 the ship *Mayflower* arrived off Cape Cod on the Massachusetts coast. The Virginia Company had been eager to have the group settle near the mouth of the Hudson River, the northernmost area of its grant. But during a rough, stormy passage, the *Mayflower* had been blown north of its course. Weary and weak from the 66-day voyage, the Pilgrims decided to stay where they were.

Because the Pilgrims had landed outside the limits of the Virginia Company, their charter did not apply. They decided to create a plan for managing their affairs. The men aboard the *Mayflower* signed an agreement, the Mayflower Compact. In it they vowed to obey any laws agreed upon for the general good of the colony. The Mayflower Compact was meant only as an informal agreement, not a permanent constitution. Still, it helped establish the idea of self-government in the Americas.

After exploring Cape Cod, the Pilgrims settled at the site named Plymouth on John Smith's map, which they carried. Plymouth had a harbor, cleared fields, and running brooks. "At least it was the best they could find, and the season and their present necessity made them glad to accept of it," wrote William Bradford. Bradford would later govern the colony and write its history.

HARD TIMES AT PLYMOUTH

Like the early settlers at Jamestown, the Pilgrims endured a starving time. That first winter, disease and death struck with such fury that "the living were scarce able to bury the dead." Half their number had died by spring.

With spring came energy, hope, and help. One day an Indian clad only in a loincloth walked up to a group of settlers. To their astonishment, he called out, "Welcome, Englishmen." This was Samoset, a Pemaquid Indian who had learned to speak English from European fishermen.

Samoset introduced the settlers to a Patuxet Indian named Squanto. Squanto was the last remaining member of the Patuxet, a nearby tribe that had been wiped out by disease. Earlier Squanto had been captured as a slave and then had returned as a sailor on a trading ship. Finding his kin all dead, Squanto set about helping the English plant corn, beans, and pumpkins in the tribal lands. He also acted as interpreter to local Indian tribes. Thanks to Squanto, the Pilgrims and Indians lived in peace for years.

While the corn grew, the men began trading with the Indians for furs and preparing clapboard (lumber used in building houses) to ship back to England. The Pilgrims had agreed to develop products to pay back the Virginia Company for its support.

Sometime in the fall of 1621—no one knows when—the Plymouth settlement cele-brated the blessings of a good harvest by holding a three-day celebration. This feast, giving thanks to God, was the first Thanksgiving. The only description of it is in a letter written back to England. According to the letter writer:

> Our harvest being gotten in, our governor sent four men on fowling, that so we might after a more special manner rejoice together, after we had gathered the fruit of our labors. They four in one day killed as much fowl as, with a little help beside, served the company almost a week. At which time . . . many of the Indians [came] amongst us . . . whom for three days we entertained and feasted. . . .

Life for the infant colony, however, was still difficult. There was not enough corn to last the year. Some people disliked the arrangement in which each person worked for the whole and shared equally in the produce. Among them were women, who did not like to cook and wash for men other than their husbands. "They deemed it a kind of slavery," Bradford wrote.

Bradford thus decided to give each family a piece of land for its own use. In Plymouth, as in Jamestown, the switch to private property led to greater prosperity for the colony and its people.

SECTION REVIEW

1. KEY TERMS Separatist, Mayflower Compact

2. PEOPLE AND PLACES Holland, Plymouth, William Bradford, Squanto

3. COMPREHENSION Why did the Separatists not remain in Holland?

4. COMPREHENSION Why was the first Thanksgiving held?

5. CRITICAL THINKING What is the common idea linking the establishment of the House of Burgesses and the Mayflower Compact?

In your reading you will most likely find topics that you would like to **research**—gather more information about. If you know what sources the library has available, you can locate the information you need without wasted effort.

LOCATING INFORMATION

Books of fiction are usually alphabetized on library shelves, using the last names of authors. To arrange books of nonfiction, some libraries use the **Dewey decimal system**. Under this system, subjects are organized in ten categories that are numbered from 000 to 999.

Other libraries use the **Library of Congress system** to arrange their books. This system has 21 lettered classifications.

The **card catalog** lists all the books in the library. Books are listed in three ways: by author, by title, and by subject. Any of the cards (author, title, or subject) will tell where you can find a book in the library. In the upper left-hand corner of the card, you will find the book's **call number**. Each book is identified by a different call number.

For easier access, many libraries have put their card catalogs on computer. Each entry that appears on the computer screen represents a "card."

USING REFERENCE BOOKS

A great deal of information is readily available in the reference section of the library. Reference books, such as dictionaries and encyclopedias, make facts easy to find.

Atlases (books of maps) and **gazetteers** (dictionaries of places) provide important geographical information. **Almanacs** and **yearbooks,** published yearly, give up-to-date facts on many subjects. *The Readers' Guide to Periodical Literature* lists articles that have appeared in periodicals (magazines and journals). *The New York Times Index* lists articles appearing in *The New York Times.*

PRACTICING YOUR SKILL

1. What are the Dewey decimal system and the Library of Congress system?
2. What sources are especially good for up-to-date facts and statistics?
3. What is the call number of the book listed on the card on this page? Under what other headings would you find this book listed in the card catalog?
4. What kind of reference book would you use to find out about (a) the major tributaries of the Mississippi River? (b) the mayors of the 50 largest cities in the United States?

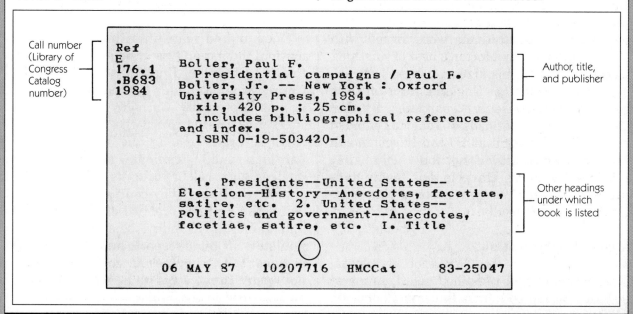

Call number
(Library of Congress Catalog number)

```
Ref
E
176.1
.B683
1984
        Boller, Paul F.
            Presidential campaigns / Paul F.
        Boller, Jr. -- New York : Oxford
        University Press, 1984.
            xii, 420 p. ; 25 cm.
            Includes bibliographical references
        and index.
            ISBN 0-19-503420-1


            1. Presidents--United States--
        Election--History--Anecdotes, facetiae,
        satire, etc.  2. United States--
        Politics and government--Anecdotes,
        facetiae, satire, etc.  I. Title


        06 MAY 87    10207716   HMCCat      83-25047
```

Author, title, and publisher

Other headings under which book is listed

3 The Settlement of New England

★ **Section Focus** ★

Key Terms Puritan ■ Great Migration ■ commonwealth ■ covenant ■ New England Way ■ dissenter ■ refuge

Main Idea The English people who settled New England hoped to build a model society based on their religious views.

Objectives As you read, look for answers to these questions:
1. Why did thousands of English people choose to migrate in the 1630s?
2. How did the Massachusetts colonists structure their society?
3. How did Massachusetts react to those who challenged their established views?

Each year the Plymouth colony sent back to England a cargo of furs and lumber. Then in 1628 the colonists sent back another kind of cargo. They sent their neighbor, Thomas Morton.

Morton had several years earlier settled north of Plymouth. Within a few years he was hunting, fishing, and trading guns to the Indians for furs. In his settlement, which he named Merrymount, Morton built an 80-foot Maypole around which he and his friends made merry with anyone who showed up.

The Maypole was a non-Christian tradition and thus offended the Plymouth colonists. Morton further angered his neighbors by welcoming "the scum of the country." How could one keep servants, Governor Bradford of Plymouth complained, if they could flee to a place like Merrymount? How could settlers feel secure if the Indians were armed with guns? Disturbed by Morton's nest of mischief, Bradford ordered his arrest.

Although sent to England, Morton was back in Massachusetts a year later. By that time, however, boatloads of religious-minded colonists had settled at Boston harbor north of Merrymount. It was not long before they cut down Morton's Maypole. His rowdy days were over. The message was clear: New England was for the godly.

UNREST IN ENGLAND

During the 1620s the population of colonial New England had remained small, numbering only about 500. This figure ballooned in the 1630s when people began fleeing unrest in England.

Some of this unrest was caused by England's struggle to change its medieval ways. Wool had become the new route to wealth. To raise sheep, landholders fenced their land and threw out the peasants who had been living there. Thousands of people drifted into the cities looking for work and for a new life. The weavers and merchants of woolen cloth did well at first. Yet when hard times hit the wool market, they too found it hard to make ends meet.

In 1625 England got a new king, Charles I. He only made matters worse. Charles I was a stubborn ruler who wanted things his own way. In particular, he insisted that the people of England all worship in the same way—his way.

One hundred years after the English Reformation, the nation was at odds over the direction the Church of England should take. The Church was not under Catholic control. Still, it had kept many Catholic traditions. The Puritans wanted to rid the Church of such "Popish" traditions as the use of statues, paintings, and instrumental music. They also disliked such celebrations as Christmas and church marriage. They considered downright sinful the English practice of playing sports and games on Sunday. The Puritans held ministers in high respect, but they resented bishops. Why, they asked, could the Church not return to the ways of the early Christians as described in the Bible?

"No way," was the essence of the king's answer. He believed that religion and the state were one. If people started to question the authority of the Church, next they might question the power of the king.

THE GREAT MIGRATION

For devout Puritans the future looked bleak, and many chose to head to America. Thus in 1630 began the Great Migration. During the next ten years thousands of people poured out of England toward the Americas.

Most of these emigrants—40,000 of them—moved to England's new colonies in the West Indies. The Caribbean was no longer a Spanish sea, and other nations were laying claim to islands there. English settlers started large farms throughout the West Indies. They raised sugar, tobacco, cotton, and dyes to sell abroad.

Another 20,000 Puritan emigrants chose New England. In 1629 the Massachusetts Bay Company had been given a royal charter to settle land in New England. Many Puritan merchants had invested in the company. It

Overcrowding and poverty in England's cities were two reasons why people migrated to the American colonies. This drawing shows the heart of London, including the Thames River and London Bridge. **HISTORY** What personal sacrifices did moving to America require?

was only natural that the company began to recruit new settlers from among English Puritans.

The leader of the Great Migration to New England was John Winthrop, a pious Puritan. A victim of the king's crackdown on Puritans, Winthrop had been fired from his job as an attorney in the king's courts. The Massachusetts Bay Company knew of Winthrop's leadership skills and convinced him to become governor. Winthrop then recruited wealthy Puritan families to migrate to New England.

In March 1630 the migration began. A fleet of 11 ships carried 700 passengers, 240 cows, and 60 horses. The arrival of the fleet more than doubled the white population of New England.

MASSACHUSETTS BAY COLONY

As governor for most of the next nineteen years, Winthrop helped set the course for the colony. In a sermon on his flagship, the *Arbella,* he had expressed the hopes of the enterprise. Theirs would be a society, he said, of justice and mercy. It would be a commonwealth, a community in which people work together for the good of the whole. It would be a model for the whole world:

> For we must consider that we shall be like a City upon a Hill; the eyes of all people are on us. If we deal falsely with our God in this work we have undertaken and so cause Him to withdraw His present help from us, we shall be made a story and a byword throughout the world.

The Massachusetts settlers believed they had a covenant, or agreement, with God to build a holy society. They also believed that they had a covenant with each other to work toward such a society. Covenants, whether written or unwritten, were important to the Puritans as a way to define and work for goals.

With Winthrop as their leader, the Puritans set out to create their model society, their "city on a hill." To give it form, they used the charter of the Massachusetts Bay Company.

The Massachusetts Bay charter was really a business arrangement. The men who had invested in the company had absolute power to rule both company and colony as long as their laws did not contradict those of England. The investors were to meet in a General Court four times a year to make laws. Once in Massachusetts, however, they gave up such power. Instead, they granted membership in the company to all adult male church members. These men then elected the governor and the representatives to the General Court. The result was a commonwealth controlled by male church members.

TOWNS IN COLONIAL NEW ENGLAND

The basic unit of the commonwealth was the congregation—a group of people who belong to the same church. Each congregation set up its own town. Towns were built around an open field called a common. Encircling the common were public buildings, as well as family houses. New England farmers lived in the towns and went out each day to work in the fields. At night they returned to their homes in town.

The most important building in each town was the meetinghouse, where people met for town meetings. At the town meeting, people made laws and other decisions for the community. They could grant land to newcomers, determine fees for laborers, and even set the price for ale. They could also appoint people to perform tasks necessary to the community —repairing fences, operating a ferry, serving in the militia. When the town's population grew too large for the meetinghouse, the congregation was likely to divide and start a new town.

THE NEW ENGLAND WAY

The meetinghouse was also used for church services. By law, everyone in the town had to attend church. The church service was a solemn event. The meetinghouse had no heat, and the hard benches were uncomfortable. The men sat in one part of the church, and the women and girls in another. The boys usually sat together in the balcony. If there was any noise, the offenders were punished in front of the whole congregation.

★ **Historical Documents**

A Model of Christian Charity (1630)

John Winthrop's sermon on board the Arbella powerfully stated the ideas on which the Puritan migration to America was based. Reminding the Puritans of their religious ideals, Winthrop declared his hope that the colony would be an example of Christian life for the entire world.

. . . The Lord will make our name a praise and glory, so that men shall say of succeeding plantations: "The Lord make it like that of New England." For we must consider that we shall be like a City upon a Hill; the eyes of all people are on us.

If we deal falsely with our God in this work we have undertaken and so cause Him to withdraw His present help from us, we shall be made a story and a byword throughout the world; we shall open the mouths of enemies to speak evil of the ways of God and all believers in God; we shall shame the faces of many of God's worthy servants and cause their prayers to be turned into curses upon us, till we are forced out of the new land where we are going.

From *Winthrop Papers,* The Massachusetts Historical Society, 1931.

ANALYZING HISTORICAL DOCUMENTS

1. According to Winthrop, what would happen to the Puritans if they failed?
2. What "worthy servants" might Winthrop have been referring to?
3. How might the Puritans' belief in the importance of their mission have affected their actions in America?

The raised platform called the pulpit was the central feature of the meetinghouse. There stood the minister, an important and respected man whose words carried great weight. From the high-rising pulpit he delivered the sermons that were the core of the New England church service.

The sermon provided instruction in the New England Way. This was the term used by the Puritans to describe both their beliefs and the society they were building. It was a society that emphasized duty, godliness, hard work, honesty, and moderation in all things. Such amusements as dancing and playing games were considered temptations to laziness and sin.

The maintenance of the New England Way depended on education. The Puritans believed that the Bible was the source of truth. Therefore each person should be able to read it. The General Court passed laws requiring that each child learn to read. (It was not necessary, however, to know how to write.) Puritan life also depended on a well-educated ministry to explain Biblical teachings. To provide a future supply of ministers, Harvard College was founded in 1636.

The Massachusetts Puritans extended their influence by building towns in an ever-widening radius from Boston. Some Puritan congregations, however, set up colonies independent of Massachusetts. In the quest for more fertile land, the minister Thomas Hooker and his congregation moved in 1636 to settle in the gentle Connecticut Valley. There they wrote and adopted The Fundamental Orders of Connecticut. In effect, these laws were a constitution, the first in the American colonies.

CONFLICT WITH INDIANS

As colonists moved westward, to Connecticut and elsewhere, relations with Indians grew unfriendly. Most Indians had welcomed the first English settlers, teaching them how to survive in the wilderness. Soon, however, they realized that the English posed a threat to their way of life.

Indians depended on the game they hunted for food and clothing. They saw the frontier settlers taking over land for farms, cutting down the forests, and wiping out game. As more and more pioneers moved to the frontier, the Indians began to fight back. Settlers,

In the spring of 1636, Thomas Hooker and his followers left Massachusetts for Connecticut. Landscape artist Frederick Edwin Church painted Hooker's journey 210 years later. CULTURE If the artist had described Hooker's journey in words instead of a painting, what do you think he might have said?

in turn, feared and distrusted the Indians, whom they regarded as savages.

Warfare flared up from time to time along the frontier. In the 1630s a series of battles took place between the colonists and the Pequot Indians. A group of Puritans, seeking revenge for an earlier raid, attacked a Pequot fort in 1637. The colonists surrounded the fort at night and then struck, burning it to the ground. Hundreds of Pequot men, women, and children burned to death.

In 1675 several New England Indian groups joined together to attack the English colonists. The Indians were led by the Wampanoag Chief Metacomet, known to the colonists as King Philip. In a series of attacks called King Philip's War, the Indians destroyed about 25 settlements in what is now Massachusetts, New Hampshire, and Maine. The colonists fought back savagely and in time killed or drove west most of the New England Indians. Still, fighting continued for many years, and the bloodshed moved westward with the frontier.

CHALLENGES TO THE PURITANS

The Puritans did not bring freedom of religion to New England. They came to the Americas to worship in their own way. They were intolerant of dissenters. (A dissenter is someone who challenges the generally accepted views of Church or society.)

The first important dissenter was Roger Williams, a minister from Salem. Massachusetts leaders thought it bad enough when Williams said that the king of England had no right to give away Indian land. They were outraged, however, when he claimed that government should have no power over religious matters. That challenged the very heart of the commonwealth. As a result, the General Court ordered him shipped back to England. Quickly, Williams slipped away in the winter snows to Narragansett Bay. With a small group of followers, he founded a colony there in 1636 that would become Rhode Island. There, Williams helped found the first Baptist congregation in North America.

BIOGRAPHY

JOHN WINTHROP (1588–1649) was the dominant figure in the early history of Massachusetts. Winthrop was drawn to Puritanism while still a teenager in England. Fearing that King Charles's anti-Puritan policies would harm his career, Winthrop agreed to lead the journey to New England in 1630. There he remained a leading citizen until his death, serving many years as governor of the colony. While Winthrop was involved in controversies, such as the conflict with Anne Hutchinson, his piety and honesty were never questioned.

Soon Massachusetts faced another radical dissenter, Anne Hutchinson. At weekly meetings she explained her belief that a person could find inner truth and divine guidance without the help of the ministry.

By challenging the religious leaders, Hutchinson was also challenging the basis of the commonwealth. This was treason, and she was brought to trial. At trial, pregnant with her sixteenth child, Hutchinson refused to change her views.

The court banished her from the colony. In 1638 she left for Rhode Island. Rhode Island, called "Rogue Island" in Massachusetts, had become a refuge—a place of protection—for anyone seeking freedom of religion.

A generation later the commonwealth was again challenged. This time it was the Quakers, a radical Puritan sect that had arisen in England in the 1650s. The Quakers believed that each person could know God directly through an "inner light." Because all people were equal before God, they said, neither ministers nor the Bible was needed.

Such beliefs caused the Quakers to be persecuted both in England and in Massachusetts. In Massachusetts the laws against Quaker missionaries were harsh. Authorities whipped the Quakers and threw them in prison. They cropped their ears, and bored their tongues with hot irons. When those methods did not stop the Quakers, Massachusetts began to hang them. The king himself had to order the practice stopped.

The Puritan commonwealth lasted just three generations. In 1691 the Crown forced a new charter on Massachusetts. As a result, the governor was chosen by the Crown, rather than elected by church members. Also, the right to vote was tied to ownership of property—not church membership. Finally, Massachusetts had to tolerate Baptists and Quakers.

SECTION REVIEW

1. KEY TERMS Puritan, Great Migration, commonwealth, covenant, New England Way, dissenter, refuge

2. PEOPLE Charles I, John Winthrop, Roger Williams, Anne Hutchinson

3. COMPREHENSION What caused the Great Migration?

4. COMPREHENSION Who held political power in Massachusetts? When did this situation change?

5. CRITICAL THINKING Why were the Puritans, who had migrated to North America in search of religious freedom, intolerant of religious dissenters?

4 More Colonies, New People

Section Focus

Key Terms tidewater ■ proprietor

Main Idea The colonies that became part of England's expanding American empire were distinct in many ways.

Objectives As you read, look for answers to these questions:
1. How did geographical factors influence life in the Chesapeake Tidewater?
2. How did New Netherland pass from Dutch to English rule?
3. What new English colonies were created?

By the mid-1600s, there were two clusters of English colonists in America. One cluster was in New England. The other cluster was in the lowlands around the Chesapeake Bay. This area, in present-day Maryland and Virginia, is called the Chesapeake Tidewater. (A tidewater is a region of low coastal land, whose rivers are affected by ocean tides.)

Both clusters of English colonists had about the same number of people. The Chesapeake Tidewater had about 23,000 people, and New England about 22,000. A New Englander visiting the Chesapeake Tidewater, however, might ask where the people were. In the Chesapeake Tidewater, people did not live in towns as in New England.

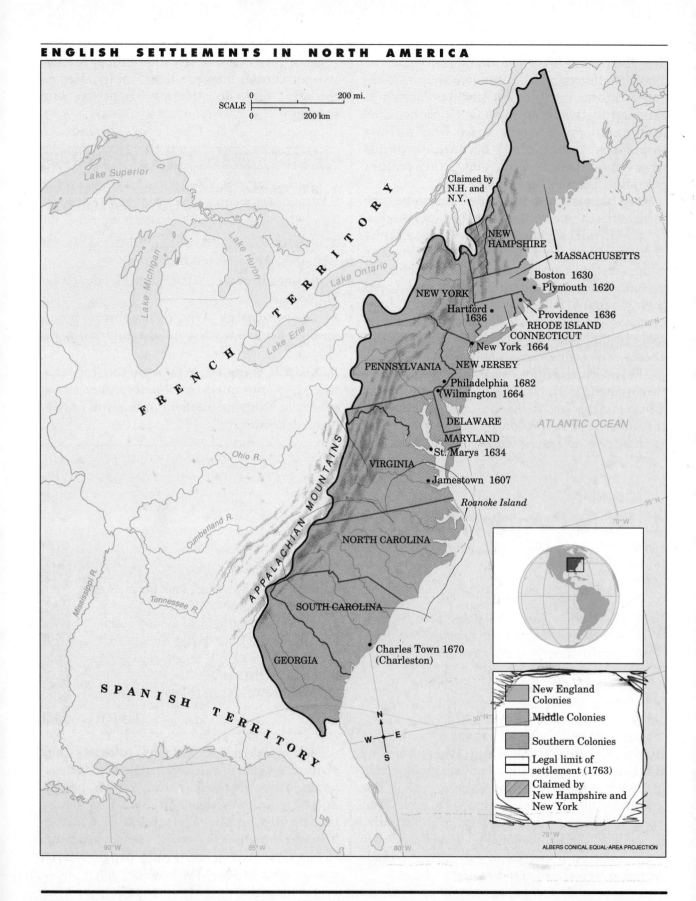

SCALE

0   200 mi.

0   200 km

Lake Superior

Lake Michigan

Lake Huron

Lake Erie

Lake Ontario

FRENCH TERRITORY

Ohio R.

Cumberland R.

Tennessee R.

Mississippi R.

APPALACHIAN MOUNTAINS

SPANISH TERRITORY

Claimed by
N.H. and
N.Y.

NEW
HAMPSHIRE

MASSACHUSETTS

• Boston 1630
• Plymouth 1620

NEW YORK

Hartford •
1636

Providence 1636
RHODE ISLAND
CONNECTICUT

• New York 1664

PENNSYLVANIA

NEW JERSEY

• Philadelphia 1682
• Wilmington 1664

DELAWARE

MARYLAND
• St. Marys 1634

VIRGINIA

• Jamestown 1607

Roanoke Island

NORTH CAROLINA

SOUTH CAROLINA

GEORGIA

• Charles Town 1670
(Charleston)

ATLANTIC OCEAN

40°N

35°N

30°N

70°W

75°W

90°W   85°W   80°W

N
W   E
S

New England
Colonies

Middle Colonies

Southern Colonies

Legal limit of
settlement (1763)

Claimed by
New Hampshire and
New York

ALBERS CONICAL EQUAL-AREA PROJECTION

THE CHESAPEAKE TIDEWATER

Twenty-five years after its founding in 1607, Virginia's population had reached 2,500, and tobacco sales had soared. Through trial and error, the Virginia colonists had learned how to prosper in the Chesapeake Tidewater. In doing so, Virginia set the pattern for its new neighbor, Maryland.

Maryland was founded in 1634 by Lord Baltimore as a refuge for Catholics fleeing persecution in England. Yet the number of Catholics was small. To attract settlers, Lord Baltimore gave religious toleration to Protestants. During the Great Migration thousands of Puritans moved to Maryland, where they soon outnumbered the Catholics.

The large tobacco farms of the Chesapeake Tidewater were strung out along the region's many waterways. To the dock of each farm came ships that brought manufactured goods from England and in turn carried the tobacco to market. Towns were not needed because there was no need for a place to buy and sell goods. Because the farms were scattered, ministers found it hard to enforce Church rules of behavior. As a result the Church had far less influence there than in New England.

Life for the early Chesapeake settlers was hard. Before tobacco could be planted, fields had to be cleared of trees and the stumps pulled. The planting and harvesting of tobacco demanded back-breaking labor. Within three or four years tobacco used up the nutrients in the soil. Thus a tobacco farmer was always clearing new land. When there was no more land to clear, the farmer moved upriver and started over again.

Disease took a high toll on Chesapeake settlers. Half of all children died. Even those who lived to age twenty could expect to live only half as long as New Englanders.

MAP SKILLS

English settlers established colonies along the North American coast. What were the two earliest English settlements? What natural feature formed the colonies' western boundary? CRITICAL THINKING Why were the settlements located on or near the coast?

For much of the 1600s, therefore, scores of immigrants came in response to the labor demands of the tobacco farms. Some were convicts sent to the colonies as punishment for their crimes. Others were jobless artisans who came in search of a better life.

Most laborers came as indentured servants. On arrival, they were auctioned off to those willing to pay their ocean passage. After their time of servitude, those who had survived would be given a hoe and a new suit of clothes and freed.

NEW NETHERLAND

Between New England and the Chesapeake Tidewater was New Netherland. This colony of the Dutch West India Company included the Hudson River valley, Long Island, and land along the Delaware River.

The Dutch company had profited from fur-trading at Fort Orange (Albany) and New Amsterdam (New York City), but it had few settlers. It was ruled by a cranky and strong-willed governor, Peter Stuyvesant. Stuyvesant used a wooden peg to replace a leg lost in battle, thereby earning the nickname "Pegleg Peter."

Though small, the population of New Amsterdam was more varied than that of its neighbors. Eager to attract and keep settlers, the colony had welcomed different kinds of people. From its founding in 1625 the colony had included African indentured servants. By the 1660s one-eighth of New Amsterdam was African American.

The colony also included settlers from Scandinavia. In 1655 Peter Stuyvesant had taken over the neighboring colony of New Sweden, whose residents had built trading posts along the Delaware River. From their homeland the Swedes introduced the log cabin to the North American continent. The simple, sturdy log cabin could be built quickly and with only an axe for a tool. It was so practical that it became the symbol of the American frontier.

Puritans moving down from Massachusetts also settled in New Netherland, particularly on Long Island. Among the colony's Puritan settlers was Anne Hutchinson. She had moved to New Netherland from Rhode Island after her husband died.

Peter Stuyvesant was willing to accept Africans, Scandinavians, and English Puritans into his colony. He was not so pleased in 1654 when 23 Jewish settlers arrived. Stuyvesant did allow the Jews to land, but then he wrote the Dutch West India Company asking what he should do. The company responded: Let the Jews remain there. The Jews were to have the same rights as other settlers of New Netherland.

SEIZURE OF NEW NETHERLAND

English colonization stopped in the middle of the 1600s as a result of civil war in England. The war started in 1642 and ended in 1649 when an army of Puritans defeated Charles and beheaded him. The Puritans ruled England until 1660. In that year Charles II reclaimed his father's throne. Stability was restored. The second Charles, known as the "Merry Monarch," was very popular with the English. Colonization resumed when the king decided to expand England's American empire.

The first thing to do, the king decided, was drive out the Dutch. He gave the assignment to his brother, the Duke of York, by telling him he could have what he could take. When the duke's ships appeared off New Amsterdam in August 1664, the colony surrendered without a fight—much to the disgust of Peter Stuyvesant. The Duke of York was now the proprietor, or owner, of New Netherland, which was renamed New York.

NEW JERSEY AND PENNSYLVANIA

The Duke of York was now the largest single landowner in America. He gave a chunk of his claim, the province of New Jersey, to two friends. These were Sir George Carteret and Lord John Berkeley. They encouraged settlers to come to their new land by promising freedom of religion, large grants of land, and a representative assembly.

The Duke of York gave up an even larger part of his estate in 1681 when he paid off a debt to William Penn. Years before, the Duke of York had borrowed money from Penn's father. Penn, an active Quaker, was seeking a refuge for Quakers being persecuted in England. By reminding the duke of the debt,

The Dutch settlement of New Amsterdam later became New York City. This painting shows Manhattan Island as it appeared around 1650. At the time, about 1,000 people lived in New Amsterdam. **GEOGRAPHY** What other areas were part of New Netherland?

Quakers were among the many religious groups who found a home in the American colonies. There is no minister at a Quaker meeting. In the scene above, a Quaker speaks his mind while others pray silently. **CULTURAL PLURALISM** Why did Pennsylvania become a home to many Quakers?

Penn was granted the tract of land that became Pennsylvania in 1682. He later bought still more land from the Duke of York, the three counties that became Delaware.

Because the Quakers believed that all people are equal, they welcomed different religions and ethnic groups. Pennsylvania thus kept an open door to the world. This policy, as well as the colony's fertile land, would make Pennsylvania one of the wealthiest colonies.

Land was of no use to a proprietor as wilderness. Settlers were needed to work the land. Thus William Penn, after first throwing open Pennsylvania to the Quakers, went off to Germany to find more immigrants. In time, thousands of Germans arrived in Pennsylvania. They brought with them craft skills and productive farming techniques that helped the colony thrive.

In the 1700s a large new group of immigrants began landing on Philadelphia's docks. These were the Scots-Irish. Like other immigrants, they felt both the push from the old world and the pull of the new world. The Scots-Irish were Scottish Protestants, mostly small farmers and weavers, who had settled in northern Ireland as part of England's effort to control that island. Rising rents and several years of poor crop yields provided the "push" to leave. The "pull" was American land and opportunity. On arrival, most of the Scots-Irish fanned out to the frontier, where land was cheap. They were a practical, restless people who valued liberty, religion, and responsibility.

THE CAROLINAS AND GEORGIA

When Charles II became king, he owed a debt of gratitude to a number of people. Eight of them asked Charles for a grant of land between Virginia and Spanish Florida. This was to be Carolina (a feminine form of the name Charles). In 1663 Charles granted their request. The first settlers built Charles Town (Charleston) in 1670 and busied themselves cutting timber, raising cattle, and trading with the Indians for deerskins.

Charleston soon lost its frontier character. In 1685 the king of France began persecuting the French Protestants, known as Huguenots (page 77). Thousands were forced to leave France, and a number found a new home in Carolina. There they began to farm the lowlands and turn Charleston into one of the most attractive and charming cities of the colonies. They achieved this prosperity, however, by heavy use of slave labor.

Meanwhile, some tobacco farmers from Virginia had moved south into present-day North Carolina. Their settlements were far apart, and the people had little contact with each other. As a result, in 1729 the Crown took direct control of the two Carolina colonies, North and South.

In 1732 one more colony, Georgia, was founded. The English government saw it as a military outpost and buffer against Spanish Florida. James Oglethorpe, founder of the colony, saw it as an opportunity to establish a model society. Oglethorpe had long been upset by the number of people thrown into English prisons for debt. He hoped that in

In 1734 Pierre Fourdrinier made this sketch of Savannah for the planners of the Georgia colony. The planners used the sketch to attract settlers and investors. **ECONOMICS** What features might have encouraged people to settle or to invest in the colony?

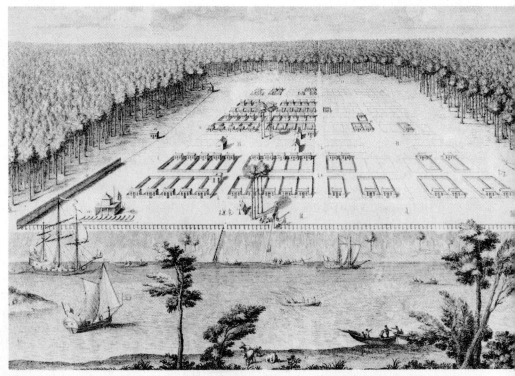

Georgia debtors could start life anew by gaining economic freedom and self-respect. He formed a charitable organization to help debtors. This organization in turn received a charter to settle Georgia. Oglethorpe and other officers of the organization had complete authority over the colony.

Oglethorpe used his authority to set strict rules dealing with the operation of the colony. He limited the amount of land each settler could own. He outlawed trade with the Indians in order to avoid conflict. He also banned both slavery and alcohol. Many settlers came to resent the strict rules, and complained bitterly. By 1750 the rules had been overturned. With large farms and slavery allowed, the colony grew rapidly.

CHAPTER 5 SUMMARY AND TIMELINE

1. Despite many hardships, an English colony at Jamestown, Virginia, survived to become the first successful English colony in the Americas. By raising tobacco for export to England, Jamestown prospered.

2. The colony of Plymouth was started by Separatists who had fled England to escape religious persecution. Landing outside the area of their charter, the Separatists established a form of self-government. Starvation and disease threatened to destroy the infant colony. Yet with the aid of nearby Indians, Plymouth survived.

3. New England was settled by Puritans who tried to build a society based on their religious beliefs. The Puritans left England during the 1630s because of unrest. They built communities in which all laws were based on their interpretation of the Bible.

4. English colonies outside New England differed from one another in many ways. For example, unlike New England, colonists in the Chesapeake Tidewater lived on scattered farms rather than in towns. By the early 1700s, there were thirteen English colonies along the east coast of North America.

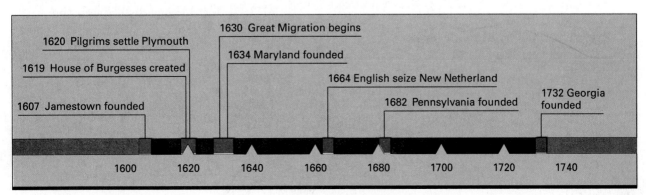

1620 Pilgrims settle Plymouth
1630 Great Migration begins
1619 House of Burgesses created
1634 Maryland founded
1664 English seize New Netherland
1607 Jamestown founded
1682 Pennsylvania founded
1732 Georgia founded

1600　1620　1640　1660　1680　1700　1720　1740

Chapter 5 REVIEW

PLACES TO LOCATE

Match the letters on the map with the places listed below. Write your answers on a separate sheet of paper.

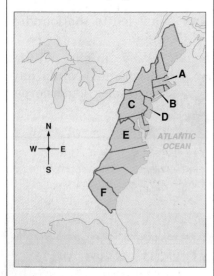

1. Connecticut
2. Georgia
3. Massachusetts
4. New Jersey
5. Pennsylvania
6. Virginia

KEY TERMS

Use the following terms to complete the sentences.

**Great Migration
House of Burgesses
Mayflower Compact
New England Way
Puritan
Separatist**

1. A _____ was one of the English Protestants who founded Plymouth.

2. The movement of English people to the American colonies during the 1630s is known as the _____.
3. The _____ was the term used by Puritans to describe their beliefs and the society they were building.
4. A _____ was one of the founders of Massachusetts Bay Colony.
5. The _____ was formed in 1619 to give the settlers of Jamestown a voice in their own affairs.
6. The _____ was an agreement among Plymouth's settlers to obey laws created for the common good.

PEOPLE TO IDENTIFY

Match each of the following people with the correct description.

**Lord Baltimore
Anne Hutchinson
William Penn
Roger Williams
John Winthrop**

1. Dissenter banished from Massachusetts.
2. Founder of Maryland.
3. Founder of Rhode Island.
4. First governor of Massachusetts.
5. Founder of Pennsylvania.

REVIEWING THE FACTS

1. Why were such colonies as Jamestown and Plymouth

financed by joint-stock companies rather than private individuals?
2. What problems did the Jamestown settlers face?
3. How did John Smith help save Jamestown?
4. Why did the Separatists move to the Americas?
5. What were the relations between the Plymouth settlers and the nearby Indians? Why?
6. Describe the conflict between the Puritans and King Charles I.
7. What agreement did the Massachusetts settlers think that they had with God?
8. What values did the New England Way represent?
9. Why was there such a great demand for labor in the Chesapeake Tidewater?
10. Briefly describe the founding of (a) Maryland, (b) New Netherland, (c) New Jersey, (d) Pennsylvania, (e) the Carolinas, (f) Georgia.

CITIZENSHIP

1. What qualities and skills did settlers at Jamestown need to have? How, if at all, did these differ from the qualities and skills needed of citizens today?
2. Why was Roger Williams's claim that government had no control over religious matters a challenge to Puritan society?

PRACTICING YOUR SKILL

Suppose you wanted to do research to find out more about the settlement at Jamestown. The following questions deal with researching that topic. Answer the following questions on a separate sheet of paper, choosing from this list of reference books: dictionary, biographical dictionary, encyclopedia, atlas, gazetteer, almanac, *Readers' Guide to Periodical Literature, New York Times Index.*

1. In which sources would you look to find out more about the geography of the Jamestown area?
2. In which sources might you find more information about the life of John Smith?
3. What source could tell you about any recent magazine articles dealing with Jamestown?

CRITICAL THINKING SKILLS

1. IDENTIFYING SIGNIFICANCE Explain why it was important that the Pilgrims landed outside the boundary of the Virginia Company's land in the Americas.

2. ANALYZING A QUOTATION What did John Winthrop mean when he said that the Puritan settlement in Massachusetts would be "a city upon a hill"? What might he have aimed to accomplish in describing the settlement in these terms?

3. STATING BOTH SIDES OF AN ISSUE State (a) the argument that the governor of Massachusetts might have given for banishing Roger Williams or Anne Hutchinson and (b) the reply that the dissenters might have given.

4. INFERRING Why did many English laborers agree to work as indentured servants in the colonies?

5. MAKING A GENERALIZATION Using such colonies as New Jersey, Pennsylvania, and the Carolinas as examples, explain the importance of personal relationships in the founding of colonies.

PROJECTS AND ACTIVITIES

1. DEVELOPING A PLAN Imagine that you and a group of colonists are about to begin a settlement in North America in the 1600s. Make up a plan of government to guide your colony. Include the rights and responsibilities of the colonists. Share your plan with the rest of the class.

2. DEFENDING OPINIONS With several other students, present a panel discussion about religious freedom in New England in the 1600s. Some students should take the parts of Puritan ministers. Others should take the parts of challengers such as Roger Williams and Anne Hutchinson. The class can represent townspeople and ask questions of the panel.

3. ORGANIZING INFORMATION ON A CHART Make a chart showing the religious groups that came to the English colonies. Include the following headings in the chart: "Religious Group," "Colony They Settled," "Date They Came," "Where They Came From," and "Other Information." Include at least five groups on your chart.

WRITING ABOUT TOPICS IN AMERICAN HISTORY

1. CONNECTING WITH LITERATURE A selection from *The Serpent Never Sleeps* by Scott O'Dell appears on pages 635–637. Read it and answer the questions. Then answer the following question: Why was England's ability to resupply its American colonies important for the colonists' morale?

2. APPLYING THEMES: PLURALISTIC SOCIETY Support the following statement in an essay of at least two paragraphs: "By the early 1700s, the American colonies already contained a wide variety of peoples from different backgrounds."

Gilbert Stuart painted this portrait of Mrs. Christian Bannister and her son, of Rhode Island. Families like the Bannisters benefited from the colonies' growing prosperity.

6 English Colonial Life (1630–1763)

1 Colonial Patterns and the Growth of New England

Section Focus

Key Terms   raw materials ■ Navigation Acts ■ triangular trade ■ smuggling ■ surplus ■ apprentice ■ commerce ■ Salem Witchcraft Trials ■ deism ■ Great Awakening

Main Idea   Aided by the success of fishing and trade, New England grew and prospered.

Objectives   As you read, look for answers to these questions:
1. What geographic and economic features did the English colonies have in common?
2. Why did New Englanders turn to the sea for a living?
3. What religious trends developed in New England?

In the mid-1700s a Frenchman, <u>Michel Guillaume Jean de Crèvecoeur</u> (krev–KUR), settled in the colony of New York. He later wrote a book full of praise for colonial life:

> [Here a visitor] beholds fair cities, substantial villages, extensive fields, an immense country filled with decent houses, good roads, orchards, meadows, and bridges, where a hundred years ago all was wild, woody, and uncultivated!

By Crèvecoeur's time, English colonial life was established. Three main regions had emerged: the New England Colonies, the Middle Colonies, and the Southern Colonies. Each had its own distinct features. Yet these regions also had important things in common.

THE GEOGRAPHY OF THE COLONIES

The eastern seaboard varies in geography and climate. To the north it is <u>rockier</u> and colder,</u> to the south <u>flatter</u> and <u>warmer</u>. The coastal plain in the <u>north is narrow,</u> while in the <u>south it is wide.</u> Yet when the first colonists arrived, all of the land seemed wild. Indians lived there, but there were few of them and they generally did not settle the land as their own property.

Thus settlers worked to tame the wilderness and make it their own. This was a hard job. The land had to be cleared for farming, and food had to be grown or gathered.

The colonies shared a common western boundary, the Appalachian Mountains. This long, north-south range formed a barrier to western settlement. At first, settlers had little reason to leave the flatter lands near the coast. Farming was easier there, as was transportation. Settlers could move by boat along the coast or up the many rivers stretching inland. There were few good roads, so rivers became the first highways of the colonies and the main routes to inland settlement.

Throughout the colonies, the waterfront was the center of activity. It was where cargo was sold and where travelers arrived. Ship captains carried both the latest news and the mail. Ships and boats were the economic lifeblood that connected the colonies to England and to each other.

The most important cities in 1700—Boston, Newport, Philadelphia, New York City, and Charleston—had developed around deep, safe harbors. Boston was still the leading city in the 1740s, with a population nearing 15,000.

THE COLONIAL ECONOMIES

The colonies all followed the rules of mercantilism (page 68). This policy held that the colonies existed to benefit the parent country. Colonies were supposed to supply England with raw materials—natural resources used to make other goods—and to buy English manufactured goods. Thus the colonies sent their tobacco, indigo, furs, grain, and timber to England. In return they bought factory-made goods such as clothes, dishes, weapons, and tools.

To protect this trade, the English Parliament had passed a series of laws known as Navigation Acts beginning in 1651. These acts required the colonies to sell certain items only to England or other colonies. This trade had to be carried out on ships built in England or in the colonies. On the other hand, these laws did boost the colonial shipbuilding industry.

Colonial merchants developed a series of trade routes known as the triangular trade. On one such route, rum and iron from New England were sent to Africa and exchanged for slaves and gold. The slaves and gold were shipped to the West Indies and traded for sugar and molasses. Finally, the sugar and molasses were brought to New England and made into rum.

On another triangular trade route, colonial grain, lumber, and other goods were shipped to the West Indies and exchanged for sugar, molasses, and fruit. These goods were taken to England and traded for manufactured items. On the last leg of this route, the manufactured items were shipped to New England.

To increase their profits, colonial merchants often broke English trade laws. For example, one law required traders to buy sugar and molasses only from English colonies in the West Indies. The demand for these goods was so great, though, that colonial merchants illegally bought sugar and molasses from the French, Dutch, and Spanish. Such illegal importing of goods is called smuggling.

In the early days of settlement, the colonists had little time to make their own goods. Yet as the colonies became more wealthy, people began to make products in their homes. Colonial manufacturing became a threat to the sale of English-made products. As a result, Parliament passed laws restricting manufacturing in the colonies.

Under these laws, colonists could make certain goods for their own use but not for sale in other colonies or countries. In 1699, for example, Parliament passed the Woolen Act. This law prohibited the colonies from sending wool to England or to other colonies. The Iron Act of 1750 was passed to keep the colonists from making their own iron goods. The colonies had to send their raw iron to England and buy finished products from English iron mills.

FARMING AND FISHING IN NEW ENGLAND

Most settlers in the New England Colonies—Massachusetts, New Hampshire, Connecticut, and Rhode Island—had come with the idea of farming the land. They soon learned, however, that the area was not well suited to farming. The land was hilly and heavily forested, and boulders dotted the thin, rocky soil. The climate did not help either. The winters were long and harsh, and the summer growing season was short. As a result, farmers were able to raise only a limited number of crops.

Through hard work, though, farmers in New England were able to grow enough

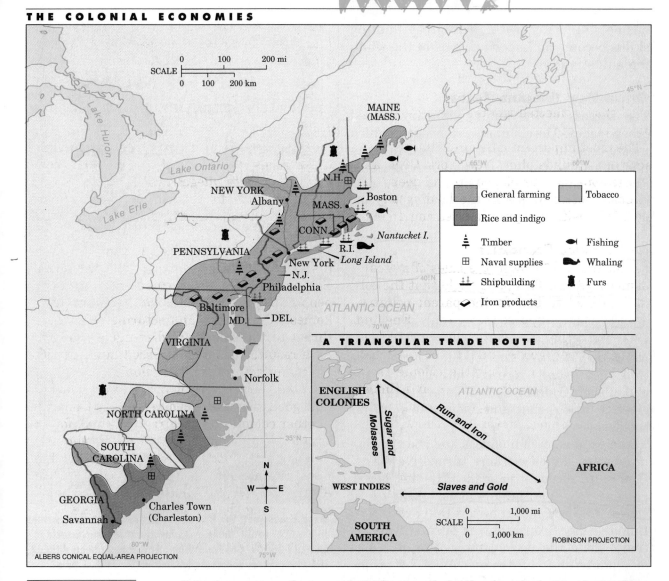

A TRIANGULAR TRADE ROUTE

MAP SKILLS Natural resources and overseas trade (inset map) played major roles in the colonies. Where was shipbuilding important? What items did colonists trade for African slaves?

CRITICAL THINKING Why did the colonies produce more raw materials than finished goods?

grains and vegetables to support their families. Eventually, some of them were even able to build up a surplus—an extra amount—to trade or sell.

New Englanders soon realized that their region showed much greater promise for another activity: fishing. The jagged coast was cut with many natural harbors in which boats could dock. Not far off the coast lay some of the world's richest fishing grounds, home to huge numbers of codfish, halibut, and other kinds of fish.

Thus, many New Englanders turned to fishing for their livelihood. They traded surplus fish to other colonies or to the West Indies. By 1765 Massachusetts alone was exporting 35 million pounds of fish a year, mainly cod. Massachusetts recognized its debt to the "sacred cod" when in 1784 it hung a carved codfish five feet long in the State House in Boston.

In the 1600s New Englanders also began to hunt for whales, which provided oil for lamps. By 1700 whaling had grown into a profitable business. Indians, with their great hunting skills, became an important part of the whaling industry.

OTHER NEW ENGLAND TRADES

The success of the fishing industry helped other trades. More ships were needed, which meant that lumber, sails, rope, and anchors had to be produced. New Englanders became excellent shipbuilders. Skilled workers also began to make furniture and household goods for sale.

Many New England workers learned their trades by serving as apprentices. An apprentice was a young person who learned a skill or trade from a master worker—a sailmaker, a carpenter, or a blacksmith, for example. Apprentices signed a contract to live with the master's family for several years while they learned their trade. During this time they usually received no wages. At the end of their training period, apprentices were given a little money and allowed to work for themselves.

The expansion of business and the growing number of skilled workers turned New England into a center of trade. By the 1700s, commerce—the buying and selling of goods—had become an important part of New England life. Seaport towns bustled with activity along the docks and in the offices of merchants and shipowners. As these people prospered, they built large and elegant homes. Many merchants' homes had expensive furnishings that rivaled those in the great houses of England.

WOMEN IN NEW ENGLAND

For the most part, women in New England (and throughout the colonies) did not play a leading role in business or public life. In some cases, however, women did take over and run the family business when their husbands or fathers died. Many women worked as shopkeepers. Others were teachers, lawyers, blacksmiths, and shoemakers, among other trades. Before 1776, ten newspapers in the colonies were published by women.

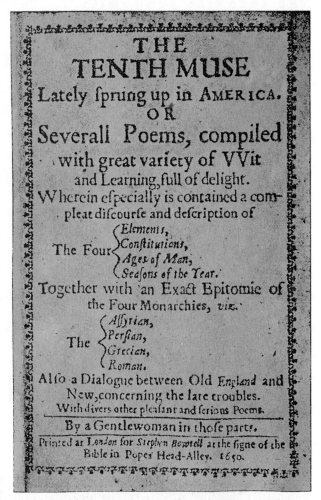

THE
TENTH MUSE
Lately fprung up in AMERICA.
OR
Severall Poems, compiled
with great variety of VVit
and Learning, full of delight.
Wherein efpecially is contained a compleat difcourfe and defcription of

The Four { Elements,
Conftitutions,
Ages of Man,
Seafons of the Year.

Together with an Exact Epitomie of the Four Monarchies, viz.

The { Affyrian,
Perfian,
Grecian,
Roman.

Alfo a Dialogue between Old England and New, concerning the late troubles. With divers other pleafant and ferious Poems.

By a Gentlewoman in thofe parts.

Printed at London for Stephen Bowtell at the figne of the Bible in Popes Head-Alley. 1650.

Anne Bradstreet, the first important American poet writing in English, wrote about everyday life in Massachusetts in the mid-1600s. CULTURE Why might it have been difficult for a woman to become a leading writer at that time?

In general, though, women worked at home, taking care of the household and raising a family. New England farm women tended the livestock and vegetable garden. They made cheese and butter as well as the family's cloth, soap, and candles. Taking care of the children was a major task. Families were large, with an average of nine children in early colonial days. It was not uncommon for a child to have twelve or even fifteen brothers and sisters.

Girls were not allowed to attend grammar school or college. Many New Englanders chose to educate their daughters at home. As a result, many girls learned to read and write. Some, such as Anne Bradstreet, became accomplished authors.

AFRICAN AMERICANS IN NEW ENGLAND

More free black colonists lived in New England than in any of the other colonies. Free black men became merchants, soldiers, sailors, printers, and carpenters. African Americans were allowed to own land in New England. Some African American families ran their own farms.

Slavery remained legal in New England, though not many New Englanders owned slaves. One reason is that the economy did not call for large numbers of unskilled laborers. In 1700 fewer than 1,000 slaves lived in New England.

Puritan slaveowners gave their slaves religious instruction and sometimes taught them to read and write. Phillis Wheatley, a slave in the household of a Boston tailor, gained fame as a poet. A book of her poems was published in London in 1773.

CHANGES IN NEW ENGLAND SOCIETY

Puritan New England was originally a church-centered society. By the late 1600s, however, this had begun to change. Growing prosperity and the end of Puritan political control led to new ideas and values. New generations of colonists did not share the strict religious views of their parents. To these younger people, wealth and the things it could buy seemed more important than religious faith and self-sacrifice. Puritan ministers began to complain that their "city on a hill" was full of greedy merchants.

One person whose ideas reflected both the old and the new was Cotton Mather, New England's leading minister in the late 1600s. A believer in witchcraft, Mather helped cause a panic in Massachusetts in 1692. Several hundred people were accused of witchcraft. In Salem, accusations by a group of young girls led to the Salem Witchcraft Trials. As a result, nineteen persons were hanged, and another was pressed to death by heavy stones. Villagers soon began to doubt the girls, though, and the panic ended. The trials were an example of a society expressing its worries and fears by creating scapegoats.

For all his interest in witchcraft, however, Mather was not completely stuck in the past. He was also a modern man, open to new ideas. He read new scientific works and backed advanced ideas. In 1721 Mather led the campaign in New England to protect people against smallpox. This involved giving people a mild case of smallpox in order to build up a resistance to the disease. The practice was so new and controversial that someone threw a bomb at Mather's house.

Some people took Mather's belief in new ideas further. They believed that reason and an understanding of nature could lead to a knowledge of God. This view was called deism. Deists did not think that God changed earthly events through miracles. Instead, they believed that God had created the

Though twenty people were executed as a result of the Salem Witchcraft Trials, the judge and jurors later admitted that they had made errors. Massachusetts made payments to the families of the victims. CIVIC VALUES Could similiar trials occur today? Why or why not?

universe and then let it run itself. Religion thus played less of a role in their daily lives. With the growth of deism, religious zeal declined in the colonies.

THE GREAT AWAKENING

Between 1720 and 1750, however, a new wave of religious enthusiasm swept through New England and the other colonies. Ministers went from town to town, holding meetings at which they told people to return to their faith. This movement was known as the Great Awakening.

The leader of the Great Awakening in New England was Jonathan Edwards, a fiery

BIOGRAPHY

JONATHAN EDWARDS (1703–1758), minister and philosopher, was the leading American intellectual of his day. Born in Connecticut, Edwards entered Yale College when he was only twelve years old. Following graduation he became a Congregational minister in Northampton, Massachusetts. Edwards's sermons, such as the famous "Sinners in the Hands of an Angry God," helped spark the Great Awakening. Edwards later served as a missionary to Indians in western Massachusetts and as president of what became Princeton University.

George Whitefield preached "fire and brimstone" sermons during the Great Awakening. His dramatic, emotional style set a pattern for future religious revivals in America. **RELIGION** How might Whitefield's style and message account for the large crowds his sermons attracted?

preacher from Northampton, Massachusetts. Similar movements also sprang up in the other colonies. These movements came together in 1740 when George Whitefield, a well-known English preacher, traveled through the colonies.

Jonathan Edwards and other ministers preached "fire and brimstone" sermons to make people admit their sins and have a spiritual rebirth. "I think it is a reasonable thing," said Edwards, "to fright persons away from hell." During a Whitefield sermon, said one observer:

> Some were struck pale as Death, others wringing their hands, others lying on the ground, others sinking into the arms of their friends, and most lifting up their eyes toward heaven, and crying out to God.

Baptists and Methodists were two religious groups whose membership grew as a result of the Great Awakening. This watercolor from the early 1800s shows a Pennsylvania Baptist ceremony on a riverbank. **RELIGION** What are the four people on the shore at the right waiting for? What emotions does the artist show on the face of the woman being baptized?

Those who took the preachers' message to heart became known as the "New Lights." Those who remained suspicious were the "Old Lights." The "New Lights" organized into new religious groups. Among them were the Baptists, who had some 500 churches by 1775. The Methodists also emerged as a "New Light" faith.

The effect of the Great Awakening was electric. People who had drifted away from the church responded to the energetic new preachers. Along with this excitement came a new sense of equality among Americans. Everyone was equal in God's eyes, the preachers declared. Instead of looking up to someone who was wealthier or better educated, people called each other "brother" and "sister." Some colonists reached out to African Americans and Indians, trying to improve their lives.

SECTION REVIEW

1. KEY TERMS raw materials, Navigation Acts, triangular trade, smuggling, surplus, apprentice, commerce, Salem Witchcraft Trials, deism, Great Awakening

2. PEOPLE Anne Bradstreet, Phyllis Wheatley, Cotton Mather, Jonathan Edwards, George Whitefield

3. COMPREHENSION Describe in broad terms the economic relationship between the colonies and England.

4. COMPREHENSION How did New England become a center of trade?

5. CRITICAL THINKING Why is the term *Great Awakening* a fitting name for the religious revival of the 1700s?

Colonial Expressions

Many expressions that people use today come from customs and crafts that were familiar centuries ago. In colonial America, the strongest influence on both customs and language came from England. Some phrases crossed the oceans with the colonists and found a home in American speech.

In the law courts of England and the American colonies, lawyers and judges wore wigs and robes. Lawyers' wigs were short and curly. The judge wore a large wig that came to his shoulders, making him a **bigwig.**

Fashionable gentlemen and ladies also wore wigs, known as "wool," on other formal occasions. If someone jokingly **"pulled the wool over your eyes,"** you couldn't see what was going on. At dances and balls, a special **powder room** was set aside so that servants could put fresh powder on people's formal white wigs.

Hunting deer, or bucks, for their hides was big business in the colonies. Among both Indians and settlers, a person's wealth might be counted in buckskins, or **bucks.**

The Spanish silver *peso* was used widely in America in the 1600s and 1700s. For small amounts, people often cut the coin into "pieces of eight" or **bits** worth 12 1/2 cents each. Thus, **two bits** was worth a quarter of a dollar.

Blacksmiths, who made iron tools and horseshoes, had to heat the metal so it would be soft enough to bend. To work the metal, the smith had to **strike while the iron was hot.** If the blacksmith had **too many irons in the fire,** none would get hot enough to work well.

In colonial times, printers set type by hand, picking each letter from a wooden case. Capital letters were in the **upper case,** small ones in the **lower case.** Beginners could easily mix up similar letters and so were told to **"mind your p's and q's."**

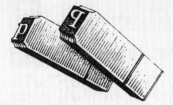

Apprentice sailors also had to be careful. Since there were more than a hundred different ropes for the sails and yards on a sailing ship, a sailor who didn't **know the ropes** could cause serious trouble.

Royal officials faced with an unruly crowd of colonists might **read them the riot act.** Under English law, once the Riot Act had been read aloud to a crowd or meeting, they had one hour in which to break up or they would be arrested.

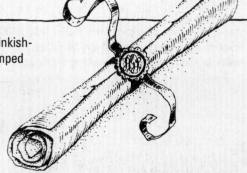

In England and France, legal documents were tied with a pinkish-red tape or ribbon, then sealed with a blob of wax and stamped with an official seal. Dealing with the government meant getting through the **red tape.**

How did Americans get the name **Yankees?** People disagree. Some people think it came from nicknames given to Dutch sailors: *Janke* (little Jan) or *Jan Kees* (a sort of Dutch John Doe). Others think it came from the Indians' pronunciation of "Yengleesh" for *English.*

2 Plantation Agriculture in the South

Section Focus

Key Terms plantation ■ fall line ■ overseer ■ backcountry

Main Idea Farming and trade became important parts of the southern economy. Yet this economy relied on slave labor.

Objectives As you read, look for answers to these questions:
1. How and why did farming thrive in the Southern Colonies?
2. Why did slavery expand in the Southern Colonies?
3. What was life like for southerners?

The Southern Colonies—the Carolinas, Georgia, Maryland, and Virginia—were a study in contrasts with New England. Not just their climate, but also their population, economy, and society, all differed from those in New England. As early as the 1700s a unique way of life was emerging in the South.

GEOGRAPHY AND THE SOUTHERN ECONOMY

Unlike New England, the Southern Colonies had rich soil and a warm climate. The tidewater coastal area, with its flat, rich land, sharply contrasted with New England's rocky coast. By the mid-1600s plantations, or large farms, had spread through the tidewater regions of the South.

Tobacco was the South's first and most important product, dating back to the James-town settlement. It was grown mostly in the Chesapeake region, where goods could be carried easily by river. Later, plantations growing rice and indigo—a plant used to make blue dye—dotted the coastal plains of South Carolina and Georgia. The ocean port of Charleston was the most important trading center for these southernmost colonies.

Tobacco, rice, and indigo were in great demand in Europe. Growing them for export thus proved profitable. The Southern Colonies kept up a lively trade with England into the 1770s. Many plantation owners, known as planters, became very rich. By and large they did not trade among themselves, though, or with the other colonies.

Nor did the Southern Colonies bother to develop much manufacturing. Instead, they im-

Baltimore, Maryland, a leading Southern town in the mid-1700s, was founded as a trading center for the tobacco plantations of southern Maryland. ECONOMICS List three ways shown in the picture in which people are making a living.

This watercolor, painted by a British sailor in 1846, records the inhumane conditions below deck on a slave ship. **ETHICS** How might slave traders justify their treatment of slaves? How would you respond to those arguments?

ported the goods they needed from England. One visitor wrote:

> They become so lazy that they send to England for clothes, linen, hats, women's dresses, shoes, iron tools, nails, and even wooden furniture (although their own wood is very fine to work on and they have loads of it).

GROWTH BEYOND THE SEABOARD

At first, people throughout the colonies depended on water transport. In New England, where there were fewer large rivers, that meant that people stayed close to the coast. The South, however, developed differently.

In the Chesapeake Tidewater, for example, there were no coastal cities. Tobacco farmers, always in search of good farmland, spread inland along the rivers. The people and the government followed. Jamestown, Virginia's first capital, became a ghost town when Williamsburg was made the capital in 1699. Williamsburg also faded, however, giving way to the new town of Richmond. Located on the James River, Richmond was built on the river's fall line—the point at which a river passes from high land to the low, coastal plains.

Large boats could not navigate beyond the fall line. Therefore, farmers farther inland could not do business from a plantation dock. They had to use wagons or small boats to carry their tobacco and other goods to a trading center. At Richmond, farmers built warehouses to hold the cargo before moving it to oceangoing boats. Stores were built to supply the farmers with manufactured goods.

Farther south, rice and indigo farmers also moved inland along rivers, giving rise to new towns. With the exception of Charleston, the major towns of the South developed at the fall line in the 1700s. They included Baltimore, Maryland; Columbia, South Carolina; and Augusta, Georgia.

EXPANDING THE SLAVE TRADE

Raising such crops as tobacco took a large number of unskilled workers. By the 1660s, however, the supply of English indentured servants was steadily dropping. To make up the difference, the planters turned to African slaves. The slave trade began to boom after 1700. In 1706, 24 slaves were brought into South Carolina. In 1735 eleven ships docked in Charleston with a human cargo of 2,641 Africans.

Behind such numbers lies a story of human tragedy. Olaudah Equiano was eleven years old when he was kidnapped from his African home and sold into slavery. Later, after he

This advertisement announces the sale of newly arrived Africans as slaves.
CULTURAL PLURALISM How did Africans resist slavery?

bought his freedom, he wrote the story of his life. The most frightening part of the story was the journey across the Atlantic.

Equiano's first fear was that he was "to be eaten by those white men with horrible looks, red faces, and long hair." Assured not, he then feared death, for "the white people looked and acted, as I thought, in so savage a manner; for I had never seen among any people such instances of brutal cruelty." On shipboard the slaves were so crowded together that one "had scarcely room to turn himself." The air became so foul and stinking that many died. "The shrieks of the women, and the groans of the dying, . . . rendered the whole a scene of horror almost inconceivable." People were whipped for not eating. If they tried to jump overboard, they were whipped "unmercifully for . . . attempting to prefer death to slavery."

The importation of slaves swelled the population of the Southern Colonies. By 1750, 40 percent of the people in these colonies were of African descent.

THE CONDITIONS OF SLAVERY

Those Africans who survived the terrible conditions of the slave ships faced a life of forced labor. Most slaves were field hands, though some slave women were also used as cooks, maids, and household servants. Field hands received orders from an **overseer, or supervisor of slaves**. Overseers punished the slaves, usually by whipping them, for breaking rules. On some large plantations, the slaves were allowed to learn skilled trades.

As slave laborers became important to the economy, the Southern Colonies passed harsh slave codes. They decreed that Africans and their children would be slaves for life, even if they were Christians. The planter had the right to sell a slave's children and to sell husbands and wives away from each other. Marriages between whites and blacks were illegal. The slaves had no legal status, no rights as people. In sum, the slave codes turned Africans into property of no more status than cattle.

African American men and women resisted slavery in a number of ways. From time to time they rose in open revolt, even at the risk of severe punishment. Slaves more often resisted by slowing down work, damaging goods, or carrying out orders incorrectly. Some ran away and tried to pass as free blacks in other colonies. Because other colonies did not ban slavery until after the American Revolution, runaway slaves had nowhere to turn. They were usually caught and returned to their owners.

PLANTATION LIFE

Plantations formed the basis of life in the South. On a typical plantation, the largest building was the Great House, home to the planter and his family. The Great House had a parlor for visitors, a library, and many bedrooms. The rich planters sought to live in the style of the wealthy landowners of England. Thus their homes, filled with fine furniture and paintings brought from Europe, resembled English manor houses. The planters also adopted the sports of the English upper class, such as horse racing and fox hunting.

William Byrd II of Virginia led the sort of easy life that was common among wealthy planters. Byrd's father was a London silversmith who had moved to Virginia and struck it rich in tobacco. Byrd went to school in England. After his return he played a leading role in Virginia politics. Byrd became one of the richest men in the colony and built a large mansion on his plantation at Westover.

An amateur scientist and writer, Byrd left a detailed account of his daily life. In his diary for June 6, 1709, he wrote:

> I rose at 5 o'clock and read a chapter in Hebrew and some Greek. . . . I said my prayers and ate chocolate for breakfast. . . . I walked about the plantation. In the evening the boat returned and brought some letters from England, with an invoice of things sent for by my wife which are enough to make a man mad. It put me out of humor very much. I neglected to say my prayers, for which God forgive me.

A typical day for Byrd also included a round of social activities—playing cards, or eating with friends.

Life was not always so easy, though. Running a plantation took a lot of attention. Even wealthy planters like Byrd faced disease, mosquitoes, and blistering heat.

On a typical plantation, the slaves lived in rough cabins not far from the Great House. Near the slaves' cabins were the blacksmith shop, the stables, and other necessary buildings. Thus the plantation might look like a small town.

Planters' wives helped run the family plantation. They supervised the slaves in the house, garden, dairy, and poultry yard. They took care of sick family members and slaves and prepared medicines themselves. Sometimes they led prayers on the plantation and educated the children. Women also ran farms

Rice Hope, this 20,000-acre plantation, belonged to Jonathan Lucas, who received the property in a royal grant. Lucas invented machines for milling rice, South Carolina's most important export in colonial times. ECONOMICS What other crops were important in the colonial South?

or plantations when their husbands or fathers were absent.

One planter's daughter, Eliza Lucas of South Carolina, had a major impact on the southern economy and southern life. In 1738, when Eliza was seventeen, her father went away on military duty and left her in charge of the family's three plantations. During his long absence, she experimented with new crops, including indigo. Through her efforts, indigo became one of the South's principal crops. She later married and, after her husband's death, managed vast plantations scattered across South Carolina.

SMALL FARMERS

Only a few southern colonists owned huge plantations. Small landowners made up a large middle group in southern society. Some of these people owned one or more slaves, but most owned none. Many small landowners lived much like the farmers of New England.

One southerner, Devereux Jarratt, left an account of life on a small family farm in the South. Jarratt was born in rural Virginia in 1733. His parents were hard-working and honest people, he wrote, "free from real want, and above the frowns of the world." They "always had plenty of plain food and raiment [clothing] . . . suitable to their humble station." All their food was grown on the farm, "except a little sugar, which was rarely used." Shoes, just about the only clothes his mother did not make herself, were worn only "in the winter season."

Jarratt learned to read and write, and later became a minister. Still, he never forgot the social barrier that separated small farmers from wealthy planters. As a young man, Jarratt wrote, the sight of a planter riding his horse down the road "would so alarm my fears . . . that, I dare say, I would run off as for my life."

THE BACKCOUNTRY

Another group in white southern society were those people who owned no land. Most were tenant farmers, working on land owned by others. They had little chance to get an education or to better their lives.

To claim their own land, many tenant farmers and other poor settlers moved inland to the hilly frontier region known as the backcountry. This area, located between the fall line and the Appalachian Mountains, remained sparsely settled until the mid-1700s. The people who came to the backcountry were fiercely independent and often rough-mannered. At first they cleared small patches of land and built rough log cabins. In time, wider areas were cleared, and the settlers raised larger crops of grains, potatoes, and fruit. The backcountry grew into a land of farm villages and orchards.

By the 1760s a 700-mile-long road, known as the Great Wagon Road, stretched through the backcountry from Pennsylvania to Georgia. Southward along this road rolled covered wagons full of settlers and their belongings. Northward went the grain and cattle the settlers produced for northern markets. It was the busiest highway in America. In 1766, the governor of North Carolina wrote, "I am of the opinion this province is settling faster than any on the continent." Before long, backcountry residents like Daniel Boone would be pushing west across the Appalachian Mountains into the future states of Tennessee and Kentucky.

SECTION REVIEW

1. KEY TERMS plantation, fall line, overseer, backcountry

2. PEOPLE AND PLACES Charleston, Richmond, Olaudah Equiano, Eliza Lucas

3. COMPREHENSION What kinds of crops were grown in the South? Where were these crops sold?

4. COMPREHENSION How did life in the backcountry differ from life on the plantations?

5. CRITICAL THINKING Do you think the southern plantations could have survived without slavery? Why or why not?

How do you say this?

I placed four new boxes on the floor near the door.

Whatever you said sounded natural to your ear, but it is not how every American might say it. Did your *four* sound like *for,* or did it sound more like *foh–uhr*? Did you pronounce *door* more like *doh–ah* or *doh* or *dor*? Does your *new* sound more like *noo* or *nyu*?

As many as a dozen regional dialects, or speech patterns, make up the American language. Dialects reflect differences in vocabulary as well as pronunciation. For example, in the South people call a paper container a *sack,* while people in other areas call it a *bag.* In different regions you may hear a large sandwich described as a *hoagie, hero, sub,* or *grinder.*

The three major American dialects are New England, Southern, and Midland. The Midland dialect, which is also called General American, is spoken by about two-thirds of the population. These three dialects emerged from the major colonial regions: New England, the Southern Colonies, and the Middle Colonies.

NEW ENGLAND

Most New England colonists came from southeastern England. Today New England speech sometimes resembles English as it was spoken in that part of England three centuries ago. Some New Englanders are likely to pro-

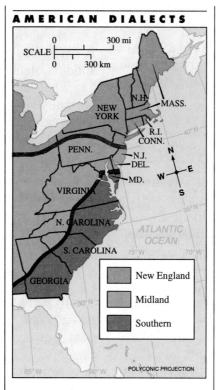

AMERICAN DIALECTS

SCALE 0 — 300 mi
0 — 300 km

New England
Midland
Southern

POLYCONIC PROJECTION

nounce the *a* in *can't* or *class* as *ah.* They also are likely to drop *r* sounds so that *car* sounds like *cah* and *farmer* sounds like *fahmah.* When pronouncing the words *box* or *not,* New Englanders round their lips to make the *o* sound more like *aw.*

SOUTHERN

The distinctive drawl of southern speech reveals the influence of both Scots-Irish and Africans. The southern use of *you-all* and *we-all* reflects a speech pattern the Scots-Irish carried from northern Ireland. African slaves held on to much of the vocabulary and rhythm of African language even when they learned English. Because

slaves often took care of white children, their language pattern influenced that of white southerners.

The southern dialect today features a slow-breaking vowel that is like a bridge between syllables. Southerners will pronounce *class* as *clay–is. Yes* is pronounced *yay–is.* Southerners are also likely to drop the final consonant so that *floor* sounds like *flo* and *running* becomes *runnin.*

MIDLAND

The Midland dialect emerged from the diverse ethnic traditions of the Middle Colonies. Speakers of this dialect sound a strong *r* when they say *car* or *farmer.* They use a short, flat *a* in words such as *class* and *can't.* The word *hot* is pronounced *haht.* Where there is a pair of vowels, Midland speakers stress the first vowel. The result is that *four* sounds the same as *for* and *hoarse* sounds like *horse.*

Over time, influences such as television may cause the regional dialects to become different or even disappear. Language is like a river; it appears the same but is ever changing.

CRITICAL THINKING QUESTIONS
1. How do you think the lack of good transportation among the colonies affected the development of regional dialects?
2. What influences besides television might change regional dialects in the future?

3 Farming and Manufacturing in the Middle Colonies

Section Focus

Key Term   cash crop

Main Idea   The economies of the Middle Colonies benefited from good farming conditions, harbors for shipping, and the growth of manufacturing.

Objectives   As you read, look for answers to these questions:
1. Why was farming important in the Middle Colonies?
2. What factors encouraged the growth of trade and manufacturing?
3. What kinds of people settled in the Middle Colonies?

Thomas Jefferson once wrote that a visitor to America could predict the character of the colonists based on where they lived. Northerners, he said, were cool and businesslike. Southerners were emotional and generous. In Pennsylvania, "the two characters seem to meet and blend and to form a people free from the extremes both of vice and virtue."

Indeed, the Middle Colonies—Pennsylvania, Delaware, New Jersey, and New York—combined features of both New England and the South. Like the South, the Middle Colonies had rich soil, a good growing season, and a number of large rivers. Farming thus flourished in the region. At the same time, like New England, the Middle Colonies developed trade and manufacturing. Towns and cities grew more rapidly than in the South.

THE "BREAD BASKET COLONIES"

As in New England and in the South, the first settlers in the Middle Colonies were farmers. The farmers of the Middle Colonies, however, did not live in small villages or on grand plantations. Instead, many of them

Bethlehem, Pennsylvania, on the Lehigh River, was a prosperous farming community when this view was painted in 1757. GEOGRAPHY Why was this town established by a river?

The kitchen was the most important room in a colonial home and the center for much of women's activities. Here women cooked meals, made herbal medicines, and spun and dyed flax and wool to make the family's clothing. **ECONOMICS** How did colonial women contribute to the economic well-being of their families?

lived on large farms that extended inland from the seacoast.

Farmers in the Middle Colonies gathered rich harvests of wheat, barley, rye, and other grains. Fruit and livestock flourished in New York, Pennsylvania, and New Jersey. Farmers in the Middle Colonies soon produced surplus grains. These grains were called **cash crops**—crops grown to be sold. (The tobacco, rice, and indigo of the South were also cash crops.) By 1760 New York farmers were selling more than 80,000 barrels of wheat flour a year to other colonies. Because the Middle Colonies produced so much grain, they became known as the "bread basket colonies."

TRADE AND MANUFACTURING

As the Middle Colonies prospered, the farmers had larger surpluses to trade. Other settlers had timber and fur for sale. Two seaports, New York at the mouth of the Hudson River and Philadelphia on the Delaware River, became trading centers. Goods from the Middle Colonies were sold to other colonies, to the West Indies, and to Europe.

Colonial roads were poor. In fact, shipping a load of goods across the Atlantic was cheaper than sending it overland 100 miles within the colony. As a result, a brisk European trade developed. Colonial merchants took wheat and other items to Europe and returned with foreign goods. Many merchants in the Middle Colonies grew rich from this trade. By 1768, Philadelphia had replaced Boston as the largest seaport in the colonies.

The first settlers of the Middle Colonies made the fairly simple items they needed in their homes. As the colonies prospered, however, manufacturing grew. Women and men toiled in workshops. There they made clocks, watches, guns, locks, cloth, hats, and glassware. The iron industry in Pennsylvania and New Jersey grew quickly after many skilled German workers settled there. Iron ore, mined in the Middle Colonies, was heated in forges and turned into pig iron. From pig iron, workers made nails and iron tools. All of this, of course, was illegal under the old Navigation Acts. Yet both the colonists and the English long ignored those laws.

BENJAMIN FRANKLIN: SON OF A NEW AGE

To see how prosperity affected life in the colonies, we need only look at the career of the Middle Colonies' best-known resident, Benjamin Franklin. Born in Boston in 1706, Franklin was the fifteenth child in his family. His father was a candlemaker who labored long hours at his trade in order to care for his large brood. Franklin became a printer's apprentice at age twelve. Five years later he took off to make his way in the world. He ended up in Philadelphia almost penniless. As he later wrote in his *Autobiography*:

> I was dirty from my journey; my pockets were stuffed out with shirts and stockings; I knew no soul nor where to look for lodging; I was very hungry; and my whole stock of cash consisted of a Dutch dollar and about a shilling in copper.

In Philadelphia, Franklin went to work for a printer. Later he set up his own printing shop, which soon was doing a thriving business. In his biggest-selling book, *Poor Richard's Almanack,* Franklin wrote bits of wisdom and advice that still ring true today:

> Early to bed and early to rise, makes a man healthy, wealthy, and wise.

> A penny saved is a penny earned.

> God helps them that help themselves.

> **"God helps them that help themselves."**
>
> —*Benjamin Franklin*

Franklin practiced what he preached, working hard to make his printing shop a success. Indeed, he did so well that he was able to retire at age 42 and devote himself to other tasks. He invented an iron stove known as the Franklin stove. He experimented with electricity by flying a kite in a thunderstorm.

Benjamin Franklin was a well-known printer and civic leader when this portrait was painted in 1746. He was an innovator in many areas: his newspaper was the first to publish a political cartoon and to illustrate a news story with a map. **NATIONAL IDENTITY** What American values did Franklin's life reflect?

Lightning struck the kite and passed down the wire to a key at the end, causing a spark. This proved that lightning was electricity. It led to Franklin's invention of the lightning rod.

Franklin also did many useful things for Philadelphia. He organized a fire department and convinced city leaders to pave the streets. He even helped establish the city's first public library. Finally, as you will read in later chapters, Franklin played a central role in the birth of the United States.

Franklin's life showed that with hard work, a person could rise from humble beginnings to become wealthy and famous. Franklin became the model of a new breed of colonist: curious, hard-working, and interested in personal achievement and worldly success.

SOCIETY IN THE MIDDLE COLONIES

The Middle Colonies attracted a greater variety of settlers than New England or the Southern Colonies. The Dutch and the Swedes had first settled the areas that became New York, New Jersey, and Delaware. English Quakers later founded Pennsylvania, but thousands of Germans and Scots-Irish also moved to the colony. Welsh, Irish, Scottish, and French colonists added to the variety of people in the Middle Colonies.

The Middle Colonies are sometimes called a "melting pot" because of the many groups who settled there. Each added its own customs to the colony. For example, the Dutch built brick homes with a wooden porch called a stoop. The Germans built an efficient wood-burning stove that others copied. The colonies benefited from this variety of new ideas.

The Middle Colonies became home to several different religious groups. Even if one group formed the majority in a place, it did not persecute those with different beliefs. Both the Quakers and the Dutch believed in religious toleration. The Quakers welcomed German Protestants to Pennsylvania. The Dutch allowed Catholics and Jews to settle in New York. On the other hand, Jews in New York were not allowed to build a synagogue until the 1750s.

The climate of tolerance that existed in the Middle Colonies encouraged settlers there to speak their minds. As one Philadelphia resident put it:

> The poorest laborer upon the shore of the Delaware thinks himself entitled to deliver his sentiments in matters of religion or politics with as much freedom as the gentleman or scholar. Indeed, there is less distinction among the citizens of Philadelphia, than among those of any civilized city in the world. Riches give none. For every man expects one day or another to be upon a footing with his wealthiest neighbor.

SOCIAL HISTORY
Famous Firsts

1639	First printing press in English colonies established by Stephen Daye.
1650	Anne Bradstreet, first woman author in America, publishes a volume entitled *The Tenth Muse*.
1728	Botanic garden established by John Bartram in Philadelphia. It is still in existence in its original location.
1731	First circulating library, Philadelphia.
1750	Conestoga wagon developed by German craftsmen in Pennsylvania.
1755	Verses to "Yankee Doodle" written.

The Middle Colonies had fewer schools and colleges than did New England. Religious groups ran most of the early schools. The Dutch Reformed Church in New York, Quakers in Pennsylvania, and Catholic priests in Maryland all started schools. Religious groups also formed some of the colleges, such as Princeton and Rutgers, that grew up in the Middle Colonies in the mid-1700s. Princeton had been founded during the Great Awakening to serve as a training center for "New Light" ministers. As in the other colonies, women and African Americans could not attend college.

SLAVERY IN THE MIDDLE COLONIES

Slavery was legal in the Middle Colonies until the Revolutionary War. Yet fewer slaves lived in the Middle Colonies than in the South. As in New England, the grain crops grown in the Middle Colonies required only seasonal labor. Fewer workers were needed. In contrast, the cash crops of the South needed heavy, year-round labor.

The movement to free the slaves began in the Middle Colonies. In 1688 the Quakers in Germantown, Pennsylvania, drew up the earliest American protest against slavery.

The movement continued under Quaker leaders like John Woolman, who was born in 1720. When still a boy, Woolman had killed a small bird with a rock. Feeling tremendous guilt, Woolman became convinced that people must "exercise goodness toward every living creature."

As an adult, Woolman focused on the plight of the slaves. "I believe liberty is their right," he wrote in his journal, "and I see they are not only deprived of it, but treated in other respects with inhumanity in many places." He worked tirelessly to convince Quakers to free their slaves. As a result of Woolman's efforts, Quakers were among the first to join the antislavery cause.

SECTION REVIEW

1. KEY TERM cash crop

2. PEOPLE AND PLACES New York, Philadelphia, Benjamin Franklin, John Woolman

3. COMPREHENSION Why were the Middle Colonies called both a bread basket and a melting pot?

4. COMPREHENSION What different religious groups settled in the Middle Colonies? What role did religious groups play in education?

5. CRITICAL THINKING How did the lack of cheap inland transportation influence trade in the Middle Colonies?

4 The Development of Self-Government

Section Focus

Key Terms search warrant ■ Magna Carta ■ jury ■ Petition of Right ■ English Bill of Rights ■ limited monarchy ■ libel

Main Idea Working from English ideas about government, colonists in America took steps to achieve self-government.

Objectives As you read, look for answers to these questions:
1. How did people in England win recognition of their basic rights?
2. What kinds of government grew up in the English colonies?
3. What issues caused political conflict in the colonies?

It was sunny, but very cold, that day in February 1761 as Boston's leading citizens made their way to the Council Chamber of the Town Hall. The governor and his council arrived, lace ruffles on their shirts and swords at their sides. Boston's foremost merchants took their seats on three long rows of chairs. In the chamber a great fire burned to chase the winter cold.

All eyes were on the five judges, splendidly garbed in scarlet robes and great wigs powdered white. "Oyez (OH–yay), oyez," the clerk called out, using the French word for "Hear ye." The court came to order.

RIGHTS AND ENGLISH LAW

The merchants had come to court to challenge a government plan to use blank search warrants to control smuggling. Signed by a judge, a search warrant gives officials the right to search a person's property for a particular object. The blank search warrants, however, would allow officials to search any place at any time for any smuggled goods.

The lawyer who spoke for the merchants argued that the blank search warrant violated the principles of English law. In English law, he said, "A man is as secure in his house as a prince in his castle." The merchants lost their case, but their cause remained. This was that English people, including English colonists, had certain rights that could not be taken away by the government.

These rights were based on three historic documents.

(1) **Magna Carta.** In the early 1200s England was ruled by King John, a harsh monarch who wished to govern as he pleased. King John taxed the people unfairly and ruled cruelly. In 1215 a group of angry nobles made him accept a document called the Magna Carta. Magna Carta is a Latin term that means "Great Charter."

The Magna Carta limited the king's power. In it, King John agreed that nobles and freemen should not be punished except by the judgment of their equals—a right we today call trial by **jury.** (A jury is a group of citizens who listen to the facts and then give judgment.) The king also agreed to consult the Great Council of nobles and church officials about taxes and other important matters. At first, the benefits of the Magna Carta applied only to nobles and freemen. Yet in time, these rights were extended to all English people.

(2) **Petition of Right.** Charles I ruled England in the early 1600s. Like King John, Charles was determined to rule as he saw fit. He rarely consulted Parliament. King Charles broke a long-standing tradition by taxing the people without Parliament's consent, or agreement. In 1628 the protests against the king became so great that Charles had to accept the Petition of Right. It stated that the people could not be taxed without the consent of Parliament.

(3) **English Bill of Rights.** Another English king, James II, ignored Parliament and the rights of the people. In 1688, in what was called the Glorious Revolution, the English people made James II leave the country. In 1689 the new monarchs, William and Mary, accepted the English Bill of Rights. It said that elections for Parliament were to be held often. It allowed citizens to bear arms, forbade cruel and unusual punishment, and asserted the right to a jury trial.

This painting of Virginia's House of Burgesses shows America's first representative legislature. The House started meeting in 1619 and included two citizens, or burgesses, from each borough of Virginia. CULTURAL PLURALISM What groups do not appear to be represented?

Magna Carta (1215)

English barons secured the Magna Carta (Great Charter) from King John in 1215. The charter provided a basis for guaranteeing the liberties of the people of England and placed English monarchs under the rule of the law. The Magna Carta was, in short, an important step in establishing the principle of limited government.

Know ye, that we, in the presence of God, . . . have confirmed for us and our heirs forever:

1. That the English Church shall be free, and shall have her whole rights and liberties inviolable. . . . We have granted moreover to all the freemen of our kingdom, for us and our heirs forever, all the liberties, to be enjoyed and held by them and by their heirs, from us and from our heirs. . . .

39. No freeman shall be seized, imprisoned, dispossessed, outlawed, or exiled, or in any way destroyed; nor will we proceed against or prosecute him except by the lawful judgment of his peers, or by the law of the land.

40. To none will we sell, to none will we deny, to none will we delay right or justice.

60. Also all these customs and liberties which we have granted to be held in our kingdom, for so much of it as belongs to us, all our subjects, as well clergy as laymen, shall observe toward their tenants as far as concerns them. . . .

63. Wherefore our will is, and we firmly command that the Church of England be free, and that the men in our kingdom have and hold the aforesaid liberties, rights, and concessions, well and in peace, freely and quietly, fully and entirely, to them and their heirs, of us and our heirs, in all things and places forever, as is aforesaid.

From J. J. Bagley and P. B. Rowley, eds., *A Documentary History of England*, Vol. 1, pp. 91–113.

ANALYZING HISTORICAL DOCUMENTS

1. Describe the relationship the Magna Carta established between England's king and its Church.
2. Explain item 39 of the charter in your own words.
3. In what ways did the Magna Carta represent a change in England's political system?

By accepting these three important documents, the English monarchs admitted that their subjects had important rights. As a result, by the late 1600s the English people had a limited monarchy—a monarchy in which the ruler does not have complete power. The English people were proud of their success in limiting the power of the Crown. They were determined to maintain their rights against anyone who tried to deny them.

AMERICAN COLONIAL RIGHTS

The English colonists who settled in America claimed the same rights as people who lived in England. Indeed, many colonists came to America because they wanted more rights. Others came because they thought their rights were not fully respected in their homeland.

The colonial charters granted by the English Crown backed the colonists' claims. The charters often declared that the English colonists in America were to have the same "liberties . . . as if born within this our realm of England."

For example, the charters promised that English colonists would have the right to a jury trial. They also guaranteed the right to bring complaints to the Crown. Finally, settlers had a voice in colonial government. Men who owned a certain amount of land usually could vote for people to serve in the

This picture shows the Old Senate chambers of the Maryland state capitol at Annapolis. The laws passed here were early examples of self-government in the colonies. **PARTICIPATION** If you were establishing a new government, what laws would you first propose?

legislature. The legislatures normally decided important questions. These included taxes and voting rights.

English colonists did not have all the rights that belong to Americans today. Many colonists, including women, slaves, indentured servants, and men with no land, could not vote. In many colonies, some religious groups were denied their rights because of their faith. Also, the rights of the Indians were generally ignored.

Nevertheless, by 1750 English colonists had more freedom than people elsewhere in the Americas or in most parts of Europe. Like other English subjects, they believed that those rights could not be taken away from them.

COLONIAL GOVERNMENT

American colonial governments were modeled on the English government. A governor headed each colonial government, just as the English monarch headed the English government. Each colony had a legislature similar to the English Parliament. These legislatures made laws for the colonies and approved taxes. Each colony also had courts like those of England.

The colonial governments usually held a great deal of power over local affairs. England always had the last word. Parliament could overrule laws passed by a colonial legislature. Laws passed by Parliament, however, had to be obeyed in the colonies.

The colonies chose their governors in different ways. In Rhode Island and Connecticut, the legislature elected the governors. This gave the people of these colonies a good deal of power. Because Rhode Island and Connecticut were governed by the terms of their charters, they were called charter colonies.

In Maryland, Pennsylvania, and Delaware, the proprietor chose the governor. For this reason, these were called proprietary colonies. In these colonies, the governor picked by the proprietor had to be approved by the Crown.

The eight remaining English colonies had been founded by trading companies or by proprietors. At first the founders had the power to choose governors. In time, however, the Crown took over these colonies and began to appoint their governors. These colonies were known as royal colonies. The people of the royal colonies did not have any voice in choosing their governors.

TWO TYPES OF ENGLISH COLONIAL GOVERNMENT

⬇ Appoint ⬇ Elect ⬇ Pass laws ⬇ Pass laws and reject laws passed by colonial legislature

Diagram A

Monarch — Parliament

Governor — Laws

Upper House of Legislature — Lower House of Legislature

Colonists

Diagram B

Monarch — Parliament

Laws — Colonists

Upper House of Legislature — Lower House of Legislature

Governor

As you read through this book, you will notice that historical information is sometimes presented in graphic form for quicker and easier understanding. One graphic form that historians often use is the diagram. A diagram shows how something is organized and how its parts work together.

THE PARTS OF A DIAGRAM

Diagrams A and B above show two different kinds of English colonial government. Each diagram shows the parts of government (monarch, Parliament, governor, upper and lower houses of the legislature, and colonists), the laws these parts of government create, and the relationship between the parts of government. The connecting arrows show the flow of power from one part to another. The color of each arrow represents a kind of power: to appoint, to elect, and to pass or reject laws. The direction of the arrow shows whom the power affects.

Not all diagrams use the same symbols or have the same meaning for the symbols they use. For example, in other diagrams arrows may not represent power. The meaning of the arrows will depend on the content and purpose of each diagram.

Using the diagrams on this page and the information in Section 4 of this chapter, answer the following questions.

PRACTICING YOUR SKILL

1. How is the governor chosen in Diagram A? Diagram B?
2. In both diagrams, which part of the government do the colonists have the power to elect?
3. In both diagrams, how are members of the upper house of the legislature chosen?
4. How is the governor chosen in the system shown in diagram B?
5. What powers do the monarch and the Parliament exercise in both systems of government?
6. Using your reading, name two colonies that had governments similar to the one shown in Diagram B.
7. Under which system, A or B, do the colonists have greater power? Why?

Colony	Date Founded as English Colony	Reasons Founded
New England Colonies		
● Massachusetts	1630	Religious freedom
● New Hampshire	1623	Farming; trade
● Connecticut	1636	Farming; religious freedom
● Rhode Island	1636	Religious freedom
Middle Colonies		
◖ New York	1664	Trade
◖ New Jersey	1664	Trade; farming
◖ Delaware	1664	Trade; farming
◖ Pennsylvania	1682	Religious freedom
Southern Colonies		
◖ Virginia	1607	Trade; farming
◖ Maryland	1634	Religious freedom; farming
◖ North Carolina	1663	Trade; farming
◖ South Carolina	1663	Trade; farming
◖ Georgia	1732	Home for debtors

CHART SKILLS The reasons for the establishment of colonies varied with their location and date of their founding. Which colonies were founded for religious reasons? Which were founded after 1700? CRITICAL THINKING Why might Britain have established no new colonies after 1732?

Colonial legislatures worked with the governors. Most legislatures had two houses, or branches. The upper house was smaller and less powerful than the lower house. The governor appointed the members of the upper house. Members of the lower house were elected by the voters. Each town or county in the colony could send at least one representative to this lower house. In this way, the people had a voice in the passing of laws.

Typically, voting was a public affair. Voters simply went to the polls and announced their vote to all present, including the candidates. The following exchange took place at one election:

Sheriff: "Who do you vote for, Mr. Buchanan?"

Buchanan: "For John Clopton."

Clopton: "Mr. Buchanan, I shall treasure that vote in my memory. It will be regarded as a feather in my cap forever."

All too often, candidates handed out food, drink, and other "treats" to sway the voters. The public became used to such favors. In fact, candidates who opposed the practice had little chance of winning elections.

LOCAL AFFAIRS

Decisions affecting all the colonies were made in London. Yet when it came to local affairs, colonial governments had almost complete control.

In the New England Colonies, the town was the basis of local government. At regular times, often just once a year, citizens would gather for town meetings. At town meetings in colonial New England, all citizens could voice their opinion on local affairs. However, only voters were allowed to elect town officers. These officers then carried out town business. In general, the town meeting allowed for a great deal of self-government.

Counties formed the basis of local government in the Southern Colonies. The local affairs of each county were handled by a sheriff and several justices of the peace. (A justice of the peace is an official with many duties, including judging court cases and collecting taxes.) Justices of the peace were chosen by the governor, not elected.

In the Middle Colonies, a mixture of town and county government developed. In New York, for example, the town became the common form of local government. In Pennsylvania the county type of government was used more often.

WRESTLING FOR POLITICAL POWER

As might be expected, disputes often arose between governors and colonists. Sometimes a governor acted against the wishes of the people. At other times, governors objected to

Nathaniel Bacon led farmers in an uprising against Virginia's governor. Though the rebellion was crushed, the governor was removed. **PARTICIPATION** How might an unpopular governor be removed from office today?

the legislature's handling of money. The legislature of each colony voted on tax laws and set the governor's salary. Thus it could limit the governor's power.

Another limitation on the governor was the power of a free press. An early hero in the struggle for freedom of the press was a German immigrant named John Peter Zenger. In 1733 Zenger became printer of *The New York Weekly Journal.* A year later, Zenger was thrown in jail for libel (LY–buhl), or printing statements that harm a person's reputation. Zenger's real crime was criticizing New York's royal governor. At Zenger's trial, his lawyer argued that not all printed criticism was libel, only *false* criticism. He convinced the jury that Zenger's charges against the governor were true. The jury agreed and let Zenger go free. A great victory for a free, but responsible, press had been won.

Sometimes the colonists quarreled not with the government, but among themselves. People on the frontier and those in seacoast towns often had very different interests. Some farmers and frontier settlers complained that the rich merchants in the cities had too much political power.

BACON'S REBELLION

In Virginia, conflict over political power led to violence in 1676. Frontier farmers in Virginia had several complaints. Low tobacco prices had ruined many tobacco farmers. Taxes were high. Political power lay in the hands of the royal governor, Sir William Berkeley, and a handful of his friends. No election had been held in fourteen years. Although Indian raids were killing frontier settlers, Berkeley refused to fight the Indians.

Nathaniel Bacon, a wealthy landowner, sided with the farmers. He led a group of farmers, including some free blacks, to punish the Indians. The farmers attacked and killed the first Indians they came across. These Indians happened to be peaceful, fur-trading friends of the governor. Nevertheless, many settlers on the frontier hailed Bacon as a hero.

Governor Berkeley, alarmed at news of the attack, allowed the election of a new assembly giving better representation to the farmers. Yet the frontier remained unprotected. Bacon and his followers marched on Jamestown. In an attack known as Bacon's Rebellion, they forced the governor to flee and then burned the town. Soon afterward, Bacon fell ill and died. English soldiers crushed the rebellion, and Governor Berkeley returned to power. He then ordered that 23 of Bacon's followers be hanged.

Back in England, King Charles II was dismayed at Berkeley's action. He quickly appointed a new governor, and things settled down in Virginia. Yet no later governor dared assume as much power as Berkeley had. Bacon's Rebellion was an early sign that the colonists were willing to fight for their rights.

SECTION REVIEW

1. KEY TERMS search warrant, Magna Carta, jury, Petition of Right, English Bill of Rights, limited monarchy, libel

2. PEOPLE John Peter Zenger, William Berkeley, Nathaniel Bacon

3. COMPREHENSION What rights did English colonists have? Why did they have these rights?

4. COMPREHENSION What were the three different kinds of colonial government, and how did they differ?

5. CRITICAL THINKING If England's government had not been a limited monarchy, how might American colonial rights have been different?

CHAPTER 6 SUMMARY AND TIMELINE

1. Though New England lacked good farming conditions, fishing and trading became profitable, and towns grew. The power and influence of the Church weakened as the colonies prospered, though the Great Awakening increased interest in religion.

2. Farming was king in the Southern Colonies. Such crops as tobacco and rice were grown on large plantations, where slaves performed most of the hard labor. Many white farmers had only small plots of land or no land at all. Many landless farmers moved farther inland, to the backcountry near the Appalachians.

3. In the Middle Colonies, large, prosperous farms developed. Crop surpluses allowed the Middle Colonies to sell food to other colonies. Some manufacturing also developed. Attracting people from many different nations, the Middle Colonies became a "melting pot."

4. English colonists sailing to the Americas brought with them ideas of limited government and self-rule. They kept their rights as English citizens when they moved to the colonies. Colonial governments modeled on English government were set up. Colonists had control over local affairs, but broader issues were decided by England.

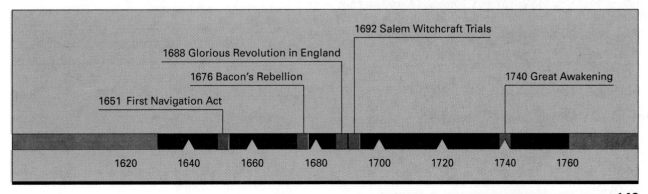

1651 First Navigation Act
1676 Bacon's Rebellion
1688 Glorious Revolution in England
1692 Salem Witchcraft Trials
1740 Great Awakening

1620 1640 1660 1680 1700 1720 1740 1760

PLACES TO LOCATE

Match each of the letters on the map with the places that are listed below.

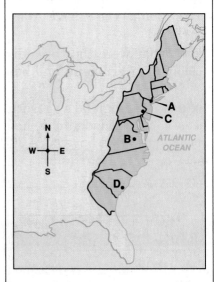

1. Charleston
2. New York City
3. Philadelphia
4. Richmond

KEY TERMS

Define the terms in each of the following pairs.

1. raw materials; surplus
2. backcountry; fall line
3. overseer; apprentice
4. Magna Carta; Petition of Right
5. triangular trade; smuggling
6. jury; libel

PEOPLE TO IDENTIFY

Match each of the following people with the correct description.

Nathaniel Bacon
Charles I
Jonathan Edwards
Olaudah Equiano
Benjamin Franklin
Eliza Lucas
John Peter Zenger

1. Printer arrested for libel but then freed.
2. American famous for his writings and scientific experiments.
3. Planter who introduced indigo to the South.
4. African captured and sold into slavery.
5. Minister who helped lead the Great Awakening.
6. Virginia landowner who led an uprising against the governor.
7. English king forced to accept the Petition of Right.

REVIEWING THE FACTS

1. Where were the first important colonial cities located?
2. How did England try to protect its trade with the colonies?
3. What economic activities prospered in New England?
4. What products did the Southern Colonies trade with England?
5. What rights did slave-owners have over slaves? What rights did slaves have?
6. What led the Middle Colonies to establish a brisk trade with Europe?
7. Why was there less slavery in the Middle Colonies than in the Southern Colonies?
8. Name and describe the three historic documents that limited the power of the English monarch.
9. Briefly describe the structure of the colonial governments.
10. In what way was the trial of John Peter Zenger a victory for freedom of the press?

CITIZENSHIP

1. Do you think the colonists had a duty to observe English laws on trade and manufacturing? Explain.
2. Why might voting rights in the English colonies have been limited to property owners?
3. Name an advantage and a disadvantage of the town meeting system of local government.
4. How does a free press help protect the rights of the people against abuses by the government?

PRACTICING YOUR SKILL

Use the diagram of colonial government below to answer the following questions.

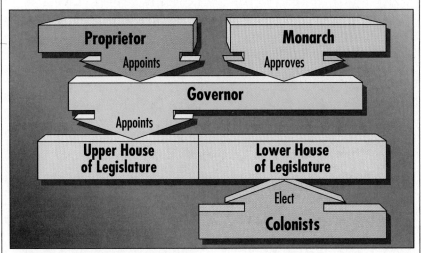

1. How is the governor chosen in the colony represented in this diagram?
2. What role does the monarch play in the organization of this colonial government?
3. How is the upper house of the legislature chosen?

4. How is the lower house of the legislature chosen?
5. What type of colonial government does this diagram represent?

CRITICAL THINKING SKILLS

1. IDENTIFYING SUPPORTING IDEAS Find three facts that support the following statement: "Despite their many differences, the colonies had important things in common."

2. ANALYZING A QUOTATION Explain what Benjamin Franklin meant by the statement, "A penny saved is a penny earned."

3. MAKING A HYPOTHESIS Why is the right to a jury trial an important safeguard of individual liberty?

PROJECTS AND ACTIVITIES

1. WRITING A REPORT Find out more about the Magna Carta, the Petition of Right, or the English Bill of Rights. Use reference books to help you determine what events led to the signing of the document you chose. Write a two-page report on your findings.

2. PERFORMING A SKIT Consider what would happen if Nathaniel Bacon stood trial in Virginia after his uprising was put down by English soldiers. With two or three other students, prepare to act out part of Bacon's imaginary trial in class. Include the parts of Bacon, the judge, a lawyer, the colonial governor, and ordinary citizens.

3. INTERPRETING INFORMATION Make a list of the issues a New England town meeting might have considered in the early 1700s. Be prepared to discuss the issues in class and to decide which of them would still be relevant today.

WRITING ABOUT TOPICS IN AMERICAN HISTORY

1. CONNECTING WITH LITERATURE A selection from the memoirs of Olaudah Equiano appears on pages 637–639. Read it and answer the questions. Then answer the following question: Why was slavery important to the economy of the Southern Colonies?

2. APPLYING THEMES: GEOGRAPHY How did the geographic features of the American colonies influence the kinds of economic activities that took place there?

France, building its own North American empire, clashed with England. Native Americans became caught up in the struggle, which ended with an English victory in 1763.

CHAPTER

7 The Clash of Empires
(1668–1763)

KEY EVENTS

1682	La Salle reaches the Gulf of Mexico
1718	New Orleans founded
1754	Albany Plan of Union proposed
1756	Seven Years' War begins
1759	British capture Quebec
1763	Treaty of Paris

1 The Expanding French Empire

Section Focus

Key Term portage

Main Idea The French explored America's great rivers and claimed a huge section of the country's interior. They competed for land and trade rights with the Spanish and British.

Objectives As you read, look for answers to these questions:
1. In what ways did French colonies in North America differ from English colonies?
2. How did the French come to rule the territory of Louisiana?

Winter was not far away that day late in 1668 as canoes of Indians paddled down the St. Lawrence River. They were headed for a French trading post just outside of Montreal. The Indians were strangers in these parts. They were Seneca Iroquois in a region dominated by the Algonquin.

At the trading post they spoke with the lean, sun-darkened Frenchman in charge. Yes, he said. The Seneca could camp there for the winter. The Frenchman was pleased at the prospect. From the Seneca he hoped to learn more about the lands to the south of the St. Lawrence.

In this year the Frenchman was 25. Born Robert Cavelier, he was known as La Salle. The son of a wealthy merchant, he had come to New France two years before to trade for furs with the Indians. La Salle had prospered as a trader. His great ambition, however, was to find a route to Asia through the interior of North America. This would be the Northwest Passage, for which European explorers had long searched in vain.

THE ST. LAWRENCE: CORE OF NEW FRANCE

New France had begun with Samuel Champlain's founding of Quebec in 1608 (page 75). Half a century later the French population in North America was about 2,000 and mostly male. They were fur traders, government officials, and missionaries.

Quebec was the capital of New France. The town sat upon rocky bluffs high above the St. Lawrence. Farther up the St. Lawrence was the French settlement of Montreal. It started as a fur trading post and continued to be the center of the fur trade.

In the 1660s the government of France became concerned about the growing number of English and Dutch colonists. They were beginning to compete with the French for the fur trade. As a result, France began to encourage French families to settle in New France. There had been few French settlers up to this point. While the English set up permanent settlements, most Frenchmen had come temporarily. Many of those who stayed married Indian women.

Often the best transportation through the thickly wooded areas of North America was by river. Here Indian canoeists portage, or carry, their canoes around some rapids, a practice adopted by the French. **CULTURE** Why did the French get along relatively well with the Indians?

Now the French planned to establish a permanent colony of farming families in the St. Lawrence River valley. These families would raise crops, livestock, and children for the colony. The increased population would serve as a line of defense against English expansion.

The plan worked in that the population of New France grew to 15,000 by 1700. New France, however, never drew the numbers of new immigrants that were flowing into the English colonies.

A TRADING EMPIRE

The French based their North American empire on trade. They had not set out to conquer and rule like the Spanish. Nor had the French transplanted themselves and their institutions as had the English. Ordinary Frenchmen could not own land in New France. Land was granted only to nobles. They in turn were responsible for bringing settlers for the land. For most French, the riches of America lay not in gold mines, nor in farmland, but in pelts and hides.

The fur trade depended on the Indians. The French got along with the Indians better than any other colonial power. French trappers and traders learned to live as the Indians did. The *voyageurs* (VOY–uh–zhur)—canoeists—and *coureurs de bois* (kuh–RUR DEH BWAH)—fur traders—often lived in Indian villages and married Indian women. French missionaries also treated the Indians with respect. They took the time to learn Indian languages. Although they hoped to convert Indians to Christianity, they did not try to force them to follow European or French ways. French missionaries needed no soldiers to protect them.

Both the French and the Indians benefited from the trading relationship. The Indians could barter fur pelts and deerskins for manufactured items: iron pots, steel knives, glass beads, even guns. In turn, the French reaped great profits when shiploads of furs reached European markets.

REACHING THE OHIO

In the 1660s the French empire in North America included the land around the Great Lakes and the St. Lawrence River valley. Within two decades France would expand this empire to the Gulf of Mexico.

La Salle was the first Frenchman to head south. That winter of 1668 La Salle took notes as the Seneca Iroquois told him about their homeland. A great river called the Ohio ran through this land, they said. The river flowed into the sea, but it took eight or nine months to reach its mouth.

La Salle could hardly contain his excitement. Was it possible that the Ohio was the Northwest Passage? He was eager to find out and set out the next spring. From Lake Ontario he headed southward until he reached a tributary of the Ohio. When he reached the great river, he followed it almost to the Mississippi. Then he realized that the Ohio was heading south and was not likely to be the Northwest Passage.

FRENCH EXPLORATION OF THE MISSISSIPPI

Meanwhile, Indians were telling of a "great water" that emptied into an even larger one. On that sea floated tall ships manned by white men. Jacques Marquette (mahr–KET), a missionary priest, and fur trader Louis Joliet (JOH–lee–et) were sent out in 1673 to find out the truth. They were also ordered to chart the course of the "great water."

Marquette and Joliet, taking two canoes

Father Jacques Marquette, pictured here with Indians of the Natchez tribe, traveled the Mississippi in 1673 with Louis Joliet. They followed the river as far south as present-day Arkansas. GEOGRAPHY What was the aim of Marquette and Joliet's mission?

and five men, paddled from Lake Michigan to the headwaters of the Fox River. There they made a portage—carrying boats overland—to the headwaters of the Wisconsin River. The Wisconsin flows in a southwest direction until it reaches the Mississippi. Marquette and Joliet followed the Mississippi as far as the Arkansas River. Then, afraid they might run into the Spanish, they returned to Lake Michigan.

LA SALLE REACHES THE GULF OF MEXICO

Back in Quebec, La Salle learned of what Joliet had found. From his explorations of the Ohio River, La Salle had begun to dream of expanding New France to the West. He envisioned the creation of permanent French settlements along the Ohio and Mississippi river valleys. Using Joliet's information, La Salle was sure he could reach the mouth of the Mississippi. He asked the French king's permission to explore the Mississippi for purposes of colonization. In 1677 Louis XIV, king of France, granted La Salle's request.

> "**I** cannot tell you the civility and kindness we received from these barbarians."
>
> —*French missionary priest*

In 1679 La Salle crossed the Great Lakes by boat. Later, in December 1681, he set out with 23 French colonists and 31 Indians. Among the Indians were ten women and three infants. From Lake Michigan the expedition portaged to the Illinois River. To do so, they dragged their canoes on sleds across the snow. Then the expedition paddled down to the Mississippi River. In the lower Mississippi Valley they met the descendants of the mound builders (page 11) and were impressed. "I cannot tell you the civility and kindness we received from these barbarians," wrote one of the priests on the expedition.

The expedition reached the Gulf of Mexico in April 1682. There, at the mouth of the Mississippi, La Salle set up a cross and a column with the French coat of arms. He then claimed "this country of Louisiana . . . in the name of the most high, mighty . . . and victorious Louis the Great, by Grace of God King of France."

La Salle defined the territory of Louisiana as the drainage of the Mississippi River from the Great Lakes to the Gulf of Mexico. This huge area stretched from the crest of the Appalachian Mountains to the crest of the Rocky Mountains. It was the heart of the North American continent.

To achieve his grand design, La Salle planned to build a string of forts from the Great Lakes to the Gulf of Mexico. Around each fort there would be a French settlement. The Mississippi would be a water highway linking the settlements from the Great Lakes to the Gulf.

A DISASTROUS EXPEDITION

La Salle was thus enthusiastic when the French king asked him to found a settlement on the Mississippi Delta. From there the king planned to threaten New Spain. In particular, the French had their eyes on the silver mines of northern Mexico.

With the king's blessing, La Salle set out from France in 1684 to establish a hold on the Mississippi Delta. He had four ships carrying over 300 colonists. The expedition was a disaster.

First of all, La Salle did not recognize the mouth of the Mississippi River when he sailed by it on the Gulf of Mexico. This happened because by the time it discharges into the Gulf, the Mississippi has split into several different rivers.

La Salle was somewhere off Matagorda Bay on the Texas coast when he realized he had overshot the mark. He was also out of food. La Salle landed at Matagorda Bay more from necessity than design. There the men and women with him built a crude fort they called Fort St. Louis.

La Salle had lost all but one of his ships during the voyage. The remaining ship was also wrecked after Indians killed its crew while ashore. La Salle had no water transportation, and he did not know exactly where he was.

With a small party he set out by land to find the Mississippi. La Salle had never been a popular or well-liked man. Now, on the hard march northward, grudges boiled over into hatred. A group of his followers rebelled. They killed La Salle north of the Brazos River in Texas. The year was 1687.

The murderers of La Salle escaped to live with the Indians. A loyal few finally did reach the Mississippi and eventually found their way back to France. As for Fort St. Louis, Spanish soldiers later found it in ruins. The only inhabitants were corpses, dead from smallpox and Indian attack.

AT THE MISSISSIPPI DELTA

For a while it looked as if La Salle's dream of a French empire in the Mississippi Valley would completely die. Shortly after La Salle's murder, the French government had ordered that "settlers should be kept together building towns and villages . . . and staying in close communication with France." Later the government ordered the French trappers and traders out of the wilderness completely. "Their privilege of going into the woods is forever abolished," read the declaration by the Crown. The interior was to remain Indian territory permanently.

La Salle's friends, however, continued to urge a settlement at the mouth of the Mississippi. They argued that such a settlement could serve several purposes. (1) It would be a base of attack against Mexico. (2) It would function as a trading post for furs and ores

A 1682 meeting in northern Louisiana between La Salle and a chief of the Taesna Indians is the subject of this painting by American artist George Catlin. HISTORY What happened to La Salle's attempt to build a settlement in the Mississippi Delta?

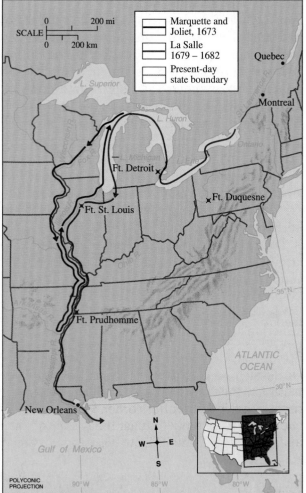

SCALE
0 — 200 mi
0 — 200 km

Marquette and Joliet, 1673
La Salle 1679 – 1682
Present-day state boundary

L. Superior
L. Huron
Ontario
Quebec
Montreal
Ft. Detroit
Ft. Duquesne
Ft. St. Louis
Ft. Prudhomme
New Orleans
ATLANTIC OCEAN
Gulf of Mexico
35° N
30° N
N W E S
POLYCONIC PROJECTION
90° W   85° W   80° W

MAP SKILLS

French explorers followed the Mississippi River through the interior of North America. In what body of water did La Salle's journey begin? In what body of water did it end? **CRITICAL THINKING** What was the significance of French control of Quebec and New Orleans?

from the interior. (3) It would keep England from taking control of the Mississippi River.

The last argument was a strong one. Already the English were planning to plant a colony on the Mississippi. In 1699, therefore, the French king approved of settlements on the lower Mississippi. The French expedition first built a fort at Biloxi, in present-day Mississippi. Jean Baptiste de Bienville (byan–VEEL) was left in charge.

Bienville began exploring the Mississippi Delta. Imagine his surprise one day to round

a bend and find an English ship laden with colonists. Was this the Mississippi? asked the captain of the English ship. No, Bienville lied. This was another river. The English believed him and turned back.

FRENCH SETTLEMENTS GROW SLOWLY

In the years to come, Bienville would oversee the building of more French settlements in southern Louisiana, including the founding of New Orleans in 1718. Other forts along the Mississippi helped link the two settled parts of New France. By the early 1700s, then, France held the two main access points to the American interior. The first of these was the St. Lawrence River, controlled by Quebec and Montreal. The second was the mouth of the Mississippi, controlled by New Orleans.

Southern Louisiana developed slowly. By 1745 about 3,200 Europeans and 2,000 African slaves lived in a thin line of settlements along the lower Mississippi and Gulf of Mexico. One reason the settlements grew so slowly was that the colonists had little freedom. They did not own their own land. Another was that the French government refused to let Protestants settle in New France. They feared the spread of Protestantism. As a result, only Catholics could emigrate, and their numbers remained small. Still, France held on to the shell of its huge empire.

SECTION REVIEW

1. KEY TERM portage

2. PEOPLE La Salle, Jacques Marquette, Louis Joliet, Jean Baptiste de Bienville

3. COMPREHENSION How did France's approach to its North American colonies differ from England's?

4. COMPREHENSION Why did the French decide to build settlements at the mouth of the Mississippi?

5. CRITICAL THINKING What factors might account for France's success in exploring the interior of the North American continent?

If you learn to develop good study habits, your chances of doing well on tests will be much improved. Information that you have memorized little by little over a period of days or weeks will stay with you longer than material you try to learn all at once on the night before a test.

To reduce the amount of work required to prepare for a test, read your assignments carefully and take notes as you read. If you have kept up with daily assignments, you can get ready for a test merely by reviewing material that you already know.

When the day of the test arrives, remember the most important rule of test-taking, "Follow the directions." Read the instructions for the test carefully. Even if you have prepared well and know the correct answers, you may lose points if you do not give the answer exactly as your teacher asks.

When you get the test, skim through it quickly to decide how much time you can spend on each part. If you cannot answer a question, go on to the next one so that you get credit for all the questions you can answer. When you have been through all the questions, go back to the ones you skipped and work on them.

There are three common kinds of questions that appear on American history tests. These are multiple-choice, matching, and essay questions.

MULTIPLE-CHOICE QUESTIONS

A **multiple-choice** question asks you to choose the correct answer from three or four possible answers. Read the question carefully and try to answer it before looking at the choices. If you are not certain of the right answer, eliminate those that you know are wrong. Then look at the remaining answers and choose the best one. Keep in mind that some tests may contain "decoy answers." These are answers that at first glance appear to be correct but actually are incorrect.

MATCHING QUESTIONS

In **matching** questions, you must match items in one column with items in a second column. Match first those items that you know with certainty. Then look for clues to the remaining answers.

ESSAY QUESTIONS

An **essay** question requires you to write a short composition in a limited time. Essay questions are often more complex than other types of questions. Read the question carefully so that you will know exactly what you are being asked to do: *list, discuss, compare, contrast,* or *summarize.* If you are asked to describe the similarities between a capitalist economy and socialist economy, for instance, do not waste time by listing the differences. On scratch paper, jot down the names, dates, facts, or terms required in your answer and arrange them in appropriate order. Write an outline if you have time. In it list the main points and supporting details you will use in your essay.

Be specific in your essay. An answer that is brief, detailed, and well-organized will receive more points than a long, rambling essay. After you have finished writing your essay, reread it and correct any errors in grammar, spelling, or punctuation.

PRACTICING YOUR SKILL

1. What is the most important rule of test-taking?

2. What is the first thing you should do when you take a test?

3. What should you do if you are not certain of the correct answer to a multiple-choice question?

4. Write four multiple-choice questions, one matching question, and one essay question for a section of this book that you have recently read. Exchange papers with a partner and see if you are able to answer each other's questions.

2 Rivalry over Furs and Land

Section Focus

Key Terms League of the Iroquois
■ balance of power ■ land speculator
■ Albany Plan of Union

Main Idea Rivalry between France and Britain took place on a global scale. The two nations fought for valuable resources in the Americas.

Objectives As you read, look for answers to these questions:
1. Why did English-French rivalry develop in North America?
2. What role did Native American tribes play in the English-French rivalry?

At the beginning of the 1700s, three powers controlled North America. England, France, and Spain each had carved out chunks of the North American mainland for themselves. Their rivalry also extended to the Caribbean.

HEMISPHERIC RIVALRY

In the West Indies, England controlled such islands as Barbados and Jamaica. British ports in the Caribbean played an important part in England's triangular trade (page 118).

France, too, claimed part of the West Indies. By the end of the 1500s most of the Spanish settlers had moved from Hispaniola

Colonial farms in the Caribbean used slaves to grow sugar cane. Freshly cut cane was crushed at a windmill and then boiled to make sugar and molasses. **HISTORY** Which European nations competed for control of the Caribbean?

to richer colonies. In 1664 France took over the western end of the island. Then it was called Domingo or St. Domingue. Today it is called Haiti (HAY–tee).

Haiti became the richest of the French possessions and one of the richest colonies in the world. French planters brought thousands of African slaves to the island. The planters grew wealthy from the slaves' labor, producing sugar and coffee.

TENSIONS ON THE TEXAS FRONTIER

France, England, and Spain all sought to expand their empires in North America. As they did so, tensions mounted along the frontier. The story of Louis de Saint-Denis (SAN duh–NEE) is an example of the conflicting goals of Spain and France.

In the fall of 1714 Saint-Denis, with a party of four Frenchmen and three Indians, crossed the Rio Grande from the north. Entering the Spanish mission of San Juan Bautista (bow–TEES–tuh), he called upon the commander of the presidio. Saint-Denis had visited San Juan Bautista ten years earlier. This time, however, he was made prisoner. The year before, the viceroy of New Spain had sent out an order: any foreigner crossing into Spanish lands was to be arrested.

A company of soldiers took Saint-Denis to Mexico City for questioning. They wanted to know what he was doing in Texas, where he had come from, what his intentions were. Saint-Denis explained that he had walked into Texas from Mobile (later in Alabama).

He said his intention was to work with the Spanish to bring Christianity to the Indians. His real intention, however, was to extend France's trading empire into New Spain.

Saint-Denis was allowed to return to San Juan Bautista as a Spanish officer. There he married the granddaughter of the commander. In 1716 the couple accompanied the expedition to establish missions in east Texas (page 67). By sending missions off to east Texas, the Viceroy hoped to hold Texas against French expansion. Saint-Denis, on the other hand, was playing the role of double agent. He secretly proposed to the French that they extend their territory to the Rio Grande. Saint-Denis also used the missions and his Spanish in-laws to increase trade between the French and Spanish. The trade violated Spanish law and mercantilist practice. Within a few years, Spanish authorities stopped the trade. Saint-Denis had to flee.

INDIAN ALLIANCES

Hostility between the rival European empires could be rather quiet, such as that between France and Spain on the Gulf of Mexico. It could also erupt into ferocious warfare. This happened on the frontier shared by the English colonies and New France. Frontier warfare between the French and English was made worse because each side recruited Indian allies. In this effort, France had allied itself with the Algonquin and Huron Indians of the lands bordering the St. Lawrence Valley. The Iroquois had been trading partners with the Dutch in the Hudson River fur trade. After England had driven the Dutch from North America, the Iroquois allied themselves with the English.

The Iroquois actually consisted of five (later six) different tribes or nations. Some time around 1500, these nations had joined together in the League of the Iroquois.

The rivalry between France and England over furs and land resulted in frontier warfare. Here, Abenaki Indians and their French allies attack the British settlement at Deerfield, Massachusetts. HISTORY How does this painting show the brutality of frontier fighting?

BIOGRAPHY

HENDRICK (1680–1755) was a Mohawk chief and a leader of the Iroquois. In 1754 Hendrick attended the meeting of colonial representatives in Albany. Hendrick called for a union of the colonies against the French. Holding three sticks in his hand, Hendrick said, "Put them together and you cannot break them. Take them one by one, you can break them easily." Hendrick died a year later, fighting for the British.

They did so to end the almost constant warfare that existed among the tribes. The League of the Iroquois would become the most powerful Indian confederation in America. Each of the member tribes held seats in a council, with each tribe having one vote. Decisions required unanimous votes.

Wars over the Fur Trade

By 1640, all the beaver in the Hudson Valley had been trapped. The Iroquois then began warring on their northern neighbors in an attempt to gain control of their fur trade. Within a decade they had defeated the Hurons. Through conquest, the Iroquois then extended their control over an area ranging from Maine to the Ohio Valley and north to Lake Michigan. By 1670, Iroquois trappers were hauling to the trading post at Albany one million pounds of beaver skins each year.

Iroquois expansion threatened the French fur trade. In 1687 France began to wage war on the League. The conflict broadened in 1689 when France and England went to war in the first of their struggles for world empire. (The wars fought in the Americas are named after the English ruler at the time.)

In King William's War (1689–1697) the Iroquois defended the English frontier against the French and their Indian allies. Neither in King William's War nor in two later wars,

Queen Anne's War (1702–1713) and King George's War (1744–1748), did the balance of power change in North America. (Balance of power among nations means that they have equal levels of strength.) One effect of the frontier wars, however, was to unleash French-sponsored Indian raids on English settlements.

Frontier Brutality

The frontier wars fostered brutality. Consider the story of Hannah Duston of Haverhill, Massachusetts. This incident happened during King William's War. In March 1697 she, her week-old baby, and a nurse were in the house when a party of twenty Indians attacked the town. Her husband, in the field nearby, ran to save his wife. But the Indians got there first.

The Indians forced Hannah Duston, her baby, and the nurse to join the other captives they had by then collected. Before "they had gone many steps, they dashed out the brains of the infant against a tree." As other captives tired, they were slain by a hatchet blow.

Duston and her nurse were assigned to an Indian family. Also with the family was a youth captured the year before. The captives accompanied the family 150 miles north to its home on the Merrimack River near present-day Concord, New Hampshire. The Indians intended to take the captives to Canada and sell them to the French. The prisoners were not guarded, for the Indians did not believe they would try to escape so far from home.

One day, Hannah Duston and her two companions rose just before daybreak. Seizing hatchets, they killed two men, two women, and six children. They had started on their way when Duston became fearful that her neighbors would not believe her story. So, they turned back, scalped the Indians, and returned to Haverhill with the bloody proof wrapped in a piece of plaid homespun.

The Search for a Secure Frontier

By the 1750s, the growing population of the English colonies helped shift the balance of

JOIN, or DIE.

Benjamin Franklin drew this first political cartoon in America to rally support for a union of the colonies. He based it on the belief that a snake cut into pieces would live again if the pieces were rejoined. The initials represent the colonies. HISTORY Why did the colonies reject Franklin's proposal?

power between France and England. In 1750, French colonists numbered nearly 80,000, compared with over 1,000,000 English. The English colonies were doubling their population every generation.

English land speculators—people who hope to make a profit from buying and selling land—began to plan for the settlement of the fertile Ohio Valley. The Ohio Company of Virginia had started to negotiate with the Indians in the Ohio Valley. Britain had already granted the company a half-million acres in the valley.

France became alarmed. A British presence along the Ohio River could threaten its control of the Mississippi Valley. France began to rim the Ohio Valley with forts in order to protect its claims.

FRANKLIN URGES UNION

Both France and Britain were building forts on the territory of the Six Nations of the Iroquois. Yet no one really knew what the boundaries of that territory were. To discuss relations with the Iroquois, the British called a meeting at Albany in 1754.

Representing Pennsylvania at the conference was Benjamin Franklin. Franklin believed the British colonies had to join together for their mutual defense. He made that point just before the conference when he published the first political cartoon in America. It pictured a snake cut into pieces with the caption "JOIN, or DIE."

Franklin went to Albany, therefore, not only to discuss matters with the Iroquois. He also intended to present a plan of union to the other colonies. Known as the Albany Plan of Union, Franklin's proposal called for each colony to send representatives to a new council. The head of the council would be a president-general appointed by the Crown. The council would have the authority to make war and peace with the Indians. It would also have other powers—to raise armies, construct forts, levy taxes, and found new settlements.

The plan devised by Franklin reflected his respect for the League of the Iroquois. It would be strange, he said, if the Six Nations could establish such a league but the colonies could not.

In the end, though, the colonies rejected the Albany Plan of Union. None of the colonies wanted to give up power to a central government. Nor did they want to pay taxes for a joint defense.

SECTION REVIEW

1. KEY TERMS League of the Iroquois, balance of power, land speculator, Albany Plan of Union

2. PEOPLE AND PLACES St. Domingue (Haiti), Louis de Saint-Denis, Benjamin Franklin

3. COMPREHENSION Over what issues did the rivalry between England and France grow in North America?

4. COMPREHENSION What was the relationship between the League of the Iroquois and the Albany Plan of Union?

5. CRITICAL THINKING How did European colonization affect the relationship among Indian tribes?

3 The French and Indian War

Section Focus

Key Terms French and Indian War ■ casualty ■ prime minister ■ Battle of Quebec ■ Treaty of Paris (1763)

Main Idea The French-English rivalry exploded in the mid-1700s. France eventually lost its North American empire to Great Britain.

Objectives As you read, look for answers to these questions:
1. What advantages did each side have in the French and Indian War?
2. How did the war affect the fate of North America?

On a spring morning in April 1754 a 22-year-old Virginian mounted his best horse. He gave a command. The drummer began his cadence, and a single file of 132 soldiers followed the leader out of Alexandria, Virginia. Their orders were clear: they were to drive the French from the upper Ohio Valley.

AT THE FORKS OF THE OHIO

The name of the young Virginian in charge was George Washington. Washington was familiar with the territory ahead. At eighteen he had helped survey a large part of what is now West Virginia. Six months earlier, he had carried a message from Virginia's governor to the French whose forts dotted the Ohio River valley. The message informed the French they were on soil claimed by Virginia and requested their "peaceable departure." Not surprisingly, the French had refused. Washington had reported to the governor that only force would make the French leave.

With the power of the British government behind him, the governor then ordered Washington to drive the French out. His first task was to secure the Forks of the Ohio. At the Forks of the Ohio the Allegheny River, flowing from the north, and the Monongahela, flowing from the south, meet to form the Ohio River. Whoever controlled this site could control access to the Ohio Valley.

An advance party of militia had been sent ahead to build a fort at the Forks. Washington was not far from the Forks when the fort commander appeared. He had just seen an armada of 350 canoes and other boats containing 1,000 Frenchmen. Faced with such power, the Virginians surrendered the fort and left. The French then expanded and strengthened the fort. They renamed it Fort Duquesne (doo–KAYN).

> **"A** charming field for an encounter."
>
> *—George Washington on the site of Fort Necessity*

While he waited for reinforcements promised by the governor, Washington put his men to work. They widened a trail into a road for carts carrying supplies and artillery. They camped in a marshy valley where two streams joined. Washington thought it "a charming field for an encounter." They surrounded the camp with a stockade of sharpened logs and called it Fort Necessity.

Historian Robert Alberts has described the scene:

> A person can stand at the edge of the clearing today, look across the sweep of land, then rougher and more swampy than it is now, and imagine the scene as it must have appeared in June of 1754. It would not have been an orderly scene by present military

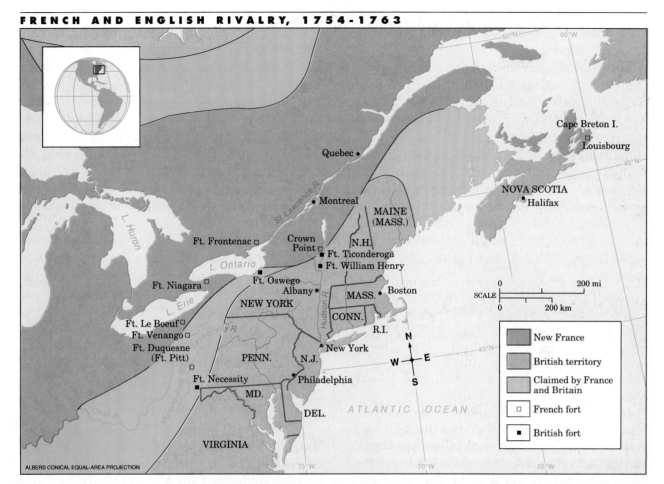

MAP SKILLS This map shows the sites of major battles in the French and Indian War. Along which river was the Battle of Quebec fought? **CRITICAL THINKING** Why might the French have had difficulty protecting their southern forts?

standards. There were cattle and horses grazing; men performing their housekeeping chores; smoke rising from the scattered cooking fires where small groups kept a pot boiling. We can picture detachments marching out with axes, saws, sledges, and rigging to work on the road; crowds gathering around any messenger [who was] newly arrived . . . and Indians wandering sharp-eyed through the camp or dozing in front of their wigwams at the edge of the woods.

THE FRENCH AND INDIAN WAR

The scene changed several weeks later. Early on a rainy July morning, French soldiers ad-

vanced on Fort Necessity. Rather than charge the fort, the French lay in the surrounding woods and fired down onto the camp. The rain came down even harder. It soaked the gunpowder. It was "an unequal fight," Washington wrote, "with an enemy sheltered behind the trees, ourselves without shelter, in trenches full of water."

There was nothing to do but retreat to Virginia. Washington had learned a lesson. Never again would he make a similar mistake in locating a camp.

The battle at Fort Necessity was the first battle of the French and Indian War. This war would in turn become part of a larger, worldwide war known as the Seven Years' War (1756–1763). Britain and France fought each other in Europe and in India as well as in North America.

The French had four major advantages in the struggle against the British. (1) France controlled more land in North America than did Britain. (2) New France had a single colonial government that could act quickly. The British, on the other hand, had to ask for help from the thirteen separate colonial governments. (3) France sent ships and professional soldiers to America rather than depending on military help from its colonists. (4) The French could count on help from such loyal Indian allies as the Huron and the Algonquin.

The British had their strong points as well. (1) Many more settlers lived in the British colonies than in New France. (2) The British colonies, concentrated along the Atlantic coast, were easier to defend. (3) Most of the English colonists were willing to fight hard to save their land, homes, and families.

In past wars the Iroquois had aided the British. They had stayed on the sidelines, however, as Britain and France faced off in the Ohio Valley. Washington's defeat at Fort Necessity cost the British their Indian allies. The Iroquois wanted to avoid being on the losing side of a battle between Europeans. Within months many Iroquois were siding with the French, burning and pillaging along the length of the frontier. Other Iroquois remained neutral.

BRADDOCK'S DEFEAT

George Washington had failed in his attempt to drive the French from the Ohio Valley. In 1755, General Edward Braddock made a second attempt. Leading an army of both Virginians and British troops, Braddock headed into the wilderness. As was common, several of the soldiers' wives traveled along with their husbands. Braddock's army arrived within ten miles of Fort Duquesne. The hard march was over. All that remained was to haul the cannons within range of the fort. Frontier forts could not withstand the bombardment of such artillery.

In desperation, the French commander at Fort Duquesne sent out his 250 soldiers dressed as Indians. Accompanying them were 600 real Indians. They lay in ambush as the British in their bright red uniforms continued their march. Then the French and Indians attacked. The ambush threw the British forces into wild confusion. They were being shot at, but they could not see an enemy to fire back at. Panic reigned. Braddock had five horses shot out from under him before he himself was killed.

After three fierce hours of fighting, the British retreated. Their casualties—the wounded and dead—amounted to about two-thirds of the army. Among the dead on the battlefield were eight women.

As a result of Braddock's defeat, the French kept control of the Ohio Valley. For the next two years the French and their Indian allies won a string of victories against the British. Then, in 1757, the picture began to change.

BRITISH VICTORIES

In 1757 a new British government was formed. William Pitt was secretary of state and the virtual prime minister—head of government. Pitt was a bold, confident leader. He poured vast amounts of money into the war, thereby throwing England into debt. Pitt also persuaded the colonies to furnish more troops and money. He sent young, vigorous generals to lead the fight against the French.

In 1758 the British captured the important French fort at Louisbourg at the mouth of the St. Lawrence. The British also took several forts in the Ohio Valley, including Fort Duquesne. They renamed it Fort Pitt in honor of William Pitt. Today it is the site of Pittsburgh, Pennsylvania.

In the end, the fate of the Ohio Valley was to be settled by the fate of Canada. The crucial year was 1759. In the summer of that year the British, under the bold leadership of James Wolfe, sailed up the St. Lawrence to attack the French stronghold of Quebec. Quebec was the head and heart of New France.

British troops led by General James Wolfe stormed the steep cliffs of Quebec, surprised the French defenders, and won a great victory that helped end the French and Indian War. This painting by an eyewitness shows the daring British assault. **GEOGRAPHY** Why might the British attack have surprised the French?

Wolfe knew if he could conquer Quebec, New France would collapse. It would not be an easy task, however. Quebec sat high on cliffs above the St. Lawrence. Strong walls and many cannons protected it.

Two hundred ships carrying 18,000 men, including some of Britain's best units, arrived at the foot of the imposing cliffs. Waiting for them were 14,000 French troops under the command of Louis Montcalm. Quebec seemed unconquerable. For three months Wolfe sailed up and down the river, while the French matched his movements on land.

Finally, a British scout found a hidden path that led up the cliffs to the grassy fields on the plateau above. On a September night, more than 4,000 British filed one-by-one up the steep passage. This daring move took the French by surprise. At daybreak the British were waiting in battle formation before the fortress. Both Wolfe and Montcalm lost their lives in the battle that followed, but the British won a decisive victory.

THE FRENCH LEAVE NORTH AMERICA

The Battle of Quebec marked a turning point in North American history. After Quebec, the British went on to capture Montreal. Thus ended the fighting in North America. The British now controlled all of New France. The war continued in other parts of the world, with Britain finally defeating France. The Seven Years' War formally ended with the Treaty of Paris (1763).

MAP SKILLS

The Treaty of Paris ended the French and Indian War and gave Great Britain control of eastern North America. What river formed the western boundary of British territory? Who controlled the Great Lakes region and the St. Lawrence River valley? **CRITICAL THINKING** Why did the outcome of the war alarm many Indians?

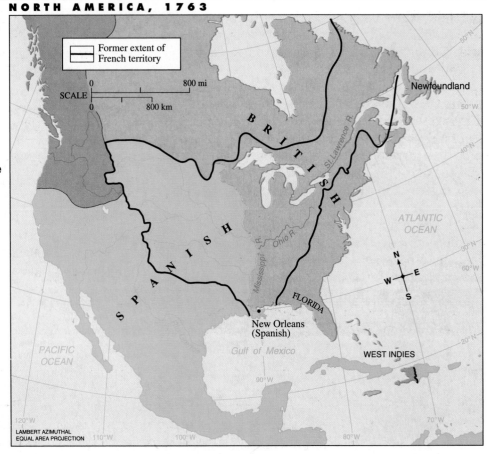

By the terms of the Treaty of Paris, Britain took from France all its land east of the Mississippi River except New Orleans. This vast territory included the core of New France—the St. Lawrence Valley and the Great Lakes—as well as the Ohio Valley.

Spain, which had sided with France in the war, was forced to give up Florida to Great Britain. To make up for this loss, France gave Spain New Orleans and all of Louisiana west of the Mississippi.

PONTIAC'S UPRISING

Britain's victory over France did not bring peace to the frontier. In fact, the opposite happened.

For years the Indian tribes of the Ohio River region had traded with the French. The French in turn had not taken Indian lands. After the British drove the French from North America, the Indians grew worried. Gone was their long-time trading partner and protector.

To many Indians, the future looked grim. Had not the English colonists steadily pushed westward? Their fences and guns had taken over Indian hunting grounds. Was it not just a matter of time before the British crossed the Appalachians?

Indians had reason to be alarmed. Jeffrey Amherst, the British officer in charge of Indian affairs, thought of the Indians as no better than wild beasts. "Could it not be contrived," he wrote the commander at Fort Pitt, "to send the Small Pox among [them]?" The commander then pretended to show good will to Indian leaders. He gave them blankets. But the blankets were a gift of death, for they came from a smallpox hospital.

British traders were no better than their

officials. They cheated and insulted the Indians. They told of the thousands of whites who would soon be crossing the mountains.

The ink on the Treaty of Paris had barely dried when an Ottawa chief and holy man named Pontiac called together the Shawnee, Delaware, Chippewa, and Ottawa tribes. Pontiac's warriors drove the British from every outpost but Fort Detroit and Fort Pitt. White settlers in the Ohio Valley were killed and their cabins burned. The Indians would keep the British at bay for two years.

The uprising showed the British that it would not be easy to govern their huge American holdings. Back in London, British leaders cast about for a way to keep peace on the American frontier. In Chapter 8, you will read how their solution started the chain of events that led to the Revolutionary War.

SECTION REVIEW

1. KEY TERMS French and Indian War, casualty, prime minister, Battle of Quebec, Treaty of Paris (1763)

2. PEOPLE AND PLACES George Washington, Fort Duquesne, Edward Braddock, William Pitt, Pontiac

3. COMPREHENSION What advantages did Britain have in its fight against the French in North America?

4. COMPREHENSION Why was the future of the Ohio Valley settled by the British victory at the Battle of Quebec?

5. CRITICAL THINKING How might history have been different had a British scout not discovered a path up the cliffs of Quebec?

CHAPTER 7 SUMMARY AND TIMELINE

1. Based on the claims of its early explorers, France set up colonies along the St. Lawrence River in the 1600s. Most early French colonists were fur trappers or traders. France sought to establish permanent settlements as English and Dutch settlements expanded. La Salle, Marquette, and Joliet used North America's river system to explore the interior of the continent.

2. Rivalry between Britain, Spain, and France grew over competition for colonies and their wealth. Britain and France competed on a worldwide scale. In North America, each side recruited Indian allies. The two countries fought a number of wars on the western frontier of Britain's colonies. Neither side had a clear advantage. British land speculators hoped to take control of the Ohio Valley.

3. The French and Indian War was a struggle for the rich lands along the Ohio River. The British suffered an early defeat at Fort Duquesne in 1755, but in 1759 they captured Quebec. This battle turned the tide of the war. In the Treaty of Paris of 1763, the French gave up their claims in North America. That same year, an Indian uprising in the Ohio Valley raised new tensions.

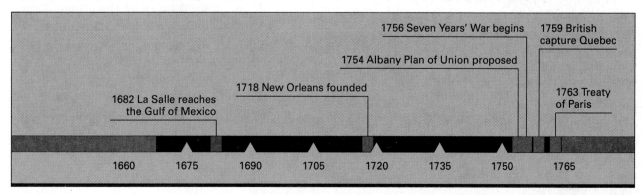

1756 Seven Years' War begins
1759 British capture Quebec
1754 Albany Plan of Union proposed
1718 New Orleans founded
1682 La Salle reaches the Gulf of Mexico
1763 Treaty of Paris

1660   1675   1690   1705   1720   1735   1750   1765

PLACES TO LOCATE

Match the letters on the map with the places that are listed below.

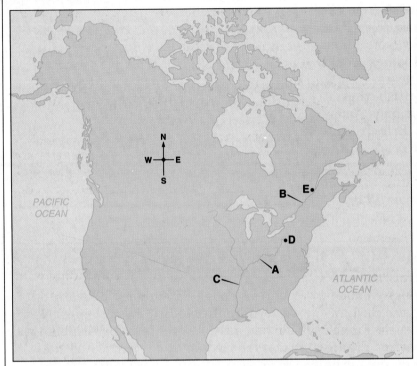

1. Fort Duquesne
2. Mississippi River
3. Ohio River
4. Quebec
5. St. Lawrence River

KEY TERMS

Define the terms in each of the following pairs.

1. balance of power; French and Indian War
2. League of the Iroquois; Albany Plan of Union
3. Battle of Quebec; Treaty of Paris (1763)

PEOPLE TO IDENTIFY

Match each of the following people with the correct description.

Edward Braddock
Louis Joliet
La Salle
William Pitt

1. French fur trader who explored the Mississippi.
2. British general killed in expedition against French fort.
3. British secretary of state in 1700s who supported war against France.
4. French nobleman who explored North America in search of a Northwest Passage.

REVIEWING THE FACTS

1. Which explorer founded New France? When?
2. What was the major source of wealth traded by the French in North America?
3. Why did France decide to establish permanent settlements in New France?
4. Who claimed the territory of Louisiana for France? When?
5. Which Caribbean island became the richest French colony?
6. Why was the League of the Iroquois formed?
7. In what region did the first battles of the French and Indian War take place?
8. What was the effect of the war on Britain's economy?
9. What was the effect of the war on France's North American empire?
10. Which country owned New Orleans and all of Louisiana west of the Mississippi after the war?

PRACTICING YOUR SKILL

Turn to the skill feature on page 153 and review the paragraphs on answering an essay question. Then write a short essay of at least two paragraphs comparing the two sides in the French and Indian War.

CITIZENSHIP

1. Why did the French government refuse to allow Protestants to settle in New France? How did this policy affect the colony?

2. What was the objection of the thirteen colonies to the Albany Plan of Union?

CRITICAL THINKING SKILLS

1. **FORMING A HYPOTHESIS** If England and France had not been at war in North America, would relations between Indian nations have been different? Why or why not?

2. **MAKING COMPARISONS** Imagine you are a citizen of Britain in 1757. Do you support William Pitt's war policy? Why or why not?

3. **DRAWING CONCLUSIONS** It has been said that the French fur trade was one reason why France lost its North American territory. Explain why this may have been so.

PROJECTS AND ACTIVITIES

1. **WRITING A PLAY** With a group of classmates, write a play dealing with one of the following topics: one of La Salle's expeditions, Louis de Saint-Denis's experience as a double agent, the Battle of Quebec.

2. **MAKING A MAP** Draw a map to illustrate the explorations of Marquette, Joliet, and La Salle in North America. On your map, use arrows to show the journeys of the explorers. Explain the arrows in a map key. Use dates to show the progress of each exploration. Label all other necessary information on the map and give the map a title.

3. **WRITING A REPORT** Research and write a report about one of the following topics: the League of the Iroquois, colonial Haiti, Braddock's defeat, the early history of New Orleans.

WRITING ABOUT TOPICS IN AMERICAN HISTORY

1. **CONNECTING WITH LITERATURE** A selection from *Northwest Passage* by Kenneth Roberts appears on pages 639–640. Read it and answer the questions. Then answer the following question: Why might the Indians in Rogers's party have been willing to participate in the raid on an Indian village?

2. **APPLYING THEMES: GLOBAL INTERACTIONS** Write an essay discussing the economic and political importance of colonies for European nations during the 1700s. Which groups benefited from colonization? Which groups were hurt? In the concluding paragraph, state your own views on the competition for colonies among European nations. Provide reasons for your conclusions.

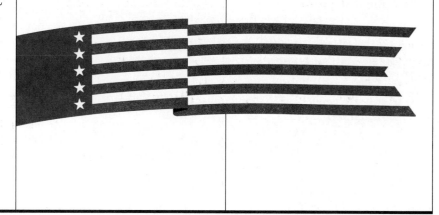

UNIT 2: American Mosaic

★ A Multicultural Perspective ★

From the beginning, the population of the American colonies has been strikingly diverse. People from many different backgrounds and different cultures helped the American colonies to expand and prosper.

Colonial women played a major role in the establishment of several settlements. **Lady Deborah Moody,** born in England late in the 1500s, moved to Massachusetts in 1639. Four years later, following a disagreement with local religious leaders, she and some followers moved to the Dutch colony of New Netherland. Together they founded a settlement on Long Island dedicated to self-government and religious freedom. Moody remained a respected leader until her death in 1659.

In Maryland the name of one colonial woman is still heard. **Anne Arundel** (left) was the wife of the colony's founder, the second Lord Baltimore. The state's largest city is named for her husband, but its capital, Annapolis, bears her name—and so does Anne Arundel County.

Mary Rowlandson (right) earned fame the hard way. The wife of a Massachusetts minister, she and her three children were captured during King Philip's War in 1676 when Indians stormed their village. Rowlandson spent the next three months in captivity, her courage bolstered by a strong Christian faith. Finally her husband won her freedom by paying a ransom. Two of her children were also released; the other had since died. Rowlandson's account of her experiences was a widely read and classic account of frontier life.

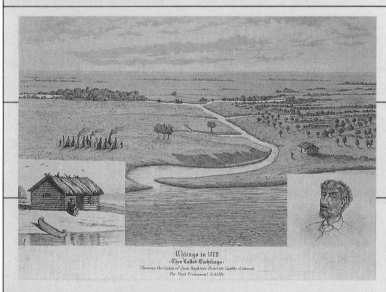

Chicago in 1779
(Then Called Eschikago)
Showing the Cabin of Jean Baptiste Point de Sable (Colored)
The First Permanent Settler

A black trader named **Jean Baptiste Point Du Sable** (bottom right of the picture) came to New France in 1765. He later built a trading post at the spot where the Chicago River empties into Lake Michigan. (Post is shown, bottom left. The main picture is of Chicago in 1779.) Du Sable, who had been educated in Paris, aroused the suspicions of the British. Recognizing his business talent, however, they hired him to run one of their own firms. In 1784 he returned to his trading post, building it into a thriving enterprise. The lakeside settlement became the mighty city of Chicago. The Indians joked that the first white man to come to Chicago was a black man!

Africans, kidnapped from their homes, did not choose to come to the Americas. Yet they contributed to their new homeland nonetheless. **Lucy Terry** grew up as a slave in western Massachusetts. She witnessed an Indian massacre there in 1746 and wrote a dramatic poem about the event, the first poem published by an African American. She married Abijah Prince in 1756, and he bought her freedom. When their son became old enough to attend nearby Williams College, Lucy Prince quoted "an abundance of law and Gospel, chapter and verse" to convince the trustees to admit him—but she was unsuccessful. She did, however, win the land dispute she reportedly argued before the United States Supreme Court. She died at 91, a widely admired member of her community.

The religious freedom of Rhode Island attracted **Jacob Rodríguez Rivera** (left) to the colony in 1748. Rivera's family had fled Spain when laws there ordered Jews to convert to Roman Catholicism, leave, or die. They ended up in the Dutch West Indies, where Rivera learned about the whaling industry. He brought that knowledge with him to Newport, introducing the industry that turned oil from sperm whales into candles and fuel for lamps. Within a few decades, whaling had become central to the New England economy.

In the early 1700s Father **Antonio Margil De Jesus** (right) traveled to East Texas hoping to bring the Indians who lived there into the Roman Catholic Church. As a young priest, Father Margil had wandered barefoot across southern Mexico and Central America, erecting crosses in the mountains to remind his converts of their new faith. In Texas he set up several missions, the most famous of which was the Mission of San José and San Miguel de Aguayo, considered by many to be the most beautiful in New Spain.

The first Filipinos to reach North America arrived in 1763, having jumped from Spanish ships that were engaged in trade between the ports of Acapulco and Manila.

HISTORIANS' CORNER

Three Views of Pontiac's "Conspiracy"

Pontiac's War, in 1763, was the last and greatest effort by Indians in the Northeast to turn back the advance of English settlers. American historians such as Francis Parkman saw Pontiac's actions as a "conspiracy" or "rebellion" by "savages." Pontiac himself, however, saw his situation in a different way. So did the English adventurer Robert Rogers, who wrote about meeting Pontiac in his 1765 book, *A Concise Account of North America.*

Francis Parkman (1870)

Each savage countenance seemed carved in wood, and none could have detected the ferocious passions hidden beneath that immovable mask.... Then Pontiac rose, and walked forward into the midst of the council.... His features ... had a bold and stern expression; while his habitual bearing was imperious and peremptory, like that of a man accustomed to sweep away all opposition by the force of his impetuous will....

Looking round upon his wild auditors he began to speak, with fierce gesture, and a loud, impassioned voice; and at every pause, deep, guttural ejaculations of assent and approval responded to his words. He inveighed against the arrogance, rapacity, and injustice of the English, and contrasted them with the French whom they had driven from the soil....

Having roused in his warlike listeners their native thirst for blood and vengeance, he next addressed himself to their superstition....

From Francis Parkman, *The Conspiracy of Pontiac*, 6th ed., Little, Brown and Company, 1902.

Pontiac (1763)

It is important, my brothers, that we drive from our lands this nation [the English], whose only object is our death....

When I visit the English chief [at Fort Detroit] and tell him of the death of any of our comrades, instead of lamenting as our French brothers used to do, they make fun of us. If I ask him for anything for our sick, he refuses, ... from which it is clear he seeks our death. We must therefore, in return, destroy them without delay.... Why should we not attack them? Are we not men? ... There is no longer any time to lose, and when the English shall be defeated, we will block the way so that no more shall return upon our lands.

Adapted from a contemporary diary quoted in Parkman, *The Conspiracy of Pontiac* (Appendix C), 6th ed., Little, Brown, and Company, 1902.

Major Robert Rogers (1765)

He [Pontiac] often intimated to me, that he could be content to reign in his country in subordination to the King of Great Britain, and was willing to pay him such annual acknowledgment as he was able in furs.... He was curious to know our methods of manufacturing cloth, iron, etc., and expressed a great desire to see England.... He assured me that he was inclined to live peaceably with the English while they used him as he deserved, and to encourage their settling in his country; but intimated that if they treated him with neglect, he should shut up the way and exclude them from it; ... he expected to be treated with the respect and honour due to a King or Emperor, by all who came into his country, or treated with him.

From Robert Rogers, *A Concise Account of North America.* Originally published 1765; reprinted 1966 by S. R. Publishers and Johnson Reprint Corporation.

Critical Thinking

1. How is Parkman's description of Pontiac culturally biased?

2. What picture of Pontiac do you get from his own words? How does this compare with the picture given by Parkman? By Rogers?

3. Rogers' account suggests the possibility of an Indian nation existing side-by-side with the English. Could this idea have worked?

UNIT THREE

A New Nation

THEMES IN AMERICAN HISTORY

Economic Development   Disagreements with Britain's economic policies helped spark the American Revolution.

Global Interactions   The cause of American independence was aided by several European nations. In turn, the American Revolution inspired independence movements around the world.

Gen. Bernardo de Gálvez
Battle of Mobile 1780

Constitutional Government   After winning independence, Americans established representative government, first under the Articles of Confederation and later under the Constitution.

Expanding Democracy   The Bill of Rights set forth Americans' basic civil liberties.

American Culture   Writers emphasized self-reliance and independence as American virtues.

By 1775 American colonists were fighting for the cause of independence. This John Trumbull painting shows Patriot Dr. Joseph Warren (center) dying at Breed's Hill.

8 The Thirteen Colonies Rebel (1763–1776)

1 Tighter British Control

Section Focus

Key Terms Proclamation of 1763
■ Quartering Act ■ revenue ■ currency
■ Stamp Act ■ Stamp Act Congress
■ Sons of Liberty ■ impressment
■ boycott ■ repeal

Main Idea After the French and Indian War, Britain passed new laws and taxes for the Americans. Colonists resented the laws and taxes and protested against them.

Objectives As you read, look for answers to these questions:
1. Why did Great Britain take measures to increase its control over the American colonies?
2. Why did the colonists object to British efforts to tax them?

Alliances often crumble when they no longer have a common enemy. The alliance between Britain and its American colonies is a case in point. British soldiers and American colonists had fought side by side against the French. Once the French had been defeated, however, old problems resurfaced and new ones arose.

HALTING WESTWARD MOVEMENT

Pontiac's uprising in 1763 (page 162) brought groans in London. British leaders wanted no more war. How, they asked, could they keep peace in America? They found the answer in the Proclamation of 1763. This law forbade colonists to settle west of the line formed by the Appalachian Mountains. That land would be for the Indians. To enforce the law, King George III decided to leave 10,000 British soldiers in America. In 1765 the Quartering Act required the colonies to quarter—house and supply—these British soldiers.

Colonists felt cheated when they heard about the Proclamation of 1763. Land ownership meant everything to a colonist. Those without land had no position in society. They could not even vote. The territory west of the Appalachians was the land of opportunity, not only for the landless but also for the young, the restless, and for those whose land was wearing out. They were angry that their own government would stop them from settling there. Many colonists ignored the proclamation and began to settle in the Ohio Valley.

WAR DEBTS AND NEW REVENUES

Britain's war with France had caused Britain to go deeply in debt. Keeping an army on the American frontier would be an added cost. To meet the cost of its empire, Britain would need more revenue—government income. Britain's prime minister, George Grenville,

SCALE
0 — 300 mi
0 — 300 km

Settled area
British fort
Proclamation Line, 1763
INDIAN GROUP

POLYCONIC PROJECTION

MAP SKILLS

The Proclamation of 1763 closed land west of the Appalachians to settlement, angering many colonists. Does the map show any settled areas west of the Proclamation Line? Were any forts west of the Ohio River? CRITICAL THINKING Why might the Proclamation have increased Indian support of the British government?

believed that the colonists should help pay Britain's war debts. After all, the wars against France had been fought partly to protect the colonists' lands. Grenville also wanted the colonies to pay half the cost of keeping the British army in North America.

The best way to raise money, Grenville thought, was to revive Britain's mercantilist policy. This policy—that colonies should earn money for the parent country—had long been ignored. Grenville's new program aimed to help British merchants, British shippers, and the British treasury. It called for:

(1) *Strict enforcement of the Navigation Acts.* Parliament had passed the Navigation Acts during the 1660s. They were designed to let England profit from colonial trade. Certain goods, such as tobacco and sugar, could be sold only to England. All goods imported to the colonies had first to pass through England. All goods, exported or imported, had to be carried in English ships.

Most colonists had ignored the acts, and for years the British had not enforced them. In 1763, however, Grenville sent new officers to the colonies to enforce the Navigation Acts. British warships began keeping a close lookout for smugglers in American waters.

(2) *The Sugar Act.* In 1764 Grenville pushed the Sugar Act through Parliament. The act taxed sugar, coffee, indigo, and molasses from anywhere but Britain. The Sugar Act thus discouraged colonists from buying Dutch, French, and Spanish goods.

(3) *The Currency Act.* Before 1764 most of the American colonies had issued their own currency—paper money—because they had little gold or silver. The Currency Act outlawed the use of paper money. It required colonists to pay all debts in gold or silver. Those who owed money were worst hurt by this new law.

(4) *The Stamp Act.* In 1765 Parliament passed the Stamp Act. Stamps sold by the British government had to be placed on a variety of items. These included legal papers, advertisements, newspapers, calendars, and playing cards.

The British government thought that the new tax laws were fair. In Britain, citizens already paid a stamp tax and other taxes. It seemed reasonable to ask the colonists in America to do the same. But what was reasonable in London was outrageous in Boston.

PROTESTS IN BOSTON

On the morning of August 14, 1765, citizens of Boston saw a straw dummy hanging from a tree by a rope. Underneath, a sign warned, "He that takes this down is an enemy to his country." The dummy was made up to look like Andrew Oliver. Oliver was the British official in charge of stamp distribution in Boston. The display was a protest against the Stamp Act. As evening fell, a crowd of colonists marched to Oliver's office and destroyed it. They went on to Oliver's home and ransacked it. Oliver quit his job the next day.

The issue for colonists like Samuel Adams, himself a former tax collector, was clear. Adams opposed taxation by Britain's Parliament because colonists had no vote there. Representatives to Britain's Parliament were chosen only by citizens of Britain. The colonists had no representative in Parliament. If Parliament could pass a stamp tax without the colonists' consent, what else might it tax in the future? "Why not our lands?" demanded Adams. "Why not the produce of our lands and everything we possess and make use of? . . . If taxes are laid upon us in any shape without our having a legal representative where they are laid, are we not reduced from . . . free subjects to slaves?"

Adams and others took up the cry of James Otis, a wealthy Boston lawyer. Otis declared that there should be "no taxation without representation." In other words, the colonists should only contribute revenue to a government that gave them a vote in how to spend that money. Otis believed that "taxation without representation" violated colonists' rights as British citizens.

> "No taxation without representation."
>
> —James Otis

RESISTANCE TO THE STAMP ACT

In October 1765, nine colonies sent delegates to the Stamp Act Congress in New York City. The Congress sent a protest to Britain. The protest stated that the colonists were loyal to Britain. It then declared that the right to tax the colonists belonged not to Parliament but to the colonial assemblies.

As public opposition to the Stamp Act grew, an organized movement emerged. In every

Colonists, shown reading about the Stamp Act, were outraged by the law. It required them to pay as much as four English pounds for a stamp on certain documents. CONSTITUTIONAL HERITAGE How might a tax on printed materials limit freedom of the press?

city, colonists formed groups called the Sons of Liberty. Members were mainly lawyers, merchants, and artisans. These groups had the most to lose from the Stamp Act.

Protests against the Stamp Act drew all those angry at the British, whatever the reason. Many resented the impressment of seamen. Impressment meant forcing American sailors to join the British navy. Was this not another violation of their rights? Americans asked.

Colonists also complained that British officials were corrupt. Customs officers, they charged, often took colonists' property without reason. One Connecticut newspaper wrote that the British "behaved more like pirates than like those appointed to protect our trade."

The Sons of Liberty discovered that their best weapon against the Stamp Act was to boycott—refuse to buy—British goods. The British government might ignore the Stamp Act Congress. It might treat colonists with contempt. It could not, however, ignore the complaints of British businessmen. As trade with America shrank, British merchants called for a change in colonial policy.

These protests weakened support for Grenville. Soon he was replaced as head of Britain's government. In March 1766 Parliament said it would repeal—overturn or withdraw—the Stamp Act. At the same time, it passed the Declaratory Act. This new law stated that Parliament had "full power" to pass laws governing the colonies "in all cases whatsoever." In other words, Parliament still claimed the right to tax the colonies if it so chose. At the time, though, all the colonists

cared about was the Stamp Act's repeal. Bells rang and crowds gathered to proclaim their loyalty to Britain. The storm seemed to have passed.

SECTION REVIEW

1. KEY TERMS Proclamation of 1763, Quartering Act, revenue, currency, Stamp Act, Stamp Act Congress, Sons of Liberty, impressment, boycott, repeal

2. PEOPLE AND PLACES Appalachian Mountains, George III, George Grenville

3. COMPREHENSION How was the Proclamation of 1763 linked to Pontiac's uprising?

4. COMPREHENSION Why did colonists call the Stamp Act "taxation without representation"?

5. CRITICAL THINKING Was Great Britain justified in thinking that the colonies should pay for part of their own defense? Why or why not?

2 Colonial Resistance Grows

Section Focus

Key Terms Townshend Acts ■ writs of assistance ■ redcoat ■ propaganda ■ Boston Massacre ■ Committee of Correspondence ■ Boston Tea Party

Main Idea Colonial leaders resisted Britain's efforts to tighten its control over the colonies. They began to organize in order to combat British policies more effectively.

Objectives As you read, look for answers to these questions:
1. Why did colonists object to British taxation policies?
2. How did colonists attempt to resist British policies?

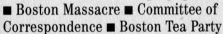
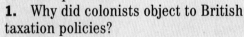

Joyful at the repeal of the Stamp Act, few colonists paid any attention to the Declaratory Act. Nor did they know that 3,000 miles across the ocean new plots were hatching. King George III was narrow-minded, prejudiced, and stubborn. He wanted to keep Americans firmly under the British thumb. Others agreed with him.

THE TOWNSHEND ACTS

Parliament wanted no more trouble like that caused by the Stamp Act. On the other hand, it still badly needed new revenues to pay for the army it was stationing in America. The king's new finance minister, Charles Townshend (TOWN–zend), told Parliament that he had found a way to tax the colonies "without offense." Parliament passed his plan, known as the Townshend Acts in 1767.

The Townshend Acts placed duties—import taxes—on glass, paper, paint, lead, and tea. These duties had to be paid in gold or silver. The money would pay for the salaries of governors and other British officers. Writs of assistance would be used to enforce the acts and to stop smuggling. A writ of assistance was a search warrant that gave officers the right to search *any* building for *any* reason.

NEW PROTESTS

Townshend had thought the laws would not upset the colonists because they imposed duties, not direct taxes. How wrong he was. The distinction meant nothing to the colonists. The new duties, they thought, were but an excuse to raise revenue. The real question was, wrote John Dickinson of Pennsylvania, "whether Parliament can legally take money out of our pockets without our consent."

The writs of assistance upset merchants who thought that homes and stores should be safe from government officials. Colonists also objected to paying officials' salaries from tax money. This would mean that the colonies no longer had to approve the officials' salaries. As a result, colonists would have less control over how the British officials did their jobs.

The colonists had learned from their fight against the Stamp Act. They used the same tactics against the Townshend Acts. Again, through town meetings, colonists organized a boycott of British goods. The Sons of Liberty regrouped. They asked shopkeepers not to sell British goods. Merchants who continued to trade with Britain were called enemies of their country. They too became the targets of boycotts.

Colonists began making their own cloth, paper, and paint. The Daughters of Liberty held spinning bees and drank herbal tea. These activities spread the goal of using only American-made products.

The boycott of British goods helped pull the colonists together. British official Thomas Hutchinson estimated that seven-eighths of the colonial towns supported the boycott. "The majority of every order of men in government," he wrote, had united with "the body of people" on the issue. Trade between Britain and the colonies once again dropped sharply.

Again, colonial leaders asked for nonviolence. Articles in the *Boston Gazette* called for "no mobs, no confusions, no tumults. . . . Constitutional methods are the best." Most colonists still had faith in British rule, even though that faith was weakening.

REDCOATS IN BOSTON

Conflict over the Townshend Acts flared when the merchant ship *Liberty* entered Boston harbor. John Hancock, a wealthy merchant, owned the ship. On board lay casks of

This engraving shows some of the British troops who occupied Boston in 1768 to enforce the writs of assistance. CIVIC VALUES Describe the attitudes of the civilians and soldiers who appear in the foreground of this picture.

Paul Revere made this engraving of the Boston Massacre and sold it together with a patriotic poem. **HISTORY** Why might this engraving be called propaganda?

Madeira wine from Portugal. The cargo had been smuggled and was illegal under British law. When customs officers tried to seize the ship, a riot broke out. A crowd forced the officers to flee.

Fearing for their lives after the riot, the officials called for British troops to keep order in Boston. In September, 1,000 British soldiers—known as redcoats for their bright scarlet jackets—arrived under the command of General Thomas Gage. The Quartering Act stated that local residents had to give them housing and supplies.

The decision to quarter troops only made things worse. The redcoats were poorly paid. They thus hired themselves out as workers at rates lower than those American workers received. American resentment boiled at the sight of outsiders taking American jobs. Even Sam Adams's shaggy dog took sides and became famous for biting only redcoats. The redcoats and street youths often taunted each other. "Lobsters for sale!" the youths would holler. "Yankees!" the soldiers jeered. *Yankee*

was intended as a term of ridicule, but colonists soon came to accept and even take pride in the name.

THE BOSTON MASSACRE

Tensions finally exploded on a snowy night in March 1770. A gang of street youths and dockworkers gathered in front of the Boston customhouse. They complained about impressment and how soldiers were taking their jobs. Others soon joined them. The soldiers guarding the customhouse looked on nervously. As the crowd grew, it began yelling insults at the soldiers. Someone rang the church bells, the signal for people to come out during a fire. Fearful of the angry crowd, one soldier and then others fired. When the smoke cleared, five men lay dead or mortally wounded. Among the dead was Crispus Attucks, an African American sailor and escaped slave.

The Sons of Liberty used the incident as propaganda—a way of spreading its political views and beliefs. They called the shooting the Boston Massacre and claimed that it showed the dangers of having British troops stationed among colonial citizens.

In a highly unpopular move, lawyers John Adams and Josiah Quincy, Jr., defended the king's soldiers against a charge of murder. The law, Adams said, should be "deaf . . . to the clamors of the populace." Their defense was successful. Six of the soldiers were acquitted—cleared of wrongdoing. Two others had their thumbs branded as a penalty for the shootings.

THE TEA ACT

Little more than a month later, Parliament repealed the Townshend Acts. The colonial boycott had hurt British trade. British businessmen were again complaining. Parliament kept only the tax on tea, to show that it still had the right to tax the colonists.

For most Americans, the crisis was over. In Boston, however, Samuel Adams continued to push for total independence from Britain. In

This 1793 engraving is the earliest known picture of the Boston Tea Party. **ECONOMICS** Why did the British pass the Tea Act? Who among the colonists most resented low-priced British tea?

1772 Adams organized a Committee of Correspondence to keep up communication among Massachusetts towns. The idea quickly spread. Soon committees in all the colonies were corresponding with each other.

Parliament then blundered again and opened up old wounds when it passed the Tea Act of 1773. This act aimed to bail the British East India Company out of financial trouble by giving it sole control over the American tea trade. The tea would arrive in the trading company's own ships and be sold by its own merchants. It would be even cheaper than smuggled tea. Colonists, however, would still have to pay a tax on tea.

American shippers and merchants opposed the new law. It hurt their business. Other colonists voiced a basic concern: If Parliament could create a monopoly on tea, what monopoly might it create next?

THE BOSTON TEA PARTY

Merchants and anti-British leaders organized against the Tea Act through the Committees of Correspondence. In Charleston, colonists unloaded the tea and stored it in damp cellars so it would rot. In New York City and Philadelphia ships carrying tea were turned away from the harbors. In Boston, the Sons of Liberty put on a tea party. George Hewes gave this account of the Boston Tea Party:

> It was now evening, and I immediately dressed myself in the costume of an Indian, equipped with a small hatchet . . . and a club. . . . [After painting] my face and hands with coal dust in the shop of a blacksmith, I [went] to Griffins Wharf, where the ships lay that contained the tea. When I first appeared in the street, after being thus disguised, I fell in with many who were dressed, equipped, and painted as I was, and [we] marched in order to the place of our destination [and boarded the ships]. . . .
>
> We then were ordered by our commander to open the hatches, and take

out all the chests of tea and throw them overboard. . . .

In about three hours from the time we went on board, we had thus broken and thrown overboard every tea chest to be found in the ship, while those in the other ships were disposing of the tea in the same way, at the same time.

On that evening in mid-December 1773, Hewes and others destroyed 342 chests of tea. Many colonists rejoiced when they heard about the Boston Tea Party. John Adams thought it "the grandest event which has ever yet happened since the controversy with Britain opened!" He believed it would show Great Britain how strongly colonists opposed taxation without representation. Other colonists doubted that destroying property was the best way to resolve the debate over the right to tax. Benjamin Franklin even offered to pay for the tea out of his own fortune. His only condition was that the British repeal the Tea Act. The British ignored him. Britain's heavy-handed response to the Boston Tea Party would feed the fires of rebellion in the thirteen colonies.

SECTION REVIEW

1. KEY TERMS Townshend Acts, writs of assistance, redcoat, propaganda, Boston Massacre, Committee of Correspondence, Boston Tea Party

2. PEOPLE Samuel Adams, Charles Townshend, John Hancock, Crispus Attucks

3. COMPREHENSION Why did colonists think the Townshend Acts violated their liberty?

4. COMPREHENSION How did colonists fight the Townshend Acts? The Tea Act?

5. CRITICAL THINKING Why was it important for colonial leaders to unite colonists against Britain? What methods did they use to accomplish this goal?

3 The Road to Lexington and Concord

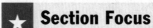

Section Focus

Key Terms Intolerable Acts ■ pamphlet ■ First Continental Congress ■ embargo ■ Minuteman ■ Patriot ■ Loyalist

Main Idea Tensions between Britain and the colonies led to armed conflict in Massachusetts.

Objectives As you read, look for answers to these questions:
1. How did Britain respond to the colonists' refusal to obey British laws?
2. What events led up to the fighting at Lexington and Concord?

When news of the Boston Tea Party reached London, King George III was furious. As the king saw it, there were two possible responses. "We must master them," the king said of the colonists, "or totally leave them to themselves and treat them as aliens." Of course, leaving the colonists to themselves was never a serious choice. Britain had invested too much money in the colonies. There was also the matter of Britain's prestige. The world's most powerful nation simply did not let a group of upstart colonists tell it what to do.

THE INTOLERABLE ACTS

In 1774 King George took the first choice: mastering the colonies. To punish the colonists of Massachusetts, Parliament passed four harsh laws. The colonists found these laws so intolerable—unbearable—they called them the Intolerable Acts. The Intolerable Acts had several parts.

(1) They closed the port of Boston until colonists paid for the destroyed tea.

(2) They gave more power to the Massachusetts royal governor. He could ban town meetings, for example, or the Committees of Correspondence.

(3) They allowed British commanders to quarter troops in private homes.

(4) They allowed British officials accused of crimes to stand trial in Britain rather than in the colonies.

To enforce the Intolerable Acts, King George sent more British troops to Boston. He named General Thomas Gage, their commander, governor of Massachusetts. In effect, the colony was under military rule.

The Committees of Correspondence circulated pamphlets—unbound, printed essays —denouncing the Intolerable Acts. The committees also sent food and money to Boston to help support the city while its port was closed.

THE FIRST CONTINENTAL CONGRESS

The Committees of Correspondence called for delegates from all thirteen colonies to meet about the crisis. In September and October of 1774, delegates from all the colonies except Georgia met in Philadelphia. Calling themselves the First Continental Congress, they agreed to support Massachusetts. They declared that they would not obey the Intolerable Acts. They organized an embargo—a ban on all trade—against Britain. To soothe those who called for a peaceful settlement, they sent a list of their grievances to Parliament. At the same time, however, the Congress called on each colony to begin training soldiers for defense.

The meeting of the First Continental Congress marked an important step in American history. Most delegates did not want independence from Britain, but they took their rights as British subjects seriously. Their meeting

broke British law and carried the risk of further punishment. It also carried the seed of a future independent government.

Before the Congress broke up, the delegates agreed to meet again in seven months. By the time the Second Continental Congress met, however, fighting with Britain had already begun.

BETWEEN WAR AND PEACE

Most colonists expected that the embargo on British goods would force Parliament to repeal the Intolerable Acts. After all, past boycotts had led to the repeal of the Stamp Act and the Townshend Acts. This time, however, Parliament stood firm. It added new limits on colonial trade and sent more troops.

Colonists force a tarred-and-feathered tax collector to drink tea in this 1774 cartoon entitled "Bostonians Paying the Excise Man." POLITICS Do you think the artist was pro- or anti-British? Why?

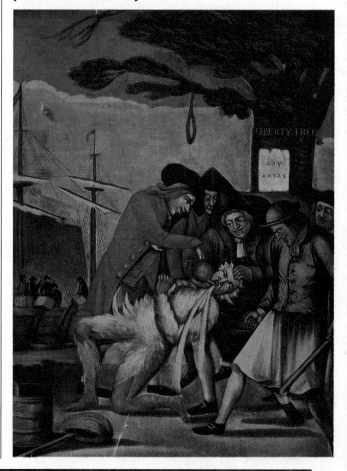

By the end of 1774, some colonists began preparing to fight. In Massachusetts, John Hancock headed a Committee of Safety with the power to call out the Minutemen. The Minutemen were members of the militia who could be ready to fight given only minutes' notice. Minutemen gathered for military drill against the orders of the governor, General Gage.

Such acts of defiance split the colonists into two camps. Those who opposed British policies were called Patriots. Those who remained loyal to Great Britain were called Loyalists.

Most Patriot leaders thought that any fight between the colonies and Britain would be short. They believed a show of force by the colonists would make the British repeal the Intolerable Acts. The Americans would then go on being loyal British subjects. Few Patriots expected a war of independence. One who did, however, was Patrick Henry of Virginia. In a stirring speech before the Virginia Convention of Delegates in March 1775, Henry declared:

> "I know not what course others may take; but as for me, give me liberty, or give me death!"
>
> —*Patrick Henry*

Gentlemen may cry, peace, peace—but there is no peace. The war is actually begun! The next gale that sweeps from the north will bring to our ears the clash of resounding arms! Our brethren are already in the field! Why stand we here idle? What is it that gentlemen wish? What would they have? Is life so dear, or peace so sweet, as to be purchased at the price of chains and slavery? Forbid it, Almighty God! I know not what course others may take; but as for me, give me liberty, or give me death!

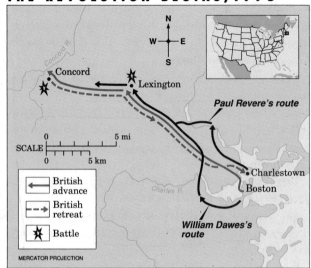

THE REVOLUTION BEGINS, 1775

MAP SKILLS

This map shows the first clashes of the American Revolution. What river did William Dawes cross? Why did Revere and Dawes hope to arrive before the British? In what city did the British retreat end? CRITICAL THINKING Why, in your opinion, did the colonists decide to fight the British?

PAUL REVERE'S RIDE

Patrick Henry's prediction of war soon proved true. The British could not stand by while the colonists defied them by gathering guns and ammunition. In April 1775 General Gage discovered that the militia had stored arms in Concord, a town eighteen miles northwest of Boston. Gage hoped to crush the rebellion before it began. On the night of April 18, Gage ordered 700 troops to march on Concord and seize the weapons. He also ordered them to capture two rebel leaders, Samuel Adams and John Hancock, at the nearby town of Lexington. General Gage hoped to arrest Adams and Hancock and send them to stand trial in Britain.

Despite the care Gage had taken to keep the raid secret, Dr. Joseph Warren, head spy of the Sons of Liberty, observed that British soldiers were on the move. Warren warned the Patriots in Concord to get their supplies out of town and hide them. Then, as the redcoats silently made their way to the edge of

Boston harbor, Warren called two trusted messengers. They were Paul Revere and William Dawes.

Revere and Dawes rode to Lexington by different routes, waking up Minutemen along the way. Revere alerted Hancock and Adams, who made their escape. In Lexington, Revere and Dawes met Dr. Samuel Prescott of Concord. The three were making their way to Concord when they were surprised by a British cavalry patrol. They quickly split up. Prescott jumped his horse over a stone fence and galloped away to wake the Minutemen at Concord. Dawes fled into the woods on foot. Revere, however, was captured and his horse taken by the British. Finally, the soldiers allowed him to go. Revere's famous midnight ride ended on foot along a moonlit country lane.

LEXINGTON AND CONCORD

At dawn, when the tired British troops reached Lexington, they found the Minutemen facing them. British officers ordered the Americans to lay down their arms. No one knows who fired the first shot, but minutes later eight Patriots lay dead. The British then marched on the town of Concord. They burned the courthouse and destroyed some of the militia's supplies. At the Old North Bridge over the Concord River, however, Minutemen forced the British to retreat.

CHART SKILLS The roots of American colonists' resentment of British rule went back more than a decade before the outbreak of the Revolutionary War. What year did colonists begin to take action against British laws they considered unfair? Before Lexington and Concord, what tactic did the colonists use to protest actions of the British Parliament? **CRITICAL THINKING** How might the Intolerable Acts be seen as a response rather than a cause?

CONFLICT WIDENS BETWEEN BRITAIN AND AMERICA

Date	Actions of the British Parliament	Reactions of the Colonists
1763	Issues the Proclamation of 1763 to close the frontier	Resent the Proclamation
1765	Passes the Stamp Act to pay for British troops in the colonies	Boycott British goods; pass Stamp Act Resolves
1766	Repeals the Stamp Act; passes the Declaratory Act to assert its authority	End the boycott
1767	Passes the Townshend Acts to raise more money from colonial imports	Organize new boycotts; clash with British troops in the Boston Massacre (1770)
1773	Passes the Tea Act, giving the East India Company a monopoly on tea trade	Protest the Tea Act by boycotting British tea and staging the Boston Tea Party
1774	Passes the "Intolerable Acts" to tighten British control over Massachusetts	Establish the First Continental Congress; boycott British goods
1775	Orders troops to Lexington and Concord, Massachusetts	Battle British troops; establish the Second Continental Congress and a Continental Army

Years later, the writer Ralph Waldo Emerson described the battle as "the shot heard round the world." Nearly 4,000 Minutemen had answered Revere's alarm. Now they lined the road from Concord back to Lexington. From behind walls and trees, they pelted the British soldiers with musketfire.

The British were unprepared for this kind of warfare. They were trained to march in closed ranks to within a few yards of the enemy. Then they would all fire their muskets at the same time. Finally, reserve troops from Boston arrived and helped the British to safety. They had over 250 casualties—dead and wounded. Fifty Americans died and another 42 were wounded. The Revolutionary War had begun.

SECTION REVIEW

1. KEY TERMS Intolerable Acts, pamphlet, First Continental Congress, embargo, Minuteman, Patriot, Loyalist

2. PEOPLE AND PLACES Thomas Gage, Lexington and Concord, John Hancock, Paul Revere, William Dawes, Samuel Prescott

3. COMPREHENSION Why did Parliament pass the Intolerable Acts?

4. COMPREHENSION What led to the battles of Lexington and Concord?

5. CRITICAL THINKING Why did the colonial embargo fail to make Parliament repeal the Intolerable Acts?

4 Declaring Independence

★ Section Focus

Key Terms Second Continental Congress ■ Battle of Bunker Hill ■ Olive Branch Petition ■ resolution ■ Declaration of Independence

Main Idea Hostilities between Britain and the colonies led colonists to form an army and declare their independence.

Objectives As you read, look for answers to these questions:
1. What decisions did colonial leaders make at the Second Continental Congress?
2. What were the arguments for and against American independence?
3. What ideas and beliefs were contained in the Declaration of Independence?

After the battles of Lexington and Concord, thousands of militiamen from New England began gathering at Patriot headquarters near Boston. Militias from other colonies prepared to join them. General Gage decided to remove his soldiers from the peninsula opposite Boston. All the British were then in Boston. Because Boston was nearly surrounded by water, a land attack against the city was almost impossible.

That same spring of 1775, a band of rowdy backwoodsmen stormed Britain's Fort Ticonderoga on Lake Champlain. These were the Green Mountain Boys. Their leaders were Benedict Arnold and Ethan Allen.

The Green Mountain Boys seized Ticonderoga "in the name of the Great Jehovah and the Continental Congress." The fort itself was not very important. Within its walls, however, lay a valuable store of artillery. That artillery would drive the British from Boston.

THE CONTINENTAL ARMY

In May of 1775 the Second Continental Congress began in Philadelphia. The delegation from Massachusetts included John

Adams, Samuel Adams, and the merchant John Hancock. Benjamin Franklin was part of the Pennsylvania delegation. From Virginia came George Washington, Richard Henry Lee, and Patrick Henry.

Henry and the two Adamses believed that the task of the Congress was to prepare for war. Other delegates hesitated. They believed in negotiation, not war. Many delegates felt unsure about Ethan Allen's action. They talked of giving Ticonderoga back to the British. "We find a great many bundles of weak nerves," John Adams wrote to Dr. Warren in Boston.

> "**W**e find a great many bundles of weak nerves."
>
> —*John Adams to Dr. Warren*

John Adams thought the troops gathering in Massachusetts needed experienced leadership. To this end he convinced his fellow delegates to set up a Continental Army and to name George Washington its leader. He pointed to Washington's experience fighting for the British during the French and Indian War. Washington had studied Indian war tactics that had worked against the redcoats. Washington was also wealthy. He had married the widow Martha Custis, one of the richest women in America. Southerners in particular considered independent wealth a requirement for leadership. Not all New Englanders agreed with Adams. They doubted their militias would obey a southerner. After two days of debate, the Congress gave George Washington the job.

THE BATTLE OF BUNKER HILL

In June 1775 Washington and his aides left on horseback for Massachusetts. They had gone less than twenty miles when a dusty messenger galloped up with news. The Battle of Bunker Hill had just been fought near Boston.

The heights of Charlestown were the location of the Battle of Bunker Hill, a British victory. American forces fought so well, however, that the British general described his casualties as "greater than we can bear." GEOGRAPHY Why might soldiers assaulting a hill suffer high casualties?

This is what happened: Patriot troops moved to occupy the peninsula recently vacated by the British. On this peninsula were two hills, Breeds Hill and Bunker Hill. Overnight, the Patriots turned the peninsula into an armed camp. Stunned, the British hurried to retake it.

General William Howe, with 2,200 men, crossed by boat to the beaches below Breeds Hill. There the redcoats formed assault lines, guns at the ready. Drums beat. Up the hill they marched. Tense, the Patriots waited. The redcoats were only fifteen paces away when the Patriots began firing.

Twice the British stormed the hill. Twice they were turned back. Then American gunpowder ran out. The British claimed the hill. In spite of their retreat, Patriots viewed the Battle of Bunker Hill as a victory. Over 1,000 redcoats had been killed or wounded. There were 400 Patriot casualties. The colonial militia had proved it could hold its own against the world's most powerful army.

PETITION AND RESPONSE

In spite of the bloody battles of Lexington and Concord and of Bunker Hill, most colonists still hoped for peace. They thought that Parliament and the king's ministers might have made some bad decisions. Even so, George III still deserved their loyalty. Like a good father, they believed, he would step in and settle the dispute.

Thus in July 1775 Congress sent off the Olive Branch Petition. Written by John Dickinson of Pennsylvania, the petition blamed Parliament for the war. It begged the king to stop the war and bring about "a happy and permanent reconciliation." John Adams was disgusted, but he signed it. What good, he thought, could it do?

No good at all, as it turned out. The king refused the petition and called the colonists rebels. He said he would blockade American shipping and send 10,000 Hessian (German) mercenaries — hired soldiers — to fight in America. "When once these rebels have felt a smart blow, they will submit," he declared.

BIOGRAPHY

ABIGAIL ADAMS (1744–1818) was the wife of John Adams, the second President, and she was the mother of John Quincy Adams, the sixth President. A champion of women's rights, she urged her husband to "remember the ladies" when drafting the nation's new legal system. Her letters give a valuable picture of her society and times.

DRIVING THE BRITISH FROM BOSTON

In Massachusetts George Washington faced the almost impossible task of forming an army without enough money, supplies, or arms. There was so little ammunition that when the British fired a cannon ball, the Patriots ran after it, shoved it into one of their cannons, and fired it back.

Help was on the way, however. Patriots were hauling artillery from Fort Ticonderoga. The job posed a great challenge, for there were no roads across the mountainous landscape. It took two months to drag 59 cannons over the snow-covered mountains to Boston.

With cannons and ammunition available at last, Washington moved his army to Dorchester Heights overlooking Boston. Then the Patriots began bombarding the city. General Howe, who was now in charge of the British forces, decided he had no choice but to get out.

In March 1776, Abigail Adams watched them go—170 sailing ships carrying 9,000 soldiers. With them went about 1,000 American Loyalists. Anti-British feeling in Boston was so strong that the Loyalists feared for their safety. Among these Loyalists were some of Abigail Adams's closest friends. Surrounded by joyous Patriots, Adams felt "positively deflated." The greatest concern of most Patriots, however, was where would the British strike next?

PUSH FOR INDEPENDENCE

Most Americans still hesitated to make the final break with Britain. Abigail Adams expressed some of their fears when she wrote:

> If we separate from Britain, what code of laws will be established? How shall we be governed so as to retain our liberties? . . . Who shall frame these laws? Who will give them force and energy?

In January 1776 a 46-page pamphlet shook Americans out of their uncertainty. The pamphlet was *Common Sense;* its author was Thomas Paine. Paine came from the British lower class. He had emigrated to Philadelphia in 1774. Paine did what no one else had been able to do: he made a bold call for independence from Britain. Many people of the time still believed that kings ruled by the will of God. Paine ridiculed this idea. He called George III "the Royal Brute" and said that all monarchies were in fact corrupt. Paine also dismissed economic arguments for remaining a British colony. "Our corn," he wrote, "will fetch its price in any country in Europe." America had its own destiny, Paine believed. "Everything that is right or reasonable pleads for separation," he said. "The blood of

BIOGRAPHY

THOMAS PAINE (1737–1809) was born in poverty in England and began working at the age of 13. He became a friend to Benjamin Franklin, who was then in London. Following Franklin's advice, Paine moved to Pennsylvania, editing a magazine and writing in support of independence. In *Common Sense,* he attacked the idea of the divine right of kings. Paine's clear, powerful writing made him perhaps the most influential figure of his day.

the slain, the weeping voice of nature cries, 'Tis time to part.'"

> "**E**verything that is right or reasonable pleads for separation."
>
> —*Thomas Paine*

Common Sense was an instant success. Never had a book sold so well in America. More and more colonists took up the call for independence.

Gaining Skill: Analyzing Primary Sources

Earlier you read that historians depend on primary sources to study the past. Documents such as letters, journals, diaries, cargo lists, wills, and tax records written at the same time as the events they describe are all primary sources.

When primary sources are printed in a book, two special kinds of punctuation are often used to save space or to make the meaning clearer. The set of dots you see here . . . is called an **ellipsis** (ih–LIP–sis). An ellipsis shows that some words have been left out. Brackets such as [these] sometimes enclose a word. A word in brackets is not part of the primary source. It either replaces words or information that have been left out or helps identify an unfamiliar word.

STEPS TO ANALYSIS

The following four steps will help you analyze primary sources:

(1) Identify who wrote the document.

(2) Note when and where the document was written.

(3) Skim the document to get an idea of its content.

(4) Read the document carefully and try to recognize the writer's opinions.

Sometimes, one person's views of an event can indicate how others were feeling at the time. Below is an excerpt from a letter to John Adams, a Patriot leader, from his wife Abigail Adams. Use the four steps just described to read this primary source. Then answer the questions that follow on a separate sheet of paper.

Braintree [Massachusetts]
14 September, 1774
. . . About eight o'clock Sunday evening there passed by here about two hundred men, preceded by a horsecart, and marched down to the powder-house, from whence they took the [gun] powder, and carried it into the other parish and there [hid] it. I opened the window upon their return. They passed without any noise, not a word among them till they came against this house, when some of them, [seeing] me, asked me if I wanted any powder. I replied, No, since it was in so good hands. The reason they gave for taking it was that we had so many Tories [people loyal to Britain] here, they dared not trust us with it. . . . This town appears as [excited] as you can well imagine, and, if necessary, would soon be in arms. Not a Tory but hides his head. The church parson [a Tory] thought they were coming after him and ran up [to his attic]; they say another jumped out of his window and hid among the corn, whilst a third crept under his board fence.

[Abigail Adams]

PRACTICING YOUR SKILL

1. When and where did Abigail Adams write this letter?

2. What event did the author of this letter witness?

3. Were the people who took the gunpowder Patriots or Tories? What evidence for this is in the letter?

4. Based on your reading of this letter, do you think the author is a Patriot or a Tory? Why do you think so?

5. What is the mood of the people as reflected in this letter?

6. What events did Abigail Adams report although she did not actually see them? What phrase gives you a clue that she did not see the events?

7. How do you think the author felt about the events reported in this letter? Cite examples to support your answer.

In John Trumbull's painting, "The Declaration of Independence," John Hancock sits at the desk and (left to right) John Adams, Roger Sherman, Robert Livingston, Thomas Jefferson, and Benjamin Franklin stand before him. **HISTORY** Why did some delegates oppose the Declaration?

A TIME OF DECISION

In June 1776 Richard Henry Lee of Virginia presented the Continental Congress with several resolutions, proposals to be voted on. Lee's resolutions called for the colonies to (1) become independent states, (2) take measures to form their own foreign alliances, and (3) prepare a plan of confederation.

Not all the delegates were prepared to vote on Lee's resolutions. The Congress went ahead anyway and appointed a committee to draft a Declaration of Independence. The committee included Benjamin Franklin, John Adams, Roger Sherman, Robert Livingston, and Thomas Jefferson. At 33, Thomas Jeffer-

son was young, but was the best writer of the group. To him, therefore, went the task of writing the Declaration. At a portable desk of his own design, Jefferson went to work. In about two weeks, he had finished most of the Declaration.

On July 1, 1776, Congress began to debate Lee's resolutions. Some delegates, including John Dickinson, were upset. How, he asked, could the states think of independence? It was "like destroying our house in winter . . . before we have got another shelter." When the vote was taken, however, the *ayes* had it. From then on, the colonies were to be independent states.

THE DECLARATION IS ADOPTED

Two days later, on July 4, 1776, Congress adopted the Declaration of Independence. The core idea of the document was that people have rights that the government cannot take away. In what was to become the Declaration's best-known passage, Jefferson wrote:

> We hold these truths to be self-evident, that all men are created equal, that they are endowed by their Creator with certain unalienable Rights, that among these are Life, Liberty, and the pursuit of Happiness.

If a government disregards these God-given rights, Jefferson explained, it loses its right to govern. The people then have the right to abolish that government, by force if necessary. They can then form a new government that will protect their rights.

When Jefferson spoke of "the people," however, he meant only free white men. In Jefferson's time it was commonly believed that some people should rule and others should be ruled. Women were thought to be weaker and less intelligent than men. They had no place in politics.

African American slaves made up 20 percent of the population. Jefferson originally included a passage condemning the slave trade. Slaveowners pressured him to drop the passage. Jefferson himself owned hundreds of slaves. The passage was struck from the final document.

Declaring independence from Britain was not a step to be taken lightly. Therefore, in powerful language, Jefferson listed the reasons for the break with Britain: the misdeeds of George III.

In conclusion, the Declaration declared the colonies to be free and independent states.

Many Americans greeted the decision to declare independence from Britain with joy and festivities. In this picture, Americans raise a liberty pole to celebrate freedom from British rule. The man standing at the booth in the right-hand corner is signing up to fight.
HISTORY What important problems did the independent states face?

This was a grave action—treason from the British point of view—and the authors of the document knew it. John Hancock warned the delegates that "there must be no pulling in separate ways; we must all hang together." "Yes," replied Benjamin Franklin, "we must all hang together, or assuredly we shall all hang separately."

The Declaration closed with the following pledge:

> And for the support of this Declaration, with a firm reliance on the protection of divine Providence, we mutually pledge to each other our Lives, our Fortunes and our sacred Honor.

Americans had declared independence. Now they had to win it.

1. KEY TERMS Second Continental Congress, Battle of Bunker Hill, Olive Branch Petition, resolution, Declaration of Independence

2. PEOPLE Ethan Allen, George Washington, William Howe, John Dickinson, Hessians, Thomas Paine, Thomas Jefferson

3. COMPREHENSION Why did some colonists question whether independence was a sensible policy?

4. COMPREHENSION Summarize Thomas Paine's arguments for independence.

5. CRITICAL THINKING Under what circumstances did Jefferson argue that it was right to overthrow an established government? Do you agree? Why or why not?

CHAPTER 8 SUMMARY AND TIMELINE

1. To pay for the French and Indian War and for maintaining troops in the American colonies, Britain revived its mercantilist policies. Among these were taxes on colonial trade and business, including the Stamp Act of 1765. The Sons of Liberty organized protests and boycotts against the Stamp Act.

2. The Townshend Acts brought more protests. British leaders sent troops to Boston. Tensions between colonists and the British erupted in 1770 with the Boston Massacre. Parliament passed the Tea Act in 1773 to gain revenue for the British East India Company. Angry colonists led boycotts and destroyed tea shipments.

3. After the Boston Tea Party, Parliament passed the Intolerable Acts. Colonial representatives organized the First Continental Congress. Colonial militias began to organize. When British troops moved to seize the militia's weapons, the two sides fought at Lexington and Concord.

4. Although many colonists remained loyal to Britain, Patriot leaders declared America's independence and prepared to fight for it. The Second Continental Congress voted to form its own army. In the Battle of Bunker Hill, Patriot forces killed and wounded over 1,000 British troops. Congress issued the Declaration of Independence in 1776.

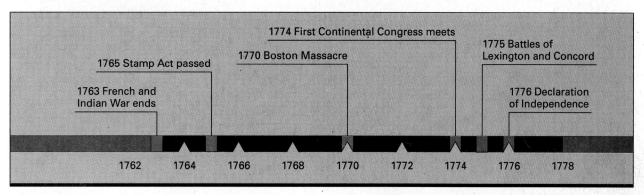

1774 First Continental Congress meets

1775 Battles of Lexington and Concord

1765 Stamp Act passed

1770 Boston Massacre

1763 French and Indian War ends

1776 Declaration of Independence

1762 1764 1766 1768 1770 1772 1774 1776 1778

PLACES TO LOCATE

Match the letters on the map with the places listed below. Write your answers on a separate sheet of paper.

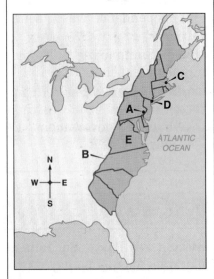

1. Boston
2. New York City
3. Philadelphia
4. Proclamation Line of 1763
5. Virginia

KEY TERMS

Match each of the following terms with its correct definition.

embargo
pamphlet
propaganda
repeal
revenue

1. An unbound, printed essay.
2. Money raised for government spending.
3. To overturn a law.
4. A way of spreading a political point of view.
5. A ban on trade.

PEOPLE TO IDENTIFY

Identify the following people and tell why each one was important.

1. Samuel Adams
2. Ethan Allen
3. George III
4. Thomas Jefferson
5. Thomas Paine
6. George Washington

REVIEWING THE FACTS

1. Why did Britain change its colonial policies after 1763?
2. What objections did colonists raise to these changes?
3. Which method proved most effective in combating the Stamp Act? Why?
4. What events led up to the Boston Massacre?
5. Describe the significance of the First Continental Congress.
6. What was the purpose of Paul Revere's famous ride?
7. How did the fighting styles of the two sides at Lexington and Concord differ?
8. How did Washington succeed in forcing British troops to leave Boston?
9. For what reasons did some Americans oppose independence from Britain?
10. How did the Declaration of Independence justify the Patriots' decision to break with Britain?

CITIZENSHIP

1. If you had been a colonist in 1775, which, if any, of Britain's policies would you have most objected to? Explain your answer.
2. In 1776, which Americans had full rights, including the right to vote?

CRITICAL THINKING SKILLS

1. IDENTIFYING ADVANTAGES AND DISADVANTAGES What were the advantages and disadvantages to the American colonists of remaining in the British Empire?

2. DRAWING CONCLUSIONS If you were an American in the mid-1700s, would you have favored independence from Britain? Why or why not?

3. STATING BOTH SIDES OF AN ISSUE Make the best case you can in support of each of the following statements: (a) Parliament had the right to govern Britain's American colonies in any way it pleased. (b) Parliament had no right to govern the colonies without colonial representation.

PRACTICING YOUR SKILL

The excerpt below is from a letter written in 1775 by C. S., an American woman living in Philadelphia. Read the excerpt and answer the questions that follow.

> I will tell you what I have done. My only brother I have sent to the camp with my prayers and blessings. . . . I am confident he will behave with honor, and emulate the great example he has before him; and had I twenty sons and brothers they should go. I have retrenched every superfluous expense in my table and family; tea I have not drunk since last Christmas, nor bought a new cap or gown since your defeat at Lexington, and what I never did before, have learnt to knit, and am now making stockings of American wool for my servants, and this way do I throw in my mite to the public good. I know this, that as free I can die but once, but as a slave I shall not be worthy of life. I have the pleasure to assure you that these are the sentiments of all my sister Americans. They have sacrificed both assemblies, parties of pleasure, tea drinking, and finery to that great spirit of patriotism. . . .

1. What specific things has C. S. done to help the American cause?

2. According to C. S., do other American women share her feelings? How can you tell?

3. Based on the excerpt, is C. S. a Patriot or a Loyalist?

4. Is C. S. writing to someone in the colonies or in Britain? How can you tell?

PROJECTS AND ACTIVITIES

1. WRITING A NEWS STORY
Write a newspaper account of the events at Lexington and Concord, Massachusetts, in April 1775. Include comments of people who might have been there.

2. DRAWING A CARTOON
Draw a cartoon or poster whose point is that America should be independent. Make another drawing that argues for Americans to remain loyal to Britain.

3. INTERPRETING A DOCUMENT
Read the preamble to the Declaration of Independence on page 192. Then rewrite the paragraph in your own words.

4. WRITING A SKIT Write a skit about the Boston Massacre or the Boston Tea Party. You may wish to work alone, with a partner, or with a small group. Then cast the characters, rehearse the skit, and perform it for the class. You may wish to liven your performance with costumes, props, or simple scenery.

5. DEBATING AN ISSUE Prepare and present arguments for a formal debate on the question: "Resolved, Great Britain could not have avoided the differences with its American colonies that led to the Declaration of Independence."

WRITING ABOUT TOPICS IN AMERICAN HISTORY

1. CONNECTING HISTORY AND LITERATURE A selection from the novel *Johnny Tremain* by Esther Forbes appears on pages 640–642. Read it and answer the questions. Then write a short essay describing the aspects of his personality that enable Johnny to succeed in his mission.

2. APPLYING THEMES: EXPANDING DEMOCRACY Read a newspaper to find out about a movement for independence taking place in the world today. Then write a report stating the reasons why the group wants independence and the difficulties the movement is facing.

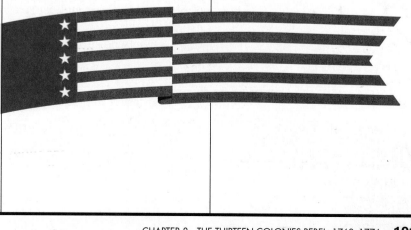

The Declaration of Independence

The first paragraph, known as the Preamble, explains why the American colonists thought it necessary to make a political break with Great Britain.

When in the Course of human events, it becomes necessary for one people to dissolve the political bands which have connected them with another, and to assume among the powers of the earth, the separate and equal station to which the Laws of Nature and of Nature's God entitle them, a decent respect to the opinions of mankind requires that they should declare the causes which impel them to the separation.*

[THE RIGHT OF THE PEOPLE TO CONTROL THEIR GOVERNMENT]

This paragraph states that all people are born with certain God-given rights that are "unalienable." In other words, these rights cannot be given away or taken away by any government. Governments get their authority from the "consent" or approval of the people they govern. If a government lacks the consent of the people, then the people have a right to change or dissolve it. The people should, however, only resort to such change when the existing government has abused its powers.

endowed provided
usurpations wrongful uses of authority
Despotism unlimited power
Tyranny unjust use of power
candid fair

We hold these truths to be self-evident, that all men are created equal, that they are endowed by their Creator with certain unalienable Rights, that among these are Life, Liberty and the pursuit of Happiness. That to secure these rights, Governments are instituted among Men, deriving their just powers from the consent of the governed, That whenever any Form of Government becomes destructive of these ends, it is the Right of the People to alter or to abolish it, and to institute new Government, laying its foundation on such principles and organizing its powers in such form, as to them shall seem most likely to effect their Safety and Happiness. Prudence, indeed, will dictate that Governments long established should not be changed for light and transient causes; and accordingly all experience hath shown, that mankind are more disposed to suffer, while evils are sufferable, than to right themselves by abolishing the forms to which they are accustomed, But when a long train of abuses and usurpations, pursuing invariably the same Object evinces a design to reduce them under absolute Despotism, it is their right, it is their duty, to throw off such Government, and to provide new Guards for their future security. Such has been the patient sufferance of these Colonies; and such is now the necessity which constrains them to alter their former Systems of Government. The history of the present King of Great Britain is a history of repeated injuries and usurpations, all having in direct object the establishment of an absolute Tyranny over these States. To prove this, let Facts be submitted to a candid world.

[TYRANNICAL ACTS OF THE BRITISH KING]

This section lists the colonial grievances against George III and his government. Each of these 27 British offenses occurred

He has refused his Assent to Laws, the most wholesome and necessary for the public good.

He has forbidden his Governors to pass Laws of immediate and

---

*In punctuation and capitalization, the text of the Declaration follows accepted sources.

between 1763 and 1776. The language of this section is often very emotional. Words such as *despotism, annihilation, ravaged,* and *perfidy* express the seriousness of the King's offenses against the colonies. The list of grievances makes it clear that King George no longer has "the consent of the governed," and so should not continue to rule the colonies.

Assent approval
relinquish give up
inestimable too valuable to be measured
formidable causing fear
fatiguing tiring
Annihilation destruction
convulsions violent disturbances
Naturalization the process of becoming a citizen
tenure term

pressing importance, unless suspended in their operation till his Assent should be obtained; and when so suspended, he has utterly neglected to attend to them.

He has refused to pass other Laws for the accommodation of large districts of people, unless those people would relinquish the right of Representation in the Legislature, a right inestimable to them and formidable to tyrants only.

He has called together legislative bodies at places unusual, uncomfortable, and distant from the depository of their Public Records, for the sole purpose of fatiguing them into compliance with his measures.

He has dissolved Representative Houses repeatedly, for opposing with manly firmness his invasions on the rights of the people.

He has refused for a long time, after such dissolutions, to cause others to be elected; whereby the Legislative powers, incapable of Annihilation, have returned to the People at large for their exercise; the State remaining in the mean time exposed to all the dangers of invasion from without, and convulsions within.

He has endeavoured to prevent the population of these States; for that purpose obstructing the Laws for Naturalization of Foreigners; refusing to pass others to encourage their migrations hither, and raising the conditions of new Appropriations of Lands.

He has obstructed the Administration of Justice, by refusing his Assent to Laws for establishing Judiciary powers.

He has made Judges dependent on his Will alone, for the tenure of their offices, and the amount and payment of their salaries.

He has erected a multitude of New Offices, and sent hither swarms of Officers to harass our People, and eat out their substance.

He has kept among us, in times of peace, Standing Armies without the Consent of our legislatures.

He has affected to render the military independent of and superior to the Civil power.

He has combined with others to subject us to a jurisdiction foreign to our constitution, and unacknowledged by our laws; giving his Assent to their Acts of pretended Legislation:

For quartering large bodies of armed troops among us:

For protecting them, by a mock Trial, from Punishment for any Murders which they should commit on the Inhabitants of these States:

For cutting off our Trade with all parts of the world:

For imposing Taxes on us without our Consent:

For depriving us in many cases, of the benefits of Trial by Jury:

For transporting us beyond Seas to be tried for pretended offences:

For abolishing the free System of English Laws in a neighboring

Arbitrary tyrannical
abdicated given up
ravaged destroyed
perfidy treachery
constrained forced
insurrections rebellions

Province, establishing therein an Arbitrary government, and enlarging its Boundaries so as to render it at once an example and fit instrument for introducing the same absolute rule into these Colonies:

For taking away our Charters, abolishing our most valuable Laws, and altering fundamentally the Forms of our Governments:

For suspending our own Legislatures, and declaring themselves invested with power to legislate for us in all cases whatsoever.

He has abdicated Government here, by declaring us out of his Protection and waging War against us.

He has plundered our seas, ravaged our Coasts, burnt our towns, and destroyed the lives of our people.

He is at this time transporting large Armies of foreign Mercenaries to compleat the works of death, desolation and tyranny, already begun with circumstances of Cruelty and perfidy scarcely paralleled in the most barbarous ages, and totally unworthy the Head of a civilized nation.

He has constrained our fellow Citizens taken Captive on the high Seas to bear Arms against their Country, to become the executioners of their friends and Brethren, or to fall themselves by their Hands.

He has excited domestic insurrections amongst us, and has endeavoured to bring on the inhabitants of our frontiers, the merciless Indian Savages, whose known rule of warfare, is an undistinguished destruction of all ages, sexes and conditions.

[EFFORTS OF THE COLONIES TO AVOID SEPARATION]

This section states that the colonists tried, without success, to settle their grievances with the king. George III ignored the colonists' repeated petitions for change. The British people, too, failed to listen to the colonists' pleas. The colonists must now look on them as enemies in war and friends in peace.

Oppressions unjust uses of
 power
Petitioned for Redress asked for
 the correction of wrongs
unwarrantable jurisdiction unjust
 control
magnanimity generous nature
consanguinity blood relationship
acquiesce accept

In every stage of these Oppressions We have Petitioned for Redress in the most humble terms: Our repeated Petitions have been answered only by repeated injury. A Prince, whose character is thus marked by every act which may define a Tyrant, is unfit to be the ruler of a free people.

Nor have we been wanting in attentions to our British brethren. We have warned them from time to time of attempts by their legislature to extend an unwarrantable jurisdiction over us. We have reminded them of the circumstances of our emigration and settlement here. We have appealed to their native justice and magnanimity, and we have conjured them by the ties of our common kindred to disavow these usurpations, which, would inevitably interrupt our connections and correspondence. They too have been deaf to the voice of justice and of consanguinity. We must, therefore, acquiesce in the necessity, which denounces our Separation, and hold them, as we hold the rest of mankind, Enemies in War, in Peace Friends.

[THE COLONIES ARE DECLARED FREE AND INDEPENDENT]

The final paragraph states that the colonies are now free and independent states. All political ties between the United States of America and Great Britain are broken. The United States now has the power to declare war, make peace treaties, form political alliances, and establish trade. In the last sentence, the delegates (signers) pledge their support of the Declaration of Independence. They express their reliance on the protection of God.

rectitude honesty
Absolved freed
divine Providence God's
   guidance

We, therefore, the Representatives of the United States of America, in General Congress, Assembled, appealing to the Supreme Judge of the world for the rectitude of our intentions, do, in the Name, and by Authority of the good People of these Colonies, solemnly publish and declare, That these United Colonies are, and of Right ought to be Free and Independent States; that they are Absolved from all Allegiance to the British Crown, and that all political connection between them and the State of Great Britain, is and ought to be totally dissolved; and that as Free and Independent States, they have full Power to Levy War, conclude Peace, contract Alliances, establish Commerce, and to do all other Acts and Things which Independent States may of right do. And for the support of this Declaration, with a firm reliance on the protection of divine Providence, we mutually pledge to each other our Lives, our Fortunes and our sacred Honor.

Signers of the Declaration

NEW HAMPSHIRE
Josiah Bartlett
William Whipple
Matthew Thornton

MASSACHUSETTS
John Hancock
Samuel Adams
John Adams
Robert Treat Paine
Elbridge Gerry

RHODE ISLAND
Stephen Hopkins
William Ellery

CONNECTICUT
Roger Sherman
Samuel Huntington
William Williams
Oliver Wolcott

NEW YORK
William Floyd
Philip Livingston
Francis Lewis
Lewis Morris

NEW JERSEY
Richard Stockton
John Witherspoon
Francis Hopkinson
John Hart
Abraham Clark

PENNSYLVANIA
Robert Morris
Benjamin Rush
Benjamin Franklin
John Morton
George Clymer
James Smith
George Taylor
James Wilson
George Ross

DELAWARE
Caesar Rodney
George Read
Thomas McKean

MARYLAND
Samuel Chase
William Paca
Thomas Stone
Charles Carroll of Carrollton

VIRGINIA
George Wythe
Richard Henry Lee
Thomas Jefferson
Benjamin Harrison
Thomas Nelson, Jr.
Francis Lightfoot Lee
Carter Braxton

NORTH CAROLINA
William Hooper
Joseph Hewes
John Penn

SOUTH CAROLINA
Edward Rutledge
Thomas Heyward, Jr.
Thomas Lynch, Jr.
Arthur Middleton

GEORGIA
Button Gwinnett
Lyman Hall
George Walton

The difficult and perilous American struggle for independence brought to the fore our nation's greatest hero, General (and later President) George Washington.

9 The War for Independence (1776–1783)

1 Perilous Times

Section Focus

Key Terms Battle of Saratoga ■ alliance

Main Idea Inexperienced Patriot forces struggled with a lack of supplies and a divided society in the war with the British.

Objectives As you read, look for answers to these questions:
1. What difficulties did Washington face as head of the American army?
2. What were the major battles of the war in the North?
3. How did foreign nations affect the war?

New Englander Mercy Otis Warren used her wit against the British. In 1776 she published *The Blockheads,* a play set in Boston during the British occupation. In the play a British officer, General Puff, complains:

> Well, gentlemen, a pretty state for British generals and British troops— the terror of the world become mere scarecrows to themselves. We came to America, flushed with high expectations of conquest, and curbing these sons of riot. . . . But how are we deceived? Instead of this agreeable employ, we are shamefully confined within the bounds of three miles, wrangling and starving among ourselves.

General Puff's complaint reflects the British situation throughout the Revolutionary War. The British were able to take and hold every city, except for Boston, that they chose

to. They could do so because of their superior firepower, trained troops, and supply ships from Britain. However, British troops went into the countryside at their peril. As another character in Warren's play observed: "These Yankee dogs . . . divert themselves by firing at us, as at a flock of partridges. A man can scarcely put his nose over the entrenchments without losing it."

THE COUNTRY DIVIDED

The Americans had problems of their own. Only a minority of Americans actively supported the Revolution. About two-fifths of them were active Patriots. One-fifth were active Loyalists. The remainder were neutral.

The American Revolution was thus a war that bitterly split families and neighbors. Patriots and Loyalists both came from all walks of life and from all parts of America. In general, however, New England and Virginia had the greatest share of Patriots. Loyalists were most numerous in New York State, among Scottish immigrants of the Carolinas, and in cities near the coast. Loyalists were often employees of the British government or clergy of the Church of England. Those who stayed neutral included Quakers and the German population of Pennsylvania.

Colonists loyal to Britain suffered harsh treatment at Patriot hands. Many were tarred and feathered. Millions of dollars' worth of their property was seized without payment. In all, 80,000 Loyalists fled to Britain's other North American colony, Canada.

Most Indians sided with the British during the Revolution. They believed that if the Patriots won, they would be pushed off their land by swarms of land-hungry settlers. Indeed, the Congress had offered Indian land to men who enlisted. The Indians hoped a British victory would allow them to live in peace.

LACK OF MONEY AND EQUIPMENT

George Washington had formed the Continental Army from the ranks of local militias. Throughout the war Washington would face the challenge of how to hold his army together. The soldiers needed everything. Basic supplies such as shoes, soap, and food were scarce, as were guns and ammunition. How, Washington worried, could a war be fought without guns, let alone wagons, horses, clothes, and tents?

Washington looked in vain to the Continental Congress, which had authorized the army. To raise funds, the Congress issued paper money. The British, however, were paying for goods in silver and gold. As the war dragged on, Continental paper money lost so much value that suppliers refused to accept it. The expression *not worth a Continental* came to mean "worthless."

AMERICANS AT WAR

Washington also had trouble getting men to enlist for long terms. As a result, he was often dealing with inexperienced troops. Many American soldiers were poor farmers. They were attracted by the promise of land after the war. They also hoped to gain money and social standing by soldiering for a year or so.

One group of Americans stood out in their eagerness to enlist for longer periods. These were free black men. At first Washington, a slaveholder himself, opposed enlistment by African Americans. He and others feared that arming African Americans could threaten the slave system. Washington became alarmed, however, when the British governor of Virginia, Lord Dunmore, promised freedom to slaves who fought for the king. Washington then announced that the Patriot forces would welcome free black soldiers. In all, about 5,000 African Americans would serve in the Continental Army.

Know that there were black men of courage in every major battle, on land and at sea. At the Battle of Bunker Hill, for instance, Patriots Salem Poor and Peter Salem had distinguished themselves. When 14-year-old James Forten, a powderboy in the navy, was captured, he refused the British offer to go to England. "I am here a prisoner for the liberties of my country," he said. "I never, never, shall prove a traitor to her interests."

The army's problems would have been still worse were it not for Patriot women. Martha Washington was the most famous of those who followed their husbands in the army.

Here Mary Ludwig Hays takes over her fallen husband's cannon. For her wartime services, she was awarded a pension by the government. **CULTURAL PLURALISM** In what other ways did women help the revolutionary cause?

Others did so because they had no other way to survive. Women busied themselves with soldiers' washing, cooking, nursing, sewing, and mending. A few women even joined their men on the battlefield. Mary Ludwig Hays continued to load and fire a cannon even after her husband had collapsed from the heat.

Women served in other ways as well. They gave up their pewter plate to be melted into musket balls. They spied. They forced merchants to set fair prices and not profit from wartime scarcity. Like Mercy Otis Warren, they also used their pens.

THE NORTHERN CAMPAIGNS, 1776–1778

The British had left Boston in March 1776. Washington guessed that they would reappear in New York City. If they seized control of the nearby Hudson Valley, the British could divide the country in two.

Acting on his hunch, Washington hastened with his raw army to New York. There he stationed troops on both Manhattan and Long Island. In July 1776, Britain's General Howe finally made his move. He arrived from Nova Scotia with the largest seaborne army ever launched. The ships were so numerous that New York harbor resembled a forest of stripped trees.

British troops, including some 8,000 Hessian mercenaries, forced Washington from Long Island and then from Manhattan. By November his ragged army, with Howe at its heels, was retreating into New Jersey. By December, another British general, Lord Cornwallis, had chased Washington across the Delaware River into Pennsylvania.

It was now winter—and a cold one. Leaving the Hessians in New Jersey, Howe returned to the warmth and gaiety of New York. After all, a proper army did not fight in winter. Besides, Howe reasoned, winter just might destroy what was left of Washington's army.

Patriot spirits fell as low as the thermometer. Many volunteers went home. The army fell from 20,000 to a few thousand. To rekindle the patriotic fire, Thomas Paine wrote *The Crisis.* "These are the times that try

★ **Historical Documents**

The Crisis (1776)

A former customs collector who became one of the most controversial people of his day, Thomas Paine vigorously rejected keeping any ties with Britain. In his pamphlet entitled The Crisis, *Paine's fiery words convinced thousands of colonists to support the struggle for independence.*

These are the times that try men's souls. The summer soldier and the sunshine patriot, will, in this crisis, shrink from the service of their country, but he that stands by it *now* deserves the love and thanks of man and woman. . . . Britain, with an army to enforce her tyranny, had declared that she has the right, not only to tax, but "to *bind* us in *all cases whatsoever*"; if being bound in that manner is not slavery, then there is not such a thing as slavery upon earth. . . .

Not a place upon earth might be so happy as America. Her situation is remote from all the wrangling world, and she has nothing to do but trade with them. . . . America will never be happy till she gets clear of foreign domination.

From Thomas Paine, *The Crisis* (1776)

ANALYZING HISTORICAL DOCUMENTS

1. Why does Paine advocate independence from Britain?
2. What is Paine's vision for an independent American nation?
3. How might citizens in Britain have viewed Paine and his arguments?

men's souls," Paine declared. "The summer soldier and the sunshine patriot will, in this crisis, shrink from the service of his country; but he that stands by it *now,* deserves the love and thanks of man and woman."

With the situation desperate, Washington was willing to gamble. "Victory or Death" was the choice, he said. Late on December 25, 1776, Patriot troops rowed across the icy Delaware River to the New Jersey shore. From there they marched in the bitter pre-dawn cold to catch the Hessians at Trenton sleeping off their Christmas revels. The Patriots captured or killed over 1,000 Hessians. In addition they acquired a great quantity of supplies, guns, and ammunition.

To boost Patriot morale, Washington marched his prisoners through the streets of Philadelphia. There was a near riot as Patriot citizens called for revenge on the enemy.

Washington's victories at Trenton and at Princeton a week later gave the Patriots new hope. The army attracted new recruits.

BRITISH BLUNDERS

Their losses at Trenton and Princeton did not greatly discourage the British. The Patriot army still consisted of a mere 4,000 men. In the summer of 1777, Howe began a campaign to take Philadelphia. He hoped that seizing the Patriots' capital and largest city would destroy their will to fight. Howe easily captured the city, but he failed to behead the Patriot cause. The Continental Congress just picked up and moved to the town of York, located in the countryside.

Howe's Philadelphia campaign, however, did wreck the grand British plan to split the colonies. In the summer of 1777, a British army under General John Burgoyne started south from Canada. At the same time, a second British force was supposed to move east from Lake Ontario. Howe was to march north from New York. The three armies would meet in Albany, securing the Hudson Valley. However, Howe had already decided to take Philadelphia. He thus ignored the orders to march north.

Meanwhile, Burgoyne's army moved south from Canada. The redcoats recaptured Fort

This famous painting of Washington crossing the Delaware River to attack the British forces at Trenton dates from 1851. The artist has changed Washington's stance for dramatic effect. HISTORY What was the significance of the surprise attack?

BATTLES IN THE MIDDLE STATES, 1776–1777

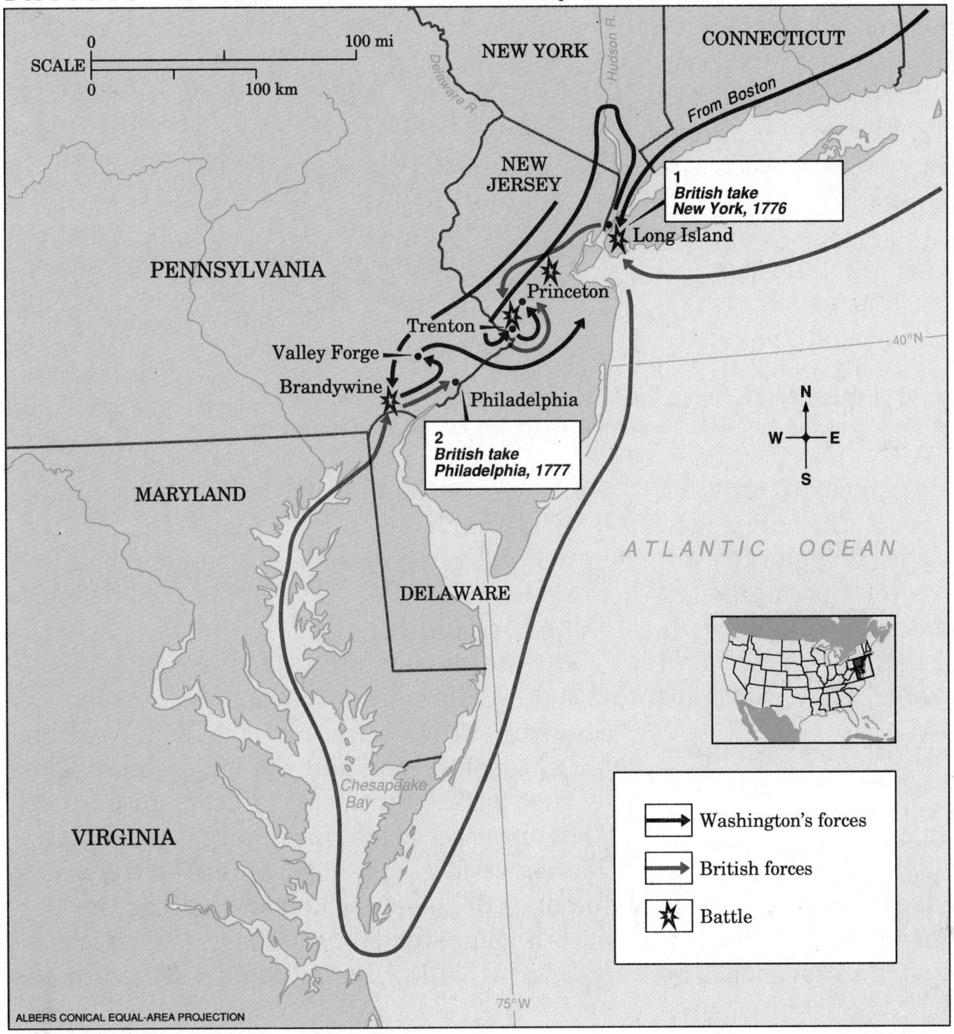

SCALE

0 — 100 mi
0 — 100 km

NEW YORK

CONNECTICUT

From Boston

NEW JERSEY

PENNSYLVANIA

1 *British take New York, 1776*

Long Island

Princeton

Trenton

Valley Forge

Brandywine

Philadelphia

2 *British take Philadelphia, 1777*

MARYLAND

DELAWARE

ATLANTIC OCEAN

40°N

N
W E
S

Chesapeake Bay

VIRGINIA

→ Washington's forces
→ British forces
✸ Battle

ALBERS CONICAL EQUAL-AREA PROJECTION

75°W

MAP SKILLS

Naval power enabled the British to seize American seaports. In 1776 British forces occupied New York City. What route did British troops take from New York to Philadelphia? In what state was the Battle of Trenton fought? **CRITICAL THINKING** Why might the capture of Philadelphia be described as a failure for the British?

Ticonderoga. Burgoyne's confidence grew. Nicknamed "Gentleman Johnny" by his soldiers, he liked to travel slowly and throw lavish parties between battles. His slow pace gave the Patriots the chance to cut down trees across his road. They also burned crops and drove off cattle, leaving the countryside bare of supplies.

Burgoyne thought his army could live off the countryside. Patriot forces, however, destroyed his raiding party of Hessians at the Battle of Bennington in Vermont. As Burgoyne's weakened army approached Albany, it faced a powerful American army under Horatio Gates. Howe should have been closing in behind Gates, but he was back in Philadelphia. At the Battle of Saratoga in October

1777, Gates and Benedict Arnold crushed Burgoyne. "Gentleman Johnny" surrendered his entire force of almost 6,000 troops.

HELP FROM ABROAD

The American victory at Saratoga persuaded France to back the Patriot effort. France had long wanted revenge on its old enemy, Britain, for its defeat in the Seven Years' War. It had not, however, wanted to join in a losing cause. Now it recognized America's independence and entered an alliance with the new nation. (An alliance is an agreement by two or more nations to act together in a cause.) France also persuaded its ally, Spain, to join the American side. Spain and France donated more badly needed funds.

Washington and his troops camped in Valley Forge during the bitter winter of 1777–1778.
HISTORY How does the painting show that the Americans were not equipped for winter weather?

Hearing news of the alliance, George III declared war on France. Soon other European nations were drawn into the struggle. Britain declared war on Holland after Dutch bankers loaned money to the Americans. Dutch merchants had been helping the Patriot cause all along. Lured by huge profits, they sold gunpowder to the Continental Army.

A Bitter Winter

Driven from Philadelphia by Howe, Washington spent the winter of 1777–1778 at nearby Valley Forge. The name would come to stand for the hunger and suffering the Patriots endured. "No pay, no clothes, no provisions, no rum," soldiers grumbled.

Over the winter, nearly a quarter of the soldiers at Valley Forge died from the cold, from smallpox and typhoid, and from lack of food. Many soldiers deserted because of the terrible conditions. "The want of clothing, added to the misery of the season," wrote Washington, "has occasioned them to suffer such hardships as will not be credited but by those who have been spectators."

There was some good news, however. The Patriot cause received a boost from Europeans who came to America to fight. The nineteen-year-old Marquis de Lafayette (mahr–KEE DUH lah–fee–ET) was among these volunteers. Lafayette, a French noble, asked to serve without pay under Washington. Lafayette would become one of the army's most popular leaders.

Leaders of the fight for independence in Poland also arrived to lend their talents. Casimir Pulaski (puh–LAS–kee) and Thaddeus Kosciusko (kahs–ee–US–ko) planned defenses along the Hudson River.

The spring saw a changed army. A professional soldier from Germany, Baron von Steuben (STOO–buhn), had drilled Washington's troops throughout the long winter. They learned about European military formations. They practiced making charges with bayonets—two-foot-long steel knives—attached to the ends of their muskets. By spring the German drillmaster felt satisfied. The American troops at Valley Forge could fight with the best.

SECTION REVIEW

1. KEY TERMS Battle of Saratoga, alliance

2. PEOPLE AND PLACES Lord Dunmore, Princeton, John Burgoyne, Valley Forge, Marquis de Lafayette, Thaddeus Kosciusko, Baron von Steuben

3. COMPREHENSION What difficulties did the Continental Army face?

4. COMPREHENSION How did British strategy fail at Saratoga? What was the importance of this battle?

5. CRITICAL THINKING Why might a country fighting for independence seek alliances with other nations?

Gaining Skill: Reading a Flow Chart

A useful way to present historical information clearly is on a flow chart. Sometimes a flow chart shows a sequence of events or decisions. Other times it shows how power, information, or supplies flow from one place to another.

The flow chart below shows how information flowed between the Continental Congress and the ordinary soldiers who made up the Continental Army. The solid red lines show pathways for orders or commands. They appear as arrows, because orders only flow one way—from the person who gives orders to the one who receives them. The broken lines show pathways for administrative information—information needed to carry out commands. For example, the commander-in-chief might want to know when supplies for his troops will arrive. This administrative information would help the commander decide what commands to give.

One historically significant point about the flow chart below is that the Continental Congress stood at the top of the power structure.

That is, even though George Washington was commander-in-chief of the Continental Army, he had no authority over the Continental Congress. Congress had appointed him to his position and could, if it wished, dismiss him. The principle of civilian control over the military has remained an important safeguard of democracy throughout American history.

PRACTICING YOUR SKILL

1. Members of what body could give commands to the commander-in-chief of the Continental Army?

2. According to the flow chart, from what three sources could the Continental Congress get administrative information?

3. What groups shown on the chart neither received nor gave commands?

4. How many levels of command separated the commander-in-chief from ordinary soldiers?

5. Who had the larger command in the Continental Army—the leader of a brigade or the leader of a regiment?

THE CONTINENTAL ARMY

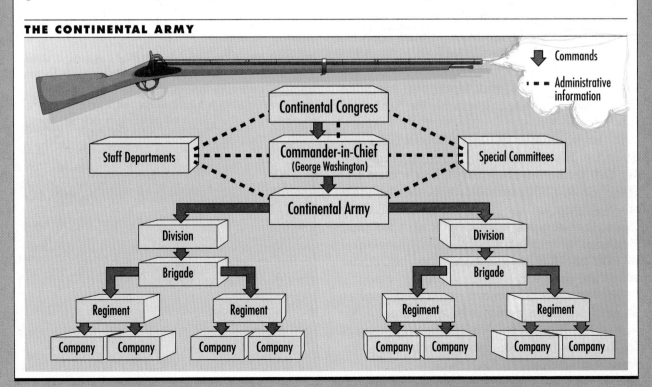

2 The British Defeated

★ **Section Focus**

★ **Key Terms**   partisan ■ Battle of Yorktown

★ **Main Idea**   The war's focus shifted from the North to three other areas: the frontier, the sea, and the South. It was in the South that the final battles of the war would be fought.

Objectives   As you read, look for answers to these questions:
1. Why did much of the worst fighting of the war take place in the South?
2. What events led to the end of the war?

In 1778 a 26-year-old explorer walked into the offices of Virginia's governor, Patrick Henry. He had come, he said, to argue for the defense of the land on America's western frontier. Virginia had claimed land in Indiana and Illinois. It therefore should defend the land against the British. "If a country is not worth protecting," he declared, "it is not worth claiming." Governor Henry was impressed with the red-haired young man with black, sparkling eyes. The governor gave him money and authorized him to raise an army to capture Illinois from the British.

WAR ON THE FRONTIER

The young man's name was George Rogers Clark. He was well qualified to lead such an expedition. At the age of nineteen he had explored both sides of the Ohio River valley. He had seen that the land there was valuable and wanted to make it available for American settlement.

In the summer of 1778, Clark traveled down the Ohio River with 175 Virginians. After 900 miles on the river, Clark's men left their boats. They started on foot for the town of Kaskaskia on the Mississippi River. Once there, they slipped inside the town's fort and captured it without a fight. Clark moved on to take the fort at Vincennes (vin–SENZ) on the Wabash River.

That winter, however, British forces under Henry Hamilton recaptured Vincennes. Hamilton was known as "Hair Buyer" because of the rewards he was supposed to have paid for American scalps.

Clark was determined to retake Vincennes. He did not, however, have enough soldiers to fight the British in a regular battle. Instead, he relied on surprise. Clark's men set out from Kaskaskia in February of 1779. They slogged through miles of flooded swamps known as the "drowned lands," caught the British defenders off-guard, and took the "Hair Buyer" prisoner. Clark was not a merciful man. He scalped the Indians who fought with the British and ruled the territory he conquered as a near dictator.

Clark's victory gave the Americans a hold on the vast Great Lakes–Ohio region—an area over half the total size of the thirteen states. Fort Detroit, however, remained in British hands.

Marching his soldiers through miles of swampland, George Rogers Clark defeated the British at Vincennes to secure American control of the West. HISTORY Why did Clark want to expel Britain from Indiana and Illinois?

Bernardo de Gálvez, the Spanish governor of Louisiana, aided the Patriot cause. A stamp issued in 1980 honored him. **GEOGRAPHY** Why was Gálvez's capture of the British forts at Natchez and Baton Rouge an important boost for the Americans?

USA 15c
Gen. Bernardo de Gálvez
Battle of Mobile 1780

BERNARDO DE GÁLVEZ, SPANISH HERO

The man who helped make Clark's victories possible was the Spanish governor of Louisiana, Bernardo de Gálvez. Clark lacked money to buy ammunition and supplies. He also had to buy gifts for those Indian tribes whose support he needed. Even before Spain declared war on Britain in 1779, Gálvez supplied him with funds. Gálvez also led an amazing series of raids on British forts on the lower Mississippi and Gulf of Mexico.

Gálvez's troops included Spaniards, Africans, and a few Irishmen and French Canadians. In 1779, they forced the British out of their Mississippi Delta forts at Natchez and Baton Rouge. As a result, the Mississippi was opened to American ships. At a cost of only three casualties, Gálvez's men had captured over 1,000 enemy soldiers. They also had seized three forts, eight warships, and 1,300 miles of rich Mississippi land.

In March of 1780 Gálvez captured the port of Mobile on the Gulf of Mexico. He then turned his attention to the nearby port of Pensacola in the territory of West Florida. Pensacola served as the base of the British Royal Navy. The entrance to the port was guarded by a fort set high on a cliff. From this position, the British could send 32-pound cannonballs raining down on enemy ships.

Gálvez tried to persuade Spain's officials in Cuba and Mexico to lend him ships and men to attack Pensacola. His request was refused. Finally, Gálvez sent the admiral of the Spanish fleet a present. It was a cannonball fired from the Pensacola fort. To the cannonball,

Gálvez had attached a message: "Whoever has honor and valor will follow me." The admiral agreed to join Gálvez. Together, their forces numbered 7,000 men.

> # "Whoever has honor and valor will follow me."
>
> *—Bernardo de Gálvez*

The Spanish sailors dodged the fire from the 150 cannons that blazed at them on their way into Pensacola harbor. On shore, they faced a stubborn defense by British troops and Loyalists. After a two-month siege, a deserter revealed where the British stored their gunpowder. A Spanish shell found the spot and set off a huge explosion.

With his victory at Pensacola in the spring of 1781, Gálvez had won another huge stretch of land for Spain. He had helped the Patriots by creating a second war front and thus taking some of the pressure off the American army. In addition, Gálvez's offensive prevented Britain from attacking the United States from the southwest. The Texas city of Galveston was later named in honor of his contribution to the Patriot cause.

WAR AT SEA

The poster called on "All gentlemen seamen and able-bodied landsmen who have a mind to distinguish themselves in the glorious cause of their country and make their fortunes." It informed them that "An opportunity now offers." The job was sailing aboard John Paul Jones's privateer *Ranger*. (Remember from Chapter 4 that privateers were privately owned, armed ships that captured enemy merchant vessels.)

Jones had joined the British merchant marine at age 12. Now he commanded the *Bonhomme Richard*, named after the French version of Ben Franklin's character, Poor Richard. Jones and other privateer captains rejoiced at the news of France's entry into the war. Now they could use French ports as bases from which to attack British ships in British waters.

Patrolling along the British coast, Jones bore down on a fleet of merchant ships guarded by two British warships. Jones chose the *Serapis*, the larger of the two, to attack first. He deftly edged the *Bonhomme Richard* alongside the British vessel. His crew then lashed the two ships together. With the muzzles of their guns almost touching, the two warships blasted away at each other at point-blank range. Seeing Jones's damaged ship begin to sink, the British commander called out, "Have you surrendered?" In words that have become famous, Jones supposedly replied, "I have not yet begun to fight!" and went on shooting. After a bloody three-hour battle, the mainmast of the *Serapis* cracked and fell, and its captain surrendered.

> # "I have not yet begun to fight!"
>
> *—John Paul Jones*

Jones, however, was one of the few American captains who took the war into British waters. The Continental Navy was simply too small to make a big difference in the outcome of the war.

WAR IN THE SOUTH, 1778–1781

After three years of fighting, the British faced some tough decisions. The battles in the North had brought them no nearer to victory than they had been in 1775. In addition, France's entry into the war had forced Britain to defend the rest of its empire. For example, the British had to move troops from the American colonies to defend the West Indies.

British generals, therefore, decided on a new strategy. They would shift the focus of the war to the South. There they hoped to benefit from the many southern Loyalists. They also (correctly) expected slaves to join them in large numbers. Pursuing the promise

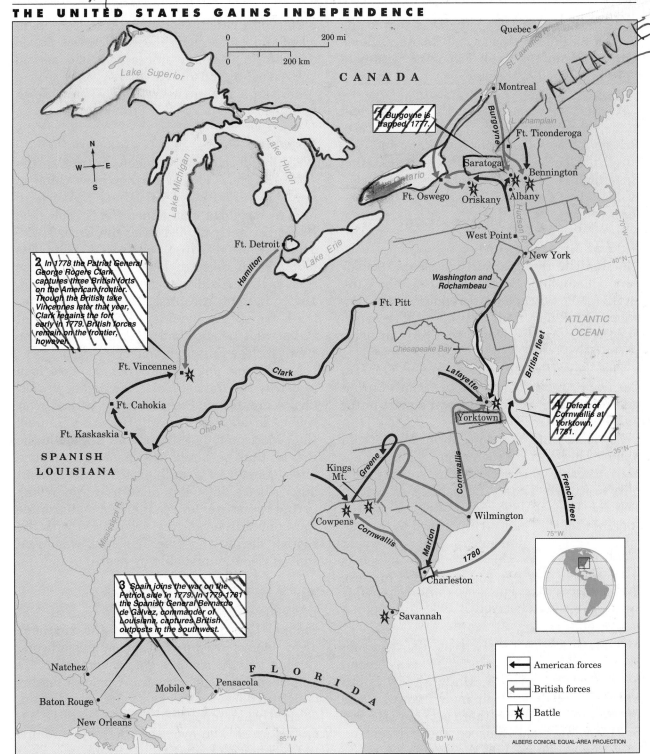

1 Burgoyne is trapped 1777.

2 In 1778 the Patriot General George Rogers Clark captures three British forts on the American frontier. Though the British take Vincennes later that year, Clark regains the fort early in 1779. British forces remain on the frontier, however.

3 Spain joins the war on the Patriot side in 1779. In 1779-1781 the Spanish General Bernardo de Gálvez, commander of Louisiana, captures British outposts in the southwest.

4 Defeat of Cornwallis at Yorktown, 1781.

Washington and Rochambeau

⟵ American forces
⟵ British forces
✶ Battle

ALBERS CONICAL EQUAL-AREA PROJECTION

American victories at Saratoga, Vincennes, and Yorktown led to independence. What was the role of the French fleet at Yorktown? What other European nation aided America?
CRITICAL THINKING In what part of the country did the British concentrate their attacks later in the war? Why?

of freedom, at least 50,000 slaves served the British as guides, spies, and laborers. Some saw action in the field. From the winter of 1778 to the end of the war, nearly all the major battles took place in the South.

At first it seemed that the British had made the right decision. In November 1778, British forces sailed from New York and captured the port of Savannah, Georgia. Using Savannah as a base, the British soon controlled all of Georgia. Repeated efforts to dislodge them failed.

PATRIOT SETBACKS

The British then captured a second major port: Charleston, South Carolina. When the city's 5,500 defenders surrendered, the Patriots lost almost their entire southern army. For the Americans, it was the worst disaster of the war.

The new British forces under General Cornwallis set out to secure the South Carolina countryside. Some of the war's most bitter fighting followed.

Loyalists and Patriots formed guerrilla bands. They carried out vicious raids against each other in which all existing rules of warfare were cast aside. The policies of British Colonel Banastre Tarleton, known as the "butcher" of the countryside, added to the violence. Tarleton announced that he would "give no quarter"—show no mercy—to rebels he captured. The Patriots responded in kind. At the battle of Kings Mountain, Patriots shouted "Tarleton's Quarter" as they killed Loyalist captives.

Francis Marion, known as the "Swamp Fox," led a band of Patriot partisans—members of guerrilla forces. Marion knew South Carolina's coastal swamplands from when he had hunted and fished there as a boy. He and his men launched raids on the British and then fled to the swamps for safety.

The Americans lost again at Camden, South Carolina. Washington had asked General Gates, the victor at Saratoga, to form a new southern army. Gates's new recruits lacked training. At Camden, on meeting experienced British troops, the Americans panicked and ran. Among those killed was Baron de Kalb, a German officer who had served with Washington at Valley Forge. A second American army in the South had gone down to defeat.

SPIES AND PLOTS

With the disaster at Camden, Patriot spirits sank to a new low. A further blow came in September 1780. General Benedict Arnold, a hero at Saratoga, had joined the British side. He had secretly agreed to let the British take over the fort at West Point, New York. His plot was discovered, however, and the fort was saved. Historians believe that Arnold, deeply in debt, accepted a large payment for his betrayal. Arnold was also resentful that Gates, and not he, had received most of the credit for the Saratoga victory.

Arnold was not the only famous American to betray the Patriot cause. Benjamin Franklin's secretary in Paris secretly turned over American plans to Britain. Historian Samuel Eliot Morison found that Ethan Allen told the British that he would stop fighting in return for a quarter of a million acres of Vermont land. Allen's defenders believe he was trying to put pressure on Congress to guarantee Vermont statehood. Any negotiation with the British during the war, however, was treason—a crime punishable by death.

THE TIDE TURNS IN THE SOUTH

In 1780 Washington put a new general, Nathanael Greene, in charge of the southern army. One of Washington's most able officers, Greene was the son of a Quaker preacher. He had been expelled from the Quakers for his belief in armed struggle against Britain. Greene began a policy of mercy toward Loyalists. He also won over the Cherokee Indians to the American side.

Greene's forces avoided full-scale battles. Instead, they let the British chase them around the countryside and wear themselves out. When they fought, even if they retreated, they made sure the British suffered heavily.

George Washington appears to the left of the American flag in this scene of the 1781 surrender of Cornwallis at Yorktown, Virginia. The artist, John Trumbull, painted many scenes of the American Revolution. HISTORY What was the significance of the British surrender?

"Another such victory will destroy the British army," grumbled a British leader on hearing of a costly battle.

THE END OF THE WAR

The war dragged into its sixth year. In London, opposition grew to Britain's war policies. Some British leaders began to think American independence would not be so bad.

The last year of the war was fought mostly in Virginia. Britain's Lord Cornwallis had set up a base at Yorktown on Chesapeake Bay. From there he could receive supplies by ship from New York.

Meanwhile, French forces came to the Americans' aid. Almost 6,000 well-trained, well-supplied troops landed in Rhode Island under the command of General Jean Rochambeau (roh–shahm–BOH). Washington had planned to use them to retake New York City. Washington then learned that a large French fleet had also arrived from the West Indies. Here was an opportunity. He could use the French fleet to cut Yorktown off from resupply. Cornwallis would then be trapped on land.

Washington and Rochambeau marched swiftly south with their armies. When British ships tried to reach Cornwallis, French ships drove them back. The American and French troops began to bombard Yorktown. Cornwallis realized his situation was hopeless. On October 19, 1781, he sent up the white flag and surrendered his army of 8,000.

Back in London, British leaders took the news hard. "It is all over!" gasped Lord North again and again. Indeed, he and other British leaders were soon forced to resign. Their defeat at the Battle of Yorktown convinced Britain's new leaders to begin peace talks with the Americans.

SECTION REVIEW

1. KEY TERMS partisan, Battle of Yorktown

2. PEOPLE George Rogers Clark, Bernardo de Gálvez, John Paul Jones, Banastre Tarleton, Nathanael Greene, Lord Cornwallis, Jean Rochambeau

3. COMPREHENSION Why did the fighting shift to the South in the last stage of the war?

4. COMPREHENSION Describe the events that led to the British defeat at Yorktown.

5. CRITICAL THINKING What difficulties might the United States have faced if France had not declared war on Britain?

3 Peace and Independence

In November 1783, over eight years after the Battle of Lexington and Concord, the last British troops sailed from New York City. As they left, American troops marched in. Benjamin Tallmadge, an American colonel, noted "the joy of meeting friends, who had long been separated by the cruel rigors of war." George Washington took leave of his officers at a New York tavern. After toasting them, Washington said, "I cannot come to each of you, but shall feel obliged if you will come and take me by the hand." Washington had finished the job assigned to him. Now, he said, he would "retire from the great theatre of action."

WHY THE AMERICANS WON

As you have read, Patriot forces faced many obstacles in the Revolutionary War. They lacked training and experience. They were ill-equipped. They were loosely organized. By contrast, British forces ranked among the best trained and equipped in the world. They were professional soldiers, not volunteers.

The Patriots won the war in spite of these disadvantages. Several factors aided them:

(1) British generals made errors in judgment. Many had been promoted through political connections rather than because of their ability. Their overconfidence caused crucial blunders at Saratoga and Yorktown.

Washington, on the other hand, proved to be an excellent leader. He had valuable experience from the French and Indian War. He also kept his spirit through difficult times, such as the winter at Valley Forge.

(2) Britain's rivals helped the Patriots. Loans and military aid from these nations proved essential to the American victory.

BIOGRAPHY

JOHN JAY (1745–1829) was a delegate to the First and Second Continental Congresses. He favored resistance to Britain, but not independence. Once independence was declared, however, Jay supported the Revolution. In 1779 Congress sent Jay to persuade Spain to recognize America's independence, but he failed. In 1782 Jay helped negotiate the treaty ending the Revolution. George Washington later made Jay the first Chief Justice of the United States.

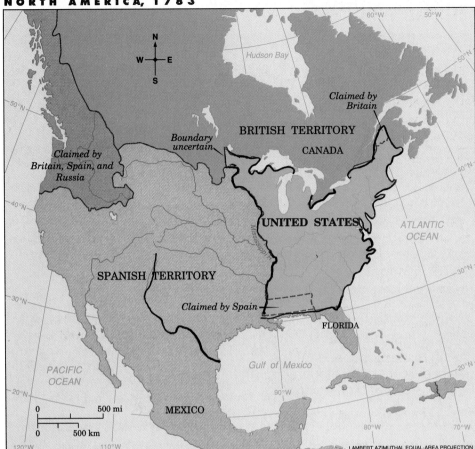

By signing the Treaty of Paris in 1783, Britain recognized American independence. What natural feature formed the western boundary of the United States at the time? Which nation claimed most of the land in the West? **CRITICAL THINKING** What indications does the map give that additional conflicts with Britain lay ahead?

(3) The British could not control the countryside. Though their navy allowed them to take cities on the coast, it could not bring complete victory.

(4) The Patriots had more to fight for. At stake were their property and their ideals. Far from their homes, the British and Hessians fought with less motivation.

THE COST OF THE WAR

About 25,000 Americans and 10,000 British lost their lives in the fighting. Many Americans died in prison after being captured by the British. Others starved or froze to death in military camps. Many of the survivors left the army penniless. They had received little or no pay while they served. After the war, many sold the titles to the western land they had received in order to have enough to eat.

The United States went deeply into debt to finance the war. Congress later gained the power to tax American trade and used such taxes to help pay off its war debts.

THE TREATY OF PARIS

In the year after the Battle of Yorktown, John Adams, Benjamin Franklin, and John Jay met with British and French diplomats in Paris. They hoped to negotiate a three-way peace treaty. However, the Americans did not trust the French. They believed France wanted American land for itself and its ally, Spain. As Jay put it, the United States could count on nobody "except on God and ourselves." The Americans therefore dealt separately with the British. After an agreement had been reached, Franklin tried to smooth things over with the French.

The final peace treaty was very favorable to the United States. The Treaty of Paris (1783) established that:

(1) The United States was independent.

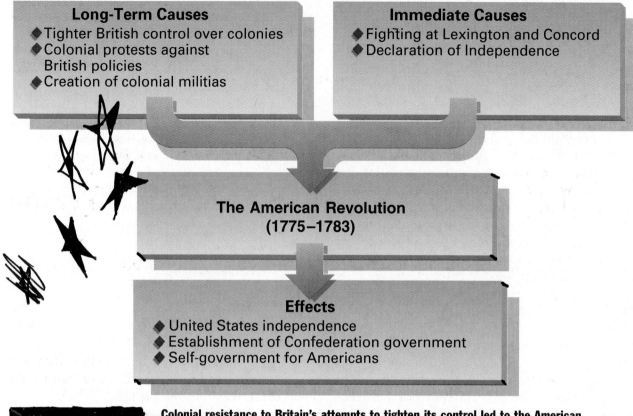

Long-Term Causes	Immediate Causes
◆ Tighter British control over colonies ◆ Colonial protests against British policies ◆ Creation of colonial militias	◆ Fighting at Lexington and Concord ◆ Declaration of Independence

The American Revolution (1775–1783)

Effects
◆ United States independence
◆ Establishment of Confederation government
◆ Self-government for Americans

Colonial resistance to Britain's attempts to tighten its control led to the American Revolution. **CRITICAL THINKING** Could the Revolution have been avoided? Why or why not?

(2) The boundaries of the United States would extend west to the Mississippi River. The nation would border Canada to the north and Spanish Florida to the south (map, page 211). The exact locations of these last two boundaries, however, would remain in dispute for some time.

(3) The United States would receive fishing rights off Newfoundland and Nova Scotia.

(4) Each side would repay debts owed from before the war.

(5) The British would return any slaves they had captured.

(6) Congress would recommend that states give back property taken from Loyalists.

Franklin's diplomatic skills impressed the French. He was proud when they titled him "the Washington of negotiations." Some Americans, however, were less impressed. Virginia tobacco planters, for example, owed Britain millions of dollars. They resented having to pay their debts. "If we are now to pay debts due the British merchants," complained George Mason, "what have we been fighting for all this while?"

Neither Britain nor the United States fully lived up to the terms of the Treaty of Paris. Americans did not repay their prewar debts to British merchants. Neither did they return Loyalist property.

For their part, the British refused to give up military outposts in the Great Lakes, such as Fort Detroit. Britain's continued presence on the western frontier would be a source of tension in the years to come.

THE WAR AND SOCIAL CHANGE

The Revolutionary War brought about important changes in American society. One of the most important came in land ownership. After Britain's defeat, the Proclamation of 1763 was null and void. As Native Americans had feared, white settlers rushed to seize land west of the Appalachians.

In addition, revolutionary leaders enriched themselves by taking over Loyalist property. In Pennsylvania, the state took over land belonging to the Penn family and paid the Penns but 13 percent of its value. The states also gave property to landless Americans. More Americans with land meant more Americans who could vote.

The new landowners took their power to the ballot box, pushing states to pay for education. Slavery was also affected. Massachusetts and New Hampshire had abolished it by 1784. Other northern states began moving toward emancipation—freeing of slaves.

EFFECTS OF THE AMERICAN REVOLUTION

The effects of the American Revolution spread around the world like ripples in a pond. As you will read in Chapter 12, the French Revolution of 1789 was inspired by the ideals set forth in the Declaration of Independence. Crushing debt from French efforts

to defeat Britain also helped bring on France's revolution. Another European nation, Poland, had long fought to preserve its independence from its neighbors, Austria and Prussia. Thaddeus Kosciusko, who had fought with the Americans, returned to Poland to lead its struggle for freedom.

The effects were not limited to the 1700s. Even in our own time, groups fighting against oppression and colonialism refer to the ideals of the American Revolution.

SECTION REVIEW

1. KEY TERM Treaty of Paris (1783)

2. PEOPLE John Jay

3. COMPREHENSION Describe some of the social changes following the Revolution.

4. COMPREHENSION In what ways did the American Revolution affect other independence movements in the world?

5. CRITICAL THINKING Of the factors that led to America's victory over Britain, which do you think was most important? Why?

CHAPTER 9 SUMMARY AND TIMELINE

1. The Revolutionary War divided American society. Washington's troops faced hardships and an experienced enemy. Yet the Americans won an important victory at Saratoga and gained the support of France.

2. Fierce fighting on many fronts, at sea as well as on land, led to Britain's defeat. The

tide turned against Britain when French and American forces combined to defeat the British at Yorktown.

3. In 1783 Britain signed a peace treaty recognizing United States independence. The American Revolution helped inspire other independence movements worldwide.

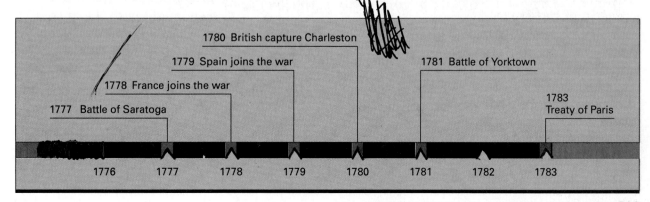

1777 Battle of Saratoga
1778 France joins the war
1779 Spain joins the war
1780 British capture Charleston
1781 Battle of Yorktown
1783 Treaty of Paris

1776 1777 1778 1779 1780 1781 1782 1783

PLACES TO LOCATE

Match each of the letters on the map with the places that are listed below. Then explain the importance of each place.

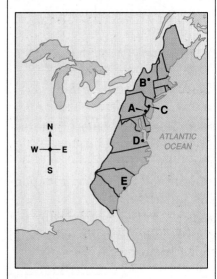

1. Charleston
2. Philadelphia
3. Saratoga
4. Trenton
5. Yorktown

KEY TERMS

Use the following terms to complete the sentences.

alliance
Battle of Saratoga
Battle of Yorktown
partisans ✓
Treaty of Paris (1783)

1. During the war in the South, bands of ____ on both sides fought bitterly.

2. The ____ convinced Britain to end the war.
3. Their ____ with France greatly aided the cause of the Patriots.
4. The boundaries of the United States were redrawn under the ____.
5. The French joined the Revolutionary War after the ____.

PEOPLE TO IDENTIFY

Identify the following people and tell why each one was important.

1. George Rogers Clark
2. Lord Cornwallis
3. Bernardo de Gálvez
4. Nathanael Greene
5. John Jay
6. Marquis de Lafayette

REVIEWING THE FACTS

1. What were some of the problems that George Washington faced as commander of the Patriot forces?
2. Why did Washington consider Lord Dunmore a threat during the Revolutionary War?
3. Why is the Battle of Saratoga considered to be the turning point of the war?
4. Which diplomat helped persuade France to become America's ally during the Revolutionary War?

5. Why did privateers join the fight against the British navy?
6. What was Spain's role in the war?
7. Which Patriot military leader took a bribe from the British?
8. How was Cornwallis forced to surrender at Yorktown?
9. What were the major effects of the Revolutionary War?
10. What aspects of the Treaty of Paris did each side fail to live up to?

CITIZENSHIP

1. Only a minority of the colonists supported the Revolution against Britain. Do you think they had a right to act for the equally large minority of colonists who did not take sides? Explain your answer.
2. Explain George Washington's statement that "A free-man, contending for liberty on his own ground, is superior to any slavish mercenary on earth."
3. A number of free black men fought with the Patriot forces. What special reason might they have had for backing the Patriot cause?

PRACTICING YOUR SKILL

Use your skill in interpreting flow charts to answer the questions about the chart below:

```
┌─────────────────────────┐
│   Second Continental    │
│    Congress Meets       │
│     May 10, 1775        │
└─────────────────────────┘
            │
            ▼
┌─────────────────────────┐
│   Delegates Discuss     │
│        Issues           │
└─────────────────────────┘
            │
            ▼
┌─────────────────────────┐
│   Richard Henry Lee     │
│  Proposes Independence  │
│      June 7, 1776       │
└─────────────────────────┘
            │
            ▼
┌─────────────────────────┐
│   Committee Draws Up     │
│ Declaration of Independence │
└─────────────────────────┘
            │
            ▼
┌─────────────────────────┐
│     Delegates Vote      │
│  to Adopt Declaration   │
│      July 4, 1776       │
└─────────────────────────┘
```

1. What did the delegates do first?

2. How long after the delegates' first meeting was independence from Great Britain proposed?

3. Who proposed that the United States become independent?

4. When was the Declaration of Independence adopted?

CRITICAL THINKING SKILLS

1. ANALYZING How did Thomas Paine's *The Crisis* influence Americans during the Revolutionary War? Which books have influenced you? Why?

2. MAKING A JUDGMENT Explain the choices facing slaves during the Revolutionary War. If you had been a slave at the time, which side would you have supported? Why?

3. IDENTIFYING CAUSE AND EFFECT Make a diagram showing the events that led to the Battle of Saratoga. Also show how this battle affected the course of the war.

4. FORMING A HYPOTHESIS Other nations aided the Patriot cause. Could the Patriots have won the Revolutionary War without such aid? Use facts to support your answer.

PROJECTS AND ACTIVITIES

1. GIVING AN ORAL REPORT Find out about one of the following topics: African American soldiers, Valley Forge, Hessians, women in the war, the U.S. Navy. Present an oral report to the class.

2. WRITING DIALOGUE Write a dramatic scene between two members of the same family who support opposite sides in the Revolutionary War.

3. WRITING A DIARY Imagine that you are a soldier at Valley Forge during the winter of 1777–1778. Write down your experiences in the form of several diary entries.

WRITING ABOUT TOPICS IN AMERICAN HISTORY

1. CONNECTING WITH LITERATURE A selection from *Sarah Bishop* by Scott O'Dell appears on pages 642–643. Read it and answer the questions. Then answer the following question: Would it have been difficult to remain neutral if you were a colonist during the events of 1775? Why or why not?

2. APPLYING THEMES: AMERICAN CULTURE During the American Revolution, states ended the practice of supporting churches with government-collected taxes. Do research and write a report about the separation of church and state in Virginia.

Having won their independence, Americans set forth in the 1780s to build a new nation. This George Caleb Bingham painting shows famed pioneer Daniel Boone.

10 A Union of Thirteen States (1781–1787)

KEY EVENTS

1781 Articles of Confederation adopted

1783 Treaty of Paris

1783 Massachusetts outlaws slavery

1785 Ordinance of 1785 adopted

1787 Northwest Ordinance adopted

1 Forging a Republic

 Section Focus

Key Terms republic ■ democracy ■ legislative ■ executive ■ judicial ■ confederation ■ Articles of Confederation ■ ratify ■ republicanism

Main Idea With independence, Americans faced the difficult task of creating stable governments.

Objectives As you read, look for answers to these questions:
1. What important ideas lay behind the state constitutions?
2. What were the powers and structure of the first national government?
3. How did the American Revolution encourage social change?

The words of Thomas Paine had urged Americans on in their fight for liberty. Now his words hailed the peace: "The times that tried men's souls are over and the greatest and completest revolution the world ever knew gloriously and happily accomplished."

> **"Y**ou and I did not imagine when the first war with Britain was over that the revolution was just begun."
>
> —*Harrison Gray Otis*

So it must have seemed for those who fought for one goal—independence. Americans, joyful at their country's freedom, were less aware of the new struggles beginning to take shape. These struggles centered on how

to bring to life the ideals of the Declaration of Independence.

Harrison Gray Otis, a future leader of Massachusetts, was eighteen when the peace treaty with Britain was signed. Years later he wrote a friend, "You and I did not imagine when the first war with Britain was over that the revolution was just begun."

THE AMERICAN REPUBLIC

Most Americans agreed that their new nation should be a republic. In a republic the people choose representatives, who make the laws. Their republic would be based on democratic principles. A democracy is a system of government by the people. Never again would a king tell the Americans what to do.

The form of most colonial governments had been shaped by charters. These were written contracts between the Crown and proprietors or between the Crown and a corporation.

Written compacts such as the Mayflower Compact also had a long tradition in America. It was only natural that Americans wanted to write down how their government should work.

Between 1776 and 1780, during the Revolution, eleven of the thirteen former colonies drew up a constitution, a plan for government. Connecticut and Rhode Island reworded their colonial charters. Never before in history had people written down the rules under which they were to be governed. Several principles underlay these constitutions. One was the idea of compact, of people making an agreement for the common good. Another was that good government is based on the consent of the people. A third was that there are fundamental laws that differ from ordinary laws. These fundamental laws are so basic they cannot be changed by mere lawmakers.

States based their governments on these principles. In all thirteen states, the duties of governing were divided among three branches. The most powerful of these branches was the legislative branch, which made the laws. The executive branch, made up of a governor or council, enforced these laws. Interpreting laws and punishing lawbreakers was the job of the judicial branch.

THE QUESTION OF THE WEST

While the states set up their own governments, they debated the way the country should be run. In 1776 the Continental Congress had begun work on a plan for a national government. Members proposed that the states should join together in a loose union, or confederation. They drew up a plan called the Articles of Confederation. The Articles of Confederation described a structure, already in effect, in which the states held most of the power.

By 1779, twelve states had ratified—approved—the Articles. Maryland refused. Its people were upset over the huge chunks of western lands claimed by other states. Control of this fertile land between the Appalachians and the Mississippi River would more

than double the size of some states. People in Maryland saw this growth in size and power as a threat to their small state. They said that the western lands had been won by the "common blood and treasury of the thirteen states." Before ratifying the Articles, Maryland insisted that these lands be turned over to the nation.

States such as New York and Virginia opposed Maryland's demands. Still, these large states understood the need for a central government. Virginia declared itself willing to "make great sacrifices to the common interests of America." One by one the larger states gave up their claims. In March 1781, seven months before the victory at Yorktown, Maryland adopted the Articles. The new government was established.

THE FIRST NATIONAL GOVERNMENT

Each state sent between two and seven delegates to the Congress. No matter the number of delegates, each state had only one vote. As a result, small states had as much say in the government as large states.

Many Americans were suspicious of central government, preferring power to be left to the states. The Articles of Confederation sharply limited the Congress's powers. For instance, only the states had the power to tax and enforce laws. Congress, however, had more power over foreign affairs. It could wage war and make peace. It could also govern trade with the Indian nations. To create laws or make any other major decisions, nine of the thirteen states had to agree. All thirteen states had to vote in favor of any change in the Articles themselves.

Americans had learned to fear the power of kings and royal governors. For this reason, the executive branch was not run by one person. A three-person committee, chosen by Congress, led that branch. Like the Congress itself, the committee's powers were limited. In sum, the Articles of Confederation created a league of independent states. The system set up to govern this league had very limited authority over the states.

THE STATES' WESTERN LAND CLAIMS

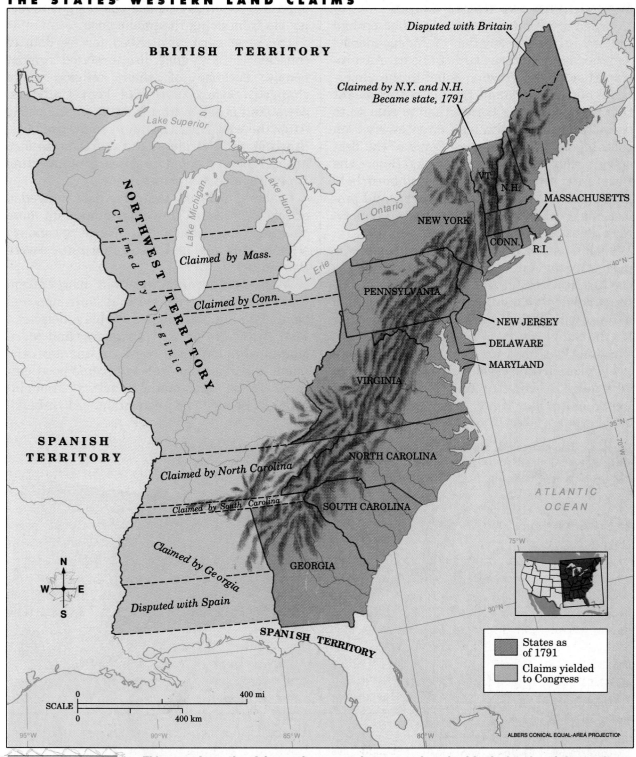

BRITISH TERRITORY

Disputed with Britain

Claimed by N.Y. and N.H.
Became state, 1791

VT.

N.H.

MASSACHUSETTS

Lake Superior

Lake Michigan

Lake Huron

L. Ontario

NEW YORK

CONN.

R.I.

NORTHWEST TERRITORY

Claimed by Virginia

Claimed by Mass.

L. Erie

Claimed by Conn.

PENNSYLVANIA

NEW JERSEY

DELAWARE

MARYLAND

VIRGINIA

SPANISH
TERRITORY

Claimed by North Carolina

NORTH CAROLINA

ATLANTIC
OCEAN

Claimed by South Carolina

SOUTH CAROLINA

Claimed by Georgia

GEORGIA

75°W

Disputed with Spain

SPANISH TERRITORY

N
W E
S

40°N

35°N

70°W

States as
of 1791

Claims yielded
to Congress

30°N

SCALE

0   400 mi

0   400 km

95°W   90°W   85°W   80°W

ALBERS CONICAL EQUAL-AREA PROJECTION

MAP SKILLS This map shows the claims various coastal states made to land in the interior of the continent. Which states did not have western land claims? Which state disputed its claims with Spain? **CRITICAL THINKING** How did the states' decision to give up their claims help unify the country?

REPUBLICANISM AND SOCIAL CHANGE

"All men are created equal . . ." Jefferson had written in the Declaration of Independence. Americans took these words to heart. As a result, they held a growing belief in the importance of the individual. For many this meant that no person was born either to rule or to obey. In the army the men often insisted on choosing their own leaders. Some of the best officers thus came from the ranks. Before the Revolution only the rich and well-born held public office. After the war, artisans and professionals achieved a new position in society. Many served in the new state legislatures.

This sense of equality among people was part of **republicanism**. Republicanism was the idea that, for the country to thrive, its citizens needed certain virtues. These included a sense of equality, simplicity, and sacrifice for the public good.

Republicanism wore many faces. It was a lawyer complaining about the great wig worn by a judge. It was Benjamin Franklin hoping his daughter would not wear jewelry. It was opposing theaters because they might divert people from doing the public good.

The new spirit also called for freedom of conscience. Laws that discriminated against people because of their religion were changed. Some states had kept Catholics, Jews, and atheists from holding public office. After the war, states began to end those laws. Starting with Virginia, state after state also struck down the old practice of supporting churches with tax money.

Leaders believed that the nation needed educated citizens. They helped open up more chances for education. New secondary schools, colleges, and state universities were started.

Women's education received more attention. The new spirit held that both men and women had important roles to play in society. Men were to be breadwinners and decision-makers. Women were to manage the home and raise children to become good citizens. To be wise mothers, it was thought, women needed an education. As Abigail

The new nation guaranteed the rights of Jews and Roman Catholics. The nation's oldest synagogue (left) stands in Newport, Rhode Island, and the first major Catholic cathedral (right) was built in Baltimore. **RELIGION** How did republicanism support freedom of religion?

Adams, a supporter of women's rights, explained, "If we mean to have heroes, statesmen, and philosophers, we should have learned women." New England towns began holding summer schools for girls while the boys worked in the fields. Other schools added "female departments." Some women opened private schools for girls.

> "**I**f we mean to have heroes, statesmen, and philosophers, we should have learned women."
>
> —*Abigail Adams*

CHANGES FOR AFRICAN AMERICANS

Americans also reconsidered the institution of slavery. The feeling grew that slavery was not in keeping with the ideals of the new nation. "It did, indeed, at least become very hard for us to listen each year to the preamble to the Declaration of Independence and still remain the owners and users and catchers of slaves," wrote a southern planter.

The antislavery movement grew with the Revolution. Vermont (not yet a state) banned slavery in a constitution it adopted in 1777. Rhode Island and Connecticut had restricted the slave trade in 1774. Virginia, Pennsylvania, and Maryland followed their lead. Virginia, Delaware, and Maryland also passed laws saying that an owner could free a slave without gaining the approval of the government.

In Massachusetts, a slave woman named Elizabeth Freeman went to court, demanding her freedom on the grounds that the state constitution declared, "All men are born free and equal." The jury agreed with her. Slavery ended in the state in 1783.

THE AFRICAN AMERICAN CHURCH

Church groups were among the first to reach out to African Americans. Quakers in Pennsylvania made that state a center of antislav-

ery activity. The number of Baptists had swelled during the Great Awakening. Now they began to license African American preachers, both slave and free.

With independence, free blacks too began to think of themselves differently. A leader of the free black community in Philadelphia was Richard Allen. Born a slave, Allen had been allowed to hire himself out for wages. He finally saved enough money, $2,000, to buy his freedom. He became a traveling Methodist preacher. Then in 1786 he decided to settle in Philadelphia. There he became

BIOGRAPHY

ELIZABETH FREEMAN (1744–1829), also known as Mumbet, was a slave whose husband had fought and died for the Patriot cause. One day Freeman was struck by her owner with a hot kitchen shovel. She left the house, refusing to return. She had heard about Massachusetts's new constitution and was determined to win her rights. Freeman took the case against slavery to court. Her victory in 1781 led to the end of slavery in the state. She lived the rest of her long life as a free woman and a respected member of the community.

This painted tray portrays Reverend Lemuel Haynes, who fought in the Revolution at Concord and Ticonderoga, preaching to a New England congregation. CULTURAL PLURALISM How did churches help the African American community in the late 1700s?

one of the founders of the Free African Society. The Free African Society was the first self-help organization for African Americans. It gave African Americans a way to meet and work on their problems. The Society also helped the needy and paid for the education of black children.

In 1793 yellow fever swept through Philadelphia. The few doctors who remained healthy could not deal with the numbers of sick and dying. The Free African Society offered its services to the whole community. Blacks then nursed the sick as well as buried the dead. In doing so, they risked, and sometimes lost, their lives. They nursed "with a degree of patience and tenderness that did them great credit," wrote Dr. Benjamin Rush.

In 1794 Richard Allen started a Methodist church for African Americans. Until then no such church existed. Allen's church, with its push for educating adults and children, became a model for other African American churches.

SECTION REVIEW

1. KEY TERMS republic, democracy, legislative, executive, judicial, confederation, Articles of Confederation, ratify, republicanism

2. PEOPLE AND PLACES Virginia, Elizabeth Freeman, Richard Allen, Philadelphia

3. COMPREHENSION What three ideas were expressed in the new state constitutions?

4. COMPREHENSION Why did Americans want a weak executive branch?

5. CRITICAL THINKING How did the experience of the Revolution contribute to the popularity of republicanism?

Many people begin the task of writing by developing an outline. An outline is a collection of notes organized by their importance. It is often most useful when arranged into three categories: main ideas, subtopics that support the main ideas, and details that add more information. A good outline provides a framework for the writer to follow. It summarizes important information and shows how ideas and facts are related.

Outlining is useful for readers too. Outlining what you read will give you clear notes about the main ideas, subtopics, and details.

FIRST STEPS IN OUTLINING

To outline Section 1 of this chapter, begin by writing the title, "Forging a Republic," on a piece of paper. Then look for the main ideas of the section. Check the six main headings to see if they express the main ideas. If you use the heading titles as the source for main ideas and label them with Roman numerals, your outline will look like this:

Forging a Republic

I. The American Republic
II. The Question of the West
III. The First National Government
IV. Republicanism and Social Change
V. Changes for African Americans
VI. The African American Church

Now identify the subtopics under main topic I. One possibility is to look for the main idea of each paragraph. For example, the first paragraph describes the system of government Americans wanted and could be summarized "Americans form a republic based on democratic principles." Label subtopics with capital letters and list them below the main topic.

Then read the paragraph to find the supporting details. Briefly list details under the subtopic, numbering each detail with an Arabic numeral. When paragraphs are short, you may want to combine them under one head. For example, information from the third and fourth paragraphs may both be listed under "Ideas of state constitutions." The first part of the outline should look something like this:

Forging a Republic

I. The American Republic
  A. Americans form a republic based on democratic principles
    1. Choose representatives
    2. Government by the people
  B. Colonial governments
    1. Charters—written contracts
    2. Compacts
  C. Ideas of state constitutions
    1. Compact
    2. Power comes from the people
    3. Fundamental laws
  D. State governments divided into three branches
    1. Legislative makes laws
    2. Executive enforces laws
    3. Judicial interprets laws

PRACTICING YOUR SKILL

Reread the parts of Section 1 (pages 217–222) in this chapter that relate to main ideas II, III, IV, V, and VI. Then answer these questions on a separate sheet of paper.

1. Which of the following would *not* be included as a subtopic under main idea II, "The Question of the West"?
  a. Planning for a national government
  b. Western lands double states' size
  c. Articles of Confederation ratified

2. Which details support the subtopic "Confederation Congress"?
  a. Each state has one vote
  b. Nine states must agree to all important decisions
  c. Republicanism and social change

3. "Richard Allen was a founder of the Free African Society." Under which main idea would that detail go?
  a. Republicanism and Social Change
  b. Changes for African Americans
  c. The African American Church

2 Organizing the Western Lands

Section Focus

Key Terms Northwest Territory
■ ordinance ■ survey ■ Northwest
Ordinance

Main Idea The laws passed to deal with
the western lands were the greatest
achievement of the Congress under the
Articles of Confederation.

Objectives As you read, look for the answers to these questions:
1. How did the Confederation Congress organize western lands?
2. How could a territory become a state?
3. What civil rights did the Northwest Ordinance protect?

On a spring day in 1775, 30 men gathered in the mountains of Virginia. Their leader was Daniel Boone, a famous woodsman and scout. He had been hired to build a road to Kentucky. Following Boone's orders, the axmen chopped down trees, connected trails, and widened buffalo paths. Working through the spring and summer, they created a wagon road over the Appalachian Mountains. This was the Wilderness Road.

The Wilderness Road led through the Cumberland Gap into the land the Iroquois called *Kentake* ("meadowland"). Daniel Boone had first crossed into the Kentucky River valley in 1769. The region teemed with game—buffalo, deer, beaver. The Indians warned Boone

Trailblazer Daniel Boone travels to Kentucky in this painting by William Ranney. GEOGRAPHY Why might it have been difficult for settlers to travel on the trail shown in the painting?

Courtesy of Time-Life Books Inc.

THE ORDINANCE OF 1785

Public lands were divided into townships

Ohio

Each township was divided into 36 sections

One section reserved to support schools

6	5	4	3	2	1
7	8	9	10	11	12
18	17	16	15	14	13
19	20	21	22	23	24
30	29	28	27	26	25
31	32	33	34	35	36

6 miles

← 6 miles →

Each section could be divided into smaller lots

Half section (320 acres)

Quarter section (160 acres)

Half quarter

1 mile

← 1 mile →

CHART SKILLS

The Ordinance of 1785 established a system, shown in this diagram, for dividing up public lands in the Northwest Territory. How did the Ordinance divide up townships? CRITICAL THINKING Why were few settlers able to buy an entire section? Who ended up buying many of the sections?

to stay away, but he paid no heed. When he tried to settle there with his family, the Indians attacked and killed his oldest son.

Now it was 1775. Revolution was in the air. Restless Americans no longer felt bound by the Proclamation of 1763 (page 171). The Virginia militia had crossed the mountains and defeated the Indians in battle. In the peace treaty that followed, the Indians gave up their claim to Kentucky. The ink on the treaty was not dry before Boone had been hired to make a road. In 1775 Kentucky had 100 white settlers. In 1780 there were about 20,000.

THE NORTHWEST TERRITORY

The Treaty of Paris (1783) granted the United States the land between the Appalachians and the Mississippi River. In effect, this was the eastern drainage of the Mississippi River valley. This region is cut in two by the Ohio River. The Ohio itself is a major river—one of the largest within the United States.

Although thousands of pioneers had settled south of the Ohio, few had moved north of it. For one thing, the Indians there remained strong and determined to keep their land. For another, it was a land of no government.

States had claimed the region north of the Ohio, but in name only. Then, in order to pass the Articles of Confederation, they had given up their claims. This region, the Northwest Territory, now belonged to the national government.

What was the best way to govern these lands? Among the proposals was one by Thomas Jefferson, now a member of the Congress. Jefferson wanted to divide the region into fourteen territories, with names like Polypotamia and Michigania. When the population of a territory equaled the population of the smallest state, it would be able to join the Union.

Congress never passed Jefferson's plan. Westerners did not like the plan because it called for rectangular boundaries. They wanted state boundaries based on natural features such as rivers and mountains. Easterners objected to the number of states. The West, they said, would soon gain control of Congress. They also doubted that settlers could rule themselves. New lands needed the firm hand of authority, they argued.

From these debates emerged new laws on settling and governing the Northwest Territory. These new laws were described as ordinances—government regulations.

THE ORDINANCE OF 1785

The first of these ordinances had more to do with selling the land than governing it. Members of Congress were eager to raise money to pay off the nation's debts. In 1785 they

The Northwest Ordinance (1787)

The Northwest Ordinance outlined a governmental structure for the Northwest Territory, the land north of the Ohio River and westward to the Mississippi River. Provisions in the Ordinance for freedom of religion, civil liberties, and free public education would eventually be incorporated into the constitutions of state governments across the nation.

That the following articles shall be considered as articles of compact between the original States and the people in the said territory, and forever remain unalterable, unless by common consent, to wit:

Article 1. No person . . . shall ever be molested on account of his mode of worship or religious sentiments. . . .

Article 2. The inhabitants of the said territory shall always be entitled to the benefits of habeas corpus, and of trial by jury. . . . No man shall be deprived of his liberty or property, but by the judgment of his peers or the law of the land. . . .

Article 3. Religion, morality, and knowledge being necessary to good government and the happiness of mankind, schools and the means of education shall forever be encouraged. The utmost good faith shall always be observed toward the Indians; their lands and property shall never be taken from them without their consent. . . .

Article 4. The said territory, and the States which may be formed therein, shall forever remain a part of . . . the United States of America. . . .

Article 5. There shall be formed in the said territory, not less than three nor more than five States.

Article 6. There shall be neither slavery nor involuntary servitude in the said territory, otherwise than in the punishment of crimes. . . .

From F. N. Thorpe, ed., *Federal and State Constitutions,* Vol. II, p. 957.

ANALYZING HISTORICAL DOCUMENTS

1. What does the Northwest Ordinance specify about slavery in the Northwest Territory?

2. Which part of the Northwest Ordinance shows the influence of the Magna Carta?

3. If you were a settler, would you want to live in the Northwest Territory? Why, or why not?

---

passed an ordinance calling for the land to be surveyed. (To survey means to measure land to determine its exact boundaries.)

The goal of this survey was to divide the Northwest Territory into squares, called townships. Six miles long and six miles wide, each township was further divided into 36 equal sections. Five of these sections remained federal land. One section belonged to the people, to be used to pay for public schools. This plan showed the value the young nation placed on education.

The Ordinance of 1785 called for each of the remaining 30 sections to be sold to the highest bidder for not less than one dollar an acre. Each section was 640 acres in size. In those days $640 was a big sum of money, and few people could afford to buy a section. Instead, groups of investors in the East pooled their money to buy the land. Then they divided their sections into smaller lots. They sold these lots to settlers at a profit.

THE NORTHWEST ORDINANCE

Congress next turned its attention to governing the Northwest Territory. In 1787 it passed the Northwest Ordinance. This law stated that the Congress would choose a governor and three judges to rule the territory. Over time, the Northwest Territory was to be carved into not fewer than three and not more than five states.

The Ordinance described the way a territory could become a state.

(1) The first step was for 5,000 free men to settle in the territory. Those settlers could then elect an assembly that would work with the governor and judges.

(2) When the population of an area topped 60,000 free citizens, they could ask to join the Union. If Congress voted to admit the area, it would become a state "on equal footing with the original states in all respects whatsoever."

The Northwest Ordinance set three other important conditions.

(1) The citizens in those lands would have freedom of religion and speech, the right to trial by jury, and protection from unfair punishments.

(2) Settlers had to treat Indians fairly.

(3) Slavery was banned in the territory. This meant that the future states of Wisconsin, Indiana, Ohio, Illinois, and Michigan would never know human bondage.

The Northwest Ordinance proved to be a good plan that lasted longer than the Confederation. It protected settlers' freedom and allowed frontier governments to change as the population changed. As the United States grew, the Northwest Ordinance became a model for the settlement of other territories.

MAP SKILLS

The Northwest Territory was eventually divided into five states, with the western portion becoming part of a sixth state, Minnesota. What physical feature made up the western border of the territory? The southern border? The northern border? CRITICAL THINKING How might settlers from the eastern part of the country have traveled to the Northwest Territory?

THE NORTHWEST TERRITORY

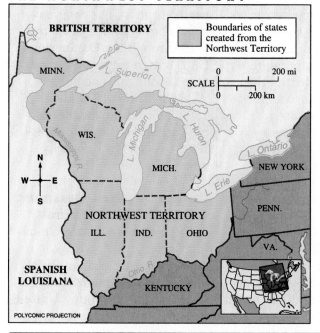

BRITISH TERRITORY

Boundaries of states created from the Northwest Territory

MINN.

L. Superior

SCALE 0 — 200 mi
0 — 200 km

WIS.

L. Michigan

L. Huron

Mississippi R.

MICH.

L. Ontario

NEW YORK

N W E S

L. Erie

PENN.

NORTHWEST TERRITORY

ILL. | IND. | OHIO

VA.

Ohio R.

SPANISH LOUISIANA

KENTUCKY

POLYCONIC PROJECTION

SECTION REVIEW

1. KEY TERMS Northwest Territory, ordinance, survey, Northwest Ordinance

2. PEOPLE AND PLACES Daniel Boone, Wilderness Road, Ohio River

3. COMPREHENSION According to the Ordinance of 1785, how were township sections distributed?

4. COMPREHENSION Under the Northwest Ordinance, how could a region become a state?

5. CRITICAL THINKING How were republican values expressed in the way Congress organized and governed the Northwest Territory?

Soon after the first English colonies were set up, settlers began to move inland from the Atlantic coastal plains. The rugged Appalachian Mountains, however, were a serious barrier to these moves.

Compared with the Rocky Mountains or the Sierra Nevada of the West, the Appalachian Mountains are not very high. The tallest peak in the range, which stretches from Canada to Alabama, is less than 7,000 feet. Yet for the early English colonists, these rugged highlands were like a wall, blocking movement westward.

Some pioneers were able to take advantage of a broad lowland, the Great Valley, which runs down the center of the Appalachians from New York to Georgia. Following the course of the Shenandoah and other rivers, the Indians' Great Trading Path and the settlers' Great Valley Road went through this valley. Pioneers traveled southwest from Pennsylvania along these trails.

GATEWAYS TO THE WEST

Rivers also cut paths through the mountains. The Mohawk River valley connected the Hudson River with lowlands leading to the Great Lakes. This was of little help to settlers, however, since the path ran through Iroquois land.

From the Middle Colonies, the Ohio River was the main route westward. To get to the

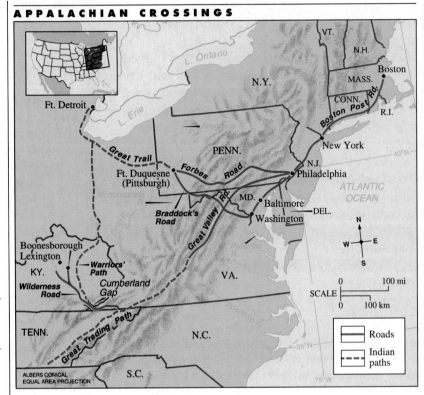

APPALACHIAN CROSSINGS

river, settlers followed troop trails over the Appalachians. At the point where the Allegheny and Monongahela rivers join to become the Ohio, the French had build Fort Duquesne. In their campaign to capture this fort during the French and Indian War, British troops cut two roads through the mountains.

THE WILDERNESS ROAD

In the southern Appalachians, a steeply cut "notch" called the Cumberland Gap provides a natural pass. An Indian trail, the Warriors Path, went through the gap, connecting Cherokee towns in the Carolinas with Indian settlements in the Ohio Valley.

In 1775 an investors' group made an agreement with the Cherokee for land in present-day Kentucky. The company hired Daniel Boone to clear a trail through the Cumberland Gap. With a crew of 30 woodsmen, Boone marked out the Wilderness Road. By about 1800, more than 200,000 people had taken the Wilderness Road to settle in Kentucky and Tennessee.

CRITICAL THINKING QUESTIONS

1. What physical features helped settlers who were moving west?

2. Why was settlement west of the Appalachian Mountains important to the young United States?

3 Problems at Home and Abroad

★ Section Focus

Key Terms   inflation ■ debtor ■ creditor

Main Idea   The weakness of the central government under the Articles of Confederation led to tensions between states and to problems with currency, debt, and trade.

Objectives   As you read, look for answers to these questions:
1.   What economic problems did the new national government face?
2.   How did Britain and Spain threaten the security of the new nation?
3.   What tensions existed between states under the Articles of Confederation?

The Northwest Ordinance was the greatest triumph of the Confederation Congress. In dealing with other matters, however, Congress did poorly. George Washington, at home in Mount Vernon, read newspaper stories about quarrels between states and about Congress's inaction. It seemed that the country had lost sight of the ideals for which he had fought. In a letter to John Jay he told of his despair: "From the high ground we stood upon, from the plain path which invited our footsteps, to be so fallen! So lost!"

MONEY TROUBLES

The issues that worried Washington were not all political. Many were financial. Americans carried several different kinds of bills in their purses. A person might have bills issued by the national government, bills issued by the states, and foreign coins. The confusion caused many merchants to stop accepting paper money issued by other states. They could not be sure of the value of these bills.

The merchants' distrust was often well-placed. Both Congress and the states issued paper money without hard currency—gold or silver coin—to back it. As a result, the money lost value.

The result of all this worthless money was high inflation. In a time of inflation, prices rise because the value of money is dropping. This helps debtors, people who borrow money. Debtors gain if they can pay back a debt with money worth less than the original loan.

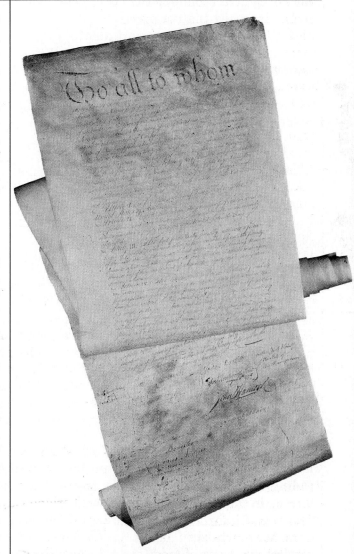

The Articles of Confederation, shown above, described the structure of the first government of the United States. **CONSTITUTIONAL HERITAGE** Which was more powerful under the Articles, the states or the national government?

Creditors lend money. They include merchants and the well-to-do. No creditor wants to be repaid in money that is worth less than the original loan. In each state, debtors and creditors battled over the amount of paper money issued by the government.

THE DEBT PROBLEM

Perhaps the greatest problem facing Congress was that it could not tax. It depended entirely on the states to give it the money it needed. The states had their own expenses and rarely sent money to the Congress. Some people proposed that Congress be allowed to raise money through an import duty, a tax on imported goods. Resistance from the states killed the plan.

Without money, the new nation found itself unable to pay its debts. The largest debt was the one that remained from the Revolution. Congress had borrowed large sums to fight the war. France, Holland, Spain, and European banks had made some of those loans.

The United States owed money to its own citizens as well. Many of the soldiers who had served in the war had not been paid. As prices rose, so did their demands for their wages. In June 1783 several hundred soldiers surrounded the state house in Philadelphia. The soldiers cursed and threatened the members of Congress meeting inside. Angry soldiers thrust their bayonets through the windows. Forced to flee, members of Congress showed how powerless they were.

INTERNATIONAL PROBLEMS

Congress also found that it did not have the power to earn the respect of other nations. Having fought their way out of the British Empire, Americans were now shut out of old trading patterns. Britain made it hard for American ships to trade with the West Indies. Britain also refused to give up its forts in the West. The new nation did not have the military muscle to remove those forts.

Spain and the United States quarreled over the boundary of Florida. Like Britain, Spain blocked American shipping in the West In-

WEAKNESSES OF THE ARTICLES OF CONFEDERATION

Congress

▶ Had one house
▶ Laws were difficult to pass (needed approval of nine out of thirteen states)
▶ Had no power to collect taxes, regulate trade, coin money, or establish armed forces
▶ Congress was responsible to the state legislatures, not to the people

Executive

▶ No President or Chief Executive

Courts

▶ No system of national courts

CHART SKILLS

Which branches of government did not exist under the Articles? CRITICAL THINKING How might the absence of these branches have weakened the national government?

dies. Even worse, Spain threatened to restrict American use of the lower Mississippi River. Development of the western lands depended on this water link with world markets.

THE NOT-SO-UNITED STATES

With the Revolution over, the threat of a common enemy no longer united the thirteen states. The Confederation Congress did not provide that unity. Just gathering enough delegates for a vote was hard. Getting them to agree was harder still.

No courts existed to settle disputes among member states. Pennsylvania and Connecticut nearly went to war over a disputed piece of land. Arguments and bad feelings also grew as each state began to pursue its own trade policy. The northern states imposed duties on imported goods. Delaware and the southern states did not. Many states placed heavy taxes on products from other states.

Thomas Jefferson saw that the states were growing more and more apart. Worried that they might go to war with each other, he wrote, "I find . . . the pride of independence taking deep and dangerous hold on the hearts of individual states."

Yet for several reasons the Articles of Confederation were not a complete failure.

(1) Americans had wanted a weak government and would have rejected a stronger one.

(2) The years after the war were difficult times—it would not have been easy for any government to rule.

(3) Given the problems the nation faced then, people might have been unhappy with any government in power.

(4) The Confederation had made wise and lasting decisions with respect to western lands.

The Confederation filled an important role in the years after the Revolution. As time went on, however, growing numbers of Americans began to agree that the Confederation Congress needed more power. If not, they feared that the thirteen states might become thirteen nations. These small countries could become prey to the armies of Britain and Spain. The United States had won the war. But could it survive the peace?

CHAPTER 10 SUMMARY AND TIMELINE

1. After independence, Americans set out to create governments based on the republican ideals of equality, religious freedom, and education. The Articles of Confederation set up a weak national government, leaving most power to the states.

2. The Confederation Congress passed the Ordinance of 1785, which organized the land between the Appalachians and the Mississippi River. Its greatest achievement was the Northwest Ordinance, which established the procedure for new lands to become states.

3. The weakness of the national government created by the Articles of Confederation led to economic problems, disputes between states, and difficulties standing up to foreign countries. Many Americans began to think they needed a stronger government.

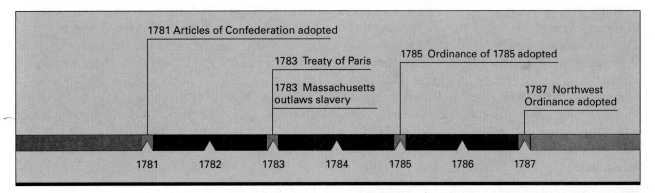

1781 Articles of Confederation adopted

1783 Treaty of Paris

1783 Massachusetts outlaws slavery

1785 Ordinance of 1785 adopted

1787 Northwest Ordinance adopted

1781 1782 1783 1784 1785 1786 1787

Chapter 10 REVIEW

Places to Locate

Match each of the letters on the map with the places that are listed below.

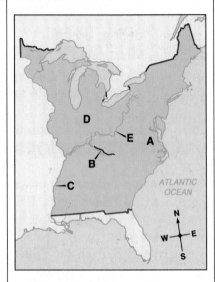

1. Mississippi River
2. Northwest Territory
3. Virginia
4. Wilderness Road
5. Ohio River

Key Terms

Use the following terms to complete the sentences.

Articles of Confederation
creditor
debtor
executive
judicial
Northwest Ordinance
ratify
republicanism

1. Inflation is better for a ____ than for a ____.

2. The ____ branch of government is responsible for enforcing laws.
3. In the early days of the United States, the ____ set up a weak national government.
4. A sense of equality and the virtue of working together for the common good are parts of ____.
5. The ____ set up a system for turning western territories into states.
6. Maryland refused to ____ the Articles of Confederation until other states gave up their western land claims.
7. The ____ branch of government interprets the nation's laws.

People to Identify

Identify the following people and tell why each one was important.

1. Richard Allen
2. Daniel Boone
3. Elizabeth Freeman

Reviewing the Facts

1. What three principles underlay state constitutions?
2. Why did it take nearly four years to ratify the Articles of Confederation?
3. Describe the organization of the government under the Articles of Confederation.
4. How did republican ideals affect African Americans?

5. What objections were made to Thomas Jefferson's plan for the Northwest Territory?
6. How was the Northwest Territory divided and sold? Who ended up buying much of the land? Why?
7. What rights were guaranteed by the Northwest Ordinance?
8. Why was the Confederation Congress unable to pay its debts?
9. What hostile acts did Great Britain make toward the United States after the Revolution?
10. Give three reasons why the Confederation was not a complete failure.

Citizenship

1. Find out when your state constitution was adopted, and then read a copy of it. Write a summary of the rights of citizens in your state.
2. Write a speech that Elizabeth Freeman might have given in court, arguing her right to be a free citizen of Massachusetts.
3. Create a chart showing the structure and powers of the government under the Articles of Confederation.
4. Do you think the spirit of republicanism is still strong in the United States today? Give examples to support your answer.

PRACTICING YOUR SKILL

Copy the outline below onto a separate sheet of paper. Complete the outline by replacing each blank item with one of the topics from the list below.

Trial by jury
Population tops 60,000
Rights in the Territory
Indians treated fairly
Congress agrees

The Northwest Ordinance

I. Steps to Statehood

  A. 5,000 free men settle

  B. _____

  C. Territory requests admission

  D. _____

II. _____

  A. Freedom of speech and religion

  B. _____

  C. Protection from unfair punishment

  D. _____

  E. No slavery

CRITICAL THINKING SKILLS

1. MAKING COMPARISONS How were state governments stronger than the federal government under the Articles of Confederation?

2. RECOGNIZING BIAS In the 1780s, what groups of Americans were not included in the declaration "All men are created equal"?

3. IDENTIFYING RELEVANT INFORMATION How were republican ideals reflected in the laws of the Ordinance of 1785 and the Northwest Ordinance?

4. STATING BOTH SIDES OF AN ISSUE List three arguments in favor of keeping the Articles of Confederation and three arguments in favor of changing them.

PROJECTS AND ACTIVITIES

1. CONDUCTING AN INTERVIEW With another member of the class, write a script of an imaginary interview with Richard Allen for a radio talk show. Perform the broadcast for the class.

2. KEEPING A JOURNAL Think about what life was like for settlers as they crossed the Appalachians. Write down the journal entries for one week in the life of someone traveling west on the Wilderness Road.

3. CREATING AN IMAGE Make a collage, diorama, or scrapbook of your idea of what the Northwest Territory was like 200 years ago.

4. MAKING A POSTER Pick one of the problems Americans faced under the Confederation government, and create a poster illustrating that problem.

WRITING ABOUT TOPICS IN AMERICAN HISTORY

1. CONNECTING WITH LITERATURE A selection from *The Trees* by Conrad Richter appears on pages 644–646. Read it and answer the questions. Then answer the following question: How did the early settlers in the Ohio Valley make a living?

2. APPLYING THEMES: ECONOMIC DEVELOPMENT In a short essay, answer the following: How might continued high inflation hurt the future of a nation's economy? In what ways would a government's inability to pay its debts affect the economy?

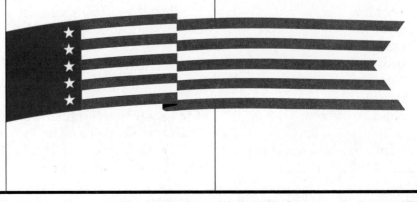

When the government under the Articles of Confederation proved unable to secure peace and prosperity, the states sent representatives to Philadelphia. There they drew up a new plan of government—the Constitution of the United States.

Creating the Constitution (1786–1791)

1 The Call for Change

Section Focus

Key Terms Shays' Rebellion ■ arsenal ■ convention ■ Constitutional Convention ■ Founding Fathers

Main Idea Believing that national government and even liberty itself were in crisis, political leaders assembled in Philadelphia in 1787 to strengthen and restructure the national government.

Objectives As you read, look for answers to these questions:
1. Why did farmers in Massachusetts rebel against the authorities?
2. Why did some Americans of the mid-1780s want changes in their government?
3. What were the men like who gathered to restructure the national government?

Imagine a trip through the United States of the mid-1780s. When you cross a state border, you have to pay import duties on goods from another state. Paying for items with one kind of bill, you might get change in another currency. Everywhere you go you also hear farmers bitterly complaining: "How can we pay our debts?"

The United States was in trouble. The country seemed to be breaking apart. Americans were free of British rule, but could they preserve their liberty and stay united? That was the challenge facing the new nation.

SHAYS' REBELLION

In 1781 paper money in Massachusetts could buy very little. Lawmakers voted to outlaw it, thereby forcing people to pay debts and taxes in hard currency. This law hurt farmers, because farming brought in little gold or silver. Unable to pay their debts, many farmers lost their land. In those days, people who owed

money could go to prison until they paid their debts. In one Massachusetts county, 80 percent of the men in jail were debtors.

In the fall of 1786, mobs of Massachusetts farmers began to march on the courts. They used threats and violence to stop the sale of farms for nonpayment of debts. These scattered protests later became known as **Shays' Rebellion**. (Daniel Shays, a former soldier in the American Revolution, was one of the leaders of the movement.)

The movement had little focus. One of Shays' men had urged on a rebellious mob by saying:

> My boys, you are going to fight for liberty. If you wish to know what liberty is, I will tell you. It is for every man to do what he pleases, to make other people do as you please to have them, and to keep folks from serving the devil.

State leaders in Boston declared that the rebels must obey the majority. They told farmers to use their votes, not their guns, to change things. At the same time, wealthy towns and merchants raised funds to send the state militia after the rebels.

Early in 1787 Shays and several hundred followers marched to Springfield, in the central part of the state. They planned to seize the United States arsenal, a storehouse for weapons. Challenged by the state militia, the rebels fled. Some 150 rebels were captured, while others, including Shays, escaped.

When spring came, the voters elected a new state government. The new leaders promised to change the strict laws against debtors. For governor they chose John Hancock, who pardoned the leaders of the revolt.

In 1786 bands of Massachusetts farmers, angered by tough economic times and court seizures of many farms, took part in Shays' Rebellion. HISTORY Though the protests were small and scattered, Shays' Rebellion sent a shock wave through the country. Why?

REACTION TO THE REBELLION

Shays' Rebellion sent a shock wave through the country. It showed how weak the national government was. In Virginia, George Washington noted that the national government had done nothing to end the rebellion. He wrote to Henry Lee, one of Virginia's delegates to Congress:

> You talk, my good Sir, of employing influence to appease the present tumults in Massachusetts. . . . *Influence* is not *government.* Let us have a government by which our lives, liberties, and properties will be secured, or let us know the worst at once.

People also worried about future revolts. Most Americans were farmers, and farmers everywhere had problems paying debts. These farmers might feel free to take the law into their own hands. John Locke, the British philosopher, had said, "Wherever law ends, tyranny begins." Had Americans thrown off the tyranny of the British king for the tyranny of mob rule?

A CALL FOR A CONVENTION

Tensions among the states over trade issues also worried many Americans. Lawmakers from Virginia called for a meeting of all the states to discuss trade disputes. This meeting of delegates, called a convention, was to be held at Annapolis, Maryland, in September 1786.

When the convention met, though, delegates from only five states showed up. Among the delegates were Alexander Hamilton from New York and James Madison from Virginia. An aide to George Washington during the war, Hamilton was a man who dressed and spoke well. He was a lawyer and a delegate to the Confederation Congress. Madison, short and soft-spoken, was another delegate to the Confederation Congress. Together with Hamilton, Madison persuaded the other delegates at the Annapolis Convention that little could be done since so few of the states were represented.

Hamilton went a step further. He wrote a report noting what was wrong with the Articles of Confederation. The Confederation could not negotiate trade treaties, the report said. It could not pay its debts. It could not resolve disputes between the states. Nor could it tax. To solve these problems, the report called for a special convention to consider ways to strengthen the Union. The delegates at Annapolis voted to support Hamilton's report.

It was about this time that news of Shays' Rebellion swept through the states. Until then, problems of trade and taxes had been the best arguments against weak government. Shays' Rebellion convinced many people that a stronger government was needed for another important reason: to keep order. From his home at Mount Vernon, George Washington wrote:

> No morn ever dawned more favourable than ours did—and no day was ever more clouded than the present! ... Without some alteration in our political creed, the superstructure we have been seven years raising at the expense of much blood and treasure, must fall.

Responding to the national feeling that something had to be done, Congress called for a convention. Delegates would meet, Congress said, "for the sole and express purpose of revising the Articles of Confederation." The convention would begin the second Monday in May 1787 in Philadelphia.

THE CONVENTION DELEGATES

Twelve states responded to the call to send delegates to Philadelphia, to what we call the Constitutional Convention. Only Rhode Island refused to attend.

The 55 delegates who went were among the most educated and experienced men in America. About half were lawyers. Others included successful planters, merchants, and doctors. Three-fourths of them had sat in the Continental Congress. Many had been members of

Hamilton, James Wilson, Madison, and Franklin appear from left to right in this mural of the Constitutional Convention. **CONSTITUTIONAL HERITAGE** What was the aim behind the meeting of the Convention?

their state legislatures and had helped write their state constitutions. Several were state governors and judges. Along with other American leaders of the time, these delegates are sometimes referred to as the Founding Fathers.

For all their experience, the delegates were a young group. Although the average age was 43, most were under the age of 40. (Today, the average age of Congress is over 50.) It was mainly the younger men who took on the challenge of putting the new nation on a firmer footing.

Alexander Hamilton, for example, was only about 30 when the Constitutional Convention started. Hamilton had been raised on the Caribbean island of Nevis. Unlike many Americans whose first loyalty was to their native state, Hamilton was interested in a strong and wealthy nation.

Gouverneur Morris, representing Pennsylvania, was also in his thirties. He had a wooden leg and could not use one arm, but his mind was keen and alert. Morris was a clear and graceful writer. His words, more than any other's, would be used in the document drawn up at the Convention.

GOUVERNEUR MORRIS (1752–1816) became a lawyer at age 19. In 1776 he helped draft a constitution for New York State. When Morris was 28, he lost a leg in a carriage accident. Such a handicap did not prevent him from becoming an important leader. As a delegate from Pennsylvania, Morris wrote the final draft of the Constitution. An eloquent and persuasive speaker, Morris favored a powerful, centralized government controlled by the wealthy.

Not all the delegates were young men. The oldest, Benjamin Franklin, was 81. Franklin brought his much-needed experience, wisdom, and humor to the Convention. During the meetings he moved around the room, giving good advice and calming delegates. He often cooled hot tempers by making a joke at the right moment.

Some leaders did not go to the Convention. Patrick Henry of Virginia was one. Henry feared that the Convention would do more than simply alter the Articles of Confederation. He refused to attend, reportedly saying that he "smelt a rat."

Other leaders were out of the country. John Adams was representing the nation in London, and Thomas Jefferson was in Paris. The news of Shays' Rebellion had not disturbed Jefferson. He wrote "I hold it, that a little rebellion, now and then, is a good thing. . . . It is a medicine necessary for the sound health of government."

THE CONVENTION ASSEMBLES

On May 25, 1787, rain poured down in Philadelphia. At the Pennsylvania State House, now called Independence Hall, 29 delegates from 7 states gathered. The rest would slowly arrive over the following weeks.

The first order of business was electing a president of the Convention. Robert Morris of Pennsylvania nominated George Washington. All the delegates voted for the 55-year-old hero of the Revolution.

Over six feet tall and weighing about 210 pounds, Washington had the dignity and presence of a great leader. He rose to make his acceptance speech. The delegates sat before him, grouped around tables in the East Room of the State House. It was in this room a dozen years before that Washington had been named commander-in-chief of the Continental Army. In the same room the Declaration of Independence had been signed. Now the nation faced another crisis.

Washington was not very hopeful. "It is too probable that no plan we propose will be adopted," he said. "Perhaps another dreadful conflict is to be sustained." Nevertheless, he urged the Convention "to raise a standard to which the wise and the honest can repair [rally around]." He concluded, "The event is in the hand of God."

> "**T**he event is in the hand of God."
>
> —*George Washington, 1787*

THE HISTORICAL RECORD

Having chosen the president and other officers, the Convention then decided on rules for its meetings. Delegates voted that all deliberations would be secret. To keep discussions from being overheard, the windows were nailed shut throughout the Convention. The resulting heat proved a terrible hardship when summer hit full force.

Delegates also agreed that votes were not binding. In other words, a majority could vote in favor of a particular plan, but then, as a result of later discussions, go back and reconsider the vote. This would happen often during the Convention.

The Convention had chosen a secretary, William Jackson, but his records were not very complete. Historians have relied more on the notes of James Madison. Each day the Convention met, Madison sat at a desk in front of the president's chair. Using his own shorthand system, he recorded all that was said.

Madison's notes have been important to later generations. They have allowed us to get past the secrecy of the Convention. We know something of the passions, the debates, and the compromises that went into the making of the Constitution.

Madison lacked the commanding presence of George Washington. He had neither the wit of Benjamin Franklin nor the force of Patrick Henry. Instead, he used reason and quiet leadership. Many of the principles of the Constitution are based on his ideas. Without James Madison, the United States as we know it might never have come about. Historians call Madison the "Father of the Constitution" because of the role he played.

SECTION REVIEW

1. KEY TERMS Shays' Rebellion, arsenal, convention, Constitutional Convention, Founding Fathers

2. PEOPLE AND PLACES Daniel Shays, Springfield, George Washington, Annapolis, Alexander Hamilton, James Madison, Philadelphia

3. COMPREHENSION What issues led to the call for a constitutional convention?

4. COMPREHENSION In what ways were the delegates to the Convention similar in outlook and experience?

5. CRITICAL THINKING Many Americans feared that if people took the law into their own hands, the result would be tyranny. Explain how this could happen.

2 Conflict and Compromise

★ **Section Focus**

Key Terms Virginia Plan ■ compromise ■ Great Compromise ■ impeach ■ Electoral College

Main Idea Through an intense process of debate and compromise, the Philadelphia delegates devised the mechanisms of a new form of government.

Objectives As you read, look for answers to these questions:
1. What was the basic structure of government adopted by the Constitutional Convention?
2. Why did states disagree so strongly about the make-up of the legislative branch?
3. Why is the Constitution a document of compromises?

The Convention was but a few days old when the governor of Virginia rose to speak. Edmund Randolph was a tall man who wore his hair loose and unpowdered. He looked squarely at the delegates and said:

Let us not be afraid to view with a steady eye the perils with which we are surrounded. . . . Are we not on the eve of war, which is only prevented by the hopes from this convention?

Views on Government

Few delegates that hot summer of 1787 disagreed with Randolph that the nation was in peril. They were less sure about the solution. For weeks the delegates argued how best to create a good and stable government.

The delegates had many beliefs in common. They surely agreed with the "truths" set forth in the Declaration of Independence. One of these is that people have certain natural rights, among which are "life, liberty, and the pursuit of happiness." The delegates also agreed that people's natural rights could not exist without government. Government, therefore, was necessary to liberty.

The delegates also agreed that governments should be based on the consent of the governed. Yet they were aware that government officials might use power for their own ends rather than for the people.

Back in 1776, in the flush of republican enthusiasm, many of the delegates had believed that a successful republic depended on a virtuous people. By 1787, events had changed their minds. As George Washington said, "We have, probably, had too good an opinion of human nature in forming our confederation." And, as Madison would write, "If men were angels, no government would be necessary. If angels were to govern men, neither external nor internal controls on government would be necessary." The delegates now assumed that people are by nature selfish.

The challenge was great. The delegates had to design a republic that would protect liberty and yet *not* depend on the virtue of people.

The Virginia Plan

Just four days after the meetings began, Governor Randolph of Virginia presented a plan to the Convention. The Virginia Plan, as it was called, was drawn up chiefly by James Madison. It proposed a national government made up of three parts.

(1) Congress, which was the legislative branch, would make the laws.

(2) An executive branch would carry out the laws.

(3) United States courts would see that justice was done under the laws.

The Virginia Plan was more than just a slight change to the Articles of Confederation.

This engraving from 1799 shows the back of Philadelphia's State House. The city's location on the Delaware River gave its merchants an outlet to the Atlantic Ocean and helped it prosper during the 1700s. The State House, known today as Independence Hall, was the site of the Constitutional Convention in 1787. **CONSTITUTIONAL HERITAGE** According to the delegates, on whose consent should governments be based?

The Declaration of Independence, the Articles of Confederation, and the Constitution were all signed in the Assembly Room of Independence Hall. **CONSTITUTIONAL HERITAGE** Why did the Virginia Plan mark a change in the purpose of the Convention?

It was a plan for a whole new form of national government. Delegates voted to expand the original goal of the Convention and consider the plan.

THE DEBATE BEGINS

The Virginia Plan called for Congress to be made up of two houses. The people would elect one house directly. That house would then elect the second house.

Some delegates were unhappy with this plan. They believed that ordinary people could not be trusted to elect good representatives. These delegates thought that the state governments should choose members of Congress. Elbridge Gerry, from Massachusetts, noted that it was ordinary people who had caused Shays' Rebellion. "The evils we experience flow from the excess of democracy," Gerry said.

Many delegates disagreed with Gerry. James Wilson of Pennsylvania argued that government drew strength from the involvement of citizens. The more people who took part in choosing Congress, the stronger it

would be, he said. Madison held that for a government to be free, the people must elect representatives. Disagreements over direct elections continued throughout the Constitutional Convention.

LARGE STATES VERSUS SMALL

Another part of the Virginia Plan sparked even hotter debate. The plan had called for Congress to have representation based on population. A state such as Delaware, for example, might have only one representative because it had so few people. A state with many people, such as Virginia, might have ten or more representatives.

Delegates from smaller states were unhappy with this part of the plan. They worried that the large states would end up ruling the rest. William Paterson of New Jersey was dramatic in his attack. "[I would] rather submit to a monarch, to a despot," he warned, "than to such a fate."

Paterson offered another plan to the Convention, the New Jersey Plan. This plan called for a legislature with only one house.

The issue of slavery was raised at the Constitutional Convention, as northern and southern delegates disagreed over counting slaves as part of a state's population. Like other issues, this was resolved by compromise, with each slave being counted as three-fifths of one free person. HISTORY Why did southern states favor including slaves in population figures?

Each state, regardless of its population, would send the same number of representatives to Congress. This way a small state would have just as many votes as a large state. The New Jersey Plan described a legislature very much like the one that existed under the Articles of Confederation.

THE GREAT COMPROMISE

By now the hot, humid days of summer had come to Philadelphia. Many said it was the worst heat they could remember. Northerners sweated out the days in wool clothing. The southern delegates were more comfortable in their lightweight suits.

For days delegates argued, feelings often running as high as the temperature. The future of the Convention seemed unclear. Watching Washington leave the hall, a former French officer reported, "The look on his face reminded me of its expression during the terrible months we were in Valley Forge Camp."

The end to the arguments would come only with both sides giving in a little. This way of settling a problem is called a compromise.

The best suggestion for compromise came from Connecticut's Roger Sherman. He offered the Great Compromise or the Con-

necticut Compromise. The Great Compromise called for the *people* to be represented in the lower house. This would be the House of Representatives. The *states,* meanwhile, would be equally represented in the upper house, the Senate. In other words, population would determine how many representatives the people of a state would elect to the lower house. In the upper house, however, each state would have two votes.

The compromise also solved the problem of who would elect members of Congress. The people would vote for members of the lower house. The upper house would be chosen by state lawmakers.

OTHER DEBATES, OTHER COMPROMISES

Having agreed to the Great Compromise, the delegates moved on to other matters.

(1) *Slavery.* The southern states had many more slaves than the northern states. Northerners argued that because slaves could not vote, they should not be counted. Southerners wanted to include slaves in the figures determining representation in Congress.

To settle this matter, delegates worked out the Three-Fifths Compromise. They decided that five slaves would count as three persons for the purposes of representation.

(2) *Trade.* The delegates debated how much power Congress should have over trade. All of them agreed that the national government should control trade between states. The northern states wanted Congress to control foreign trade as well. Because many northerners made a living by shipping, they wanted the same trade laws in force everywhere. Southerners, however, preferred to let each state set its own rules. Southerners exported large amounts of rice, tobacco, and indigo. They worried about losing foreign customers if Congress taxed these goods.

The South also feared that Congress might stop the slave trade. Many northerners opposed slavery. Even southerners who owned slaves, such as George Mason, questioned the practice. "Every master of slaves is born a petty tyrant," he said. "They bring the judgment of heaven upon a country."

> "**E**very master of slaves is born a petty tyrant."
>
> —*George Mason*

Once more, both sides compromised. The delegates gave Congress the power to control trade with other countries. Congress could tax imports but not exports. The delegates also said that Congress could end the slave trade in twenty years.

(3) *The Executive.* The Convention turned its attention to the executive branch. Should the executive be one person? Or should it be a committee? Most delegates expected that the first executive would be George Washington, and they believed that he would use his powers wisely. They decided the executive branch would be headed by a single person, a President. To keep that person from becoming too powerful, Congress would have the power to impeach the President. (To impeach is to bring an official to trial for misconduct.)

Some delegates did not trust the judgment of the people to choose a President. To lessen

FEDERAL POWERS INCREASE UNDER THE CONSTITUTION

Articles of Confederation	United States Constitution
● Declare war; make peace	✔ ✔
● Organize and direct an army and navy	✔
● Regulate trade with the Indians; manage Indian affairs	✔
● Set standards of weights and measures	✔
● Establish postal services	✔
● Borrow money to pay expenses	✔
● Manage foreign affairs	✔
● Prevent the states from issuing money	✔
● Impose taxes	✔
● Call out state militia	✔
● Regulate trade between the states and with foreign nations	✔
● Organize a system of courts	✔
● Protect copyrights and patents	✔
● Govern the capital city and territories of the United States	✔
● Take other action, as needed, to carry out the above powers	✔

CHART SKILLS

The Articles of Confederation granted the federal government certain powers. This chart shows that in addition to those powers, the Constitution granted the federal government several more. **CRITICAL THINKING** Why did the delegates believe they needed to increase the federal government's powers?

their fears, the Convention decided against direct election of the President. Instead, each state would choose electors—qualified voters. A state would have as many electors as it had senators and representatives. These electors would form the Electoral College, which elected the President and the Vice President.

THE FINAL TOUCHES

The delegates worked all summer to hammer out their differences. Often, when tempers began to rise or agreement seemed out of the question, Benjamin Franklin would tell a story. A favorite was the tale of a French-woman who argued with her sister: "I don't know how it happens, Sister, but I meet with nobody but myself that's always in the right." The delegates would laugh, and discussion—without anger—would continue.

Finally, delegates to the Convention thought that they had done the best possible job. They gathered for the last time on September 17, 1787. Of the 42 present, 39 signed the Constitution. Now it was up to special state conventions to vote on the document.

Before the delegates parted, Benjamin Franklin rose to speak. Pointing to George Washington's chair, which had a half-sun carved into the high wooden backrest, he noted:

> I have often and often in the course of this session looked at that [sun] without being able to tell whether it was rising or setting. But now at length I have the happiness to know that it is a rising and not a setting sun.

1. KEY TERMS Virginia Plan, compromise, Great Compromise, impeach, Electoral College

2. PEOPLE Edmund Randolph, William Paterson, Roger Sherman, Benjamin Franklin

3. COMPREHENSION What issues did the Great Compromise resolve?

4. COMPREHENSION How was the President to be chosen?

5. CRITICAL THINKING The delegates to the Constitutional Convention believed that people are by nature selfish. How does the Constitution deal with this problem?

3 Ratifying the Constitution

Section Focus

Key Terms federalism ■ Federalist ■ Antifederalist ■ *The Federalist*

Main Idea Strong and spirited debate was part of the process of approving the Constitution. In the end the Constitution was approved with the understanding that a bill of rights be added to protect individual liberties.

Objectives As you read, look for answers to these questions:
1. How did the Constitution become law?
2. What were the concerns of the opponents of the Constitution?
3. How did supporters of the Constitution compromise in order to win its approval?

Within two days of its signing, the Constitution was front-page news. A Philadelphia paper printed the first words, "We the People of the United States," in large bold type.

The Convention debate had been held in secret. This was not the case for the debate over final approval. In the fall, each state called a special convention to decide whether or not to ratify, or accept, the new form of government. If nine of the thirteen states gave their approval, the Constitution would become "the supreme law of the land."

A FEDERAL SYSTEM OF GOVERNMENT
The Philadelphia Convention had created something very different from before. "This

government is so new, it wants a name," said Patrick Henry. It was no longer a loose league of powerful states. Neither was it a government that denied the states any power. It was a mixture of the two, known as federalism. Federalism is the sharing of power between a central government and its political subdivisions, in this case the states. The Constitution of 1787 was the first to provide for a federal system of government.

The Constitution became the hottest political topic in the country. Some people, known as Federalists, strongly favored the new plan of government. Others, who were called Antifederalists, were against it.

CONCERNS OF THE ANTIFEDERALISTS

The Antifederalists had two main fears:

(1) They thought, first of all, that the Constitution gave too much power to the national government.

(2) They feared that, under the Constitution, the national government would swallow up the states. This, they reasoned, would mean a loss of freedom. Liberty, they thought, could only survive in a small republic. In a small republic it is easier for people to keep a close watch over their leaders.

Patrick Henry, who had refused to attend the Convention, criticized the Constitution:

This proposal of altering our federal government is of a most alarming nature. . . . You ought to be extremely cautious, watchful, jealous of your liberty; for instead of securing your rights, you may lose them forever. If a wrong step be now made, the republic may be lost forever.

> "**I**f a wrong step be now made, the republic may be lost forever."
> —*Patrick Henry*

Thomas Jefferson, in France at the time, was not so doubtful. When he received a copy of the Constitution, he approved of much of it. He also saw important weaknesses. In a letter to James Madison he expressed his views:

I like the organization of the government into legislative, judiciary, and executive [branches]. I like the power given the [Congress] to levy taxes, and . . . I approve of the greater House being chosen by the people directly. . . . I will now tell you what I do

---

CHART SKILLS

The Federalists believed that the United States needed a strong central government. Antifederalists feared that a strong central government might oppress the people. **CRITICAL THINKING** Explain how both positions reflected the lessons of past experience.

FEDERALISTS VERSUS ANTIFEDERALISTS

Policies favored by the Federalists

▶ Strong national government

▶ Government controlled by wealthy and educated citizens

▶ Policies favorable to trade, business, and finance

▶ A national bank

▶ Protective tariffs

▶ Strong ties with Britain, but not with France

Policies favored by the Antifederalists

▶ Limited national government

▶ Government controlled by ordinary citizens

▶ Policies favorable to farmers, artisans, and skilled workers

▶ State banks

▶ Free trade

▶ Strong ties with France, but not with Britain

The Federalist, No. 10 (1787)

The basis of American government is representative government, rather than direct democracy. In The Federalist, No. 10, *James Madison put forth his arguments in support of electing representatives to Congress.*

The two great points of difference between a democracy and a republic are: first, the delegation of the government, in the latter, to a small number of citizens selected by the rest; secondly, the greater number of citizens and greater sphere of country, over which the latter may be extended.

The effect of the first difference is, on the one hand, to refine and enlarge the public views, by passing them through the medium of a chosen body of citizens, whose wisdom may best discern the true interest of their country and whose patriotism and love of justice will be least likely to sacrifice it to temporary or partial considerations. . . .

By enlarging too much the number of electors, you render the representative too little acquainted with all their local circumstances and lesser interests; as by reducing it too much, you render him unduly attached to these, and too little fit to comprehend and pursue great and national objects. . . .

Extend the sphere and you take in a greater variety of parties and interests; you make it less probable that a majority of the whole will have a common motive to invade the rights of other citizens.

From J. and A. McLean, eds., *The Federalist: A Collection of Essays*, Vol. I, No. 10.

ANALYZING HISTORICAL DOCUMENTS

1. Which form of government does James Madison prefer, a democracy or a republic? What reasons does he give for his choice?

2. Which body in our present-day government corresponds to Madison's "chosen body of citizens"?

3. What counter-arguments could be made against Madison's position?

not like. First, [there is no] bill of rights, providing clearly . . . for freedom of religion, freedom of the press, protection against standing armies, . . . and trials by jury in all matters [that may be tried] by the laws of the land. . . . Let me add that a bill of rights is what the people are entitled to against every government on earth. . . .

THE FEDERALISTS RESPOND

In answer to those attacks, Federalists insisted that citizens' rights were safe. After all, each state constitution already had a bill of rights. Also, the House of Representatives was to be elected by the people. Members would be sure to protect the people's rights.

The Federalists argued their views in town meetings, newspapers, and pamphlets. The best-known writings were 85 essays collected under the title *The Federalist*. These essays were the work of James Madison, Alexander Hamilton, and John Jay—all supporters of a strong central government. They clearly explained the Constitution and presented strong reasons for approving it. The 85 essays were written under the pressure of newspaper deadlines. Still, they have become classics of American political thought. Even today they remain the best explanation of federalism.

THE STATES DECIDE

Among the first states to ratify the Constitution were the small states. Delaware, New Jersey, Georgia, Maryland, and Connecticut quickly approved it.

In Massachusetts, public opinion was divided. To gain support for the Constitution, Federalists came up with a plan. The state should ratify the Constitution. At the same time, it should recommend that a bill of rights be added. Supporting that plan, Massachusetts voted to ratify.

New Hampshire was the ninth state to approve the Constitution, in June 1788. Nine states were needed to make it the law of the land. Yet New York and Virginia had still not approved. Without Virginia, the new government would lack the support of the largest state. Without New York, the nation would be separated into two parts. From his home

Noted painter John Trumbull painted this portrait of Alexander Hamilton in the 1790s. A delegate at the Constitutional Convention, Hamilton wrote parts of *The Federalist,* which urged ratification of the Constitution. **HISTORY** On what condition did New York approve the Constitution?

at Mount Vernon, George Washington wrote his old friend Lafayette, "The plot thickens fast. A few short weeks will determine the political fate of America."

At last, the promise of a bill of rights convinced Virginia to accept the Constitution. A month later, New York narrowly approved it. North Carolina and Rhode Island did not ratify the Constitution until more than a year later. By then, the framework of government under which we live today was in place.

SECTION REVIEW

1. KEY TERMS federalism, Federalist, Antifederalist, *The Federalist*

2. PEOPLE Patrick Henry, Alexander Hamilton, James Madison, John Jay

3. COMPREHENSION In what way is a federal system of government a mixed government?

4. COMPREHENSION What were the two main reasons for opposition to the Constitution?

5. CRITICAL THINKING How did the Antifederalists have an impact on the Constitution?

Historians examine the documents, letters, journals, and pictures from a specific time. They analyze these **primary sources** to come up with a discussion of an event or period. Though they are based on facts, these discussions are interpretations of history. The discussion is often influenced by the historian's education, background and experience. This **frame of reference** helps shape the historian's point of view.

Keep that fact in mind when you study history. Remember that historians pick and choose which facts to include and which to stress. Note the judgments they make about those facts.

ONE VIEW OF THE CONSTITUTION

The selection below was written by Roger Wilkins, a professor of history at George Mason University. Wilkins presents an African American's response to the 200th anniversary of the signing of the Constitution. Read the selection. Answer the questions that follow to identify Wilkins's frame of reference.

The celebration of the 200th anniversary of the Constitution is, on one level, about pictures and memories. The dominant pictures are those of a group of contemplative people dressed in 18th-century clothing in a room in Philadelphia 200 summers ago. . . . A black American born in the 20th century cannot avoid noticing that the people in the pictures are white and male. . . . After all, his American memory contains the possibility that one or more of the men in the picture actually owned one or more of his black ancestors. . . .

The Constitution is a lot of things. . . . I viewed the Constitution as a Promise, a basket . . . of things I'd heard about. . . . All of that added up, in my young mind, to promises of freedom and equality and justice to all of us "We the people," in a country great enough to dream up those promises in the first place.

Roger Wilkins

PRACTICING YOUR SKILL

1. What, according to Roger Wilkins, is the most powerful picture connected to the Constitution?
2. How does Wilkins describe himself? How does that description contrast with the picture of those who drew up the Constitution?
3. As a young man, did Wilkins have a positive or negative view of the Constitution?
4. What does Wilkins mean by the statement "I viewed the Constitution as a Promise, a basket . . . of things I'd heard about"?
5. Consider Wilkins's frame of reference. In your opinion, with which of the Constitutional Convention's decisions would he most likely disagree?

4 A More Perfect Union

Section Focus

Key Terms separation of powers ■ checks and balances ■ veto ■ unconstitutional ■ amendment ■ Bill of Rights ■ due process ■ elastic clause ■ Cabinet

Main Idea The Constitution created a strong and balanced government with separated powers and the flexibility to adjust to the nation's growth and changing needs.

Objectives As you read, look for answers to these questions:
1. How does the Constitution divide power among the branches of the federal government and between the states and the federal government?
2. What is the purpose of the Bill of Rights?
3. How does the Constitution provide for change?

Every year thousands of people visit the National Archives in Washington, D.C. There, in the main hall, carefully displayed, is the Constitution. People can still make out the words on this more than 200-year-old document.

The message remains strong. "We the people . . . establish this Constitution for the United States of America." These opening lines declare that the United States is not ruled by a king, queen, or other individual. Instead, the Constitution has created a country in which the supreme power rests with the nation's citizens.

THE STRUCTURE OF GOVERNMENT

The Virginia Plan, presented to the Constitutional Convention, outlined a new form of government. There were problems with the plan, and some of its points were changed before the Constitution was signed. Yet the basic structure of government it described remained intact.

The nation's capital, Washington, D.C., houses the three branches of government as well as historic documents of our nation's past. In the foreground is the Capitol. The National Archives is located along Pennsylvania Avenue, at the upper right. Other government buildings line both sides of the Mall, which leads to the Washington Monument. **CONSTITUTIONAL HERITAGE** Why is it important that the Constitution begins with the words "We the people"?

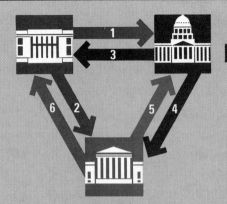

THE EXECUTIVE BRANCH
(The President)

1 **Checks on Congress**
- Can veto acts of Congress
- Can call special sessions of Congress
- Can suggest legislation and send messages to Congress

2 **Checks on Court**
- Appoints Supreme Court justices and other federal judges
- Can grant reprieves and pardons

THE LEGISLATIVE BRANCH
(Congress)

3 **Checks on President**
- Can impeach and remove the President
- Can override the President's veto by a two-thirds vote
- Controls appropriation of money
- Senate can refuse to confirm presidential appointments
- Senate can refuse to ratify treaties

4 **Checks on Court**
- Can impeach and remove federal judges
- Can refuse to confirm judicial appointments
- Establishes lower federal court
- Can propose constitutional amendments to overturn court decisions

THE JUDICIAL BRANCH
(The Supreme Court)

5 **Checks on Congress**
- Can declare acts of Congress unconstitutional

6 **Checks on President**
- Can declare executive acts unconstitutional
- Appointment for life makes judges free from executive control

CHART SKILLS The system of checks and balances was designed to prevent any one branch of government from becoming all-powerful. **CRITICAL THINKING** Does the system work? What might be some of its flaws?

The plan called for the power of government to be divided into three separate branches.

(1) The legislative branch makes laws. It consists of the Senate and the House of Representatives. Senators are elected for six years, while representatives serve for two.

(2) The executive branch enforces the laws. The President and the Vice President, who serve four-year terms, head it. Today this branch includes such federal departments as the Department of Education.

(3) The judicial branch, which interprets the laws, consists of the Supreme Court and other federal courts.

This separation of powers keeps any one branch from becoming too powerful. Imagine if one person or group of people had all the power of government in their hands. They could make a law and then arrest you if you broke it. If you appeared in court and claimed

the law was unfair, you would be making your arguments to the same group that wrote the law.

Separation of powers reduces the chance of cruel government. It does not, however, prevent any branch of the government from misusing its power. For example, Congress could pass laws favoring one state over another. The executive branch and the federal courts could also act unfairly.

To prevent such events from taking place, the Constitution gives each branch some powers over the others. These checks keep the parts in balance. This principle of checks and balances limits the power of the three branches by having each branch watch the others.

For example, the President must approve a proposed law, or bill, that Congress passes before it can take effect. If the President chooses to veto—reject—the bill, it does not become law. The President can also check the power of the judicial branch. It is the President who appoints federal judges.

The Senate, however, must approve the President's choices for judges. This is one way Congress checks both the executive and the judicial branches. In addition, Congress may overturn a presidential veto. Congress also has the power to remove a President or judge who seriously misbehaves.

Federal courts have the power to strike down laws and actions of the other two government branches. The Supreme Court may decide that a law passed by Congress goes against the Constitution. The Court then declares the law unconstitutional.

THE FEDERAL SYSTEM

In writing the Constitution, delegates took care that not all the power rested in the federal (national) government. The federal government was given power over issues that concern the country as a whole. For example, only Congress can make treaties, coin money, tax imports, and declare war.

Yet the Constitution also allows for some powers to be shared by the federal and state governments. Both can tax. Both can borrow money, control banking, build roads, and maintain courts. The state militias (today's National Guard) are under the control of both the states and Congress. The Constitution makes sure, however, that federal law is supreme. If conflicts arise between state and national laws, the states must follow the national laws.

States do have powers that are theirs and theirs alone. Each state can make its own laws about education and about trade within its borders. Each state can also set its own punishments for most crimes. The Constitution lists the responsibilities of the federal government. All other powers "are reserved to the states respectively, or to the people."

Think of how this division of power works. On the news, you see the President meet with

---

THE FEDERAL SYSTEM

Powers of the Federal Government	Powers Shared by Federal and State Governments	Powers of State Governments

Federal Powers

Maintain army and navy

Establish a postal system

Set standards for weights, measures, copyrights, and patents

Regulate trade between states and with foreign nations

Declare war

Shared Powers

Impose taxes

Establish courts

Regulate banks

Borrow money to pay expenses

Build roads

Provide for general welfare

State Powers

Establish local government

Establish schools

Regulate state commerce

Make regulations for marriage

Establish and regulate corporations

CHART SKILLS
Americans live under both federal and state governments. This chart shows the powers each level possesses under the federal system. Which level of government has the power to regulate marriages? Which level may declare war? Which level may impose taxes? **CRITICAL THINKING** State powers are sometimes called *reserved powers*. Why is this term appropriate?

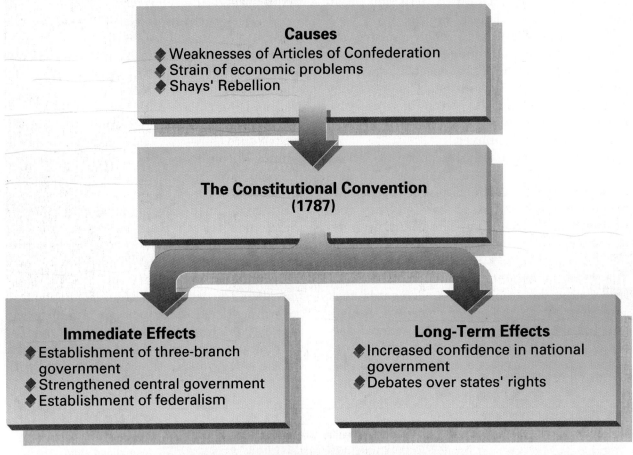

Causes
- Weaknesses of Articles of Confederation
- Strain of economic problems
- Shays' Rebellion

The Constitutional Convention (1787)

Immediate Effects
- Establishment of three-branch government
- Strengthened central government
- Establishment of federalism

Long-Term Effects
- Increased confidence in national government
- Debates over states' rights

CHART SKILLS This chart shows how the Constitutional Convention dealt with the severe problems facing the new nation. CRITICAL THINKING What is meant by *federalism*?

foreign leaders to discuss trade. The Constitution says that only the federal government can "regulate commerce with foreign nations..." (Article I, Section 8, Clause 3). Your state's governor is banned from signing a treaty with another country. Yet your governor, like the President, can pardon a criminal. That is because the states, like the federal government, have the power to punish people who have broken its laws. Still, a prisoner who broke a state law cannot be pardoned by the President. Only the governor has power in that case.

THE BILL OF RIGHTS

When it came time to ratify the Constitution, many Americans thought the government was too powerful. The memory of British injustice was fresh in their minds. "What will keep Congress from passing laws against public criticism?" they asked. "How can we be sure we will get a fair trial?"

In many states, these questions became a demand. Some states would approve the Constitution only if a list of guaranteed rights were added. The Constitution had provided for additions, called amendments, to be made. In 1791 the first ten were added. They are known as the Bill of Rights because they describe the rights Americans have under their government.

The First Amendment guards some of the liberties we cherish most. It protects freedom of religion, freedom of speech, and freedom of

The Supreme Court, the nation's highest court, meets in the room shown here. Also pictured is the Court's first woman justice, Sandra Day O'Connor. She joined the Court in 1981. **CONSTITUTIONAL HERITAGE** What is the relationship between the Supreme Court and the Bill of Rights?

the press. It also says that citizens may meet peacefully in groups. In addition, it gives people the right to ask the government to hear their complaints.

The next seven amendments guarantee other freedoms. These include the right to bear arms and the right to a fair trial. The Bill of Rights also protects us from having our property taken or homes searched without reason. It states that people accused or convicted of crimes must always be treated fairly and according to the law. This is called due process.

The first eight amendments are specific lists of what the government cannot do. The last two amendments in the Bill of Rights make it clear that there are many more re-

strictions on government actions. They grant to the states and to the people any powers not mentioned in the Constitution.

THE FLEXIBILITY TO CHANGE

The delegates to the Constitutional Convention traveled to Philadelphia on horses. They communicated with the families they left behind through letters. Today the United States is a country where citizens zoom between towns in cars and jets. Telephones, computers, and fax machines send messages in seconds. Yet the Constitution continues as the framework of our government.

The reason is that a plan for making changes is built into the Constitution. Article V describes how to amend the Constitution.

The Supreme Court's 1954 decision in the case *Brown v. Board of Education of Topeka* outlawed the practice of separating public schoolchildren by race. The Court ruled that this practice discriminated against African American students. HISTORY How did the Court's decision mark a change from an earlier ruling?

Congress or state conventions can propose an amendment. It then goes to the states to be approved.

The addition of the Bill of Rights was the first time the Constitution was amended. James Madison, whose ideas inspired the Constitution, wrote most of the Bill of Rights. He must have suspected that the future would bring more amendments. "In framing a system which we wish to last for ages," he said, "we should not lose sight of the changes which the ages will produce." (However, in more than 200 years the Constitution has been amended only 26 times.)

Besides amendments, the Constitution can be changed in more subtle ways. One of these ways is through the Supreme Court. The language of the Constitution is often general. It is the Court's job to interpret that language. In one clause of the Constitution, Congress is given the power to make any laws "necessary and proper" for carrying out its duties.

The Supreme Court has applied this clause to many different situations over the years. For example, the Constitution says nothing about the airline business. Yet it does give Congress the right to control interstate trade. Therefore, the Court decided that Congress can also regulate airlines. Because this clause has allowed the powers of Congress to expand, it is called the elastic clause.

CHANGE OVER TIME

The Supreme Court can also change its interpretations as times change. In 1892 a conductor in Louisiana told Homer Plessy to get off a railway car marked "for whites only." Plessy, an African American, had to sit in a separate car for blacks. The Court decided this was constitutional (page 545).

As time passed, the idea of treating African Americans differently became less acceptable. In 1954 the Supreme Court declared that making white and black children go to separate schools was wrong. It struck down laws separating people on the basis of race.

Custom also affects the Constitution. Certain practices have been followed so long they have become an unwritten part of government. For example, all Presidents appoint a Cabinet—a formal group of advisers. The Constitution makes no mention of such a group. It simply says that the President may set up departments to help run the government. The President may also name people to run the departments. It is by custom, not by law, that the Cabinet has become an official part of the executive branch.

The Constitution continues to change through new customs, court decisions, and amendments. Yet its principles remain unchanging. The United States is ruled not by the whims of its leaders, but by a set of laws. These laws unite a diverse and changing population. As historian Richard B. Morris notes:

> The Constitution is the mortar that binds the fifty-state edifice: . . . it is the symbol that unifies . . . 250 million people of different origins, races, and religions into a single nation.

SECTION REVIEW

1. KEY TERMS separation of powers, checks and balances, veto, unconstitutional, amendment, Bill of Rights, due process, elastic clause, Cabinet

2. COMPREHENSION What powers do the states and federal government share?

3. COMPREHENSION What does the Bill of Rights protect?

4. COMPREHENSION How has Congress achieved powers not specifically assigned to it by the Constitution?

5. CRITICAL THINKING The system of checks and balances discourages government officials from acting rapidly. How might this be an advantage? How might it be a drawback?

CHAPTER 11 SUMMARY AND TIMELINE

1. Shays' Rebellion, combined with complaints about the government's inability to tax and control commerce, led to the calling of a convention to revise the Articles of Confederation.

2. The Constitution was forged from a series of compromises. Delegates debated proportional versus state representation in Congress and direct election by the people versus states' choosing representatives. Southern and northern delegates disagreed over the issue of slavery. Delegates also reached compromises on the details of the executive branch.

3. Antifederalists feared that the Constitution gave too much power to the federal government. The arguments of Federalists and the promise of a bill of rights helped convince such states as Virginia and New York to ratify the Constitution. By mid-1788 the Constitution was the law of the land.

4. The Constitution has provided a strong but flexible framework for the American republic. This framework is based on a division of powers between the federal and state governments, separation of powers within the federal government, and a system of checks and balances.

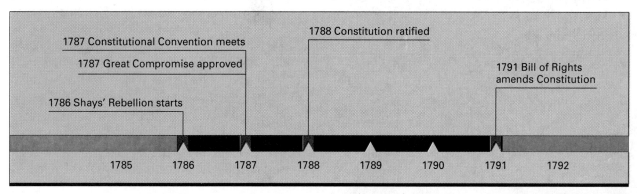

1787 Constitutional Convention meets

1787 Great Compromise approved

1786 Shays' Rebellion starts

1788 Constitution ratified

1791 Bill of Rights amends Constitution

1785 1786 1787 1788 1789 1790 1791 1792

PLACES TO LOCATE

Match each of the letters on the map with the places that are listed below.

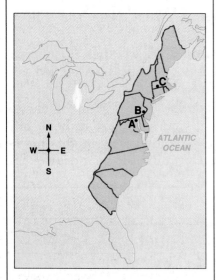

1. Philadelphia, Pennsylvania
2. Springfield, Massachusetts
3. Annapolis, Maryland

KEY TERMS

Use the following terms to complete the sentences. Write your answers on a separate sheet of paper.

   amendments
   Cabinet
   compromise
   Constitutional Convention
   federalism
   veto

1. American leaders gathered at the ____ in Philadelphia in 1787.
2. Delegates with opposing views had to ____ to reach an agreement.
3. Under the Constitution's system of checks and balances, the President can ____ laws passed by Congress.
4. Under the system of ____, states share power with the central government.
5. The Bill of Rights consists of the first ten ____ to the Constitution.
6. The Constitution does not mention the President's ____; it is a custom that has developed over time.

PEOPLE TO IDENTIFY

Identify the following people and tell why each one was important.

1. Benjamin Franklin
2. Alexander Hamilton
3. Patrick Henry
4. James Madison
5. Edmund Randolph

REVIEWING THE FACTS

1. What caused Shays' Rebellion? What were the consequences of the rebellion?
2. What problems in the 1780s led some Americans to call for revisions in the Articles of Confederation?
3. What goals and values did all of the delegates to the Constitutional Convention share?
4. What issues caused the greatest controversy in the debate over the legislative branch? How were they resolved?
5. What issues caused the greatest controversy in the debate over the executive branch? How were they resolved?
6. What was the process by which the Constitution became the law of the land?
7. What were the concerns of the Antifederalists?
8. How can the judicial branch check the powers of the other two branches of the federal government?
9. What powers are shared by both the federal and state governments?
10. How is a plan for dealing with change built into the Constitution?

CITIZENSHIP

1. How does the separation of powers serve to protect liberty in America?
2. At the close of the Constitutional Convention, Benjamin Franklin was approached by a woman who asked, "Well, Dr. Franklin, what kind of government have you given us?" He replied, "A republic, if you can keep it." What did he mean?

PRACTICING YOUR SKILL

Alexis de Tocqueville, a French political scientist, visited and wrote about the United States in the 1830s. In the following excerpt from his book, *Democracy in America,* Tocqueville compared the United States Constitution to the state constitutions. Read the excerpt and the answer the questions that follow.

> I consider that the federal Constitution is superior to all the state constitutions. . . . The federal government is more just and moderate in its proceedings than those of the states. There is more wisdom in its views; . . . there is more skill, consistency, and firmness in the execution of its measures.

1. Why did Tocqueville prefer the United States Constitution to state constitutions?
2. During Tocqueville's time, France did not have a federal system, but was ruled almost completely at the national level. How might that fact have influenced Tocqueville's attitude toward state constitutions?

CRITICAL THINKING SKILLS

1. FORMING A HYPOTHESIS
Why did radical opponents of British rule, such as Sam Adams, condemn the actions taken by Shays and his followers? How might they have made a case that Shays' Rebellion was different from the Boston Tea Party?

2. MAKING JUDGMENTS
What, in your opinion, were the most important arguments in favor of ratifying the Constitution? What were the most important arguments against ratification? What might have happened if the Constitution had been rejected or if not all the states had ratified it?

3. IDENTIFYING SIGNIFICANCE
One of the Antifederalists' objections to the Constitution was that no one had authorized the delegates to say "We the people" instead of "We the states." What was the significance of this changed wording?

PROJECTS AND ACTIVITIES

1. PARTICIPATING IN GOVERNMENT Under our political system, the people control their representatives through their power to vote them into or out of office. Between elections, citizens inform their representatives of their concerns by writing letters. Write a letter to your representative about an issue that is important to you.

2. MAKING A MAP Make a map of the thirteen original states. Number the states to show the order in which they ratified the Constitution.

3. GIVING AN ORAL REPORT Find out more about one of the delegates to the Constitutional Convention. Share your findings with the class in an oral report.

4. CREATING A SCRAPBOOK Choose one of the rights protected by the Bill of Rights. Then gather pictures, news articles, and other images illustrating that right. Display them in an annotated scrapbook.

WRITING ABOUT TOPICS IN AMERICAN HISTORY

1. CONNECTING WITH LITERATURE A selection from *Miracle at Philadelphia* by Catherine Drinker Bowen appears on pages 646–647. Read it and answer the questions. Then answer the following question: Why was it so important to the future of the country that Virginia ratify the Constitution?

2. APPLYING THEMES: CONSTITUTIONAL GOVERNMENT The Constitution is frequently described as a "living document." Cite examples illustrating the ways the Founding Fathers ensured that the Constitution would remain valid in changing times. What reasons might explain why the Constitution has been formally amended only 26 times?

Constitution Handbook

The framers of the Constitution wanted to create a government powerful enough to protect the rights of citizens and defend the country against its enemies. They did not want a government, however, so powerful that it could become a tyranny. As James Madison observed, "In framing a government . . . the great difficulty lies in this: you must first enable the government to control the governed; and in the next place oblige it to control itself." As you study the Constitution, you will discover the many ways the framers sought to balance these diverse goals.

PRINCIPLES OF THE AMERICAN SYSTEM OF GOVERNMENT

The United States is dedicated to the proposition that people have the capacity to make wise decisions and govern themselves. Our country is a *republic* because we choose representatives to act for us in governing. It is also a democracy because all qualified citizens have the privilege of voting and therefore determining the kind of government we have. French historian Alexis de Tocqueville studied systems of government in the 1830s. Compared to other forms of government, Tocqueville concluded, republics "will be less brilliant, less glorious, and perhaps less strong, but the majority of the citizens will enjoy a greater degree of prosperity, and the people will remain quiet . . . because it is conscious of the advantages of its condition."

What are some features of our form of government? Under the Constitution, states share power with the federal (national) government. Some powers are given only to the federal government; others belong to the states; some are held jointly. This division of powers, known as federalism, encourages each side to protect its special powers against intrusion by the other.

The Constitution provides for separation of powers within the federal government as well. Only the legislative branch of the government can make laws. The executive branch administers them. The judicial branch interprets laws when disagreements arise over their meanings.

In order to guard against any one branch of the federal government becoming too powerful, the Constitution specifies a system of checks and balances. Each branch of government possesses the power to check, or limit the actions of, the other two branches.

THIRTEEN ENDURING CONSTITUTIONAL ISSUES

Our Constitution is the world's oldest written constitution. In the two centuries since its ratification, the Constitution has been changed through custom and through amendment, though these changes have been remarkably few. Arguments over how to interpret the language of the document, however, have been continual. When disputes over the Constitution's meaning arise, the Supreme Court interprets and decides the issue. Supreme Court interpretations have changed over the years, and many unresolved issues remain. The following thirteen issues have been sources of ongoing debates among legislators, legal scholars, and concerned citizens. The course of these debates shapes our system of government and the society in which we live.

1. National Power

The framers of the Constitution carefully limited the power of the federal government. However, over time, the government has expanded its authority at the expense of sectional interests. In the course of the nation's expansion, the federal government has also taken possession of territories such as Puerto Rico, the Panama Canal, the Philippines and other Pacific islands, and land belonging to American Indian tribes. During national emergencies, the government has tried to take over some businesses and forced others to close. Has the expansion of federal power gone too far? Or is the federal government too weak to deal effectively with complex problems that the nation faces as it nears the twenty-first century?

2. Federalism

The framers of the Constitution divided power between the state governments and the federal government to avoid the dangers of centralized authority. In doing so, however, they created what John Quincy Adams called "the most complicated government on the face of the earth."

The boundaries between state and federal power have been the subject of many lawsuits. Supporters of states' rights argue that state governments should have final authority within their state. Federalists believe that many state policies and laws involve national issues and should be under the authority of the federal government. The Supreme Court has claimed the power to declare state laws unconstitutional.

In addition, the federal government controls most tax revenues. State governments depend on federal aid to carry out many of the powers reserved to them in the Constitution. The federal government has used the threat of withholding this aid to change state policies. Is the increased power of the federal government necessary to enforce justice throughout the nation? Or does it endanger our liberties by destroying the balance of power in the federal system?

3. The Judiciary

The Supreme Court is unique because it decides fundamental social and political questions. These include the boundaries between church and state, between legislative and executive power, and even between racial groups. The Court has the power to declare the acts of governors, Congress, or the President to be unconstitutional. Tocqueville called this power of judicial review "one of the most powerful barriers that have ever been devised against the tyranny of political assemblies." But its opponents have challenged judicial review repeatedly since *Marbury v. Madison* established it in 1803.

In the twentieth century, Supreme Court decisions have helped shape government policies in controversial areas such as desegregation and abortion. Some scholars believe it is the Court's responsibility to act when Congress or the state legislatures do not. Others support "judicial self-restraint," claiming that the activism of the unelected federal judiciary represents a threat to the separation of powers and to democracy itself.

4. Civil Liberties

The first ten amendments to the Constitution are known as the Bill of Rights. The First Amendment guarantees individual liberties such as freedom of speech, religion, and assembly. Questions of limits on these individual liberties have been frequently and heatedly debated. For example, should the First Amendment right to freedom of speech prevail if it offends the values of the majority? What if it is racist speech? To what extent should human and civil rights be limited in the name of national security?

5. Suspects' Rights

How can the government balance the rights of persons accused of crimes and the public's right to safety? For example, some believe the courts should allow guilty persons to go free if crucial evidence against them has been obtained without a warrant, or if they were not specifically informed of their constitutional rights. Others argue that these restrictions on law-enforcement needlessly endanger the rest of the community.

Another area of debate concerns the widespread practice of "plea-bargaining" in criminal cases. In order to avoid costly trials, should prosecutors permit accused persons to plead guilty to lesser crimes? Or does this allow the guilty to escape the punishment they deserve?

6. Equality

In what ways are all Americans equal? The Constitution guarantees equality before the law, as well as equal political rights. Traditionally, discriminatory political and legal practices have thwarted these goals. Today, many people believe that the government should actively promote a more equal distribution of economic resources and benefits among citizens. For example, affirmative action programs require employers to promote a racial and sexual balance in the work force by favoring minority and female applicants. Supporters contend that without government intervention, the injustices of the past will continue to plague minorities. Opponents argue that affirmative action is a misguided attempt to guarantee equality of result rather than equality of opportunity.

7. Women's Rights

Does the Constitution adequately protect the rights of women? The document does not mention women, but neither does its use of the terms "person" and "citizen" exclude women. In recent years the nation has debated the merits of the Equal Rights Amendment. Is such an amendment necessary? Is it desirable? Short of a constitutional amendment, how can women be assured that they will not suffer from discrimination in the work force and other areas? How do Supreme Court decisions on reproductive issues affect women's rights?

8. Minority Rights

Slaves had no vote or other rights under the Constitution until passage of the Fourteenth Amendment in 1868. After World War II, the federal government took a larger role in protecting minority groups from discrimination. In *Brown v. Board of Education of Topeka* (1954), the Supreme Court redefined racial boundaries by outlawing school segregation. Often, government decisions involving minority rights met fierce resistance from people who felt that their own rights and the principle of majority rule were threatened. Then, in the 1980s, there appeared to be a reversal of government policy. Critics of Supreme Court decisions argued that minority gains from earlier decades were fast being eroded. Despite some gains, many minorities still suffer from discrimination. What is the federal government's role in protecting minority rights? What is the proper balance between majority rule and minority rights?

9. Foreign Policy

Under the Constitution, Congress alone has the power to declare war, but the President is commander-in-chief of the armed forces. How should the government handle the conduct of war and foreign policy? Should the President have the power to send troops into combat without a declaration of war, as was done in Korea and Vietnam? Some people argue that the President needs to be able to act decisively to protect national security interests. Others take the view that without popular support, in the form of a congressional vote, military actions are misguided and illegitimate. In passing the War Powers Act of 1973, which limited the President's ability to use military power, did Congress unconstitutionally infringe on presidential power?

10. Separation of Powers

Does the separation of powers make the federal government too inefficient to meet modern-day challenges? The framers deliberately pitted the branches of government against one another and, in effect, lessened their efficiency in order to guard against abuses. Some critics argue that these safeguards are not worth the price we pay for them in governmental inefficiency and delay. Others contend that the history of abuse of governmental power proves the worth of the system of checks and balances.

11. Representation

Our government is based on a system of representation. Does our current system of government provide fair and effective representation of our citizenry? The twentieth century has seen the growth of thousands of special interest groups, which often have political clout beyond the size of their memberships. Do these groups protect the rights of minorities? Or are they unacceptable limitations of democracy?

12. Government and the Economy

Does the Constitution's encouragement of business and commerce help all Americans, or does it favor the interests of the wealthy? In the twentieth century, reformers have urged the government to limit the exercise of free enterprise in order to protect the public from a variety of abuses. These abuses include unfair pricing, unsafe products, and environmental destruction.

13. Constitutional Change

How flexible is the Constitution? The framers included Article V so that the Constitution could be revised to suit future conditions. However, they deliberately made the amendment process difficult so that the Constitution would be more than temporary law. Does the requirement of a two-thirds vote of Congress and a three-quarters vote of the state legislatures or state conventions benefit the nation by making its political system more stable? Or does it harm America by preventing the Constitution from adapting to changing times? If, in accordance with Article V, the states called a second constitutional convention, would the delegates have the right to frame an entirely new constitution?

STUDYING THE CONSTITUTION

These thirteen enduring issues involve basic questions of law and policy. It is useful to keep them in mind as you study the Constitution, since they demonstrate the document's importance in the lives of American citizens.

The complete text of the Constitution of the United States begins on the next page. The actual text of the Constitution appears in the inside column on each page, while the other column explains specific parts or provisions.

Headings and subheadings have been added to the Constitution to help you find specific topics. Those parts of the Constitution that are no longer in effect are in lighter type. Some spellings and punctuation have been modified for modern readers.

A Directory of the Constitution

The Constitution of the United States

The Preamble states the purposes for which the Constitution was written: (1) to form a union of states that will benefit all, (2) to make laws and establish courts that are fair, (3) to maintain peace within the country, (4) to defend the nation against attack, (5) to ensure people's general well-being, and (6) to make sure that this nation's people and their descendants remain free.

The opening words of the Constitution make clear that it is the people themselves who have the power to establish a government or change it.

The first branch described is the legislative, or law-making, branch. Congress is made up of two houses—the Senate and the House of Representatives.

Section 2
Note that the states establish qualifications for voting. Any person who has the right to vote for representatives to the state legislature has the right to vote for the state's representatives in the House of Representatives. This is the only qualification for voting listed in the original Constitution. It made sure that the House would be elected by the people themselves.

Preamble

We the people of the United States, in order to form a more perfect union, establish justice, insure domestic tranquility, provide for the common defense, promote the general welfare, and secure the blessings of liberty to ourselves and our posterity, do ordain and establish this Constitution for the United States of America.

ARTICLE I Legislative Branch

SECTION 1   Congress

All legislative powers herein granted shall be vested in a Congress of the United States, which shall consist of a Senate and House of Representatives.

SECTION 2   The House of Representatives

Clause 1. Election and term of members   The House of Representatives shall be composed of members chosen every second year by the people of the several states, and the electors in each state shall have the qualifications requisite for electors of the most numerous branch of the state legislature.

Clause 2. Qualification of members   No person shall be a representative who shall not have attained to the age of twenty-five years, and been seven years a citizen of the United States, and who shall not, when elected, be an inhabitant of that state in which he shall be chosen.

Clause 3. Appointment of representatives and direct taxes Representatives [and direct taxes] shall be apportioned among the several states which may be included within this Union, according to their respective numbers, [which shall be determined by adding to the whole number of free persons, including those bound to service for a term of years, and excluding Indians not taxed, three-fifths of all other persons]. The actual enumeration shall be made within three years after the first meeting of the Congress of the United States, and within every subsequent term of ten years, in such manner as they shall by law direct. The number of representatives shall not exceed one for every thirty thousand, but each state shall have at least one representative; [and until such enumeration shall be made, the State of New Hampshire shall be entitled to choose three; Massachusetts, eight; Rhode Island and Providence Plantations, one; Connecticut, five; New York, six; New Jersey, four; Pennsylvania, eight; Delaware, one; Maryland, six; Virginia, ten; North Carolina, five; South Carolina, five; and Georgia, three].

Clause 4. Filling vacancies When vacancies happen in the representation from any state, the executive authority thereof shall issue writs of election to fill such vacancies.

Clause 5. Officers; impeachment The House of Representatives shall choose their Speaker and other officers; and shall have the sole power of impeachment.

SECTION 3 The Senate

Clause 1. Number and election of members The Senate of the United States shall be composed of two senators from each state, chosen [by the legislature thereof,] for six years; and each senator shall have one vote.

Clause 3
Several amendments have changed these provisions. All the people of a state are now counted in determining the number of representatives a state shall have, based on a census taken every ten years. The House of Representatives cannot have more than one member for every 30,000 persons in the nation. But each state is entitled to one representative, no matter how small its population. In 1910 Congress limited the number of representatives to 435.

Amendment 16 made the income tax an exception to the rule against direct taxes not based on population.

Clause 4
When a state does not have all the representatives to which it is entitled—for example, when a representative resigns or dies—the governor of the state may call an election to fill the vacancy.

Clause 5
Only the House can impeach, that is, bring charges of misbehavior in office against a U.S. official.

Section 3
Senators are no longer chosen by state legislatures but elected by the people (Amendment 17).

Senators in the 1st Congress were divided into three groups so that their terms would not all end at the same time. Today all senators are elected for six-year terms, but only one-third are elected in any election year.

A bird's-eye view of the nation's capital in 1880, when the Washington Monument was still being built.

Daniel Webster in a tense Senate debate, 1850.

Clauses 6 and 7

The Senate tries the case when a federal official is impeached by the House of Representatives. The Senators must formally declare that they will be honest and just. If the President of the United States is on trial, the Chief Justice presides over the Senate. Two-thirds of the senators present must agree that the charge is true for the impeached person to be found guilty.

If the Senate finds an impeached official guilty, the only punishment is removal from office and disqualification for ever holding a government job again. Once out of office, however, the former official may be tried in a regular court and, if found guilty, punished like any other person.

Clause 2. Choosing senators Immediately after they shall be assembled in consequence of the first election, they shall be divided as equally as may be into three classes. [The seats of the senators of the first class shall be vacated at the expiration of the second year, of the second class at the expiration of the fourth year, and of the third class at the expiration of the sixth year,] so that one-third may be chosen every second year; [and if vacancies happen by resignation, or otherwise, during the recess of the legislature of any state, the executive thereof may make temporary appointments until the next meeting of the legislature, which shall then fill such vacancies.]

Clause 3. Qualifications of members No person shall be a senator who shall not have attained to the age of thirty years, and been nine years a citizen of the United States, and who shall not, when elected, be an inhabitant of that state for which he shall be chosen.

Clause 4. Senate President The Vice President of the United States shall be President of the Senate, but shall have no vote, unless they be equally divided.

Clause 5. Other officers The Senate shall choose their own officers, and also a President pro tempore, in the absence of the Vice President, or when he shall exercise the office of President of the United States.

Clause 6. Impeachment trials The Senate shall have the sole power to try all impeachments. When sitting for that purpose, they shall be on oath or affirmation. When the President of the United States is tried, the Chief Justice shall preside; and no person shall be convicted without the concurrence of two-thirds of the members present.

Clause 7. Impeachment convictions Judgment in cases of impeachment shall not exceed further than to removal from office, and disqualification to hold and enjoy any office of honor, trust, or profit under the United States; but the party convicted shall nevertheless be liable and subject to indictment, trial, judgment, and punishment, according to law.

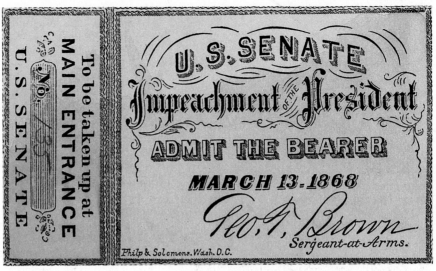

A visitor's ticket to the Senate gallery for the 1868 impeachment trial that acquitted President Johnson.

SECTION 4   Congressional Elections and Meetings

Clause 1. Elections   The times, places, and manner of holding elections for senators and representatives shall be prescribed in each state by the legislature thereof; but the Congress may at any time by law make or alter such regulations, [except as to the places of choosing senators.]

Clause 2. Meetings of Congress   The Congress shall assemble at least once in every year, [and such meeting shall be on the first Monday in December, unless they shall by law appoint a different day.]

SECTION 5   Organization and Rules

Clause 1. Organization   Each house shall be the judge of the elections, returns, and qualifications of its own members, and a majority of each shall constitute a quorum to do business; but a smaller number may adjourn from day to day, and may be authorized to compel the attendance of absent members, in such manner, and under such penalties as each house may provide.

Clause 2. Rules   Each house may determine the rules of its proceedings, punish its members for disorderly behavior, and with the concurrence of two-thirds, expel a member.

Clause 3. Journal   Each house shall keep a journal of its proceedings, and from time to time publish the same, excepting such parts as may in their judgment require secrecy; and the yeas and nays of the members of either house on any question shall, at the desire of one-fifth of those present, be entered on the journal.

Section 4
The legislature of each state has the right to determine how, when, and where senators and representatives are elected, but Congress may pass election laws that the states must follow. For example, a federal law requires that secret ballots be used. Congress must meet at least once a year. Amendment 20 made January 3 the day for beginning a regular session of Congress.

Andrew Johnson, the only U.S. President impeached.

Clause 3
Each house of Congress keeps and publishes a record of what goes on at its meetings. The *Congressional Record* is issued daily during sessions of Congress. Parts of the record that the members of Congress believe should be kept secret may be withheld. How members of either house vote on a question may be entered in the record if one-fifth of those present wish it.

Clause 4

When Congress is meeting, neither house may stop work for more than three days without the consent of the other house. Neither house may meet in another city without the consent of the other house.

Section 6

Senators and representatives are paid out of the United States Treasury and have a number of other privileges.

Until their terms have ended, senators or representatives may not hold offices created by the Congress of which they are members. The same restriction applies to jobs for which Congress has voted increased pay. No person may be a member of Congress without first giving up any other federal office he or she may hold.

Section 7

Bills for raising money for the federal government must start in the House of Representatives, but the Senate may make changes in such bills. Actually, the Senate now has as much influence over revenue bills as does the House. Other bills may start in either the Senate or the House of Representatives. However, exactly the same bill must be passed by a majority vote in both houses of Congress.

President Gerald Ford signs a tax bill into law.

Clause 4. Adjournment Neither house, during the session of Congress, shall without the consent of the other adjourn for more than three days, nor to any other place than that in which the two houses shall be sitting.

SECTION 6 Privileges and Restrictions

Clause 1. Pay; Congressional immunity The senators and representatives shall receive a compensation for their services, to be ascertained by law, and paid out of the Treasury of the United States. They shall in all cases, except treason, felony, and breach of the peace, be privileged from arrest during their attendance at the session of their respective houses and in going to and returning from the same; and for any speech or debate in either house, they shall not be questioned in any other place.

Clause 2. Restrictions No senator or representative shall, during the time for which he was elected, be appointed to any civil office under the authority of the United States which shall have been created, or the emoluments whereof shall have been increased during such time; and no person holding any office under the United States shall be a member of either house during his continuance in office.

SECTION 7 Method of Passing Laws

Clause 1. Revenue bills All bills for raising revenue shall originate in the House of Representatives; but the Senate may propose or concur with amendments as on other bills.

Clause 2. How bills become law Every bill which shall have passed the House of Representatives and the Senate shall, before it become a law, be presented to the President of the United States; if he approves he shall sign it, but if not he shall return it, with his objections, to that house in which it shall have originated, who shall enter the objections at large on their journal, and proceed to reconsider it. If after such reconsideration two-thirds of that house shall agree to pass the bill, it shall be sent, together with the objections, to the other house, by which it shall likewise be reconsidered, and if approved by two-thirds of that house, it shall become a law. But in all such cases the votes of both houses shall be determined by yeas and nays, and the names of the persons voting for and against the bill shall be entered on the journal of each house respectively. If any bill shall not be returned by the President within ten days (Sundays excepted) after it shall have been presented to him, the same shall be a law, in like manner as if he had signed it, unless the Congress by their adjournment prevent its return, in which case it shall not be a law.

Clause 3. Presidential approval or disapproval Every order, resolution, or vote to which the concurrence of the Senate and House of Representatives may be necessary (except on a question of adjournment) shall be presented to the President of the United States; and before the same shall take effect, shall be approved by him, or being disapproved by him, shall be repassed by two-thirds of the Senate and House of Representatives, according to the rules and limitations prescribed in the case of a bill.

SECTION 8   Powers Granted to Congress

The Congress shall have power
Clause 1. To lay and collect taxes, duties, imposts, and excises; to pay the debts and provide for the common defense and general welfare of the United States; but all duties, imposts, and excises shall be uniform throughout the United States;

Clause 2. To borrow money on the credit of the United States;

Clause 3. To regulate commerce with foreign nations, and among the several states, and with the Indian tribes;

Clause 4. To establish a uniform rule of naturalization, and uniform laws on the subject of bankruptcies throughout the United States;

Section 8
This section lists the many delegated powers of Congress.

Clause 3
Under this "commerce clause," the national government has broadened its powers.

The harbor at Philadelphia — an important center for American commerce and shipping — in 1800.

Clause 5. To coin money, regulate the value thereof and of foreign coin, and fix the standard of weights and measures;

Clause 6. To provide for the punishment of counterfeiting the securities and current coin of the United States;

Clause 7. To establish post offices and post roads;

Clause 8. To promote the progress of science and useful arts by securing for limited times to authors and inventors the exclusive right to their respective writings and discoveries;

Clause 9. To constitute tribunals inferior to the Supreme Court;

Clause 10. To define and punish piracies and felonies committed on the high seas and offenses against the laws of nations;

Clause 11. To declare war, grant letters of marque and reprisal, and make rules concerning captures on land and water;

Clause 12. To raise and support armies, but no appropriation of money to that use shall be for a longer term than two years;

Clause 13. To provide and maintain a navy;

Clause 14. To make rules for the government and regulation of land and naval forces;

Clause 15. To provide for calling forth the militia to execute the laws of the Union, suppress insurrections, and repel invasions;

Clause 16. To provide for organizing, arming, and disciplining the militia, and for governing such part of them as may be employed in the service of the United States, reserving to the states respectively the appointment of the officers and the authority of training the militia, according to the discipline prescribed by Congress;

Clause 8
Congress may pass copyright and patent laws that make it illegal for a person to use the work of an artist, musician, author, or inventor without permission.

U.S. gold "quarter eagle" coins, minted in 1796.

Clauses 11–16
These provisions ensure civilian control of the military.

The first American dollar bill, an 1862 "greenback."

Clause 17. To exercise exclusive legislation in all cases whatsoever over such district (not exceeding ten miles square) as may, by cession of particular states and the acceptance of Congress, become the seat of the government of the United States, and to exercise like authority over all places purchased by the consent of the legislature of the states in which the same shall be for the erection of forts, magazines, arsenals, dock-yards, and other needful buildings; and

Clause 18. To make all laws which shall be necessary and proper for carrying into execution the foregoing powers, and all other powers vested by this Constitution in the government of the United States, or in any department or officer thereof.

SECTION 9   Powers Denied to the Federal Government

Clause 1. [The migration or importation of such persons as any of the states now existing shall think proper to admit shall not be prohibited by the Congress prior to the year one thousand eight hundred and eight, but a tax or duty may be imposed on such importation, not exceeding ten dollars for each person.]

Clause 2. The privilege of the writ of habeas corpus shall not be suspended, unless when in cases of rebellion or invasion the public safety may require it.

Clause 3. No bill of attainder or ex post facto law shall be passed.

Clause 4. No capitation or other direct tax shall be laid, unless in proportion to the census or enumeration herein before directed to be taken.

Clause 5. No tax or duty shall be laid on articles exported from any state.

Clause 6. No preference shall be given by any regulation of commerce or revenue to the ports of one state over those of another; nor shall vessels bound to or from one state be obliged to enter, clear, or pay duties in another.

Clause 7. No money shall be drawn from the treasury, but in consequence of appropriations made by law; and a regular statement and account of the receipts and expenditures of all public money shall be published from time to time.

Clause 8. No titles of nobility shall be granted by the United States; and no person holding any office of profit or trust under them shall, without the consent of Congress, accept of any present, emolument, office, or title, of any kind whatever, from any king, prince, or foreign state.

Clause 17
Congress has the power to make laws for the District of Columbia, the national capital. Congress also makes laws regulating the use of all other property belonging to the national government—forts, arsenals, national parks, etc.

Clause 18
The "necessary and proper" clause, or elastic clause, is the basis for the implied powers.

Section 9
This is the first list of prohibited powers—those denied to the federal government.

Clause 1
Congress could not take action against slavery until 1808, when it prohibited further importation of slaves.

The shelling of Ft. McHenry, Baltimore, in 1814, which inspired the words of the "Star-Spangled Banner."

Clause 8
The United States may not grant a title of nobility. Federal officials may not accept titles, gifts, or honors from any foreign ruler or government unless Congress gives its permission.

Section 10
This is the listing of powers prohibited to the states.

Clause 2
States cannot tax goods leaving or entering their territory but may charge fees to cover the costs of inspection. Any profit from such inspection fees must be turned over to the United States Treasury. Congress has the power to change the inspection laws of a state.

Clause 3
Unless Congress gives permission, a state may not tax ships entering its ports, keep an army or navy—except the militia — in time of peace, make treaties with other states or foreign countries, or make war except when it is invaded.

The second branch is the executive branch, which carries out the laws.

GENERAL ANDREW JACKSON.
The Hero, the Sage and the Patriot.

Clause 2
This provision sets up the Electoral College: The President and Vice President are elected by electors chosen by the states according to rules established by the legislatures. Each state has as many electors as it has senators and representatives in Congress.
This clause did not work well in practice and was changed by Amendment 12.

SECTION 10 Powers Denied to the States

Clause 1. No state shall enter into any treaty, alliance, or confederation; grant letters of marque and reprisal; coin money; emit bills of credit; make any thing but gold and silver coin a tender in payment of debts; pass any bill of attainder, ex post facto law, or law impairing the obligation of contracts; or grant any title of nobility.

Clause 2. No state shall, without the consent of the Congress, lay any imposts or duties on imports or exports, except what may be absolutely necessary for executing its inspection laws; and the net produce of all duties and imposts, laid by any state on imports or exports, shall be for the use of the treasury of the United States; and all such laws shall be subject to the revision and control of the Congress.

Clause 3. No state shall, without the consent of Congress, lay any duty of tonnage; keep troops or ships of war in time of peace; enter into any agreement or compact with another state or with a foreign power; or engage in war, unless actually invaded or in such imminent danger as will not admit of delay.

ARTICLE II Executive Branch

SECTION 1 President and Vice President

Clause 1. Term of office The executive power shall be vested in a President of the United States of America. He shall hold his office during the term of four years, and, together with the Vice President chosen for the same term, be elected as follows:

Clause 2. Electoral College Each state shall appoint, in such manner as the legislature thereof may direct, a number of electors, equal to the whole number of senators and representatives to which the state may be entitled in the Congress; but no senator or representative, or person holding an office of trust or profit under the United States, shall be appointed an elector.

[The electors shall meet in their respective states and vote by ballot for two persons, of whom one at least shall not be an inhabitant of the same state with themselves. And they shall make a list of all the persons voted for and of the number of votes for each; which list they shall sign and certify, and transmit sealed to the seat of government of the United States, directed to the President of the Senate. The President of the Senate shall, in the presence of the Senate and House of Representatives, open all the certificates, and the votes shall then be counted. The person having the greatest number of votes shall be the President, if such number be a majority of the whole number of electors appointed; and if there be more than one who have such majority, and have an equal number of votes, then the House of Representatives shall immediately choose by ballot one of them for President; and if no person have a majority, then from the five highest on the list the said house shall in like manner choose the President. But in choosing the President the votes shall be taken by states, the representation from each state having one vote; a quorum for this purpose shall consist of a member or members from two-thirds of the states, and a majority of all the states shall be necessary to a choice. In every case, after the choice of the President, the person having the greatest number of votes of the electors shall be the Vice President. But if there should remain two or more who have equal votes, the Senate shall choose from them by ballot the Vice President.]

Clause 3. Time of elections   The Congress may determine the time of choosing the electors, and the day on which they shall give their votes; which day shall be the same throughout the United States.

Clause 4. Qualifications for President   No person except a natural-born citizen, [or a citizen of the United States, at the time of the adoption of this Constitution] shall be eligible to the office of President; neither shall any person be eligible to that office who shall not have attained the age of thirty-five years, and been fourteen years a resident within the United States.

Clause 5. Succession   In case of the removal of the President from office or of his death, resignation, or inability to discharge the powers and duties of the said office, the same shall devolve on the Vice President; and the Congress may by law provide for the case of removal, death, resignation, or inability, both of the President and Vice President, declaring what officer shall then act as President; and such officer shall act accordingly, until the disability be removed or a President shall be elected.

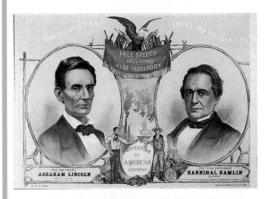

An 1860 poster for candidates Lincoln and Hannibal Hamlin.

Clause 3
Congress determines when electors are chosen and when they vote. The day is the same throughout the United States. The popular vote for electors takes place on the Tuesday after the first Monday of November every four years. In mid-December the electors meet in their state capitals and cast their electoral votes.

Clause 5
If the presidency becomes vacant, the Vice President becomes the President of the United States. If neither the President nor the Vice President is able to serve, Congress has the right to decide which government official shall act as President. Amendment 25 practically assures that there always will be a Vice President to succeed to the presidency.

The White House — the presidential mansion — in 1848.

Section 2
Presidential powers are described very generally (unlike those of Congress).

Clause 1
The President is commander-in-chief of the armed forces and of the militia when it is called out by the national government. This is another provision to ensure civilian control of the military. No provision is made in the Constitution for the Cabinet or for Cabinet meetings, but the existence of executive departments is implied in this clause.

Clause 2
The President is the nation's chief diplomat, with the power to make treaties. All treaties must be approved in the Senate by a two-thirds vote of the senators present. The President also can appoint important government officials, who must be approved in the Senate by a majority.

Past and future Presidents and their families at the inauguration of John F. Kennedy. (The front row includes the Eisenhowers, Lady Bird Johnson, Jacqueline Kennedy, Lyndon Johnson, Richard Nixon, and the Trumans.)

Clause 6. Salary The President shall, at stated times, receive for his services a compensation, which shall neither be increased nor diminished during the period for which he shall have been elected, and he shall not receive within that period any other emolument from the United States, or any of them.

Clause 7. Oath of office Before he enter on the execution of his office, he shall take the following oath or affirmation: "I do solemnly swear (or affirm) that I will faithfully execute the office of President of the United States, and will to the best of my ability, preserve, protect, and defend the Constitution of the United States."

SECTION 2   Powers of the President

Clause 1. Military powers; Cabinet; pardons The President shall be Commander-in-Chief of the Army and Navy of the United States, and of the militia of the several states, when called into the actual service of the United States. He may require the opinion, in writing, of the principal officer in each of the executive departments, upon any subject relating to the duties of their respective offices, and he shall have power to grant reprieves and pardons for offenses against the United States, except in cases of impeachment.

Clause 2. Diplomatic powers; appointments He shall have power, by and with the advice and consent of the Senate, to make treaties, provided two-thirds of the senators present concur; and he shall nominate and, by and with the advice and consent of the Senate, shall appoint ambassadors, other public ministers and consuls, judges of the Supreme Court, and all other officers of the United States, whose appointments are not herein otherwise provided for, and which shall be established by law; but the Congress may by law vest the appointment of such inferior officers as they think proper in the President alone, in the courts of law, or in the heads of departments.

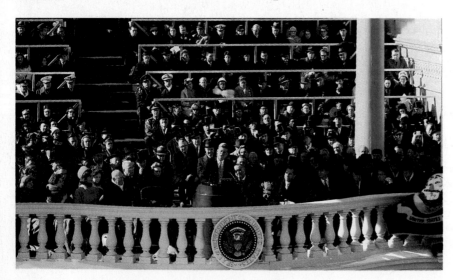

Clause 3. Filling vacancies The President shall have power to fill up all vacancies that may happen during the recess of the Senate, by granting commissions which shall expire at the end of their next session.

SECTION 3 Duties of the President

He shall from time to time give to the Congress information of the state of the Union, and recommend to their consideration such measures as he shall judge necessary and expedient; he may, on extraordinary occasions, convene both houses, or either of them, and in case of disagreement between them with respect to the time of adjournment he may adjourn them to such time as he shall think proper; he shall receive ambassadors and other public ministers; he shall take care that the laws be faithfully executed, and shall commission all the officers of the United States.

SECTION 4 Impeachment

The President, Vice-President, and all civil officers of the United States shall be removed from office on impeachment for, and conviction of, treason, bribery, or other high crimes and misdemeanors.

Clause 3
If the Senate is not meeting, the President may make temporary appointments to fill vacancies.

Section 3
The Constitution imposes only a few specific duties on the President. One is to give a "State of the Union" message, which Presidents now deliver once a year.

Section 4
This section makes all Federal officials subject to the impeachment process described in Article I.

The Supreme Court held its first two sessions in this New York building, known as the Exchange.

ARTICLE III Judicial Branch

SECTION 1 The Federal Courts

The judicial power of the United States shall be vested in one Supreme Court and in such inferior courts as the Congress may from time to time ordain and establish. The judges, both of the Supreme and inferior courts, shall hold their offices during good behavior and shall, at stated times, receive for their services a compensation which shall not be diminished during their continuance in office.

Article III gives the power to interpret the laws of the United States to the third branch, the judicial, which includes the Supreme Court and the other federal courts established by Congress. District courts and courts of appeal are now part of the regular court system. Federal judges are appointed by the President with the approval of the Senate.

Section 2

The federal courts have jurisdiction in certain kinds of cases.

Roger B. Taney, Chief Justice of the United States in the crucial years between 1836 and 1864.

Section 3

The Constitution defines treason and places limits on how it can be punished.

The Supreme Court building today.

SECTION 2 Federal Court Jurisdiction

Clause 1. Federal cases The judicial power shall extend to all cases, in law and equity, arising under this Constitution, the laws of the United States, and treaties made, or which shall be made, under their authority; to all cases affecting ambassadors, other public ministers, and consuls; to all cases of admiralty and maritime jurisdiction; to controversies to which the United States shall be a party; to controversies between two or more states; [between a state and citizens of another state;] between citizens of different states; between citizens of the same state claiming lands under grants of different states, and between a state, or the citizens thereof, and foreign states, citizens, or subjects.

Clause 2. Supreme Court jurisdiction In all cases affecting ambassadors, other public ministers, and consuls, and those in which a state be a party, the Supreme Court shall have original jurisdiction. In all the other cases before mentioned, the Supreme Court shall have appellate jurisdiction, both as to law and fact, with such exceptions and under such regulations as the Congress shall make.

Clause 3. Trial rules The trial of all crimes, except in cases of impeachment, shall be by jury; and such trial shall be held in the state where the said crimes shall have been committed; but when not committed within any state, the trial shall be at such place or places as the Congress may by law have directed.

SECTION 3 Treason

Clause 1. Definition Treason against the United States shall consist only in levying war against them or in adhering to their enemies, giving them aid and comfort. No person shall be convicted of treason unless on the testimony of two witnesses to the same overt act, or on confession in open court.

Clause 2. Punishment The Congress shall have power to declare the punishment of treason, but no attainder of treason shall work corruption of blood, or forfeiture except during the life of the person attainted.

ARTICLE IV The States and the Federal Government

SECTION 1 State Records

Full faith and credit shall be given in each state to the public acts, records, and judicial proceedings of every other state. And the Congress may by general laws prescribe the manner in which such acts, records, and proceedings shall be proved, and the effect thereof.

SECTION 2 Rights of Citizens

Clause 1. Privileges and immunities The citizens of each state shall be entitled to all privileges and immunities of citizens in the several states.

Clause 2. Extradition A person charged in any state with treason, felony, or other crime who shall flee from justice and be found in another state shall, on demand of the executive authority of the state from which he fled, be delivered up, to be removed to the state having jurisdiction of the crime.

[**Clause 3. Fugitive workers** No person held to service or labor in one state, under the laws thereof, escaping into another shall, in consequence of any law or regulation therein, be discharged from such service or labor, but shall be delivered upon claim of the party to whom such service or labor may be due.]

SECTION 3 New States and Territories

Clause 1. Admission of new states New states may be admitted by the Congress into this Union; but no new state shall be formed or erected within the jurisdiction of any other state; nor any state be formed by the junction of two or more states, or parts of states, without the consent of the legislatures of the states concerned, as well as of the Congress.

Clause 2. Federal territory The Congress shall have power to dispose of and make all needful rules and regulations respecting the territory or other property belonging to the United States; and nothing in this Constitution shall be so construed as to prejudice any claims of the United States, or of any particular state.

SECTION 4 Federal Duties to the States

The United States shall guarantee to every state in this Union a republican form of government, and shall protect each of them against invasion; and on application of the legislature, or of the executive (whom the legislature cannot be convened), against domestic violence.

Dakota Territory applying to Uncle Sam for statehood, in an 1880's cartoon.

Article V sets up two ways of amending the Constitution and two ways of ratifying amendments.

ARTICLE V Amending the Constitution

The Congress, whenever two-thirds of both houses shall deem it necessary, shall propose amendments to this Constitution, or, on the application of the legislatures of two-thirds of the several states, shall call a convention for proposing amendments, which, in either case, shall be valid to all intents and purposes, as part of this Constitution, when ratified by the legislatures of three-fourths of the several states or by conventions in three-fourths thereof, as the one or the other mode of ratification may be proposed by the Congress; provided that [no amendments which may be made prior to the year one thousand eight hundred and eight shall in any manner affect the first and fourth clauses in the ninth section of the first article; and that] no state, without its consent, shall be deprived of its equal suffrage in the Senate.

Article VI makes the Constitution the "supreme law of the land." If state law is in conflict with national law, it is the national law that must be obeyed.

ARTICLE VI Supremacy of National Law

Clause 1
The framers of the Constitution agreed that the United States would be responsible for all debts contracted by the government under the Articles of Confederation.

Clause 1. Public debt All debts contracted and engagements entered into, before the adoption of this Constitution, shall be as valid against the United States under this Constitution as under the Confederation.

Clause 2. Supreme law of the land This Constitution, and the laws of the United States which shall be made in pursuance thereof, and all treaties made, or which shall be made, under the authority of the United States, shall be the supreme law of the land; and the judges in every state shall be bound thereby, anything in the Constitution or laws of any state to the contrary notwithstanding.

Clause 3. Oath of office The senators and representatives before mentioned, and the members of the several state legislatures, and all executive and judicial officers, both of the United States and of the several states, shall be bound by oath or affirmation to support this Constitution; but no religious test shall ever be required as a qualification to any office or public trust under the United States.

Present-day courtroom, Newport, Rhode Island.

The signing of the Constitution, September 17, 1787.

ARTICLE VII Ratification of the Constitution

The ratification of the conventions of nine states shall be sufficient for the establishment of this Constitution between the states so ratifying the same.

Article VII established that the Constitution would go into effect when nine states voted to accept it. This occurred on June 21, 1788, with New Hampshire's ratification.

George Washington —
President and
delegate
from Virginia

New Hampshire
John Langdon
Nicholas Gilman

Massachusetts
Nathaniel Gorham
Rufus King

Connecticut
William Samuel
Johnson
Roger Sherman

New York
Alexander Hamilton

New Jersey
William Livingston
David Brearley
William Paterson
Jonathan Dayton

Pennsylvania
Benjamin Franklin
Thomas Mifflin
Robert Morris
George Clymer
Thomas FitzSimons
Jared Ingersoll
James Wilson
Gouverneur Morris

Delaware
George Reed
Gunning Bedford, Junior
John Dickinson
Richard Bassett
Jacob Broom

Maryland
James McHenry
Daniel of St. Thomas
Jenifer
Daniel Carroll

Virginia
John Blair
James Madison, Junior

North Carolina
William Blount
Richard Dobbs
Spaight
Hugh Williamson

South Carolina
John Rutledge
Charles Cotesworth
Pinckney
Charles Pinckney
Pierce Butler

Georgia
William Few
Abraham Baldwin

AMENDMENTS to the Constitution

Amendments 1–10 make up the Bill of Rights.

Amendment 1 protects citizens from government interference with their freedoms of religion, speech, press, assembly, and petition. These are the basic civil liberties.

AMENDMENT 1 Freedom of Religion, Speech, Press, Assembly, and Petition (1791)

Congress shall make no law respecting an establishment of religion or prohibiting the free exercise thereof; or abridging the freedom of speech, or of the press; or the right of the people peaceably to assemble, and to petition the government for a redress of grievances.

Amendment 2 guarantees that the federal government cannot deny states the right to enlist citizens in the militia and to provide them with training in the use of weapons.

AMENDMENT 2 Right to Bear Arms (1791)

A well-regulated militia being necessary to the security of a free state, the right of the people to keep and bear arms shall not be infringed.

Amendment 3 was included because of the troubles caused when the British sought to quarter and supply their troops in colonists' homes. The amendment guarantees that in time of peace the federal government may not force people to have soldiers live in their homes. Even in time of war, people cannot be compelled to do this unless Congress passes a law requiring it.

AMENDMENT 3 Quartering of Soldiers (1791)

No soldier shall, in time of peace, be quartered in any house without the consent of the owner, nor in time of war, but in a manner to be prescribed by law.

AMENDMENT 4 Search and Seizure (1791)

Amendment 4 extends the people's right to privacy and security by setting limits on authorities' power to search property and seize evidence.

The right of the people to be secure in their persons, houses, papers, and effects, against unreasonable searches and seizures, shall not be violated, and no warrants shall issue but upon probable cause, supported by oath or affirmation and particularly describing the place to be searched and the persons or things to be seized.

AMENDMENT 5   Rights of the Accused (1791)

No person shall be held to answer for a capital or otherwise infamous crime, unless on a presentment or indictment of a grand jury, except in cases arising in the land or naval forces, or in the militia, when in actual service in time of war or public danger; nor shall any person be subject for the same offense to be twice put in jeopardy of life or limb; nor shall be compelled in any criminal case to be a witness against himself, nor be deprived of life, liberty, or property, without due process of law; nor shall private property be taken for public use without just compensation.

Amendment 5 ensures certain rights for people accused of crimes. It says that no person may be tried in a federal court unless a grand jury decides that the person ought to be tried. (Members of the armed forces may be tried in military court under military law.) Other provisions guarantee due process of law. Finally, a person's private property may not be taken for public use without a fair price being paid for it.

AMENDMENT 6   Requirements for Jury Trial (1791)

In all criminal prosecutions, the accused shall enjoy the right to a speedy and public trial by an impartial jury of the state and district wherein the crime shall have been committed, which districts shall have been previously ascertained by law, and to be informed of the nature and cause of the accusation; to be confronted with the witnesses against him; to have compulsory process for obtaining witnesses in his favor; and to have the assistance of counsel for his defense.

Amendment 6 lists additional rights of an individual accused of a crime. A person accused of a crime is entitled to a prompt public trial before an impartial jury. The trial is held in the district where the crime took place. The accused must be told what the charge is. The accused must be present when witnesses give their testimony. The government must help the accused bring into court friendly witnesses. The accused must be provided with legal counsel.

AMENDMENT 7   Rules of Common Law (1791)

In suits at common law, where the value in controversy shall exceed twenty dollars, the right of trial by jury shall be preserved, and no fact tried by a jury shall be otherwise reexamined in any court of the United States than according to the rules of common law.

Amendment 7 is somewhat out of date. Today, cases involving lawsuits are not tried before federal courts unless large sums of money are involved.

The draft of the Bill of Rights — twelve amendments sent to the states in 1789 — only ten of which were approved.

Amendment 8 provides that persons accused of crimes may in most cases be released from jail if they or someone else posts bail. Bail, fines, and punishments must be reasonable.

Amendment 9 was included because of the impossibility of listing in the Constitution all the rights of the people. The mention of certain rights does not mean that people do not have other fundamental rights, which the government must respect. These include the right to privacy.

Amendment 10 establishes the reserved powers. It states that the powers that the Constitution does not give to the United States and does not deny to the states belong to the states and to the people.

This amendment was the first that was enacted to override a Supreme Court decision. It confirms that no federal court may try a case in which a state is being sued by a citizen of another state or of a foreign country. Amendment 11 changes a provision of Article III, Section 2.

AMENDMENT 8   Limits on Criminal Punishments (1791)

Excessive bail shall not be required, nor excessive fines imposed, nor cruel and unusual punishments inflicted.

AMENDMENT 9   Rights Kept by the People (1791)

The enumeration in the Constitution of certain rights shall not be construed to deny or disparage others retained by the people.

AMENDMENT 10   Powers of the States and the People (1791)

The powers not delegated to the United States by the Constitution, nor prohibited by it to the states, are reserved to the states respectively, or to the people.

AMENDMENT 11   Lawsuits Against a State (1798)

The judicial power of the United States shall not be construed to extend to any suit in law or equity commenced or prosecuted against one of the United States by citizens of another state or by citizens or subjects of any foreign state.

A southern jury in 1867 included blacks who, for the first time, had the rights of citizens.

AMENDMENT 12 Election of President and Vice President (1804)

The electors shall meet in their respective states and vote by ballot for President and Vice President, one of whom, at least, shall not be an inhabitant of the same state with themselves; they shall name in their ballots the person voted for as President, and in distinct ballots the person voted for as Vice President, and they shall make distinct lists of all persons voted for as President, and of all persons voted for as Vice President, and of the number of votes for each, which lists they shall sign and certify, and transmit sealed to the seat of the government of the United States, directed to the President of the Senate; the President of the Senate shall, in the presence of the Senate and House of Representatives, open all the certificates and the votes shall then be counted; the person having the greatest number of votes for President shall be the President, if such number be a majority of the whole number of electors appointed; and if no person have such majority, then from the persons having the highest numbers not exceeding three on the list of those voted for as President, the House of Representatives shall choose immediately, by ballot, the President. But in choosing the President, the votes shall be taken by states, the representation from each state having one vote; a quorum for this purpose shall consist of a member or members from two-thirds of the states, and a majority of all the states shall be necessary to a choice. And if the House of Representatives shall not choose a President whenever the right of choice shall devolve upon them, [before the fourth day of March next following] then the Vice President shall act as President, as in the case of the death or constitutional disability of the President. The person having the greatest number of votes as Vice President shall be the Vice President, if such number be a majority of the whole number of electors appointed, and if no person have a majority, then from the two highest numbers on the list, the Senate shall choose the Vice President; a quorum for the purpose shall consist of two-thirds of the whole number of senators, and a majority of the whole number shall be necessary to a choice. But no person constitutionally ineligible to the office of President shall be eligible to that of Vice President of the United States.

Amendment 12 changed the Electoral College procedure for choosing a President. The most important change made by this amendment was that the presidential electors would vote for President and Vice President on separate ballots. In 1800, when only one ballot was used, Thomas Jefferson and Aaron Burr received the same number of votes, and the election had to be decided by the House of Representatives. To guard against this possibility in the future, Amendment 12 calls for separate ballots.

Thomas Jefferson, third President of the United States.

AMENDMENT 13 Slavery Abolished (1865)

Section 1. Abolition of slavery Neither slavery nor involuntary servitude, except as a punishment for crime whereof the party shall have been duly convicted, shall exist within the United States or any place subject to their jurisdiction.

Section 2. Enforcement Congress shall have the power to enforce this article by appropriate legislation.

Amendment 13 is the first of three amendments that were a consequence of the Civil War. It states that slavery must end in the United States and its territories.

Congress may pass whatever laws are necessary to enforce Amendment 13. This statement, called an *enabling act,* is now commonly included in amendments.

By the definition of citizenship in Amendment 14, black Americans were granted citizenship. The first section provides that all persons born or naturalized in the United States and subject to this country's laws are citizens of the United States and of the state in which they live. State governments may not deprive anyone of due process of law or equal protection.

This section abolished the provision in Article 1, Section 2, which said that only three-fifths of the slaves should be counted as population.

Section 3 was designed to bar former leaders of the Confederacy from holding federal office.

Following emancipation, most Southern blacks became sharecroppers, working land owned by others.

AMENDMENT 14   Civil Rights Guaranteed (1868)

Section 1. Definition of citizenship   All persons born or naturalized in the United States, and subject to the jurisdiction thereof, are citizens of the United States and of the state wherein they reside. No state shall make or enforce any law which shall abridge the privileges or immunities of citizens of the United States; nor shall any state deprive any person of life, liberty, or property, without due process of law; nor deny to any person within its jurisdiction the equal protection of the laws.

Section 2. Apportionment of representatives   Representatives shall be apportioned among the several states according to their respective numbers, counting the whole number of persons in each state, [excluding Indians not taxed.] But when the right to vote at any election for the choice of electors for President and Vice President of the United States, representatives in Congress, the executive and judicial officers of a state, or the members of the legislature thereof, is denied to any of the [male] inhabitants of such state, [being twenty-one years of age] and citizens of the United States, or in any way abridged, except for participation in rebellion, or other crime, the basis of representation therein shall be reduced in the proportion which the number of such [male] citizens shall bear to the whole number of [male] citizens [twenty-one years of age] in such state.

Section 3. Restrictions on holding office   No person shall be a senator or representative in Congress, or elector of President and Vice President, or hold any office, civil or military, under the United States, or under any state, who, having previously taken an oath as a member of Congress, or as an officer of the United States, or as a member of any state legislature, or as an executive or judicial officer of any state, to support the Constitution of the United States, shall have engaged in insurrection or rebellion against the same, or given aid or comfort to the enemies thereof. But Congress may by vote of two-thirds of each house remove such disability.

Black members of Congress elected after the Civil War.

Section 4. Valid public debts of the United States The validity of the public debt of the United States, authorized by law, including debts incurred for payment of pensions and bounties for services in suppressing insurrection or rebellion, shall not be questioned. But neither the United States nor any state shall assume or pay any debt or obligation incurred in aid of insurrection or rebellion against the United States, or any claim for the loss or emancipation of any slave; but all such debts, obligations, and claims shall be held illegal and void.

Section 5. Enforcement The Congress shall have power to enforce by appropriate legislation the provisions of this article.

This section was included to settle the question of debts incurred during the Civil War. All debts contracted by the United States were to be paid. Neither the United States nor any state government, however, was to pay the debts of the Confederacy. Moreover, no payment was to be made to former slave owners as compensation for slaves who were set free.

AMENDMENT 15   Black Voting Rights (1870)

Section 1. The right of citizens of the United States to vote shall not be denied or abridged by the United States or by any state on account of race, color, or previous condition of servitude.

Section 2. The Congress shall have power to enforce this article by appropriate legislation.

Amendment 15 sought to protect the right of citizens, particularly former slaves, to vote in federal and state elections.

AMENDMENT 16   Income Tax (1913)

The Congress shall have power to lay and collect taxes on incomes, from whatever source derived, without apportionment among the several states and without regard to any census or enumeration.

Amendment 16 authorizes Congress to tax incomes. An amendment was necessary because in 1895 the Supreme Court had decided that an income tax law, passed by Congress a year earlier, was unconstitutional.

Amendment 17 changed Article I, Section 3, to allow the direct election of senators by popular vote. Anyone qualified to vote for a state representative may vote for United States senators.

Amendment 18 forbade the manufacture, sale, or shipment of alcoholic beverages within the United States. Importing and exporting such beverages was also forbidden. Amendment 18 was later repealed by Amendment 21.

Federal agents destroying a still to enforce Prohibition.

AMENDMENT 17 Direct Election of Senators (1913)

Section 1. Election by the people The Senate of the United States shall be composed of two senators from each state, elected by the people thereof, for six years; and each senator shall have one vote. The electors in each state shall have the qualifications requisite for electors of the most numerous branch of the state legislatures.

Section 2. Senate vacancies When vacancies happen in the representation of any state in the Senate, the executive authority of such state shall issue writs of election to fill such vacancies: provided that the legislature of any state may empower the executive thereof to make temporary appointments until the people fill the vacancies by election as the legislature may direct.

Section 3. Effective date This amendment shall not be so construed as to affect the election or term of any senator chosen before it becomes valid as part of the Constitution.

AMENDMENT 18 Prohibition (1919)

[Section 1. After one year from the ratification of this article the manufacture, sale, or transportation of intoxicating liquors within, the importation thereof into, or the exportation thereof from the United States and all territory subject to the jurisdiction thereof for beverage purposes is hereby prohibited.

Section 2. The Congress and the several states shall have concurrent power to enforce this article by appropriate legislation.

Section 3. This article shall be inoperative unless it shall have been ratified as an amendment to the Constitution by the legislatures of the several states, as provided in the Constitution, within seven years from the date of the submission hereof to the states by the Congress.]

AMENDMENT 19   Women's Voting Rights (1920)

Section 1.   The right of citizens of the United States to vote shall not be denied or abridged by the United States or by any state on account of sex.

Section 2.   The Congress shall have power to enforce this article by appropriate legislation.

AMENDMENT 20   Terms of Office and Presidential Succession (1933)

Section 1. Terms of office   The terms of the President and Vice President shall end at noon on the 20th day of January, and the terms of senators and representatives at noon on the 3rd day of January, of the years in which such terms would have ended if this article had not been ratified; and the terms of their successors shall then begin.

Section 2. Sessions of Congress   The Congress shall assemble at least once in every year, and such meeting shall begin at noon on the 3rd day of January, unless they shall by law appoint a different day.

Section 3. Presidential succession   If, at the time fixed for the beginning of the term of the President, the President-elect shall have died, the Vice President-elect shall become President.   If a President shall not have been chosen before the time fixed for the beginning of his term, or if the President-elect shall have failed to qualify, then the Vice President-elect shall act as President until a President shall have qualified; and the Congress may by law provide for the case wherein neither a President-elect nor a Vice President-elect shall have qualified, declaring who shall then act as President, or the manner in which one who is to act shall be selected, and such person shall act accordingly until a President or a Vice President shall have qualified.

Section 4. House election of President   The Congress may by law provide for the case of the death of any of the persons from whom the House of Representatives may choose a President whenever the right of choice shall have devolved upon them, and for the case of the death of any of the persons from whom the Senate may choose a Vice President whenever the right of choice shall have devolved upon them.

Section 5. Effective date   Sections 1 and 2 shall take effect on the fifteenth day of October following the ratification of this article.

[**Section 6. Ratification**   This article shall be inoperative unless it shall have been ratified as an amendment to the Constitution by the legislatures of three-fourths of the several states within seven years from the date of its submission.]

Amendment 19 provides that women citizens may not be denied the right to vote in a federal or state election.

A suffragist rally.

When the Constitution was written, transportation and communication were slow. There was a long period, therefore, between the President's election (November) and inauguration (March). One purpose of Amendment 20 was to shorten that waiting period. The amendment established that the terms of the President and Vice President end at noon on January 20 following a presidential election. The terms of one-third of the senators and of all representatives, meanwhile, end at noon on January 3 in years ending in odd numbers. The new terms begin when the old terms end.

Section 2 provides that Congress must meet at least once a year, with the regular session beginning on January 3 unless Congress sets a different day.

Section 3 provides ways of filling the office of President in several emergencies.

Because the House of Representatives chooses the President if no candidate receives a majority of the electoral votes, Section 4 also gives Congress power to make a law to decide what to do if one of the candidates dies.

Amendment 21 repealed Amendment 18, putting an end to Prohibition. It was the only amendment submitted to special ratifying conventions instead of state legislatures.

Section 2 allows states or local governments to continue prohibition if they wish.

Amendment 22 set limits on the time a President may serve. No person may be elected President more than twice. A person who has served more than two years in the place of an elected President may be elected President only once. This limitation did not apply to President Truman, who was in office when Amendment 22 was proposed.

Presidents Washington, Jefferson, and Madison set the pattern of serving only two terms in office. Although Ulysses S. Grant and Theodore Roosevelt sought third terms, the precedent of serving only two terms was not broken until 1940, when Franklin D. Roosevelt was elected for a third term.

AMENDMENT 21   Repeal of Prohibition (1933)

Section 1.   The eighteenth article of amendment to the Constitution of the United States is hereby repealed.

Section 2. State laws.   The transportation or importation into any state, territory, or possession of the United States for delivery or use therein of intoxicating liquors, in violation of the laws thereof, is hereby prohibited.

[**Section 3.**   This article shall be inoperative unless it shall have been ratified as an amendment to the Constitution by conventions in the several states, as provided in the Constitution, within seven years from the date of the submission hereof to the states by the Congress.]

AMENDMENT 22   Limits on Presidential Terms (1951)

Section 1.   No person shall be elected to the office of the President more than twice, and no person who has held the office of President, or acted as President, for more than two years of a term to which some other person was elected President shall be elected to the office of the President more than once. But this article shall not apply to any person holding the office of President when this article was proposed by the Congress, and shall not prevent any person who may be holding the office of President, or acting as President, during the term within which this article becomes operative from holding the office of President, or acting as President during the remainder of such term.

[**Section 2.**   This article shall be inoperative unless it shall have been ratified as an amendment to the Constitution by the legislatures of three-fourths of the several states within seven years from the date of its submission to the states by the Congress.]

A victorious Franklin D. Roosevelt with congratulatory mail after his sweeping 1936 election victory.

Celebrating the bicentennial of the Constitution, 1987.

AMENDMENT 23 Voting in the District of Columbia (1961)

Section 1. The District constituting the seat of government of the United States shall appoint, in such manner as the Congress may direct:

A number of electors of President and Vice President equal to the whole number of senators and representatives in Congress to which the District would be entitled if it were a state, but in no event more than the least populous state; they shall be in addition to those appointed by the states, but they shall be considered, for the purposes of the election of President and Vice President, to be electors appointed by a state; and they shall meet in the District and perform such duties as provided by the twelfth article of amendment.

Section 2. The Congress shall have power to enforce this article by appropriate legislation.

This amendment gave the residents of the District of Columbia the right to vote in presidential elections. Before Amendment 23 was adopted, residents of the District of Columbia had not voted for President and Vice President because the Constitution provided that only states should choose presidential electors.

AMENDMENT 24 Poll Tax Illegal (1964)

Section 1. The right of citizens of the United States to vote in any primary or other election for President or Vice President, for electors for President or Vice President, or for senator or representative in Congress, shall not be denied or abridged by the United States or any state by reason of failure to pay any poll tax or other tax.

Section 2. The Congress shall have power to enforce this article by appropriate legislation.

Amendment 24 prohibited using the poll tax to deny voting rights in federal elections. (The poll tax was a device used in some southern states to keep black voters from the polls.) In 1966, the Supreme Court ruled that payment of poll taxes was also an unconstitutional precondition for voting in state and local elections.

AMENDMENT 25 Presidential Disability (1967)

Section 1. Vice President In case of the removal of the President from office or of his death or resignation, the Vice President shall become President.

Amendment 25 clarifies Article 2, Section 1, which deals with filling vacancies in the presidency. It also establishes procedures to follow when the President is too ill to serve and when there is a vacancy in the office of Vice President.

With ratification of the 26th Amendment, the voting age was lowered to eighteen years.

Section 2. Replacing the Vice President Whenever there is a vacancy in the office of the Vice President, the President shall nominate a Vice President who shall take office upon confirmation by a majority vote of both Houses of Congress.

Section 3. Presidential inability to act Whenever the President transmits to the President pro tempore of the Senate and the Speaker of the House of Representatives his written declaration that he is unable to discharge the powers and duties of his office, and until he transmits to them a written declaration to the contrary, such powers and duties shall be discharged by the Vice President as Acting President.

Section 4. Determining presidential disability Whenever the Vice President and a majority of either the principal officers of the executive departments or of such other body as Congress may by law provide, transmit to the President pro tempore of the Senate and the Speaker of the House of Representatives their written declaration that the President is unable to discharge the powers and duties of his office, the Vice President shall immediately assume the powers and duties of the office as Acting President.

Thereafter, when the President transmits to the President pro tempore of the Senate and the Speaker of the House of Representatives his written declaration that no inability exists, he shall resume the powers and duties of his office unless the Vice President and a majority of either the principal officers of the executive department or of such other body as Congress may by law provide, transmit within four days to the President pro tempore of the Senate and the Speaker of the House of Representatives their written declaration that the President is unable to discharge the powers and duties of his office. Thereupon, Congress shall decide the issue, assembling within forty-eight hours for that purpose, if not in session. If the Congress, within twenty-one days after receipt of the latter written declaration, or, if Congress is not in session, within twenty-one days after Congress is required to assemble, determines by two-thirds vote of both Houses that the President is unable to discharge the powers and duties of his office, the Vice President shall continue to discharge the same as Acting President; otherwise, the President shall resume the powers and duties of his office.

AMENDMENT 26   Voting Age (1971)

Section 1. The right of citizens of the United States who are eighteen years of age or older to vote shall not be denied or abridged by the United States or by any state on account of age.

Section 2. The Congress shall have power to enforce this article by appropriate legislation.

AMENDMENT 27   Congressional Pay (1992)

No law, varying the compensation for the services of the Senators and Representatives, shall take effect, until an election of Representatives shall have intervened.

Review of the Constitution

KEY TERMS

Match the following words with the numbered definitions below: *ratification, impeachment, appropriation, jurisdiction, judicial review, democracy, Bill of Rights.*

1. Charges of crimes or misdeeds in office brought against a government official.
2. Money granted by a legislature to be used for a specific purpose.
3. The first ten amendments to the Constitution.
4. System in which people elect the government either directly or through representatives.
5. The act of giving approval to a document such as a treaty.
6. The limits within which a government body (such as a court) may act and make decisions.
7. The power of the court system to decide whether laws are constitutional.

REVIEWING THE FACTS

1. Who holds the office of President of the Senate? When can the President of the Senate cast a vote? Which house of Congress introduces bills needed to raise money for the government?
2. Name six of the specific powers given to Congress by the Constitution. What is the "elastic clause"?

3. According to Article 2, what happens if the President dies in office? How did the Twenty-fifth Amendment provide additional measures in case of this event?
4. How are federal judges chosen? For how long do they hold office?
5. What freedoms are guaranteed by the First Amendment?
6. Under what circumstances may the Constitution be amended?
7. How does the Constitution limit the President's power to make treaties?
8. What three constitutional amendments were passed soon after the Civil War? What issues caused these amendments to be added?
9. Which branch of government has the power to declare war?

CRITICAL THINKING SKILLS

1. **MAKING JUDGMENTS** The Founding Fathers sought both to create and to limit government power. Is this a contradiction in terms? Did they achieve their goal? Explain your answer.

2. **STATING BOTH SIDES OF AN ISSUE** How would you respond to someone who said, "Only the President has the information required to make decisions about war. Often he receives this information in secret. Therefore, we should not question his actions"?

3. **MAKING JUDGMENTS** Supporters of constitutional protections for criminal suspects claim that it is better if some guilty people go free than if innocent people are convicted. Do you agree or disagree? Explain your reasons.

4. **FORMING A HYPOTHESIS** Does testing for drug use and AIDS violate Fourth Amendment restrictions on search and seizure? How might a lawyer make a case in favor of these tests?

WRITING ABOUT THEMES IN AMERICAN HISTORY

1. **ISSUES** Find out what constitutional amendments are currently under consideration. Write a report explaining the arguments both for and against two of the proposed amendments.

2. **PARTICIPATION** Research the following Supreme Court decisions on civil rights: *Dred Scott v. Sanford* (1857), *Plessy v. Ferguson* (1896), *Brown v. Board of Education of Topeka* (1954). Write a report describing how constitutional interpretation changed in each case.

3. **CONSTITUTIONAL HERITAGE** Research the history of the War Powers Act (1973). How does it illustrate the tension between the executive branch and the legislative branch under the separation of powers?

UNIT 3: American Mosaic

★ *A Multicultural Perspective* ★

A number of famous heroes emerged during the turbulent times of the Revolution and the first years of the nation. Yet there were many lesser-known Americans who played important roles in creating the new country. These people accurately reflected the diversity of the young nation.

DEBORAH SAMPSON.
Published by H. Mann. 1797.

Robert Shurtleff, a brave and loyal Continental soldier, fought at Yorktown and was wounded twice. Shurtleff hid these wounds, though. When Shurtleff was forced into the hospital with a high fever in June 1783, doctors discovered why. Robert Shurtleff was actually **Deborah Sampson** (left), a Massachusetts woman who had disguised herself as a man in order to fight for her country. She was forced to leave the army, but General George Washington ordered that she be given an honorable discharge. Congress later awarded Sampson veterans' benefits.

The Revolution forced all Americans—including Native Americans—to choose sides. Mohawk leader **Joseph Brant** (above) fought for the British, taking part in successful raids against Patriots in upstate New York. Brant's older sister had married the British Superintendent of Indian Affairs in 1753, and the couple helped educate the boy. When the time came for the Iroquois League to decide whom to support, Brant argued in favor of the British. The League split, and Brant and his followers found themselves on the losing side. After the war they moved to Canada, where Brant spent much of his time translating the Bible into the Mohawk language.

During the Revolutionary War **James Armistead** (right), a slave from Virginia, crossed British lines several times on spy missions for General Lafayette. The military information that Armistead gathered helped the Patriot cause so much that, after the war, Lafayette asked Virginia's legislature to grant Armistead his freedom. It did so in 1786, praising the actions he had taken "at the peril of his life."

As a young man, **Gaspar de Portolá** joined Spain's army. He then came to Spain's American colonies and was asked to lead an expedition into then-unknown territory in northern California. Shown here setting out from Father Junípero Serra's mission in San Diego in 1769, Portolá (on horseback, pointing) and his men rode north to Monterey Bay and finally reached San Francisco Bay. They became the first Europeans to see this strategic natural harbor. Portolá was also the first white man to establish contact with California's Salinas Indians.

Kamehameha I (right) conquered several of Hawaii's islands in the late 1700s and became their ruler. Kamehameha encouraged trade with the outside world and the adoption of modern technology. At the same time, he insisted on preserving traditional Hawaiian customs and beliefs. Once admitted, however, the outside world proved difficult to keep at bay. After Kamehameha's death, for example, missionaries converted many of the islanders to Christianity.

Bishop Museum

Moses Sash was an African American veteran of the Revolutionary War. After the war, Sash helped lead Shays' Rebellion in Massachusetts. Sash was jailed when the rebellion failed, but was later pardoned by Massachusetts governor John Hancock.

Gregory Shelikof established Russia's first settlement in Alaska in 1784.

Nancy Ward was a member of the Wolf clan of Indians who lived in Tennessee. She married a Cherokee and, in 1755, gained fame fighting alongside him in a battle against rival Creek forces. Her husband was killed in the battle, but Ward helped turn the tide in favor of the Cherokee. As a result, she was elected to the tribal council. Ward worked to make peace between the Cherokee and their white neighbors, and she supported the Patriots during the Revolution. Her efforts did not prevent the Cherokee's land being taken from them, but Ward became a legendary figure whose dignity and wisdom commanded respect from Indians and settlers alike.

HISTORIANS' CORNER

Constitutional Critics and Admirers

To some people, the federal system created by the new Constitution seemed dangerously radical. One harsh critic was Mercy Otis Warren, a writer and historian. She listed her objections in "Observations on the New Federal Constitution," issued in 1788 under the pen-name "a Columbian Patriot." In the 1830s, however, the French political writer Alexis de Tocqueville admired how well this unique form of federalism worked in practice.

Mercy Otis Warren

[2] There is no security in the proffered system either for the rights of conscience or the liberty of the press. . . .

[3] There are no well-defined limits to the judiciary powers. . . .

[4] The executive and the legislative [branches] are so dangerously blended as to give just cause for alarm. . . .

[9] There is no provision for a rotation nor anything else to prevent the perpetuity of [political] office in the same hands for life; which by a little well-timed bribery will probably be done. . . .

[14] There is no provision by a bill of rights to guard against the dangerous encroachments of power in too many instances to be named. . . .

[15] The difficulty . . . of exercising the equal and equitable powers of government by a single legislature [Congress] over an extent of territory that reaches from the Mississippi to the Western lakes, and from them to the Atlantic Ocean, is an insuperable objection to the adoption of the new system. . . .

[16] Not one state legislature in the United States had the most distant idea, when they first appointed members for a convention . . . that they would . . . presume on so bold and daring a stride as ultimately to destroy the state governments. . . .

From Mercy Otis Warren, *Observations on the New Federal Constitution and on the Federal and State Conventions.* Published in Boston by Isaiah Thomas, 1788.

Alexis de Tocqueville

This Constitution [of the United States], which at first sight one is tempted to confuse with previous federal constitutions, in fact rests on an entirely new theory, a theory that should be hailed as one of the great discoveries of political science in our age.

In all confederations previous to that of 1789 in America, the peoples who allied themselves for a common purpose agreed to obey the injunctions [orders] of the federal government, but they kept the right to direct and supervise the execution of the union's laws in their territory.

The Americans who united in 1789 agreed not only that the federal government should dictate the laws but that it should itself see to their execution. In both cases the right is the same, and only the application thereof different. But that one difference produces immense results. . . .

In America the Union's subjects are not states but private citizens. . . . It does not borrow its power, but draws it from within. It has its own administrators, courts, officers of justice, and army. . . .

Here the central power acts without intermediary on the governed, administering and judging them itself, . . . but it only acts thus within a restricted circle.

From *Democracy in America* by Alexis de Tocqueville, translated by George Lawrence, and edited by J. P. Mayer. Copyright English translation © 1966 by Harper & Row Publishers. Reprinted by permission of HarperCollins Publishers.

Critical Thinking

1. What are Warren's main fears about the new system? How might Tocqueville have answered her?

2. Why, in Tocqueville's view, is the U.S. Constitution successful?

3. What do you think was Warren's attitude toward adding a Bill of Rights to the Constitution?

UNIT FOUR

The Growing Nation

THEMES IN AMERICAN HISTORY

 Constitutional Government Supreme Court decisions upheld federal authority and strengthened the federal judiciary.

 Economic Development The creation of a national bank helped put the United States on a sound economic footing. During the first half of the 1800s, the coming of industry and the building of transportation links brought new prosperity.

 Geography The Louisiana Purchase of 1803 marked a giant step in America's westward expansion.

 Pluralistic Society Slavery became a central feature of life in the South.

 Global Interactions Tensions with Britain led to war in 1812.

By 1789 the United States had a new constitution and its first President. Terence Kennedy's Political Banner combined several symbols of the young nation.

KEY EVENTS

1789	Washington becomes President
1794	Whiskey Rebellion
1797	John Adams becomes President
1798	Alien and Sedition Acts
1800	Capital moves to Washington, D.C.

1 The Government Takes Shape

Section Focus

Key Terms   inaugurate ■ precedent ■ public debt ■ bond ■ interest ■ capitalism ■ strict construction ■ loose construction ■ tariff

Main Idea   President Washington and his Treasury Secretary, Alexander Hamilton, designed financial policies that would strengthen the credit and authority of the government.

Objectives   As you read, look for answers to these questions:
1. What steps did Congress take to organize the new government?
2. What views did Alexander Hamilton hold about money and business?
3. What financial policies did Washington adopt?

New York City was festive on the last day of April 1789. At dawn thirteen cannons boomed. The streets were strung with banners. Church bells rang. Crowds gathered in front of Federal Hall, the temporary home of Congress. This was the day in which the first President of the United States would be sworn into office, or inaugurated.

At noon George Washington arrived. He was in formal dress: white silk stockings, silver buckles on his shoes, sword at his side, hair powdered white. His new suit was of a rare material: brown cloth made in the United States. Washington took the oath of office on a balcony of Federal Hall. When the short ceremony ended, the crowd shouted, "God bless our President."

Washington soon began the task of leading the new republic. "I walk on untrodden ground," he wrote. "There is scarcely any part of my conduct which may not hereafter be drawn into precedent." (A precedent is an example that becomes standard practice.) Washington knew his actions would help define the office of President for generations to come.

> "**I** walk on untrodden ground."
>
> —*George Washington*

LAUNCHING THE GOVERNMENT

Washington had been elected only a few months before, after members of the Electoral College had prepared their ballots. Each elector had written down two names. The top vote-getter would become the new President. The runner-up would be named Vice President. Washington's name was on every single ballot. He was the unanimous choice for President.

A cheering crowd in New York City greets George Washington as he rides to Federal Hall to be sworn in as the first President of the United States. **CIVIC VALUES** In your opinion, why was Washington the unanimous choice for President?

The choice for Vice President was less clear. Alexander Hamilton, an influential political leader, believed the government would need the support of New England. He backed John Adams, a Massachusetts man. Many electors, however, wanted men from their own states. Adams was elected Vice President—but fewer than half the electors named him on the ballot.

The country now had a President, a Vice President, and the Congress. The Constitution also called for a Supreme Court and other courts. Yet it left many questions unanswered. How many judges should there be on the Supreme Court? How many other courts were needed by the federal government? The Constitution also mentioned executive departments to help the President. What should they be? The first task of the new Congress was to fill in the blanks left by the Constitution.

To set up a system of courts, Congress passed the Federal Judiciary Act. This act declared that the Supreme Court would consist of five justices—judges—plus a Chief Justice. (Over time, that number has gone up to nine.) Washington decided to appoint John Jay, the lawyer who had negotiated the 1783 Treaty of Paris, as Chief Justice. The law also set up several other federal courts.

Congress created three departments to help the President. Washington chose talented men to run these departments. Thomas Jefferson, who had served as a diplomat in France, headed the Department of State. This office handled relations between the United States and other countries. Henry Knox, a trusted soldier during the Revolution, became Secretary of the War Department. (Today, military matters are handled by the Department of Defense.) Alexander Hamilton ran the Treasury Department. He had responsibility for raising money and handling government finances.

Washington named Edmund Randolph as Attorney General. Randolph's job was to advise the government on legal matters. The three department heads and the Attorney General made up Washington's Cabinet. Over the years, the number of departments has grown. Today there are fourteen members of the Cabinet.

ECONOMIC DIFFICULTIES

The new government's most pressing problem was financial. The government needed a source of income, and it needed to pay its debts. The United States still had large debts from fighting the Revolution. The country owed millions of dollars to France, the Netherlands, and Spain. The government had also borrowed from private citizens. Individual states had borrowed, too, to pay for the Revolution. Together these debts were the public debt—the money owed by government.

When a government borrows, it gives the lender a bond—a paper promising to repay the loan at a certain time. When the bond becomes due, the government returns the sum it borrowed, plus interest. Interest is an extra payment in return for the use of money loaned.

By 1789 the United States owed more than $52 million. The states owed another $25 million. To gain the confidence of its people, the country needed to be able to pay this money back. "What are we to do with this heavy debt?" asked Washington.

> ## "What are we to do with this heavy debt?"
> —*George Washington*

Few Americans understood finance. Hard coins in one's pocket, a profit selling a piece of land—these the people understood. Most did not understand how a bank worked. After all, there were only three banks in the United States.

For help, the President turned to his young Secretary of the Treasury, Alexander Hamilton. Hamilton believed in a strong central government that encouraged business and industry. Born poor, but now rich, Hamilton had little faith in ordinary people. As he saw it, a strong nation depended on a strong class of merchants and manufacturers.

THE INFLUENCE OF ADAM SMITH

Hamilton's ideas showed the influence of Adam Smith. Smith, a Scottish economist,

President Washington (right) chose leading political figures to run federal departments. These men, the nation's first Cabinet, were (from right to left) Secretary of State Thomas Jefferson, Secretary of the Treasury Alexander Hamilton, Secretary of War Henry Knox (seated), and Attorney General Edmund Randolph. **CONSTITUTIONAL HERITAGE** In which branch of government is the Cabinet included?

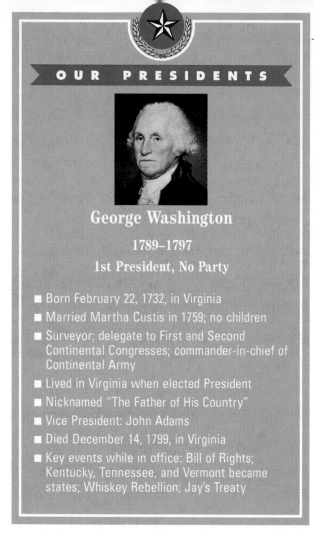

George Washington

1789–1797

1st President, No Party

- Born February 22, 1732, in Virginia
- Married Martha Custis in 1759; no children
- Surveyor; delegate to First and Second Continental Congresses; commander-in-chief of Continental Army
- Lived in Virginia when elected President
- Nicknamed "The Father of His Country"
- Vice President: John Adams
- Died December 14, 1799, in Virginia
- Key events while in office: Bill of Rights; Kentucky, Tennessee, and Vermont became states; Whiskey Rebellion; Jay's Treaty

published his *Wealth of Nations* in 1776. In it Smith described capital—money available for investment. Capital can produce wealth, Smith said. Smith pointed out that money that lies under a mattress does not make money. It is just being stored. On the other hand, money that is invested or lent produces wealth.

Banks help circulate money by paying people interest for putting their savings in the bank. Then the banks lend the savings out to other people. A bank might lend money to a manufacturer, for instance, to build a factory. The factory makes goods that are sold. Some of the money collected from those sales goes to wages for the factory's employees. Employees buy goods with some of their wages and put some of it into the bank. The bank

also gets money from the factory, because the factory must pay back the loan with an additional interest charge. The borrowed money thus "works" to create more money. Smith therefore favored the development of banking and of paper money.

Adam Smith also favored private enterprise over mercantilism. He thought the government should set as few limits as possible over business, trade, and manufacturing. Today Adam Smith's ideas go by the name of capitalism. This economic system has two main features:

(1) Most businesses are privately owned and operated.

(2) Competition and the free market primarily determine what will be produced and at what price it will sell.

HAMILTON'S FINANCIAL PLAN

In January 1790 Hamilton presented a plan to Congress. He wanted to combine all state and federal debts into one large debt. The government could issue new bonds for all the money owed. It could then pay off these bonds with tax money it would collect. Hamilton argued that if the nation did not pay off its debts, no one would lend it money in the future.

Many people doubted the fairness of Hamilton's plan. As they saw it, only the rich would benefit. Poorer people—often farmers and veterans of the Revolution—had sold off their bonds at very low prices during the years of Confederation. Many of those bonds were bought by wealthy people willing to risk small sums in the hope of large profits. Under Hamilton's plan these buyers would benefit greatly.

Southerners hated Hamilton's plan. Most buyers of government bonds lived in northern states. Southerners worried that the North would grow rich at the expense of the South. Southerners also saw no reason for the national government to pay all state debts. Every state had borrowed to meet the war costs. Some southern states, however, had already repaid their debts. It was only fair, they argued, that the other states repay their debts themselves.

Secretary of State Thomas Jefferson came from Virginia, a state that had repaid its debts. Though not in Congress, Jefferson had great influence there. Southern farmers such as Jefferson thought the best kind of wealth was land. Jefferson was suspicious of people who earned money in any other way. He dreamed of a country of small, independent farmers. He hated the idea of people getting rich by buying and selling bonds. He feared such a class of people could threaten the country's liberty.

A Compromise

One morning in July 1790 Jefferson went to President Washington's home. On his way up the steps he was stopped by Hamilton. Hamilton was worried that, without Jefferson's help, the plan to solve the debt problem would never pass. He needed to convince Jefferson to back his plan.

Jefferson wanted Hamilton's plan to fail, but he wanted something else more. The capital of the country at that moment was in New York. Northerners wanted it to stay there or to move to Philadelphia. Jefferson hoped it would move south, to the banks of the Potomac River. So did his fellow Virginian, James Madison, a leader in Congress.

Jefferson considered Hamilton's plea for help. At dinner the next day he discussed a compromise with Madison. Southerners should vote for Hamilton's plan to solve the debt problem, suggested Jefferson. In exchange, Hamilton would push for a capital in the South.

Hamilton accepted the compromise and Congress passed Hamilton's plan. It also voted to locate the nation's capital between Maryland and Virginia. These states gave some of their land along the Potomac River to the federal government. The area was called the District of Columbia in honor of Christopher Columbus.

The new capital city, Washington, was designed by a French-born engineer, Pierre

L'Enfant (lahn–FAHN). He worked with Benjamin Banneker, an African American mathematician and surveyor. Banneker had been publishing an almanac, which so impressed Thomas Jefferson that he sent a copy to the French Academy of Sciences. In 1790 Banneker was chosen to serve on the planning commission for the new capital. He played a major role in deciding where the White House, the Capitol, and other public buildings were to be located.

The Bank Debate

Solving the public debt problem was a first step for Hamilton. He also wanted to set up a national chain of banks. Presenting his plan to Congress, Hamilton called for a central bank in Philadelphia with branches in other

BIOGRAPHY

BENJAMIN BANNEKER (1731–1806), a free black tobacco farmer, educated himself with the help of books loaned by a Quaker mill owner. He was a brilliant astronomer, and became famous for compiling a series of six almanacs. Banneker sent Jefferson a copy, and included a letter calling for the abolition of slavery. Much impressed by Banneker's scientific ability, Jefferson recommended Banneker for the job of helping lay out the nation's new capital, Washington, D.C.

This illustration shows the Philadelphia headquarters of the Bank of the United States, founded in 1791 through the efforts of Alexander Hamilton. **ECONOMICS** Why did southern planters, including James Madison and Thomas Jefferson, oppose the bank's creation?

cities. These banks would give the government a safe place to keep its money. The banks could also loan money to the United States Treasury and to American businesses.

The bank proposal brought forth howls of protest from Madison, Jefferson, and other Southerners. These men argued that the bank would create a class of moneyed men. Once again, they said, Hamilton was helping wealthy northern merchants at the expense of southern farmers.

Madison and Jefferson also believed in strict construction of the Constitution. That is, they thought that the government has only the powers that the Constitution specifically gives it. The Constitution mentioned nothing about a national bank. The government had no right to establish one, argued Madison and Jefferson.

Hamilton held a different interpretation of the Constitution. Hamilton's view supported a loose construction of the Constitution. According to this view, the government can do anything the Constitution does not say it cannot do. Hamilton pointed to the elastic clause (page 254), arguing that the bank was "necessary and proper" to carrying out the government's duties.

Jefferson and Hamilton went to President Washington. Each argued the rightness of his point of view. Hamilton won the argument, convincing Washington—and Congress. The first Bank of the United States was established in 1791.

Where would the government get the money to put in the bank? To raise funds, Congress had passed a tariff, a tax on imported goods. For example, nails brought into the United States were taxed one cent a pound. Molasses, which came from the islands of the West Indies, was taxed two and a half cents a gallon.

The tariff did more than raise money. It made foreign goods more expensive than American goods. That encouraged Americans to buy from Americans, not from foreigners. Some imported goods, however, were not yet made in the United States. While northerners made most of the goods they needed, southerners relied more on imports. Therefore, the tariff hit the South's economy hardest. Tariffs became another source of disagreement between southern farmers and northern merchants.

SECTION REVIEW

1. KEY TERMS inaugurate, precedent, public debt, bond, interest, capitalism, strict construction, loose construction, tariff

2. PEOPLE AND PLACES Alexander Hamilton, New York City, George Washington, Thomas Jefferson, Adam Smith, Potomac River, Benjamin Banneker

3. COMPREHENSION What were the first executive departments of the United States?

4. COMPREHENSION What economic problems did the new government face?

5. CRITICAL THINKING A year after agreeing to support Hamilton's plan in exchange for a capital on the Potomac, Jefferson wrote to Washington. He said, "Of all the errors of my political life, this has occasioned me the deepest regret." Why might he have felt that way?

When studying history—as well as many other subjects—it is often useful to compare information. For instance, you might want to know the value of the goods that the United States traded with Great Britain, France, and Spain in the late 1700s. By comparing these figures, you could tell which of these countries was the leading trading partner of the United States.

One of the clearest ways to show this kind of information is in a table. In a table, information is arranged in columns (going down) and rows (going across). With a glance at a row or column, you can do a quick comparison of the information presented.

RULES FOR READING TABLES

To read a table, follow these guidelines. First, look at the title of the table. This tells you what information is presented in the table. Next, carefully read the column headings to see what kind of information is contained in each column and how the columns are arranged. (Often the information in the column is presented in alphabetical order. Other tables are arranged in time order, by date.) Finally, compare and contrast the information presented in the table.

The table on this page shows the results of the first official population count, or **census**, of the United States. It was taken in 1790. The census was used to determine how many seats each state would have in the House of Representatives. Since that time, a census has been taken every ten years. Though it is still used to determine representation, the census affects many other government programs today as well.

PRACTICING YOUR SKILL

Study the table and answer the following questions.

1. In what kind of order are the states in this table listed?

THE 1790 CENSUS

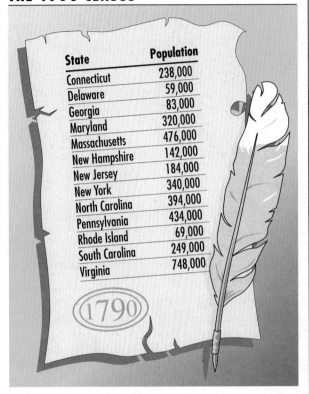

State	Population
Connecticut	238,000
Delaware	59,000
Georgia	83,000
Maryland	320,000
Massachusetts	476,000
New Hampshire	142,000
New Jersey	184,000
New York	340,000
North Carolina	394,000
Pennsylvania	434,000
Rhode Island	69,000
South Carolina	249,000
Virginia	748,000

2. What was the population of South Carolina in 1790?

3. Which state had the smallest population in 1790?

4. In which state did more people live in 1790, Connecticut or New Jersey?

5. According to the table, which two states had the largest populations in 1790? What fact concerning the early English colonization of North America might explain why these two states had more people than the other states?

6. Create another table using the 1790 census figures, and arrange this new table by population size.

7. Which five states would be entitled to the greatest number of seats in the House of Representatives as a result of the figures collected in the 1790 census?

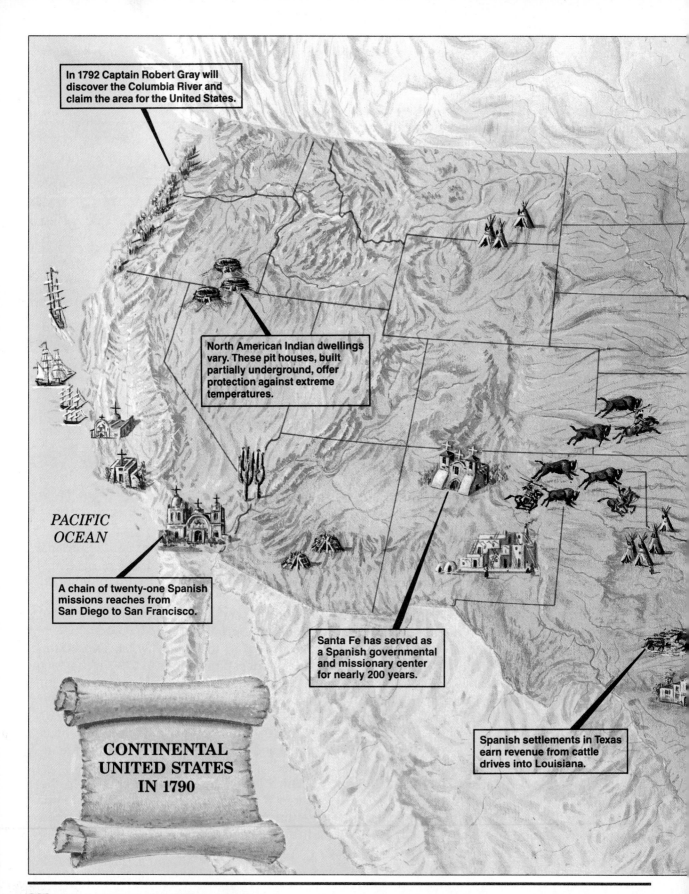

In 1792 Captain Robert Gray will discover the Columbia River and claim the area for the United States.

North American Indian dwellings vary. These pit houses, built partially underground, offer protection against extreme temperatures.

PACIFIC OCEAN

A chain of twenty-one Spanish missions reaches from San Diego to San Francisco.

Santa Fe has served as a Spanish governmental and missionary center for nearly 200 years.

Spanish settlements in Texas earn revenue from cattle drives into Louisiana.

CONTINENTAL UNITED STATES IN 1790

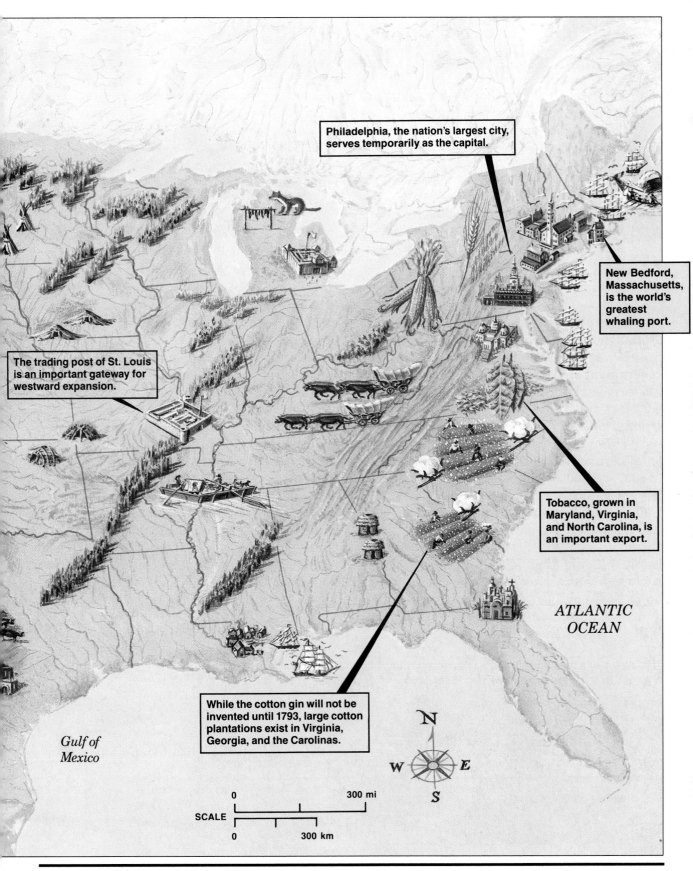

Philadelphia, the nation's largest city, serves temporarily as the capital.

New Bedford, Massachusetts, is the world's greatest whaling port.

The trading post of St. Louis is an important gateway for westward expansion.

Tobacco, grown in Maryland, Virginia, and North Carolina, is an important export.

While the cotton gin will not be invented until 1793, large cotton plantations exist in Virginia, Georgia, and the Carolinas.

ATLANTIC OCEAN

Gulf of Mexico

N
W E
S

0   300 mi
SCALE
0   300 km

2 Securing the West and Avoiding War

The United States today is powerful and respected. It has a large army and navy, modern weapons, a strong economy, and is on good terms with its neighbors. It may be hard to imagine, but 200 years ago the United States was thought of as weak. The federal government had a hard time controlling its western lands. Canada, our northern neighbor, was ruled by Great Britain. Spain governed the land west of the Mississippi River. Both these great European powers hungered for American territories. Even France, an old friend, wanted to pull the United States into larger conflicts.

President Washington and his young government were faced with a tough job. How should the United States react to events in Europe? Could they keep the West safe for American settlers? Was it possible to stand up to Spain and Britain without being drawn into war? It was to take all of Washington's skill to answer those questions.

THREATS TO THE WEST

In the spring of 1788, a group of 47 Americans moved west, passing beyond Pittsburgh and the frontier towns of Pennsylvania. They floated down the Ohio River, stopping where the Muskingum River joins the Ohio. There, they built a town, Marietta. That town served as the capital of the Northwest Territory. Farther down the Ohio River other settlers founded Cincinnati. In under two years that town had about 900 residents.

These settlers were part of a stream of Americans heading west. By the Treaty of Paris (1783), Great Britain had granted the United States the land east of the Mississippi from the Great Lakes in the north to the 31st parallel in the south. The Northwest Ordinance had organized more than half of that land. (See Chapter 10.)

Yet, despite the treaty, the British still had some forts north of the Ohio River. In fact, the governor of Canada was plotting with the

This sketch of a New Orleans marketplace reveals the city's ethnic diversity. GEOGRAPHY Why was New Orleans considered vital to the economic development of the West?

In this illustration, General Anthony Wayne accepts the surrender of Miami leader Little Turtle after the Battle of Fallen Timbers. HISTORY What was Little Turtle hoping to gain by preventing the United States from taking control of the Northwest Territory?

Indians to attack Americans in the Northwest Territory.

Spain, too, was urging Indians to resist Americans. Neither the Indians nor Spain felt they needed to honor the Treaty of Paris. Spain claimed much of North America west of the Mississippi. It also controlled Florida and the port of New Orleans. New Orleans was important to westerners. They had only one way to get their goods to market: by flatboat down the Mississippi to New Orleans. Spain wooed westerners with the idea that their interests lay with Spain, not the United States.

THE BATTLE OF FALLEN TIMBERS

Washington knew that the security of the West was important to the growth of the nation. In 1790 and 1791 he sent troops into the Northwest Territory. Both armies were badly defeated by Indians led by the Miami chief Little Turtle. The second defeat was one of the worst ever dealt the United States Army. Westerners were terrified. Indians now hoped that an Indian nation north of the Ohio was possible.

Washington sent another army west, this one headed by Anthony Wayne. A hero in the Revolution, Wayne was both experienced and shrewd. Known for his reckless courage, Wayne was called "Mad Anthony." At his headquarters near Cincinnati, he turned his raw recruits into a well-trained force.

In Canada, the British governor announced that he would help the Indians. British troops built a new fort, Fort Miami, on the Maumee River in Ohio. Expecting British help, Indian warriors from all over the Northwest Territory gathered near Fort Miami to prepare for battle.

Washington realized that General Wayne's troops were greatly outnumbered. He also knew that the United States risked war with Britain. Yet Washington felt that the safety of the West was at stake. Learning that the war drums were beating that summer of 1794, Washington ordered Wayne to march toward Fort Miami.

As many as 2,000 Shawnee, Ottawa, and Chippewa Indians planned to ambush Wayne's smaller force. The site they had chosen was littered with trees struck down by a tornado. As Wayne drew closer to Fort Miami, however, he stopped his march. Wayne knew that it was an Indian custom not to eat before a battle. The warriors waited three days for Wayne, all the time growing weaker and hungrier. When they finally met, Wayne soundly defeated the Indians at the Battle of Fallen Timbers.

The Indians fled to Fort Miami, but the British closed the gates to them. Despite their talk, the British would not help the Indians if it meant risking a war with the United States. The Battle of Fallen Timbers crushed the Indians' hopes of keeping their land. They signed the Treaty of Greenville, agreeing to surrender their homelands and move west.

TROUBLE ON THE FRONTIER

While Wayne fought in Ohio, trouble was brewing in western Pennsylvania. It had begun when Alexander Hamilton proposed a tax on certain American-made goods. At his suggestion, Congress taxed all whiskey made and sold in the United States.

The tax on whiskey angered frontier farmers. These farmers had trouble taking their crops to market because of poor roads. To get around this problem, they made their grain into whiskey. Whiskey was easier than grain to carry and brought a better price in the East. Backcountry settlers had little cash with which to buy goods, let alone pay the tax. They often used whiskey like money to buy salt, sugar, nails, and ammunition. The whiskey tax, then, came as a hard blow.

To many, the whiskey tax seemed as unfair as British taxes had been. Some feared that even more taxes would follow. James Jackson, a representative from Georgia, spoke out in Congress. "The time will come," he warned, "when a shirt shall not be washed without an excise [tax]."

George Washington, the only President to lead troops into battle while in office, reviews the forces assembled at Fort Cumberland, Maryland, to crush the Whiskey Rebellion. **CONSTITUTIONAL HERITAGE** What effect did Washington's handling of the rebellion have on federal authority?

This painting shows the beheading of France's king in 1793 during the French Revolution. **HISTORY** Why were many Americans attracted to the cause of the French revolutionaries?

A group of farmers in western Pennsylvania refused to pay the tax. In an outbreak called the Whiskey Rebellion, the farmers took up arms. They chased away the tax collectors. Some marched on Pittsburgh. Amid rumors that there would soon be taxes on plows and babies, the farmers spoke of separating from the United States.

The farmers were poorly organized. Their threat to the Union was slight. However, Hamilton wanted to prove the federal government's strength. He convinced Washington that troops were needed to put down the uprising. That fall President Washington himself—with Hamilton as his aide—led an army of 13,000. They crossed the Appalachians into western Pennsylvania.

The army was made up of troops from several states. Those from New Jersey sang about how they would put down the uprising. They called the rebellion sedition—saying or doing anything to bring down the government.

> To arms once more our hero cries,
> Sedition lives and order dies;
> To peace and ease then bid adieu
> And dash to the mountains, Jersey
>   Blue.

These soldiers never got a chance to fight. Many of the rebels fled to Kentucky. By the time the army reached western Pennsylvania, the rebellion had ended. As Thomas Jefferson said, "An insurrection was announced and proclaimed and armed against, but could never be found." The troops, however, did make a difference. They proved that the federal government had the power and will to enforce its laws.

JOLTS FROM THE FRENCH REVOLUTION

Americans thought of France as a friend. The French had helped the United States win independence. Then, in 1789, France had its own revolution. The French rose up against their king, demanding liberty and equality.

Many Americans supported the French Revolution. They thought the French were following the American lead. Thomas Paine traveled to France to sit on their councils. Thomas Jefferson wrote a proposed bill of rights for the new French government.

By 1793, however, the French Revolution had grown cruel. The ruling group executed thousands of people, including the king and queen. Liberty and law seemed to disappear. The monarchs of Europe feared that the revolution would spread. They joined to defeat

France and stamp out its revolution. Britain was a leader in this fight against France.

Events in Europe divided the American people. Growing numbers opposed the turn the French Revolution had taken. They agreed with Alexander Hamilton that the United States had to stay on good terms with Britain. British trade was too important to the American economy to risk. On the other hand, Thomas Jefferson and others remained pro-French. Jefferson believed that the cause of liberty was closely linked to the French Revolution.

George Washington had a different point of view. For him, it was most important that the United States be neutral, or take no one's side. In the spring of 1793 he announced that the government would be "friendly and impartial" to both sides in the war. Congress followed that up with a law forbidding Americans to help either side.

The French were not happy with the American decision. They sent Edmond Genêt (zhuh–NAY) to the United States. The Frenchman claimed he had come to improve relations between the two countries. What he really hoped for was American support. Secretly helped by Jefferson, Genêt traveled around the country. Crowds met him with feasts and cheers. Wherever he went, he enlisted Americans in the French cause.

Despite Genêt's efforts, Washington maintained his policy of neutrality. This greatly frustrated Genêt. Believing he had massive support, Genêt threatened to go over Washington's head to the American people. That was an insult that angered even Jefferson. Washington demanded that France recall Genêt.

By then a new government had taken power in France. If Genêt returned, he would be arrested. Rather than send Genêt home to certain death, Washington allowed him to stay as a private citizen.

MAINTAINING NEUTRALITY

With Europe armed and fighting, Washington worried about American defenses. Wash-

ington had not thought a navy necessary. He had held to this view even when pirate states on the Barbary Coast of North Africa captured American ships. Then Britain seized 250 American trading ships in the West Indies. In 1794 the President urged Congress to start a navy and to buy warships. These warships—called frigates—turned out to be the best and fastest of their type on the seas.

Still, Washington wanted to keep the peace. He sent John Jay, who was Chief Justice, to London to settle the differences between Britain and the United States. Jay's main goal was to get the British to withdraw from the Northwest Territory. During the talks, news came to London of the American victory at Fallen Timbers (page 305). The news gave Jay more clout at the bargaining table. The result was Jay's Treaty, signed in late 1794.

In Jay's Treaty, Britain agreed to leave the Ohio Valley. Britain also agreed that under certain conditions, American ships could trade in the West Indies. Other issues, such as illegal captures of ships, were to be settled by joint commissions (special committees).

The treaty with Britain was followed by a treaty with Spain. Thomas Pinckney arranged the treaty. Pinckney's Treaty al-

At President Washington's urging, Congress authorized the creation of the U.S. Navy in 1794. This etching by William Birch shows shipbuilders working on the *Philadelphia,* a naval warship.
GLOBAL AWARENESS What overseas event raised Washington's concern over American defenses?

lowed American ships on the Mississippi. For three years Westerners also had the right of deposit in New Orleans. They were allowed, in other words, to store goods in New Orleans awaiting ocean transport. The Spanish also agreed to accept the 31st parallel as the southern boundary of the United States. They promised not to help the Indians fight Americans.

Together, Jay's Treaty and Pinckney's Treaty had far-reaching effects. The United States managed to avoid war and keep its boundaries safe. The treaties allowed Americans to move west without fear of European attacks. Furthermore, they helped cement frontier settlers' loyalty toward the federal government.

SECTION REVIEW

1. KEY TERMS Whiskey Rebellion, sedition, French Revolution, neutral, Jay's Treaty, Pinckney's Treaty, right of deposit

2. PEOPLE AND PLACES Ohio River, Northwest Territory, New Orleans, Little Turtle, Anthony Wayne, Edmond Genêt

3. COMPREHENSION What military and diplomatic actions secured the West?

4. COMPREHENSION How did the French Revolution divide the American people?

5. CRITICAL THINKING Do you think that neutrality was a good policy in the 1790s? Why or why not?

3 The Federalists in Charge

Section Focus

Key Term political party

Main Idea The split between Alexander Hamilton and Thomas Jefferson led to the creation of political parties, which grew in importance after George Washington left the presidency.

Objectives As you read, look for answers to these questions:
1. What were the goals of the Federalist and the Democratic-Republican parties?
2. What was Washington's farewell message to the nation?
3. What were John Adams's strengths and weaknesses as a leader?

As members of President Washington's Cabinet, Hamilton and Jefferson repeatedly locked horns over the course of the new nation. They had disagreed on the correct way to interpret the Constitution. They had disagreed over a plan for national finance and banking. When war broke out between Great Britain and France, Hamilton had favored Britain while Jefferson favored France. Finally, they each had a different vision of what the United States should be. Hamilton foresaw an America of manufacturing, industry, and cities. Jefferson wanted a country of small, independent farmers.

Tensions between the two continued to mount. Each found it hard even to be in the same room as the other. Meanwhile, each man attracted followers. These followers formed *political parties*, groups that work for certain goals and candidates. The conflict between these two groups was to play a major role in the politics of the new nation.

The Growth of Political Parties

By 1793 Thomas Jefferson was fed up. Tired of President Washington's support of Hamilton's ideas, Jefferson quit his job as Secretary of State. He believed that Hamilton was making the government too powerful and too favorable toward business. With the help of James Madison, he formed the Democratic-Republican Party. This name showed their strong belief in democracy and in the republican system.

Jefferson's followers were mainly farmers and artisans. They were often called Republicans (but they are not connected to today's Republican Party). Low taxes and small government was their aim. They supported strict construction of the Constitution. Republicans believed that ordinary people and state lawmakers—not the United States Congress—should control most government matters. The Republicans, for example, opposed the idea of a national bank.

Hamilton, on the other hand, wanted a strong national government. A strong national government could take steps, such as establishing banks, that would benefit the economy. Hamilton's ideas appealed mostly to business people from the Northeast. Hamilton and Vice President John Adams together formed the Federalist Party. The Federalists believed in a loose construction of the Constitution.

Washington Retires

Both the Federalists and the Republicans held President Washington in great respect. Washington had hoped to leave after serving four years in office. It was clear, however, that he was needed to keep the country united. "North and South will hang together if they have you to hang on," Jefferson wrote to the President. In 1792 Washington was re-elected President.

Four years later, Washington decided that the time had come to leave office. In the sum-

Thomas Jefferson believed that the future of the country depended on its being a land of small farmers, like those shown above. Alexander Hamilton wanted a nation of manufacturing and cities. POLITICS Which man would you have supported? Why?

mer of 1796 he published his Farewell Address, stating he would not run again. The tradition of serving no more than two terms as President would continue for almost 150 years. (Franklin Roosevelt ran for a third and fourth term in 1940 and 1944 and won both times.) The 22nd Amendment to the Constitution (1951) stated that no person may be elected President more than twice.

In his Farewell Address, Washington urged Americans to avoid party politics. (See page 312.) Political parties, he said, could harm the national interest. Despite this advice, parties became a permanent part of American politics.

The nation paid more attention to Washington's advice on foreign policy. In his Farewell Address, Washington advised the country to stay neutral. He warned against making long-term pacts with foreign nations. The United States would follow this principle for the next 150 years.

As Washington made his plans to return to Mount Vernon, the question of who would be the next President took center stage. John Adams, the Vice President, was the Federalist choice. His running mate was Thomas Pinckney, famous for his treaty with Spain. Republicans backed Jefferson for President and Aaron Burr for Vice President.

Washington's Farewell Address (1796)

At the end of his second term as President, George Washington spoke of three dangers facing the nation: the rise of political parties, sectionalism, and involvement in European affairs. He urged Americans to steer a neutral course in foreign relations.

A solicitude for your welfare which cannot end with my life . . . urges me on an occasion like the present . . . to recommend to your frequent review some sentiments which are the result of much reflection. . . .

The name of American, which belongs to you . . . must always exalt the just pride of patriotism. . . . You have in a common cause fought and triumphed together. The independence and liberty you possess are the work of joint councils and joint efforts, of common dangers, sufferings and successes. . . . Every portion of our country finds the most commanding motives for carefully guarding and preserving the union of the whole. . . .

This government, the offspring of our own choice, . . . completely free in its principles, in the distribution of its powers, uniting security with energy, and containing within itself a provision for its own amendment, has a just claim to your confidence and your support. Respect for its authority, compliance with its laws, acquiescence in its measures, are duties enjoined by the fundamental maxim of liberty. . . .

Against the insidious wiles of foreign influence, the jealousy of a free people ought to be constantly awake, since history and experience prove that foreign influence is one of the most baneful foes of republican government. . . . The great rule of conduct for us in regard to foreign nations is in extending our commercial relations to have as little political connection as possible. . . . It is our true policy to steer clear of permanent alliances, with any portion of the foreign world. . . .

From J. D. Richardson, ed., *A Compilation of the Messages and Papers of the Presidents,* Vol. I, p. 213.

ANALYZING HISTORICAL DOCUMENTS
1. In this address, what does George Washington praise about the American government?
2. What is Washington's position on relations between the United States and foreign governments?
3. What does Washington mean when he says "foreign influence is one of the most baneful foes of republican government"? What reasons might he have for holding this belief?

Jefferson was very popular among Americans. The French liked him too and openly backed him. Americans, however, resented foreign meddling in their elections. As a result, Jefferson won only 68 electoral votes to Adams's 71. In those days, the candidate with the second highest electoral vote became Vice President. For the first and last time, the country had a President from one party and a Vice President from another.

JOHN ADAMS TAKES OFFICE
John Adams was an experienced statesman. He had served as a diplomat, representing the United States in Great Britain. Though admired for his honesty, Adams was considered cold, even rude at times.

One of Adams's greatest assets was his wife, Abigail. Well-read and intelligent, Abigail Adams had strong opinions and let her husband know them. Her most famous piece

The Adamses moved into an unfinished White House in 1800. Here, Abigail Adams watches a servant hang out laundry in the East Room. Today the East Room is open to the public. **NATIONAL IDENTITY** What has the White House come to symbolize?

of advice—ignored by John Adams—had to do with women's rights. When he served in the Continental Congress she wrote to him:

> By the way in the new Code of Laws which I suppose it will be necessary for you to make I desire you would Remember the Ladies and be more generous and favorable to them than your ancestors.

The Adamses were the first presidential family to live in Washington, D.C. President Washington had chosen the spot on the Potomac River in 1791. Nine years later, the capital moved to the unpaved and muddy city. Members of Congress lived in wooden boarding houses around the Capitol.

Abigail Adams described the city she moved to in November 1800. "Houses scattered over a space of ten miles, and [many] trees and stumps . . . with a castle of a house," she wrote. She was living in the still unfinished White House, hanging her washing to dry in the East Room. She had only to put up with the discomforts of Washington for a short time. In less than a year, her husband would be out of office.

SECTION REVIEW

1. KEY TERM political party

2. PEOPLE AND PLACES Thomas Jefferson, Alexander Hamilton, John Adams, Abigail Adams, Washington, D.C.

3. COMPREHENSION How did the first two political parties differ?

4. COMPREHENSION Why did Washington want the United States to avoid foreign alliances?

5. CRITICAL THINKING Do you think a person like John Adams could be elected President today? Explain.

4 Trouble at Home and Abroad

★ ★ ★ ★

Section Focus

Key Terms XYZ Affair ■ alien ■ Alien and Sedition Acts ■ states' rights

Main Idea A near-war with France triggered a Federalist effort to stamp out Republican opposition.

Objectives As you read, look for answers to these questions:
1. What caused tensions with France?
2. How did Federalists respond to criticism of their policies?
3. What was the Republican response to the Alien and Sedition Acts?

In the fall of 1797 relations between the United States and France were tense. France was angry that the United States and Britain had signed Jay's Treaty. The French were still fighting the British, and France resented American friendliness to Britain. The French navy began capturing American ships, keeping them from carrying goods to the enemies of France. In a short time the French had seized more than 300 American vessels.

Earlier in the decade British ships had hurt American trade. Now France was doing the same. John Adams, the new President, faced the same problem George Washington had. How could he protect American interests without going to war?

THE XYZ AFFAIR

President Adams wished to follow in Washington's footsteps. Negotiations and treaties, he hoped, would end tensions. To this end, Adams sent Charles Pinckney, Elbridge Gerry, and John Marshall to Paris, the capital of France. There they hoped to meet with Maurice de Talleyrand (TAL–uh–RAND), the French Minister of Foreign Affairs.

For weeks the three Americans sat in waiting rooms, ignored by the French. Then three

This American cartoon of the XYZ Affair shows France as a five-headed monster. American diplomats resist its demands for money, declaring, "Cease bawling, monster! We will not give you sixpence!" HISTORY What other negative images of France are included in the cartoon?

In the undeclared war with France of the late 1790s, American merchant ships, such as the *Planter* shown here, battled French privateers. **CONSTITUTIONAL HERITAGE** Why was the United States not officially at war?

of Talleyrand's agents—later referred to as X, Y, and Z—approached them. The minister would speak with them about a treaty, the agents said. First, however, he wanted the United States to "loan" France $12 million, and pay him $250,000. Pinckney, like the other Americans, realized he was being asked for a bribe. Somewhat deaf and unable to believe his ears, Pinckney answered "No, no, not a sixpence."

> "**M**illions for defense, not one cent for tribute!"
>
> —*Popular slogan during the XYZ Affair*

The Americans sent a full report of the XYZ Affair to President Adams. When Adams told Congress, the country exploded in anger. Pinckney's words were transformed into a popular slogan, "Millions for defense, not one cent for tribute!" In other words, they would rather fund and fight a war than pay a bribe. In 1798 Congress canceled the treaties

it had made with France. It began to recruit an army and prepare for war. Washington even agreed to lead the army, if need be.

The situation grew so tense that fighting broke out at sea. At the time, the American navy included only 22 ships. They attacked and captured French ships whenever they could. In less than three years, the French lost 84 ships. Yet neither Congress nor the French government ever declared that a state of war existed.

THE ALIEN AND SEDITION ACTS

Meanwhile the Republicans were attacking Adams and the Federalists. The critics disliked the new federal taxes and the expanded army and navy. They were also sympathetic to France.

Feelings on both sides ran strong. Republicans were accused of being "democrats, mobocrats, and all other kinds of rats." Republican newspapers fired back. One called Adams "the blasted tyrant of America." Adams was furious at such criticism in a time of near-war. He blamed the Republican newspapers and the thousands of new immigrants. Most of the new immigrants were Republicans. They included about 25,000 newcomers

John Adams

1797–1801

2nd President, Federalist

- Born October 30, 1735, in Massachusetts
- Married Abigail Smith in 1764; 5 children
- Lawyer; delegate to First and Second Continental Congresses; Vice President under Washington
- Lived in Massachusetts when elected President
- Vice President: Thomas Jefferson
- Died July 4, 1826, in Massachusetts
- Key events while in office: XYZ Affair; Alien and Sedition Acts; Washington, D.C., became the nation's capital

from France as well as thousands of Irish. Immigrants who were not yet citizens were **aliens**, or foreigners.

To silence Republican critics, the Federalist Congress passed the **Alien and Sedition Acts** in 1798. Until that time, it had taken five years to become a United States citizen. The new laws set fourteen years as the waiting period. In this way, Congress hoped to maintain Federalist power. One had to be a citizen to vote. The fewer immigrants who could become citizens, the fewer votes the Republicans were likely to get in the election.

The Alien and Sedition Acts gave the President power to arrest disloyal immigrants or order them out of the country. The acts also outlawed sedition, which they defined as false or critical speech about the government. Federalists used this law to silence their crit-

ics. About 25 Republican newspaper editors were arrested and 10 sent to jail. One congressman was also locked up for speaking out against the President. In this way, the law restricted freedom of speech and of the press.

THE REPUBLICAN RESPONSE

Republicans believed that liberty itself was at stake. Thomas Jefferson was horrified by the Alien and Sedition Acts. Republicans charged that the aim of the Federalists was:

> To frighten . . . all presses which they consider as contrary to their views; to prevent a free [exchange] of opinion; . . . and, through those means, to [keep] themselves in power.

Jefferson and James Madison challenged the new laws, using a theory that came to be called **states' rights**. This theory claimed that states had the right to judge whether a law passed by Congress was unconstitutional. The Kentucky and Virginia legislatures agreed. In 1798–1799 they passed resolutions written by Jefferson and Madison. The Kentucky and Virginia Resolutions declared that the Alien and Sedition Acts had no legal force because they violated the Bill of Rights.

No other states sided with Kentucky and Virginia. Within a few years a new Congress changed the laws or let them expire. Yet the issue of states' rights would reappear in later years, most notably in the decades leading to the Civil War.

PEACE WITH FRANCE

The Federalists continued to call for war against France. Adams dragged his feet. He doubted that the French would invade. Then, in 1799, the French stopped seizing American ships. Americans would be welcome in France, said Talleyrand. Adams saw this as proof that the country need not go to war. "The end of war is peace, and peace was offered me," he said.

When Federalists scoffed at the French offer, Adams broke with the Federalist Party and sent another peace mission to France. By this time a new French leader, Napoleon Bonaparte, had come to power. Napoleon had no wish to continue fighting with the United States. The two countries signed an agreement to stop all naval attacks. This agreement, the Convention of 1800, cleared the way for American and French ships to sail the ocean in peace.

President Adams was proud of having saved the country from unnecessary bloodshed. Although the Federalists accused Adams of weakness, the President believed that he had served his country well. He later said that he wished to be remembered as "John Adams, who took upon himself the responsibility of peace with France."

SECTION REVIEW

1. KEY TERMS XYZ Affair, alien, Alien and Sedition Act, states' rights

2. PEOPLE John Adams, Charles Talleyrand, Napoleon Bonaparte, James Madison

3. COMPREHENSION What caused trouble between the United States and France during John Adams's presidency?

4. COMPREHENSION Why did Congress pass the Alien and Sedition Acts? What was the response of Kentucky and Virginia?

5. CRITICAL THINKING Why did Adams choose not to declare war on France?

CHAPTER 12 SUMMARY AND TIMELINE

1. President Washington worked to establish a strong federal government. Alexander Hamilton arranged to pay federal and state debts, started a national bank, and introduced tariffs to produce revenue and to protect American manufacturers.

2. The new government secured the West after battling Indians in Ohio and rebellious farmers in western Pennsylvania. Though the French Revolution divided Americans, Washington was able to improve relations with Britain and Spain through negotiation and passage of Jay's and Pinckney's treaties.

3. Hamilton and Jefferson formed rival political parties. The Federalists, led by Hamilton, favored business interests and a powerful federal government. Jefferson's Democratic-Republican Party argued for the interests of ordinary citizens and the states. After Washington left office, John Adams became President and the capital moved to Washington, D.C.

4. The conflict between the United States and France became an undeclared war. At the same time, Federalists in Congress passed the Alien and Sedition Acts, which, critics charged, violated the Constitution. Thomas Jefferson and James Madison responded by writing the Virginia and Kentucky Resolutions.

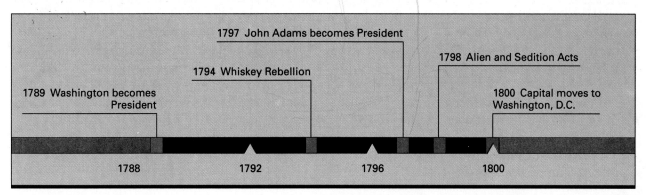

1789 Washington becomes President

1794 Whiskey Rebellion

1797 John Adams becomes President

1798 Alien and Sedition Acts

1800 Capital moves to Washington, D.C.

1788 1792 1796 1800

PLACES TO LOCATE

Match each of the letters on the map with the places that are listed below.

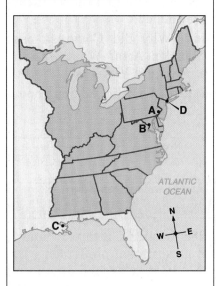

1. Washington, D.C.
2. New York City
3. New Orleans
4. Philadelphia

KEY TERMS

Match each of the following terms with its correct description.

Alien and Sedition Acts
bond
neutral
political party
states' rights
tariff
Whiskey Rebellion

1. Paper promising to repay a loan at a certain time.
2. Tax on imports.
3. Uprising of farmers against a federal tax.

4. Taking no side in a dispute.
5. Group that works for certain goals and candidates.
6. Laws that lengthened the time necessary to become a citizen and made it illegal to say anything false or critical about the government.
7. Theory that seeks to protect the powers of the states against those of the federal government.

PEOPLE TO IDENTIFY

Use the following names to complete the sentences.

Abigail Adams
Alexander Hamilton
Little Turtle
James Madison
Adam Smith
Charles Talleyrand

1. To win support for his economic policies, ____ agreed to move the capital to the banks of the Potomac River.
2. In his book, *The Wealth of Nations*, ____ described the capitalist system.
3. ____ was defeated at the Battle of Fallen Timbers.
4. An early supporter of women's rights, ____ moved into the White House in 1800.
5. Agents of ____ asked the three members of the American mission to France for a bribe.

6. Angered by the Alien and Sedition Acts, ____ helped write a resolution calling the acts unconstitutional.

REVIEWING THE FACTS

1. What questions, left open by the Constitution, were addressed by the Federal Judiciary Act?
2. What financial problems did the new nation face? How did Alexander Hamilton propose to solve them?
3. Describe the disagreement between those who believed in a strict construction of the Constitution and those who supported a loose construction.
4. What problems did the United States face in the West in the 1790s? How did President Washington deal with them?
5. How did Americans view the French Revolution?
6. What problems did Jay's Treaty address? Pinckney's Treaty?
7. What groups of Americans supported Jefferson and the Democratic-Republican Party? What groups supported Hamilton and the Federalists?
8. What advice did Washington give the nation in his Farewell Address?
9. What was the XYZ Affair?
10. Why did Federalists pass the Alien and Sedition Acts? Why did John Adams support those laws?

PRACTICING YOUR SKILL

The table below shows the value of American trade over a 70-year period. The "Imports" column tells how many millions of dollars Americans spent on goods from abroad. The "Exports" column shows income from the sale of goods to foreign countries. Study the table and answer the following questions.

VALUE OF UNITED STATES TRADE, 1790 - 1860

Year	Imports (in millions)	Exports (in millions)
1790	$24	$20
1810	89	67
1820	74	70
1830	63	72
1840	100	124
1850	180	144
1860	368	334

1. What was the value of American exports in 1790? In 1820?
2. What was the value of American imports in 1790? In 1840?
3. Which had greater value in most years—imports or exports? Which years are the exceptions?
4. Did trade generally increase, decrease, or remain steady over the years shown? Why?

CITIZENSHIP

1. Research the organization of the federal court system, set up by the Federal Judiciary Act, and create an organization chart describing that court system.
2. In your opinion, which group won the debate over how to interpret the Constitution—those who supported strict construction or those who supported loose construction? Cite examples to support your answer.
3. Pennsylvania farmers took up arms to protest taxes they considered unfair. What are ways that today's Americans protest taxes with which they disagree?

CRITICAL THINKING SKILLS

1. **ANALYZING A QUOTATION** "Merchants have no country. The mere spot they stand on does not constitute so strong an attachment as that from which they draw their gains." Who probably spoke these words, Jefferson or Hamilton? Explain your answer.

2. **RECOGNIZING FRAME OF REFERENCE** What might Washington have meant when he called the formation of political parties dangerous?

3. **IDENTIFYING CAUSE AND EFFECT** Why did the British aid American Indians in the West?

PROJECTS AND ACTIVITIES

1. **CREATING A CHART** Do research on the French Revolution, and design a chart comparing and contrasting the American and French revolutions.

2. **BUILDING A MODEL** Referring to the picture on page 299 and other sources, create a model of the Capitol, White House, or other structure from the early years of Washington, D.C.

3. **EXPRESSING POINTS OF VIEW** Imagine that you and your classmates are members of Congress in the 1790s. President Adams has just told you about the XYZ Affair. Discuss how you should respond.

WRITING ABOUT TOPICS IN AMERICAN HISTORY

1. **CONNECTING WITH LITERATURE** A selection from *The Glorious Conspiracy* by Joanne S. Williamson appears on pages 647–648. Read it and answer the questions. Then answer the following question: How might Federalists have responded to Greenleaf's criticisms?

2. **APPLYING THEMES: ECONOMIC DEVELOPMENT** Find out more about the ideas of Adam Smith. Which of Smith's ideas did Hamilton use in his policies?

The stormy seas of European conflict brought about war with Britain in 1812. The victory of the U.S.S. Constitution over the British frigate Guerrière symbolized Americans' determination to defend their rights.

13 The United States Becomes Stronger (1800–1815)

1 The Impact of Thomas Jefferson

Section Focus

Key Terms   radical ■ administration

Main Idea   In 1800 the Republicans gained power with the election of Thomas Jefferson, who proceeded to overturn Federalist programs.

Objectives   As you read, look for answers to these questions:
1. Why was the election of 1800 significant?
2. What qualities did Thomas Jefferson have?
3. What policies did Jefferson pursue?

The year 1800 marked the beginning of a new era for the United States. The 1800s would be the century in which the nation would expand to the Pacific Ocean. It was the century in which American democracy began to flower. The man elected President in 1801 had a powerful influence on these developments.

THE ELECTION OF 1800

The election of 1800 was a contest between John Adams and Thomas Jefferson. It was also a bitter face-off between Federalists and Republicans.

Each party accused the other of endangering the Constitution and the American republic. The Republicans saw themselves as saving the nation from tyranny and monarchy. Again and again they stressed that the Alien and Sedition Laws violated the Bill of Rights.

The Federalists thought that the nation was about to be undone by non-religious radicals. (A radical is someone who takes an extreme position). Fresh in the memory of the Federalists were the excesses of the French Revolution—thousands killed, the Church stripped of power.

When the returns came in, Jefferson had defeated Adams, 73–65. Yet there was a problem. Under the Constitution, electors cast two votes for President and the runner-up became Vice President. However, Aaron Burr, the Republican candidate, had received the same number of electoral votes as Thomas Jefferson.

BREAKING THE TIE

Aaron Burr was the grandson of the fiery preacher Jonathan Edwards (page 122). Burr had fought with distinction during the Revolution. Like Alexander Hamilton, he was now a New York lawyer and politician.

According to the Constitution, the House of Representatives would have to break the tie between Burr and Jefferson. Republicans, it was clear, intended Jefferson to be President. The Federalists, however, held a majority in Congress. Thus the Federalists, not the Republicans, would have the power to decide on the new President.

The Federalists were divided over whom to support. Some Federalists so feared Jefferson that they supported Burr. Alexander Hamilton, however, urged Jefferson's election. "[Burr] is as unprincipled and dangerous a man as any country can boast," Hamilton wrote. "If there be a man in the world I ought to hate, it is Jefferson. . . . But the public good must be paramount to every private consideration."

The House deadlocked on 35 ballots. On the 36th ballot three Federalists decided to follow Hamilton's advice and withdrew their support from Burr. Jefferson thus became the new President, and Burr the Vice President.

The mass of people were overjoyed by Jefferson's election. A newspaper in Philadelphia reported, "The bells have been ringing, guns firing, dogs barking, cats mewling, children crying, and [Republican radicals] getting drunk ever since the news of Mr. Jefferson's election arrived in this city."

The 1800 election led to the ratification of the Twelfth Amendment in 1804. It called for separate ballots for the President and Vice President. In the future it would be clear which office each candidate was to fill.

THE MANY TALENTS OF THOMAS JEFFERSON

Our nation, in its more than 200 years of existence, has had more than 40 Presidents. They have included great leaders and men of good judgment. None of our Presidents, however, has matched Thomas Jefferson in the variety of his achievements.

You have already read about some of what Jefferson did. He wrote the Declaration of Independence. He served as ambassador to France and Secretary of State under Washington. He was leader of the Republican Party and Vice President under Adams. Yet Jefferson accomplished far more.

Jefferson was still a young lawyer when he also became an architect. Inspired by the buildings of classical Greece and Rome, he designed his home, Monticello. For this elegant and graceful mansion Jefferson invented a dumbwaiter (elevator for food dishes), storm windows, and a seven-day clock. Our nickel honors Jefferson's achievement. On one side of the nickel is the image of Thomas Jefferson. On the other side is the image of Monticello.

Thomas Jefferson designed and built Monticello, his home on a hilltop outside Charlottesville, Virginia. Monticello took many years to construct.
HISTORY What does Monticello tell us about the abilities of Thomas Jefferson?

The look of the nation's capital also reflects Jefferson's interest in classical architecture. From the time the Potomac site was chosen, Jefferson worked closely with the architects and designers of Washington, D.C.

Jefferson was also a musician who loved to play the violin. An eager reader, he had one of the best libraries in America. After he died, his library became the core of the new Library of Congress.

Jefferson wrote only a few books, but one—*Notes on the State of Virginia*—is a classic. In this book Jefferson carefully described the state's geography, wildlife, population, and government. He also expressed his own views. "Those who labor in the earth are the chosen people of God," he wrote. The land, Jefferson believed, fostered virtue and the basic goodness of people.

> "**T**hose who labor in the earth are the chosen people of God."
>
> —*Thomas Jefferson*

As President, Jefferson dressed and behaved like a gentleman farmer. He refused to follow city fashions. He often wore green corduroy breeches, a red vest, and yarn stockings. Jefferson also did not like ceremony and show. Instead of riding in a fancy carriage to his inauguration, he walked. He entertained at the White House with friendly dinners instead of grand parties. He signed his invitations "Mr. Jefferson" rather than "The President of the United States."

OVERTURNING THE FEDERALIST PROGRAM

For President Jefferson the first order of business was quieting the nation's political passions. In his Inaugural Address, therefore, he called for unity. "Let us unite with one heart and one mind," he urged the nation. "Every difference of opinion is not a difference of principle. We are all Republicans, we are all Federalists."

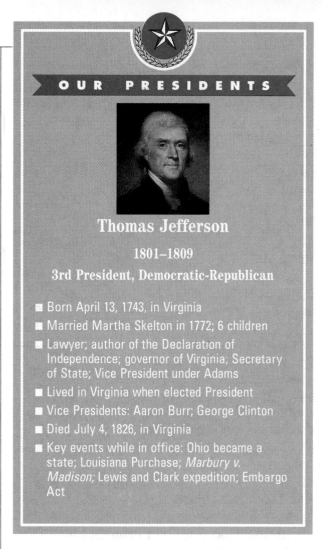

Despite his words, Jefferson was no Federalist. He disagreed with Federalist ideas about a strong, active government. Jefferson believed in a strict construction of the Constitution. In Jefferson's mind, the federal government should have a limited role in people's lives. At his inauguration, he said Americans needed a wise government "which shall [keep] men from injuring one another, which shall leave them otherwise free to regulate their own pursuits. . . ."

Jefferson undid as much of the Federalist program as he could. In this his ally was the new Congress, now controlled by Republicans. At his urging, Congress allowed the Alien and Sedition Acts to expire. Jefferson released from prison any persons convicted under the Sedition Act. Congress also ended internal taxes, including the tax on whiskey.

In effect, Jefferson wanted to destroy the finance system set up by Hamilton. Hamilton's system depended on a certain amount of public and private debt. Jefferson opposed debt in any form. "Banking establishments are more dangerous than standing armies," he said. "The principle of spending money to be paid by posterity [future generations] . . . is but swindling . . . on a large scale." Jefferson had no sympathy for industry, manufacturers, or cities. Instead, he believed, government should encourage farming.

Jefferson's repeal of most taxes reduced the government's income. To cut government spending, Jefferson trimmed the number of its employees. He also took aim at the military. With Congress's approval, he reduced the size of the navy and stopped the building of new ships. He slashed the army from 4,000 to 2,500 soldiers.

A FEDERALIST JUDICIARY

The thorn in Jefferson's side was the judicial branch of government. Between the election of 1800 and Jefferson's inauguration, Adams had worked to place Federalists as judges. When the Chief Justice resigned, Adams had appointed John Marshall to the job.

Marshall was a Virginian and a distant relative of Thomas Jefferson. He had little formal schooling. Indeed, there was hardly time for school. Until he turned twenty, Marshall helped raise his fourteen younger brothers and sisters on their family farm. Marshall then served in the Continental Army and spent the winter of 1777 with Washington at Valley Forge. After the war Marshall served in Congress and as Secretary of State under Adams. As a staunch Federalist, he disagreed heartily with Jefferson.

Jefferson often felt frustrated by Federalist control of the courts. Yet there was little he could do. Judges were appointed for life. As he once remarked about judges, "Few die and none resign."

One reason Adams had chosen Marshall was that he was "in the full vigor of middle age." Thus, Adams reasoned, Marshall would be around a long time to check the Republicans. Adams guessed right. Marshall would serve as Chief Justice until his death in 1835. During that time, he did much to shape American government and law.

A STAND AGAINST PIRACY

To Jefferson, small government did not mean weak government. This he proved early in his administration—term in office. At the time, the United States enjoyed a healthy trade with Europe. Shipping goods on the Mediterranean Sea, however, involved risks. Pirates from the Barbary Coast—the North African states of Morocco, Algiers, Tunis, and Tripoli —preyed on merchant ships.

THE BARBARY COAST

MAP SKILLS

Refusing to pay tribute to Barbary Coast pirates, Jefferson sent warships to the Mediterranean in 1801. In what continent were the Barbary states located? CRITICAL THINKING Why might Jefferson's use of force have surprised some people?

In 1804 a raid led by 25-year-old Stephen Decatur burned the *Philadelphia,* a captured American ship in Tripoli harbor. HISTORY When did piracy finally end in the Mediterranean?

For years, American and European governments had paid tribute to the Barbary pirates to leave their ships alone. Jefferson had opposed this policy. "Weakness provokes insult and injury," he argued.

In 1800 the ruler of Tripoli demanded more "protection money" from the United States. Jefferson reacted in 1801 with a show of force. He sent a fleet of warships to the Mediterranean to protect American merchant ships.

For the next four years, America's small navy clashed with enemy ships in the Mediterranean. Early in 1804, Stephen Decatur led a bold raid against an American ship, the *Philadelphia,* that Barbary pirates had earlier captured. Decatur's crew burned the ship, thus keeping the pirates from using it. The following year the ruler of Tripoli signed a treaty. In it he promised not to interfere with American ships. The other Barbary states later did the same.

Piracy in the Mediterranean did not really end, however, until 1815. In that year Britain and Holland also refused to pay tribute to the pirates. The pirate kingdoms then collapsed.

SECTION REVIEW

1. KEY TERMS radical, administration

2. PEOPLE AND PLACES Thomas Jefferson, Aaron Burr, John Marshall, Barbary Coast

3. COMPREHENSION What weakness in the Constitution did the election of 1800 reveal? How was it corrected?

4. COMPREHENSION How and why did the Republicans try to undo Hamilton's financial system?

5. CRITICAL THINKING What did Jefferson mean when he said, "weakness provokes insult and injury"? What examples in history support Jefferson's view?

2 Jefferson Looks West

Section Focus

Key Term Louisiana Purchase

Main Idea By 1800 the movement of people was bringing rapid change to the continent of North America. Jefferson's foreign policy, weighted toward the concerns of westerners and southerners, resulted in the purchase of new lands for the United States.

Objectives As you read, look for answers to these questions:
1. What changes were taking place on the Pacific coast? What changes were taking place on the Great Plains?
2. How did events in the West Indies affect the course of American history?
3. What effect did the frontier have on Jefferson's foreign policy?

"This is a great country, the most peaceful and quiet country in the world," a new arrival wrote home. "One lives better here than in the most cultured court in Europe." The new arrival was Diego de Borica (bor–EE–kuh), appointed by Spain in 1794 to be governor of its colony in California. Borica probably knew little about the struggling new republic on the other side of the continent. Yet that country—the United States—was becoming more interested in events beyond its borders.

The entire continent of North America was changing in 1800. This was caused by European rivalry, movements of people, new trading patterns, and new ideas. Americans were involved in much of this change.

THE PACIFIC COAST IN 1800

Spain had once claimed the entire Pacific coast. In the 1700s, however, other nations challenged this claim.

The first Europeans to move into the Pacific Northwest were the Russians. In the 1740s the Russians set up trading posts on the Alaska coast. In search of sea otter and seal furs, they slowly moved southward.

Spain had become nervous about the Russian move toward its territory. Spain had claimed California 200 years before. Not until 1770, however, did the Russian threat cause Spain to begin settlement of Alta (Upper) California.

The first mission settlement was set up in 1769 at San Diego by Captain Gaspar de

Father Junípero Serra established a series of missions along the California coast. The Franciscan mission church at San Diego, founded in 1769, appears above. United States forces took control of San Diego in 1846.
HISTORY Why did Spain decide to colonize California?

Portolá (por–taw–LAH) and Father Junípero Serra. In 1776 Juan Bautista de Anza selected sites for both a presidio and mission in San Francisco. By 1800 a chain of twenty-one mission outposts stretched from San Diego to San Francisco.

In addition to the missions, the Spanish founded towns at Los Angeles, Monterey, San

Map: Spanish Settlement of California

Legend:
- ⛪ Mission
- Area settled by 1820

Labels on map:
- Sacramento R.
- SIERRA NEVADA
- San Joaquín R.
- Salinas R.
- Colorado R.
- Ft. Ross (Russian)
- San Francisco de Asís
- Santa Clara de Asís
- Monterey
- San Carlos Borromeo
- San Antonio de Padua
- San Luís Obispo
- MOJAVE DESERT
- San Buenaventura
- Los Angeles
- San Gabriel Arcángel
- San Juan Capistrano
- San Diego de Alcalá
- El Camino Real
- PACIFIC OCEAN
- SCALE: 0 — 100 mi / 0 — 100 km
- ALBERS CONICAL EQUAL-AREA PROJECTION

MAP SKILLS

The Spanish called the road connecting their California missions El Camino Real, or the King's Highway. The road began in the south at San Diego and followed the coast north to San Francisco. CRITICAL THINKING Why might Spain have limited its settlement north of San Francisco?

Jose, and San Francisco. Los Angeles, for instance, was founded in 1781. The new settlers were poor people from Mexico. An ethnic "rainbow," the first settlers included Spaniards, Africans, Indians, mestizos, and possibly some Filipinos. Each settler was given clothes, saddles, tools, and livestock with which to start a new life.

Meanwhile the British Canadians were pushing westward. In 1793 the great explorer Alexander MacKenzie became the first white man to cross North America on land and reach the Pacific. As a result, the British also laid claim to the Pacific Northwest.

American traders were also reaching for the Northwest, but by sea. New England merchant ships sailed around the southern tip of the Americas at Cape Horn. Like the Russians, they wanted furs and pelts. In 1792 Captain Robert Gray discovered the great river that now divides the states of Washington and Oregon. He named the river "Columbia" after his ship. Gray also claimed the region for the United States. By 1800 so many New Englanders were trading along the Oregon coast that the Indians there called all white men "Bostons."

CHANGES ON THE GREAT PLAINS

Spain claimed most of the North American interior, but in name only. Except for Spanish settlements in southeast Texas and the Rio Grande Valley, Spanish influence was absent. Meanwhile, rapid change was taking place on the Great Plains. This change was caused by the horse.

The first Spanish explorers, such as Coronado, had left horses behind. For a time bands of horses roamed wild. Gradually the Indians learned to master the horse and use it for their own. The result was a social and economic revolution among the Indians that bordered the Great Plains. As tribe after tribe learned to ride, they moved onto the Plains. With the horse, the Plains Indians could easily follow the buffalo herds. Horses also made it easier to chase down and kill buffalo. Hunting buffalo took far less effort than farming. As a result, buffalo became the principal food of the Plains Indians.

With more leisure time, the Plains Indians turned to art. The men painted tepees and shields. The women made beautiful clothing decorated with beadwork and quills. It was the golden age of Plains culture.

The new horse-using cultures sometimes migrated far from their traditional homelands. The Comanche, for instance, moved southward from Wyoming. As they did so, the Comanche waged war on other Plains Indians and on Spanish settlements in New Mexico and Texas. In 1758 the missionaries

George Catlin's painting suggests the importance of buffalo hunting to the Plains Indians' way of life. After American settlers moved westward, the buffalo herds almost disappeared. **CULTURAL PLURALISM** How did the Indians come to depend on the buffalo?

in northeast Texas sent out a call for help. At the Battle of Red River in 1759, however, the Comanche crushed a force of Spanish soldiers. As a result, Spain decided to leave northern Texas to the Indians and closed down the frontier missions.

AMERICAN PIONEERS MOVE WESTWARD

The Plains Indian culture would be doomed by another development taking place at this time. This was the steady westward movement of Americans. Settlers by the thousands were spilling over the Appalachians. By 1800 Kentucky and Tennessee were both states. Ohio would enter the Union in 1803.

As the numbers of westerners grew, so did their political influence. For instance, every state with a large frontier population had voted for Jefferson for President. In 1800 westerners had also pressured Congress to sell public land cheaply. Cheap land, and plenty of it, continued to be part of the American dream.

The new frontier west of the Appalachians differed from earlier frontiers. The frontier family was as distant in travel time from Boston or New York as those cities were from London or Paris. Far from the traditions and attitudes of the East Coast, frontier people developed their own.

"The Mississippi boatman and the squatter on Indian lands were perhaps the most distinctly American type then existing," wrote historian Henry Adams. "Their language and their imagination showed contact with Indians." As an example he quoted two boatmen getting ready to fight:

> "I am a man; I am a horse; I am a team," cried one voice; "I can whip any man in all Kentucky, by God!" "I am an alligator," cried the other; "half man, half horse; can whip any man on the Mississippi, by God!" "I am a man," shouted the first; "have the best horse, best dog, best gun, and hand-

somest wife in all Kentucky, by God!" "I am a Mississippi snapping-turtle," rejoined the second; "have bear's claws, alligator's teeth, and the devil's tail; can whip *any* man, by God."

Most pioneers lived in crude log cabins set on an acre or two of cleared land. There was always the chance of Indian attack. Fever and sickness were almost certain. Those who had moved west because they were poor often stayed to build a life for themselves. Their small communities began to show up as new dots on the map. Those who wanted adventure and independence were likely to pick up and move on as soon as they could see the smoke from a neighbor's chimney.

A Shifting Foreign Policy

When Jefferson became President, American foreign policy made a small but important shift. The concerns of the West and South carried more weight than the commercial interests of the North. An example was the change in policy toward Hispaniola.

The Federalists had helped the North by encouraging trade. More than one-third of American trade was with the West Indies, and within those islands the most important market was Hispaniola. France controlled the western half of the island (now Haiti). Spain controlled the eastern half (now the Dominican Republic).

The French colony on Hispaniola was the jewel of the French empire. Its production of sugar, coffee, indigo, and cotton formed two-thirds of France's total commerce. This rich commerce in turn depended on the labor of half a million African slaves.

The French Revolution caused turmoil on French Hispaniola. Inspired by the ideals of liberty and equality, the colony's slaves rebelled in 1791. By 1793 they had seized Haiti and declared their freedom. In this their leader was Toussaint L'Ouverture (too–SAN loo–vayr–TOOR). Toussaint was born a slave but was the grandson of an African chief.

The Federalists saw opportunity in the revolt on Hispaniola. They gave Toussaint military aid in exchange for trading rights. With such help, Toussaint then conquered the Spanish part of Hispaniola. By 1801 he ruled the whole island.

The news that slaves had rebelled and were governing Hispaniola unnerved American slaveowners. As a slaveowner himself, Jefferson felt little sympathy for Toussaint L'Ouverture. He was also an admirer of France. Thus, when Napoleon asked for American help in putting down the rebellion, Jefferson said yes. (Nothing, however, was to come from this promise.)

As more settlers headed west of the Appalachians, businesses arose to meet their needs. Here is an Iowa trading post, where pelts and other items could be exchanged for staple goods. **ECONOMICS** Why would trading posts be so important for frontier settlers?

BIOGRAPHY

TOUSSAINT L'OUVERTURE (1743–1803) was the liberator of Haiti and one of history's great generals. Toussaint was a slave until age 48, when he led the first successful slave revolt in history. When Napoleon sought to re-establish slavery, Toussaint's armies defeated the French, but Toussaint himself was captured and died in prison.

FRANCE REGAINS LOUISIANA

What Jefferson did not know was that Napoleon's plans went further than Hispaniola. Napoleon controlled most of Europe, and Spain was in his grip. In a secret treaty signed in 1800, Spain agreed to return Louisiana to France. Napoleon planned first to re-establish white rule on Hispaniola. His next move would be to send an army to occupy Louisiana.

Meanwhile, Jefferson grew alarmed over an issue dear to the heart of every westerner. This was free navigation of the Mississippi and the right of deposit at New Orleans. In late 1802 the right of deposit was cut off, and westerners responded with a howl of outrage. Jefferson sought to preserve neutrality. Yet he had to protect the rights of Americans on the Mississippi.

THE LOUISIANA PURCHASE

To preserve peace, Jefferson sent ministers to France with an offer to buy New Orleans. Behind the offer was a threat. If France should take possession of New Orleans, he had written, "we must marry ourselves to the British fleet and nation."

The French, meanwhile, were still fighting to restore slavery to Hispaniola. Even though Toussaint had been captured, resistance on Hispaniola continued. To crush the rebellion, Napoleon had sent an army of nearly 34,000 men. Heavy fighting and an outbreak of yellow fever had reduced the French force to 4,000. Disgusted with the whole venture, Napoleon decided to withdraw from Hispaniola. He also decided to sell Louisiana—all of it. Thus it was that for $15 million the United States made the Louisiana Purchase in 1803. This purchase doubled the area of the United States.

Jefferson agonized over the purchase. Was it legal? he asked. Jefferson believed in strict construction of the Constitution. Yet the Constitution said nothing about whether the President had the authority to buy land. Among those urging Jefferson to accept a loose interpretation of the Constitution was that old revolutionary, Thomas Paine. Paine wrote Jefferson that acquiring Louisiana did not change the Constitution. Instead, he argued, "It only extends the principles of it over a larger territory."

The purchase of Louisiana was the most important act of Jefferson's years as President. As a result of the purchase, the United States gained the western part of the Mississippi River basin. This was all the land between the Mississippi River and the Rocky Mountains. At the time no American knew how large the territory was, or even what it looked like.

SECTION REVIEW

1. KEY TERM Louisiana Purchase

2. PEOPLE AND PLACES Alaska, California, Alexander MacKenzie, Robert Gray, Columbia River, Hispaniola, Toussaint L'Ouverture, Napoleon

3. COMPREHENSION What reason did Spain have for deciding to colonize Upper California in the 1770s?

4. COMPREHENSION What events led to the Louisiana Purchase?

5. CRITICAL THINKING Why did Jefferson threaten that if France occupied New Orleans, the United States would ally itself with Britain?

3 Exploring the Far West

★ **Section Focus** ★

★ **Key Term**   Lewis and Clark expedition ★

★ **Main Idea**   In the early 1800s American explorers acquired valuable information about the West. ★

Objectives   As you read, look for answers to these questions:
1. Why did President Jefferson encourage western exploration?
2. What regions of the West were explored during the early 1800s?
3. What were the effects of these western expeditions?
★

In early 1801 Meriwether Lewis was an officer with the army at Detroit when he received a letter from Thomas Jefferson. Would Lewis, Jefferson asked, come to Washington as his private secretary? The new President explained that he wanted a secretary who had knowledge of both the army and the "Western Country."

If Jefferson had really wanted a secretary, he would not have chosen Lewis. Lewis had a limited education and was a poor speller. Jefferson actually was looking for someone who would explore the West for him.

THE FIRST AMERICAN SCIENTIFIC EXPEDITION

For years Jefferson had dreamed of an American expedition to explore beyond the Mississippi. Now, as President, Jefferson had the chance to make his dream come true. In Jefferson's map-lined study, Jefferson and Lewis began to plan the trip. They called it the Corps of Discovery.

The Corps of Discovery was the first American scientific expedition. The explorers were expected to return with detailed information about the land, the plants and animals, and the Indians. For this they needed scientific instruments, books, maps, and paper. For camping and traveling, they needed guns, ammunition, kettles, clothing, fishhooks, and oil lamps. To trade with the Indians, they packed such things as beads, fabric, needles, scissors, axes, and sheets of copper.

Lewis also decided he needed a partner who could recruit and oversee the volunteer force. He turned to his old friend, William Clark. Clark was an able mapmaker, outdoorsman, and leader. He was the younger brother of George Rogers Clark, who had made a name for himself during the Revolution. With Clark sharing the lead, the Corps of Discovery became known as the Lewis and Clark expedition.

Accompanying Clark was York, his African American servant. York was a large, strong man skilled at hunting and at charming the Indians. York was to play an increasingly important role in the expedition. He went exploring with Clark on several small side trips. The first black man that many Indians had ever seen, York became a celebrity among western Indian nations.

The expedition was almost ready when news came that France was going to sell all of Louisiana to the United States. The purchase made it more urgent than ever to explore the West. Lewis and Clark set out in the summer of 1803, and by winter had reached St. Louis.

St. Louis sits on the western bank of the Mississippi, near the junction with the Missouri River. Because people preferred water routes over land routes, St. Louis would become the gateway to the West. In 1803, however, St. Louis was just an outpost with 180 houses. Many of the town's citizens were French settlers who had lived for years under Spanish rule.

Lewis and Clark spent the winter at St. Louis. There they waited for the ceremony to

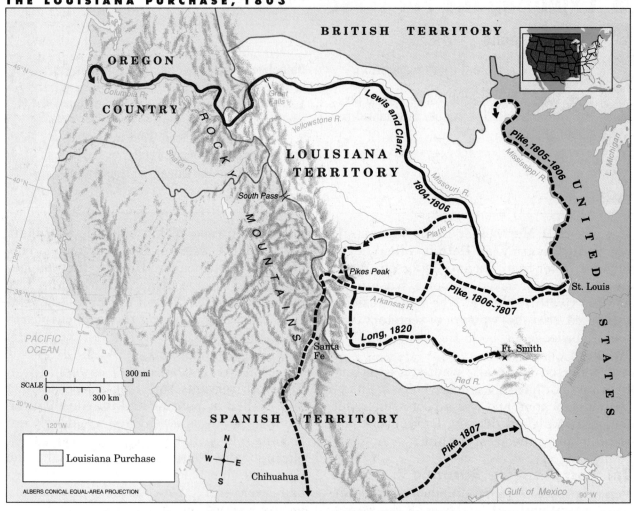

BRITISH TERRITORY

OREGON COUNTRY

LOUISIANA TERRITORY

ROCKY MOUNTAINS

UNITED STATES

PACIFIC OCEAN

SPANISH TERRITORY

Columbia R.
Great Falls
Yellowstone R.
Snake R.
South Pass
Lewis and Clark
1804–1806
Missouri R.
Mississippi R.
L. Michigan
Pike, 1805–1806
Pikes Peak
Platte R.
Arkansas R.
Pike, 1806–1807
St. Louis
Long, 1820
Ft. Smith
Santa Fe
Red R.
Chihuahua
Pike, 1807
Gulf of Mexico

45°N
40°N
35°N
30°N
125°W
120°W
90°W

SCALE
0 — 300 mi
0 — 300 km

Louisiana Purchase

ALBERS CONICAL EQUAL-AREA PROJECTION

N W E S

MAP SKILLS This map shows the Louisiana Territory and the routes taken by Lewis and Clark, Zebulon Pike, and Stephen Long. What natural features made up the eastern and western borders of the territory? CRITICAL THINKING Which rivers did Lewis and Clark follow? Why?

mark the transfer of Louisiana to the United States. In March 1804, the Stars and Stripes were raised over St. Louis. Several days later the former commander at St. Louis called an Indian powwow. "Your old Fathers, the Spaniard and the Frenchman, grasp by the hand your new Father, the Head Chief of the United States," he said. "By an act of their good will, and in virtue of their last treaty, I have delivered up to them all these lands."

UP THE MISSOURI RIVER

By May 1804 the expedition was finally on its way. About 40 men headed up the Missouri in one flat-bottomed riverboat and two

pirogues (pih–ROHGS). A pirogue was shaped like a canoe but was much larger. Both pirogues were 40 feet long, one painted red and one painted white.

By then Lewis knew by memory the President's instructions. The Corps of Discovery was to explore the Missouri River and its tributaries. The explorers hoped to find a practical water route across the continent for the purpose of trade. At the same time they were to maintain friendly relations with the Indians and to gather scientific data.

The expedition slowly made its way up the Missouri. Sometimes it was necessary to pull, rather than row or sail, their big boats

In this painting, Lewis and Clark, with their guide Sacajawea and their servant York, stand at the Great Falls of the Missouri River in 1805. Lewis and Clark recorded their expedition in this notebook bound with elkskin. **CULTURAL PLURALISM** Why did Lewis and Clark include Sacajawea in the expedition?

against the current. In late October they reached the Mandan Indian villages in what is now North Dakota.

The expedition built a small fort and wintered at the Mandan villages. There they met a handful of French Canadian trappers and traders. The Frenchmen acted as translators, but they were not happy to see the Americans come. They suspected—and rightly—that the Americans would soon elbow in on the rich trade in beaver furs.

In the spring of 1805 the expedition set out again. In the company now was a Frenchman named Toussaint Charbonneau (shar–buhn–NO), his wife, Sacajawea (sa–kuh–juh–WEE–uh), and their baby. Sacajawea was a Shoshone Indian who had been kidnapped from her people years before. Lewis and Clark planned for Sacajawea to be their interpreter when they reached her people in the Rocky Mountains.

As they proceeded upriver, Lewis and Clark were awed by the variety of wildlife. Their journals are full of sightings of buffalo, antelope, elk, deer, wolves, coyotes, beaver, and birds. One of Clark's journal entries noted:

Although the game is very abundant and gentle, we only kill as much as is necessary for food. . . . Beaver are very

abundant. The party kill several of them every day. The eagles, magpies, and geese have their nests in trees adjacent to each other. . . . The bald eagles are more abundant here than I ever observed them in any part of the country.

ON TO THE PACIFIC

The expedition's upriver passage was stopped abruptly at the Great Falls of the Missouri. This cascading water was really a series of waterfalls ten miles long. To get around the falls, they had to make an eighteen-mile portage. To do so, they crafted wheels of cottonwood and attached them to the canoes. Even with wheels, the trek took almost two weeks. Their moccasins were not sturdy enough to withstand cactus spines. Rattlesnakes, bears, and even a severe hail storm slowed their passage.

As they came to the Rocky Mountains, Sacajawea pointed out Shoshone lands. Eager to make contact with the Indians, Lewis and a small party went overland. Their route led to the headwaters of the Missouri. There they could stand with a foot on each bank.

The Thomas Gilcrease Institute of American History and Art, Tulsa, Oklahoma.

Lewis found the Shoshone, whose chief recognized Sacajawea, his sister. The Shoshone willingly traded horses to Lewis and Clark. Sinking their canoes for safekeeping, Lewis and Clark then followed Shoshone guides across the mountains to the Snake River.

On reaching the Snake, the group built new canoes and headed downriver. The Snake flows into the mighty Columbia River, which empties into the Pacific Ocean. Lewis and Clark reached the mouth of the Columbia in November 1805. There they spent a rain-soaked winter before returning the next year to St. Louis.

The Lewis and Clark expedition brought back large amounts of scientific and geographic information. Americans began to have a sense of what lay to the far west. The expedition also reinforced the American claim to the Pacific Northwest.

INTRIGUE IN THE WEST

Lewis and Clark had set out to explore the northern part of the Louisiana Purchase. Two years later an expedition led by an army officer, Zebulon M. Pike, took a more southerly route. Scientific curiosity was not the only reason, however, for Pike's trip. Pike's main mission was to uncover information that might help Aaron Burr take control of the Southwest.

Burr, you remember, had tied Jefferson for the presidency in 1800. Alexander Hamilton had urged Jefferson over Burr because, he said, Burr could not be trusted. Hamilton continued to block Burr, and Burr's outrage grew. While still Vice President, Burr challenged and then killed Hamilton in a duel in 1804. Though formally charged with murder, Burr remained Vice President until his term ended in 1805.

After leaving office, Burr began to pursue a vision of himself as a western Napoleon. He planned not only to rule Louisiana but to seize Mexico from Spain.

To do that, Burr needed more information about New Spain. He plotted with General James Wilkinson, governor of the Louisiana Territory. Wilkinson, who was working as a double agent for Spain, planned an expedition to find the headwaters of the Red River. The Red River was supposed to be the boundary between New Spain and Louisiana.

Pike was put in command of the expedition. His orders were to make treaties with the Indians, collect scientific information, and probe the defenses on New Spain's northern frontier.

From St. Louis, Pike's party of two dozen men headed westward across the Plains. In what is now Kansas, Pike learned from the Pawnee Indians that the Spanish had recent-

In 1806–1807 Zebulon Pike led an expedition across the Plains to the Rocky Mountains. This colored engraving from 1822 shows Pike's party as it approached the Front Range of the Rockies. HISTORY What was the purpose of Pike's expedition?

ly been there looking for him. Pike coolly followed their trail to the southern Rockies. While he was still 150 miles away, Pike could see the peak that today bears his name, Pikes Peak.

Pike's exploring party proceeded to head into mountains frosted by winter. They suffered dreadfully from hunger and severe frostbite. Pike finally set up a small camp in the San Luis Valley. Running south through the valley was a small river. It was the upper Rio Grande.

SUCCESS AND FAILURE

Pike was in Spanish territory, and Spanish troops arrested him and his men. Since that was Pike's intention, he did not resist. The Americans were taken south to Santa Fe. From there the governor sent them on to Chihuahua, Mexico, for further questioning. The following year, Pike and his men were returned through Texas and released in American territory.

Pike had not even come close to the Red River. Still, he had achieved his larger purpose. Pike's account of his expedition and his description of New Spain were important. They provided the first information in English on the Great Plains and the Rio Grande Valley.

Burr and Wilkinson, on the other hand, failed miserably in their attempt to control Louisiana and Mexico. Wilkinson betrayed Burr to Jefferson. Burr was tried for treason and found not guilty. Pike was cleared of any involvement in the scheme.

ANOTHER SEARCH FOR THE RED RIVER

In 1820 Stephen H. Long tried to find the Red River. Both scientist and explorer, Long followed the Platte River westward from the Missouri River. He mapped the Plains, climbed Pikes Peak, and then headed south to find the Red River. To his great disappointment, however, the river he followed eastward was the Canadian River, not the Red River. The Red River was located farther to the south. (See map, page 332.)

EFFECTS OF THE EXPLORATIONS

The first American explorations of the West were more than tales of individual heroism. The knowledge they gained had effects that would be felt for years to come.

(1) The combined efforts of Lewis and Clark, Pike, and Long produced the first accurate maps of the Louisiana Purchase. These maps would become invaluable to later explorers.

(2) Pike had called the Great Plains the "Great American Desert." Long seemed to agree that the region had no value for settlement. For decades, Americans believed that the Great Plains were fit only for Indians and were unsuitable for farming. Thus was born the idea that all Indians should move (or should be forced to move) from east of the Mississippi to the Plains.

(3) Interest in the fur trade led a German-born businessman named John Jacob Astor to establish a trading post at Astoria, at the mouth of the Columbia River in present-day Oregon. In the next decades American mountain men—hunters and trappers—added to the knowledge of the West as they searched for new routes and new game.

SECTION REVIEW

1. KEY TERM Lewis and Clark expedition

2. PEOPLE AND PLACES Meriwether Lewis, William Clark, St. Louis, Missouri River, Sacajawea, Aaron Burr, Zebulon M. Pike, Santa Fe, Stephen H. Long

3. COMPREHENSION What was the purpose of the Lewis and Clark expedition? What route did it follow?

4. COMPREHENSION What was the principal effect of Pike's expedition?

5. CRITICAL THINKING How were Thomas Jefferson's aims in sending Lewis and Clark to the American West similar to the aims of Ferdinand and Isabella in supporting Christopher Columbus's voyages to the new world? How were they different?

Western explorers in the early 1800s saw the contrasts of an awe-inspiring landscape: deep canyons, towering peaks, broad rivers, near-desert.

Traveling westward from the last settled towns, they crossed the original "tall grass" prairie. Here were hundreds of miles of gently waving shoulder-high grasses, dotted with starflowers and other wildflowers. Clumps of trees grew along rivers where there was enough water.

Farther west, where less rain falls, the prairie grasses were shorter. Trees were fewer. The western edge of the Great Plains is the arid region that Zebulon Pike named the "Great American Desert."

REACHING THE WEST

Meriwether Lewis and William Clark left St. Louis and followed the Missouri River northwest across the prairies. Once they had tracked the Missouri to its source high in the mountains of Montana, Lewis and Clark crossed the northern Rockies on horseback. On the western side lay a dramatic landscape created by ancient volcanoes. The Snake and Columbia rivers cut valleys out of the rock of the Columbia Plateau.

Though this plateau was formed by ancient lava flows, the Northwest still contains active hot springs and geysers. The mountains of the Cascade Range feature the distinctive cone shape of volcanic peaks.

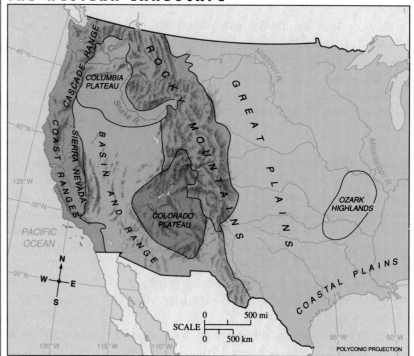

THE WESTERN LANDSCAPE

Most of these volcanoes have been quiet for many years except for small amounts of smoke or ash.

The first Europeans to see the Southwest came long before Zebulon Pike. In the 1540s, members of an expedition from Mexico led by Francisco de Coronado looked in wonder on the Colorado River and the Grand Canyon.

The Southwest's dramatic scenery is mainly a result of the region's dry climate. The high plateau between the Rockies and the Pacific coast lies in a "rain shadow." Coastal mountain ranges capture all the moisture from the air that blows inland from the ocean. The land on the opposite side of the mountains receives hardly any water.

Farther north, in present-day Utah and Nevada, is the "Basin and Range" area. Here smooth-floored valleys, or basins, lie between small mountain ranges.

Early explorers returned with exciting descriptions of the western landscape. Later explorers and settlers would discover even more about this immensely varied and beautiful region.

CRITICAL THINKING QUESTIONS

1. What geographical forces shaped the Southwest and the Pacific Northwest?

2. How were rivers essential to westward exploration?

4 The War of 1812

Section Focus

Key Terms   War of 1812
■ Non-Intercourse Act ■ War Hawk
■ blockade ■ Treaty of Ghent
■ secession ■ Hartford Convention

Main Idea   The clamor of westerners pushed the country into war with Britain in 1812. Although the war did little to settle issues, the United States successfully resisted British invasions.

Objectives   As you read, look for answers to these questions:
1. What were the causes of the War of 1812?
2. What was the outcome of the War of 1812?
3. Why were Americans divided over the war?

It ofttimes has been told, that the
British seamen bold
Could flog the tars of France so neat
and handy, O;
But they never met their match till
the Yankees did them catch,
O the Yankee boys for fighting are the
dandy, O!

This popular song of 1812 expresses the fighting spirit of many Americans as they again went to war with Britain. This was the War of 1812.

DRIFTING TOWARD WAR

The resentments that led to the War of 1812 started on the high seas. In 1803 France and Britain were once more at war. Each was trying to prevent the other from getting food and supplies. Thus both France and Britain seized American ships and cargoes sailing toward the enemy's ports. Britain also stepped up the impressment of American sailors into the British navy.

Jefferson, re-elected for a second term in 1804, could not ignore the British and French attacks. He wanted to avoid war. Yet how could he force European nations to respect the rights of American ships at sea?

TRADE AS A WEAPON

Jefferson decided to pressure Great Britain and France by using a government order to stop foreign trade. The Embargo Act, passed in 1807, banned American ships from sailing to *any* foreign ports. It also closed American ports to ships from other countries.

The act was folly. The growing wealth of the nation was tied to commerce. The government's income depended on import duties. To stop foreign trade was to cripple the United States.

Americans went without sugar, tea, and other imported goods. Farmers suffered from the loss of their foreign customers. Sailors and shipbuilders had little work.

Many merchant ships chose to ignore the embargo and sailed for Europe anyway. In doing so, of course, they risked seizure.

The embargo became a major issue in the election of 1808. Jefferson declined to run a third time. Instead he passed the Republican Party torch to his old friend James Madison. Madison won. It was clear, however, that the embargo was causing the party to lose popularity. The Republicans cast about for something to replace the embargo.

Their solution to the problem was the Non-Intercourse Act of 1809. This law allowed merchants to trade with any country *except* France and Britain. Trade with these countries would resume when they agreed to respect American ships. However, the Non-Intercourse Act was no more effective than the embargo.

Meanwhile the American temper was becoming more warlike, particularly toward

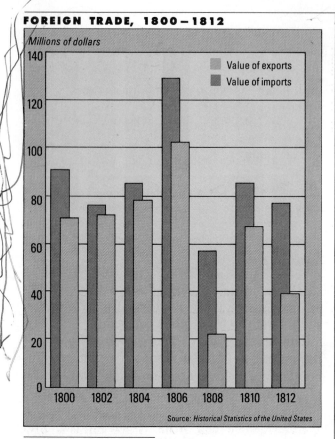

FOREIGN TRADE, 1800–1812

Millions of dollars

Value of exports
Value of imports

1800 1802 1804 1806 1808 1810 1812

Source: *Historical Statistics of the United States*

CHART SKILLS

This bar graph shows the value of American imports and exports from 1800 to 1812. Which were greater during the period shown, imports or exports? What was the value of exports in 1806? By how much did exports decrease between 1806 and 1808? **CRITICAL THINKING** What caused the drop in exports between 1806 and 1808?

Great Britain. Calls for war came, not from eastern merchants, but from westerners. They blamed their Indian problems on the British.

TECUMSEH'S PURSUIT OF INDIAN UNITY

In the West, young Indian warriors resented losing large parcels of land given up by their chiefs. One of those who hated this loss of Indian lands was Tecumseh (tih–KUM–suh). Tecumseh was the son of a Shawnee chief. His brother, known as the Prophet, was a shaman, or medicine man. The Prophet had once taken credit for causing the sun to stop during an eclipse. Ever since, the Shawnee had believed in his magical powers. The

headquarters of Tecumseh and the Prophet was Prophetstown, on Tippecanoe Creek in central Indiana.

To understand white people better, Tecumseh learned English. He read the Bible, Shakespeare, and history books. From his reading, he concluded that the Indians had to do what white Americans had done: unite.

In 1809 William Henry Harrison, governor of the Indiana Territory, persuaded a few tribes to sign a treaty selling land in the heart of the Indiana Territory. The Indians sold about 3 million acres for less than one-half cent per acre. Tecumseh declared the treaty meaningless. In a speech he said:

> The white people have no right to take the land from the Indians, because the Indians had it first. It is theirs. The Indians may sell, but they must join together. Any sale not made by all is not valid.

Tecumseh traveled from the Gulf Coast to the Great Lakes urging the Indians to form a confederation. Tecumseh's warriors were itching to fight. After all, they argued, the Prophet had promised to make the Americans' bullets harmless. No, Tecumseh said. They were not to fight unless attacked first.

> "**The white people have no right to take the land from the Indians, because the Indians had it first. It is theirs.**"
>
> —*Tecumseh*

In 1811 Tecumseh set out to rally the Indians south of the Ohio. In his absence, Harrison marched with 1,000 soldiers toward Prophetstown. He camped outside of the town. At dawn, on November 7, 1811, the Indians attacked. After two hours of fighting, Harrison defeated the Indians and the next day burned their village. This was the Battle of Tippecanoe. It destroyed Tecumseh's dream of an Indian confederation.

THE WAR HAWKS OF THE WEST

Harrison and others blamed the British for helping Tecumseh and encouraging Indian unity. The British had had nothing to do with Tecumseh's efforts. After Tippecanoe, however, Tecumseh and his warriors found a warm welcome in Canada. At that point the British and Indians became allies.

Tecumseh's welcome in Canada raised even further the anti-British feelings on the frontier. Western leaders such as Henry Clay of Kentucky called for war. Those westerners were dubbed War Hawks. Not only did they want British aid to the Indians stopped, they wanted the British out of Canada altogether.

The British attacked American ships and removed sailors the British claimed were deserters. **HISTORY** What issues besides impressment led to war with Britain?

"I am not for stopping at Quebec," said Clay, "but would take the whole continent."

Urged on by the War Hawks, Congress declared war on Britain on June 18, 1812. The reasons given were (1) the impressment of American sailors, (2) violations of American rights at sea, and (3) British encouragement of the Indians.

THE FIRST PHASE OF THE WAR

The War of 1812 had two phases. During the first phase, from 1812 to 1814, Britain was still absorbed in its fight against Napoleon in Europe. Therefore Britain conducted a limited war in North America. It defended Canada from American attacks and conducted hit-and-run raids along the coast. In addition, the British set up a blockade. That is, the British navy blocked ships from entering or leaving American ports.

Most American efforts during this first phase met with failure. The American army had fewer than 7,000 men at the war's start. Its leadership was poor. State militias provided help, but only for defense.

The actions of the navy, on the other hand, gave Americans something to cheer about. The navy's volunteer crews were dedicated. Its officers had experience fighting the French and the Barbary pirates. Its frigates (warships) were the fastest afloat. The frigates *Constitution, United States,* and *President* won stirring victories on the high seas. The most important naval victory, however, took place on Lake Erie.

In the winter of 1812–1813 the Americans had begun to build a fleet of boats on the shores of Lake Erie. The man put in charge of the infant fleet was Oliver Hazard Perry. The son of a sea captain, Perry was an experienced and brave seaman.

In September 1813 the small British fleet on the lake set out to destroy the American fleet. Perry lifted anchor and sailed out to meet it. Perry's ship, the *Lawrence,* flew a banner: "Don't give up the ship."

For two hours the two sides exchanged cannon shots. Perry's ship was demolished, the guns put out of action, the rigging destroyed. Perry could have surrendered with honor. Instead, he grabbed the ship's banner and jumped into a rowboat. Then, under a hail of shot, he and five others rowed to another ship. Taking command of the second ship, Perry proceeded to destroy two British vessels. The British surrendered. "We have met the enemy, and they are ours," he scribbled to William Henry Harrison.

> ## "We have met the enemy, and they are ours."
>
> —*Oliver Hazard Perry*

Harrison was waiting with an army of 3,000 soldiers on the Ohio shore of Lake Erie. When he received Perry's note, he made his move. Harrison ferried his army across Lake Erie to Detroit. By the time Harrison arrived, however, the British had retreated into Canada. Harrison followed. At the Battle of the Thames in October 1813, Harrison defeated the British and their Indian allies. One of the battle dead was Tecumseh.

ATTACK ON WASHINGTON AND BALTIMORE

The second phase of the war began with the British defeat of Napoleon in April 1814. With that war ended, the British turned their full attention to the Americans. The new British strategy was to invade the United States by pushing south from Canada and north from New Orleans. To keep the Americans off balance, the British kept up their hit-and-run attacks on American ports.

The most spectacular of these attacks was against the nation's capital. In August 1814, the British sailed into Chesapeake Bay. From the Maryland shore, the British marched overland toward Washington, D.C. The British quickly overpowered the thousand or so soldiers protecting the capital. As the British entered one side of the city, government officials and citizens fled from the other side. Among them was the President's wife. Fortunately, Dolley Madison did not flee the White House empty-handed. She took with her some important papers and a famous painting of George Washington.

According to one story, British officers ate the dinner laid out for President Madison. Then the British torched public buildings, including the White House and Capitol.

This illustration shows British troops putting the torch to buildings in Washington, D.C., in 1814. **HISTORY** How did the raid on Washington fit into British strategy against the United States?

Historians—in fact, any person who studies history—must be able to recognize points of view. Points of view are **subjective**. They involve a person's opinions, beliefs, and feelings. They can affect how a person "sees" the world. When historians study primary sources, they have to be able to judge when a point of view has colored the facts.

One clue to a historian's point of view is the use of **positive language**. For example, a writer who described Washington as "useful and virtuous" probably had a high opinion of him. That writer's description of events surrounding Washington may have been affected by that opinion. **Negative language** indicates an unfavorable point of view. When Thomas Paine called King George III the "Royal Brute," he made his negative feelings clear.

Most writers have their own point of view on subjects that they care about. Some writers, however, have a sharply slanted point of view known as **bias**. A bias is a strong personal preference that prevents objective reporting. Historians must be wary of accepting information from sources that are biased.

DIFFERENT VIEWPOINTS

The quotations that follow show two different points of view of the War of 1812. The first is from President Madison's War Message to Congress.

> The conduct of [Britain's] Government presents a series of acts hostile to the United States as an independent and neutral nation.
> British cruisers have been in the continued practice of violating the American flag on the great highway of nations, and of seizing and carrying off persons sailing under it. . . .
> Under pretended blockades, . . . our commerce has been plundered in every sea. . . .
> We behold . . . on the side of Great Britain a state of war against the United States, and on the side of the United States . . . peace toward Great Britain.

A very different point of view was expressed by George IV, who was then ruling Great Britain as Prince Regent. Read this leader's statement and then answer the following questions.

> The earnest endeavours of the Prince Regent to preserve the relations of peace and amity with the United States of America having unfortunately failed, his Royal Highness . . . deems it proper publicly to declare the causes, and origin of the war, in which the government of the United States has compelled him to engage. . . .
> His Royal Highness can never acknowledge any blockade whatsoever to be illegal. . . . His Royal Highness can never admit, that . . . the . . . right of searching neutral merchant vessels in time of war, the impressment of British seamen, when found therein, can be deemed any violation of a neutral flag. . . .
> Such are the causes of war which have been put forward by the government of the United States. But the real origin of the present contest will be found in that spirit, [found in] the councils of the United States: their marked partiality in . . . assisting the aggressive tyranny of France. . . .

PRACTICING YOUR SKILL

1. What three charges does President Madison make against the British?

2. Why, according to George IV, did the United States declare war?

3. In Madison's first paragraph, what kind of language is used to describe Britain's actions? Give an example.

4. What kind of language does George IV use in his first paragraph to describe Britain's actions? Give an example.

5. How do the two points of view presented in these quotations differ?

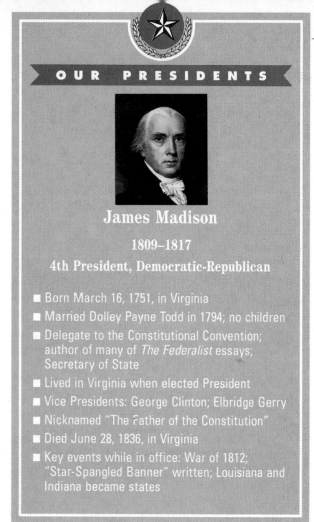

James Madison

1809–1817
4th President, Democratic-Republican

- Born March 16, 1751, in Virginia
- Married Dolley Payne Todd in 1794; no children
- Delegate to the Constitutional Convention; author of many of *The Federalist* essays; Secretary of State
- Lived in Virginia when elected President
- Vice Presidents: George Clinton; Elbridge Gerry
- Nicknamed "The Father of the Constitution"
- Died June 28, 1836, in Virginia
- Key events while in office: War of 1812; "Star-Spangled Banner" written; Louisiana and Indiana became states

This act was in revenge for an American attack on the Canadian city of York. In that attack, American troops had burned several government buildings.

Washington was still burning the next day when a great hurricane struck. Trees were uprooted, roofs were torn off, and buildings blown down. At the first calm, the British hastened back to their ships.

The British next attacked Fort McHenry at Baltimore. The fort's commander had earlier requested a flag "so large that the British will have no difficulty in seeing it." The huge flag inspired the writing of our national anthem. Held prisoner on a British ship, Francis Scott Key watched the all-night battle. At dawn he was thrilled to see that the flag still flew. On an old envelope he wrote a poem, "The Star-Spangled Banner."

FAILED BRITISH INVASIONS

Meanwhile, the British were planning two full-scale invasions of American territory. In September 1814 the British sent a force from Canada across Lake Champlain. Their goal was to push south through the Hudson Valley and cut New England off from the rest of the country. This plan failed when American ships defeated the British at the Battle of Lake Champlain. The British were forced to withdraw to Canada.

The next British move was at New Orleans. By December 1814 dozens of ships carrying 7,500 British troops were approaching Louisiana. Waiting for them was Andrew Jackson.

BIOGRAPHY

DOLLEY MADISON (1768–1849) was born a Quaker in North Carolina. She hosted many White House functions while her husband, James Madison, served as Secretary of State under Thomas Jefferson, a widower. When her husband became President, she continued the role of First Lady. During the British attack on Washington, D.C., in 1814 she rescued state papers and George Washington's portrait from the White House.

"The Star-Spangled Banner" (1814)

During the British attack on Fort McHenry in 1814, a young American lawyer named Francis Scott Key wrote the words to "The Star-Spangled Banner." In 1931 Congress made "The Star-Spangled Banner" the national anthem of the United States.

O say! can you see, by the dawn's early
    light,
What so proudly we hail'd at the twi-
    light's last gleaming,
Whose broad stripes and bright stars,
    thro' the perilous fight,
O'er the ramparts we watch'd were so
    gallantly streaming?
And the rockets' red glare, the bombs
    bursting in air,
Gave proof thro' the night that our flag
    was still there.
O, say, does that Star-Spangled Banner
    yet wave
O'er the land of the free and the home of
    the brave?

From Francis Scott Key, "The Star-Spangled Banner," 1814.

ANALYZING HISTORICAL DOCUMENTS

1. In your own words, explain the events described in "The Star-Spangled Banner." Whose point of view is recorded? Where is the narrator?
2. Why, in your opinion, did "The Star-Spangled Banner" become so popular?
3. How do flags and anthems serve to promote nationalistic feelings?

Lean and tough, Jackson was a self-made man of the frontier. Earlier that year he had defeated the Creek Indians, who had sided with the British, at the Battle of Horseshoe Bend in Alabama. Now, with a hodgepodge army of frontier militiamen, Indians, African Americans, and pirates, Jackson prepared to defend New Orleans. To do so, the army built a ditch and, behind it, an earthen wall.

In crisp formation, the British attacked on January 8. From behind their wall, the Americans mowed down the advancing redcoats. It was a great victory for Jackson. American casualties were 21; the British, about 2,030.

The Battle of New Orleans made Jackson a hero of the West. Yet the war had already ended. Neither side at New Orleans knew that a peace treaty between Britain and the United States, the Treaty of Ghent, had been signed two weeks earlier. The treaty reflected the lack of a clear winner in the war. No territory changed hands. Border and trade disputes were resolved in later talks.

Because everything turned out well, it is easy to forget that the War of 1812 was a serious crisis. If the British strategy had worked, the United States might not have survived.

STATES' RIGHTS IN NEW ENGLAND

Jackson's victory at New Orleans and the peace treaty affected political developments within the United States. One effect was to undermine a states' rights movement in New England.

New England merchants and shippers had bitterly opposed the War of 1812. They saw it as proof that the Republicans were willing to destroy trade in favor of the interests of the West and South. They even called the war "Mr. Madison's War." Resentments festered as the war went on. Some in New England began to talk of secession (withdrawing from the Union) and a separate peace with Britain.

Peace seemed far away when Massachusetts issued a call to neighboring states to meet at Hartford, Connecticut. In December 1814, at the Hartford Convention, Federalist moderates steered the talk away from secession. Instead they proposed new constitutional amendments. The amendments would have limited the power of Congress to impose embargoes, restrict trade, make war, or admit new states. To undercut the power of the South, the convention wanted to set aside the Three-Fifths Compromise. By this

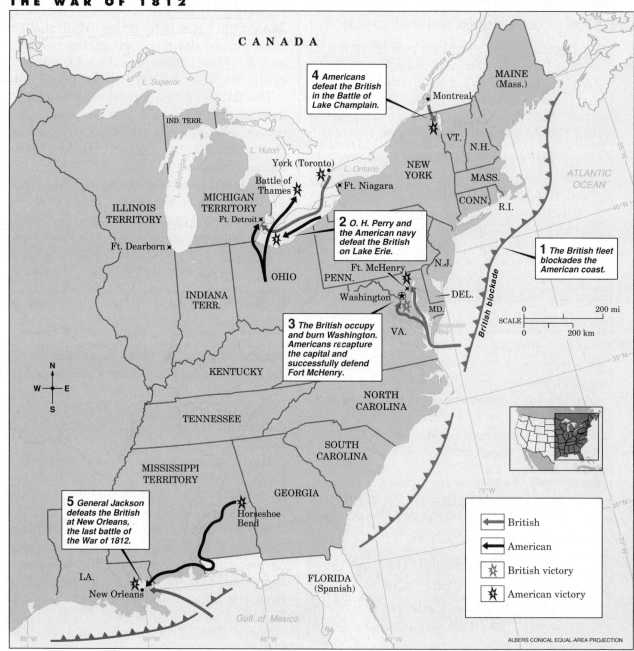

CANADA

4 Americans defeat the British in the Battle of Lake Champlain.

MAINE (Mass.)

Montreal

St. Lawrence R.

L. Superior

IND. TERR.

L. Huron

VT.

N.H.

York (Toronto)

L. Ontario

NEW YORK

MASS.

ATLANTIC OCEAN

Battle of Thames

× Ft. Niagara

CONN.

R.I.

ILLINOIS TERRITORY

MICHIGAN TERRITORY

Ft. Detroit ×

2 O. H. Perry and the American navy defeat the British on Lake Erie.

Ft. Dearborn ×

OHIO

1 The British fleet blockades the American coast.

N.J.

Ft. McHenry

PENN.

INDIANA TERR.

Washington ⊛

DEL.

MD.

British blockade

SCALE

0   200 mi

0   200 km

3 The British occupy and burn Washington. Americans recapture the capital and successfully defend Fort McHenry.

VA.

Chesapeake Bay

KENTUCKY

N
W ← → E
S

NORTH CAROLINA

TENNESSEE

SOUTH CAROLINA

MISSISSIPPI TERRITORY

GEORGIA

5 General Jackson defeats the British at New Orleans, the last battle of the War of 1812.

Horseshoe Bend

LA.

New Orleans

FLORIDA (Spanish)

Gulf of Mexico

75°W

30°N

70°W

→ British

← American

✷ British victory

✷ American victory

ALBERS CONICAL EQUAL-AREA PROJECTION

95°W   90°W   85°W   80°W

MAP SKILLS The belt below, given by Tecumseh to the British, symbolizes Britain's alliance with the Indians, which was one cause of the War of 1812. What American victory prevented the British from invading the northeastern United States? **CRITICAL THINKING** How does the map show Britain's wide use of seapower in the war?

agreement, slaves were included as part of a state's population (page 242). Following the lead of the Kentucky and Virginia Resolutions of 1798–1799 (page 316), the convention also said the states had the right to repeal acts of Congress.

The convention chose three people to carry its message to President Madison. When they arrived in Washington, the city had just learned of the peace treaty and of Jackson's victory at New Orleans. This news touched off a wild celebration in the capital.

The Federalists felt completely out of place. So, the delegation slipped quietly out of town. Little more was heard from New England on the subject of states' rights. And not much more was heard from the Federalist Party. It lost support and soon withered into nothing.

SECTION REVIEW

1. KEY TERMS War of 1812, Non-Intercourse Act, War Hawk, blockade, Treaty of Ghent, secession, Hartford Convention

2. PEOPLE AND PLACES James Madison, Tecumseh, William Henry Harrison, Oliver H. Perry, Lake Erie, Detroit, Dolley Madison, Andrew Jackson

3. COMPREHENSION Why did westerners insist on a war with Britain?

4. COMPREHENSION How were the two phases of the War of 1812 different?

5. CRITICAL THINKING The War of 1812 has been called "the unnecessary war." Do you agree or disagree? Explain.

CHAPTER 13 SUMMARY AND TIMELINE

1. Thomas Jefferson, elected President in 1800, cut taxes, reduced the armed forces, and kept the federal government's activity to a minimum. He also ordered American forces to fight Barbary pirates who threatened shipping in the Mediterranean.

2. The West Coast became a region of outside interests in the late 1700s with the growth of Spanish settlements, British exploration, and American trade. At the same time, the introduction of horses brought a golden age to the Plains Indians. When France, unable to stop a slave revolt in Haiti, offered to sell its western landholdings, President Jefferson made the Louisiana Purchase.

3. Jefferson sent Meriwether Lewis and William Clark to explore and study the West. Later expeditions explored the southern Rockies. These explorations produced more accurate maps, fostered an interest in the fur trade, and led Americans to believe that the Great Plains were unsuitable for farming.

4. The War of 1812 began primarily because of British violation of American sea rights and aid to western Indians. Though some British attacks were successful, the United States won victories at sea and several land battles. The war quieted Indian resistance and led to the end of the Federalist Party.

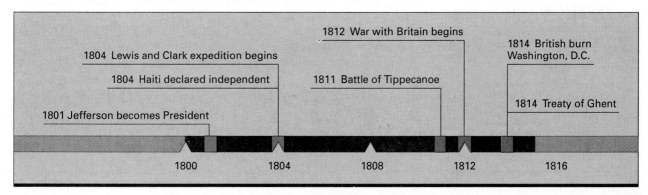

1804 Lewis and Clark expedition begins
1804 Haiti declared independent
1801 Jefferson becomes President
1812 War with Britain begins
1811 Battle of Tippecanoe
1814 British burn Washington, D.C.
1814 Treaty of Ghent

1800   1804   1808   1812   1816

PLACES TO LOCATE

Match each of the letters on the map with the places that are listed below.

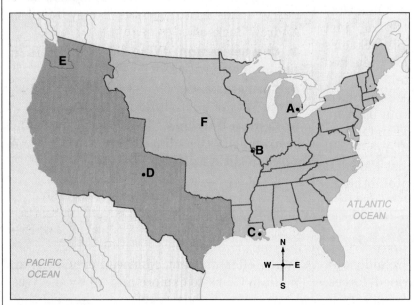

1. Columbia River
2. Detroit
3. Missouri River
4. New Orleans
5. St. Louis
6. Santa Fe

KEY TERMS

Choose the term in parentheses that best completes each sentence.

1. During Thomas Jefferson's (*administration / secession*) the size of the army was dramatically reduced.
2. The (*Lewis and Clark expedition / Louisiana Purchase*) doubled the size of the United States.
3. The British set up a (*blockade / embargo*) to prevent American ships from entering or leaving their ports.
4. The (*Hartford Convention / Treaty of Ghent*) expressed Federalist opposition to the War of 1812.

PEOPLE TO IDENTIFY

Match each of the following people with the correct description.

Aaron Burr
Thomas Jefferson
Meriwether Lewis
Sacajawea
Toussaint L'Ouverture

1. Republican Party leader.
2. Leader of uprising against the French on Hispaniola.
3. A Republican candidate in the 1800 election who nearly became President.
4. Leader of first American expedition into Louisiana Territory.
5. Shoshone Indian who served as a guide for the Corps of Discovery.

REVIEWING THE FACTS

1. What events led to the passage of the Twelfth Amendment?
2. What changes in the federal government did Thomas Jefferson make when he became President?
3. What nations were competing for influence in California during the 1790s?
4. How did the introduction of horses change life for Indians on the Great Plains?
5. Why did Napoleon sell the Louisiana Territory to the United States?
6. What were the goals of the Lewis and Clark expedition? Was the expedition successful in achieving them?
7. What were the goals of Zebulon Pike's explorations? Was he successful in achieving them?
8. How did Jefferson try to avoid war with Britain?
9. In which section of the country did people support the War of 1812 most strongly? Why?
10. Why can it be said that the War of 1812 destroyed the Federalist Party?

PRACTICING YOUR SKILL

The passages below express different points of view on land ownership. The first is from a letter by President Thomas Jefferson to Meriwether Lewis. The second is from a speech by Tecumseh. Read the passages and answer the following questions.

> The Indian tribes residing within the limits of the United States have . . . been growing more and more uneasy at the constant diminution [decrease] of the territory they occupy. . . . Experience and reflection will develop to them the wisdom of exchanging what they can spare and what we want for what we can spare and they want.
> —*Thomas Jefferson*

> The spirit within me . . . tells me that until lately there was no white man on this continent. Then, it all belonged to red men, placed on this continent by the Great Spirit that made them, to keep it, to travel across it, to enjoy its production. . . . That race has since been made miserable by the white people, who are never contented, but always want more.
> —*Tecumseh*

1. Does Thomas Jefferson believe that the Indians will be willing to sell their land? What part of the passage supports your answer?
2. What is Tecumseh's attitude toward white people? What part of the passage supports your answer?
3. Based on these quotes, would you have predicted increased or decreased tensions between whites and Indians? Explain your answer.

CITIZENSHIP

1. What was Jefferson's philosophy of government? Did the Louisiana Purchase and Embargo Act contradict that philosophy? Why or why not?
2. Do you think that the Hartford Convention was an effective way for citizens to protest government actions? Explain your answer. In what other ways might New Englanders have protested the War of 1812?
3. Do you think Jefferson was wise to make cutbacks in the military when he became President. Why or why not? How heavily do you think the nation should spend for military purposes today? Explain.

CRITICAL THINKING SKILLS

1. ANALYZING A QUOTATION Jefferson once wrote, "Were it left to me to decide whether we should have a government without newspapers, or newspapers without a government, I should not hesitate a moment to prefer the latter." Do you agree? Explain your answer.

2. INFERRING How did the Lewis and Clark expedition strengthen the American claim on the Pacific Northwest?

3. IDENTIFYING CAUSE AND EFFECT Why did the British aid American Indians on the frontier?

PROJECTS AND ACTIVITIES

1. RESEARCHING PLACE NAMES Use an atlas to find out how many places in the United States bear the names of people mentioned in this chapter.

2. MAKING A TIMELINE Find out the dates of important battles and events during the War of 1812. Make a timeline to show this information.

3. DESIGNING A POSTER Imagine that you are a War Hawk in 1811 or a New England Federalist in 1814. Design a poster to express your views.

WRITING ABOUT TOPICS IN AMERICAN HISTORY

1. CONNECTING WITH LITERATURE A selection from *Great River* by Paul Horgan appears on pages 648–649. Read it and answer the questions. Then answer the following question: How did a son's coming of age on the frontier reflect "an extension of the national ideal of equality and democratic opportunity"?

2. APPLYING THEMES: GEOGRAPHY Imagine that you are traveling west with Lewis and Clark. Write a letter home describing your experiences.

Americans, buoyed by their success against Britain, had new confidence after the War of 1812. Artists' depictions of the United States' natural beauty reflected this mood.

CHAPTER

14 National Confidence and Economic Expansion (1815–1850)

KEY EVENTS

1817	Erie Canal begun
1819	Adams-Onís Treaty
1823	Monroe Doctrine
1831	Nat Turner's Rebellion

1 A Spirit of Nationalism

★ Section Focus

Key Terms *Marbury v. Madison*
■ judicial review ■ American System
■ National Road

Main Idea A burst of nationalism and an expanding transportation system characterized the United States after the War of 1812.

Objectives As you read, look for answers to these questions:
1. What were some examples of social, economic, and political nationalism?
2. How did the Supreme Court strengthen the power of the federal government?
3. What effect did the Erie Canal have on the nation's economic development?

The War of 1812 achieved none of the demands of the War Hawks. Yet Americans celebrated the end of the war as a victory. Why? What had they gained? A Vermont newspaper summarized the answer:

The fear of our late enemy;
The respect of the world; and
The confidence we have acquired in ourselves.

THE RISE OF NATIONALISM

Until 1815 it was not clear that the United States would survive. Wars in Europe and strife at home were real threats to the republic. By 1815, however, Americans had fought what some called a Second War of Independence. The war gave rise to a new and growing spirit of nationalism.

Nationalism was a mix of beliefs and feelings. It was patriotic pride in the achieve-

ments of the whole country. It was also a belief that Americans were unique and did not have to follow the lead of other countries. History textbooks of the early 1800s stressed the superiority of the United States, comparing it to "worn-out" Europe. Books and newspapers earnestly preached patriotism. Noah Webster, a former teacher and newspaper editor, published a dictionary in 1806. It modified the way British words were spelled, used, and pronounced. Webster's dictionary went on to sell millions of copies. It helped create a distinctly *American* version of the English language.

Symbols of the nation also promoted patriotism. The bald eagle, for example, became the national bird in the 1780s. By the 1800s, eagles decorated chinaware, furniture, magazines, watch chains—nearly everything. Artisans stamped the bird's image on the nation's coins as well.

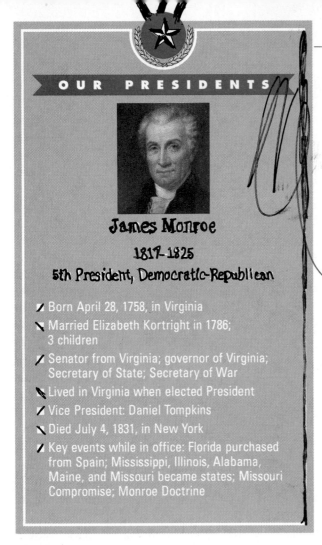

James Monroe

1817–1825

5th President, Democratic-Republican

- Born April 28, 1758, in Virginia
- Married Elizabeth Kortright in 1786; 3 children
- Senator from Virginia; governor of Virginia; Secretary of State; Secretary of War
- Lived in Virginia when elected President
- Vice President: Daniel Tompkins
- Died July 4, 1831, in New York
- Key events while in office: Florida purchased from Spain; Mississippi, Illinois, Alabama, Maine, and Missouri became states; Missouri Compromise; Monroe Doctrine

A GROWING SENSE OF UNITY

As nationalist feelings spread, people felt more loyalty toward the federal government and less toward state governments. For a while the issue of states' rights faded. The focus changed to the nation as a whole. The political strife of earlier years gave way to what a Boston newspaper called the Era of Good Feelings.

Party politics in the years after the War of 1812 reflected this sense of national unity. In 1816 the Republicans swept to an easy victory. James Monroe, James Madison's Secretary of State, became President. The Federalist Party, weakened by participation in the Hartford Convention (page 343), made such a poor showing in the election of 1816 that it soon dissolved.

THE SUPREME COURT AND FEDERAL POWER

Federal power grew through the decisions of an old Federalist, John Marshall. Marshall served as Chief Justice of the United States for 34 years—an all-time record. Under his guidance, the Supreme Court upheld federal authority and strengthened the power of the federal judiciary.

The first of the Marshall Court's landmark decisions came in the case of *Marbury v. Madison* (1803). In it, Marshall declared that an act passed by Congress back in 1789 was unconstitutional. This meant it was not in accord with the Constitution and thus was invalid. "The Constitution," declared Marshall, "is superior to any ordinary act of the legislature . . . and must govern."

Of course the Constitution was "the supreme law of the land." It states so itself. The question was: Who finally decides whether an act is constitutional or unconstitutional? The Supreme Court does, Marshall answered. This power of the federal courts is called judicial review.

Judicial review gave the Supreme Court the final say in interpreting the Constitution. Using the concept of judicial review, the Marshall Court, in decision after decision, chipped away at the limits on federal power.

One of the court's key decisions was made in *McCulloch v. Maryland* (1819). At issue was the right of the state of Maryland to tax a federal bank. The state even questioned the right of Congress to form a federal bank. The Court declared, however, that since this power was not prohibited outright by the Constitution, it was legal. Marshall favored, in other words, a loose construction of the Constitution. He believed federal power went beyond what the Constitution specifically called for. The government could exercise other, unnamed powers if the Court decided they achieved legitimate goals. Marshall also declared that the federal government was a government of people, not of states. Therefore, it had power over the states.

In *Gibbons v. Ogden* (1824), the Marshall Court ruled that states could not regulate

JOHN MARSHALL (1755–1835) was known as the "Great Chief Justice" because of his tremendous impact on the United States judicial system. A Virginian and a distant relative of Thomas Jefferson, Marshall had little formal schooling. His influence helped ensure that the judicial branch of the federal government would have equal authority with the executive and legislative branches.

commerce between states. Only the federal government would have that power.

Marshall also developed a friendly climate for American business. In *Dartmouth College v. Woodward* (1819), the Court upheld the rights of property owners and contract holders. This decision would later help corporations, which depend on the rights granted in their charters.

THE AMERICAN SYSTEM

In Congress, John C. Calhoun of South Carolina and Henry Clay of Kentucky promoted the nationalist point of view. Both were lawyers who were elected to Congress at an early age. Both had been War Hawks. Clay and Calhoun wanted a self-sufficient nation that did not need foreign products or foreign markets. The United States would thus be a "world within itself."

The self-sufficiency Clay and Calhoun hoped for had already begun. During the War of 1812, Americans had begun to produce goods once imported from Britain. With the return of peace, Congress wanted to protect these new industries. In 1816 it passed tariffs that made goods from Europe more costly. The result was to discourage Americans from buying foreign goods. Instead, they bought more goods made in American factories.

The new tariffs to protect American industry were part of a program, advanced by Henry Clay, called the American System. The other two features of the plan were (1) a national bank that would strengthen the country's financial system, and (2) improved transportation to help trade within the country.

The transportation problems facing the nation were as huge as the country itself. Only a few roads for coaches and wagons stretched between the states. Coaches and wagons also moved slowly. The 260-mile journey from New York to Boston, for example, took 39 hours by stagecoach. The only other ways to travel or move goods were by small boats, on horseback, or on foot. Slow, costly transport was bad for business. It could isolate Americans in one region from those in another.

> "**L**et us bind the Republic together with a perfect system of roads and canals. Let us conquer space."
>
> —*John Calhoun*

"Let us bind the Republic together with a perfect system of roads and canals," Calhoun said. "Let us conquer space." National roads were not a new idea. In 1806 Congress had

CANALS CONNECT RIVERS AND LAKES

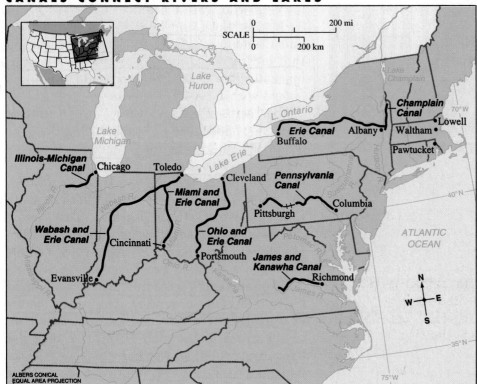

MAP SKILLS

Between 1820 and 1860 many canals were built linking major waterways. According to the map, how many canals linked the Great Lakes with the Ohio River? What other rivers were linked directly to the Great Lakes by canals? **CRITICAL THINKING** Which region of the country benefited the most from canals? Explain your answer.

pledged to fund the building of a paved road linking Ohio with the East. By 1815, however, only 20 miles of it had been finished. With prodding from the nationalists, Congress then voted more money for the road. Within three years the Cumberland Road, or National Road, had crossed the Appalachians, connecting Cumberland, Maryland, with Wheeling, on the Ohio River. By 1833 it would reach Columbus, Ohio. As the country's main east-west route, the road was soon jammed with everything from mail coaches to herds of cattle going to market.

When Congress voted to fund other transportation projects, however, President Madison vetoed the bill. Spending federal money on internal improvements—projects involving major construction—was unconstitutional, he said. As a result, states took on the challenge of building roads and canals.

THE ERIE CANAL

The most successful, and most daring, improvement of this period was the Erie Canal.

Paid for by New York State, it made possible an all-water route from New York City to the Great Lakes. Few people in the early 1800s believed the project was possible. Even the far-sighted Thomas Jefferson declared that "talk of making a canal of 350 miles through the wilderness is little short of madness."

> "**T**alk of making a canal of 350 miles through the wilderness is little short of madness."
>
> —*Thomas Jefferson,*
> *on the Erie Canal*

The man who held on to the dream of the canal was DeWitt Clinton, New York's governor. He recognized the problems but was confident they could be overcome. Clinton was an example of the energy and confidence that now swept over America. At Clinton's urging, the citizens of New York voted to build the "big ditch."

The builders of the "big ditch" did indeed face huge problems. The water level in Lake Erie is over 550 feet higher than that of the Hudson River. There were forests to clear and deep valleys to cross. No one had ever built such a canal. To overcome the problem of elevation, American engineers designed a system of more than 80 locks. Locks are "water elevators" that enable boats to be raised or lowered to different levels of a canal.

To meet other problems, engineers invented new machines. One machine pulled a tree down from its top. Another machine pulled roots from the ground.

As important as the machines were, most of the canal was dug by thousands of men using pickaxes, shovels, and wheelbarrows. Work on the canal drew thousands of Irish immigrants to America. The canal wage was 80 cents a day plus room and board. That was three times the rate in Ireland.

At times the work could be dreadful. One account tells of problems the workers faced in marshy areas:

> The first day in the marshes, the men joked about the easy digging. But the next morning their jokes had turned sour because the soft mud they shoveled out had . . . flowed back in the ditch. There was little sign of the channel dug the day before. . . . But the worst did not come until . . . the mosquito season. The insects, enormous clouds of them, fell on the men in such savage numbers that hands swelled and eyes were puffed almost shut. . . . By early August, workers by the hundreds were coming down with chills and with fevers. . . . Soon work stopped completely and there was dark talk about giving up the whole project. But when autumn came, the sickness disappeared with the mosquitoes—and the work went ahead once again.

In 1825, after eight years of labor, the task was done. The Erie Canal soon became the most important route between the Atlantic seaboard and the West. From New York City, passengers and cargo traveled northward up the Hudson River to Albany. Then they moved westward on the canal to Buffalo. On the return trip, boats brought products from the West to markets in New York City and beyond.

Before the canal opened, freight costs between Buffalo and New York City ran about $100 per ton. The canal sliced this cost to $10. In addition, the time needed to send goods fell to less than half that of pre-canal days.

The Erie Canal opened the upper Ohio Valley and the Great Lakes region to settlement. Thousands of immigrants traveled the canal to homesteads in Ohio, Indiana, Illinois, and Michigan. Farm products from this rich region flowed eastward on the canal. Such a surplus of farm products made it possible for the population of eastern cities to grow. Fed by the West, easterners could concentrate on trade and manufacturing. In turn, the westerners bought the manufactured goods of the East.

Trade on the canal drew more people to New York City and helped it become the nation's largest city. Between 1820 and 1830, the city's population swelled from less than 125,000 to more than 200,000.

The success of the Erie Canal encouraged canal-building in other sections of the country. So many canals were built between 1825 and 1850 that the period has been called the Canal Era.

THE DEVELOPING WEST

Improved transportation helped Americans push west in search of new lands to farm. American victories during the War of 1812 had also crushed most Indian resistance east of the Mississippi. In addition, there was a spirit of confidence and restlessness in the air. People were on the move just to be on the move. "Old America seems to be breaking up and moving westward," a traveler on the National Road wrote in 1817. "We are seldom out of sight, as we travel on this grand track, towards the Ohio, of family groups before and behind us."

Families on the move often used flatboats—large, raftlike barges—for transportation. One observer wrote in 1828:

> We have seen [flatboats] fitted up for the descent of families to the lower country, with a stove, comfortable apartments, and beds. . . . We see in them ladies, servants, cattle, horses, sheep, dogs, and poultry; all floating on the same bottom, and on the roof the looms, ploughs, spinning wheels and domestic equipment of the family.

The movement westward brought four new states into the Union in just four years. Two states—Indiana (1816) and Illinois (1818)—came from the Northwest Territory. The new states of Mississippi (1817) and Alabama (1819) had been part of the Mississippi Territory.

SECTION REVIEW

1. KEY TERMS *Marbury v. Madison,* judicial review, American System, National Road

2. PEOPLE Noah Webster, John Marshall, John C. Calhoun, Henry Clay

3. COMPREHENSION What effects did the decisions of the Marshall Court have on the power of the federal government?

4. COMPREHENSION Describe the effect of the Erie Canal on the development of the West.

5. CRITICAL THINKING Cite some examples of nationalism in the United States today. How are they similar to or different from the nationalism of the early 1800s?

---

2 A Bold New Foreign Policy

★ **Section Focus** ★

Key Term Monroe Doctrine

Main Idea After the War of 1812, the United States gained land from Spain, and it developed an independent foreign policy.

Objectives As you read, look for answers to these questions:
1. How did United States foreign policy change following the War of 1812?
2. What changes took place in Spain's American colonies?

At the age of ten, John Quincy Adams set sail for France with his father, John Adams. While his father worked as a diplomat in Europe, young "Johnny" went to school in Paris and Amsterdam. At fourteen, he went to St. Petersburg as secretary to the first American ambassador to Russia. After his father became President, John Quincy Adams served as ambassador to Russia and later to Great Britain. His most important work, however, was still to come.

Adams's main challenge was to come from Latin America. Spain's role in the Western Hemisphere changed dramatically as a spirit of independence took hold of the region. Adams served as President James Monroe's

MAP SKILLS

Great changes took place in Latin America in the early 1800s. Which European nation lost all its territory there? CRITICAL THINKING Why did most people in the United States support Latin American independence?

(BRITISH RULE)

	Independent states
	Spanish rule
	French rule
	British rule
	Dutch rule
★	Capital

UNITED STATES

ATLANTIC OCEAN

Gulf of Mexico

MEXICO
★ Mexico City

CUBA
SANTO DOMINGO
JAMAICA
PUERTO RICO
BR. HONDURAS
HAITI
Caribbean Sea
GUATEMALA
EL SALVADOR
HONDURAS
NICARAGUA
UNITED PROVINCES OF
CENTRAL AMERICA
COSTA RICA
PANAMA

PACIFIC OCEAN

Equator

N
W   E
S

Caracas
★
VENEZUELA
Bogotá ★
GREAT COLOMBIA
GUIANAS
COLOMBIA
ECUADOR

PERU
★ Lima

EMPIRE OF BRAZIL

BOLIVIA

Rio de Janeiro ★
PARAGUAY

ARGENTINA
United Provinces
of La Plata
URUGUAY
CHILE
Buenos Aires ★

PATAGONIA
(Unexplored)

SCALE
0   1,000 mi
0   1,000 km

VAN DER GRINTEN PROJECTION

Inset map:

(BRITISH RULE)

UNITED
STATES

ATLANTIC OCEAN

Mexico ★
ST. DOMINGUE
Caribbean Sea

PACIFIC OCEAN

GUIANAS
★ Bogotá

N
W   E
S

★ Lima
BRAZIL

Rio de Janeiro ★

★
Buenos Aires ★

LATIN AMERICA ABOUT 1800

	Spanish rule
	Portuguese rule
	French rule
	British rule
	Dutch rule
★	Capital

SCALE
0   1,000 mi
0   1,000 km

Artist Juan O'Gorman painted this dramatic mural of important events in the struggle for Mexican independence. **CULTURAL PLURALISM** According to this mural, which groups in Mexican society were involved in this struggle?

Secretary of State during those years. He needed all his experience as a diplomat to chart a new, independent course for American foreign policy. That policy reflected the nationalist spirit in the United States.

REVOLUTION IN THE SPANISH COLONIES

As you have read in Chapter 3, Spain founded many colonies in the Americas at the height of its power. Events in those colonies affected relations between Spain and the United States.

Spain's hold over its Latin American colonies crumbled in the wake of the American and French Revolutions. Inspired by the spirit of liberty, Creoles and mestizos began to call for reform. These groups had been kept out of power by the home government in Spain. Now, like the American colonists, they demanded a say in how they were governed.

Starting in the 1780s, Latin American colonies fought wars of independence against Spain. One of the early leaders was a Venezuelan Creole named Francisco de Miranda (mee–RAHN–duh). Miranda had fought against the British in Florida and in the Bahamas during America's Revolutionary War. Later, he also fought for revolution in Venezuela, and was taken prisoner by the Spanish.

Spain became caught up in European conflicts in the early 1800s. In 1808 Napoleon, the new ruler of France, conquered Spain. As a result, Spain was too weak to hold on to power in the colonies. Now was the moment for its colonies to break away. Simón Bolívar (boh–LEE–vahr), a follower of Miranda, formed an army to fight the Spanish. "I will give no rest to my arm or repose to my soul," Bolívar swore, "until I have broken the chains that oppress us."

> "**I** will give no rest to my arm or repose to my soul, until I have broken the chains that oppress us."
>
> —*Simón Bolívar*

Bolívar had help from a military genius, José de San Martín (SAHN mahr–TEEN) of Argentina. Bolívar's forces drove the Spanish army from the northern part of South America. Then San Martín's troops advanced from the south. They met in Peru, the center of Spain's American empire. In 1824 Bolívar defeated the last Spanish forces. All of Spanish South America became independent.

THE UNITED STATES GAINS FLORIDA

Trouble was brewing for Spain in Florida as well. When the United States bought Louisiana from France, neither country was sure of the exact boundaries of the purchase. Spain kept a narrow strip of land along the Gulf of Mexico (West Florida) as well as the large peninsula then called East Florida (map, below). It had gained this land partly through the efforts of General Bernardo de Gálvez during the Revolutionary War (page 205). The United States claimed some of the land in West Florida near the Mississippi River. West Florida also had useful ports on the Gulf of Mexico that the United States was eager to obtain.

In 1810 President Madison took advantage of a rebellion in West Florida to declare part of it to be United States land. During the War of 1812, the United States occupied more of West Florida. Spain was too weak to fight these claims. By 1815 Spanish strength was limited to three forts at St. Marks, Pensacola, and St. Augustine.

Seminole Indians lived in much of the rest of Florida. The Seminole tried to prevent white settlers from taking over their land by raiding white settlements in Georgia. They also welcomed escaped slaves. American troops crossed into Spanish Florida to hunt down the Indians and recapture slaves. By 1816 a state of war existed between the United States and the Seminole.

In late 1817 President Monroe sent Andrew Jackson, a hero of the War of 1812, to Georgia with orders to crush the Seminole. Jackson was told to cross into Spanish territory if need be and to attack the Seminole there. He was told not to attack if the Indians took shelter at a Spanish post. Jackson was a passionate nationalist who hated both the Spanish and the Indians. He wrote President

MAP SKILLS

The addition of East and West Florida gave the United States important outlets to the Gulf of Mexico. Which port cities did the United States gain? Which of these cities was occupied by the United States before being ceded by Spain? **CRITICAL THINKING** Why was control of the Floridas important to the development of Georgia and Alabama?

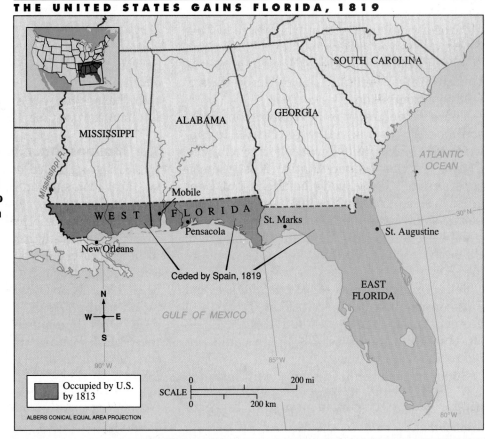

THE UNITED STATES GAINS FLORIDA, 1819

SOUTH CAROLINA

MISSISSIPPI

ALABAMA

GEORGIA

ATLANTIC OCEAN

Mobile

WEST FLORIDA

St. Marks

Pensacola

St. Augustine

New Orleans

Ceded by Spain, 1819

EAST FLORIDA

30° N

N
W—E
S

GULF OF MEXICO

90° W

85° W

80° W

Occupied by U.S. by 1813

SCALE

0 — 200 mi

0 — 200 km

ALBERS CONICAL EQUAL AREA PROJECTION

The Monroe Doctrine (1823)

President Monroe's message to Congress in 1823, later to be called the Monroe Doctrine, proclaimed the pre-eminence of the United States in the Western Hemisphere. The Monroe Doctrine has continued to influence American foreign policy to the present day.

The American continents, by the free and independent condition which they have assumed and maintain, are henceforth not to be considered as subject for future colonization by any European powers. . . .

The political system of the [European] powers is essentially different . . . from that of America. . . . We owe it, therefore, to candor . . . to declare that we should consider any attempt on their part to extend their system to any portion of this hemisphere as dangerous to our peace and safety. . . .

Our policy in regard to Europe, which was adopted [many years ago], nevertheless remains the same, which is, not to interfere in the internal concerns of any of its powers.

From J. D. Richardson, ed., *A Compilation of the Messages and Papers of the Presidents*, Vol. II, p. 207.

ANALYZING HISTORICAL DOCUMENTS

1. What position does the Monroe Doctrine take regarding European political influence in the Western Hemisphere?
2. How does the Monroe Doctrine try to justify this position?
3. Explain the significance of the third paragraph.

Monroe a reply urging that "the whole of East Florida be seized and held." "If the possession of the Floridas would be desirable to the United States," wrote Jackson, "in 60 days it will be accomplished."

There was no reply from Washington. Jackson took this as a signal to go ahead. He captured St. Marks and Pensacola and claimed Florida for the United States. Most Americans applauded Jackson's boldness, but Congress was angry that he had acted without permission. Spain and other European nations were outraged. They said the seizure of Spanish territory had broken international law.

John Quincy Adams defended Monroe and Jackson against their critics at home and abroad. The United States had invaded Florida, Adams argued, because Spain could not police its own territory.

Spain in turn realized that it was better to sell Florida than to have it seized. In the Adams-Onís Treaty of 1819, Spain gave East and West Florida to the United States. As part of the treaty, Spain also gave up its claim to the Oregon region. The United States, meanwhile, dropped a $5 million claim against Spain and stopped insisting that Texas had been bought as part of the Louisiana Purchase.

THE MONROE DOCTRINE

In 1815 an alliance of Britain, Austria, Russia, and Prussia had defeated Napoleon. The king of Spain had regained his throne. Now he wanted his American empire back as well. The king looked to other monarchs in Europe to help him crush the Latin American rebellions. Most European monarchies agreed to help. They feared that the "infection" of revolution might spread from the Americas to Europe. Only one monarchy, Britain, opposed their plan. Britain wanted the Latin American nations to stay independent so it could trade with them.

In the United States, nationalists such as President Monroe and Secretary of State John Quincy Adams wanted to keep potential rivals out of the Americas. Such rivalry seemed possible not only in Latin America but also in the West. Russia, for example, claimed Alaska and set up fur trading posts there in the 1790s. By 1812 Russian trading posts along the Pacific coast reached as far south as Fort Ross, just north of San Francisco.

In 1823 President Monroe delivered the Monroe Doctrine. "The American continents," Monroe stated, "are henceforth not to be considered as subject for future colonization by any European powers." In sum, the United States told Europe to keep out of the Americas.

It was one thing to declare the Monroe Doctrine. It was another to enforce it. The United States was able to take a tough stand be-cause Britain, with its giant navy, stood behind it. Today the Monroe Doctrine is still a keystone of American foreign policy.

SECTION REVIEW

1. KEY TERM Monroe Doctrine

2. PEOPLE John Quincy Adams, Francisco de Miranda, Simón Bolívar, José de San Martín

3. COMPREHENSION Describe United States foreign policy in the period after the War of 1812.

4. COMPREHENSION What were some of the reasons for the revolutions in Latin America?

5. CRITICAL THINKING How might European nations have viewed the Monroe Doctrine?

3 The Industrial Revolution in the North

Section Focus

Key Terms textile industry ■ Industrial Revolution ■ interchangeable parts

Main Idea During the late 1700s and early 1800s, inventions changed the way people lived and worked. The Northeast became the industrial center of the United States.

Objectives As you read, look for answers to these questions:
1. How did industry come to the United States?
2. How did the Industrial Revolution change peoples' lives?

In the 1830s a man traveling by stagecoach through New England wrote this comment about Lowell, Massachusetts:

Suddenly the stage stops amidst a throng of people of all tongues, the noise of rushing waters, and the rattling of a thousand machines. Driver, what city is this? There was nothing here 25 years ago. "No nor fifteen, sir. But it is no city; it is the village of Lowell." A village! It should be a

city. . . . What a bustle! What a scene of activity! . . . Here, Industry throws her shuttle, and out springs a [cloth], which is destined to travel over half the globe.

What was taking place in Lowell was typical of changes occurring in other northeastern towns. Factories, built along rivers and streams that provided water power, began to churn out goods at a terrific rate. People moved from the countryside to work in the

In this picture, women spin yarn in their home using a spinning wheel. The hand-operated wheel produced a single thread at a time. The thread was then woven into cloth, which was sold to merchants. This system of home production was known as a cottage industry. **ECONOMICS** Why might merchants have welcomed improvements in the cottage industry system?

factories. Villages grew into towns and cities. These changes had their origins in the Industrial Revolution.

THE INDUSTRIAL REVOLUTION

The growth of manufacturing in this country owed much to events that took place earlier in Britain. There, in the late 1700s, machines were first used on a large scale to produce goods once made by hand. The first industry to be affected was the textile industry—the large-scale production of woven fabric.

Before the mid-1700s, almost every house had a spinning wheel (for making thread and yarn) and a hand loom (for weaving cloth). Both, however, were very slow. It took many hours to produce fabric at home.

Then, in the 1760s, James Hargreaves built the first spinning jenny. It could spin eight threads at a time instead of one. In a few years another Englishman, Edmund Cartwright, invented a power loom, run by water power.

Richard Arkwright's inventions led to the setting up of the first factory. He put several spinning jennies and looms in one large building and hired workers to run them. Soon, workers in factories all over Britain were turning out more cloth than ever before.

The factories changed the way people lived and worked. Before the invention of the spin-

ning jenny and the power loom, craftsworkers had spun and woven fabrics in their own homes. They sold the finished goods directly to local merchants. Now families no longer worked together at home or set their own hours and goals. Workers left for factories in the morning. Their hours were set by the factory owner. They also had to meet the owner's production goals. Taken together, these changes in the production of goods revolutionized society. For this reason, historians call them the Industrial Revolution.

FACTORIES IN THE NORTHEAST

The textile industry became so important to Britain's economy that Britain tried to keep the process a state secret. The British government outlawed the sale of the new machines to other countries. It even passed a law forbidding textile workers to leave the country. A man named Samuel Slater, however, did just that.

While working for a British spinning mill, Slater memorized its plan in detail. Then, with hopes of making his fortune, he set sail for America. Slater built a small spinning mill in Pawtucket, Rhode Island, in 1790. He then found investors willing to back construction of a full-scale spinning factory. Slater's mill opened in 1793. The Industrial Revolution had come to the United States.

Two decades after Slater's first mill, a Boston merchant named Francis Cabot Lowell moved the textile industry a giant step further. After viewing the power looms in Britain, Lowell teamed up with a gifted mechanic to make the first American power looms. Then in 1813 he built a factory at Waltham, Massachusetts. Lowell's factory combined all the steps of textile production. Raw cotton entered one end of the plant and emerged at the other end as finished goods. This factory would be the model for other textile operations and later for other industries as well.

Early factories used water power to run the machines. The first factories, therefore, were near the swiftly moving streams outside of Philadelphia and in New England. Of the two regions, New England would end up as the manufacturing center of the United States. It had not only water power but ships for transportation and a large labor force.

New England's first factory workers were farm families. Tired of wresting a living from New England's stony fields, they looked to the factories with hope of a better life. Two employment systems developed. In the Rhode Island system whole families were hired and housed. Even the young children worked in the mills.

Francis Cabot Lowell introduced the Waltham system. He brought together young women from nearby farms to work in the factories. The "Lowell Girls," as they were called, made up around 90 percent of the factories' workforce. Although some were as young as ten or eleven years old, most were between fifteen and thirty.

The young mill women entered the mills for different reasons. According to one mill girl's report:

> One . . . is in the factory because she hates her mother-in law . . . [another] has a wealthy father, but like many of our country farmers, he is very [stingy], and he wishes his daughters to maintain themselves. . . . The next has a "well-off" mother, but she is very

This painting of Slater's spinning mill shows its location by the Pawtucket Falls on Rhode Island's Blackstone River. Early factories depended on the force of rapidly flowing water to turn the huge wheels that provided power. **TECHNOLOGY** How did relying only on water power limit the development of factories?

American manufacturers copied British spinning and weaving machines. This picture shows one of those machines in an American mill. **HISTORY** How did the new technology affect traditional ways of life and work?

pious and will not buy her daughter so many pretty gowns and collars and ribbons . . . as she likes. . . . The next one has a horror of domestic service. The next one has left a good home, because her lover, who has gone on a whaling voyage, wishes to be married when he returns, and she would like more money than her father will give her.

The young women lived in dormitories under the watchful eyes of company matrons. During the early years of the mills, workers were encouraged to read and attend "mind-lifting" lectures. However, the owners' kindly attitudes toward mill workers gradually changed. To increase output, workers had to rise at five in the morning and work until seven at night with hardly a break. Employers neglected working conditions. Fast-paced production, loud noise, and a suffocating lack of fresh air became the norm. At the end of the long day, the mill girls' supper often consisted only of bread and gravy.

Women workers in the mills were the first to experience the pain of the Industrial Revolution. In addition to enduring dismal working conditions, they were paid half as much as men. By 1830 a male worker at Lowell earned 85 cents to $2 a day. A female worker earned 40 to 80 cents. Women would be among the first in New England to organize into labor unions and demand better working conditions and wages.

ADVANCES IN PRODUCTION

An important factor in the growth of American industry was the use of standardized, interchangeable parts. In 1798 the United States government needed guns to supply its armed forces. It hired the inventor Eli Whitney to make the guns. Whitney's task was to make 10,000 muskets in two years. Until that time, skilled gunsmiths had started work on a new gun only after finishing the one before. Each gun differed slightly. If a part broke, a new one had to be custom-made to replace it.

By 1800 Eli Whitney had not yet delivered the guns. He was called to Washington to explain the delay. Whitney arrived with a box containing piles of musket parts—barrels, stocks, triggers, and so on. He entered a room where Vice President Jefferson and other officials were waiting. As they watched, Whitney took one part at random from each pile and assembled a complete musket in seconds. Eli Whitney had not wasted his time. He had spent the two years developing precise machines that could make parts that were exactly alike. For example, the trigger from one of Whitney's muskets would fit any of the other muskets.

These interchangeable parts speeded up production and made repairs easy. Using an assembly line, Whitney could produce hundreds of muskets in the time it took a gunsmith to make one. In addition, Whitney's machines could be run by unskilled workers. Interchangeable parts became the norm for goods and machinery.

THE IMPORTANCE OF THE STEAM ENGINE

America's first factories began by using water power. It was not long, however, before they switched to steam power. More than any other invention, the steam engine is a symbol of the early Industrial Revolution. The steam engine was first invented in the early 1700s to pump water from Britain's coal mines. With time steam power took over from animal, wind, and water power.

The steam engine carried America into the modern world. It made possible a revolution in transportation. The idea of putting a steam engine on a boat had been around since the 1780s. Robert Fulton, however, was able to apply the idea successfully. Fulton came from a poor family in Pennsylvania. He became an artist and made a living selling his paintings. At 21 he went to Europe to study art, but he soon became fascinated by machines.

Fulton wanted to invent a steam-powered boat that could move against the current or a strong wind. His attempts failed until he designed the steamship *Clermont*. On the *Clermont* the steam engine turned a side paddle wheel, which pushed the boat through the water. People who watched it being built in New York City called the boat "Fulton's Folly." They said it would never work.

Fulton launched the *Clermont* on the Hudson River in 1807. It made the 300-mile round-trip from New York to Albany in 62 hours. After the journey Fulton wrote, "The morning I left New York there were not 30 persons in the city who believed the boat would ever move one mile."

> "There were not 30 persons in the city who believed the boat would ever move one mile."
>
> —*Robert Fulton, on his steamship* Clermont

In 1811 the *New Orleans* became the first steamship to travel down the Ohio and Mississippi rivers. Its engines, however, were not powerful enough to return against the river

BIOGRAPHY

ROBERT FULTON (1765–1815) was an inventor, engineer, and artist. He created machines for making rope and spinning flax, as well as an experimental submarine. His most famous invention, the *Clermont*, was the first commercially successful steamship.

current. The man who solved this problem was Henry Miller Shreve. This Mississippi trader designed a more powerful engine. He installed it on a double-decker boat with the paddle wheel in the back. Shreve's design opened up a new era of trade and transportation on the Mississippi. By 1820, 60 steamboats moved up and down the Mississippi and its tributaries. Steamboats turned New Orleans into a center of trade second only to New York City.

The steamboat made possible speedy, two-way travel on America's rivers and lakes. Steamboat travel, though, had its dangers. Hidden rocks and sandbars, swift currents, and exploding boilers often caused accidents. Sparks from the smokestacks could cause fires. Rival steamships sometimes collided as they raced each other. In spite of these dangers, steamboats were fast, comfortable, and cheap. They were, therefore, very popular.

After their introduction in the 1830s, railroads rapidly became the nation's most important form of transportation. Linking East and West, coal-burning steam locomotives hauled passengers, mail, and freight at speeds boats could not match. **TECHNOLOGY** In your opinion, what is the most important form of transportation today? Explain your answer.

RAILROADS TAKE OVER

In the 1830s inventors adapted steam power to another means of transportation—the steam-powered locomotive. In a famous race near Baltimore in 1830 the locomotive *Tom Thumb* raced a horse—and lost. The railroad's supporters, however, did not give up.

The first railroads were not exactly models of comfort. One passenger recalled an 1831 trip:

> The [coaches] were coupled together with chains, leaving from two to three feet slack . . . and in stopping, came together with such force as to send [passengers] flying from their seats.
>
> They used dry pitch for fuel, and . . . black smoke [filled] with sparks, coals, and cinders, came pouring back the whole length of the train. Each of the tossed passengers who had an umbrella raised it as a protection against the smoke and fire. They were found to be [but] little protection, for I think in the first mile the last umbrella went overboard, all having their covers burnt off from the flames.

Nevertheless, trains were improved, and rail service spread. In 1830 there were about 30 miles of railroad track in the United States. Ten years later there were 2,800 miles of track. By 1850 the number had jumped to 9,000 miles.

Rail transport moved people and goods faster than roads or canals. Railroads provided transportation where water travel was impossible. The new railroads also began to link the West more closely with the Northeast. The South, as you will learn in the next section, was following a different track.

SECTION REVIEW

1. KEY TERMS textile industry, Industrial Revolution, interchangeable parts

2. PEOPLE Samuel Slater, Francis Cabot Lowell, Robert Fulton

3. COMPREHENSION Why did New England become the manufacturing center of the United States?

4. COMPREHENSION What were some of the changes the Industrial Revolution made in society?

5. CRITICAL THINKING What are some arguments for and against using children as factory workers? Which side do you support? Why?

Gaining Skill: Determining Relevance

Suppose you were writing a report on how machines changed the working lives of Americans. You would probably find a huge amount of information on that subject, but not all of it would be relevant—applicable or to the point. Relevant information is essential to your understanding of your particular subject and will support any arguments you make about that subject in your report. Non-relevant information may be interesting, but it does not advance your understanding of the subject.

Determining what is relevant and what is non-relevant is very important to the study of history. It helps you make decisions about what kinds of evidence are likely to support a historical statement or theory. Also, when you are preparing for a test, determining relevance helps you decide what material you should review.

NOTING INFORMATION

Keeping in mind your task—to determine how machines changed the working lives of Americans—read the following sentences about the sewing machine. While you read, be sure to look for information that is relevant to your subject.

Elias Howe, who invented the sewing machine, was born in Scotland. The sewing machine created opportunities for women to earn wages.

The first sentence tells you where the inventor of the sewing machine, Elias Howe, was born. This information may be interesting, but it does not add anything to your understanding of how machines changed the working lives of Americans. It is non-relevant information. The last sentence, however, does contain relevant information. It points out that the sewing machine gave many women the chance to earn wages. This information is essential to understanding the effect machines had on the working lives of Americans during the first part of the nineteenth century.

PRACTICING YOUR SKILL

Now make a decision about whether each of the following statements is relevant or non-relevant to your understanding of how machines changed the working lives of Americans. Then, on a separate sheet of paper, write an **R** if you think the statement is relevant. If you think the statement is non-relevant, write an **N**.

1. Samuel Slater kept the plans of English textile machines in his head when he left the country.

2. Samuel Slater was an English textile worker who opened Slater's Mill in Pawtucket, Rhode Island.

3. The British government passed a law forbidding all textile workers from leaving the country.

4. Before Eli Whitney developed standardized, interchangeable parts, each handmade gun, for example, was different from every other handmade gun.

5. Water power, and later steam power, was used to drive the new machines.

6. Some factories employed children or families with children.

7. Although factory workers worked as long as 12 to 15 hours a day, their pay was quite low.

8. Some factory workers organized groups for the purpose of pressing for shorter hours and higher pay.

9. Before the widespread use of machines, many people worked in their homes or in small workshops.

10. Because they were all alike, the goods produced in factories did not fill the workers with as much pride as the goods they had made by hand.

4 The Changing South

Section Focus

Key Term   cotton gin

Main Idea   The invention of the cotton gin changed life in the South. Of overriding significance was the fact that slavery became important socially and economically.

Objectives   As you read, look for answers to these questions:
1.   In what way did cotton culture stimulate westward expansion?
2.   What was life like in the "Cotton Kingdom"?
3.   How did slavery affect the lives of black and white Americans?

It was 1792. At age 27 Eli Whitney had just graduated from college and was heading south to take a job as tutor on a plantation in Georgia. He then found that the job had been taken. Fate stepped in to change his life and the course of American history.

Eli Whitney's Cotton Gin

On his way south, Whitney met Catherine Greene, widow of General Nathanael Greene of Revolutionary War fame. Mrs. Greene was now struggling to make her Georgia plantation profitable.

This painting by Louis Hoppe shows the Meyenberg family farm in southeastern Texas. Most white southerners lived on small farms like this one. Working their own land with little or no slave labor, these farmers grew food and cash crops. **ETHICS** Why were so many small farmers willing to support the slavery system?

Mrs. Greene's problems were not unique. Few places in the South were prosperous. Uncertain markets and soil exhaustion had reduced profits from tobacco, indigo, and rice. Planters along the Georgia coast, however, had discovered a profitable new crop. This was sea-island cotton, which had a long staple (fiber). The new English mills had created a huge demand for cotton. Long-staple cotton could be separated from its seed by machine. Thus large amounts could be cleaned profitably. Unfortunately, sea-island cotton grew best in limited areas near the coast—mainly in South Carolina and Georgia. The only cotton that grew upland (away from the coast) was a short-staple cotton. The fibers of this cotton stuck so firmly to the seed that it had to be cleaned by hand. A worker could clean just one pound of short-staple cotton a day.

While visiting Mrs. Greene, Whitney heard planters complain about the problems of short-staple cotton. Whitney had shown skill at inventing and fixing things since he was a child. Within ten days he had designed a cotton-cleaning machine. Whitney's cotton gin was a wooden box filled with stiff wire teeth. When the teeth brushed against the cotton, they picked up the cotton fiber and left the seeds behind. By April 1793 Whitney's engine, or *gin,* was in operation. It could clean 50 pounds of short-staple cotton a day.

THE COTTON KINGDOM

The cotton gin changed life in the South in three ways:

(1) It made the uplands more valuable than the coast. Thus, it triggered a vast move westward. Cotton farming moved from the Atlantic coastal states—the so-called "Old South"—into the uplands of Alabama, Mississippi, and northern Florida. Then it crossed the Mississippi River into Louisiana and the Mexican province of Texas.

(2) Because cotton was such a valuable crop, planters put all their efforts into growing it. In the years after 1812, cotton made up one-third of all exports from the United States. By 1830 it accounted for half of

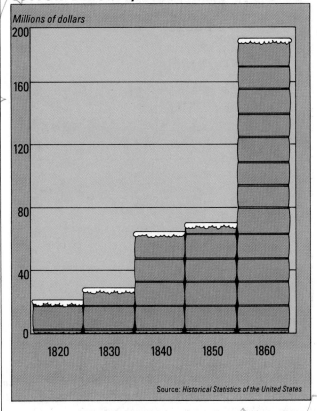

COTTON EXPORTS, 1820–1860

Millions of dollars

Source: *Historical Statistics of the United States*

all exports. The South's prosperity depended on it. Southerners said, "Cotton is King."

(3) Before the cotton gin, slavery had been dying out. Cotton culture, however, required a large work force. Instead of dying out, slavery became more important than ever as a source of workers.

PLANTATION OWNERS LEAD THE SOUTH

Cotton-growing on large plantations worked by slaves was highly profitable. Slaves cost money, however, and most white southerners could not afford to buy any. In the mid-1800s, only about one white family in four in the South could afford to own slaves. In a white population of 5,500,000, fewer than 10,000 planters owned 50 or more slaves. The

THE COTTON KINGDOM

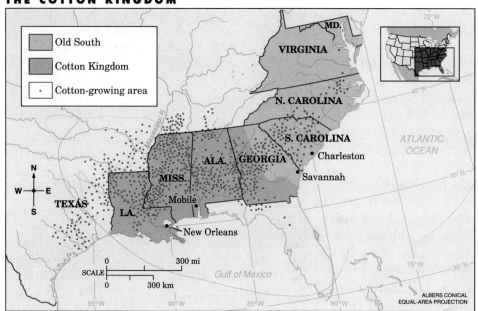

MAP SKILLS

This map shows the location of cotton-growing areas in the South around 1850. Which states made up the Cotton Kingdom? In what direction from the Old South did cotton growing spread? **CRITICAL THINKING** What effects do you think the Mississippi River had on the cotton business?

number who owned more than 100 slaves was much smaller.

Planters with many slaves and much land came to control most of the South's wealth. These men also spoke for the South in Congress. In contrast to the powerful plantation owners, most southern farmers worked small farms with their own hands. Some of them owned a slave or two. Many poor white farmers dreamed that someday they too would own vast cotton fields and many slaves. This hope of getting ahead in the world was one reason why small farmers supported the policies of the plantation owners.

COTTON AND SLAVERY

Slaves made up over one-third of the South's population. They did all the hard work on the plantation. While some worked as house servants, most were field hands. Solomon Northrup, a free black who was kidnapped and sold into slavery, told of the life slaves led:

During all the hoeings the overseer or driver follows the slaves with a whip.... The fastest hoer takes the lead row. He is usually about [fifteen feet] in advance of his companions. If one of them passes him, he [the fastest

hoer] is whipped. If one falls behind or is a moment idle, he is whipped. In fact, the lash is flying from morning until night....

When a new hand, one unaccustomed to [picking cotton], is sent for the first time into the fields, he is whipped up smartly, and made for that day to pick as fast as he can possibly. At night [what he has picked] is weighed, so that his capability in cotton picking is known. He must bring in the same weight each night following.... The hands are required to be in the cotton field as soon as it is light in the morning, and, with the exception of 10 or 15 minutes, which is given them at noon to swallow their allowance of cold bacon, they are not permitted to be a moment idle until it is too dark to see.

The day did not end with field work. There were still more tasks for slaves to do. "One feeds the mules," Northrup wrote, "another the swine—another cuts the wood." Slaves did not return to their cabins until evening. Then, before they could sleep, they had to prepare the next day's food.

Slavery made it possible for the South to ship hundreds of thousands of tons of cotton to the textile mills of the North and Europe each year. As cotton profits rose, so did the price of slaves. A male field hand was worth $300 in the 1790s. By 1840 the price rose to $1,000. Slave trading became big business. In time, one slave trading company, Franklin and Armfield, made over half a million dollars for each of its partners.

THE INSTITUTION OF SLAVERY

By 1860 nearly 4 million African American southerners were laboring as slaves. Accounts of their treatment vary. Evidence shows that some were treated as members of their owners' families. Others were treated as work animals. The following two accounts by slaves in Texas give an idea of the differences in treatment:

> After they brought us to Texas in 1859, I worked in the field, plowing and hoeing. The children didn't do much except carry water. When they got tired, they'd say they were sick and the overseer would let them lie down in the shade. He was a good man. When we did wrong, and we told him, he forgave us. He didn't whip the boys because he was afraid they'd run away. —*Phoebe Henderson*

> The overseer was Uncle Big Jake. He was black like the rest of us. But he was so mean I think the devil made him overseer. Massa Charles . . . let Uncle Big Jake whip the slaves so much that some like my papa who had spirit were all the time running away. —*Sarah Ford*

Even if all slaves had been treated well, however, they were still slaves. Slaves had no freedom of choice because they were owned by others. Their parents, their children, their brothers and sisters could all be sold away at any time, and they were helpless to prevent it. Slaves had no rights. They could be tried in court only by whites. They could offer no evidence against a white man. While it was a crime to steal a slave, it was not a crime to kill one who tried to escape.

Although slavery put whites in a position of authority, they paid a price too. The planter class tried to convince itself that slaves were

An engraving from 1861 shows white buyers at a slave auction in Virginia. **ETHICS** Judging from the picture, do you think the artist supported or opposed slavery? How can you tell?

happy and well taken care of. Many planters, however, lived in constant fear of the day their slaves might turn on them.

Other southerners were caught in a moral dilemma. They felt slavery was wrong, but they believed it was an economic necessity. Frances Anne Kemble, an English actress who had married a rice and cotton planter in Georgia, worried over her place in the system. She wrote in 1838:

> After I had been in the house a little while, I was summoned out again to receive the petition of certain poor women in the family way [pregnant] to have their work lightened. . . . They said they had already begged "massa," and he had refused, and they thought, perhaps, if "missis" begged "massa" for them, he would lighten their task. Poor "missis," poor "massa," poor woman, that I am to have such prayers addressed to me!

SLAVE CULTURE

Slaves took refuge in their own culture and in religion. Whites hoped that Christian teaching would make the slaves more accepting of their lot. White ministers often preached the virtues of obedience. However, slaves heard something else in the Bible stories: they heard about the enslavement of the Hebrews in Egypt and how Moses led the Hebrews to freedom. The story of Moses, told again and again by slave preachers, held out the hope that a new Moses would come to lead them to freedom.

A distinct African American culture had grown up by the early 1800s. Music is one example. Visitors to plantations commented on how much the slaves sang as they worked—partly because masters and overseers feared silent slaves. Most slave songs were versions of Christian hymns learned in camp meetings. The rhythms, however, came from African music, and the emotions came from the slaves' experience. Frederick Douglass recalled the importance of that music.

1825	First internal combustion engine is patented.
1828	First complete American dictionary is *An American Dictionary of the English Language* by Noah Webster.
1830	Baltimore & Ohio Railroad opens, first steam railroad to carry passengers and freight.
1831	"America" sung publicly in the Park Street Church by Boston schoolchildren (July 4). Louisiana and Arkansas are first states to make Christmas a legal holiday.
1833	First railway passenger deaths occur when a passenger car overturns in New Jersey.
1846	First steam-heated building, Eastern Hotel, opens in Boston.

[The songs] told a tale of grief and sorrow. In the most [joyful] outbursts . . . there was ever a tinge of deep melancholy. . . . Every tone was a testimony against slavery, and a prayer to God for deliverance from chains.

RESISTANCE AND REPRESSION

Slaves resisted any way they could. They sabotaged farm operations. Thousands ran away. The advertisements for these runaways are reminders of a basic cruelty of slavery—the disregard for family ties.

Richmond (Va.) Enquirer, February 20, 1838. Stop the Runaway!!!—$25 Reward. Ran away from the Eagle Tavern, a Negro fellow named Nat. He is no doubt attempting to follow his wife, who was lately sold to a speculator named Redmond.

Slaves sometimes rebelled. A large revolt took place near New Orleans in 1811. About

450 slaves gathered after a plantation revolt. Their numbers grew as they moved to other plantations. U.S. Army and Louisiana militia forces attacked the group and killed 66 slaves on the spot.

The most famous rebellion was led by Nat Turner in Virginia in 1831. Inspired by a dream of black and white angels fighting, Turner led about 60 fellow slaves on a rampage. They attacked several plantations and killed about 55 white men, women, and children. They were captured when their ammunition ran out.

Although Nat Turner was tried and hanged, his revolt sent shock waves through the South. Virginia became an armed camp. State legislatures began to pass harsh laws. As a result of these laws, slaves lost whatever freedom of movement they had. Slaves running errands, for example, now had to carry passes. In addition, whites were forbidden to teach a slave to read or write. Slaves were barred from holding religious meetings. Meanwhile, a movement begun in Virginia to abolish slavery faded after Nat Turner's Rebellion. With this action died any hope that the South itself would put an end to slavery.

SECTION REVIEW

1. KEY TERM cotton gin

2. PEOPLE AND PLACES Eli Whitney, New Orleans, Nat Turner

3. COMPREHENSION How did the cotton gin change the South?

4. COMPREHENSION In what ways did slavery deprive African Americans of basic rights?

5. CRITICAL THINKING How was the Cotton Kingdom a creation of the Industrial Revolution?

CHAPTER 14 SUMMARY AND TIMELINE

1. After the War of 1812, a nationalist mood took hold in the United States. Supreme Court rulings increased the power of the federal government. Congress pushed for higher tariffs and improved transportation. The Erie Canal and other waterways helped make westward expansion possible.

2. United States foreign policy under Monroe took a more assertive tone. The United States took advantage of revolution in Latin America to take over Spanish Florida. The Monroe Doctrine warned European nations not to interfere in the Americas.

3. The Industrial Revolution spread to the United States in the early 1800s. The textile industry boomed in the Northeast. Many families moved from their farms to work in factories. Technological advances such as interchangeable parts and steam power boosted industry and fueled the country's expansion.

4. The South became a one-crop economy after the invention of the cotton gin. Cotton profits drew settlers westward and led to a rise in slavery. Slaves tried to preserve their culture and sought freedom, but their efforts were often crushed.

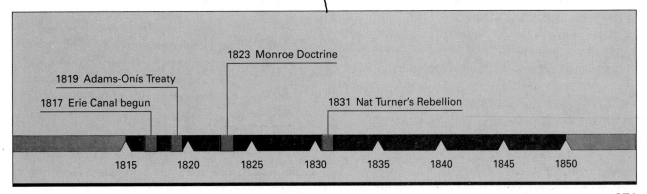

1817 Erie Canal begun
1819 Adams-Onís Treaty
1823 Monroe Doctrine
1831 Nat Turner's Rebellion

1815 1820 1825 1830 1835 1840 1845 1850

PLACES TO LOCATE

Match each of the letters on the map with the places that are listed below. Then explain the importance of each place.

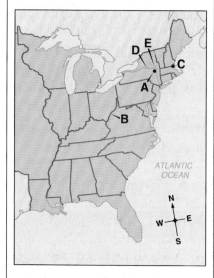

1. Hudson River
2. Lowell, Massachusetts
3. Albany, New York
4. Ohio River
5. Erie Canal

KEY TERMS

Use the following terms to complete the sentences.

cotton gin
interchangeable parts
judicial review
Monroe Doctrine
National Road

1. _____ gave the United States Supreme Court the power to declare laws passed by Congress to be unconstitutional.
2. The _____ aimed to keep European powers from interfering in the Western Hemisphere.
3. Westward movement increased with construction of the _____.
4. The invention of the _____ greatly influenced the South's economy.
5. Assembly lines using _____ could produce more goods faster than before.

PEOPLE TO IDENTIFY

Identify the following people and tell why each one was important.

1. John Quincy Adams
2. Simón Bolívar
3. Francis Cabot Lowell
4. John Marshall
5. Nat Turner
6. Eli Whitney

REVIEWING THE FACTS

1. What was the American System?
2. How did the Erie Canal improve trade?
3. By what means did the Marshall Court increase the power of the federal government?
4. How, according to Henry Clay, would tariffs help make the United States more self-sufficient?
5. What was the relationship between Latin American independence and the acquisition of Florida by the United States?
6. What was the Industrial Revolution? Which region of the United States was the first to industrialize? Explain you answer.
7. Why were large numbers of New England farm families drawn to work in factories?
8. In what ways did the invention of the cotton gin change life in the South?
9. How did slaves try to maintain their culture and dignity?
10. How did slaves actively resist slavery?

CITIZENSHIP

1. Explain how judicial review fits into the Constitution's system of checks and balances.
2. Describe the relationship between war and nationalism. Explain your answer.
3. Write a letter to the editor of a newspaper expressing your opinion on the movement for independence in Latin America.
4. Southern planters were able to control southern politics by convincing small farmers to support the policies of plantation owners. Give an example of a political group today that combines different interest groups.

PRACTICING YOUR SKILL

Read the second paragraph under the heading "Plantation Owners Lead the South," on page 368. Then determine whether the following statements are relevant or non-relevant to an understanding of relations between slaveowners and poorer white farmers. Explain your answers.

1. Slaveowners paid more in taxes than poorer farmers.
2. Plantation owners often gave food or money to poorer farmers.
3. Slaves became much more expensive after the slave trade ended.
4. Plantation owners hired slave overseers from among their poorer neighbors.

CRITICAL THINKING SKILLS

1. ANALYZING A QUOTATION Former slave Frederick Douglass said, "No man can put a chain about the ankle of his fellow man without at last finding the other end fastened about his own neck." Explain what Douglass meant.

2. STATING BOTH SIDES OF AN ISSUE Some historians have argued that slavery hurt the South economically because it did not allow the region to develop industry comparable to the North's. Present evidence both for and against this argument.

3. FORMING A HYPOTHESIS

Which Americans might have opposed the decisions of the Marshall Court? Why might the Court's decisions have met with less opposition in the Era of Good Feelings?

4. ANALYZING A QUOTATION John C. Calhoun defended slavery by saying that there has never existed a wealthy society in which one portion of the society did not live on the labor of others. Do you agree? Why or why not?

PROJECTS AND ACTIVITIES

1. GIVING AN ORAL REPORT Research one of the following topics and give an oral report to the class: steamships, Latin American independence, the Seminole War, free blacks in the South, slave rebellions.

2. DRAWING A CARTOON Draw a cartoon on the theme of how the Industrial Revolution changed the lives of working people.

3. WRITING A DIARY Suppose you are a worker in a New England textile mill. Write journal entries describing what work in the factory is like. Include the reasons why you took the job and what you hope to gain from it.

WRITING ABOUT TOPICS IN AMERICAN HISTORY

1. CONNECTING WITH LITERATURE A selection from *Jubilee* by Margaret Walker appears on pages 649–652. Read it and answer the questions. Then answer the following question: Describe the slaveholders' response to the rumor of an uprising. How does the passage reflect the fear and tension that lay below the surface of slaveholding society?

2. APPLYING THEMES: PLURALISTIC SOCIETY Write an essay explaining why slavery became a way of life in the southern United States. Include economic and political factors as well as attitudes toward African Americans that made slavery possible.

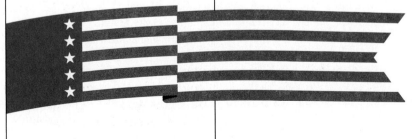

UNIT 4: American Mosaic

★ A Multicultural Perspective ★

During the early decades of the United States new opportunities for white women arose as the nation expanded and industrialized. At the same time, however, this period saw the growth of slavery and setbacks for American Indians' chances for peace and justice.

Ira Aldridge (right) was one of the most famous actors of the nineteenth century. The son of a minister, Aldridge left New York City to study drama in England. In 1833 he played the role of Othello, a black nobleman, in London's famous Covent Garden Theatre. Aldridge's powerful and dignified acting won him fame from Ireland to Russia. Because of public prejudice against seeing an African American actor appear with a white cast, Aldridge was prevented from performing in the United States.

The publication in Scandinavia of a book, *A True Account of America for the Information and Help of Peasant and Commoner*, caused a wave of immigration from Norway, Sweden, and Denmark in the late 1830s.

The first American-born saint, **Elizabeth Ann Seton** (left), grew up in an Episcopalian family in New York City. She married and had five children. Seton's husband died in 1803 during a trip to Europe. After his death, the 30-year-old Seton stayed on in Italy, where friends urged her to convert to Catholicism. Seton did so. On her return to the United States, Seton became a nun and worked to train teachers and open orphanages. Mother Seton founded the first American order of the Sisters of Charity as well as the nation's first free parochial school. Pope Paul VI declared her a saint in 1975.

Maria Mitchell (above) was born in 1818 on the Massachusetts island of Nantucket. As a child, she frequently joined her father as he studied astronomy from the roof of their house. In 1847 Mitchell made her own discovery: a new comet which was named for her and for which she received a gold medal from the king of Denmark. Mitchell became America's first female astronomer and the first female professor of astronomy. She was also the first woman elected to the American Academy of Arts and Letters.

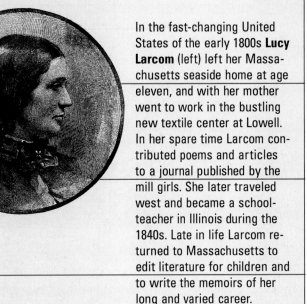

Garcia was the name of an ex-slave who, with a group of Seminole Indians and runaway slaves (one is shown above), set up a community in Florida. After the War of 1812, slaveholders demanded that force be used to keep Florida from becoming what Andrew Jackson called "a perpetual harbor for our slaves." Jackson sent forces to defeat Garcia. Jackson's men killed 250 Indians and African Americans. The survivors were forced back into slavery, and Garcia was shot.

In the fast-changing United States of the early 1800s **Lucy Larcom** (left) left her Massachusetts seaside home at age eleven, and with her mother went to work in the bustling new textile center at Lowell. In her spare time Larcom contributed poems and articles to a journal published by the mill girls. She later traveled west and became a schoolteacher in Illinois during the 1840s. Late in life Larcom returned to Massachusetts to edit literature for children and to write the memoirs of her long and varied career.

When he was sixteen years old, **Paul Cuffe** (right), part Indian and the son of an ex-slave, shipped out as a sailor on a whaling vessel. A few years later he was building his own ships. By 1806, when he was 47, Cuffe was a wealthy merchant. Cuffe's African roots were important to him, and he became a leader in the movement to settle free American blacks in West Africa. In time, opposition from other African American leaders led him to abandon the colonization movement.

The story of **Shábona** (above), a Potawatomi leader, illustrates the difficult choices Indians faced. Shábona was the great-nephew of Pontiac, leader of the 1763 fight against Britain's seizure of Indian lands. At first a supporter of Tecumseh's tribal confederacy, Shábona later argued that rather than fight hopelessly against government forces, Indians should negotiate treaties. This stance made him unpopular with some of his followers, who tried to assassinate him. In the end, Shábona's approach failed. The U.S. government broke its treaties with the Potawatomi, and Shábona's own land was taken from him.

Born into slavery in Haiti in 1766, **Pierre Toussaint** (left) was taken by his owner to New York City in 1787. There Toussaint worked as a hairdresser's apprentice and was allowed to keep some of the money he earned. Toussaint's owner died suddenly, leaving his family penniless. Toussaint secretly supported them with his own earnings for the next twenty years. In addition, Toussaint was active in the Catholic Church, raising money to help the sick and needy. For his good works and humility, the Catholic Church began in 1990 to investigate the possibility of Toussaint's becoming the first African American saint.

ISTORIANS' CORNER

Debating the Louisiana Purchase

Today the Louisiana Purchase seems an inevitable part of American history. At the time, however, serious constitutional questions were asked: Should the nation expand? Could the government acquire more land? Could the new territory become a state? These two accounts of the debate in Congress reveal some of these questions. The first is from Henry Adams' classic history published in 1889-1891, the second from a modern historian.

Henry Adams

Every speaker, without distinction of party, agreed that the United States government had the power to acquire new territory either by conquest or by treaty; the only difference of opinion regarded the disposition of this territory after it was acquired. Did Louisiana belong to the central government at Washington, or to the states?

The Federalists maintained that the central government . . . might, . . . hold the rest of America in its possession and govern it as England governed Jamaica or as Spain was governing Louisiana, but without the consent of the States could not admit such new territory into the Union. The Republicans seemed rather inclined to think that new territory acquired by war or conquest would become at once a part of the general territory mentioned in the Constitution, and as such might be admitted by Congress as a State. . . .

At the bottom, both doctrines were equally fatal to the old status of the Union. In one case the States . . . east of the Mississippi had established a government which could hold the rest of the world in despotic control, and which bought foreign people as it might buy cattle, to rule over them as their owner; in the other case, the government was equally powerful, and might besides admit the purchased or conquered territory into the Union as States. The Federalist theory was one of empire; the Republican was one of assimilation; but both agreed that the moment had come when the old Union must change its character.

From Henry Adams, *History of the United States of America During the Administration of Thomas Jefferson.* Volume arrangement, notes, and chronology copyright © 1986 by Literary Classics of the United States, Inc., New York, NY. Published by The Library of America.

Alexander DeConde

[Representative] Griswold next questioned the power of the President to incorporate territory and people into the Union as provided in the . . . Louisiana treaty. In general, even administration opponents such as Griswold and John Quincy Adams in the Senate supported expansion. They conceded that the government could acquire territory by purchase or conquest, but only to hold as a colony. They argued that neither the president nor Congress had clear authority to incorporate new territory into the Union without the consent of the states or without an amendment to the Constitution. In the Senate Timothy Pickering stated the extreme Federalist view. He argued that the government could acquire territory by conquest or purchase but could not bring it into the Union without "the assent of each individual state." A few New Englanders mumbled threats of secession if their objections were ignored.

From Alexander DeConde, *This Affair of Louisiana.* Copyright © 1976 by Alexander DeConde. Published by Charles Scribner's Sons.

Critical Thinking

1. What became the central issue on which the political parties disagreed?

2. How did regional issues influence those who wanted Louisiana to be a colony?

3. How might American history have been different if Louisiana had been kept as a colony?

Expansion and Development

THEMES IN AMERICAN HISTORY

Expanding Democracy The 1820s and 1830s saw a broadening of voting rights.

American Culture A spirit of reform, energized by a religious revival, led to movements for abolition and other causes during the 1830s and 1840s.

Geography Victory over Mexico in 1848 gave the United States vast new western lands. The discovery of gold in California triggered a large westward migration.

Constitutional Government Tensions between North and South threatened to tear apart the federal system of government.

Economic Development Economic differences among the nation's regions created tensions.

Pluralistic Society The West drew settlers of different cultural backgrounds who joined the region's Hispanic and Indian populations.

Democracy grew along with the nation, as George Caleb Bingham showed in this painting of a county election campaign. Yet widening differences among the nation's sections caused political turmoil.

1 A New Kind of Politics

Section Focus

Key Terms sectionalism ■ Missouri Compromise ■ Jacksonian democracy ■ spoils system

Main Idea Tensions between regions of the country led to disputes over new states and a political split in the election of 1824. Andrew Jackson's election in 1828 reflected the growth of democracy in the country.

Objectives As you read, look for answers to these questions:
1. What kinds of political disputes appeared in the early 1820s?
2. What conflicts arose over the election of 1824?
3. How did Andrew Jackson represent something new in American politics?

In 1819, members of the Sixteenth Congress gathered in Washington, D.C. For five years they had been unable to meet in the Capitol, which the British had burned in the War of 1812. Now the rebuilt Capitol stood ready for the new Congress. Thick red curtains hung in the Hall of Representatives. Red silk was draped above the Speaker's desk.

As the session began, it became clear that the mood of the Congress was also new. The Era of Good Feelings was coming to a close. Tensions were developing between representatives from different regions. These tensions —and the growing political power of ordinary men—were to set the course of the country for the decades to follow.

THE MISSOURI COMPROMISE

Many of the emerging divisions within the United States reflected the changing economies of the country. One-crop farming was important in the South. Southerners relied on slaves to raise the cotton that enriched the region. Manufacturing and trade were at the

Destroyed by British troops during the War of 1812, the Capitol was once again in use by 1819. HISTORY What was new about the mood of Congress as it met in 1819?

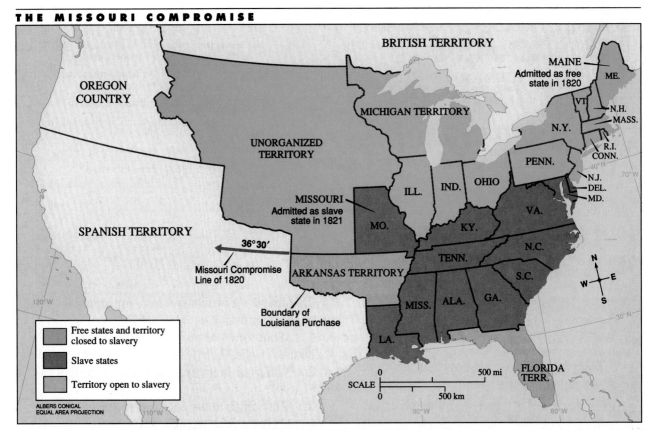

BRITISH TERRITORY

OREGON COUNTRY

MAINE
Admitted as free state in 1820

ME.

MICHIGAN TERRITORY

VT
N.H.
MASS.

N.Y.

UNORGANIZED TERRITORY

PENN.

R.I.
CONN.

ILL.
IND.
OHIO

N.J.
DEL.
MD.

MISSOURI
Admitted as slave state in 1821

MO.

VA.

KY.

SPANISH TERRITORY

36°30′

Missouri Compromise Line of 1820

N.C.

TENN.

ARKANSAS TERRITORY

S.C.

Boundary of Louisiana Purchase

MISS.
ALA.
GA.

Free states and territory closed to slavery

LA.

Slave states

FLORIDA TERR.

Territory open to slavery

0   500 mi
SCALE
0   500 km

ALBERS CONICAL EQUAL AREA PROJECTION

MAP SKILLS The Missouri Compromise of 1820 permitted slavery in Missouri and in states south of the Missouri Compromise line. What state joined the Union to balance the number of free and slave states? CRITICAL THINKING Why was the Missouri Compromise only a temporary solution to the problem of sectionalism?

center of the Northeast's wealth. In the West, settlers on the expanding frontier wanted cheap land and good transportation. The interests of these three sections of the country were often in conflict. Loyalty to local interests is called sectionalism. Sectionalism began to replace nationalism as the dominant mood of Congress.

Sectionalism burst into the open when Missouri applied for statehood. People there wanted to allow slavery in their state. At the time, the United States was evenly split into eleven slave states and eleven free states. A new state would tilt the balance of power in Congress.

In Congress, James Tallmadge of New York proposed that slavery be banned in Missouri. Southerners were angry. They asked: Did the Constitution give Congress

the power to ban slavery? If nonslave states ever formed a majority in Congress, might they ban slavery altogether? "It is a most unhappy question, awakening the sectional feelings, and exasperating them to the highest degree," Henry Clay wrote. Clay, from Kentucky, was now Speaker of the House.

For months the debate raged. Meanwhile, Maine declared itself ready for statehood. Clay saw a chance for compromise. He suggested that Missouri be admitted as a slave state and Maine as a free state. Congress passed Clay's plan, known as the Missouri Compromise of 1820. The compromise maintained the balance of power between slave states and free states. It also called for slavery to be banned from the Louisiana Territory north of the parallel 36°30′, Missouri's southern border.

Thomas Jefferson, nearing 80 and living quietly in Virginia, was not happy with the Missouri Compromise. He worried that sectionalism would tear the country apart. "This momentous question, like a firebell in the night, awakened and filled me with terror," he wrote. "I considered it the [death] knell of the Union."

This momentous question, like a firebell in the night, awakened and filled me with terror."

—*Thomas Jefferson, on the Missouri controversy*

THE ELECTION OF 1824

Jefferson's fears were not groundless. Just four years later, sectional differences led to a fight over the presidency. The Republican Party split apart, with four men seeking to replace Monroe as President. John Quincy Adams, Monroe's Secretary of State and an excellent diplomat, was New England's choice. The South supported William Craw-ford of Georgia. Clay, the "Great Compromiser," and Andrew Jackson of Tennessee were backed by westerners.

Jackson won the most electoral votes, but he did not win a majority. Under the Constitution, in such a case the House of Representatives chooses the President from the top three vote-getters. Clay had come in fourth and was out of the running. He threw his support behind Adams, who won the House vote. The new President then named Clay his Secretary of State.

Jackson was furious with his fellow westerner. He pointed to the Biblical story of the betrayal of Jesus to describe his feelings about Clay. "So you see the *Judas* of the West has closed the contract and will receive the thirty pieces of silver," Jackson wrote.

No evidence exists that Clay and Adams had made a deal. Yet Jackson's supporters charged that money and power had defeated liberty. Jackson resigned his Senate seat and returned to Tennessee.

John Quincy Adams was not a likable man. Stern and stubborn like his father, our nation's second President, Adams did not bargain easily. He did little to ease the resentment of Jackson's friends in Congress.

The House of Representatives, shown in this painting by Samuel F. B. Morse, decided the 1824 presidential election after none of the candidates received a majority of electoral votes. The House chose John Quincy Adams to be President. HISTORY What accusation did Andrew Jackson make after Adams's election?

John Quincy Adams

1825–1829

6th President, National Republican

- Born July 11, 1767, in Massachusetts
- Married Louisa Catherine Johnson in 1797; 4 children
- Lawyer; senator from Massachusetts; ambassador to Russia and to England
- Lived in Massachusetts when elected President
- Vice President: John C. Calhoun
- Died February 23, 1848, in Washington
- Key event while in office: Erie Canal opened

Adams ended up spending much of his four years as President jousting with Congress. The able diplomat was unable to lead.

A New Democratic Spirit

In 1828 all eyes were on the coming rematch between Jackson and Adams. Democrats saw the election as a chance for average people to show their political strength. They viewed Adams as corrupt, a man who worked for the rich. Adams's backers attacked Jackson as a gambler and drunkard.

Jackson won the election of 1828 in a landslide. His victory has been called a triumph for democracy. That victory reflected changes in the country. Many states had once required that a man own property before he could vote. Members of the Electoral College

had been chosen by state legislatures. Now, in the new western states, every adult white male could vote. Older states were lowering property requirements for voting. In all but two states, the people, rather than their lawmakers, voted for presidential electors.

There was a fresh democratic spirit in the United States. Historians call this new spirit Jacksonian democracy. The mass of people once had been content to let their "betters" run the government. Andrew Jackson's election signaled new thinking in the land. Americans no longer thought of themselves as having betters.

An American Hero

On March 4, 1829, Washington, D.C., was seething with excitement. Andrew Jackson was to be sworn in as President. From all over the country, people poured into the capital. "I never saw such a crowd before," observed Daniel Webster, senator from Massachusetts. "Persons have come 500 miles to see General Jackson, and they really seem to think that the country is rescued from some dreadful danger!"

Why was Jackson so popular? Americans saw him as one of them, a person who had risen above hardship and poverty. His father, a Scots-Irish immigrant, had died shortly before he was born. The Jacksons had managed to get by, farming on the Carolina frontier. In 1780, at the age of thirteen, Jackson had joined the militia. Taken prisoner by the British, he refused to shine the boots of an officer. The officer struck the boy with a sword, leaving a scar that Jackson bore for the rest of his life.

As a young man, Jackson moved to the Tennessee frontier and became a wealthy planter. He studied and then practiced law, becoming a frontier prosecutor. After Tennessee became a state, he served as a member of Congress. He led troops against the British in the War of 1812. His victories made him a war hero.

Jackson's nickname was "Old Hickory," after one of the hardest woods in the forest. He

Married to Andrew Jackson for more than three decades, Rachel Jackson died shortly before his inauguration as President. HISTORY How did the inauguration ceremony symbolize the new democratic spirit in the nation?

was tough. He was honest and courageous. He got things done. He also had a quick temper and had fought a number of duels. Loyal toward his friends, he could be bitter toward his enemies.

> "I had rather be a doorkeeper in the house of God, than to live in that palace at Washington."
>
> —*Rachel Jackson*

JACKSON TAKES OFFICE

Jackson looked thin and sad at his inauguration. His wife, Rachel, had died less than a month after his victory. Political life had been hard on her. "I had rather be a doorkeeper in the house of God," she had often said, "than to live in that palace at Washington."

The inauguration took place without the outgoing President. Bitter in defeat, John Quincy Adams had left the city. The ceremony was held outdoors so that the thousands present could witness it. In the White House, long tables had been set with punch and cakes for those invited to the reception. Lack of invitations, however, did not stop the crowd. People pushed through the doors, breaking furniture and surrounding the food. "The reign of KING MOB seemed triumphant," a Supreme Court justice complained. The mob finally left, some through the windows, when punch and liquor were moved out to the lawn.

A NEW POLITICAL ERA

Jackson launched a new era of politics. He fired large numbers of government officials, many of them members of the upper classes. Jackson said that the duties of public office were so simple, any smart person could do the work. He followed an old saying, "To the victor belong the spoils [rewards]." Members of his own party were given the jobs of those he had dismissed. This practice of giving government jobs to political backers is called the spoils system. Although subject to abuse, the spoils system did break the upper class's hold on government jobs.

SECTION REVIEW

1. KEY TERMS sectionalism, Missouri Compromise, Jacksonian democracy, spoils system

2. PEOPLE AND PLACES Missouri, Henry Clay, Maine, John Quincy Adams, Andrew Jackson

3. COMPREHENSION Why was the outcome of the election of 1824 decided in the House of Representatives?

4. COMPREHENSION Why did Americans admire Andrew Jackson?

5. CRITICAL THINKING Why did Jefferson believe that the Missouri controversy was a sign of future disaster for the nation?

2 Jackson's Harsh Indian Policy

In the 1820s the Cotton Kingdom was steadily moving westward. The United States' rising demand for cotton was creating a great demand for new soil in which to grow it. Southern cotton planters looked greedily at the fertile lands then being held by the Indian tribes of the Southeast.

THE CHEROKEE NATION

Since the War of 1812, it had been the policy of the United States government to encourage the Indians to move west of the Mississippi River. Working on behalf of the government in 1817, Andrew Jackson had offered each Cherokee the choice of moving west or settling down on 640 acres of land. To his surprise, and probably to his dismay, most had decided to adopt the white person's way of life. Not only did the Cherokee acquire vast herds of cattle, they also had cotton gins, spinning wheels, and looms. Furthermore, the Cherokee owned African American slaves.

An important leader of the Cherokee during these years was Sequoya. Also known as George Guess, he was the son of a white trader and a Cherokee woman. Sequoya decided that Indian survival depended on literacy—being able to read and write. Sequoya developed an alphabet for the Cherokee language. Within a few months of its introduction, the Cherokee were reading and writing in their own language. Among their reading materials were Sequoya's newspaper, *The Cherokee Phoenix,* and the Bible.

To convince whites that they were no barbarians, the Cherokee went even further. They adopted a constitution, based on the United States Constitution, for a Cherokee Republic. Sadly though, the Cherokee did not realize that nothing they did would win the respect of white society. No matter how the Indians behaved, no matter what they accomplished, white people considered them inferior simply because they were Indians. Most importantly, white people wanted Indian land, no matter what.

The southeastern states were often ruthless as they tried to pry Indians from their land. The state of Georgia signed a phony treaty with the Creek Indians. When the Creek protested, John Quincy Adams refused to honor the treaty. His protection of Indian rights angered many people, both southerners and westerners.

BIOGRAPHY

SEQUOYA (1770?–1843), a Cherokee Indian, devised an 85-character alphabet that represented each of the sounds in the Cherokee language. The system was easily mastered, and by 1828 there were many books and a newspaper written in Cherokee. Sequoya also helped keep peace between his people and the United States government.

Once in office, Jackson reversed the government's stand. He proposed to Congress that the southeastern Indians be forced to move. Although religious and political groups protested, Congress passed the Indian Removal Act in 1830. The new law called for the Indians to move to public lands west of the Mississippi. The area had less rain and fewer trees than the Southeast and was considered by many to be worthless.

The Democrats said they were acting in the Indians' best interests. In the words of the historian Robert Remini, however, the law "was harsh, arrogant, racist—and inevitable."

INDIAN RESISTANCE

Not all Native Americans peacefully accepted the move west. The Sauk and Fox Indians of southern Wisconsin and northern Illinois

Osceola led the Seminole Indians in their battles against the United States during the 1830s. Seminole resistance continued after Osceola's capture, but the Seminoles lost their determination when they lost their leader. ETHICS Defend or criticize the means used to capture Osceola.

were forced to move into the Iowa Territory. In 1832 a Sauk chief named Black Hawk tried to lead his people back to their original homes. The United States Army and the Illinois militia quickly crushed this uprising. The Black Hawk War was the last Indian war of the Midwest.

> "**I**f suddenly we tear our hearts from the homes around which they are twined, our heart-strings will snap."
>
> —*Seminole response when ordered to leave Florida*

In 1835 the Seminole Indians refused to leave their lands in Florida. Told they must move west, they answered, "If suddenly we tear our hearts from the homes around which they are twined, our heart-strings will snap." A young chief named Osceola (ahs–ee–OH–luh) became their leader. He declared that his people would fight "till the last drop of Seminole blood has moistened the dust of his hunting ground."

In 1837 an American general raised a flag of truce to discuss peace with Osceola. During the meeting, the chief and his men were put in chains. Sent to prison, Osceola died of disease. Many Americans were shocked by the trick that had been used to capture him.

The Seminole fought for seven years, until they were almost wiped out. Some retreated into the swamps of the Everglades. Most of those that remained moved west.

THE TRAIL OF TEARS

The Cherokee also resisted leaving their homes—but not by fighting. When Georgia decided to take over their lands, the Cherokee appealed to the Supreme Court. They pointed to the treaty, made with the federal government, guaranteeing their lands. A state, they argued, could not overrule a federal treaty.

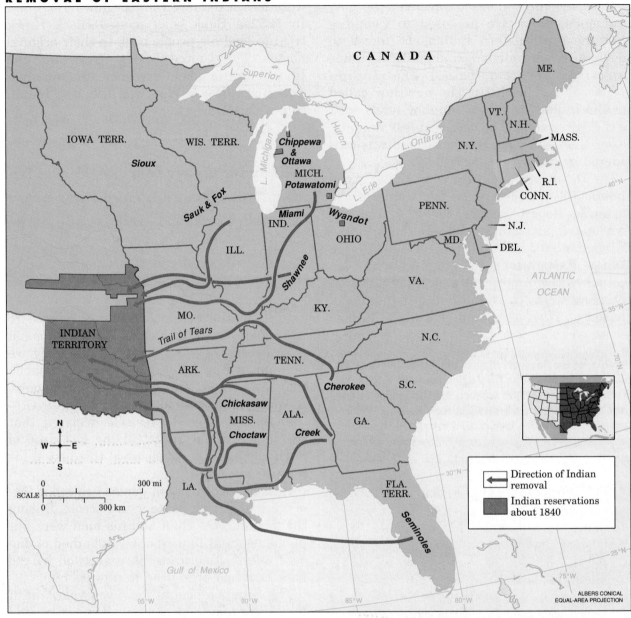

MAP SKILLS Starting in 1830, the United States forced most Eastern Indians onto government-run reservations in what is now Oklahoma. Other tribes were also moved west of the Mississippi River. **CRITICAL THINKING** Why was the Supreme Court unable to prevent the relocation?

In 1832 Chief Justice John Marshall ruled in favor of the Cherokee. He declared that Georgia had no right to force the Cherokee to relocate, or move. Under the Constitution, President Jackson should have obeyed the Supreme Court decision. Instead he chose to ignore it. "John Marshall has made his decision," Jackson said. "Now let him enforce it."

Some Cherokee gave up and moved west to the Indian Territory, now Oklahoma. Most remained in Georgia. In 1838 federal troops rounded up the 15,000 remaining Cherokee. The troops moved the men, women, and children west. Forced to march in the cold and rain of winter, the Cherokee sickened and starved. One survivor remembered reaching

Endless Trail, a painting by Jerome Tiger, shows the forced migration of Indian people.
HISTORY What hardships did the Cherokee suffer?

the icy Mississippi River and seeing "hundreds of sick and dying penned up in wagons or stretched upon the ground."

The harsh journey became known as the Trail of Tears. Nearly one quarter of the unwilling migrants died. A settler moving westward wrote of what he saw:

On Tuesday evening we fell in with a detachment of the poor Cherokee Indians . . . about 1,100 Indians—60 wagons—600 horses, and perhaps 40 pairs of oxen. We found them in the forest camped for the night by the road side . . . under a severe fall of rain accompanied by heavy wind. With their canvas for a shield from the . . . weather, and the cold wet ground for a resting place, . . . they spent the night. . . . Many of the aged Indians were suffering extremely from the fatigue of the journey, and the ill health consequent upon it. . . . Several were then quite ill, and one aged man we were informed was then in the last struggles of death. . . .

One lady passed [with] . . . her youngest child about three years old . . . sick in her arms, and all she could do was to make it comfortable as circumstances would permit. . . . She could only carry her dying child in her arms a few miles farther, and then she must stop in a stranger-land and [give up] her much loved babe to the cold ground, and that too without pomp or ceremony, and pass on with the multitude. . . .

SECTION REVIEW

1. KEY TERMS literacy, Indian Removal Act, relocate, Trail of Tears

2. PEOPLE AND PLACES Sequoya, Black Hawk, Florida, Osceola, John Marshall, Indian Territory

3. COMPREHENSION What was the goal of Jackson's Indian policy?

4. COMPREHENSION How was Osceola captured?

5. CRITICAL THINKING Do you agree with the historian Robert Remini that forced relocation of the Indians could not be avoided? Why or why not?

3 Sectional and Financial Controversies

Section Focus

Key Terms   doctrine of nullification
■ secede ■ credit

Main Idea   As President, Andrew Jackson struggled to keep the nation from splitting apart over the issue of tariffs.

Objectives   As you read, look for answers to these questions:
1.   What differences in economic goals divided the East, South, and West?
2.   What led to the nullification controversy?
3.   On what issues did President Jackson take strong stands?

The United States Constitution was but a decade old when Congress passed the Alien and Sedition Acts. At the time, Thomas Jefferson and James Madison had introduced the idea of states' rights: that a state does not have to obey a federal law it considers unconstitutional (page 316). Shortly afterward the Republicans gained power, and the issue of states' rights died down—but not completely.

Some important questions remained unanswered. If a state had chosen to accept the Constitution and become part of the United States, could it later choose to leave the Union? Which laws were more powerful, those passed by a state or those passed by the federal government? Could a state strike down a federal law?

Today the answers may seem obvious: the states must respect federal law. In the 1830s, however, the questions were the subject of heated debate. Duels were fought and careers destroyed as Americans took sides on the issue of states' rights. It took the popularity of President Jackson and the leadership of several senators to keep the country united in those years.

RISING SECTIONAL DIFFERENCES

Conflicts among the North, South, and West had flared when Jackson first ran for office in 1824. They grew worse throughout John Quincy Adams's term. Each region had its own needs, which were often at odds with those of the other two regions. When Jackson took office, the country was divided along sectional lines. At issue were internal improvements, the sale of public land, and tariffs.

The Northeast was the region where banking, business, and manufacturing were strongest. The economic prosperity of the Northeast depended on good, cheap transportation. Good transportation was necessary for several reasons:

(1) Raw materials had to be brought to the factories.

(2) Manufactured goods had to be sent to the West.

(3) Western foodstuffs had to be carried to eastern cities.

Business leaders in the North, therefore, supported spending government money on transportation. Northern leaders also did not want western land to be sold at low prices. Cheap land in the West would attract workers from the East. With fewer workers in the East, the wages of those who remained would be forced up.

Northerners backed high tariffs. Tariffs caused imported goods to be more expensive than American-made goods. This made it easier for American manufacturers to sell their products.

In contrast, southerners were beginning to hate tariffs. Tariffs had risen steadily since 1816. In that year, Congress had passed a tariff as part of the nationalists' American System (page 351). The tariff was also the government's main source of income.

The South opposed rising tariffs because they made imported goods more expensive.

The issue of internal improvements was one question dividing Americans along sectional lines during the 1820s and 1830s. In some places, people built roads across their own lands and charged travelers a fee. The need for more roads, however, led to calls for government road-building projects. **ECONOMICS** Why did southerners oppose government funding for transportation?

Why, then, did the South not buy American-made goods? The answer is that planters usually received credit, rather than cash, for their cotton. Because they sold most of their cotton overseas, they had overseas credit. They used that credit to buy manufactured goods made overseas. Because of the tariff, those goods cost more.

Southerners did not oppose roads and canals as such. They did oppose, however, anything that might cost money and therefore might cause tariffs to rise. In Congress, southerners began to vote against any proposal for internal improvements.

Roads and canals, however, were lifelines to people on the frontier. Westerners wanted the government to build as many as possible. They also wanted public land sold at low prices. Both moves would encourage settlement of western territories. The more people who moved West, the more political power the region would have.

THE DOCTRINE OF NULLIFICATION

In the last months of John Quincy Adams's term, Congress passed a very high tariff. Adams signed it into law. The South was outraged. In South Carolina, angry lawmakers spoke of leaving the Union.

John C. Calhoun, Vice President of the United States, had been born and raised in South Carolina. He loved his home state and the South. Calhoun also believed in a strong national government. (He had supported the 1816 tariff as part of the American System.) To prevent hotheads from leading South Carolina out of the Union, Calhoun proposed the doctrine of nullification. Congress, said Calhoun, had no authority to pass laws that favored one section of the nation at the expense of another. When it did, a state had the right to declare that law null and void within the state.

The doctrine of nullification was but another version of states' rights. It raised anew an old question: How complete was the authority of the national government over the states?

THE HAYNE-WEBSTER DEBATES

Calhoun's arguments calmed southern leaders, unhappy as they still were with the high tariffs. To reduce the tariffs, southerners knew they needed help from the West. They cast about for a way to drive a wedge between the West and the Northeast. Then, in 1830 easterners called for limiting the sale of public land. Westerners protested. Here was the chance for which the South had waited!

Senator Robert Y. Hayne of South Carolina backed the West's call for a generous land policy. He argued that it was an abuse of federal power to cut off land sales. Each state had the right to make its own decisions, said Hayne.

Hayne's argument shifted the topic of debate from land sales to states' rights. He claimed that the rights of the states came before the unity of the nation. A state could nullify any federal law it judged to be unfair, he said.

Hayne was an excellent speaker. The man who rose to answer him, however, was one of the greatest speakers of his time. Daniel Webster, from Massachusetts, had dark, deep-set eyes and a thundering voice. He believed that Hayne's views threatened the future of the country. His speeches against those views were passionate and brilliant.

Webster argued that laws made by Congress were not subject to the approval of each state. Instead the laws represented the will of the people as a whole. "It is, Sir," he declared, "the people's Constitution, the people's government, made for the people, made by the people, and answerable to the people." He reminded western states that they had been created by the national government, which worked for them. Webster scolded Hayne for

This painting shows Massachusetts Senator Daniel Webster debating Senator Robert Hayne of South Carolina in 1830. The two senators argued whether states could disregard federal laws. **CONSTITUTIONAL HERITAGE** What was Webster's argument?

wanting "Liberty first, and Union afterwards." He demanded "Liberty *and* Union, now and forever, one and inseparable!"

Webster's speeches lessened western support for the South. Southerners turned to President Jackson, hoping that he would back them. They learned how he felt at the Jefferson Birthday Dinner of 1830.

> "Our Federal Union—it must be preserved!"
>
> —*Andrew Jackson*

Among the southerners attending the dinner were Vice President Calhoun and Senator Robert Hayne. Hayne was the principal speaker at the dinner. He reminded his audience that Thomas Jefferson had first raised the issue of states' rights in the Kentucky and Virginia Resolutions of 1798. After the speech, Jackson was invited to give a toast. He rose, looked squarely at Calhoun, and said, "Our Federal Union—it must be preserved!" The room was silent. Calhoun's hand shook. He was called on to make the second toast. He replied, "The Union—*next to our liberty,* the most dear!"

South Carolina's Threat

Jackson understood the South's objection to high tariffs. He recommended that the tariff be lowered, and in 1832 Congress did so. South Carolina's legislature still thought the tariff too high and voted to nullify the law. If the federal government tried to enforce the tariff, the legislators said, South Carolina would secede—withdraw—from the Union.

Jackson was furious when he learned what South Carolina had done. Calhoun defended his state. Since the state chose to join the Union, explained Calhoun, it could choose to leave the Union. Jackson's reply was swift: "To say that any state may at pleasure secede from the Union is to say that the United States is not a nation."

Jackson announced in December that he would enforce the tariff laws. He prepared to send an army to South Carolina. "If one drop of blood be shed [in South Carolina] in defiance of the laws of the United States," he said, "I will hang the first man of them I can get my hands on to the first tree I can find."

Calhoun successfully ran for election to the Senate from South Carolina. Then he resigned as Vice President. Armed conflict seemed possible. South Carolina readied

This cartoon criticized John C. Calhoun's support for the doctrine of nullification by showing Calhoun ordering the sun to stand still. **POLITICS** What issue led South Carolina to threaten to secede in 1832?

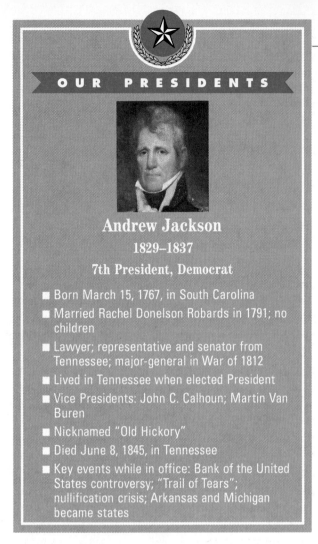

Andrew Jackson

1829–1837

7th President, Democrat

- Born March 15, 1767, in South Carolina
- Married Rachel Donelson Robards in 1791; no children
- Lawyer; representative and senator from Tennessee; major-general in War of 1812
- Lived in Tennessee when elected President
- Vice Presidents: John C. Calhoun; Martin Van Buren
- Nicknamed "Old Hickory"
- Died June 8, 1845, in Tennessee
- Key events while in office: Bank of the United States controversy; "Trail of Tears"; nullification crisis; Arkansas and Michigan became states

troops to repel any federal "invasion." At this point Henry Clay stepped in with a compromise. He suggested that tariff duties be lowered gradually over a period of ten years. Congress passed the Compromise Tariff in March 1833, and President Jackson signed it into law. South Carolina stayed in the Union.

JACKSON AND THE NATIONAL BANK

The greatest controversy of Jackson's presidency was his fight against the Bank of the United States. The fight began in 1832.

The original Bank of the United States had been Alexander Hamilton's idea. He saw a national bank as a way to unify and control the country's financial system. He convinced Congress to charter the bank in 1791 (page 300). That charter had run out in 1811.

After the War of 1812, the country's finances were a mess. Once again, Congress chartered a national bank. The Second Bank of the United States was owned largely by eastern business leaders. The federal government had almost no power to control it.

Like most westerners, Jackson distrusted the prosperous bank. He believed that powerful bank officers were influencing Congress to pass laws friendly to it. He thought that the bank's high interest rates made it hard for the average person to borrow money.

Henry Clay and Daniel Webster supported the bank. Both opposed Jackson in his bid for re-election. Though the bank's charter did not run out until 1836, Webster and Clay convinced the bank's president to ask for renewal in 1832. They hoped that the fight over the bank would end Jackson's chances of remaining in office. With Webster's and Clay's support, Congress voted to renew the charter of the bank.

JACKSON'S BANK VETO

Jackson was sick in bed when he heard the news. The old soldier gathered strength at the thought of a battle against his rivals. "The Bank is trying to kill me," he declared, "but I will kill it." With the help of his advisers, Jackson wrote a powerful veto message.

The bank, he said, was a monopoly that was creating a special class of privileged men. It helped the few at the expense of the many. The message continued:

> There are no necessary evils in government. Its evils exist only in its abuses. If it would confine itself to equal protection, and, as Heaven does its rains, shower its favors alike on the high and the low, the rich and the poor, it would be an unqualified blessing.

Jackson's veto of the bank was the first time a President had vetoed a bill on other than constitutional grounds. In effect, Jack-

In the above cartoon, President Jackson (at left) attacks the many-headed Bank of the United States with a weapon labeled "VETO." Vice President Van Buren (in the middle) assists Jackson. The monster's heads represent bank branch directors. **CONSTITUTIONAL HERITAGE** How was Jackson's veto of the bank bill a "first"?

son stated that a President had the right to veto any law for any reason. He thus thrust the power of the presidency into the process of making a law. From then on, Congress had to consider a presidential veto whenever it proposed a law.

As planned, the bank veto became a central issue in the election of 1832. Yet Jackson used it to his advantage. He charged that the bank was a monster. He presented himself as the defender of the American people against that monster.

Jackson won the election. He took this as a sign that the public approved of his war on the bank. In his second term he set out to destroy its power.

THE PET BANKS

The bank's charter did not run out until 1836, but Jackson wanted to starve it to death in the meantime. To do so, he ordered all government money withdrawn from the bank. These funds were then deposited in 29 state banks that became known as "pet banks." The pet banks began to offer **credit**—money on loan—on easier terms. They also printed paper money representing far more cash than what they had on deposit.

Many of the pet banks were in the West. Jackson found it hard to ignore western bankers who had supported him. Often the banks were not soundly managed.

This transfer of a large portion of government funds to western banks had several important results.

(1) Easy money in the West fueled an increase in land speculation. Western land prices shot up.

(2) As land prices went up, so did government land revenues. The government made $5 million from land sales in 1834 and $25 million in 1836.

(3) More government money created the need for more pet banks. The number of pet banks rose to 89. These banks eagerly loaned out the government funds on deposit to more speculators.

By 1836 it was clear to Jackson that it was unhealthy for speculators to buy government land with credit from state banks. In the Specie Circular, therefore, he ordered that land bought from the government be paid for in gold or silver. (*Specie* refers to coined money.) The order would go into effect after the election of 1836.

SECTION REVIEW

1. KEY TERMS doctrine of nullification, secede, credit

2. PEOPLE AND PLACES South Carolina, John C. Calhoun, Robert Y. Hayne, Daniel Webster

3. COMPREHENSION Why did the Northeast and the South disagree over tariffs?

4. COMPREHENSION What reasons did Andrew Jackson have for opposing the Bank of the United States?

5. CRITICAL THINKING Do you think that the states should have had the right to nullify federal laws? Why or why not?

While reading newspapers or magazines, you may have noticed political cartoons. These drawings are often funny, but they always express the cartoonist's point of view. Some political cartoons call attention to issues or problems. Some make fun of public figures and their decisions. Any political cartoon, however, expresses an opinion on an important issue of the day. Political cartoons are meant to influence as well as inform.

USING EXAGGERATION

To make their viewpoint clearer or more forceful, cartoonists often exaggerate the facts. They also may use exaggeration to create figures that can be easily recognized. For example, Abraham Lincoln was very tall. Many cartoonists used to draw him with very long legs and a tall stovepipe hat. When the public saw a drawing of a tall, thin man with a tall, thin hat they knew the cartoonist was showing Lincoln. A drawing that exaggerates certain features of a person for effect is called a **caricature**.

USING SYMBOLS

Cartoonists also use symbols to make their point. For example, a dove is often used to represent peace. A skull and crossbones usually means death. Maps are often used to stand for countries and parts of the world. To understand a political cartoon fully, you must study its symbols.

ANALYZING A CARTOON

The cartoon on this page was published in the 1830s, when Andrew Jackson was President. Jackson, a forceful and strong-willed Chief Executive, was a highly controversial public figure and thus was the subject of many political cartoons. The drawing serves as a commentary on the cartoonist's opinion of Jackson, his leadership style, and his policies. In order to get his point across, the cartoonist used common tools, such as exaggeration and symbolism, as well as a caption.

King Andrew I

PRACTICING YOUR SKILL

1. How is Andrew Jackson dressed? How does the way he is dressed explain the cartoon's caption?

2. Was the comparison of Jackson to a king meant as praise or criticism? Explain.

3. What paper is Jackson holding in his hand? What incident is the cartoonist referring to with that paper?

4. What pieces of paper are lying on the floor beneath Jackson? To what incidents might these objects refer?

5. What do you think the cartoonist thought of Jackson? Explain.

6. How, in your opinion, was the cartoonist trying to influence American public opinion toward Jackson?

4 Prosperity and Panic

Section Focus

Key Terms panic ■ Panic of 1837 ■ depression

Main Idea After Andrew Jackson left office, the nation suffered from an economic downturn and a lack of strong political leadership.

Objectives As you read, look for answers to these questions:
1. What political parties developed in the 1830s?
2. What caused the Panic of 1837?
3. How was William Henry Harrison elected President in 1840?

Andrew Jackson was nearly 70 years old the day he left office. Frail and thin, he watched Martin Van Buren sworn in as the new President. Van Buren spoke to the crowd that had gathered in front of the Capitol. Then Jackson, now a private citizen, turned and faced the crowd. He walked down the steps, took off his hat, and bowed. A giant cheer rose up from the people. A senator described the cheer and the moment: "It was affection, gratitude, and admiration . . . the acclaim of posterity. . . . I felt an emotion which had never passed through me before."

Jackson no longer governed the nation. Yet he remained a towering figure. His influence in the development of political parties continues to affect us today. Jackson is considered the founder of the modern Democratic Party.

NEW POLITICAL PARTIES

The country's first political parties had been founded in the 1790s: the Federalists and the Democratic-Republicans (page 310). The Federalist Party died out soon after Monroe's election. That left the Democratic-Republicans as *the* political party in the country.

The election of 1824 split the party in two (page 381). Jackson's followers called themselves Democratic-Republicans. During the 1830s they became known simply as Democrats. Adams and those who backed him were National Republicans. Once again, the country had a two-party system.

Jackson's party was linked to the ideals of Thomas Jefferson. Democrats stressed their ties to the common people and were against a

strong federal government. The party came to stand for low tariffs and states' rights. For these reasons, it attracted many voters in the South and West.

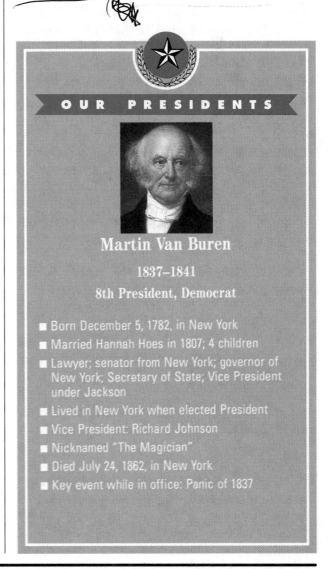

OUR PRESIDENTS

Martin Van Buren

1837–1841
8th President, Democrat

■ Born December 5, 1782, in New York
■ Married Hannah Hoes in 1807; 4 children
■ Lawyer; senator from New York; governor of New York; Secretary of State; Vice President under Jackson
■ Lived in New York when elected President
■ Vice President: Richard Johnson
■ Nicknamed "The Magician"
■ Died July 24, 1862, in New York
■ Key event while in office: Panic of 1837

The National Republicans were Federalist at the core. Party leaders resented Jackson's personal popularity, calling him "King Andrew I." They called themselves Whigs after the political party in Britain that opposed the British king. The Whig Party stood for high tariffs and strong national government. Most of its supporters lived in the Northeast.

In 1836 the Whigs ran three different candidates, including Daniel Webster, for President. The Democrats backed Vice President Martin Van Buren. Short and plump, Van Buren had been a loyal follower of Jackson's but had few followers of his own. Still, Jackson was able to use his own popularity to win the election for Van Buren. Jackson retired content, knowing his party was still in power. To a friend he admitted he had only two regrets—he had been unable to shoot Henry Clay and hang John C. Calhoun.

PROSPERITY BECOMES PANIC

Most of the nation had prospered during the last years of Jackson's administration. More money was available as a result of easy credit and the paper money printed by state banks. It was a time of inflation. A confident spirit was in the air. People freely spent money on luxury goods, most of which were foreign made. For example, imports of silk more than doubled between 1831 and 1836.

Jackson left office proud of the nation's prosperity. But it was a puffed-up prosperity. Like a balloon, it had little substance. Jackson's Specie Circular of 1836 was the pinprick that deflated it.

Soon after President Van Buren took office in 1837, a panic—an economic crisis—spread throughout the country. Worried by the Specie Circular, people began taking their paper money to the banks and demanding hard cash in exchange. Each bill was supposed to be worth a certain amount of gold or silver. The banks quickly exhausted their small supplies of gold and silver.

Paper money quickly lost its value. When the government tried to get back its money from the state banks, the banks could not

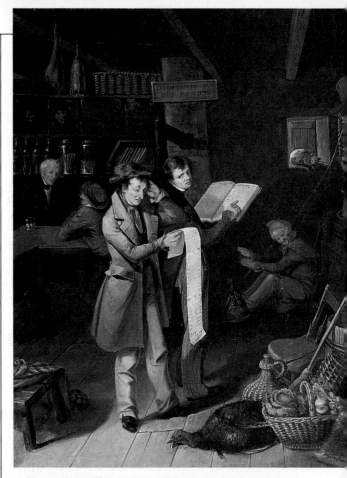

The prosperity of the early 1830s turned suddenly to panic and depression in 1837. Here a merchant wonders how he will pay a bill for unsold merchandise. **ECONOMICS** What caused the Panic of 1837?

pay. Banks failed like falling dominoes. The collapse of the nation's money system triggered the Panic of 1837. The Panic of 1837 was one of the first depressions—periods of economic hardship—in American history.

Because people no longer had money, manufacturers no longer had markets for their goods. Almost 90 percent of the nation's factories closed down within the year.

Workers, out of jobs, had no way of buying food or paying rent. In New York City workers gathered in front of City Hall to demand cheaper food. Urged on by a speaker, the crowd stormed a flour merchant. A newspaper described what happened:

Barrels of flour, by dozens, fifties and hundreds were tumbled into the street

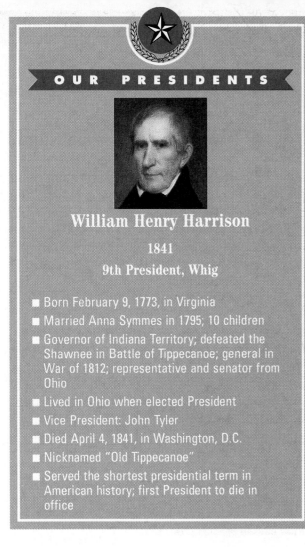

from the doors, and thrown . . . from the windows. . . .

Amidst the falling and bursting of the barrels and sacks of wheat, numbers of women were engaged . . . filling the boxes and baskets with which they were provided, and their aprons, with flour, and making off with it. . . .

Night had now closed upon the scene, but the work of destruction did not cease until strong bodies of police arrived, followed, soon afterward, by detachments of troops. . . .

The panic also spread to England. There, exporters of luxury goods could not collect money owed by Americans. The failure of the exporters spread to the cotton mills, which closed down. When English cotton mills closed, American planters no longer had a market for their cotton. Without money from cotton, they could not buy food from the West. Every section of the country suffered.

The depression was hardest on those who lived in the cities. In 1837 about 10 percent of the population lived in cities of more than 2,500 people. Farmers were hurt less because they could at least grow their own food. Future economic depressions would become increasingly painful as more of the population took factory jobs.

THE ELECTION OF 1840

In the late 1830s, Senators Henry Clay and Daniel Webster argued that the government needed to step in and help the economy through the difficult economic times. President Van Buren disagreed. He believed that the economy would improve if left alone. Interference by the federal government in the nation's economy was not only unwise, said Van Buren, it was unconstitutional. Van Buren argued that "the less government interferes with private pursuits the better for the general prosperity."

The hungry, the poor, and the unemployed did not care for Van Buren's theories. They wanted help. Many Americans blamed Van Buren for the Panic of 1837, though he had taken office only weeks before it started. Stories of expensive new furniture at the White House angered them even more.

The Whigs made use of this shift in public opinion in the election of 1840. They chose William Henry Harrison of Ohio to run for President and John Tyler of Virginia to run for Vice President. Harrison had commanded the army that defeated the Indians at Tippecanoe in 1811 (page 338). He had also fought

bravely in the War of 1812. The Whigs made the most of Harrison's military record and his nickname, "Old Tippecanoe." "Tippecanoe and Tyler too!" became their slogan.

In the election of 1840, image was much more important than issues. Harrison was the son of a Virginia plantation owner. Because he had settled on a farm in Ohio, however, the Whigs said Harrison was a true westerner. They used the log cabin and hard cider of the frontier as the symbols of the Harrison campaign. The Whigs accused Van Buren of wearing "corsets and silk stockings." In noisy parades and stirring rallies they shouted their slogans.

THE RISE AND FALL OF THE WHIG PARTY

Harrison won, the first member of the Whig Party to be elected President. He also became the first President to die in office. An elderly man, he had been worn out by the campaign. He died of pneumonia only one month after taking the oath of office.

"He plows his own ground, and feeds his own hogs," boasted a Whig campaign jingle about William Henry Harrison. These claims, as well as the log cabin used in Whig advertisements such as the one at left, presented Harrison as a rough-hewn man of the frontier. Harrison was, in fact, a wealthy easterner. Still, he and Tyler won the 1840 election. **HISTORY** How did Tyler become President?

John Tyler took his place. Tyler had been nominated for Vice President chiefly to win electoral votes in the South. Tyler had been a popular Virginia governor and senator, as well as a member of the House of Representatives. As President, however, he failed to get along either with Whig Party leaders or with Congress. These quarrels led the Whig Party to nominate Henry Clay instead of Tyler for the election of 1844. James K. Polk, a Democrat, won. The Whigs were back in power in 1849 when Zachary Taylor became President, but that was their last victory. In the 1850s the Whig Party disappeared from the American political scene. The Democratic Party continues to this day.

IAJ's ideas were good enough to continue 200 years

SECTION REVIEW

1. KEY TERMS panic, Panic of 1837, depression

2. PEOPLE Martin Van Buren, William Henry Harrison, John Tyler

3. COMPREHENSION What happened to the Republican Party in 1824? What new parties were later formed?

4. COMPREHENSION What methods did Harrison's supporters use to win the election of 1840?

5. CRITICAL THINKING How did Jackson's economic policies help cause the Panic of 1837?

CHAPTER 15 SUMMARY AND TIMELINE

1. Tensions between regions of the country led to disputes over the admission of new states, which the Missouri Compromise of 1820 temporarily resolved. These disputes led to the break-up of the old Republican Party and election of John Quincy Adams to the presidency in 1824. The election of Andrew Jackson as President in 1828 reflected the expansion of the democratic spirit in the United States.

2. Though several Indian groups resisted the Indian Removal Act, President Jackson used the army to enforce his policy of making American Indians relocate west of the Mississippi River.

3. South Carolina threatened to nullify the tariff laws and to secede from the Union if necessary, but a compromise tariff ended that threat. President Jackson battled with Congress over the Bank of the United States. He vetoed the renewal of the bank's charter, withdrew government funds from it, and deposited the money in state banks.

4. The end of easy credit led to the Panic of 1837, a period of high unemployment in the cities and bank failures all over the country. William Henry Harrison won the election of 1840, but he died after only one month in office. Vice President John Tyler became President.

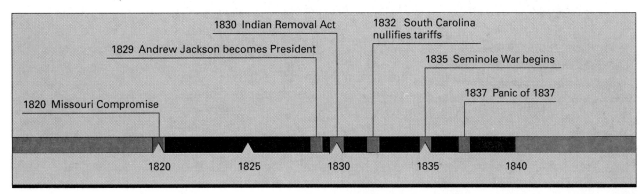

1820 Missouri Compromise
1829 Andrew Jackson becomes President
1830 Indian Removal Act
1832 South Carolina nullifies tariffs
1835 Seminole War begins
1837 Panic of 1837

1820   1825   1830   1835   1840

PLACES TO LOCATE

Match each of the letters on the map with the places that are listed below.

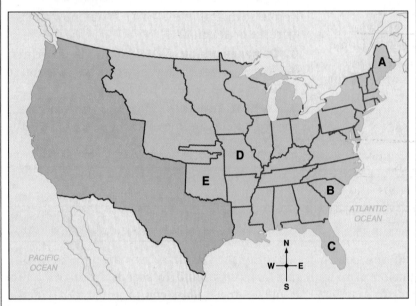

1. Florida
2. Indian Territory
3. Maine
4. Missouri
5. South Carolina

KEY TERMS

Use the following terms to complete the sentences.

credit
Panic of 1837
relocate
secede
sectionalism
Trail of Tears

1. In the 1820s the mood of Congress changed, and the spirit of nationalism gave way to ____.
2. The Cherokee Indians, forced to ____, traveled to Indian Territory on a journey now known as the ____.
3. South Carolina threatened to ____ over the issue of high tariffs.
4. The pet banks offered easy ____, fueling western land speculation.
5. Paper money lost its value and the country's money system collapsed, leading to the ____.

PEOPLE TO IDENTIFY

Identify the following people and tell why each was important.

1. John C. Calhoun
2. Henry Clay
3. Osceola
4. Sequoya
5. Daniel Webster

REVIEWING THE FACTS

1. What controversy did the Missouri Compromise resolve? How did it resolve that controversy?
2. What changes in the United States did Jackson's election signal?
3. What steps did the Cherokee take to become accepted by white society?
4. What arguments did the Cherokee make to the Supreme Court to counter Georgia's plan to take their lands? What was the Court's decision? How did President Jackson respond?
5. Why did the Northeast support government spending to improve transportation? Why did the South oppose tariffs?
6. How did Daniel Webster respond to Robert Hayne's argument that the states had the right to nullify federal laws?
7. What steps did Jackson take to destroy the Second Bank of the United States?
8. What policies did the Democratic Party of the 1830s support? What was the platform of the Whig Party?
9. How did the Specie Circular trigger the Panic of 1837?
10. What was the strategy of the Whigs in the election campaign of 1840?

PRACTICING YOUR SKILL

The political cartoon below comments on the election of 1824. Study the cartoon and answer the questions that follow.

1. What do the two steamships symbolize?
2. Which candidate appears to be ahead? What has happened to his chances of being elected? Who will end up winning?
3. Do you think that the cartoonist was pleased or disappointed by the outcome of the election of 1824? Explain your answer.

CITIZENSHIP

1. What are the advantages and disadvantages of the spoils system? Does this system still exist today?
2. During the 1830s and 1840s the major political parties were made up of a variety of groups who often had different political goals.

To what degree are our major political parties today made up of political factions?

CRITICAL THINKING SKILLS

1. **IDENTIFYING TRENDS** Why has Andrew Jackson sometimes been called "the maker of the modern presidency"?

2. **MAKING A VALUE JUDGMENT** Andrew Jackson's years as President are sometimes called the Age of Jackson. Is it possible today for one individual to stamp his or her image on an entire age in the same manner as Jackson? Who in the United States today might have such a profound impact?

PROJECTS AND ACTIVITIES

1. **ORGANIZING A CHART** Make a chart with two columns to show the arguments for and against the doctrine of nullification.

2. **MAKING A TIMELINE** Identify the amendments to the

Constitution concerned with the right to vote. Then create a timeline illustrating the expansion of that right.

3. **DRAWING A POLITICAL CARTOON** Review the Indian Removal Act of 1830 and draw a political cartoon representing your opinion of that law.

WRITING ABOUT TOPICS IN AMERICAN HISTORY

1. **CONNECTING WITH LITERATURE** A selection on the Trail of Tears by Elizabeth Sullivan appears on page 652. Read it and answer the questions. Then answer the following question: What other alternatives, besides forced relocation, might the United States have pursued to end conflicts between settlers and Indians?

2. **APPLYING THEMES: ECONOMIC DEVELOPMENT** Write an editorial expressing your opinion of Van Buren's response to the Panic of 1837.

Energized by newly arrived immigrants and by a variety of reform movements, American society during the mid-1800s became more diverse and more democratic.

16 Changes in American Life (1820–1860)

1 The Impact of Immigration

★ Section Focus

Key Terms   steerage ■ famine ■ tenement ■ nativist

Main Idea   In the mid-1800s millions of immigrants made new homes in cities and on the farms of the United States, leading to a wave of anti-immigrant feeling.

Objectives   As you read, look for answers to these questions:
1.   Why did immigration from Europe to the United States increase in the 1800s?
2.   What problems did German and Irish immigrants face in the United States?
3.   Why did many native-born Americans oppose immigration?

In the mid-1800s, the harbors of American cities were busy, crowded places. Outgoing ships were being loaded with lumber, tobacco, and cotton for export. Many of the incoming ships carried a different kind of cargo. On the lowest deck, far from fresh air and light, were hundreds of people. They spoke the languages of Europe or they spoke English with accents of the British Isles. The travelers carried all their belongings as they left the ships. Stepping on land, they looked around at the country that was to be their new home.

These people were part of a great wave of immigration. Between 1815 and 1860, 5 million immigrants arrived in the United States. Most of these immigrants came from northern European countries such as Ireland and Germany. About 40,000 came from China. These newcomers would enrich the country with their labor and cultures. The poet Walt Whitman described their impact on American

society: "Here is not merely a nation but a teeming nation of nations."

> "**H**ere is not merely a nation but a teeming nation of nations."
>
> —*Walt Whitman*

CHANGES IN IMMIGRATION

Immigration to America did not start in the 1800s. People from many different countries were among the first settlers of the colonies. Yet more than 100 years of English rule had led to a dominant English culture. By the time of the Revolution, most people spoke English, were members of a Protestant church, and followed the customs of England.

In the first decades after the birth of the United States, a steady trickle of immigrants

This picture shows immigrants to North America waiting to board ships at Cork, Ireland. **HISTORY** Why did so many immigrants travel in steerage, the lowest deck of the ship?

arrived. Some 25,000 came from France in the 1790s, fleeing the French Revolution. Most immigrants, however, were from England, Scotland, Wales, and Ireland.

This began to change in the 1800s, as Europe began to change. Advances in technology sparked rapid population growth. Land became overcrowded and opportunities shrank. Poor harvests caused hardships in some places. In addition, new political ideas swept through the continent, threatening the old order. Many people found themselves persecuted for their political and religious beliefs.

These problems led millions of Europeans to leave their homes and move to the United States. Many were attracted by advertisements from American employers who needed cheap labor. Others were persuaded to move by letters from immigrants who had left earlier. These immigrants described their new country in glowing terms. One Norwegian wrote:

Now for the first time am I able to breathe freely. . . . No one is persecuted here because of his religious faith. . . . Norway can no more be compared with America than a desolate waste with a garden in full bloom.

These happy letters ignored the hardships of getting to the United States. Immigrants traveled by ship, most often in steerage, the lowest deck. Hundreds were packed in this space for weeks at a time. The stench became so bad that harbor masters could smell these ships from miles away. Diseases spread rapidly. About 5 percent of the passengers never finished the miserable trip, dying along the way.

GERMANS IN AMERICA

One of the largest groups of immigrants came from Germany. Some fled after the failure of revolutions that had tried to make Germany more democratic. Others came after several years of poor harvests.

Unlike immigrants from the British Isles, these newcomers did not speak English. Many were educated, however, and came with money and skills. Some moved to the Midwest, traveling along the Erie Canal to the Great Lakes. Large German communities grew in Ohio, Indiana, Illinois, Iowa, and Wisconsin. Belleville, Illinois, for example, had a German mayor, German city councilors, and three German newspapers.

Among the Germans who came to the United States before 1860 was a large community of German Jews. Many moved west, becoming peddlers and storekeepers on the frontier. One of the most famous German Jewish immigrants was <u>Levi Strauss</u>, who came to the United States in 1847. He opened a business in San Francisco. His company pioneered the production of work clothes, including blue jeans.

Some Germans went south, to Missouri and Texas. New Braunfels (BRAWN–fuhlz), near San Antonio, was started by a group of German nobles. They bought land in order to sell small sections to Germans interested in

BIOGRAPHY

CARL SCHURZ (1829–1906) and **MARGARETHA MEYER SCHURZ (1833–1876)** were two of the most famous German-born immigrants. They arrived in the United States in 1852 after Carl, who had helped lead the German Revolution of 1848, had to flee when the revolution was suppressed. The Schurzes moved to Wisconsin and became active in politics. Carl was elected senator in 1869 and became Secretary of the Interior in 1887. Margaretha, who had been trained in Germany by the founder of the kindergarten system, started the first kindergarten in the United States in 1856.

immigrating to America. At first, disease, Indian attacks, and poor harvests killed many. New waves of German immigrants who landed on the Texas coast helped keep the settlement going. In 1853 a German festival was held in New Braunfels. The following year San Antonio hosted a German convention.

Many of the Germans in Texas had fled Germany because they supported greater equality there. In the United States they opposed slavery, which brought them into conflict with their English-speaking neighbors.

Germans differed from settlers in other ways as well. A German farmer in Missouri in 1835 described how his outlook was at odds with that of others on the frontier:

> The American farmer has no love for home, such as the German has. I am building a smokehouse, a kitchen, a milk-house . . . a stable for the horses and one for the cows. My American neighbors say that I am building a town. . . .

SCANDINAVIAN IMMIGRANTS

Another group of immigrants came from the Scandinavian countries of Sweden, Denmark, and Norway. Like Germans, they moved west. Used to long, cold winters, many settled in the north. A Swedish writer, Frederika Bremer, explained the attraction:

> What a glorious new Scandinavia might not Minnesota become. Here would the Swede find his clear romantic lakes. . . . The climate, the situation, the character of the scenery agrees with our people better than any other of the American states.

Life in their new country was far from a paradise, however. Most homes were small, crowded cabins. Fevers and other diseases were common. Farming in the harsh climate was difficult. Some new immigrants were tricked into buying land that did not exist. A

In this painting of an Illinois scene, hard-working Swedish farmers are shown sowing their crops. **GEOGRAPHY** Why did many Scandinavian immigrants move to the Upper Midwest?

deep religious faith and strong sense of community helped Scandinavian immigrants survive these tough times.

THE IRISH EXPERIENCE

In the 1840s Ireland was a poor country. Most people there were farmers, but few owned land. They grew wheat, which they used to pay rent on the land they farmed. For food, the Irish depended on potatoes. Some people lived on as little as a few potatoes and a cup of milk a day.

Then, starting in 1845, a disease struck the potato plants. Potatoes rotted in the fields, leading to **famine**. People throughout Ireland began to starve, and thousands died. A visiting Englishman noted that "the weekly returns of the dead were like the bulletin of a fierce campaign."

Thousands of poor Irish fled the country. More than a million came to the United States. Few could afford to move west. Most stayed in the cities where their boats had docked—such centers as New York, Boston, and Philadelphia.

The poor of Ireland were farmers with few other skills. In their new country, the Irish took what jobs they could get. They dug ca-nals, laid railroad tracks, and worked in the mills that were springing up in the Northeast. Irish women took in washing and sewing or worked as cooks and servants. These newcomers worked long days, six days a week, and were often paid less than a dollar a day. "Waterpower, steam power, and Irish power" run the United States, a newspaper declared in 1850. "The last works hardest of all."

The Irish usually lived crowded into shacks and **tenements**—apartment buildings designed to house large numbers of people as cheaply as possible. Few cities had decent sewer systems. Drinking water in the slums was often polluted. Deadly diseases spread quickly.

THE ROLE OF POLITICS AND THE CHURCH

To improve their situation, the Irish banded together. They formed aid societies to help the newest arrivals. Their knowledge of English and of the English political tradition attracted them to politics. Most joined the Democratic Party, which they considered the party of the ordinary person.

Some Irish quickly became local political leaders. In exchange for votes, these leaders

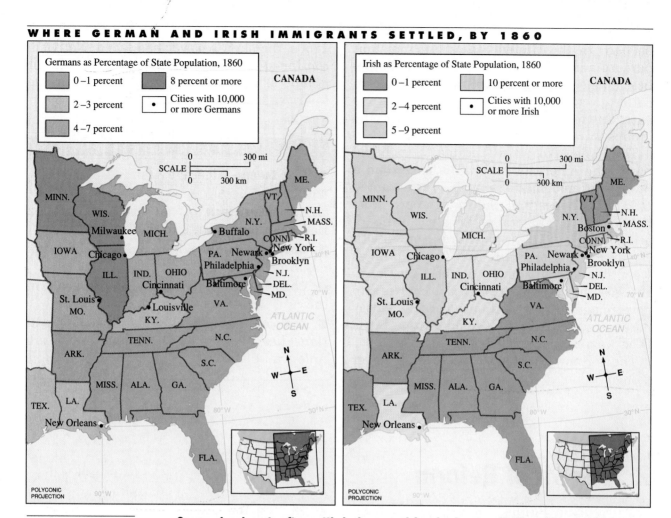

Germans as Percentage of State Population, 1860
- 0–1 percent
- 2–3 percent
- 4–7 percent
- 8 percent or more
- Cities with 10,000 or more Germans

Irish as Percentage of State Population, 1860
- 0–1 percent
- 2–4 percent
- 5–9 percent
- 10 percent or more
- Cities with 10,000 or more Irish

MAP SKILLS German immigrants often settled where good farmland was available, while most Irish clustered in the cities. Which cities had large numbers of Irish and German immigrants in 1860? CRITICAL THINKING Which region appeared to have the fewest immigrants? Why might that have been true?

helped residents with small favors—getting them jobs, finding them homes, paying for funerals, and so on.

Religion was an even more powerful force in Irish neighborhoods. Almost all the Irish immigrants of the 1850s were members of the Roman Catholic Church. The Church was part of home for them, giving charity and spiritual comfort to those in need. The Church also ran schools, where immigrant children were educated.

THE NATIVIST REACTION

The Irish, Germans, and other immigrants served as much-needed workers for the growing economy of the United States. Yet some native-born Americans saw these newcomers as a threat. These nativists worried that immigrants would take jobs from Americans. They saw the differences in customs and religion as proof that immigrants would never be "real" Americans.

Some people refused to hire immigrants, putting up signs such as "No Irish Need Apply." Others became violent. A convent school was burned in Boston, and mobs attacked churches. In cities such as New York and Boston, nativists formed secret societies. Members promised not to support any Catholics or immigrants running for public office.

One such group was the Supreme Order of the Star-Spangled Banner. Members had to be born in the United States of Protestant parents and could not be married to Catholics. Like other nativist groups, they took an oath to answer questions about the group with the reply, "I know nothing." Soon the groups were called the Know-Nothings.

The Know-Nothings became a political party, the American Party. The party had a number of undemocratic goals. They wanted to ban Catholics and the foreign-born from holding office. They called for a cut in immigration and a 21-year wait to become a citizen. With this program, the Know-Nothings were able to gain support on the East Coast. In 1854 they won control of Baltimore's city government. Know-Nothings became governors in several New England states. Some even won election to Congress.

The Know-Nothings, however, never gained strength in the West. By the late 1850s, the party's power had faded. Nativism continued—but so did immigration. Other groups of immigrants arrived, and continue to arrive today.

| SECTION REVIEW |

1. KEY TERMS steerage, famine, tenement, nativist

2. COMPREHENSION What factors attracted European immigrants to the United States?

3. COMPREHENSION Where did most Irish immigrants settle?

4. COMPREHENSION What were the goals of the American Party?

5. CRITICAL THINKING Why might some historians have said that the immigrants *were* American history?

2 A Spirit of Reform

Section Focus

Key Terms Second Great Awakening
■ lyceum ■ rehabilitate ■ temperance
■ utopia

Main Idea In the 1830s and 1840s a broad range of reform movements reflected the interest of Americans in improving society.

Objectives As you read, look for answers to these questions:
1. What role did religion play in the reform movements of the early 1800s?
2. What were the interests of the early labor movement?
3. What movements for social reform arose in the 1800s?

In 1801 Cane Ridge, Kentucky, was near the edge of the frontier. Yet in August more than 10,000 people gathered there, camped in the woods near a large clearing. Every day for a week these people would meet to hear sermons and sing religious songs. Many would leap up and cry out a new-found faith in God.

The camp meeting at Cane Ridge was part of the Second Great Awakening, a revival of religious faith in the early 1800s. All over the country, in large and small meetings, Americans listened to Baptist, Methodist, and Presbyterian preachers. They were told that every person could be saved. Christ would come again, the preachers said. First, Americans must root out evil and create a heaven on earth.

It was a message Americans took to heart. Full of confidence in their country, many thought they had a chance to make a perfect

Many reform movements trace their roots to the religious revivals of the early 1800s. Traveling preachers turned frontier camp meetings into emotionally charged religious experiences. **RELIGION** What impression does this picture give of a revival meeting?

society. Others looked at the changes brought by the Industrial Revolution and immigration, and worried about the future. The cities were growing more crowded, creating a whole new set of problems. Americans believed they needed to solve these problems, and religion gave them faith that they could.

From the Second Great Awakening came a spirit of reform. At first the reform took place within churches, with women taking a more active role. They established Sunday schools and supported newly founded missionary societies. By the 1830s and 1840s women were often leaders in the efforts to reform other parts of society.

A Better Work Place

One of the biggest changes taking place was in the way people worked. In earlier times, a worker learned a trade with the hope of becoming a master artisan. Artisans worked for themselves. In the factory system, workers did not learn a craft. They remained relatively unskilled, with little hope of ever becoming self-employed.

In addition, factory work was often noisy, boring, and unsafe. It was far different from the farm work many laborers had once known. Though farming was hard, workers were not cooped up for long hours. They were used to the freedom of working outside. One woman who worked in a New England textile mill recalled how hard it was to give up that freedom: "In sweet June weather I would lean far out of the window, and try not to hear the unceasing clash of sound inside."

By the 1830s workers had begun to organize. The young women who worked the mills in Lowell, Massachusetts, started the Factory Girls' Association. In 1836 the mill owner raised the rent of the boarding houses where these women lived. About 1,500 of them went on strike. Harriet Hanson, eleven years old, was working in the mill when she heard that workers were walking out. She recalled what happened when the workers in her area of the mill hesitated:

> I who began to think they would not go out, after all their talk, became impatient, and started on ahead. . . . I marched out, and was followed by the others. As I looked back at the long line that followed me, I was more proud than I have ever been since.

Sarah Bagley, another Lowell worker, became a leader of the movement for a ten-hour day. Other workers began to strike for higher wages. Male workers had also become voters, and so set up the Workingman's Party to win their goals. Then the Panic of 1837 hit (page 396). It caused so much unemployment that the young labor movement crumbled. It would not reappear for another generation.

Nevertheless, the early labor movement had achieved a few of its stated goals. Some health-and-safety laws were passed. In 1840 President Van Buren backed a ten-hour day for all public workers. By the 1850s private employers were following the government's example.

SCHOOL FOR ALL

An important goal for workers was education for their children. Americans had long valued schooling, believing that a democracy needed well-informed citizens. Yet, in the early 1800s, few American children were able to get a good education. New England schools had been neglected since the Revolutionary War. Buildings were run down, and teachers were poorly trained. Conditions were worse in the West. Families had to work so hard to make a living that there was little time or money left for schooling. In the South, education was often limited to the children of wealthy planters.

In many states, public schools required parents to pay part of the cost of their children's education. Poor children could attend only if their parents declared that they had

Public education had a unifying effect on the United States, even when provided in a one-room schoolhouse like this one in a painting by Winslow Homer. **CIVIC VALUES** Why is education important in a democracy?

The class of 1885 at Ohio's Oberlin College included one African American woman. Both men and women attended Oberlin. **CULTURAL PLURALISM** Why might women have been refused the same educational opportunities as men?

no money to give the school. Most poor people kept their children out of school rather than suffer that shame.

During the 1830s Americans began to demand better public education for their children. Massachusetts set up a State Board of Education, the first in the country. Its head was Horace Mann, a leader in the fight for free elementary schools.

Mann called free public education "the great equalizer," saying that it united the rich and the poor. Leaders in other states joined Mann in working for public education. By 1850 elementary schools supported by public taxes were common in the North.

CHANGES IN HIGHER EDUCATION

During this time of change, more young people gained the chance to attend high school and college. Boston established the first public high school in 1821. Other northern cities soon followed its example. Some states founded universities and provided them with public funds.

Many new colleges were founded by churches, particularly in the states carved from the Northwest Territory. They included Northwestern, Antioch, Oberlin, and Notre Dame. Private colleges began to offer a wider range of subjects, adding law, medicine, and business training.

Young women were barred from public high schools and most colleges. Some attended private high schools known as seminaries. Wesleyan College, the first American women's college, opened in Macon, Georgia, in 1836. The following year another women's college, Mount Holyoke, opened in Massachusetts. Ohio's Oberlin College was unusual in its decision to accept women as well as men. For most women, however, higher education would remain out of reach until the 1880s.

EDUCATION FOR AFRICAN AMERICANS

In northern states, African American families were required to pay taxes to support public schools. Their children, however, were often barred from those schools. A few elementary schools for African Americans were opened in northern cities and in Washington, D.C. Most free black children, however, were educated at home or not at all. In slave states, there were no schools for slave children. Teaching a slave to read had been illegal since Nat Turner's Rebellion (page 371).

Few colleges would accept African Americans. Those colleges that did often took only one or two black students at a time. College-educated blacks often became teachers, ministers, and other leaders of the community. One of the first black college graduates was John Russwurm, who finished his studies at Bowdoin College in Maine in 1826. Russwurm was one of the founders of the first African American newspaper in the United States.

A FORUM FOR REFORM

The growth of public schools led to a growth in the number of people who could read. At the same time, technology opened up the choice of reading material. Newspapers had once been expensive and available only to the few. In the 1830s cheaper newsprint and the invention of the steam-driven press brought the price down to a penny. These "penny papers" made news and information available to the average American. By 1833 there were three times as many newspapers in the United States as in England.

Hundreds of new magazines also appeared. One such magazine was *Godey's Lady's Book.* Edited by Sarah Hale, *Godey's Lady's Book* set standards of conduct, manners, and dress for American women. The magazine also advanced the new notion that there was a woman's sphere and a man's sphere, equally important but different. A woman's sphere was the home and the world of "human ties." A man's sphere was politics and the business of earning a living.

The reform age also stressed adult learning. Organizations called lyceums (ly–SEE–uhms) sponsored lectures by celebrities and reformers. Without the lyceums, none of the reform movements could have gathered the strength they did.

CARING FOR THE NEEDY

In 1841 Dorothea Dix, daughter of a wealthy Boston family, was teaching Sunday school at a women's prison. She discovered a group of insane women being kept in an unheated part of the prison. Upset by this cruel treatment, Dix began visiting jails and poorhouses. She learned that in many cases the mentally ill were kept "in cages, closets, cellars, stalls, pens! Chained naked, beaten with rods and lashed into obedience!"

Dix appealed to states to improve the care of the mentally ill. Her tireless efforts led to the founding of 32 hospitals. She became one of the best-known and most successful reformers in the country.

Dix was also a leader in the call for prison reform. Prisons in those days were not well organized. Long-time criminals, debtors, and children who had committed crimes were all housed together.

Reformers called attention to these conditions. They demanded that special jails be set up for children. They wanted those prisons to train young offenders so that they could get

BIOGRAPHY

DOROTHEA DIX (1802–1887) was a Massachusetts teacher. Shocked by the conditions in which the mentally ill and prisoners were kept, she began a lifelong crusade for better treatment for them. Her work led to the founding or improvement of 32 hospitals in 15 states. One of these, Harrisburg State Hospital, appears in her portrait.

These students at the Perkins Institute for the Blind are reading geography textbooks in Braille. The school also taught trades. **ETHICS** How might better treatment of the disabled improve society as a whole?

jobs when released. Reformers also called for more humane prisons for adults. New prisons were built with the goal of **rehabilitating** prisoners—helping them return to normal, useful lives.

Reformers also worked to improve conditions for disabled people. Samuel G. Howe founded a school that became the Perkins Institute for the Blind, in Boston. There Howe trained blind people to earn their living and to lead independent lives. Another reformer, Thomas H. Gallaudet (gal–uh–DET) worked with the deaf. In 1817 he started the first American school for deaf children.

The Temperance Movement

Hard drinking was common and accepted in the United States in the early 1800s. Some workers spent most of their wages on rum

and beer, leaving their families with little on which to live. Children could buy alcohol as easily as adults.

Reformers blamed alcohol for increasing the misery of the life of the poor. They called for **temperance**—giving up drinking alcoholic beverages. Well organized, the temperance movement sent speakers around the country. Preaching their message with fervor, the speakers urged people to sign pledges promising never to drink alcohol. By 1843, a total of 500,000 pledges had been signed.

Temperance societies had political success as well. Maine passed a law banning the sale of liquor in 1846, and twelve other states soon followed. Many people opposed these laws, however, and most of them were repealed. The movement to ban alcohol nevertheless remained a powerful force.

Utopian Societies

Most of the reform movements were practical attempts to make a better world by improving society. Other reformers believed a whole new society was needed. They tried to set up ideal communities, called **utopias**.

Religious principles were at the root of some utopian communities, such as those started by the Shakers. The founder of the Shakers, Ann Lee, came to the United States from England in 1774. She preached that all people were equal and should share in all aspects of life. In the next decades, Shakers set up communities in New York, New England, and on the frontier.

Life in these communities followed very strict schedules. Men and women lived apart, eating at different tables and sleeping in separate dormitories. They worked hard, farming and making simple and useful furniture. On Sunday they worshipped, expressing deep religious emotions. A witness described the services as filled with trembling, shaking, dancing, and singing.

The Shakers did not believe in marriage or bearing children. To grow, they relied on converts. By the mid-1800s thousands had joined their communities. Over time, however, the number of converts declined. Today only a handful of Shakers remain.

Economic reform was behind the community founded by Robert Owen, a successful British manufacturer. Owen was unhappy with the low wages and poor living conditions of factory workers. In 1825 he came to the United States and bought the land, houses, and factories of a town called Harmony, in Indiana. Renaming it New Harmony, he invited people to share equally in owning the property and working in the factories. Instead of wages, each family earned goods and services from the common store.

Owen's experiment failed. Workers grumbled that the organization was unfair. Though some factories made money, others were unsuccessful. In 1827 Owen dissolved the community.

Brook Farm, started in Massachusetts in 1841, was another attempt to create a new and better society. Members rejected city life, which they felt was based on competition and greed. They valued equality and personal responsibility. One of the most famous members was the writer Nathaniel Hawthorne. At the height of its popularity, about 100 people lived and worked at Brook Farm. Yet, like other utopias, the social experiment at Brook Farm was unsuccessful. The community broke up in 1847.

SECTION REVIEW

1. KEY TERMS Second Great Awakening, lyceum, rehabilitate, temperance, utopia

2. PEOPLE AND PLACES Sarah Bagley, Horace Mann, Sarah Hale, Dorothea Dix, Thomas Gallaudet, New Harmony, Brook Farm

3. COMPREHENSION How was the labor movement a response to problems created by the Industrial Revolution?

4. COMPREHENSION How were most African American children educated in the early 1800s?

5. CRITICAL THINKING Why might women have played a leading role in the reform movements of the early 1800s?

3 The Call for Equality

Section Focus

Key Terms   caucus ■ abolitionist ■ Underground Railroad ■ suffrage

Main Idea   The spread of democracy to almost all white men led to a call for freedom for slaves and equality for women.

Objectives   As you read, look for answers to these questions:
1. How did democracy expand in the 1800s?
2. How did abolitionism develop?
3. What was the origin of the movement for women's rights?

In 1831 a young Frenchman stepped off a boat onto United States soil. The Frenchman, Alexis de Tocqueville, (tohk–VEEL) had been sent to study United States prisons. For one year he traveled all over the country, noting what he saw.

Though he visited jails, Tocqueville was much more interested in the political life of the country. He marveled at the deep faith Americans had in their democracy. Visiting the West, he noted how the hardships of survival made each individual count. He saw that on the frontier, ability was more important than family background. "The great advantage of the Americans," he later wrote, "is . . . that they are born equal instead of becoming so."

After returning to France, Tocqueville wrote a book about his experiences, called *Democracy in America*. In it, he linked Americans' belief in equality with the success of their democracy. Tocqueville noted:

> Although the revolution that is taking place in the social condition, laws, ideas, and feelings of men is still far from coming to an end, yet its results are already incomparably greater than anything which has taken place in the world before.

EXPANDING DEMOCRACY

When Tocqueville arrived in the United States, most white men could vote. Almost all states had changed earlier laws restricting the vote to property owners.

States also passed laws allowing voters more control of the government. For example, state governors were once chosen by the legislature. In the 1830s and 1840s, laws were changed to allow voters to choose the governor in a direct election. Also, certain government officials who had once been appointed were now elected.

Until the 1830s, each political party chose its candidate in a closed caucus—a meeting of important party members. Ordinary people had little say in their political parties. In 1831 and 1832, however, the major parties held national conventions to choose candidates. Party members in each state elected delegates to represent them at the convention. These delegates then chose the party candidates for President and Vice President. Conventions gave ordinary people a stronger voice in the party's nominations.

EQUALITY VERSUS SLAVERY

African Americans were not included in the political life of the country. Almost all still worked as slaves in the South. Increasing numbers of Americans, mostly in the North, thought that slavery was wrong. They believed it went against Christianity and against the basic principles of the country.

A group of reformers called abolitionists sought to abolish, or put an end to, slavery. William Lloyd Garrison was perhaps the best-known of these abolitionists. Son of a

African Americans escaping slavery in the South stop at an Indiana farmhouse in this 1850s painting by Charles T. Weber. ETHICS Why might white Americans have helped slaves escape to freedom?

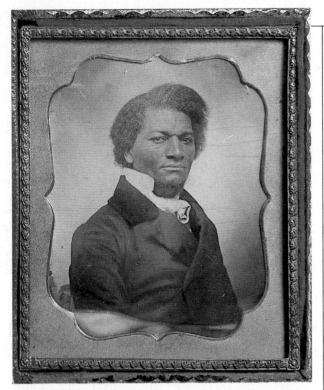

As a slave, Frederick Douglass secretly taught himself to read and write. He believed that education was the first step toward freedom. **CIVIC VALUES** Why might slaveowners have wanted to prevent slaves from being able to read and write?

New England sea captain, Garrison was working as a writer and printer in Boston when he met Benjamin Lundy. For years Lundy had preached against slavery. Lundy thought that slaves should be freed and then sent back to Africa to set up their own colony. Lundy invited Garrison to work on his newspaper in Baltimore.

> "**I** am in earnest—I will not retreat a single inch—*and I will be heard.*"
>
> —*William Lloyd Garrison*

Once in Baltimore, Garrison decided that the real issue was not a colony in Africa but the freeing of all slaves—*now*. Garrison and Lundy split up. Garrison returned to Boston to start his own paper. On January 1, 1831, he published the first issue of *The Liberator.*

In it he thundered, "I am in earnest—I will not retreat a single inch—*and I will be heard.*" For the next three decades Garrison's paper was a bugle call for freedom.

Many of the other leaders of the abolitionist movement were free blacks who had escaped from slavery. Frederick Douglass was one such leader. Born into slavery in Maryland, Douglass fled to Massachusetts when he was a young man. He went to an antislavery meeting there, speaking about what freedom meant to him. Douglass so impressed the audience that he was hired to lecture about his experience as a slave. A powerful speaker, Douglass also attacked the injustices faced by free blacks. He started a newspaper, *The North Star.* In later life, Douglass served as the United States' representative to Haiti.

Sojourner Truth was among the first African American women to speak publicly against slavery. Originally named Isabella Baumfree, she was born a slave in New York. She gained her freedom after New York abolished slavery in 1827. She changed her name, vowing to tell the truth about slavery. Traveling widely through the North, Sojourner Truth was a tireless crusader for justice.

Though the antislavery movement was strongest in the North, there were some southern abolitionists. Sarah and Angelina Grimké were raised on a South Carolina plantation. There the Grimké sisters saw clearly the contradictions between slavery and Christianity. Moving north, they joined the Quakers and became active members in the American Anti-Slavery Society. They wrote appeals to southern women to act against slavery. They spoke against slavery at lyceums and thus became the first "respectable" women to speak in public. They won over thousands of converts to the abolitionist cause.

THE UNDERGROUND RAILROAD

People who opposed slavery joined local antislavery societies. By 1840, more than 2,000 such societies stretched across the North.

These societies had a membership which included both blacks and whites.

For many, merely joining a group or listening to speeches against slavery was not enough. These people took action by helping slaves escape to freedom. They formed an informal system, called the Underground Railroad, that moved runaway slaves north. Traveling the Underground Railroad, the former slaves moved at night and stayed during the day in hiding places called *stations*. The people who led the runaways to freedom were known as *conductors*.

The most famous conductor was a slave who had escaped to freedom herself, Harriet Tubman. Tubman risked her life and freedom at least nineteen times by returning to the South to help others escape. Her efforts helped more than 300 slaves gain freedom.

THE CALL FOR WOMEN'S RIGHTS

In 1840 leaders of the antislavery movement gathered in London, England. Among the Americans attending were Lucretia Mott, Elizabeth Cady Stanton, and several other women. These women had been active in the struggle to end slavery and had much to say about their work. Yet when they tried to take part in the meeting, they found themselves silenced. Men angrily claimed that it was not a woman's place to speak in public. They voted not to allow the women delegates to play a role in the meeting. Instead, the women were forced to sit behind a heavy curtain.

The outlook of those men was not unusual for the time. Many people believed that women should not play a role in public life. In the 1800s women had few legal or political rights. Women could not vote, sit on juries, or hold public office. Many laws treated women—especially married women—as children. In most states, a husband controlled any property his wife inherited and any wages she earned. A husband could also punish his wife, as long as he did not seriously harm her.

Single women had greater freedom. They had more control over their own lives and could manage their own property.

Elizabeth Cady Stanton (left) and Susan B. Anthony (right) were two important leaders of the early struggle for women's rights. **CIVIC VALUES** Anthony once wrote "Cautious, careful people . . . never can bring about a reform." Do you agree? Why or why not?

Mott, Stanton, and the Grimké sisters believed the laws limiting women's rights were unfair. In Sarah Grimké's words, "All I ask our brethren is that they will take their heels from our necks and permit us to stand upright on that ground which God designed us to occupy."

Reformers who had called for equality for African Americans now began to urge equality for women as well. Lucy Stone was one of those to speak on women's rights in churches and at public meetings. A small woman who weighed barely 100 pounds, Stone was sometimes attacked during her speeches. At different times, she was hit by a book, drenched with water, and assaulted by a mob. Yet she continued to argue for women's rights.

THE SENECA FALLS CONVENTION

In 1848 Lucretia Mott and Elizabeth Cady Stanton called for a meeting at Seneca Falls, New York. Some 100 men and women gathered to discuss women's rights. Stanton delivered a speech, "Declaration of Sentiments." Modeled on the Declaration of Independence, the speech declared that "all men and women are created equal." The convention delegates

The Seneca Falls Declaration of Sentiments (1848)

For her opening address at the Seneca Falls Convention, Elizabeth Cady Stanton prepared a "Declaration of Sentiments." She modeled this appeal for women's rights on the Declaration of Independence.

When in the course of human events, it becomes necessary for one portion of the family of man to assume among the people of the earth a position different from that which they have hitherto occupied, but one to which the laws of nature and nature's God entitle them, a decent respect to the opinion of mankind requires that they should declare the causes that impel them to such a course.

We hold these truths to be self-evident: that all men and women are created equal; that they are endowed by their Creator with certain inalienable rights . . . that to secure these rights governments are instituted, deriving their just powers from the consent of the governed. . . .

The history of mankind is a history of repeated injuries and usurpations on the part of man toward woman, having in direct object the establishment of an absolute tyranny over her. . . .

Now, in view of not allowing one half the people of this country to vote, of their social and religious degradation . . . and because women do feel themselves aggrieved, oppressed, and fraudulently deprived of their most sacred rights, we insist that they have immediate admission to all the rights and privileges which belong to them as citizens of the United States.

In entering upon the great work before us, we anticipate mistaken ideas, misrepresentations, and ridicule; but we shall make every effort within our power to secure our object.

From E. C. Stanton, S. B. Anthony, and M. J. Gage, eds., *The History of Woman Suffrage,* Vol. I, p. 70.

ANALYZING HISTORICAL DOCUMENTS

1. What are some of Elizabeth Cady Stanton's goals for women?

2. What arguments does Stanton make in favor of women's rights? Do you agree or disagree? Why?

3. Why did Stanton choose to model the Seneca Falls Declaration on the Declaration of Independence?

voted their approval of this declaration. They went on to demand equality for women at work, school, church, and before the law. They also called for women's suffrage—the right to vote.

Many people found the idea of women's rights ridiculous. At a meeting in Ohio, a minister suggested that women were weak and helpless. Therefore, he said, women should not be allowed to vote. Sojourner Truth, who had spoken so well against slavery, spoke out for women:

That man over there says women need to be helped into carriages and lifted over ditches, and to have the best place everywhere. Nobody ever helps me into carriages or over puddles, or gives me the best place. And ain't I a woman? Look at my arm! I have ploughed and planted and gathered into barns. . . . And ain't I a woman? I could work as much and eat as much as a man—when I could get it—and bear the lash as well! And ain't I a woman? . . . I have borne thirteen children, and seen most of them sold off into slavery, and when I cried out with my mother's grief, none but Jesus heard me! And ain't I a woman?

Women, like those shown here, voted in New Jersey until the practice was outlawed in 1807.
CONSTITUTIONAL HERITAGE In the 1800s, what did the Constitution say about women's right to vote?

In the 1850s many national women's rights conventions took place. Among those who joined the movement was Susan B. Anthony. A Quaker, Anthony had been active in the temperance and antislavery movements. Anthony, a skilled organizer, soon became the most influential leader in the suffrage movement. She also worked to secure equal pay for women teachers and the right of women to control their property. Anthony even tried to vote in the presidential elections of 1872—and was arrested and fined for breaking the law.

The reform movement that began at Seneca Falls did help women gain some ground. Progress, however, was slow. A few states gave married women control over their property and earnings. Many women also made gains from increasing educational opportunities. Still, women were denied many rights—including the right to vote—for years to come.

SECTION REVIEW

1. KEY TERMS caucus, abolitionist, Underground Railroad, suffrage

2. PEOPLE AND PLACES William Lloyd Garrison, Baltimore, Frederick Douglass, Sojourner Truth, Sarah and Angelina Grimké, Harriet Tubman, Elizabeth Cady Stanton, Seneca Falls, Susan B. Anthony

3. COMPREHENSION By what means did abolitionists seek to influence public opinion?

4. COMPREHENSION What was the relationship between the abolitionist movement and the women's rights movement?

5. CRITICAL THINKING Some of the abolitionists thought that women should have waited until slavery had been abolished before starting the movement for women's rights. Why might they have thought that way? Do you agree with them? Explain your answer.

An essay is a short composition on a single subject, usually giving the writer's personal view of that subject. An essay consists of three parts: the introduction, the body, and the conclusion. Each part is made up of one or more paragraphs. Study the diagram on this page as you read the following guidelines for writing an essay.

The Parts of an Essay

An essay begins with an **introduction**. The introduction has two main purposes. First, it should interest people in reading the whole essay. Second, it should state the general subject of the essay and the author's particular view or opinion on the subject. The rest of the essay is developed to support this viewpoint or opinion.

The **body** of the essay consists of one or more development paragraphs. These paragraphs present arguments and evidence—facts and examples—that support the specific point or opinion in the introduction. For example, suppose an abolitionist were writing an essay in support of freeing all slaves. One argument for abolition might be that the Declaration of Independence declares "All men are created equal" and slavery denies equality.

Another way to support an opinion is to present an opposing viewpoint and then use evidence to disprove it. Here is an example of such a tactic, using the same essay about the antislavery movement:

Those who support slavery say that freeing slaves would destroy the economy of the South. Nothing could be further from the truth. Slavery in the South has led people there to make almost all their money from selling cotton. If cotton prices go down, the whole region will suffer. In the North, free workers produce many different kinds of goods. That protects the economy against a drop in prices for any one product.

PLAN FOR AN ESSAY

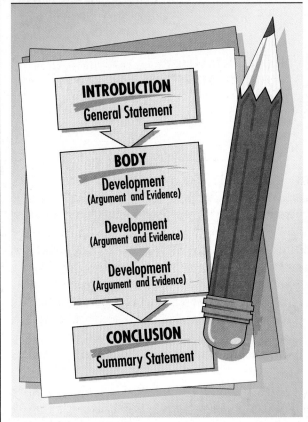

Remember that each paragraph in an essay should be linked to the next paragraph by a **transition**. A transition is a sentence that relates one idea to the next. An essay should end with a **conclusion** that, in one paragraph, restates and supports the writer's opinion.

Practicing Your Skill

Now write your own essay. Choose between these subjects:

1. Nominating conventions versus caucuses
2. The Underground Railroad
3. Women's rights

When you have enough information to begin writing, organize it into an outline. Then write your essay, using the guidelines. When you have finished the first draft, revise your essay. Finally, check for grammar and spelling errors.

4 A New American Culture

Section Focus

Key Terms   transcendentalism ■ passive resistance

Main Idea   A new pride in their country spurred American writers and artists to create works reflecting American culture and concerns.

Objectives   As you read, look for answers to these questions:
1.   What was the inspiration for the styles and subjects of American writers and artists before the 1820s?
2.   Who were some leading New England writers in the mid-1800s?
3.   How did painters change their style to reflect new attitudes toward the nation?

In 1818 a critic wrote an article on American culture in a British magazine. The critic, Sydney Smith, concluded that there was none. Americans were too busy clearing land and building settlements to write books or create art, Smith wrote. After all, he added:

> In the four corners of the globe, who reads an American book? Or goes to an American play? Or looks at an American picture or statue?

Smith's article angered Americans. Still, they could not argue with it. Though the United States had writers and artists in those years, most looked to Europe for ideas for their work. They saw their own country as rude and backward. The only way to produce great work, they thought, was to copy European styles and subjects.

The spirit of democracy and equality that swept through the country in the mid-1800s changed that attitude. American artists and

This painting, *The Return of Rip Van Winkle*, illustrates one of the most famous stories of early American literature. Written by Washington Irving, the story describes a man who falls asleep during colonial times and wakes up twenty years later, after the Revolution has been won. CULTURE What symbols of American independence can you find in this picture?

painters began to take pride in their country and its unique way of life. American history and scenery became subjects of their work. These books and paintings are still respected today.

EARLY AMERICAN LITERATURE

In the first decades after the Revolution, American writers borrowed English styles. They usually limited their writings to formal essays, such as *The Federalist* (page 246). American fiction developed slowly. Eager readers had to wait for new novels to arrive from England.

The first truly "American" writer of fiction was Washington Irving. He was also the first to be admired outside the United States. Irving was from New York and wrote about the Dutch-English heritage of his state. He first became popular in 1809 with a spoof of New York history and politics known as *Knickerbocker's History of New York.* Eleven years later, when he published a book of short stories including "Rip Van Winkle" and "The Legend of Sleepy Hollow," his fame was assured.

James Fenimore Cooper went even further toward creating truly American literature. In *The Leatherstocking Tales,* a collection of five novels, he wrote about a frontier character named Natty Bumppo. These books were published between 1823 and 1841. In them, Cooper portrayed American Indians as noble and showed the ways settlers misused the wilderness.

Edgar Allan Poe, one of the greatest of the early American writers, edited magazines and wrote poems, short stories, and mysteries. His horror stories continue to terrify readers. Poe's series of stories about a French private detective made him the father of the modern detective story.

NEW ENGLAND AUTHORS

By the 1840s, American writers were taking pride in their country's culture. They were moving to produce a uniquely American philosophy and style. The man who led that movement was Ralph Waldo Emerson. Born in Boston and educated at Harvard, Emerson was a minister for several years. In 1832 he resigned, and he spent the rest of his life lecturing and writing.

Emerson's message was based on Jacksonian ideals and the realities of American life. He taught that it was important for people to truly understand themselves. Americans needed to be self-reliant to survive in the new cities and on the frontier, he believed. In a speech made in 1837, Emerson urged American scholars to free themselves from their European roots and develop their own way of thinking. Emerson's ideas became part of a new, American philosophy which became known as **transcendentalism**.

This philosophy attracted many young writers and thinkers. They made New Eng-

This sketch of Henry David Thoreau's cabin by Walden Pond was drawn by his sister. It appeared in the 1854 edition of *Walden,* his book about life in the woods. NATIONAL IDENTITY Why might an American have been one of the first to write about protecting the environment?

MARGARET FULLER (1810–1850), a famous journalist and author, was one of the earliest feminists in the United States. She traveled to Europe in 1848 for the New York Tribune, serving as America's first woman foreign correspondent. There, she and her husband participated in the Italian revolution. She drowned when her ship back to America sank off the coast of New York.

land a center for American literature. Many were involved in the utopian community at Brook Farm. Nathaniel Hawthorne, who joined Brook Farm in 1841, wrote powerful novels about spiritual conflict. The most famous of these, *The Scarlet Letter,* was set in Puritan Massachusetts.

American history was an important theme in the work of a New England poet, Henry Wadsworth Longfellow. Another Massachusetts poet, John Greenleaf Whittier, wrote celebrations of country life. He also used his poetry to attack slavery.

POLITICS AND LITERATURE

One of the most original thinkers of the time was Henry David Thoreau (THOR–oh), a man who took strong political stands. A student of Emerson's, Thoreau believed in simplicity and in living in harmony with nature. In 1845 Thoreau moved to the quiet shores of Walden Pond, in the woods near Concord, Massachusetts. He explained why:

> I went to the woods because I wished to live deliberately, to front only the essential facts of life, and see if I could not learn what it had to teach, and not, when I came to die, discover that I had not lived.

For two years Thoreau lived alone, writing about his life and the nature around him. The book of these writings, *Walden,* has influenced many environmentalists.

Perhaps Thoreau's most powerful message was contained in his essay "Civil Disobedience." In it, he said that people should not obey laws they consider unjust. They should not protest with violence, he wrote, but by peacefully refusing to obey. Thoreau practiced what he preached. Rather than pay taxes to support the Mexican War (Chapter 18), Thoreau went to jail. This practice of passive resistance influenced future world leaders such as Mohandas K. Gandhi in India and Martin Luther King, Jr., in the United States.

> "**W**e would have every . . . barrier thrown down. We would have every path laid open to Woman as freely as to Man."
>
> —*Margaret Fuller*

Margaret Fuller was another New England writer whose work touched on political themes. Her cause was women's rights. Fuller was a friend of Emerson's and edited a literary magazine, *The Dial*. She published a best-selling book, *Women in the Nineteenth Century,* which angered many. To others, the book was a rallying cry. "We would have every . . . barrier thrown down," she wrote. "We would have every path laid open to Woman as freely as to Man."

1820	First antislavery magazine, *The Emancipator,* published in Tennessee.
1824	First black woman admitted to a convent in Loretto, Kentucky.
1837	First magazine for the blind is published in Philadelphia.
1847	Michigan abolishes capital punishment.
1849	Elizabeth Blackwell, first woman doctor of medicine, graduates from Geneva Medical College of Western New York.
1852	Elisha Graves Otis invents the safety elevator.
1866	Y.W.C.A. organized.

Fuller, like so many other literary figures of the time, lived near Emerson. Two of the most original writers of the 1850s, however, were not part of the New England scene. Herman Melville lived in New York. Having been a sailor as a young man, he once wrote, "A whale-ship was my Yale College and my Harvard." Melville drew on that experience in his books. *Moby-Dick, or The Whale,* published in 1851, is considered by many to be one of the greatest American novels of all time.

Walt Whitman, a New York poet, wanted to create a special literature that would reflect the character of the country. His collection of poems, *Leaves of Grass,* expresses his faith in democracy and in the young American nation. In his introduction he wrote, "The United States themselves are essentially the greatest poem."

THE VISUAL ARTS

Before the 1800s most American painters tried to make their art look European. Great artists such as John Singleton Copley and Benjamin West painted portraits of famous leaders and the wealthy. Their paintings of great, heroic scenes ignored American scenery and the lives of ordinary people.

Around 1825 Thomas Cole began painting landscapes in a simple, direct style. Cole became the leader of a group of American artists who often painted the Hudson River valley in New York state. Called the Hudson River School, this group of painters mainly drew quiet scenes of natural beauty.

George Caleb Bingham's pictures, on the other hand, reflected the energy of life on the frontier. He painted scenes of the Mississippi Valley. Other American artists began painting landscapes of the western plains and mountains.

John James Audubon used his talents to detail the birds and animals of America. Raised

John James Audubon was famous for his paintings of American birds in their natural setting, such as this one of a pelican. **CULTURE** Name other important American artists of the 1800s.

in France, Audubon moved to the United States at the age of eighteen. He worked as a merchant, lost all his money, and went to jail for debt in 1819. When he got out, he decided to devote himself to art. Audubon was fascinated by the birds of his adopted country and spent every free moment sketching them. Unlike the naturalists of his time, Audubon did not draw the birds stiffly sitting. Instead, he captured them in flight or movement, giving nature a truly natural feel.

Unable to find a publisher interested in his work, Audubon went to Britain in 1826. People there recognized his genius and produced his *Birds of America*. These engravings, along with his drawings and paintings, remain American masterpieces.

SECTION REVIEW

1. KEY TERMS transcendentalism, passive resistance

2. PEOPLE AND PLACES Edgar Allan Poe, Ralph Waldo Emerson, Henry David Thoreau, Walden Pond, Margaret Fuller, Walt Whitman, Hudson River, John James Audubon

3. COMPREHENSION Why did early American writers follow European styles?

4. COMPREHENSION How did Audubon's paintings of birds differ from paintings by other naturalists?

5. CRITICAL THINKING Why are Thoreau's ideas still powerful today?

CHAPTER 16 SUMMARY AND TIMELINE

1. In the mid-1800s famine and political and economic changes in Europe sent millions of immigrants to the farms and cities of the United States. In response, some native-born Americans organized groups that opposed immigration.

2. The Second Great Awakening began an era of reform that flourished in the 1830s and 1840s. Reformers pushed for improvements for the labor force, free public education, better care for the mentally ill and disabled, rehabilitation for prisoners, and temperance.

3. Many states ended property requirements for voters and gave more people a say in government. The abolitionist movement grew, calling for an end to slavery, and the Underground Railroad was set up to help slaves escape to freedom. Women involved in the abolitionist movement began to question their own lack of rights. At the Seneca Falls Convention they called for women's suffrage.

4. The new spirit of democracy and pride in their country led American artists and writers to turn away from European styles and subjects and present scenes and stories of American life. These artists and writers produced works of international and lasting significance.

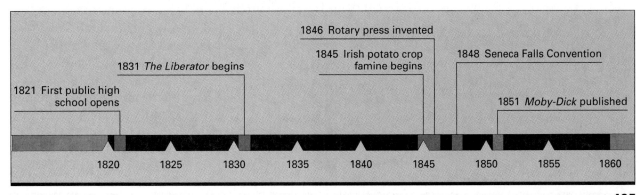

1846 Rotary press invented

1845 Irish potato crop famine begins

1848 Seneca Falls Convention

1831 *The Liberator* begins

1821 First public high school opens

1851 *Moby-Dick* published

1820   1825   1830   1835   1840   1845   1850   1855   1860

PLACES TO LOCATE

Match each of the letters on the map with the places that are listed below.

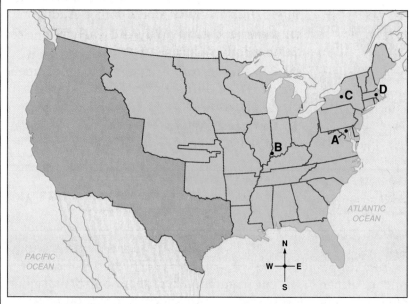

1. Baltimore
2. Brook Farm
3. New Harmony
4. Seneca Falls

KEY TERMS

Use the following terms to complete the sentences.

nativists
steerage
suffrage
transcendentalism
utopia

1. Most immigrants traveled on ships in ____, the lowest deck of the ship.
2. ____ opposed immigration.
3. An ideal community is a ____.
4. Susan B. Anthony worked to secure ____ for women.
5. The philosophy of Ralph Waldo Emerson is called ____.

PEOPLE TO IDENTIFY

Match each of the following people with the correct description.

Margaret Fuller
William Lloyd Garrison
Horace Mann
Sojourner Truth
Harriet Tubman

1. Leader of the movement for free public education.
2. Conductor of the Underground Railroad.
3. Abolitionist who founded *The Liberator*.
4. African American female abolitionist who also worked for women's rights.
5. Editor of *The Dial*.

REVIEWING THE FACTS

1. What attracted European immigrants to the United States in the mid-1800s?
2. What steps did nativists take against immigrants in the mid-1800s?
3. What obstacles in education did African Americans face in the 1800s?
4. How were prisoners and the mentally ill treated in the 1840s? What changes did reformers seek to make in those conditions?
5. Why did reformers start the temperance movement?
6. What steps were taken in the 1830s and 1840s to broaden democracy in the United States?
7. How did Frederick Douglass become a leader of the abolition movement?
8. How did the abolition movement give rise to the women's rights movement?
9. What was Ralph Waldo Emerson's message to American writers and scholars?
10. How did John James Audubon's paintings differ from those of other painters?

PRACTICING YOUR SKILL

The following sentences are part of an essay on the Seneca Falls Convention. Decide if they should go in the essay's introduction (I), its body (B), or its conclusion (C).

1. Elizabeth Cady Stanton lived in Seneca Falls.
2. In the years to come, the drive for suffrage would be the main goal of the women's movement.
3. In the reform movements of the 1800s, perhaps no event stands out as dramatically as the Seneca Falls Convention.
4. The women who attended were mostly educated, white, and financially secure.

CITIZENSHIP

1. What kinds of reformers are active in American society today? What aspects of American life do they believe are in need of improvement, and what are their goals?
2. Horace Mann once said that democracies need an educated citizenry more than do other forms of government. Do you agree? Why or why not?
3. Some abolitionists called for militant action—such as armed rebellion—in the mid-1800s. Do you think militant action was necessary? Why or why not?

4. Find out how political parties in your state choose delegates to their nominating conventions.

CRITICAL THINKING SKILLS

1. **RECOGNIZING CAUSE AND EFFECT** How did religious revivalism influence the reform movement?

2. **MAKING JUDGMENTS** Reformers called for changes in the treatment of prisoners. Do you think these reforms were necessary?

3. **PARAPHRASING A QUOTATION** Reread the quotation by Thoreau on page 423 and, in your own words, explain why Thoreau moved to Walden Pond.

PROJECTS AND ACTIVITIES

1. **WRITING A FICTIONAL ACCOUNT** Imagine you are a slave escaping on the Underground Railroad. Describe your reasons for escaping and the experiences you have along the way.

2. **RESEARCHING LOCAL HISTORY** Find out what effect, if any, the movement for public education had in your state. When was the first public high school founded? What was your state's first public institution of higher learning? Take notes as you do research.

3. **ANALYZING LITERATURE** Use the library to find a poem by Henry Wadsworth Longfellow, John Greenleaf Whittier, or Walt Whitman. In front of the class, read the poem and then explain what it means to you.

4. **CREATING AN ART EXHIBIT** Collect copies of pictures illustrating American visual arts in the 1800s. Write short notes about each picture, including who the artist was and why the painting is important.

WRITING ABOUT TOPICS IN AMERICAN HISTORY

1. **CONNECTING WITH LITERATURE** A selection from *The Autobiography of Frederick Douglass* appears on pages 653–654. Read it and answer the questions. Then answer the following question: Based on this selection, what other reform movements, besides abolitionism, might Douglass have supported? Explain your answer.

2. **APPLYING THEMES: AMERICAN CULTURE** Write a short essay on how the reform movements of the mid-1800s influenced the writers and artists of that time.

La Sta Da Carlota
Caspe y Rodriguez.
de edad de 10. aᶳ

Texas, *like the rest of the Southwest, moved from Spanish to Mexican control with Mexico's independence in 1821. This portrait reflects the region's Spanish heritage.*

17 Changes in Spanish-Speaking North America (1810–1836)

1 Mexican Independence

Section Focus

Key Terms *Tejano* ■ *Grito de Dolores*

Main Idea The people of Mexico, unhappy with Spanish rule, launched a series of revolts in the early 1800s. By 1821 Mexico was an independent nation.

Objectives As you read, look for answers to these questions:
1. What complaints did the northern provinces of Mexico have against Spain?
2. What were the goals and achievements of the revolt led by Father Miguel Hidalgo?
3. How did Mexico gain independence?

In 1821 the United States flag displayed 24 stars on its field of blue. Almost all the states represented by those stars lay east of the Mississippi River. Only Louisiana and Missouri lay west of the river.

Just 30 years later the United States had seven more states. Land added through war and negotiation stretched the country from "sea to shining sea." Bustling ports on the Pacific Ocean welcomed settlers. Thousands of others made their way west on trails across the plains and through the mountains. In these decades the Spanish traditions of the Southwest were added to the country.

SPANISH NORTH AMERICA

In 1809 Spain's American empire dominated the Western Hemisphere. Spain controlled Florida as well as islands in the Caribbean. It held land stretching from the southern tip of South America to the northern border of present-day California, Nevada, and Utah. Yet, as you have read in Chapter 14, that empire was beginning to crumble. The French ruler Napoleon had invaded Spain the year before. South Americans, sure of Spanish weakness, began their drive for independence from Spain.

Mexico was also ripe for revolt. Indians and mestizos there had few chances for education. The viceroy—the local ruler appointed by the Spanish king—held most decision-making powers. Only Spaniards born in Spain could hold high office. On top of all this, taxes were burdensome. Meanwhile, the ideals that underlay the American and French revolutions were spreading into Mexico. The ideal of political independence was particularly embraced by the Creoles—persons of Spanish ancestry born in Spanish America.

PROBLEMS IN SPAIN'S NORTHERN PROVINCES

The thinly settled northern provinces of Mexico—California, New Mexico, and Texas—had their own complaints. They had poor roads and little industry. Spain's tariffs and trade restrictions prevented these borderlands from trading with their neighbors, the Americans. (In one sense, all people who live in the Americas are *Americans*. In this book, however, that term refers to citizens of the United States.)

In 1809 *Tejanos* (teh–HAH–nohs), native Mexicans living in Texas, asked the Spanish government for help. They wanted measures to encourage agriculture and cattle raising. They asked for an end to the tariff on cotton and wool so that textile mills could be built. A college too was needed.

Like Texas, New Mexico also asked Spain for a college, as well as public schools. It requested that New Mexican settlers who served in the military be paid, as they were elsewhere. New Mexicans also wanted a court of justice to be established at Chihuahua in northern Mexico. As it was, all court cases had to be tried in Mexico City, which was located 1,500 miles away.

Spain ignored these requests. Furthermore, Spanish leaders were blind to the growing discontent throughout Mexico. Priests as well as politicians were questioning Spain's right to rule Mexico. Many met in secret societies to discuss ideas of freedom and to lay plans for Mexican independence.

THE FIRST CALL FOR REVOLT

Father Miguel Hidalgo (hih–DAHL–goh) had served for years as a parish priest in Dolores, a small town north of Mexico City. One of his goals was to improve the economic life of his Indian parishioners. He taught them, for instance, to make tile, keep honey bees, raise silkworms, tan leather, and make wine. Such activities, however, were against Spanish law. Remember that under the principle of mercantilism the colonies' role was to produce only raw materials. All manufactured products had to come from Spain. To enforce the law, Spanish officials had visited Dolores and put an end to Hidalgo's enterprises.

This experience caused Father Hidalgo to favor independence. Therefore he joined with like-minded Creoles to plan an uprising. But news of their plan leaked out. Warned that the Spanish were about to arrest them, Hidalgo and his fellow conspirators had a choice: flee or fight. They decided then and there to light the fire of revolt.

Early on September 16, 1810, Hidalgo rang the bells of the church in Dolores. Then he stood before a crowd of townspeople. "Will you make the effort to get back from the hated Spaniards the land stolen from your forefathers three centuries ago?" he asked.

Spanish missionaries founded San Antonio in 1718. During the mid-1800s, when this picture was made, San Antonio was home to about 4,000 people. Today it is one of the ten largest cities in the United States. **ECONOMICS** Judging from the picture, what do you think was San Antonio's main economic activity?

Known as the *Grito de Dolores*, or "Cry of Dolores," Hidalgo's speech was the first call for revolt.

Hidalgo demanded independence and the return of lands that had been taken from the Indians. Thousands of Indians and mestizos rallied to his cry. As they began to march south toward the capital, their numbers grew.

> "**W**ill you make the effort to get back from the hated Spaniards the land stolen from your forefathers three centuries ago?"
>
> —*Father Miguel Hidalgo*

The Army of the Americas, as Hidalgo called his followers, swelled to 80,000. Most were untrained and armed only with knives and slingshots. The political revolt turned into a social revolt as the mass of Indians and mestizos turned on the Spanish in deadly hatred. In the silver-mining town of Guanajuato, for instance, they killed 500 Spaniards. Nearing Mexico City, Hidalgo decided for unknown reasons not to enter the capital. Instead he began a retreat to the north. Hidalgo may have retreated because he feared what might happen if he totally lost control of his large and unruly force.

As the Spanish army pursued, most of Hidalgo's followers faded away. Hidalgo headed for Texas, hoping for safety there. He was less than 150 miles from the Rio Grande when the army attacked and crushed his force. Captured, Hidalgo was later executed. Today, the anniversary of the *Grito de Dolores,* September 16, is celebrated as Mexican Independence Day.

THE REVOLUTION SUCCEEDS

Despite the failure of Hidalgo's movement, Mexico continued to seethe. Another village priest, José María Morelos (moh–RAY–lohs),

took over leadership of the revolution. Unlike Father Hidalgo, Morelos set out to train his troops. By 1813 his small army was in control of much of southern Mexico.

Morelos declared independence and drew up a constitution. He promised equality for all people, the end of special rights for the Church and the army, and the breakup of large estates. These ideas cost Morelos the support of many Creoles. They feared the loss of their wealth. After a series of defeats by the Spanish army, Morelos was captured and killed in 1815.

In 1821 a new leader stepped forward. He was Agustín de Iturbide (ee–toor–BEE–day). Iturbide, a Creole, offered a three-point plan. It called for: (1) independence from Spain,

Miguel Hidalgo led 80,000 Mexicans in a revolt against Spain in 1810. Though the revolt was crushed and Hidalgo executed, Hidalgo is remembered as the father of Mexican independence. **RELIGION** How might Hidalgo's work as a priest have influenced his political ideas?

In May 1822, before an assembled crowd, Agustín de Iturbide declared himself Emperor of Mexico. Several months earlier, Iturbide had united the Mexican people against Spain by calling for independence, equality of all Mexicans, and support for the Catholic Church. **HISTORY** How and when was Iturbide overthrown?

(2) full equality for Spaniards and Creoles, and (3) continuing the Catholic Church as Mexico's state religion.

Iturbide had so much support from the Mexican people that Spain could do nothing. "He won his revolution with an idea," historian Paul Horgan said. "Not a shot was fired." On September 27, 1821, Iturbide's army entered Mexico City, making Mexico a free and independent nation.

In 1822 Iturbide declared himself the nation's new emperor. He soon had a revolt on his hands. The revolt was led by an army officer named Antonio López de Santa Anna. Santa Anna brimmed with ambition. He called for a republic, and by early 1823 had overthrown Iturbide. Mexico then got its own constitution. The new government, patterned after the United States, was a federation of states. Santa Anna was named its president. The fiery leader would rule Mexico off and on for the next 30 years.

SECTION REVIEW

1. KEY TERMS *Tejano, Grito de Dolores*

2. PEOPLE AND PLACES Chihuahua, Mexico City, Miguel Hidalgo, Agustín de Iturbide

3. COMPREHENSION What improvements did New Mexico request from Spain in 1809?

4. COMPREHENSION Why did Father Hidalgo issue the *Grito de Dolores*?

5. CRITICAL THINKING In your opinion, why was Iturbide successful in achieving independence, while Hidalgo and Morelos were not?

2 Changes on the Borderlands

★ **Section Focus**

Key Terms   *vaquero* ■ *empresario*
■ Santa Fe Trail

Main Idea   With Mexican independence
from Spain, the northern provinces of
Texas, New Mexico, and California experienced rapid change.

Objectives   As you read, look for answers
to these questions:
1. What new policies toward the northern provinces did the Mexican government
put into effect?
2. What steps did Moses Austin and Stephen Austin take to establish a colony in
Texas?
3. How did Anglo-Americans change
Texas, New Mexico, and California?

The sentries at the presidio in San Antonio scanned the horizon carefully for rising dust trails. Dust trails were often the first signs of visitors, welcome and unwelcome. Welcome visitors included *Tejano* settlers bringing cattle and crops for sale. Unwelcome, and feared, were the bands of Comanche Indians that often swept down on the town.

In one sense the Comanche were the real rulers of Texas, the lords of the Plains. Their power lay in their superb horsemanship. The first Spaniards on the Plains had left horses behind. In time, bands of wild mustangs thrived and multiplied on the grasslands. As did other Plains Indians, the Comanche had learned to master the wild horse. On horse-back, they roamed at will over the southern plains. In 1820 their warriors alone amounted to an estimated 18,000—more than all the *Tejanos*.

AUSTIN'S PROPOSAL

On December 23, 1820, the visitors that approached San Antonio were neither *Tejanos* nor Indians. They were Moses Austin of Missouri and his black servant Richmond.

Austin was an Anglo-American—a North American whose native language is English. A New Englander, Austin had settled in Missouri while it still belonged to Spain. There he became a Spanish citizen. In 1819 his mining business went bankrupt. Now he had come to Texas with a proposal. Might he have

permission to plant a colony of 300 families in Texas, provided they become Catholics, swear allegiance to Spain, and observe Spanish law? Within a month he had his answer: yes.

Spain had granted Austin's request for its own reasons. Officials thought that if some Anglo-Americans were given large land grants they could help defend the province both from illegal American settlers and from Indians.

Moses Austin did not see his dream come true. On the difficult journey home he caught pneumonia. Dying, he pleaded with his son Stephen, then 27, to take over responsibility for the new colony. Within months Stephen Austin was in San Antonio pursuing his father's dream.

Erasmo Seguín, a wealthy *ranchero* (rancher) escorted Austin into San Antonio. Seguín would later represent Texas in Mexico's Congress and would help write its constitution.

THE *TEJANOS* AND THE CATTLE BUSINESS

In 1821 Stephen Austin found a sparsely populated Texas of about 2,500 *Tejanos*. By then most of the mission settlements had been abandoned. The towns were few. San Antonio and La Bahía (Goliad) were on the San Antonio River in south Texas. Nacogdoches (NAK–uh–DOH–chiz) was the only settlement in east Texas.

This painting from 1877 shows Mexican *vaqueros* in a horse corral. North American cowhands adopted *vaquero* techniques and equipment, notably lariats, sombreros, riding boots and spurs, and leather chaps. **HISTORY** Which European explorers introduced horses into the Americas?

Thomas Gilcrease Institute of American Art, Tulsa, Oklahoma.

Tejanos such as Erasmo Seguín had prospered by rounding up wild cattle. These cattle—the Texas longhorns—were descendants of cattle the Spanish had brought to the region in the early 1700s. The cattle had thrived on the grasslands and brushlands of south Texas. With horns that could span five feet, they could fight off wolves, pull mistletoe from trees, or sweep thorned branches from their way. The longhorns were a tough breed. They could go 60 miles without water, run fast, and survive intense heat and cold.

The *Tejano* ranchers might drive a herd of cattle to settlements as far away as Louisiana. Often, however, they killed the cattle for their hides, which were far easier to transport than live animals. (Not until the 1860s did ranchers drive cattle to railroad yards in the North.) To identify their animals, the ranchers used a system of brands.

On the ranches the *vaqueros* (vah–KAYR–ohs) did the work. These cowhands worked on the open range, herding cattle from horseback and using lariats to rope them. At annual round-ups the *vaqueros* learned to tackle and throw ("bulldog") the calves for branding. They wore practical clothes. On their heads were wide-brimmed sombreros to keep off the sun and rain. Leather *chaparreras,* or chaps, protected their legs from thorny brush.

High-heeled riding boots with spurs made the *vaqueros* more effective in the saddle. The cowboys of the American West were to borrow many of the methods and clothing styles of the *vaqueros.*

THE AUSTIN GRANT

For his colony, Stephen Austin chose land between the Brazos and Colorado rivers. Austin chose the site because it had rich soil, timber, and water. It was close to the Gulf Coast and far from the Comanche Indians.

Austin and the first group of settlers were busy carving out farms and homes from the wilderness when the news of Mexican independence arrived. For Austin, the news meant that his grant would need the approval of the new government.

Alone, Austin made the difficult journey to the capital. To avoid robbers, he dressed as a beggar. Once in Mexico City, Austin asked Emperor Iturbide to recognize the proposed colony. Austin eventually won the right to proceed with his colony in east Texas.

The colony boasted 1,800 persons by 1825. Austin summarized his success: "The conquest of the wilderness was well begun; the Indians were becoming respectful; food crops were abundant; comfortable cabins were building."

This painting shows Stephen Austin and Baron De Bastrop, an old friend of Austin's father, issuing titles to land in Austin's Texas colony. HISTORY Why did Austin need Mexico's permission to start the colony?

TEXAS OPENS ITS BORDERS

Spanish policy had forbidden foreigners to trade or settle in New Spain. (The grant to Moses Austin had been an exception.) An independent Mexico now reversed those policies and opened its borders to trade and to immigration. The result was major change throughout the borderlands.

A new law established the guidelines for immigration. New settlers must come under the sponsorship of an *empresario*—a person awarded a large grant of land in return for bringing in settlers. By law, each family on an *empresario*'s grant was to receive 177 acres of farming land and 4,428 acres of grazing land. The Mexican government set two conditions for all immigrants to Texas: they had to become citizens of Mexico and join the Roman Catholic Church.

Most new immigrants came to Texas from the cotton states. Westward-moving pioneers from the South had settled Missouri and Arkansas. West of these states, however, lay the unfamiliar treeless land of the Great Plains. This land was mistakenly thought to be unfit for farming. Stopped in their movement west, the sons and daughters of the South began to look to Texas. The land across the Sabine and Red rivers looked good. It had the same familiar landscape of pines and gentle hills. The soil was good in east Texas, and the rainfall of 40 inches a year was just right for raising cotton and corn.

Texas boomed as a result of the Mexican *empresario* policy. By 1830 the population had swelled to about 10,000. Anglo-Americans greatly outnumbered *Tejanos*. Free blacks were among the Texas settlers, but nine out of ten African Americans in Texas were held as slaves.

BIOGRAPHY

LORENZO DE ZAVALA (1788–1836) was one of the few native Mexican *empresarios* in Texas. A political leader, Zavala served as governor of the state of Mexico and as Mexico's minister to France. In 1835 he returned to play a key role in the struggle for Texas independence. He was a signer of the Texas Declaration of Independence as well as an author of the Texas Constitution.

While some African Americans moved to Texas as free citizens, the majority were slaves. Many farmers from the South brought their slaves to Texas and continued to use them as farm laborers. **GEOGRAPHY** What part of Texas was well suited for farming? Why?

"GONE TO TEXAS"

Noah Smithwick was nineteen years old when an *empresario* showed up in Kentucky to recruit settlers for Texas. The *empresario* described a land overflowing with game, wild fruits, and nuts, and with a climate so mild "that houses were not essential." Smithwick was entranced. "So," he wrote, "I started out from Hopkinsville, Kentucky, with all my worldly possessions, which consisted of a few dollars in money, a change of clothes, and a gun, of course, to seek my fortune in this . . . paradise."

Many pioneers were as entranced as Smithwick. They left their old homes, it is said, posting only a simple sign on the door—GTT. Everyone knew that it meant "Gone to Texas."

Until the newcomers could build even a small log cabin, they lived in tents. Nighttime music in the strange new land included the drone of mosquitoes, the howl of wolves, the hoot of owls, and, most fearful of all, the bellow of alligators.

Smithwick found farming easy and game plentiful on the colony of Green DeWitt in southeast Texas. "Men talked hopefully of the future; children reveled in the novelty of the present," he recalled.

But the women—ah, there was where the situation bore heaviest. . . . They talked sadly of the old homes and friends left behind, . . . of the hardships . . . they were undergoing and the dangers that surrounded them. They had not even the solace of constant employment. The spinning wheel and loom had been left behind. There was, as yet, no use for them—there was nothing to spin. There was no house to keep in order. . . . There was no poultry, no dairy, no garden, no books, or papers as nowadays—and if there had been, many could not read—no schools, no churches—nothing to break the dull monotony of their lives. . . .

The Anglo-Americans carried their traditions and attitudes with them into Texas. You could see this in the look of their towns. The Mexican towns followed a traditional grid, with a plaza and church in the center. Their buildings were of stone or adobe bricks plastered with mud. The Anglo-Americans, in contrast, lived in log cabins with a chimney rising at one end. Their towns had no overall plan. They had the look of the ever-moving western frontier.

RISING TENSIONS

Anglo-Americans also held on to strong ideas about their freedoms, and did not want officials in faraway Mexico City meddling in their affairs. They were especially upset when the Mexican government ended slavery in 1829. Austin lobbied successfully for Texas to be exempt from the new law.

The Mexican government grew nervous about the outspoken and numerous Americans. It began to have second thoughts about its settlement policy. In 1830 Mexico closed the Texas frontier to Anglo-American settlers and banned the introduction of more slaves. It also placed sky-high tariffs on imports of goods from the United States. Despite these measures, Mexico was unable to stop the Anglo-American population from growing. Illegal immigrants from the United States continued to stream across the border into Texas.

THE SANTA FE TRAIL

Anglo-Americans were also crossing the border into New Mexico. In 1806 Zebulon Pike had been a Spanish prisoner in New Mexico (page 335). Later, he described the great trading opportunities that existed in Santa Fe. When Spain controlled New Mexico, the only imported goods in the region came from Veracruz, 1,500 miles away. American traders who had ventured into New Spain before 1821 were jailed or expelled.

The news of Mexican independence excited William Becknell of Franklin, Missouri. With four companions, he set out for Santa Fe. They led pack animals carrying such goods as cloth, needles, and china. He made a handsome profit and earned the reputation as father of the Santa Fe Trail.

In 1822 Becknell became the first western trader to carry his goods in Conestoga wag-

The traders who followed the Santa Fe Trail from Independence, Missouri to Santa Fe took along wagonloads of merchandise to exchange with Mexican traders. Here a caravan arrives at Santa Fe. HISTORY Who created the trail, and why?

ons. The huge wagons had first been used in Pennsylvania. In the West they were known as "covered wagons" or "prairie schooners." Each one could carry 5,000 pounds. Three pairs of oxen, mules, or horses were needed to pull a loaded wagon.

Most traders who took the Santa Fe Trail traveled on to Chihuahua, Mexico. Late each spring, traders set out from Missouri. They crossed the Plains and then the southern Rockies to reach Santa Fe. Leaving the Santa Fe Trail, they headed to El Paso and then went straight south to Chihuahua. Traders were paid in gold and silver for their merchandise. On the return trip in the fall, they brought back furs, wool, blankets, buffalo rugs, and herds of mules and burros. Barring bad luck, the traders were back in Missouri before winter.

Many traders who crossed into New Mexico's Rio Grande Valley decided to stay. The new American settlers were fine artisans, good with their hands. They built brick kilns and water-powered mills. So many of these enterprising foreigners entered the upper Rio Grande Valley that the Spanish-speaking New Mexicans grew resentful.

RANCHES REPLACE MISSIONS IN CALIFORNIA

Mexican independence brought great changes to California as well, especially to the mission system. Spain had never considered the missions to be permanent. When the Indians had learned both farming and Christianity, the missions were supposed to close. Parish priests would replace missionaries and the lands would be returned to the Indians.

In California, however, the missionaries had resisted the pressure to turn over mission lands. The Indians were not ready, they said. Of course, the missionaries had done little to encourage Indian independence.

In 1833 the Mexican Congress ordered the missions to give half their property to the Indians. Most Indians could not hold on to their land. Instead, the mission land ended up in the hands of *rancheros*. These landowners lived on *ranchos*, large land grants awarded

James Walker's painting *Patrón* shows a *Californio* on horseback inspecting his ranch. After Mexico's independence from Spain, large ranches in California were created out of mission land. ECONOMICS What role did Indians play in the new ranches?

by the government. Most of the mission Indians ended up working on the *ranchos* for no more than food, clothing, and shelter. The *ranchos* resembled feudal estates, or the old encomiendas (page 40). The Indians did the hard work, tending fields and herds.

A person with any Spanish ancestors was a *Californio*. These frontier people, in isolated California, had to cooperate and help each other. "Few ever lacked food, shelter, or other basic needs," according to the historian Albert Camarillo. Family ties were also very important. Extended family networks of cousins, aunts, and uncles gave strength and support in the frontier society.

The *Californios* thus led a life that centered around community and family activities. Visiting and entertaining neighbors were common. Such entertaining usually included lively singing and dancing. Rodeos, or round-ups, and fiestas drew neighbors from miles around.

Californios went everywhere by horseback. "Walking was a lost art," according to one account. "It was much easier to catch a passing horse, ride it where one wished to go, and turn it loose again." Children were but toddlers when they learned to ride and were experts by age ten. Boys also became expert with a lasso. A boy proved himself a man when he went into the hills to lasso and ride a wild mustang. Yet such an encounter could be dangerous, and not every boy survived.

THE CALIFORNIA TRADE

Like the other Mexican provinces, California moved toward freer trade after independence. Yankee ships began to arrive regularly on the California coast. From New England these "floating department stores" brought a cargo of all kinds of manufactured goods. They exchanged these goods for hides and tallow. The Yankees sold the tallow to Peruvians for candles and cooking. The hides became the foundation of New England's shoe industry.

The *Californios* greeted the Yankee ships with wonder and excitement. Prudencia Higuera was twelve years old when her father brought her some big brass buttons from a trading ship. They had eagles on them, like military buttons. Prudencia treasured her buttons so much that she refused to trade a half dozen of them for a beautiful black colt a friend offered her.

On board one Yankee trading ship was a college student, Richard Henry Dana. He described his experiences in a book, *Two Years Before the Mast,* published in 1840. Dana's account stirred American interest in California. In his view, the *Californios* were not taking advantage of their region's resources. He wrote, "In the hands of an enterprising people, what a country this might be!"

SECTION REVIEW

1. KEY TERMS *vaquero, empresario,* Santa Fe Trail

2. PEOPLE AND PLACES Stephen Austin, William Becknell, Santa Fe

3. COMPREHENSION What factors contributed to the rapid growth of the Anglo-American population of Texas in the 1820s?

4. COMPREHENSION What contributions did traders make to New Mexico?

5. CRITICAL THINKING How does trade bring about change, even if not intended?

3 The Texas Revolution

Section Focus

Key Terms   Battle of San Jacinto ■ annex

Main Idea   Texans, led by Sam Houston, revolted against Mexico in 1835. After heavy fighting, Texas established an independent republic in 1836.

Objectives   As you read, look for answers to these questions:
1.   What caused the crisis in relations between Texas and Mexico?
2.   How did the Texans achieve independence from Mexico?
3.   Why did Texas not immediately join the United States?

In 1832 Sam Houston moved to Texas, settling down in Nacogdoches in eastern Texas to practice law. The politics of this town were radical. Here, three years before, an attempt to declare Texas a separate republic had failed. The new resident of Nacogdoches would help that idea become reality.

SAM HOUSTON

Houston had been born in the Blue Ridge Mountains of Virginia in 1793. Like many at the time, his parents had come from the eastern part of the state. Like countless others, they planned to move on to the Tennessee

frontier. Houston's father died before the move to Tennessee, but that did not stop Houston's strong and spirited mother. In 1807 she and her brood of nine children journeyed to Tennessee in two Conestoga wagons. Houston was then fourteen.

By all accounts young Sam Houston was a moody youngster, who left home at sixteen to live with the neighboring Cherokee Indians. He spent most of the next three years with the Cherokee. Adopted into their tribe, he learned their customs and their language. For the rest of his life, Houston would be a friend to the Indians.

Born in Virginia in 1793, Sam Houston would become one of Texas's greatest heroes. Houston helped Texan forces win independence from Mexico and later held several important political positions. HISTORY Why was Texas in turmoil when Houston moved there in 1832?

At age nineteen Houston re-entered white society. When the War of 1812 broke out, Houston joined the army. He distinguished himself, and was wounded, fighting under Andrew Jackson at the Battle of Horseshoe Bend (page 343). Jackson took a liking to the young man. They would remain friends for life.

After five years of service, Houston left the army to study law in Nashville. In just six months, he was a lawyer. A talented public speaker, Houston was elected at age 30 to the United States House of Representatives. In 1827 he became governor of Tennessee, serving until 1829.

RISING TENSIONS IN TEXAS

When he moved to Texas in 1832, Sam Houston found it in upheaval. Life under the ever-changing Mexican government was neither easy nor predictable. Some people were upset that Texas was not a state by itself within Mexico. Texas was only part of the Mexican state of Texas-Coahuila. The capital of Texas-Coahuila was far south in the town of Saltillo. Anglo-Americans were unhappy with the law that official documents had to be in Spanish. They objected to the demand that they become Roman Catholics. They fiercely resented the 1830 laws that banned American immigration and placed tariffs on American goods.

Although unhappy, people could not agree on the best course of action. Most recent immigrants were for war, for splitting from Mexico altogether. In this, they had strong hopes the United States would come to their aid. On the other hand, there were those who listened to the calm, patient voice of Stephen Austin. He took seriously his promise to obey the Mexican government. He would not support the disloyal talk of separation. Instead he hoped for peaceful change.

Austin went to Mexico City to ask that Texas become its own state. He also asked the Mexican government to reverse its 1830 ban on immigration from the United States. President Santa Anna decided to grant the second request. Restrictions on immigration were lifted.

The legislature of Texas-Coahuila, meanwhile, voted to act on other complaints. Lawmakers extended local self-government, approved the use of English in public documents, set up more courts, and guaranteed religious toleration. Such moves might have kept the Texans happy, but Santa Anna triggered a crisis.

TEXAS DECLARES INDEPENDENCE

By early 1835 Santa Anna had become a dictator. As a result, pockets of rebellion flared like wildfire across Mexico. Santa Anna was able to stamp them all out. Then he abolished federalism throughout Mexico. That meant there were no more states or state governments. The constitution of Mexico had been overturned.

This was too much for the patient Stephen Austin. He called for a return to the constitu-

Two free blacks, Hendrick Arnold and Greenbury Logan, gained fame fighting against Mexico in the Texas Revolution. Along with other Texans, Arnold and Logan drove the Mexicans from the Alamo in San Antonio in December 1835. **HISTORY** How did Santa Anna react to the Texan victory at San Antonio?

tion. Austin, like many Texans, remained loyal to Mexico. From Santa Anna's viewpoint, however, the Texans were traitors. At that point, war was inevitable.

In October 1835 a group of Texans meeting at San Felipe de Austin declared themselves willing to fight to restore the Mexican constitution. The Texas Revolution had begun.

For Santa Anna, this was just one more prairie fire to stamp out. He sent an army to San Antonio. In December the Texans drove the Mexican forces from the Alamo, the old mission in San Antonio that was used as a fortress. In response, Santa Anna swept into Texas at the head of a large force. The Texans, scattered in small groups, were not prepared to meet the Mexican challenge.

THE FIGHT FOR THE ALAMO

William B. Travis with about 150 men held the Alamo. The small force included such famous frontiersmen as Davy Crockett and Jim Bowie. Another 400 Texans were 100 miles away at Goliad under James W. Fannin.

Sam Houston was chosen to lead the Texan army because of his army experience. When put in command, he had no real power. He ordered both Travis and Fannin to withdraw from their positions. Both refused.

On February 23, 1836, Santa Anna and his troops bore down on San Antonio. Santa Anna flew a red banner: the sign that no mercy would be shown, no prisoners taken, unless the Texans surrendered at once. Travis answered the demand with a cannon shot. The siege against the Alamo began the next day. More men, one with a family, slipped into the Alamo to help with its defense.

Many legends of the Alamo have developed over the years. One story about the siege says that on the tenth day Colonel Travis gathered his slim forces. Standing before them, he took his sword and drew a line on the ground. If you wish to stay and defend the Alamo, he said, cross the line. It was a choice for almost certain death—and all but one of the defenders crossed the line. Even Jim Bowie, it was said, too sick with fever to walk, had himself carried over the line.

Gaining Skill: Comparing Primary and Secondary Sources

So far in this textbook, you have read excerpts from a number of **primary sources**—records from the past such as newspapers, letters, diaries, and government documents. You have also read **secondary sources**, accounts of an event by someone who did not witness or take part in it. The "Historians' Corner" feature, for example, is a secondary source. So is the main narrative of this textbook.

Both primary and secondary sources are important to the study of history. Primary sources often give detailed accounts of past events and record how people reacted to these events at the time they took place. Secondary sources are usually based on a study of a variety of primary sources. They are also written after the events took place. For these reasons, secondary sources very often provide a clearer picture of the causes and effects of past events.

DESCRIPTIONS OF THE TEXAS REVOLUTION

The excerpts on this page illustrate some differences between primary and secondary sources. Both concern the siege of the Alamo. Read the excerpts carefully. Then answer the questions that follow.

Excerpt A

I am besieged, by a thousand or more of the Mexicans under Santa Anna. I have sustained a continual Bombardment and cannonade for 24 hours and have not lost a man. The enemy has demanded a surrender at discretion, otherwise, the garrison are to be put to the sword, if the fort is taken. I have answered the demand with a cannon shot, and our flag still waves proudly from the walls. *I shall never surrender nor retreat.* Then, I call on you in the name of Liberty, of patriotism and everything dear to the American character, to come to our aid, with all dispatch. The enemy is receiving reinforcements daily and will no doubt increase to three or four thousand in four or five days. If this call is neglected, I am determined to sustain myself as long as possible and die like a soldier who never forgets what is due to his own honor and that of his country.
VICTORY OR DEATH

Excerpt B

[James Fannin] was an adventurer, . . . now in Texas looking for promotion to general, and reluctant to throw his forces into the Alamo, not because of cowardice or fear of death, but rather because if he were to do so, he would lose his command and be forced to serve under the despised amateur Colonel Travis.

On his visit to Goliad, Lieutenant Bonham had pleaded with all the considerable moral force he could muster for Fannin to march to the relief of the Alamo. Fannin had given an equivocal answer: he would go, he would not go, he would consider it. Six days later, on the twenty-third, he was still weighing alternatives after Santa Anna had surrounded the Alamo, so that reinforcements would now encounter serious trouble if they tried to enter.

PRACTICING YOUR SKILL

1. Which of the two excerpts is the primary source? Which is the secondary source? How do you know?
2. What are some of the different kinds of primary sources that the author might have used to write the account in the secondary source?
3. In your opinion, what was the purpose of the first excerpt? Who was its author?
4. Would reading the primary source have helped the author of the secondary source in his or her research?
5. How do both the primary source and the secondary source help a reader understand the events at the Alamo?

The fierceness of the hand-to-hand fighting at the Alamo can be seen in this painting by Robert Onderdonk. In the center, with his rifle raised overhead, stands the famous frontier hunter and scout Davy Crockett. Crockett and some 180 others died defending the Alamo. **HISTORY** In what way did their defeat at the Alamo aid the Texans' cause?

Whether that story is true or not, we do know that Travis penned a letter as the siege began. "Our flag still waves proudly from the walls," he wrote. "I shall never surrender nor retreat."

> "**I** shall never surrender nor retreat."
>
> —*William B. Travis*

On March 2, 1836, Texas leaders declared their independence at Washington-on-the-Brazos. Four days later, on the thirteenth day of the siege, an angry Santa Anna ordered his men to go over the walls. The Texans greeted the attackers with a rain of cannon and rifle fire. The air was full of sounds—of guns, cannon booms, and the groans of dying men. In a room within the Alamo, Andrea Candalaria worked bravely among the wounded and dying in an effort to ease their suffering.

Then it became suddenly quiet. The Texans had run out of ammunition. As the Mexicans poured over the Alamo walls, the Texans fought on in hand-to-hand combat. At day's end 187 defenders of the Alamo were dead.

Susanna Dickinson, wife of one of the defenders, left San Antonio with the sad news.

Women and children had been spared. Candalaria, however, was wounded with a sword when Mexican soldiers stabbed Jim Bowie. He had died from fever the day before, Candalaria said, but the Mexicans thought he was still alive.

Santa Anna's victory at the Alamo was costly. His losses were 1,800 dead and wounded. Many Mexicans considered it an unnecessary loss of men. A Mexican officer also pointed out, "The massacres of the Alamo convinced the rebels that no peaceable settlement could be expected, and that they must conquer or die."

THE DEFEAT OF SANTA ANNA

Soon after the fall of the Alamo, Mexican troops attacked Fannin's force at Goliad. Although the Texans surrendered, Santa Anna ordered them all killed. Santa Anna's officers objected to the order, but Santa Anna insisted. It was the only way, he thought, to destroy Texas resistance. More than 300 prisoners were shot. Santa Anna's cruelty further aroused all Texans.

Next, Santa Anna pursued the remaining force led by Sam Houston. This force included both Anglo-Americans and *Tejanos*. Leading

Following the defeat of Mexico in 1836, Texas established an independent republic. Austin, the new capital of Texas, was named after Stephen Austin. This is how Austin appeared around 1840. **POLITICS** Why did northerners in Congress oppose Texas's request to be admitted to the Union?

one *Tejano* company was Juan Seguín, son of Erasmo Seguín. Like many *Tejanos,* both father and son helped Texas in its struggle for independence.

Houston drew the Mexican army into east Texas. On April 21, 1836, Santa Anna's force had camped near the San Jacinto (SAHN hah–SEEN–toh) River, which flowed into Galveston Bay. Santa Anna had expected Houston to attack at dawn, but the attack never came. The Mexicans relaxed, and by afternoon much of the camp was sound asleep. Then at four o'clock the Texans quietly advanced. When close to the camp, they came running and firing. "Remember the Alamo! Remember Goliad!" they screamed in fury.

> **"R**emember the Alamo!"
>
> —*Texan battle cry*

Santa Anna woke up to find the camp in turmoil. The Mexicans were quickly defeated, and Santa Anna himself was captured. With the Battle of San Jacinto, Texas won independence. Houston became a hero and a leader of the new Texas.

THE LONE STAR REPUBLIC

In December 1836 Texas adopted a flag with a single star. Adopting the nickname the Lone Star Republic, they proclaimed Texas to be an independent, self-governing country. Sam Houston became the first president of Texas. Later, the capital of Texas was established at a site on the Colorado River. Called Austin, it honored Stephen Austin, the "Father of Texas."

Many Texans did not plan to remain independent for long. They considered themselves Americans, and they wanted Texas to be a part of the United States. They also felt unsafe because Mexico had refused to recognize their independence. In 1836 Texas asked to be annexed—added—to the Union.

Many northerners objected to admitting Texas into the Union. Texas, they argued, would become a slave state. With its entrance into the Union, slave states would outnumber free states. This would give them a voting advantage in the Senate. Some government leaders also feared that annexing Texas would mean war with Mexico. Congress thus refused Texas's request. As a result, Texas would remain an independent republic for almost ten years.

GROWTH OF INTOLERANCE

After independence, the culture of Texas became increasingly intolerant of the region's Mexican heritage. Anglo-American immigrants ignored the contributions *Tejanos* had made to independence. The brutal excesses of

The Geographic Perspective: Texas Wins Independence

In 1836, after grim defeats at the Alamo and Goliad, things looked bleak for the small Texas army. For a while Sam Houston played for time. Then he learned that Santa Anna was moving east toward Harrisburg, where he hoped to capture the Texas government. Santa Anna had about 800 soldiers and he was expecting reinforcements.

SETTING THE TRAP

Houston moved for a showdown. He took his army quickly eastward along Buffalo Bayou, a fast, muddy rain-filled stream. The only ways to cross the bayou were a ferry at Harrisburg and the wooden Vince's Bridge.

To gain an advantage over the larger Mexican army, Houston planned a trap. Early on April 20, 1836, he made camp in a grove where the bayou met the San Jacinto River. The Texans took control of the ferry.

When Santa Anna arrived, he was shocked to find the Texans already there. He had his men set up barricades on the far side of the open prairie. All through the night and into the morning of April 21, Houston waited, while 500 more Mexicans arrived.

Now Houston was ready. He had his men destroy Vince's Bridge. Texans and Mexicans were now trapped together on a bit of prairie nearly surrounded by marshy rivers and bayous.

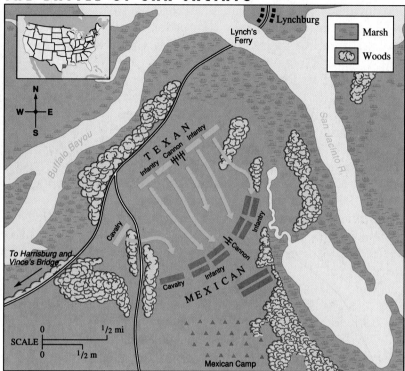

THE BATTLE OF SAN JACINTO

Marsh
Woods

"REMEMBER THE ALAMO"

Houston placed his troops carefully. In the woods on his right were 60 mounted horsemen, led by Mirabeau B. Lamar (later president of the Texas Republic). Lamar's cavalry blocked escape to the west. In the center, Houston lined up his riflemen facing the Mexican camp across the prairie. His two cannons were in the middle of the line.

At Houston's signal, the infantry moved quietly through the grass. Mexican sentinels did not spot them till they were nearly at the camp. While the Mexicans barely had time to reach their guns, the Texans' guns and knives were deadly at close range.

The angry shout went up, "Remember the Alamo!"

In less than twenty minutes, the surprised Mexican troops were defeated. More than 600 were killed in brutal hand-to-hand fighting; the rest were captured the next day. Santa Anna himself fled the battle but was found hiding in a cottonwood tree, wearing red carpet slippers and an ordinary soldier's uniform. The war was over.

CRITICAL THINKING QUESTIONS

1. Why did Houston order his men to destroy Vince's Bridge?

2. How did Houston use the natural features at San Jacinto to set his trap?

Santa Anna and the fight against Mexico nurtured a spirit of revenge toward all ethnic Mexicans. Don Martín de León, for instance, was a Mexican-born *empresario* who had been loyal to the Texan cause. According to his biographer, "This family like other loyal Mexican families were driven from their homes, their treasures, their cattle and horses, and their lands. . . ."

Juan Seguín, a hero at San Jacinto, maintained a leadership role in the new Texas, but only for a while. He served as mayor of San Antonio from 1840 to 1842. In the face of threats against his life and family, Seguín moved to Mexico in 1842. Texas honored Seguín in 1976 when his body was moved to its present grave in Seguin, Texas.

BIOGRAPHY

SUSANNA DICKINSON (1818?-1883), was eighteen years old when the Texas Revolution began. Along with her daughter, Angelina, she stayed at the Alamo while her husband, Almaron Dickinson, fought there. He was killed, and she and Angelina were two of only fourteen survivors of the Battle of the Alamo. Santa Anna spared her life and sent her to deliver the message to Sam Houston that any further revolt would be harshly put down.

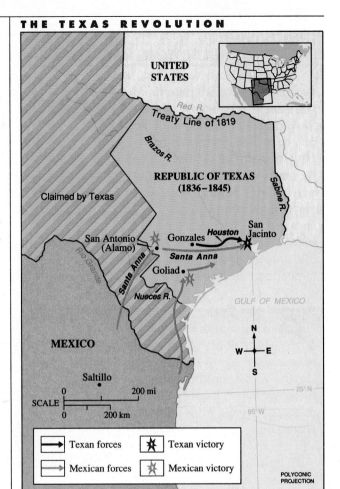

MAP SKILLS

Despite Mexican victories at the Alamo and Goliad, Texans won independence in 1836 by defeating Santa Anna at San Jacinto. What rivers did the Mexicans cross to reach San Antonio and Goliad? In what direction did the Texans march to reach San Jacinto? CRITICAL THINKING **How does the map suggest that tensions between Texas and Mexico continued after the war?**

THE TEXAS RANGERS

After independence, Texas faced the constant threat of a new war with Mexico. In addition, Mexican raiders and Plains Indians attacked Texas settlements. Among their targets was the republic's new capital, at Austin. The one-story capitol building was protected by a sturdy stockade against Indian raids.

The Texans were not content, however, to protect themselves with stockades alone. To defend the frontier, they depended on the

Texas Rangers—units of mounted and armed men. The Texas Rangers were excellent horsemen. They were swift, capable, and hardy. It was said that "a Texas Ranger can ride like a Mexican, trail like an Indian, shoot like a Tennessean, and fight like a very devil."

The Texas Rangers were the first to adopt a new kind of gun, the "six-shooter," a revolver invented by Samuel Colt in 1835. The Rangers had found the long rifle too awkward to use when firing at a full gallop. A Ranger with a Colt revolver, however, became a match for the Comanche warrior with a bow and arrow. In the decades to come, the Texas Rangers challenged the power of the Plains Indians, defending the expanding Anglo-American frontier.

CHAPTER 17 SUMMARY AND TIMELINE

1. Economic inequality, official neglect, and the influence of the French and American revolutions increased Mexican discontent with Spanish rule. After failed attempts at independence led by Father Miguel Hidalgo and Father José Morelos, Mexico achieved independence in 1821.

2. Life in the northern provinces changed after Mexico gained independence from Spain in 1821. American settlements were established in Texas, and the Santa Fe Trail expanded American trade with New Mexico.

Furthermore, American trade and interest in California grew.

3. Rising tensions between the Mexican government and Anglo-American settlers in Texas led to the Texas Revolution in 1835. After bloody defeats by Mexican forces at the Alamo and Goliad, Texans won a decisive victory at San Jacinto in April 1836. They then created a new nation, the Republic of Texas. Because the United States government refused Texas's request to join the Union, Texas remained independent.

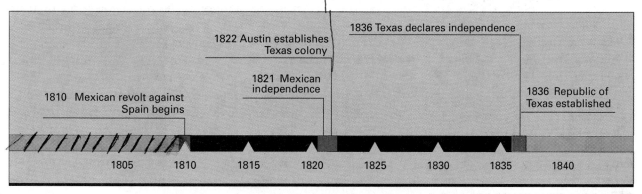

1810 Mexican revolt against Spain begins

1821 Mexican independence

1822 Austin establishes Texas colony

1836 Texas declares independence

1836 Republic of Texas established

1805 · 1810 · 1815 · 1820 · 1825 · 1830 · 1835 · 1840

Chapter 17 REVIEW

PLACES TO LOCATE

Match each of the letters on the map with the places that are listed below.

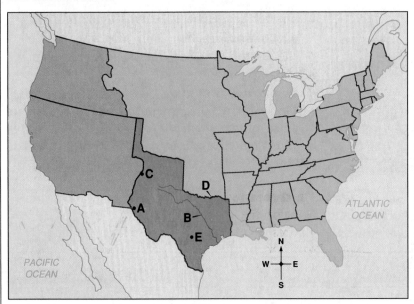

1. Brazos River
2. Red River
3. El Paso
4. San Antonio
5. Santa Fe

KEY TERMS

Use the following terms to complete the sentences.

annex
Battle of San Jacinto
Santa Fe Trail
Tejano
vaqueros

1. Traders in the 1820s and 1830s carried goods to Mexico along the ____.
2. In Texas, the system of herding and branding cattle was developed by ____.
3. Westerners wanted the United States to ____ Texas and make it a state.
4. A Spanish-speaking native of Texas was called a ____.
5. At the ____, Sam Houston led Texan forces to victory.

PEOPLE TO IDENTIFY

Match each of the following people with the correct description.

Stephen Austin
William Becknell
Sam Houston
Agustín de Iturbide
Santa Anna
William Travis

1. Mexican emperor.
2. Brought the first American settlers to Texas.
3. Leader of the Texas army during its victory at the Battle of San Jacinto.
4. Known as the father of the Santa Fe Trail.
5. Led Texas forces at the Alamo.
6. Leader of Mexican forces against Texans.

REVIEWING THE FACTS

1. Why were Mexicans unhappy with Spanish rule?
2. What were Father Hidalgo's demands of the Spanish government?
3. How did Santa Anna change Mexico's government in 1823?
4. Why did Spain grant Moses Austin the right to create a settlement in Texas?
5. What two conditions did foreigners have to meet to be allowed land grants in Mexican territory?
6. What goods were carried along the Santa Fe Trail?
7. What was the relationship between the Indians and the *rancheros*?
8. Why did Americans in Texas decide to seek independence?
9. How did Houston win the Battle of San Jacinto?
10. Why did some Americans object to admitting Texas to the Union?

PRACTICING YOUR SKILL

Read each of the following excerpts. Then answer the questions.

Excerpt A

The door to Texas was opened officially in 1823, and in the next 12 years nearly 28,000 Americans poured through it. Most of them came legally, under the auspices of Austin and other *empresarios.* But more and more of the new-comers [were] . . . illegal . . . squatters and fugitives.

Excerpt B

You wish to know my opinion, if it will do for all sorts of people to emigrate to Texas. . . . On this point, I should say, in-dustrious farmers will certain-ly do well, and cannot fail of success; that is to say, if abun-dant crops, and a ready mar-ket with high prices, will satisfy them.

1. Which of the two excerpts is the primary source? Which is the secondary source? How do you know?
2. What sorts of primary sources might the author have used to write the sec-ondary source?

CITIZENSHIP

1. Compare the course and results of the Mexican move-ment for independence with those of the American Revo-lution. In what ways were they similar? In what ways were they different?

2. Identify areas of conflict between Anglo-Americans in Texas and the Mexican gov-ernment. Do you think Americans should always have followed Mexican law? Explain your answer.
3. A number of prominent *Tejanos* supported Texas's movement for independence from Mexico. Imagine that you are one of those *Tejanos,* and write a letter to Santa Anna explaining your posi-tion.

CRITICAL THINKING SKILLS

1. ANALYZING A QUOTATION Reread the quotation from the *Grito de Dolores* on page 430. Explain to whom Hidal-go is addressing that ques-tion and what historical action he is describing. Why might this speech have moved his audience to revo-lution?

2. INFERRING Why might Texans have demanded that Texas become a separate state within Mexico?

3. MAKING CONTRASTS What advantages and disadvan-tages did Texan forces have in the Texas Revolution? What were the advantages and disadvantages of Mexi-can forces in that war?

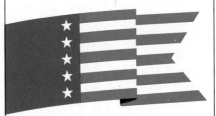

PROJECTS AND ACTIVITIES

1. DRAWING A PICTURE Draw a picture of a *vaquero* at work, based on the descrip-tion on page 434. Label the *vaquero*'s clothes and tools.

2. MAKING A CHART Create a chart that summarizes the settlement of Texas by Anglo-Americans. Include what Texas offered people from the United States, what conditions they had to ac-cept, and why conflicts arose between Anglo-American settlers and the Mexican government.

WRITING ABOUT TOPICS IN AMERICAN HISTORY

1. CONNECTING WITH LITERA-TURE A selection from *Texas* by James Michener appears on pages 655–656. Read it and answer the questions. Then identify one of the battles or people for whom a county in Texas was named and write a short essay on the significance of that battle or person.

2. APPLYING THEMES: GEOG-RAPHY Write a short essay describing how the physical features of Texas, New Mexi-co, and California led to United States interest in trade with and settlement of these areas.

As rugged as the lands they explored, mountain men such as Jedediah Smith traveled the American West. Others followed, trekking westward in search of land and gold.

18 From the Mississippi to the Pacific (1820–1853)

KEY EVENTS

1825	Jim Bridger reaches Great Salt Lake
1845	Texas annexed
1846	Mexican War begins
1847	Mormon migration to Utah
1848	Treaty of Guadalupe Hidalgo
1849	California Gold Rush
1853	Gadsden Purchase

1 Heading West

Section Focus

Key Terms   South Pass ■ Oregon Country ■ emigrant ■ Oregon Trail

Main Idea   Mountain men found routes across the West that later became trails for wagon trains of settlers.

Objectives   As you read, look for answers to these questions:
1. What qualities did a mountain man need?
2. What was the Oregon Country like in the 1820s?
3. What was life like on a wagon trail west?

In 1822 St. Louis was a raw young settlement. Sixteen years after the Lewis and Clark expedition, St. Louis had mushroomed into a town of 6,000 persons. On the very edge of the frontier, it was the place to go if you were heading west. If you wanted strong, able-bodied men for fur trapping, it was the place to advertise.

In February 1822 a small advertisement appeared in the St. Louis paper:

> The subscriber wishes to engage ONE HUNDRED MEN, to ascend the river Missouri to its source, there to be employed for one, two, or three years.

The ad was signed by William H. Ashley. Ashley headed one of four American fur-trading companies that had been formed after the Louisiana Purchase.

Sometime after that ad appeared, Jedediah Smith, aged 23, knocked at Ashley's door.

Born in New York State, Jedediah Smith had moved with his family first to western Pennsylvania and then to Illinois. Now, Smith told Ashley, he wanted to become a good hunter, learn about the Indians, explore the West, and make a living while doing so. Ashley hired him, and Smith became a mountain man.

THE MOUNTAIN MEN

Mountain men was the name given to the adventurers who trapped furs and traded goods in and around the Rocky Mountains. Their lives were molded by hardship and constant danger. A mountain man spent much of the year alone or with a few companions, trapping animals such as mink, otter, and especially beaver. Beaver fur was especially valued for men's hats, both in the East and in Europe. To survive, the mountain men became skilled trackers and pathfinders.

James Beckwourth, probably born a slave, became a leading explorer, hunter, trapper, and scout in the West. **CULTURAL PLURALISM** Why might the West of the mid-1800s have offered more opportunities for African Americans than other regions of the country?

Each spring mountain men packed their furs and headed for the rendezvous (RAHN–day–voo), or meeting place. Held each summer, the rendezvous took place at a location that was convenient for both fur trappers and traders. As many as 100 trappers and up to 5,000 Indians gathered at the rendezvous. For two or three weeks they swapped tall tales, caught up on the latest news, and enjoyed the rare chance to be sociable before returning to the wilderness trails.

One of the earliest mountain men of the Missouri Country was Manuel Lisa, a Spaniard born in New Orleans. In 1807 Lisa built the first trading post on the upper Missouri in what is now Montana. Lisa depended on Edward Rose as guide and interpreter. An African American, Rose was "as cunning as a prairie wolf," wrote one who knew him.

He was a perfect woodsman. He could endure any kind of fatigue and privation as well as the best trained Indians. He studied men. . . . He knew all that Indians knew. He was a great man in his situation.

Jim Beckwourth was another of Ashley's mountain men. Like Rose, Beckwourth was also an African American. He was adopted by the Crow Indians, who renamed him Bloody Arm in recognition of his fighting ability. Eventually he became their chief. After a time Beckwourth left the Crow, becoming an army scout in Florida. Years later he discovered an important mountain pass into California, the Beckwourth Pass.

Jim Bridger, one of the most famous mountain men, explored the Great Basin. The Great Basin is the desert region between two great mountain ranges, the Rocky Mountains on the east and the Sierra Nevada on the west. In 1825 Bridger came upon a remarkable lake some 80 miles long and 50 miles wide. It was the Great Salt Lake, the largest lake west of the Mississippi. Bridger was the first non-Indian to see the lake.

Such were the mountain men—tough, able to get along with the Indians, independent. There were many famous mountain men, remembered today in place names of mountains, mountain passes, forests, and counties throughout the west. Jedediah Smith stands out as a prime example.

JEDEDIAH SMITH

In the fall of 1823 Smith led a party of hunters to western Wyoming. It had not been difficult to cross the plains and reach the Crow villages there. To the west, however, towered the jagged peaks of the Teton Mountains. In the winter snow Smith tried to cross the Tetons, but had to give up and return to the Crow. Was there no other way west? he asked. Yes, they said. On a map Smith sculpted out of sand, the Crow pointed out a pass through the Rocky Mountains. It was south of the Tetons.

Excited, Smith and his party set out. Braving a mid-winter blizzard, they found South Pass. Unlike the more northern routes across the Rocky Mountains, South Pass was relatively low and open. It was a pass a wagon could manage. In the decades to come, thousands of travelers would go through Wyoming's South Pass on their way west.

Several years later Smith was the first to cross the desert between the Great Salt Lake and southern California. On his trip back from California, he made the first recorded crossing of the Sierra Nevada. Smith headed to California again in 1827. Attacked by Indians while crossing the desert, Smith lost ten men. When he sought help in California, the Mexicans were suspicious of his reasons for exploring the area. They jailed him as a spy.

Released in 1828, Smith's party headed northward along the coast toward Oregon. Along the way most of the party were killed by Umpqua Indians. Smith and three others finally straggled into Fort Vancouver on the Columbia River.

THE OREGON COUNTRY

In the early 1800s, Britain and the United States claimed the Oregon Country—the land drained by the Columbia, Snake, and Fraser rivers. Spain had given up its claim to Oregon in the Adams-Onís Treaty of 1819 (page 358). In 1811 John Jacob Astor's American Fur Company had established a fur-trading post at Astoria, at the mouth of the Columbia River. The British soon took it over, however, in the War of 1812. After the war, the British and the Americans agreed to joint occupation of Oregon.

By the 1820s the Hudson's Bay Company of Canada had Oregon firmly in its control. Managing the company's fur-trading business in the Pacific Northwest was John McLoughlin. The huge, white-haired Scotsman ruled the territory with great firmness and fairness. The Indians so respected him that they called him "White Eagle." McLoughlin was able to recover the furs and

horses the Umpqua Indians had stolen from Jedediah Smith.

Smith was impressed with McLoughlin's kindness to him at Fort Vancouver. He was also impressed with the country. With fellow survivors David Jackson and William L. Sublette, Smith wrote a letter to the United States Secretary of War. The letter described the rich wheat crop, the fruit trees, and the fat livestock of Fort Vancouver. The writers also stressed the quantity of furs passing through Fort Vancouver.

The British, Smith concluded, were taking over the Oregon Country even though Americans could legally settle there. Smith also pointed out that it was possible for Americans to cross the continent by wagon and thus reach the rich Oregon Country.

THE OREGON TRAIL

In the fall of 1831 a small group of Nez Perce Indians made a special trip to St. Louis. Through sign language, the Nez Perce tried to explain what they wanted. They had come in search of the "secret medicine" that allowed non-Indians to make such goods as guns, tools, and beads. The Indians believed that they could acquire this power through religious instruction.

The story of these Indians appeared in a Methodist newspaper in 1833. The Methodists leaped into action to send a missionary to Oregon. Jason Lee, their first missionary, settled in Oregon's fertile Willamette Valley in 1834. Later missionaries included Marcus and Narcissa Whitman, who settled at Walla Walla. This site was near the junction of the Snake and Columbia rivers.

In many ways, the Methodist missions were like those of the Spanish Catholics. Both tried to teach Indians the ways of white society as well as religion. The Methodist missionaries made few conversions among the Indians. Their glowing reports of the fertility of Oregon, however, had an impact.

The trickle of emigrants—people migrating out of one place to another—turned into a flood starting in 1843. In that year Marcus

NARCISSA WHITMAN (1808–1847) was one of the first white women to cross the Rocky Mountains. Leaving Liberty, Missouri, she and her husband Marcus reached Fort Walla Walla on the Columbia River in 1836. They served as missionaries to the Indians in the American Northwest. Northwest Indian anger with the increasing numbers of white settlers reached a peak in 1847 when white migrants brought a measles epidemic to the area. In revenge for the death of Indian children, local Indians murdered fourteen whites, including Narcissa and Marcus Whitman.

Whitman led a wagon train of 1,000 men, women, and children into Oregon. Within four years, 4,000 settlers had arrived. Many of them were guided by mountain men.

LIFE ON THE OREGON TRAIL

To reach Oregon the emigrants traveled along the Oregon Trail. The Oregon Trail started at Independence, Missouri. It crossed the Great Plains by following the Platte River and continued through South Pass into what is now northeast Utah. There the trail split.

A branch of the Oregon Trail, the California Trail, headed across the desert for California. The Oregon Trail itself went north and west to the Columbia River.

As of 1845, emigrants going on the trail had a guidebook to follow. The *Emigrants Guide* explained everything. The biggest expense emigrants faced was getting a good, strong covered wagon and the animals to pull it. Oxen were preferred because they were sturdier and less likely to be taken by Indians. Spare parts, heavy rope, and grease buckets were essential. For food, the emigrants were advised to bring, per adult: 200 pounds of flour, 150 pounds of bacon, 10 pounds of coffee, 20 pounds of sugar, and 10 pounds of salt. Other supplies might include dried beef, rice, dried beans, dried fruit, vinegar, mustard, and pickles.

People did not make the long journey alone. They went in organized wagon trains. Their survival depended on cooperation. At the beginning of the journey the members of a wagon train elected one person to be in charge. Rules were laid down. Each man was expected to take turns on the night watch.

At the end of a day's travel, the wagons drew into a large circle. Within the circle the oxen were herded and tents pitched. The circle thus both contained the animals and offered protection. In the evening the travelers might gather around campfires to talk, sing, and dance.

The wagon trains usually did not travel on Sunday. The men used the day to mend wagons and harnesses. The women washed and mended clothes or cooked up a pot of beans for the days ahead.

Performing daily tasks often demanded great patience—and even a sense of humor. The emigrants had to contend with rivers in flood, hordes of insects, poisonous snakes, and storms that came without warning. One woman recalled the effects of a sudden sandstorm:

After it was over our most intimate friends could hardly have recognized

The Oregon Trail crossed many rivers, requiring wagon trains to brave the hazards of deep water and fast-flowing rapids. **GEOGRAPHY** What other physical obstacles did migrants on the Oregon Trail face on their journeys west?

us—so dirty were our faces. And our dinner! Who would have eaten it? We could not tell what it consisted of, although before the storm it looked very tempting. So we had to cook another.

The diaries also tell of tragedy and hardship. Jane Gould's diary described the sad scene in a wagon train they passed:

> They . . . were just digging a grave for another woman that was run over by the cattle and wagons when they stampeded yesterday. She lived 24 hours, she gave birth to a child a short time before she died. The child was buried with her. She leaves a little two-year-old girl and a husband. They say he is nearly crazy with sorrow.

The first travelers on the Oregon Trail were helped by the Indians. Along the way Indians often brought game into their camps to exchange for cloth, needles, or other goods. As the number of travelers increased, how-ever, the Indians, fearing the loss of their land, grew hostile. In time, deadly Indian attacks became a further danger facing emigrants on the trail.

THE MORMON MIGRATION

One wagon train that set out on the Oregon Trail in 1847 was different from the others. Led by Brigham Young, this was a party of Mormons intent on finding a new home.

The Mormons belonged to the Church of Latter Day Saints. This church had been founded by Joseph Smith in 1830. The Mormons stressed economic cooperation rather than competition. Cooperation helped the Mormons become very successful. It brought them into conflict with their neighbors, who viewed their cooperation as a form of monopoly. These neighbors were also upset by the Mormon practice of polygamy—having two or more wives at the same time.

Resentment turned to murder in 1844. An anti-Mormon mob in Illinois killed Joseph Smith. He was succeeded by Brigham Young, who decided to move his flock beyond the boundaries of the United States.

The Mormons migrated to Utah. At the time, Utah still belonged to Mexico. By settling between the mountains and the desert near the Great Salt Lake, the Mormons hoped to be far from other settlements and free to live life as they chose.

Thus a massive migration began. Mormons, many of them pulling handcarts, poured into the Great Salt Lake basin. There they built a thriving city, Salt Lake City.

Brigham Young ruled with a firm hand. He told the arrivals:

No man can ever buy land here, for no one has any land to sell. But every man shall have his land measured out to him, which he must cultivate in order to keep it. Besides, there shall be no private ownership of the streams that come out of the canyons, nor the timber that grows on the hills. These belong to the people: all the people.

MAP SKILLS

This map shows the main routes for traders and settlers heading to the American West. Use the map's scale to determine the distance between Fort Walla Walla and Fort Vancouver. What was the name of the trail leading to Salt Lake City? CRITICAL THINKING Why were forts built along these trails?

WESTWARD ROUTES

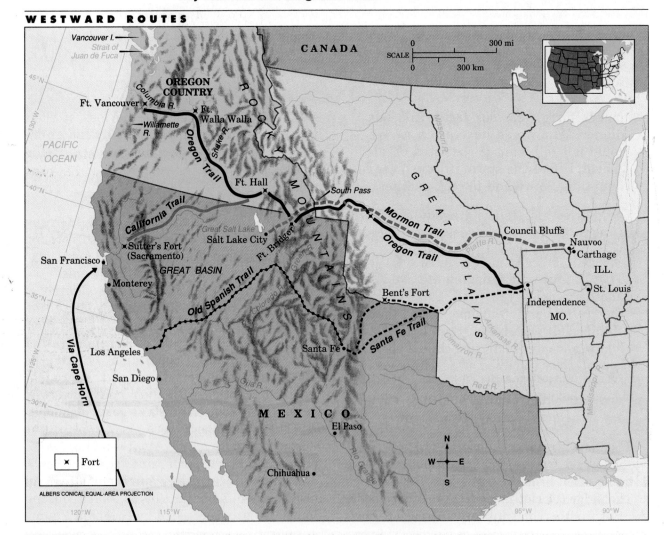

This painting shows a Mormon camp meeting at Council Bluffs, Iowa. The town, then known as Kanesville, was settled by Mormons in 1846. It was renamed in honor of Lewis and Clark's council there with local Indians in 1804. **RELIGION** Why did the Mormons make the trek to Utah?

A New Law on Water Rights

Young's rule about the need to share limited resources such as water was new to people from the East. In the eastern part of the United States, there was plenty of rain. Laws there prevented landowners from damming or diverting streams and rivers that ran through their property.

In the dry land of Utah—and in much of the western part of the country—rivers were the main source of water. To grow crops, farmers *had* to be able to divert river water. Realizing this, the Mormons developed a new set of laws governing rivers and streams. In this, the Mormons adopted ideas from Spanish and Indian water practices in the dry Southwest. These practices emphasized the good of the community over that of the individual. That philosophy still governs water laws in the West.

The Mormons became expert at desert farming. With a system of canals, they diverted mountain streams to water their fields. They were the first Anglo-Americans to cooperate in the use of water.

SECTION REVIEW

1. Key Terms South Pass, Oregon Country, emigrant, Oregon Trail

2. People and Places St. Louis, Jedediah Smith, Manuel Lisa, Jim Beckwourth, Sierra Nevada, Fort Vancouver, Marcus and Narcissa Whitman, Joseph Smith, Brigham Young, Salt Lake City

3. Comprehension How did Jedediah Smith help open up the West for the United States?

4. Comprehension What was the route of the Oregon Trail?

5. Critical Thinking How did the experience of traveling west encourage both individual achievement and cooperation?

Gaining Skill: Using a Diary as a Primary Source

A diary is a private journal, often a record of an individual's thoughts and feelings as well as the details of his or her day. For these reasons, diaries are excellent primary sources. They give historians firsthand information about people, places, and events. Diaries, because they are personal records, usually have a point of view. For this reason, historians must interpret the information presented in a diary. They read a diary with an eye to who the author was, what events are being described, and how the author feels about those events.

ANALYZING A DIARY

You, too, can master the art of gaining historical information from a diary. Begin by finding out as much as you can about the person who kept the diary. What was his or her name, family background, occupation? Where and when did he or she live? Under what circumstances was the diary kept? For example, the diary excerpted on this page was kept by a pioneer woman traveling west from St. Joseph, Missouri, on the Oregon Trail.

Once you know something about the author, read the diary. Look for factual information described in the diary. The diary of a soldier in the Revolution, for example, might mention the time of day when a certain battle was fought. The soldier might describe how far one side advanced or retreated. This kind of information helps historians reconstruct events.

EXAMINING ATTITUDES

The final step in analyzing a diary is to look for the attitudes and feelings of the writer. What personal prejudices or preferences are expressed in the diary? How does the writer feel about the event and the people who are involved? Understanding how one person felt about an event will give you a better sense of its significance.

The excerpt below is from a diary written by Lydia Allen Rudd, who traveled with her husband to Oregon in 1852. They ended their journey at Burlington, Oregon, in October. Read the diary entries and answer the questions that follow.

May 6 Left the Missouri River for our long journey across the wild uncultivated plains and uninhabited except by the red man. As we left the river bottom and ascended the bluffs the view from them was handsome! . . . But with good courage and not one sigh of regret I mounted my pony . . . and rode slowly on.

May 14 Just after we started this morning we passed four men digging a grave. . . . We passed three more graves this afternoon.

June 20 Traveled about 5 miles and obliged to stop with our sick. . . .

August 14 . . . Bought a salmon fish of an Indian today weighing seven or eight pounds. Gave him an old shirt, some bread, and a sewing needle. We have been in the most desolate looking region for a week. . . .

September 29 It is getting almost too late to try the mountains. . . . Henry is not as well tonight. . . .

October 14 . . . I am so anxious to get someplace to stop and settle that my patience is not worth much.

PRACTICING YOUR SKILL

1. What problems along the trail does Rudd note?
2. Why might the end of September be "too late to try the mountains"?
3. What is Rudd's attitude toward the trip across the country at the start of her journey? At the end?

2 President Polk and National Expansion

★ **Section Focus**

★ **Key Terms** manifest destiny
■ expansionist ■ Mexican War ■ Bear Flag
Revolt ■ Treaty of Guadalupe Hidalgo
■ cede ■ Mexican Cession

★ **Main Idea** As a result of negotiation with
Britain and war with Mexico, the United
States expanded its borders to the Pacific
Ocean.

Objectives As you read, look for answers
to these questions:
1. What new territory did the United
States acquire by negotiation?
2. What were the causes and effects of
the Mexican War?

In 1844 Henry Clay, the Great Compromiser, was running for President as the nominee of the Whig Party. People again raised the issue of annexing Texas. Clay stood against annexation. "Annexation and war with Mexico are identical," he said. Andrew Jackson, still the nation's leading Democrat, was delighted at Clay's unpopular stand. "Clay is a dead political duck," he said. Old Hickory was proved right.

> "**A**nnexation [of Texas] and war with Mexico are identical."
>
> —*Henry Clay*

POLK AND OREGON

Jackson supported the unknown James K. Polk of Tennessee, and the Democrats nominated him. Polk believed that annexation of Texas was both a necessity and a right. To gain northern support, he also urged "the re-occupation of Oregon." One of his campaign slogans was "Fifty-four forty or fight." The parallel of 54°40′ was the northern boundary of the Oregon Country.

Polk's ideas reflected a surge of feeling in the United States that it was the destiny of the nation to stretch from sea to sea. The Atlantic and the Pacific oceans, many felt, were our "natural boundaries." Acquiring Oregon, California, and Texas was, a newspaper wrote, the nation's manifest destiny. That is, expansion was not only desirable, it was bound to happen. People who believed in expanding the nation's borders were called expansionists.

Polk barely won the election. His victory, though slim, was enough to focus the nation's attention on the West. Polk prodded the British into negotiations over Oregon. In their talks each nation compromised. They agreed to divide Oregon Country at the 49th parallel. The 49th parallel was already the border between Canada and the United States from the Great Lakes to the Rocky Mountains. The agreement of 1846 extended this line of latitude west to the Pacific Ocean.

TROUBLES WITH MEXICO

After Polk's election, Congress quickly voted to annex Texas. When Texas entered the Union in December 1845, Mexico was outraged. Mexican wrath grew greater when Texas boldly claimed the Rio Grande as its southern boundary. Mexico insisted that the Texas Republic had included only the land as far south and west as the Nueces (noo–AY–sis) River.

President Polk tried to negotiate the issue with Mexico. He sent special envoy John Slidell to Mexico with an offer to set the Texas boundary at the Rio Grande. Slidell was also instructed to offer to buy New Mexico and California. Mexican officials refused even to meet with Slidell.

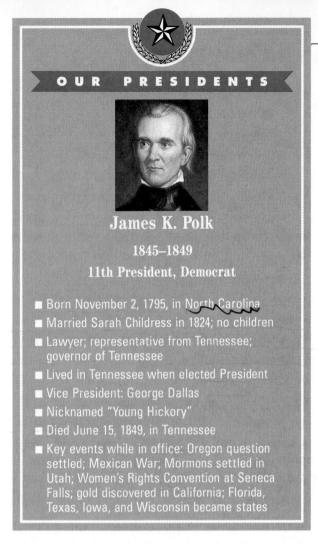

James K. Polk

1845–1849

11th President, Democrat

- Born November 2, 1795, in North Carolina
- Married Sarah Childress in 1824; no children
- Lawyer; representative from Tennessee; governor of Tennessee
- Lived in Tennessee when elected President
- Vice President: George Dallas
- Nicknamed "Young Hickory"
- Died June 15, 1849, in Tennessee
- Key events while in office: Oregon question settled; Mexican War; Mormons settled in Utah; Women's Rights Convention at Seneca Falls; gold discovered in California; Florida, Texas, Iowa, and Wisconsin became states

In January 1846 a new Mexican government came to power. It asserted that Mexican territory ended at the Sabine, meaning that it included nearly all of Texas. The new leadership announced it was ready to go to war to defend Mexico's claim. As a result, Polk became convinced that war with Mexico would be necessary.

Polk had already sent General Zachary Taylor to guard the territory near the Nueces. He ordered Taylor to take a position on the Rio Grande, inside the disputed territory. Mexico regarded that advance as an act of war.

A Mexican force crossed the river and attacked the American troops. Polk believed that the United States had to respond. Mexico "has invaded our territory and shed Ameri-can blood upon the American soil," Polk told Congress. Congress reacted in May 1846 by declaring war on Mexico.

THE MEXICAN WAR BEGINS

Most Americans in the South and West were enthusiastic about the Mexican War. In the Northeast, however, people denounced it. The Massachusetts legislature called it a war of conquest. Abolitionists saw the war as a slavery plot. The poet James Russell Lowell claimed that the expansionists just wanted "bigger pens to cram with slaves." Still, the Mexican War was not as strongly opposed as the War of 1812 had been. One reason was that the Mexican War, unlike the War of 1812, went well for the United States from the very beginning.

In the summer of 1846 a force led by Stephen Kearny (KAR–nee) headed for New Mexico from Fort Leavenworth, Kansas. New Mexico was important to Polk primarily because it was on the way to California. As the soldiers headed across the plains, they sang such verses as:

Old Colonel Kearny, you can bet,
Will keep the boys in motion,
Till Yankee Land includes the sand
On the Pacific Ocean.

The New Mexicans had been afraid the Americans would destroy their churches and take their possessions. As Kearny entered New Mexico, however, he promised to protect their rights, including freedom of religion. The Americans took Santa Fe, and with it New Mexico, without firing a shot. Kearny then headed for California.

THE BEAR FLAG REVOLT

In California, meanwhile, a handful of rough American newcomers rebelled against Mexican authority by arresting General Mariano G. Vallejo (vuh–LAY–oh) in his home at Sonoma. This rebellion was called the Bear Flag Revolt because, after Vallejo's arrest, the Americans hastily made a flag showing a grizzly bear.

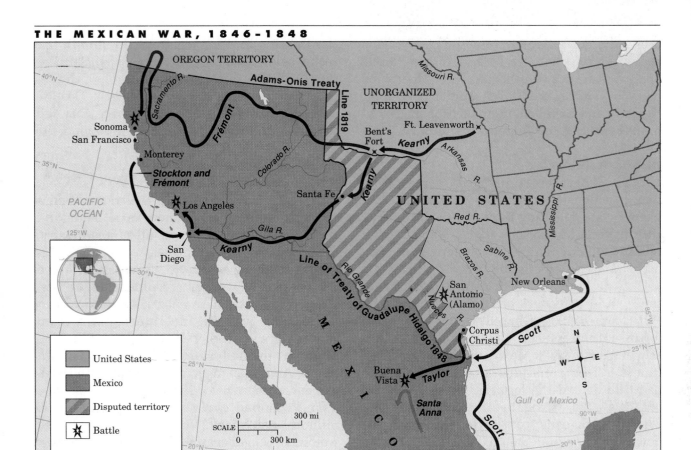

ALBERS CONICAL EQUAL-AREA PROJECTION

MAP SKILLS During the Mexican War, United States forces battled Mexicans from California to Mexico City. Who led American troops in the battle at Buena Vista? **CRITICAL THINKING** Why might southerners and westerners have supported the war while easterners opposed it?

The promoter of this affair was John C. Frémont. Frémont was an army engineer whose duties included mapping the West. Frémont had married Jessie Benton, daughter of Senator Thomas Hart Benton of Missouri. Senator Benton, an avid expansionist, had arranged for Frémont's mapping expedition to California in 1845. When Frémont's armed party of 62 arrived in California, Mexican officials became suspicious and ordered them out. Frémont tried to resist, even raising the American flag on a mountain peak. Then he gave in, leaving "slowly and growlingly," as he wrote his wife.

Frémont was in southern Oregon when he received word that war was about to break out with Mexico. He dashed back to Califor-

nia in time to give military help to the Bear Flag Revolt.

Frémont could be headstrong and foolish. He also had little knowledge of California or its people. For instance, he put General Vallejo in jail. Vallejo was probably the most respected citizen of California. Not only that, Vallejo favored United States annexation of California. For years, Vallejo had helped American settlers. His two sisters were married to "Yankees." Frémont's arrogance toward Vallejo and other *Californios* caused great—and unnecessary—bitterness.

The inhabitants of Los Angeles found American rule oppressive. Americans, for instance, tried to establish a curfew—a set time for citizens to be in their homes. Those who broke the curfew were treated harshly. This sparked a rebellion, led by José María Flores, against American authority. The Americans had to withdraw. Forces under Frémont, Kearny, and naval commander Robert Stockton recaptured Los Angeles in January 1847.

INVADING MEXICO

United States forces invaded Mexico from two directions. General Taylor moved south from Texas, defeating Santa Anna's troops at Buena Vista in February 1847. The following month General Winfield Scott landed at Veracruz and battled inland toward Mexico City.

Outside Mexico City Scott met fierce resistance from defenders of Chapultepec (chuh–POOL–tuh–pek). Chapultepec was the fortress that housed the national military school. About 1,000 Mexican soldiers and 100 cadets from the military school fought to the death to defend the fortress. Some of the cadets were as young as thirteen years old. These courageous youths fought until cut down by the final charge of United States forces. One cadet is said to have wrapped himself in the academy's flag at the end of the fighting and leaped from the fort to the rocks below. Known as *Los Niños Heroicos* (LOHS NEEN–yohs ay–ROH–ee–kohs), the cadets have become heroes of Mexico. Despite such determined resistance, Mexico City fell to Scott's troops in September 1847, and the most significant fighting was over.

The Mexican War ended with the Treaty of Guadalupe Hidalgo (gwah–duh–LOOP–ay hih–DAHL–goh) in 1848. In the treaty Mexico recognized the Rio Grande as a boundary. Mexico also ceded—gave up—New Mexico, California, and the land between them. This land, called the Mexican Cession, included the present-day states of California, Nevada, Utah, and parts of Arizona, New Mexico, Colorado, and Wyoming. In return, the United States agreed to pay Mexico $15 million in cash. The United States also paid $3.25 million to Americans who claimed that the Mexican government owed them money.

The war had cost the United States $100 million and more than 17,000 dead and wounded. A generation of officers had their first experience at battle command in the Mexican War—men such as Robert E. Lee,

This dramatic painting, by C. Escalante, shows a battle in the Mexican War at Molino del Rey, a fortress outside Mexico City where cannon and gunpowder were manufactured. The battle ended when the warehouse caught fire and the building blew up. HISTORY Why might United States forces have wanted to capture Mexico City?

Vincente Suárez (left) was only thirteen years old and Francisco Marquez (right) fourteen when they died defending their school, the Mexican Military Academy located in Chapultepec castle. Along with four other cadets killed in the battle against American forces, these young men became national heroes of Mexico. **HISTORY** What did Mexico lose as a result of the war?

Ulysses S. Grant, and Jefferson Davis. More than 25,000 Mexicans died in combat. It was a bitter defeat for Mexico, which lost almost one half of its territory.

THE GEOGRAPHY OF THE GADSDEN PURCHASE

After the Mexican War, the Gila River served as the southwest boundary of the United States. North of the Gila River lay the high peaks of the southern Rocky Mountains. South of the river, in Mexico, was a mountain pass and flatter land. Still farther south, the Gulf of California provided an outlet to the Pacific Ocean.

In 1853 James Gadsden, the United States minister to Mexico, approached Santa Anna, who was once more serving as Mexico's president. Gadsden explained that the United States wanted to buy land south of the Gila. The nation wanted the land in order to build tracks for a railroad.

Gadsden hoped to buy land that extended all the way to the Gulf of California, but Santa Anna refused. Mexico did sell the United States a strip of land in what is now southern New Mexico and Arizona for $10 million. This deal, known as the Gadsden Purchase, completed the present-day southwestern boundary of the United States. It also helped bring about the downfall of Santa Anna. Anger over the further loss of their land led many Mexicans to support Santa Anna's banishment in 1855.

SECTION REVIEW

1. KEY TERMS manifest destiny, expansionist, Mexican War, Bear Flag Revolt, Treaty of Guadalupe Hidalgo, cede, Mexican Cession

2. PEOPLE AND PLACES James K. Polk, Oregon Country, Rio Grande, Nueces River, Zachary Taylor, Stephen Kearny, John C. Frémont, Mariano Vallejo, Winfield Scott

3. COMPREHENSION How did the idea of manifest destiny lead to the acquisition of Oregon?

4. COMPREHENSION What was the American strategy for the invasion of Mexico?

5. CRITICAL THINKING Could the Mexican War have been avoided, or was it inevitable? Explain your answer.

3 California: The World Rushed In

Section Focus

Key Terms Gold Rush of 1849
■ forty-niner ■ boomtown

Main Idea The discovery of gold in California resulted in the arrival of a flood of newcomers to the region.

Objectives As you read, look for answers to these questions:
1. What cultures coexisted in California before the Gold Rush?
2. What was life like in the mining camps and gold fields?
3. What were the effects of the Gold Rush?

For a century Spain, and then Mexico, controlled the California coast below San Francisco. Although Spain claimed all of California, Spanish officials had reluctantly accepted the presence of Russian fur traders in northern California. The interior of California was, as it had been for ages, home to tens of thousands of Indians.

The Mexican War changed the flag that flew over California. The real change to the region came, however, with the discovery of gold in 1848. A title of a book on the Gold Rush summarizes that change: *The World Rushed In*. The story of that change begins almost a decade earlier, with the arrival of Johann Sutter.

SUTTER'S CALIFORNIA DREAM

In 1834 Johann Sutter, a young, bankrupt shopkeeper from Switzerland, set out for America in order to avoid debtor's prison. In the new land he hoped to make a fortune.

Johann Sutter's settlement in California's Sacramento Valley included 60 houses, 6 mills, and a tannery in 1847. The construction in 1848 of the sawmill shown here led to the discovery of gold. **CULTURAL PLURALISM** What ethnic groups lived in California in 1848?

1825   Joel R. Poinsett is named the first United States minister to Mexico.

1831   The phrase "Old Glory," used to describe the flag of the United States, was coined by an American seaman.

1832   The first American clipper ship is launched from Baltimore, Maryland.

1849   Stagecoach service provided between Independence, Missouri, and Santa Fe.

1851   The phrase "Go west, young man, go west" is first used by John B. Soule, editor of the *Terre Haute Express.*

1853   Direct rail service began between New York and Chicago.

First he settled near St. Louis and tried farming. That did not work. Then he tried making trading trips to Santa Fe. That failed too.

In New Mexico, however, Sutter met a French Canadian traveler who had spent several years in California. This man could not say enough about the region's beauty, climate, and fertility. Sutter was hooked. In 1838 he left St. Louis for California.

The Mexican governor gave Sutter permission to establish a colony in northern California. In doing so, the governor hoped that Sutter would discourage Yankees from coming over the mountains, control local Indians, and prevent the Russians from extending inland from their settlement at Fort Ross.

Sutter set up headquarters on the American River, where the city of Sacramento is now. From his base at Sutter's Fort, Sutter began to expand his land grant. In 1841 the Russians decided to abandon Fort Ross and sold their land, cattle, and farms to Sutter.

By 1847, under the American flag, California was a mix of cultures. In it lived about 9,000 *Californios* and 4,000 foreigners, including Americans. There were about 150,000 Indians. Among them were 15,000 mission Indians who worked as laborers.

THE DISCOVERY OF GOLD

Sutter contracted with James Marshall, a jack-of-all-trades, to build a sawmill on the South Fork of the American River. The mill was almost finished in January 1848. One day Marshall was inspecting the stream of water that drove the mill. Then, he said, "My eye was caught by something shining in the bottom of the ditch. I reached my hand down and picked it up; it made my heart thump, for I was certain it was gold."

> "**I**t made my heart thump, for I was certain it was gold."
>
> —*James Marshall, on the strike at Sutter's Mill*

Gold it was. Three days later he stumbled into Sutter's office. He drew out a rag from his pocket. Opening it, he showed Sutter the small gold nuggets therein.

Sutter was not happy with the find. In his words:

> During the night the thought burst upon my mind that a curse might rest upon this discovery. . . . I was convinced that it would greatly interfere with my plans. From the very beginning I knew what the outcome would be. . . .

Word of the discovery at Sutter's Mill reached San Francisco and then spread to the world beyond. Several months later a San Francisco newspaper reported:

> The whole country from San Francisco to Los Angeles and from the seashore to the base of the Sierra Nevada resounds to the sordid cry of gold, gold!, GOLD! while the field is left half planted, the house half built and everything neglected but the manufacture of shovels and pickaxes.

Women as well as men rushed to California to make their fortune. These forty-niners are shoveling gravel and mud containing gold into a wooden trough, called a sluice. The heavy gold would fall through the mud, where it was caught by bars at the bottom of the sluice. Dirt and gravel would then be washed away by water from the stream. **TECHNOLOGY** What equipment and resources were necessary for this method of mining?

THE RUSH FOR GOLD

The gold rush was on. People dreamed of instant riches. Some found them. A goldseeker wrote home, "You know Bryant, the carpenter who used to work for Ebenezer Dixon, well, he has dug more gold in the last six months than a mule can pack."

Such reports triggered the Gold Rush of 1849. Tens of thousands of forty-niners made their way to California by land and sea. Most were Americans, but people came from all over the world. By 1850 California had a non-Indian population of 93,000.

Free blacks came by the hundreds, and many struck it rich. By 1855 the African Americans living in California were the wealthiest in the country. Many used their money to establish churches. J. B. Sanderson became a reformer and used his talents to set up schools for Asian, African American, and Indian children. At the time, those students were often banned from public schools.

For Sutter, the forty-niners became a living nightmare. They shot and ate his cattle, trampled his fields, and camped on his land. The goldseekers had no respect for land titles that had been issued by the Mexican government. Sutter lost everything. "Sick at heart and body," he left California.

LIFE IN THE MINING CAMPS

Ramshackle mining camps mushroomed along the streams and rivers of the Sierra Nevada foothills. These camps acquired colorful and descriptive names that hint at the ups and downs of the miners' lives. They included Poker Flat, Hangtown, Fiddletown, Angels Camp, Whiskey Flat, Happy Camp, Murderers' Bar, Poverty Hill, and Gouge Eye.

The population of these boomtowns—towns that grow quickly—could swell almost overnight to several thousand. The population could disappear as quickly on news of a new find.

Most of the forty-niners were men. They were adventurers intent on making a fortune and returning home rich. Only a small number brought their families with the intention of staying in California. Although some women could be found laboring in the mines, most earned money by cooking, washing, and running boarding houses.

Mining for gold could be very hard. One forty-niner wrote home, "George, I tell you this mining among the mountains is a dog's life." Another wrote:

> We see nothing here but hills, mountains and rocks . . . no farming operations, no meetings, no horses and carriages or cattle, no female society—hear no music except . . . the croaking of ravens, the chattering of woodpeckers and the roaring of the [river].

The cost of goods was terribly high in the mining camps. It is not surprising, therefore, that many forty-niners made large sums of money by providing services to the miners. A newspaper reporter told this story:

> I saw a man who came to the river three weeks before my visit, without money, to dig in the dry gulch. Being very lazy, he chose a spot under a shady tree, and dug leisurely for two days without making a cent. He then gave up the place, when a little German jumped into his tracks and after a day's hard work weighed out $800. The unlucky digger then borrowed five ounces and started a boarding-house. The town increased so fast that the night I arrived he sold out his share (one third) of the concern for $1,200.

The wife of a physician in one of the camps decided to try her luck at mining. The result, she wrote, was that "I wet my feet, tore my dress, spoilt a pair of new gloves, nearly froze my fingers, got an awful headache, took cold, and lost a valuable . . . pin." For this she had earned $3.25 in gold dust. Many miners, she wrote, never earned more than "wages"—six to eight dollars a day.

THE CHINESE AND OTHER IMMIGRANTS

By the end of 1851 one-tenth of California's population was Chinese. Thousands of young Chinese men signed up as indentured servants to work in the gold fields for Chinese labor lords. They thought of California as the "Golden Mountain" and dreamed, as did others, of returning home rich.

Once in the gold fields, the Chinese met with prejudice. Their language, their food, their clothes, and their ways were all different. Most striking were their long queues (KYOOZ)—pigtails. The queue was a symbol both of Chinese manhood and of belonging to the Chinese nation. One way in which Americans harassed the Chinese was to cut off their precious queues.

Driven from the mining camps, many Chinese worked over old diggings and still made money. Some Chinese began to provide services to other miners, such as cooking and washing clothes. In later years, the Chinese served an important role in building railroads and drainage canals. Despite the prejudices they faced, the Chinese continued to see

This engraving of Chinese immigrants arriving in San Francisco also shows immigrants moving on to new homes. In 1852 California's governor called the Chinese the "most desirable of our adopted citizens." **CULTURAL PLURALISM** What forms of prejudice did the Chinese face?

Despite his arrest by American forces during the Mexican War, Mariano Vallejo supported the annexation of California. He later served as a member of the first state senate. **CULTURAL PLURALISM** Would most *Californios* have supported annexation? Why or why not?

California as the "Golden Mountain"—the land of opportunity.

The mass of goldseekers also included hundreds of immigrants from northern Mexico and Chile. Many of them ended up in the mining camp of Sonora, in the center of California. "Here were to be seen people of every nation in all varieties of costume, and speaking 50 different languages," wrote William Perkins, a Canadian forty-niner.

As growing numbers of Yankees swarmed into California, they forced foreigners out of the gold fields. Perkins, the Canadian, found Anglo-American prejudice disturbing:

> [The Yankees] are sober, do not gamble, and rarely fight except when driving off the poor Chinese, the Mexicans and the Chilenos from their coveted claims; . . . only the Yankees [act as if] none but Americans have a right to work the gold mines.

EFFECTS OF THE GOLD RUSH

Between 1849 and 1852, 240,000 people arrived in California—the largest migration in American history. The effects were enormous. San Francisco was transformed from a village into a major city. It quickly became a center of banking, manufacturing, shipping, and trade.

Most American newcomers to California held certain attitudes in common. They believed in the superiority of the white race, of the Anglo-American heritage, and of Protestant Christianity. As a result of these attitudes, they treated the *Californios* as second-class citizens. They not only overlooked the heritage of Mexican California but also had little respect for Mexican land titles. As a result of their mass migration, Anglo-American culture, enterprise, and law quickly replaced that of Mexican California.

The most disastrous effect of the Gold Rush was the devastation of the California Indians. Native Americans throughout the hemisphere had been killed by new diseases. This, too, happened in California. About 60 percent of the Indians died from disease. Large numbers of Indians, however, were purposely hunted down and slaughtered like animals. The reason for doing so was the ingrained belief that Indians stood in the way of progress. "It is as impossible for the white man and the wild Indian to live together as it is to unite oil and water," a newspaper pronounced. By 1870 the California Indian population had plummeted from 150,000 to 30,000.

Another effect of the California Gold Rush was that by 1850 California was ready for statehood. That in turn would have consequences for the rest of the nation, because California chose to be a free state.

CALIFORNIA: A FREE STATE

The forty-niners themselves were the first to decide that California should be a free territory. Among those streaming into California in the spring of 1849 were a number of slave-holders from Texas. The Texans set their slaves to work mining on the Yuba River. Other miners working the river were angry. They did not want to be doing the same work as slaves. At a mass meeting the forty-niners voted to outlaw slavery in the mines.

Meanwhile California's acting military governor called for a constitutional convention. Of the 48 delegates to this convention, eight were *Californios,* including Mariano Vallejo. As a result of their influence, the new constitution was the first in the nation to allow a married woman to retain control over her own property. That had been the law in Mexican California. (American bachelors cheerfully voted for the law because they hoped it would attract wealthy women to the new state.)

The delegates also voted unanimously to exclude slavery from California. That deci-sion would set off a heated debate among members of Congress, as these men struggled to keep the issue of slavery from tearing the nation apart.

SECTION REVIEW

1. KEY TERMS Gold Rush of 1849, forty-niner, boomtown

2. PEOPLE AND PLACES Johann Sutter, American River, James Marshall, San Francisco

3. COMPREHENSION What different peoples lived in California in the 1840s? What event brought new settlers to California?

4. COMPREHENSION How did the gold rush change California?

5. CRITICAL THINKING How might California have developed had there been no gold rush in 1849?

CHAPTER 18 SUMMARY AND TIMELINE

1. Rugged mountain men explored the West, opening trails for emigrants who traveled in wagon trains to the Oregon Territory. Mormons, moving to Utah, made up another large group of emigrants in the 1840s.

2. The United States and Great Britain agreed to divide the Oregon Country, with the southern part of the territory going to the United States. The annexation of Texas helped provoked war with Mexico in 1846. A successful invasion of Mexico resulted in an American victory.

3. Spanish culture lost its dominance in California with the Gold Rush of 1849. The population grew so fast that California entered the Union, as a free state, in 1850.

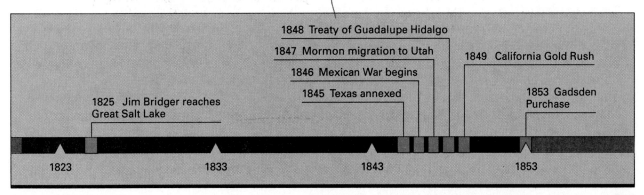

1848 Treaty of Guadalupe Hidalgo
1847 Mormon migration to Utah
1846 Mexican War begins
1849 California Gold Rush
1845 Texas annexed
1853 Gadsden Purchase
1825 Jim Bridger reaches Great Salt Lake

1823   1833   1843   1853

PLACES TO LOCATE

Match each of the letters on the map with the places that are listed below.

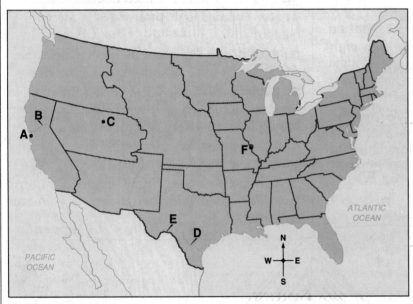

1. American River
2. Nueces River
3. Rio Grande
4. St. Louis
5. Salt Lake City
6. San Francisco

KEY TERMS

Use the following terms to complete the sentences.

**Bear Flag Revolt
emigrants
expansionists
forty-niners
manifest destiny
Oregon Trail**

1. Settlers traveled to the West on the _____.
2. People called _____, who believed in _____, thought that the United States should extend its boundaries to the Pacific Ocean.
3. _____ are people who move to a new place.
4. Americans overthrew Mexican rule in California in the _____ of 1846.
5. The _____ rushed to California to search for gold.

PEOPLE TO IDENTIFY

Choose the name in parentheses that best completes each sentence.

1. (*Jim Beckwourth, Manuel Lisa*), an African American mountain man, had been a chief of the Crow Indians.
2. (*Narcissa Whitman, Brigham Young*) chose the valley of the Great Salt Lake for a settlement.
3. A supporter of the annexation of Texas, (*Zachary Taylor, James K. Polk*) was elected President in 1844.
4. (*Mariano Vallejo, John C. Frémont*) was a *Californio* leader.
5. The Gold Rush of 1849 began after (*John Marshall, Johann Sutter*) saw gold shining in a ditch.

REVIEWING THE FACTS

1. What role did the rendezvous play in the lives of mountain men?
2. What role did mountain men play in the settlement of the Oregon Country?
3. What were the basic rules that governed wagons trains on the Oregon Trail?
4. What events led to the Mormon migration to Utah?
5. What were the immediate causes of the Mexican War?
6. What region in the United States objected to the Mexican War? Why?
7. What territory did the United States gain as a result of the Treaty of Guadalupe Hidalgo?
8. Why did Mexico give Johann Sutter permission to establish a colony in northern California?
9. What was life like in the California mining camps?
10. Why was California ready to join the Union so quickly?

PRACTICING YOUR SKILL

The following passage is an entry from the diary of Amelia Stewart Knight, who traveled to Oregon in 1853. Read the entry and answer the questions that follow.

Tuesday, May 17th We had a dreadful storm of rain and hail last night and very sharp lightning. It killed two oxen for one man. . . . As we could have no tents pitched, all had to crowd into the wagons and sleep in wet beds with their wet clothes on, without supper.

1. How did the thunderstorm described by Knight affect her wagon train?
2. How might Knight have felt about the journey west?

CITIZENSHIP

1. The writer Henry David Thoreau refused to pay taxes as a protest against the Mexican War. Do you think that was an acceptable way to protest the government's actions? What steps should the government have taken against him?
2. How did Americans' attitudes toward other ethnic and racial groups during the Gold Rush affect California? Do you think those attitudes have changed?
3. Many Americans in the 1830s and 1840s believed it was the manifest destiny of the United States to expand to the Pacific. Do you think expansion was good for the United States at that time?

Is expansionism a good attitude for a nation to have? Explain your answers.

CRITICAL THINKING SKILLS

1. IDENTIFYING CAUSE AND EFFECT How did the Mormons' sense of community help them in their attempt to colonize the Great Basin?

2. ANALYZING A QUOTATION Reread Sutter's reaction to the discovery of gold on his property on page 465. What was his attitude toward the find? Why?

3. INFERRING How did earlier westward movement pave the way for rapid expansion in the 1840s?

PROJECTS AND ACTIVITIES

1. WRITING A LETTER Write a letter from a pioneer traveling on the Oregon Trail to a relative living in the East.

2. MAKING A SPEECH Write and then deliver a campaign speech for James K. Polk, explaining why he wanted to

annex Texas and acquire all of Oregon.

3. ROLE PLAYING Imagine that you and your classmates are living in California during the gold rush days. Form a committee to discuss the crime problem your town faces and propose ways to maintain law and order.

WRITING ABOUT TOPICS IN AMERICAN HISTORY

1. CONNECTING WITH LITERATURE A selection from *Two Years Before the Mast* by Richard Henry Dana appears on pages 656–657. Read it and answer the questions. Then answer the following question: How might Dana's description of California have influenced the United States' decision to go to war with Mexico?

2. APPLYING THEMES: PLURALISTIC SOCIETY In a short essay, compare the influence of Hispanic culture on American society in the mid-1800s with Hispanic influence in the United States today.

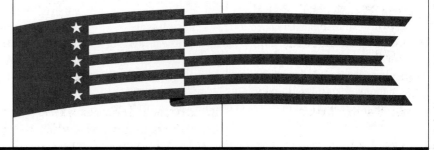

The period 1820–1860 was one of enormous growth for the United States. Talk of reform swept the nation, and the future of African Americans and Indians was debated. Meanwhile, not only did immigrants pour into the country, but the addition of territory following the Mexican War linked the Spanish heritage of Texas, California, and the Southwest to the diverse culture of the United States.

During the years of federal pressure to force the Cherokee from Georgia, the strong voice of **John Ross** (left) rose in defense of his people. (Ross, the son of a Scotsman and a Scotch-Cherokee woman, always considered himself a Cherokee.) When even the Supreme Court could not halt the removal plan, Ross led his nation on the infamous Trail of Tears. Upon arriving in Indian Territory, he helped write a constitution for the Cherokee.

José Antonio Navarro (right) was the son of Spanish immigrants to Mexico. He fought for Mexico's independence from Spain and became a legislator when independence was achieved in 1821. Around this time, Navarro formed a close friendship with Stephen Austin. For his opposition to Santa Anna's centralized government, Navarro was sent to the worst prison in Mexico. He escaped, and after Texas's annexation to the United States he became a state senator. In 1960 the state of Texas declared Navarro the "co-creator of Texas."

During the winter of 1821, **Jane Long**, her young daughter Ann, and a twelve-year old black servant named Kian lived in a small fort at Point Bolivar, Texas (above), then a part of Mexico. There they waited for Long's husband, James Long. James Long and other Texans had been fighting for freedom from Spain, which ruled Mexico. He had been killed in Mexico City, but his family did not know that and hoped for his return. Jane Long gave birth to another child that winter. She struggled to keep her family alive, fishing and hunting for food. When a band of Karankawa Indians approached the fort, Long fired a cannon and frightened them away. At last help arrived in the spring, along with the news of her husband's death. Still, Jane Long lived to see her husband's dream of an independent Texas come true. One of the first Anglo-American women to settle in Texas, she became a successful businesswoman before turning to farming. Her farm in Fort Bend County became one of the most prosperous in the state.

He started life as a member of an important *Califor-nio* family and eventually became one of the largest landowners in California. But **Pío Pico** (left) correctly saw the future when, while serving as the last Mexican governor of California, he wrote, "We find ourselves suddenly threatened by hordes of Yankee emigrants . . . whose progress we cannot arrest." Pío Pico organized resistance when the Americans invaded during the Mexican War, but in the face of a hopeless military situation he fled south. After the Treaty of Guadalupe Hidalgo in 1848, Pío Pico returned to his California ranch. In the end, through bad business decisions he lost most of his extensive holdings and died penniless.

When **Biddy Mason** (right) learned in 1851 that her owner was preparing to head for the gold fields of California, she was overjoyed. At last, here was a way out of the slave South! Even better news was to greet her upon her arrival on the West Coast. California had just outlawed slavery. When her owner threatened to move to Texas to avoid freeing her, Mason took him to court and won her freedom. She moved to Los Angeles where, through hard work and frugal living, she saved up enough money to buy land in what became downtown Los Angeles. She bought and sold other property, and became one of the state's wealthiest women. She also devoted herself to charitable work. After her death, Los Angeles honored her as one of the city's greatest humanitarians.

Thousands of free blacks were among the forty-niners who flocked to California seeking instant wealth. **George Monroe** (left) came from Georgia, but he did not make his money mining. Monroe became the best stagecoach driver in the state, ferrying tourists—including three Presidents—into the Yosemite Valley. Later, after the area had become a national park, Monroe Meadows was named in his honor.

Yung Wing

Sent to America by missionaries in China, **Yung Wing** (above) graduated from Yale University in 1854. The first Asian to graduate from an American college, he returned to China to set up a cultural exchange program between China and the United States.

Manjiro Nakahama was rescued at sea in 1841 by an American whaling ship. He was brought to Massachusetts where he was given a new name, John Mung, and sent to school. Nakahama, who returned to his homeland in 1851, is believed to be the first Japanese in America.

HISTORIANS' CORNER

Motives for Jacksonian Democracy

People often think of the Age of Jackson as a time of a new democratic spirit—a belief in the wisdom of the "common man" as opposed to the educated "aristocrats" who had earlier dominated American government. Many prominent historians of the time—such as George Bancroft—held this view, and it is still popular today. Other historians, though, see practical political reasons for the era of "Jacksonian democracy."

Arthur M. Schlesinger, Jr.

[T]he Jeffersonians . . . looked on industrial labor as an element, fortunately small, to be regarded with mistrust and abhorrence. Without property the working classes of great cities must be without independence, factious [divided] and corrupt, the prey of demagogues and tyrants. This analysis may not have been altogether inaccurate, but neither the Jeffersonians nor especially the Federalists accompanied it by serious attempts to prevent the new industrialism from spawning the class whose influence they so much feared.

The [industrial] class thus grew, for all the disapproval of the old parties, and eventually its power commanded recognition. Jacksonian democracy acted on this new political fact. Class consciousness was much greater a century ago than people imagine who believe it was invented in the Great Depression [the 1930s]. Jacksonian speeches roused it, much Jacksonian legislation was based on it, the Jacksonian press appealed to it. Democratic papers opened their columns to the defense of trade-unionism, printed reports of union meetings and assailed the enemies of labor organization.

From Arthur M. Schlesinger, Jr., *The Age of Jackson.* Copyright © 1945 by Arthur M. Schlesinger, Jr. Published by Little, Brown & Co.

George Bancroft

The absence of the prejudices of the old world [Europe] leaves us here the opportunity of consulting independent truth; and man is left to apply the instinct of freedom to every social relation and public interest. . . . We have made Humanity our lawgiver and our oracle; and, therefore, the nation receives . . . and applies principles, which in Europe the wisest accept with distrust. . . .

Such is the political system which rests on reason, reflection, and the free expression of deliberate choice. There may be those who scoff at the suggestion, that the decision of the whole is to be preferred to the judgment of the enlightened few. They say in their hearts that the masses are ignorant; that farmers know nothing of legislation; that mechanics should not quit their workshops to join in forming public opinion. But true political science does indeed venerate the masses. It maintains, not as has been perversely asserted, that "the people can make right," but that the people can DISCERN right.

From "The Office of the People in Art, Government, and Religion," speech given by George Bancroft in 1835; reprinted in *The Romantic Democracy, 1835-1855,* edited by Gilman M. Ostrander, © 1971.

Critical Thinking

1. Which of these historians holds the "romantic" belief in the wisdom and abilities of the mass of ordinary people?

2. How does Schlesinger contrast the attitudes of "Jeffersonians" and "Jacksonians" toward industrialization and the people of the working class?

3. According to Schlesinger, how did social or class divisions affect politics in the United States during the Age of Jackson?

The Nation Divided and Rebuilt

THEMES IN AMERICAN HISTORY

 Constitutional Government   By defeating the South's bid for independence, the Union reasserted the power of the federal government over the states.

 Expanding Democracy   A series of constitutional amendments helped guarantee the rights of all Americans.

 Economic Development   Following the Civil War the nation entered a period of industrial transformation and rapid growth.

 Pluralistic Society   The ending of slavery failed to eliminate the nation's racial divisions.

Slavery was the most controversial issue dividing North and South in the 1850s. This Jacob Lawrence painting shows Harriet Tubman, hero of the Underground Railroad.

19 The Nation Breaking Apart (1850–1861)

1 Growing Differences Between North and South

Section Focus

Key Terms   Mason-Dixon Line
■ homestead ■ Compromise of 1850
■ Fugitive Slave Law

Main Idea   Members of Congress, badly split over allowing slavery in new territories, looked for a compromise.

Objectives   As you read, look for answers to these questions:
1.   Why did the free states have greater economic growth than the slave states?
2.   Why did California's request for admission to the Union cause turmoil in Congress?
3.   How did North and South work out their differences?

Imagine that it is the year 1850. You are taking a trip down the length of the Ohio River. As a tourist, you are on one of the paddle-wheel steamboats that regularly travel the river. From time to time, the steamboat pulls into one of the river towns. What you see on shore, however, depends on whether the boat docks on the right bank or the left bank of the river.

If the steamboat lands on the right bank—at Cincinnati, Ohio, for example—the dock workers are likely to be white men. If the steamboat lands on the left bank, at a place such as Louisville, Kentucky, the dock workers are likely to be black slaves.

CONTRASTS BETWEEN NORTH AND SOUTH

The Ohio River—almost 1,000 miles long—was the boundary between slave and free states west of the Appalachian Mountains. (The **Mason-Dixon Line**, the border be-

tween Pennsylvania and Maryland, was the boundary east of the mountains.) On the north side of the river were the states of Ohio, Indiana, and Illinois. These were free states as a result of the Northwest Ordinance (page 226). On the south side of the river were Virginia (now West Virginia) and Kentucky. These were both slave states.

At the time of the American Revolution, slaves could be found in all the states. The northern states, however, had gradually abolished slavery. Meanwhile, slavery had grown in the cotton-growing states of the South.

In the 1830s Alexis de Tocqueville took a journey on the Ohio River "between freedom and slavery." He saw many differences between the left bank and the right bank.

On the left bank of the river the population is sparse; from time to time one sees a troop of slaves loitering through

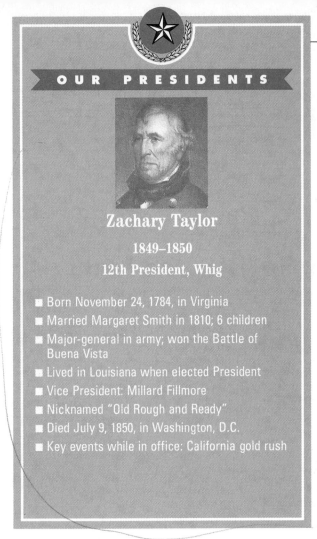

OUR PRESIDENTS

Zachary Taylor

1849–1850

12th President, Whig

- Born November 24, 1784, in Virginia
- Married Margaret Smith in 1810; 6 children
- Major-general in army; won the Battle of Buena Vista
- Lived in Louisiana when elected President
- Vice President: Millard Fillmore
- Nicknamed "Old Rough and Ready"
- Died July 9, 1850, in Washington, D.C.
- Key events while in office: California gold rush

OUR PRESIDENTS

Millard Fillmore

1850–1853

13th President, Whig

- Born January 7, 1800, in New York
- Married Abigail Powers in 1826; 2 children
- Married Caroline McIntosh in 1858; no children
- Lawyer; representative from New York; Vice President under Taylor
- Lived in New York when elected Vice President
- Vice President: none
- Died March 8, 1874, in New York
- Key events while in office: Compromise of 1850; California became a state

half-deserted fields; . . . it is nature that seems active and alive, whereas man is idle.

But on the right bank a confused hum proclaims from afar that men are busily at work; fine crops cover the fields; elegant dwellings testify to the taste and industry of the workers; on all sides there is evidence of comfort; man appears rich and contented; he works.

Why, Tocqueville asked, was there such a strong difference between one side of the river and the other? His answer was simple: slavery.

On the left bank of the Ohio work is connected with the idea of slavery, but on the right with well-being and progress; on the one side [work] is degrading, but on the other honorable; on the left bank no white laborers are to be found, for they would be afraid of being like the slaves; . . . but one will never see a man of leisure on the right bank.

Differences between North and South were nothing new. The two regions had been quite different even in colonial times. The coming of the Industrial Revolution, however, made the differences greater.

By 1850 the North and South had separate economic systems and separate cultures. Northern cities were growing rapidly as a result of industry and immigration. Starting in

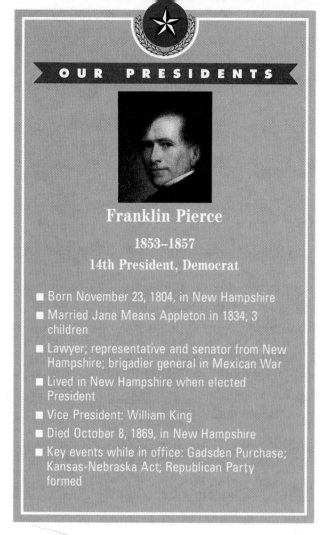
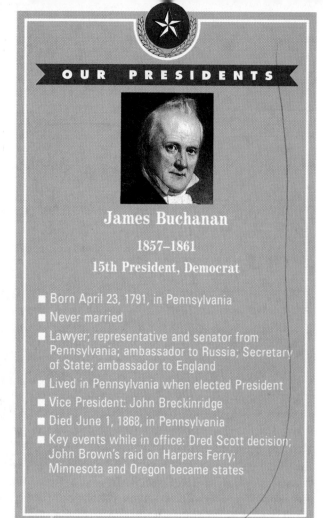
the 1840s, thousands of Irish and German immigrants landed on American shores. Most stayed in the North, for they did not choose to compete with the slave labor of the South. By 1850 the North had more wealth, more factories, more and bigger cities, and more people than the South. The South remained primarily a rural region.

SLAVERY AND RACISM

In the North, meanwhile, the abolitionist movement (page 415) had gained strength. Abolitionists wanted to end slavery because they thought it wrong and un-Christian. Other northerners had economic reasons for opposing slavery. Slavery was seen as a "blight" that "polluted" the soil and "paralyzed" economic growth.

Many southerners agreed that slavery was both a moral and an economic evil. Yet they backed slavery because they did not know any other way to live in a racially mixed society. Most white southerners, rich and poor alike, held the racist belief that white people were superior to black people. If slavery were ended, white southerners worried, the social barriers separating whites and blacks would disappear. As one white farmer put it, "Now suppose they was free, you see they'd all think themselves as good as we."

Such prejudice was not confined to the South. It existed at the very core of American society. In the North as well as the South, African Americans could not serve on juries or hold high public offices. Churches, schools, and even cemeteries would not accept them.

Debates over slavery contributed to sectional divisions during the first half of the 1800s. This scene shows slaves laboring in a cotton field. Once picked and cleaned, the cotton was taken to market. **TECHNOLOGY** What methods of transportation are shown in the painting?

Shut out of good jobs, most African Americans in the North lived in poverty. Tocqueville went so far as to write, "Race prejudice seems stronger in those states that have abolished slavery than in those where it still exists."

IMPACT OF THE MEXICAN WAR

For decades the sectional divisions over slavery had been building. Lawmakers thought they had settled the issue with the Compromise of 1820. That law had said that slavery could continue in the Louisiana Territory south of the parallel 36°30'. The issue of slavery, however, would not go away.

By 1846 the growing population of the North had tilted the balance of power in the House of Representatives toward the free states. Southerners feared that if the free states also gained control of the Senate, Congress would abolish slavery. Southern leaders reasoned, therefore, that their best defense was to extend slavery into new territories. If the territories became slave states, the slave states might then hold on to their majority in the Senate. If so, the balance of power between slave states and free states in Congress would be maintained.

In 1846 it was clear to Congress that President Polk intended to obtain California from Mexico. Gaining new territory, however, would raise the old question: slave or free? David Wilmot, a member of Congress from Pennsylvania, suggested that slavery never be allowed in any land gained from Mexico. This proposal, called the Wilmot Proviso, passed the House, but not the Senate. (The slave states were in the majority by one.)

Still, the Wilmot Proviso did not die. It came up again and again. Each time it was defeated, with northerners in favor and southerners against.

When the Wilmot Proviso failed again in 1848, some northerners formed a new political party, the Free-Soil Party. The Free-Soil Party demanded an end to slavery. It also urged Congress to give western settlers free homesteads—land on which to settle and build houses. Candidates ran for office with the slogan "Free Soil, Free Speech, Free Labor, and Free Men." The Free-Soil Party won fourteen seats in Congress in the election of 1848.

For white southerners, the success of the Free-Soil Party was one more reason for alarm. Wisconsin had just entered the Union as a free state. There were now fifteen free states and fifteen slave states. As long as that balance held, no law could pass the Senate without southern support. If new territories in the West entered the Union as free states, however, the South would lose power in Congress.

After the Mexican War ended in 1848, the dispute over slavery heated up. California asked to be admitted as a free state. Southerners wanted to divide California in half, making the southern half a slave state. Antislavery forces would have none of it.

The question of statehood for California brought matters to a head. If California became a free state, the balance of power between free and slave states would shift. Southerners would not accept that position. Talk of secession from the Union became more frequent.

THE COMPROMISE OF 1850

Henry Clay of Kentucky, though old and ailing, rose once again to present a compromise. It included admitting California as a free state.

Extremists in both the North and the South opposed such a deal. William H. Seward, a senator from New York, stated, "Slavery . . . can and must be abolished, and you and I can and must do it." He told Congress that "there is a higher law than the

The Senate debate over the Compromise of 1850 featured three great political leaders—Daniel Webster (left), Henry Clay (center), and John C. Calhoun (right). **POLITICS** Why did the issue of slavery heat up after the Mexican War?

Courtesy Time-Life Books Inc.

itution"—the law of God, in whose sight all persons are equal.

The most conservative southerners also resisted compromise. They were determined to maintain a balance between slave states and free states. When they accused Clay of deserting the South, his answer electrified the Senate. "I know my duty and coming from a slave state as I do, no power on earth shall ever make me vote for the extension of slavery over one foot of territory now free. Never.—No, Sir, NO."

> "**I** know my duty and coming from a slave state as I do, no power on earth shall ever make me vote for the extension of slavery over one foot of territory now free. Never.—No, Sir, NO."
>
> *—Henry Clay, 1850*

Daniel Webster, the Massachusetts politician, used his famous power of oratory to urge compromise:

> I wish to speak today, not as a Massachusetts man, nor as a northern man, but as an American. . . . I speak today for the preservation of the Union. Hear me for my cause.

Webster asked each side to bury the passions of the past. What was important, he said, was to preserve the Constitution. "Let us enjoy the fresh air of Liberty and Union," he urged.

It was one of Webster's most famous speeches. (American schoolchildren would recite it for years to come.) It appealed to the American people, most of whom wanted compromise. Business leaders, farmers, laborers—all were prospering. They did not want disruption. Public pressure forced Congress to vote for Clay's **Compromise of 1850**.

The **Compromise of 1850** had several important provisions:

(1) California was admitted to the Union as a free state.

(2) The rest of the Mexican Cession was divided into the territories of New Mexico and Utah. People in these territories would decide for themselves whether or not to allow slavery.

(3) The slave trade was abolished in Washington, D.C.

(4) Congress passed the **Fugitive Slave Law**. This law said that people in the free states had to help catch and return fugitive (escaped) slaves. Anyone caught aiding a runaway slave could be jailed or given a heavy fine. Under the new law, a court officer decided whether a person was a fugitive or not. Each time the officer decided in favor of the slaveholder, he received $10. For deciding in favor of the fugitive, he received only $5. In other words, the system was rigged in favor of the slaveholder.

Few Americans liked the compromise. Southerners were so upset at the admission of California that four states threatened to secede. Northerners, many of whom supported the Underground Railroad (page 417), hated the Fugitive Slave Law. Still, both sides decided to give compromise a chance.

SECTION REVIEW

1. KEY TERMS Mason-Dixon Line, homestead, Compromise of 1850, Fugitive Slave Law

2. PEOPLE AND PLACES Ohio River, California, David Wilmot, Henry Clay, Daniel Webster

3. COMPREHENSION What economic differences existed between North and South?

4. COMPREHENSION Why were passions so strong over the issue of allowing slavery in the territories?

5. CRITICAL THINKING How might the South have developed had the Founding Fathers abolished slavery?

Gaining Skill: Distinguishing Fact from Opinion

When studying history, you need both facts and opinions to get a full picture of what happened, where and when it happened, and who was involved. **Facts** are based on information that can be checked for accuracy. **Opinions,** on the other hand, express people's feelings, beliefs, and attitudes.

In this chapter, for example, the facts about the Compromise of 1850 are stated on page 482. The terms of the agreement that are described there could be checked in other sources of information and proved to be true. However, Tocqueville's statement, "Race prejudice seems stronger in those states that have abolished slavery than in those where it still exists," tells you about Tocqueville's personal beliefs and feelings about racism in the United States. The statement expresses his opinion—an opinion that may or may not prove to be accurate.

Although both facts and opinions are useful in studying history, it is important to distinguish between them. Opinions are not always based on the truth. Yet sometimes opinions are stated so strongly that they are accepted as facts. Mistaking opinions for facts can lead to misunderstandings about historical events.

When writers state facts, they use neutral language that is free of bias or personal judgments. A writer can explain a person's opinion without passing judgment on that opinion. For example, a writer might describe two opposing sides in a debate by using neutral language such as "One side claimed that . . ." and "Others responded that. . . ."

On the other hand, when writers express opinions, they use subjective language that shows their point of view. One good way to recognize opinions is to look for phrases such as "I believe" and "in my view." Such phrases tell the reader that what follows is an opinion. However, writers do not always point out when they are giving opinions rather than facts. Sometimes they simply use judgmental words, such as "smart," "best," or "unfairly."

The sentence "Thomas Jefferson was our nation's best President" may sound like a statement of fact, but it is an opinion.

The excerpt on this page is from the journal of Charlotte Forten, a sixteen-year-old free black living in Boston in 1854. She is discussing the arrest and conviction of Anthony Burns, a fugitive slave. Read the passage. Then answer the questions that follow.

> Our worst fears are realized. The [court's] decision was against poor [Anthony] Burns, and he has been sent back to a [fate] worse, a thousand times worse than death.
>
> With what scorn must that government be regarded, which cowardly assembles thousands of soldiers to satisfy the demands of slaveholders; to deprive of his freedom a man, created in God's own image, whose sole offense is the color of his skin! And if resistance is offered to this outrage, these soldiers are to shoot down American citizens without mercy; and this by the express orders of a government which proudly boasts of being the freest in the world; this on the very soil where the Revolution of 1776 began.
>
> I can write no more. A cloud seems hanging over me, over all our persecuted race, which nothing can dispel.

PRACTICING YOUR SKILL

1. In the first paragraph, what facts does Charlotte Forten give about the day's events?
2. What opinion about slavery does Forten give in the first paragraph?
3. In the second paragraph, what fact does Forten give about the orders that soldiers must follow?
4. In the second paragraph, what opinions does Forten express about the government?
5. What is the "outrage" to which Forten refers? Does the word *outrage* express a fact or an opinion?

2 The Crisis Deepens

★ **Section Focus** ★

Key Terms Kansas-Nebraska Act ■ Dred Scott case

Main Idea Several events during the 1850s increased the distrust between North and South.

Objectives As you read, look for answers to these questions:
1. How did the issue of slavery bring bloodshed to the frontier?
2. What events deepened the division between North and South?

For a brief time the Compromise of 1850 cooled hot tempers. Peace, however, did not last long. Events over the next decade caused the quarrels to become more common, more angry, and more bitter.

UNCLE TOM'S CABIN

Many fugitive slaves heading north tried to cross the Ohio River into the free states beyond. In Cincinnati, Harriet Beecher Stowe, the wife of a clergyman, watched the agony as part of the population helped slaves escape and another part tried to recapture them.

When the Fugitive Slave Law passed, Harriet received a letter from her sister. "Hattie," the letter read, "if I could use a pen as you can, I would write something that will make this whole nation feel what an accursed thing slavery is." Stowe took up the challenge.

> The heroic element was strong in me, having come down . . . from a long line of Puritan ancestry, and just now it made me long to do something, I knew not what: to fight for my country, or to make some declaration on my own account.

In 1852 Harriet Beecher Stowe published *Uncle Tom's Cabin*. The book told of a kind, hardworking slave, Uncle Tom, and his mistreatment by a cruel master. It gave a dramatic account of the sufferings of a beautiful young slave named Eliza and of her flight to freedom. The moving story touched the hearts of most northerners. The novel became an instant success, selling over 300,000 copies the first year.

Uncle Tom's Cabin affected thousands who had not thought much about slavery one way or another. As a result, it set off a tidal wave of abolitionist feeling. Stowe pointed out that slavery was not just the South's problem; it was the nation's problem. Everyone was responsible. She wrote:

> The people of the free states have defended, encouraged, and participated; and are more guilty for it, before God, than the South, in that they have *not* the apology of education or custom.

BIOGRAPHY

HARRIET BEECHER STOWE (1811–1896) won international recognition as an author and abolitionist. Born in Litchfield, Connecticut, Stowe was the daughter of a famous minister and the sister of five other clergymen. She wrote essays and stories about Puritanism, her Mayflower ancestors, and New England country life. Her later work was strongly antislavery and included three novels, the most famous of which was *Uncle Tom's Cabin.*

The nation could be saved, Stowe wrote, only "by repentance, justice, and mercy."

Angry southerners attacked the book for giving a false picture of the South. Resentful and defensive, white southerners repeated their argument that slavery was necessary and good. Planters even talked of re-opening the African slave trade.

THE KANSAS-NEBRASKA ACT

In 1854 the slavery issue once more entered the halls of Congress. The cause was a proposal to build a transcontinental railroad (a railroad running completely across the continent). Stephen Douglas, a senator from Illinois, wanted the railroad to run through Chicago. He knew, however, that a railroad heading west from Chicago would have to cross the unorganized territory of the Great Plains. He therefore proposed a new law, the Kansas-Nebraska Act.

Douglas's plan was to create two new territories, Kansas and Nebraska. Both territories would lie north of the Missouri Compromise line. By law they should have been closed to slavery. To win southern support, however, Douglas called for scrapping the Missouri Compromise in favor of the principle of popular sovereignty. That is, the people in each territory would decide whether their territory was to be slave or free.

The Kansas-Nebraska Act passed with the solid backing of the South. Northern reaction, however, was divided. Some saw it as a useful compromise. Others opposed any move to extend slavery. This group of antislavery northerners banded together and organized the Republican Party in the summer of 1854. (This is the same Republican Party that

MAP SKILLS

These maps show the changing balance between slave and free states during the mid-1800s. After the Compromise of 1850, which new territories were open to slavery? How did the Kansas-Nebraska Act overrule the Missouri Compromise? CRITICAL THINKING Why did opponents of slavery see the Kansas-Nebraska Act as a threat?

SLAVE VERSUS FREE TERRITORY IN THE WEST

AFTER MISSOURI COMPROMISE — 1820

ME
MO.
36°30'
LA

Territory acquired as part of Louisiana Purchase

Missouri Compromise Line

AFTER COMPROMISE OF 1850

OREGON TERRITORY
MINNESOTA TERR.
UTAH TERRITORY
CALIF.
NEW MEXICO TERRITORY
36°30'

Territory acquired from Mexico and Texas

AFTER KANSAS-NEBRASKA ACT — 1854

NEBRASKA TERRITORY
KANSAS TERR.

Free states and territory closed to slavery

Slave states

Territory open to slavery

ALBERS CONICAL EQUAL-AREA PROJECTION

exists today.) Its leaders shared one goal: keeping slavery out of the territories.

The new party quickly gained public support. In the 1854 congressional election, Republicans defeated 35 of the 42 northern Democrats who had voted for the Kansas-Nebraska Act.

"BLEEDING KANSAS"

Kansas became a battleground over slavery. Both proslavery and antislavery forces sent settlers to Kansas. Each side hoped to "win" Kansas in the territorial election. The antislavery settlers were more numerous. To override their votes, proslavery Missourians crossed the border to stuff ballot boxes. "We had at least 7,000 men in the Territory on the day of the election, and one-third of them will remain there," bragged a Missouri senator.

"Now let the southern men come on with their slaves."

Henry Ward Beecher, a New York clergyman and brother of Harriet Beecher Stowe, suggested that rifles might be "a greater moral agency" in Kansas than the Bible. Funds were raised to send "Beecher's Bibles," as the rifles were then called, to the antislavery settlers.

In May 1856 a group of proslavery ruffians attacked the Kansas town of Lawrence, burning homes and stores. Several people died in the blaze. An abolitionist named John Brown and several companions took revenge by killing five proslavery settlers. Several hundred settlers would die before peace was finally restored to "Bleeding Kansas." Kansas remained an antislavery territory until 1861, when it entered the Union as a free state.

The issue of slavery led to bloodshed in Kansas. In this picture, proslavery settlers armed with a cannon attack antislavery settlers at Hickory Point, a village about 25 miles north of Lawrence, Kansas. HISTORY Under the Kansas-Nebraska Act, how was the slavery issue in Kansas supposed to be decided?

THE DRED SCOTT DECISION

In 1857 a landmark case in the slavery debate came before the Supreme Court. This case concerned a Missouri slave named Dred Scott. Scott's master had taken him to live in Illinois and then in the Wisconsin Territory before returning to Missouri. After his master's death, Scott sued for his freedom. He argued that his having lived in a free territory made him a free man.

In the Dred Scott case the Supreme Court looked at three separate issues. First, was Dred Scott a United States citizen with the right to sue in the federal courts? Second, did living in free territory make Scott a free person? Third, was the Missouri Compromise constitutional?

Chief Justice Roger B. Taney (TAW–nee) handed down the Supreme Court's decision. First, Taney said, Dred Scott was not a citizen and therefore could not sue or be sued in the federal courts. Taney explained further that no person of African blood had the rights of citizenship under the United States Constitution. Taney's meaning was clear. Even if Dred Scott had been born free, he could not sue in the courts.

Taney also said that Scott's stay in free territory had no bearing on the matter. Scott was now in Missouri, and Missouri law was what mattered.

Finally, the Chief Justice said that the Missouri Compromise was unconstitutional. Congress could not ban slavery in any part of the territories. Doing so would violate slaveholders' right to own property, a right protected by the Fifth Amendment.

In other words, the territories were wide open to all settlers, including slaveholders. Once a territory entered the Union and became a state, it alone could decide whether or not to ban slavery.

Southerners cheered the Court's decision. Republicans were outraged. They decided that their best course of action was to win the presidency. By choosing new judges, a Republican President could gradually change the make-up of the Supreme Court.

THE LINCOLN-DOUGLAS DEBATES

In the 1858 congressional elections, the Republicans once again campaigned against northern Democrats willing to make a deal with the South. One of their targets was Senator Stephen Douglas, the powerful and popular Democrat from Illinois. To challenge Douglas, they chose Abraham Lincoln, a lawyer from Springfield.

Abraham Lincoln was known for his wit, his honesty, and his forceful oratory. He also was an experienced politician who had served both in the Illinois legislature and in the United States Congress. Accepting the Republican nomination for senator, Lincoln outlined the nation's dilemma:

> A house divided against itself cannot stand. I believe this government cannot endure permanently half slave and half free. I do not expect the Union to be dissolved—I do not expect the house to fall—but I do expect it will cease to be divided. It will become all one thing or all the other.

When Douglas then accused Lincoln of urging a "war of the sections," Lincoln suggested a series of debates. Douglas accepted, and in seven Illinois towns the two men debated the issue of slavery. The debates drew large crowds and were printed in national newspapers.

> "**A house divided against itself cannot stand. I believe this government cannot endure permanently half slave and half free.**"
>
> —*Abraham Lincoln, 1858*

Audiences immediately noticed outward differences between the men. The tall, thin Lincoln cared little for fashion. His coat sleeves did not reach to his wrists, nor his

Abraham Lincoln argued against slavery in new territories while debating Stephen Douglas (seated to Lincoln's right) in the 1858 Illinois Senate race. Although Lincoln lost the election, his debating skills won him national attention. **POLITICS** Why did the debates cost Douglas southern support?

trousers to his shoes. He moved awkwardly and spoke with a country accent. Douglas, on the other hand, dressed stylishly and carried himself with grace. A short man, Douglas was called "The Little Giant" because of his sturdy build and powerful voice. (In those days there were no public address systems to help a speaker be heard.) Douglas was famous throughout the nation. He even dreamed of becoming President one day.

Lincoln and Douglas differed almost as sharply in ideas as they did in appearance. Lincoln viewed slavery as "a moral, a social, and a political wrong." He did not suggest abolishing slavery where it already existed, but he opposed the spread of slavery. Douglas used the debates to defend the principle of popular sovereignty. The issue, as Douglas saw it, was not whether slavery was right or wrong. For him, the issue was the protection of democracy. The people's will was all that mattered.

Lincoln applied Douglas's reasoning to the Dred Scott decision. If the people's will is so important, he asked, could the people of a territory exclude slavery if they chose to do so? Douglas answered that a territorial legislature could exclude slavery by passing laws that were "unfriendly" to slavery. For instance, it could refuse to hire law officers to catch runaway slaves.

While the voters returned Douglas to the Senate, the debates cost him southern support. Southerners never forgave Douglas for showing how popular sovereignty could work against slavery. By losing influence in the South, Douglas lost his chance of one day becoming President. At the same time, the debates pushed the gaunt and savvy Abraham Lincoln into the national spotlight.

JOHN BROWN'S ATTACK

Sectional distrust was bad enough in 1859, but John Brown, the Kansas raider, made it much worse. By some accounts, Brown had an unbalanced mind. He was consumed with the idea of starting a slave rebellion that would sweep through the South and destroy slavery once and for all. On October 16, 1859, Brown and eighteen followers—thirteen whites and five blacks—attacked the United States arsenal at Harpers Ferry in western Virginia. Brown believed they could use the arsenal as a rallying point and supply station for a slave revolt. He was mistaken. After 36 hours of fighting, he and four survivors sur- rendered to Colonel Robert E. Lee of the United States Army. During the following weeks John Brown had been tried for murder and treason, found guilty, and hanged.

That was not the end of it. Northerners be- gan to praise John Brown for sacrificing him- self to the antislavery cause. On the day he was hanged, bells tolled and guns fired in sa- lute. Henry David Thoreau called Brown "a crucified hero." Newspapers applauded his goal even though they condemned the way he tried to achieve it.

John Brown's capture after his 1859 raid at Harpers Ferry, Virginia, ended his plans to free the slaves. This 1884 painting by Thomas Hovendon shows Brown leaving the courthouse after being sentenced to death. Brown's raid shook the nation. HISTORY Why did northerners and southerners have such different reactions to Brown's raid?

The praise that John Brown received in the North became as controversial as Brown's raid had been. Southerners had been stunned by Brown's attack on Harpers Ferry. Now they were horrified by the northern reaction to Brown's death. How, they asked, could they share the same government with people who regarded John Brown as "a martyr and Christian hero"?

For many it was the last straw. "I have always been a fervid Union man," a North Carolinian wrote, "but I confess the endorsement of the Harpers Ferry outrage . . . has shaken my [faith]." He stated that he would rather see the Union fall apart than "submit any longer to northern insolence."

3 The Drums of War

Section Focus

Key Terms border state ■ Confederate States of America

Main Idea With the election of Abraham Lincoln as President, southern states left the Union and formed their own government. The Civil War began when the South attacked Fort Sumter.

Objectives As you read, look for answers to these questions:
1. What was the main issue in the election of 1860?
2. Why did Lincoln's election cause southern states to secede?
3. What was Lincoln's attitude toward the seceding states?

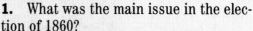
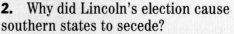
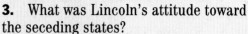

As the election year of 1860 opened, the South was in an uproar. Thousands were joining military companies. Rumors of slave revolts and abolitionist invaders abounded. Every Yankee was an enemy. Some northerners were tarred and feathered. A few were lynched.

THE ELECTION OF LINCOLN

The widening gulf between North and South ripped apart the Democratic Party. At the party convention in Charleston, South Carolina, southern Democrats insisted that the platform call for the protection of slavery in the territories. Yet Stephen Douglas, who controlled a majority of the convention delegates, refused to abandon the principle of popular sovereignty.

The convention then split. Northern Democrats chose Douglas as their candidate. Southern Democrats moved to a convention hall across town. There they chose John C. Breckinridge, Vice President and a former member of Congress from Kentucky, to run for President.

With the Democrats divided, the Republicans knew that they had a good chance of winning the election. There was great excitement at their convention hall in Chicago.

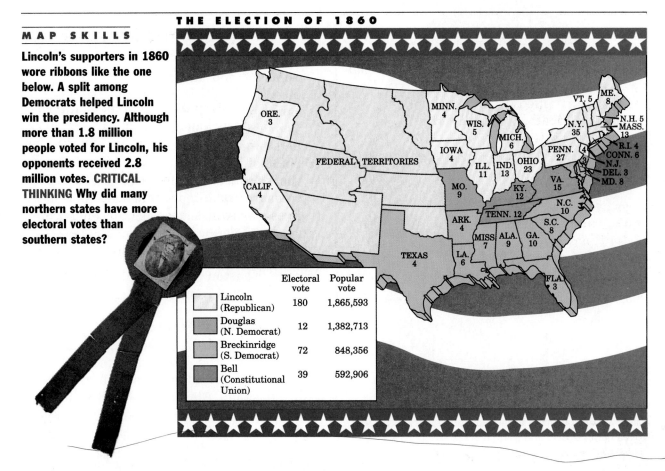

MAP SKILLS

Lincoln's supporters in 1860 wore ribbons like the one below. A split among Democrats helped Lincoln win the presidency. Although more than 1.8 million people voted for Lincoln, his opponents received 2.8 million votes. **CRITICAL THINKING** Why did many northern states have more electoral votes than southern states?

		Electoral vote	Popular vote
	Lincoln (Republican)	180	1,865,593
	Douglas (N. Democrat)	12	1,382,713
	Breckinridge (S. Democrat)	72	848,356
	Bell (Constitutional Union)	39	592,906

Spectators filled the hall and shouted for their favorite candidates. The delegates adopted a platform that called for limiting the spread of slavery. On the third ballot they nominated Abraham Lincoln as their candidate for President.

A fourth party, the Constitutional Union Party, nominated John Bell of Tennessee. Bell favored compromise as a way of saving the Union.

The election of 1860 could be seen as two different races, one in the North and one in the South. In the North the main contenders were Lincoln and Douglas. In the South they were Breckinridge and Bell. Lincoln and Breckinridge were viewed as the extremists. Lincoln was against any extension of slavery, and Breckinridge was for protecting slavery in the territories. Douglas and Bell were moderates who looked for a compromise.

The election results made it clear that the nation was no longer in a mood to compro-mise. Lincoln won with 60 percent of the northern vote. Breckinridge carried most of the South. Douglas and Bell did well only in the border states—the states between the North and South.

Mass hysteria swept through the South upon the Republican victory. Lincoln's election, many southerners were certain, meant their ruin. They feared more John Browns leading more slave revolts. They also dreaded the effect of northern majority rule in Congress. (There were now eighteen free states to fifteen slave states.) The vote for Lincoln had been, one southerner said, "a deliberate, cold-blooded insult and outrage" to southern honor.

Southern States Leave the Union

Southern radicals saw no choice but to secede from the Union. Lincoln had never called for ending slavery altogether. He had said only that it should not spread to the territories.

Jefferson Davis of Mississippi married Varina Howell in 1845. In 1861 Davis, a former senator, became president of the Confederacy. **ECONOMICS** What was Davis's view about slavery's importance to the South?

Few in the South listened. They assumed the new President planned to free the slaves.

South Carolina led the way, seceding from the Union on December 20, 1860. The South Carolina legislature feared what would happen when Lincoln took office. "The Slaveholding States will no longer have the power of self-government, or self-protection, and the Federal Government will have become their enemy," it argued. South Carolina justified its secession on the basis of states' rights. The states had voluntarily joined the Union, South Carolina argued, and therefore had the right to leave the Union.

During the next eight weeks Mississippi, Florida, Alabama, Georgia, Louisiana, and Texas voted to secede from the Union. It was a revolution fed by emotion. "You might as well attempt to control a tornado as to attempt to stop them," a southerner observed.

In Texas a number of leaders opposed secession. They included Sam Houston, the leg-endary governor of Texas. Houston warned of the conflict to come:

> Some of you laugh [at] the idea of bloodshed as the result of secession. But let me tell you what is coming. Your fathers and husbands, your sons and brothers, will be herded at the point of the bayonet. You may, after the sacrifice of countless millions of treasure and hundreds of thousands of lives . . . win southern independence . . . but I doubt it. The North is determined to preserve this Union.

Because Houston would not back secession, he was removed from office.

THE CONFEDERACY ESTABLISHED

In February 1861 the seceding states formed a new nation, the Confederate States of America. Its president was Jefferson Davis of Mississippi; Alexander H. Stephens of Georgia was the vice president. Secession, Davis stated, was necessary to maintain "the holy cause of constitutional liberty."

Yet how could the South talk about liberty while holding 3.5 million African Americans in bondage? The Confederate government answered bluntly. "Our new Government is founded . . . upon the great truth that the Negro is not equal to the white man," Stephens wrote. Liberty was for whites only.

Jefferson Davis also spoke bluntly about the South's need for slaves. Southern agriculture could not survive without slaves, Davis argued. In his words, slavery was "absolutely necessary to the wants of civilized man."

However, only about one-fourth of the white families of the Confederacy owned slaves. What about the other three-fourths? Why should they fight the battles of the slave holders? For many, the answer was to protect hearth and homeland. As one Confederate soldier told his Yankee captor, "I'm fighting because you're down here." For others, the answer was status. Even very poor whites were likely to defend a system that gave them social advantages over blacks.

Jefferson Davis's inauguration took place on the steps of Montgomery's capitol building. The Confederate government, lacking hard currency, issued paper money such as this treasury note. **NATIONAL IDENTITY** How did the Confederate states justify their secession?

THE NORTHERN RESPONSE

The idea that states had the right to defy the national government was hardly new. It had been asserted in the Kentucky and Virginia Resolutions of 1798–1799, by the Hartford Convention in 1814, and by South Carolina in 1828. Still, most northerners rejected it out of hand.

President Buchanan spoke for them. The Constitution of the United States, Buchanan said, was the supreme law of the land. If secession were allowed, the Union would become "a rope of sand." He warned that the 33 states could break up "into as many petty, jarring, and hostile republics." Abraham Lincoln, soon to take office, agreed with Buchanan. "The Union is older than any of the states," said Lincoln, "and, in fact, it created them as states."

Secession also raised the issue of democracy and majority rule. From southerners' point of view, majority rule was a threat to liberty. They believed that the North, using its advantage in numbers, would trample on their rights.

To northerners, the South's argument sounded like sour grapes. Having lost out to the majority, southerners were questioning the right of the majority to govern. "Their quarrel is not with the Republican Party, but with the theory of democracy," penned the writer James Russell Lowell.

THE FAILURE OF COMPROMISE

With war threatening, Congress made one last attempt to reach a compromise. Senator John J. Crittenden of Kentucky proposed to restore the Missouri Compromise line of 36° 30′ as the dividing line between free and slave states and territories. Lincoln, however, opposed the plan. From Springfield he wrote a friend, "The tug has to come, and better now than later." The Republicans refused to allow the spread of slavery, and the South would have no less. The deal failed.

The nation waited anxiously as Lincoln's inauguration drew near. What would he do? In his First Inaugural Address, Lincoln announced that he would not interfere with slavery in the states where it already existed. However, he also said that "the Union of these states is perpetual." No state, he declared, could lawfully leave the Union.

Lincoln said that the federal government would not abandon its property and bases in southern states. On the other hand, Lincoln did not want to start a war. "There will be no invasion," Lincoln said, "no using of force

In April 1861, Confederate troops fired on Fort Sumter, a federal outpost in Charleston, South Carolina. The Confederate capture of the fort marked the start of the Civil War.
HISTORY Why did Lincoln not withdraw the garrison at Fort Sumter before the attack?

against, or among the people anywhere." Lincoln appealed for calm. "We are not enemies, but friends," he concluded. "Though passion may have strained, it must not break our bonds of affection."

CRISIS AT FORT SUMTER

Once in office, Lincoln faced a crucial decision. What should he do about Fort Sumter in Charleston harbor and Fort Pickens in the harbor of Pensacola, Florida? Each needed supplies. In January 1861 President Buchanan had sent a ship carrying men and supplies to Fort Sumter. It had turned back when fired upon by South Carolina gunners. Now time was running out for Major Robert Anderson and his garrison at Fort Sumter. If Lincoln withdrew the garrison, he would be recognizing the Confederacy. If he supplied the garrison, he risked war. On April 6, 1861,

Lincoln announced that he was sending relief expeditions to both Fort Sumter and Fort Pickens.

Lincoln's announcement meant he intended to fight if necessary. Confederate leaders decided to attack Fort Sumter before the supply ship arrived. At 4:30 A.M. on April 12, shore guns opened fire on the island fort. For more than 30 hours the Confederates fired shells into the fort. The fort's walls crumbled. The officers' quarters caught fire. Union soldiers were choking from smoke as the fire crept toward the fort's supply of gunpowder. Anderson lowered the Stars and Stripes and surrendered. No one had been killed, but the Civil War had begun.

COULD WAR HAVE BEEN AVOIDED?

Historians have long debated the causes of the Civil War. Was slavery the only cause?

What role did economics play? Was bungling leadership responsible for the war?

For decades the South and North had been different, and for decades they had compromised to settle their differences. Compromise, however, was no longer possible in 1860 because of the nation's intense disagreement over slavery.

Could the war have been avoided? Some historians claim that better leadership could have prevented the war. The historian Arthur Schlesinger, Jr., however, disagrees.

"The unhappy fact is that man occasionally works himself into a log-jam; and that the log-jam must be burst by violence," Schlesinger has written. "Nothing exists in history to assure us that the great moral dilemmas can be resolved without pain."

CHAPTER 19 SUMMARY AND TIMELINE

1. Social and economic differences between North and South grew during the first half of the 1800s. The North, spurred by industry and immigration, prospered. The South continued to rely on agriculture and slave labor. In the Compromise of 1850, Congress tried to end the dispute over the spread of slavery to new territories. Few people were satisfied, however.

2. Events during the 1850s heightened tensions between North and South. *Uncle Tom's Cabin,* a novel published in 1852, turned many northerners against slavery. The Kansas-Nebraska Act, an 1854 compromise on the issue of slavery in the territories, brought violence to Kansas. In 1857 the Supreme Court ruled that the Constitution did not apply to African Americans. Two years later a radical abolitionist named John Brown tried to start a slave revolt. Southerners were appalled at Brown's action and at northern sympathy for Brown.

3. The election of Republican Abraham Lincoln, an opponent of slavery, as President in 1860 led southern states to leave the Union. They formed the Confederate States of America, with Jefferson Davis as president. In April 1861 Confederate forces attacked Union-held Fort Sumter, thereby beginning the Civil War.

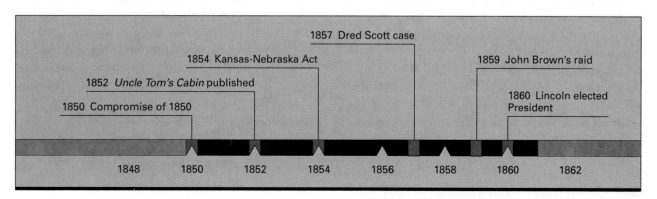

1857 Dred Scott case

1854 Kansas-Nebraska Act

1859 John Brown's raid

1852 *Uncle Tom's Cabin* published

1860 Lincoln elected President

1850 Compromise of 1850

1848 · 1850 · 1852 · 1854 · 1856 · 1858 · 1860 · 1862

PLACES TO LOCATE

Match each of the letters on the map with the places that are listed below.

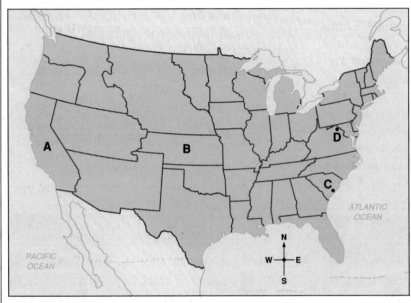

1. California
2. Fort Sumter
3. Harpers Ferry
4. Kansas Territory

KEY TERMS

Use the following terms to complete the sentences.

Compromise of 1850
Confederate States of America
Fugitive Slave Law
Kansas-Nebraska Act
Mason-Dixon Line

1. The _____, part of the Compromise of 1850, angered many northerners.
2. The _____ divided the North and South east of the Appalachians.
3. In 1861 seceding southern states formed the _____.
4. Part of the _____ was the admission of California to the Union as a free state.
5. The _____ was an attempt at compromise over slavery in the territories.

PEOPLE TO IDENTIFY

Match each of the following people with the correct description.

John Brown
Jefferson Davis
Abraham Lincoln
Harriet Beecher Stowe
Roger Taney

1. Chief Justice who wrote the Supreme Court's opinion in the Dred Scott case.
2. President of the Confederate States of America.
3. Leader of 1859 raid on Harpers Ferry.
4. Author of *Uncle Tom's Cabin.*
5. Republican elected President in 1860.

REVIEWING THE FACTS

1. Why was the Ohio River an important dividing line in the United States in the early 1800s?
2. Why did southerners want to extend slavery into new territories?
3. What were the four parts of the Compromise of 1850?
4. Why did white southerners object to *Uncle Tom's Cabin*?
5. How did passage of the Kansas-Nebraska Act lead to violence in Kansas?
6. Why was the Dred Scott decision a defeat for abolitionists?
7. What was the outcome of the debates between Abraham Lincoln and Stephen Douglas?
8. Why did the Democratic Party split in 1860?
9. Why did southern states secede after Lincoln's victory in 1860?
10. What event marked the beginning of the Civil War?

PRACTICING YOUR SKILL

The passage below expresses the reaction of former slave Frederick Douglass to the Dred Scott decision. Read the passage. Then answer the questions that follow.

[The decision] declares that Congress has no right to prohibit slavery anywhere. . . . A decision like this cannot stand. . . . The whole history of the antislavery movement is studded with proof that all measures taken to [weaken] antislavery [forces] have only made [those forces] greater and bolder. It was so with the Fugitive Slave bill. It was so with the Kansas-Nebraska bill and it will be so with this last and most shocking of all pro-slavery devices, this Taney decision.

1. Is Douglass's first sentence a fact or an opinion? How do you know?

2. Is the second sentence a fact or an opinion? How do you know?

3. What factual statement does Douglass make about the Fugitive Slave Law and the Kansas-Nebraska Act?

4. What opinions does Douglass express about the Dred Scott decision?

CITIZENSHIP

1. Consider William H. Seward's statement that "there is a higher law than the Constitution" (page 481). How might citizens in a free society deal with conflicts between their nation's laws and this "higher law"?

2. State whether you agree or disagree with the principle of popular sovereignty, and explain the reasons for your position.

CRITICAL THINKING SKILLS

1. FORMING A HYPOTHESIS Tocqueville claimed that racial prejudice was greater in states that had abolished slavery than in states where slavery still existed. Explain why this might have been so.

2. RECOGNIZING MULTIPLE CAUSATION List the events during the 1850s that led to greater tension between North and South.

3. ANALYZING FACTORS INVOLVED IN A DECISION Why did southern Democrats split from the party in the 1860 election? Why might this have been a short-sighted decision?

4. RECOGNIZING FRAME OF REFERENCE What does Jefferson Davis's statement that slavery was "absolutely necessary to the wants of civilized man" tell us about southern society in the years before the Civil War?

PROJECTS AND ACTIVITIES

1. ANALYZING PRIMARY SOURCES Find excerpts from the Lincoln-Douglas debates of 1858. Review the arguments presented and summarize them in your own words. Share your information with the rest of the class.

2. PRESENTING A READING Find a copy of *Uncle Tom's Cabin* and read all or parts of the novel. Select an appropriate scene, with dialogue, for a class reading. With a few classmates, choose parts to rehearse and present to the class. Have a narrator introduce the scene and explain what is happening.

3. MAKING A TIMELINE Arrange the important events of the chapter in a timeline that shows the coming of the Civil War. Compare your timeline with a classmate's and discuss how each event listed helped lead to war.

WRITING ABOUT TOPICS IN AMERICAN HISTORY

1. CONNECTING WITH LITERATURE A selection from *Incidents in the Life of a Slave Girl* by Harriet Jacobs appears on pages 657–659. Read it and answer the questions. Then answer the following question: How did the escape northward of southern slaves probably affect white people in the North and the South?

2. APPLYING THEMES: EXPANDING DEMOCRACY Explain how both supporters and opponents of slavery could claim that their position was consistent with democratic principles.

The Civil War was a time of unparalleled agony for the American nation. Home, Sweet Home *was Winslow Homer's ironic title for his painting of a Union army encampment.*

CHAPTER
20 The Civil War
(1861–1865)

KEY EVENTS

1861	Lincoln becomes President
1861	Civil War begins
1863	Emancipation Proclamation
1863	Gettysburg Address
1865	Confederacy surrenders
1865	Lincoln assassinated

1 The Call to Arms

★ Section Focus ★

Key Terms   antiseptic ■ anesthetic

Main Idea   By calling out the state militias, Lincoln forced the states to choose sides. Both North and South prepared for war.

Objectives   As you read, look for answers to these questions:
1. What were the strengths and weaknesses of each side?
2. How did geography affect each side's strategy for fighting the war?
3. What roles did women have in the war?

A week after the surrender of Fort Sumter, Mary Chesnut, wife of a Confederate officer, sat down to write in her diary. "I have been sitting idly today," she wrote, "looking out upon this beautiful lawn, wondering if this can be the same world I was in a few days ago."

Indeed, the battle at Fort Sumter had shattered the springtime calm. The four years of war that followed would destroy one America and witness the building of another. Yet few people that spring of 1861 knew how great a trauma the nation was about to face. Northerners and southerners alike believed that the war would last only two or three months.

People on both sides responded with energy, even excitement, to the call to arms. A young Illinois recruit wrote that "it is worth everything to live in this time." A northern woman wrote, "It seems as if we never were alive till now; never had a country till now."

In Washington, D.C., an office worker named Clara Barton took a pistol, put up a target, and blazed away.

LINCOLN CALLS OUT THE MILITIA

On April 15, 1861, President Lincoln called on the states to provide 75,000 militiamen for 90 days. Throughout the North, volunteers hurried to sign up. Yet in the South there was anger and defiance. The governor of Kentucky telegraphed, "Kentucky will furnish no troops for the wicked purpose of subduing her sister southern states." In the days that followed, Virginia, North Carolina, Tennessee, and Arkansas voted to join the Confederacy.

With Virginia on its side, the South had a much better chance for victory. Virginia was wealthy and populous. It also was the home of Robert E. Lee. A brave and able leader, Lee had been Lincoln's choice for head of the Union army. When Virginia seceded, Lee left

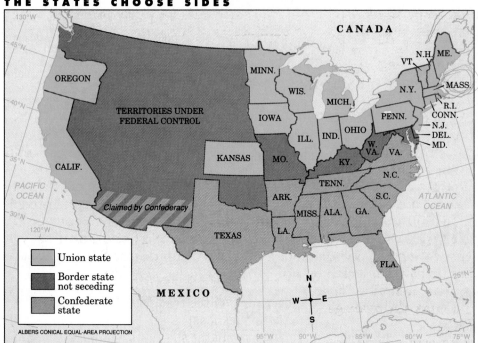

When the Civil War began, most southern states quickly joined the Confederacy. How many Union states were there? How many Confederate states? Which border states remained in the Union? **CRITICAL THINKING** What special difficulties might border states have faced?

the United States Army and joined the Confederacy. He wrote, "Save in defense of my native state I have no desire ever again to draw my sword." He soon found himself the commanding general of the Confederate forces.

> "**S**ave in defense of my native state I have no desire ever again to draw my sword."
>
> —*Robert E. Lee, 1861*

In May 1861, the Confederate Congress voted to set up its capital in Richmond, Virginia. This was a gesture of defiance against the North. The city of Richmond stood only 100 miles away from the Union capital of Washington, D.C.

CHOOSING SIDES

Both sides knew that the border states would play a key role in the war's outcome. From the Union's point of view, the most important

of the border states was Maryland. If Maryland seceded, then Washington, D.C., would be cut off from the North. The Confederates might then capture the President and destroy the government. Thus Lincoln was determined to keep Maryland in the Union. He ordered the arrest of Maryland lawmakers who backed the South. The remaining members of the Maryland legislature voted to stay in the Union.

Federal troops helped a group of western counties break away from Virginia. These counties formed the state of West Virginia and returned to the Union. Delaware and Missouri also voted to side with the Union. Kentucky at first declared itself neutral. Then a Confederate invasion prompted it to join the Union.

In the border states, war pulled families apart. This tragedy reached even into the White House. Mary Todd Lincoln, wife of the President, had four brothers and three brothers-in-law fighting for the South. Senator John Crittenden of Kentucky, who had labored for a last-minute compromise, had one son who became a Confederate general and another who became a Union general.

STRENGTHS AND WEAKNESSES OF EACH SIDE

On the face of it, the Union had huge advantages. It had 22 million people. The Confederacy had just 9 million, of whom 3.5 million were slaves. The Union had most of the mineral deposits—iron, coal, copper, and other precious metals. A full 86 percent of the nation's factories were located in the North. The North had 2.5 times the railroad mileage of the South. Almost every ship in the navy—90 of them—stayed with the Union.

The Union's greatest asset would turn out to be Abraham Lincoln. Lincoln was able to convince northerners that the survival of democracy and freedom depended on preserving the Union. "Every war has its political no less than its military side," one historian has written. "Lincoln's genius was the management of the political side."

The Confederacy had its own advantages. It began the war with better generals. One-third of the career officers in the United States Army resigned to join the Confederacy. These officers had gained experience fighting in the Mexican War. Foremost among them was Robert E. Lee.

The Confederacy had another advantage. It would be fighting a defensive war. "All we ask is to be let alone," Jefferson Davis said. An invading army is usually at a disadvantage. Invaders generally have less will to fight than soldiers defending their homes. Furthermore, maintaining the supply lines of an invading army takes great resources.

> **"All we ask is to be let alone."**
>
> —*Jefferson Davis, 1861*

The Confederate soldiers never lost a battle for lack of ammunition. Still, other needs such as food and clothing were often in short supply. At times the southerners appeared to live only on spirit and courage. Well into the war a Union officer wrote, "How such men as the rebel troops can fight as they do; that,

filthy, sick, hungry and miserable, they should prove such heroes in fight, is past explanation."

GEOGRAPHY AND STRATEGY

The two sides entered the war with different war aims and thus different strategies. The North aimed at conquering the Confederacy and bringing the southern states back into the Union. At first, Lincoln hoped to do this by smothering the South's economy. He made plans to seize Confederate strongholds along the Mississippi River. He also blockaded the Confederate coast, using the Union navy to keep ships from entering and leaving southern ports.

GRAPH SKILLS

These pie graphs show the overwhelming advantage the Union's greater population and industrialization gave it. What percentage of Americans lived in the North? CRITICAL THINKING How might the North's railways and factories have helped its armies?

UNION AND CONFEDERATE RESOURCES, 1860

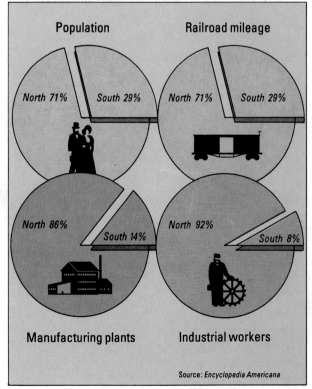

Population — North 71% South 29%

Railroad mileage — North 71% South 29%

Manufacturing plants — North 86% South 14%

Industrial workers — North 92% South 8%

Source: *Encyclopedia Americana*

The South, in contrast, did not expect to conquer the North; it aimed only at staying independent. As historian James M. McPherson pointed out, "The South could 'win' the war by not losing; the North could win only by winning." Thus the South wanted to keep its army intact by avoiding large-scale battles. Southern leaders hoped that the North would soon tire of the war and accept southern independence.

The Confederate strategy also depended on King Cotton as a way to win foreign support. When the war broke out, southern planters withheld cotton from the world market. By doing so, they hoped to force France and Britain to aid the Confederate cause in order to keep their cotton mills running. But in 1861 Europe had plenty of cotton, and this southern plan failed. By the next year southern planters were again selling cotton—if they could get it through the Union blockade. For the rest of the war they sought European support, but with little luck.

Before long, both North and South moved away from their cautious plans and looked for decisive victories on the battlefield. This happened for several reasons. People on both sides began to press their leaders for a knockout punch to end the war quickly. Also, the North came to believe that the South would give up only after its armies had been wiped out. The South, meanwhile, looked to military conquests to wreck northern morale and impress neutral Europe.

Much of the fighting took place on two fronts along the Confederacy's northern border, which stretched from Virginia to Arkansas. The eastern front lay east of the Appalachian Mountains. The western front stretched from the Mississippi River to the Appalachians. There was a third front too. It was located at sea and along the 3,500 miles of Confederate coast.

On the eastern front, the Confederate armies blocked the major routes southward. They were encamped in the Shenandoah Valley of central Virginia and on Virginia's coastal uplands.

On the western front, the main access to the South was by river. Union forces were

Mathew Brady used a new invention, the camera, to record hundreds of powerful scenes during the Civil War. This photograph shows a Union soldier from Pennsylvania whose family has joined him in camp. **HISTORY** How did women help the war effort?

based at Cairo, Illinois, at the crucial junction of the Ohio and Mississippi rivers. Not far away were the mouths of the Tennessee and Cumberland rivers. These rivers led into one of the most productive regions of the Confederacy. Here grain was grown, mules and horses bred, and iron produced. Much of the war on the western front would focus on the struggle for control of this region.

THE TWO ARMIES

In 1861 the Union was completely unprepared for war. Its forces were in high spirits but had little training. Many soldiers were city residents who had never ridden a horse or fired a gun. In contrast, the southerners had begun organizing several months before Fort Sumter. They were used to outdoor life. They knew how to handle both horses and guns.

When the war started, there were no standards for uniforms. Men came dressed as their women had outfitted them. This caused confusion in battle because troops were not always certain who was friend or foe. As the war went on, textile mills on each side began to turn out uniforms for the troops. Union soldiers wore dark blue. Confederate soldiers wore gray.

The great killer of each army was not bullets but disease and infection. By the end of the war, some 140,000 Union soldiers had been killed in action or died of wounds. Yet many more, over 220,000, died of disease and other causes. Few doctors knew that cleanliness prevented infection, and antiseptics (germ-killing drugs) were unknown. Also rare were anesthetics, or pain-killers. Most soldiers endured amputations and other operations by "biting the bullet."

WOMEN IN THE WAR

As men in the North and South enlisted in militias, the women too prepared for war. Few plans had been made for the health and general welfare of the soldiers. Women volunteered to do what the governments would not or could not do.

BIOGRAPHY

CLARA BARTON (1821–1912) was known as the "Angel of the Battlefield" for her nursing work with the wounded during the Civil War. After the war, she helped mark over 12,000 graves. In the Franco-Prussian War (1870–1871) in Europe, Barton served with the International Red Cross and later established its American branch.

Hundreds of thousands of women in the North and South organized aid societies. They raised funds for the war and made bandages and clothing for the soldiers. Clara Barton, one such woman, worked as a one-person aid society throughout the war. Thousands of other women went to the front. Many of these women, as in wars past, joined their husbands in order to cook and care for them. At least 600 Union soldiers were women who passed as men until illness or death revealed their disguise.

The women of the Soldiers' Aid Societies also formed the backbone of the Union's Sanitary Commission. Its aim was to direct the efforts of the aid societies and to help the war effort in every way. It was organized with the help of Elizabeth Blackwell, the nation's first woman doctor. Over the army's objections, the government allowed the Sanitary Commission to inspect camps and hospitals.

The Sanitary Commission's national officers, paid agents, and inspectors were men. Supporting them were women volunteers. They raised money, sent supplies to the camps, helped soldiers on leave, aided escaped slaves, and recruited nurses. The Sanitary Commission was so effective that it became a distinct advantage to the Union.

The Civil War was the first war in which several thousand women served as nurses. Some people on each side did not approve of women's taking what had been considered a man's job. Yet in 1861, women had a new heroine. She was Florence Nightingale, who had earned fame caring for British soldiers several years earlier in the Crimean War. Altogether 3,000 women would serve as official Union army nurses. The Confederacy was slower to accept women nurses, but by 1862, they too were part of the Confederate army.

Women served in other ways as well. In the absence of men, women ran plantations, farmed, and worked in factories. Women spied for the Confederacy and the Union. African American women were teachers, launderers, and cooks for the Union troops.

2 The Agony of War

Section Focus

Key Terms First Battle of Bull Run

Main Idea In the first two years of war, the Confederate army held its own on the eastern front. On the western front and at sea, however, the Union won several important victories.

Objectives As you read, look for answers to these questions:
1. What was the impact of the war's first major battle?
2. How did the Union triumph in the war at sea?
3. What was the impact of Union victories in the West?

On to Richmond! the northern papers cried. By capturing the Confederate capital, the Union might crush the rebellion in a single, swift blow. However, to win Richmond the Union army would first have to take Manassas Junction. This important railway center was only 30 miles south of Washington.

On July 18, 1861, Union troops began the march to Manassas. They were raw recruits who had signed up for only 90 days of service. It took them three days to reach the battle site.

On July 21 a group of sightseers and picnickers rode out from Washington to watch the battle. Among them were society women carrying fancy gowns in trunks. They ex-

pected the day to end with a grand ball of celebration at Richmond.

THE FIRST BATTLE

The two armies met at the stream called Bull Run, just north of Manassas Junction. The Union forces outnumbered the Confederates 30,000 to 20,000. By midday they had driven a Confederate flank back a mile. At one point, a Confederate officer rallied his troops by pointing his sword toward General Thomas J. Jackson. He is said to have cried, "There is Jackson standing like a stone wall! Rally behind the Virginians!" Thus Jackson, one of the Confederacy's most able generals, won the nickname "Stonewall Jackson." Like a

Civil War enthusiasts act out the Battle of Bull Run. The triumph of Confederate forces at Bull Run shattered northern hopes for easy victory in the Civil War. **NATIONAL IDENTITY** Why do many Americans remain fascinated by Civil War history?

stone wall, Jackson's men held fast against the Union assault.

With the arrival of fresh troops, the Confederates then launched a countercharge. Attacking the Union line, they let out a blood-curdling scream. The scream, later known as the "rebel yell," unsettled the Union troops. "There is nothing like it on this side of the infernal region," a northern veteran later recalled. "The peculiar corkscrew sensation that it sends down your backbone under these circumstances can never be told. You have to feel it."

The Union troops, discouraged, tired, and hungry, broke ranks and scattered. For raw recruits they had fought well, but they had reached their limit.

The retreating soldiers became entangled with the sightseers. Convinced that the rebels were right behind them, the whole crowd panicked. Supplies were abandoned. Horses were cut loose, and soldiers began to run. Yet the Confederate army could not take advantage of the chaos. General Joseph Johnston later explained, "Our army was more disorganized by victory than that of the United States by defeat."

The **First Battle of Bull Run** was a great shock to the North. Confident of victory, it faced defeat instead. The day after the battle, Lincoln sent the 90-day militias home and called for a real army of 500,000 volunteers serving for three years. Three days later, he called for another 500,000. Lincoln made George B. McClellan head of this army. McClellan had won distinction fighting Confederate forces in West Virginia.

News of Bull Run electrified the South. "We have broken the backbone of invasion and utterly broken the spirit of the North," the *Richmond Examiner* rejoiced. More thoughtful southerners saw that the South

In March 1862 when the Union's *Monitor* (front left) battled the Confederacy's *Virginia* (right), neither ironclad ship was able to seriously damage the other. **TECHNOLOGY** What was the advantage of ironclads over wooden ships?

had won only a battle, not the war. The victory "lulls us into a fool's paradise of conceit at our superior valor," Mary Chesnut wrote in her diary. She was right to be cautious. The war was far from over.

THE NAVAL WAR

The great battles of the Civil War would take place on land. Still, the Union's choking off of southern shipping had a decisive effect on the war's outcome.

A number of southerners entered the profitable business of blockade-running. From bases in the Caribbean, the runners carried cargoes ranging from guns to hoop skirts. They used special ships that were low in the water, fast, quiet, and painted gray. On the return voyage the blockade runners carried southern cotton.

In the first year of the war the Union blockade was practically useless. Nine out of ten ships got through. However, northern shipyards were soon busy turning out a fleet of new boats, including gunboats that could operate in shallow water and deep-sea cruisers. For the crews, blockade patrol meant months of boredom but offered the chance of riches. Each cargo captured was split between the ship's crew and the government.

Enforcing the blockade became much easier as the Union took most of the Confederacy's major harbors. By April 1862 the Union had control of almost every important Atlantic harbor. Steadily, the blockade tightened. In 1864 a runner stood one chance in three of getting captured. By 1865 it was one chance in two.

THE VIRGINIA AND THE MONITOR

The South's desire to break the northern blockade produced a revolution in naval technology: the ironclad warship. In 1861 the

Confederates took the captured Union frigate *Merrimack* and refitted it with iron sides. Sent into action off the coast of Virginia in March 1862, the *Merrimack* (now renamed the *Virginia*) destroyed two wooden Union warships and ran another one aground. On the following day the Union navy showed off its own ironclad, the *Monitor*. In the first fight ever between ironclad warships, the *Virginia* and *Monitor* hammered away at each other for two hours. Neither ship could sink the other, and the battle ended in a draw. Although both sides built ironclads for bay and river fighting, the new ships were not a decisive factor in the war. The real importance of the *Virginia* and *Monitor* is that they were the forerunners of future navies.

Union Victories in the West

Union troops in the West spent most of 1861 preparing for war. In February 1862, General Ulysses S. Grant made a bold move to take Tennessee.

Using new ironclad gunboats, Grant's forces captured two Confederate river forts. They were Fort Henry on the Tennessee and Fort Donelson on the nearby Cumberland. The seizure of Fort Henry opened up a river

During the early years, northern support for the war was strong and enthusiastic. In this painting by Thomas Nast, crowds cheer Union troops as they leave New York City for Washington, D.C. **HISTORY** What problems were caused by the sudden need to expand the armed forces?

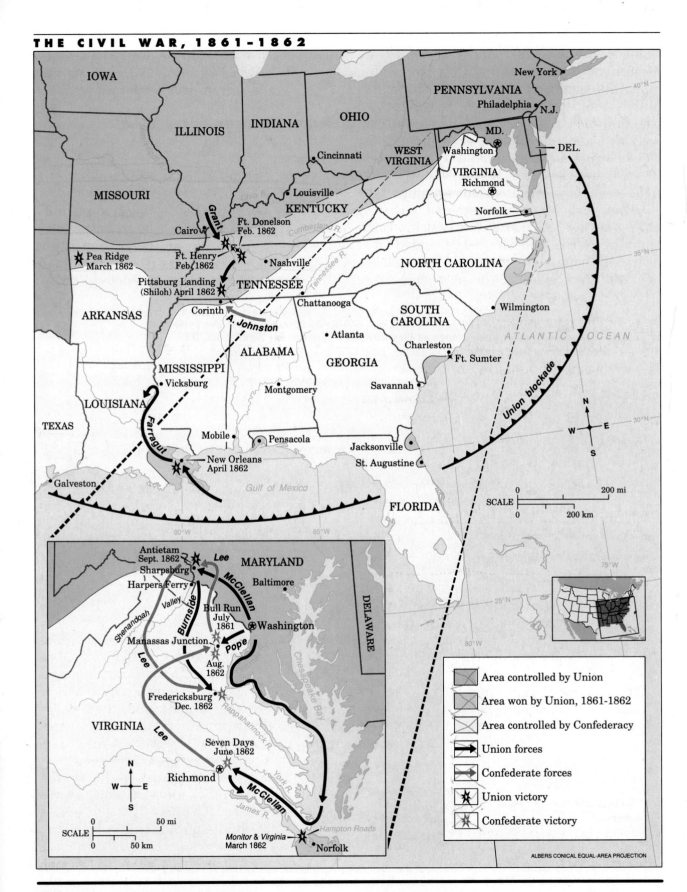

THE CIVIL WAR, 1861-1862

IOWA

ILLINOIS

INDIANA

OHIO

PENNSYLVANIA

New York

Philadelphia

N.J.

Cincinnati

WEST VIRGINIA

MD.

Washington

DEL.

MISSOURI

Louisville

KENTUCKY

VIRGINIA

Richmond

Grant

Cairo

Ft. Donelson
Feb. 1862

Norfolk

Pea Ridge
March 1862

Ft. Henry
Feb. 1862

Nashville

NORTH CAROLINA

ARKANSAS

Pittsburg Landing
(Shiloh) April 1862

TENNESSEE

Corinth

A. Johnston

Chattanooga

SOUTH
CAROLINA

Wilmington

ALABAMA

Atlanta

GEORGIA

Charleston

Ft. Sumter

ATLANTIC OCEAN

MISSISSIPPI

Vicksburg

Farragut

Montgomery

Savannah

Union blockade

LOUISIANA

N

TEXAS

Mobile

Pensacola

Jacksonville

W   E

New Orleans
April 1862

St. Augustine

S

Galveston

Gulf of Mexico

FLORIDA

SCALE

0   200 mi

0   200 km

Antietam
Sept. 1862

Lee

MARYLAND

Sharpsburg

McClellan

Baltimore

Harpers Ferry

Valley

Bull Run
July
1861

Burnside

Washington

Shenandoah

Manassas Junction

Pope

DELAWARE

Aug.
1862

Chesapeake Bay

Lee

Fredericksburg
Dec. 1862

Rappahannock R.

VIRGINIA

Lee

Seven Days
June 1862

York R.

N

Richmond

W   E

McClellan

S

James R.

Hampton Roads

SCALE

50 mi

Monitor & Virginia
March 1862

0   50 km

Norfolk

Area controlled by Union

Area won by Union, 1861-1862

Area controlled by Confederacy

Union forces

Confederate forces

Union victory

Confederate victory

ALBERS CONICAL EQUAL-AREA PROJECTION

highway into the heart of the South. Union gunboats could now travel on the river as far as northern Alabama. When the people of Nashville heard the forts were lost, they fled the city in panic. A week later, Union troops marched into Nashville. It was the first major Confederate city to be captured.

Meanwhile, Earl Van Dorn, commander of a Confederate army in Arkansas, was organizing a surprise. He planned an end run around Union troops with the aim of taking St. Louis. With 16,000 soldiers, including some Cherokee Indians, Van Dorn headed north. Between Van Dorn and St. Louis, however, stood a Union army of 11,000. On March 7, 1862, the two armies collided at Pea Ridge, near the Arkansas-Missouri border. The Confederates could not hold out against the well-drilled and well-supplied Union troops. They broke ranks, high-tailing it in all directions. It would take two weeks for Van Dorn to put his army back together.

THE BATTLE OF SHILOH

After Grant's river victories, Albert S. Johnston, Confederate commander on the western front, ordered a retreat to Corinth, Mississippi. Grant followed. By early April his troops had reached Pittsburg Landing on the Tennessee River. There he waited for more troops from Nashville. Johnston, however, was not about to wait for Grant to attack him. Marching his troops north from Corinth, on April 6, 1862, Johnston surprised the Union forces at the Battle of Shiloh (SHY-loh). It was the fiercest fighting the Civil War had yet seen.

Commanders on each side were in the thick of battle to rally their troops, most of whom had never fired at another human being. One

MAP SKILLS

Early Union advances were made mostly in the West and in southern port cities. What river is Vicksburg on? Which Union military leader tried to capture that city? **CRITICAL THINKING** Why did much of the war's fighting take place in the Virginia-Maryland region (inset map)?

Union general, William Tecumseh Sherman, had three horses shot out from under him. General Johnston was killed, and the southern command passed to General Pierre Beauregard. By the end of the day, each side believed that dawn would bring victory.

That night a terrible thunderstorm passed over the battlefield. Rain fell in torrents. Lightning lit up the battlefield, where soldiers dead and dying lay in water and mud. During that awful night, Union boats ran upriver to deliver fresh troops to Grant's camp. Grant made a surprise attack at dawn and forced the exhausted southerners to retreat.

The cost of the Union victory was dreadful. Union casualties at Shiloh were 13,000, about one-fourth of the army. The Confederates lost 11,000 out of 41,000 soldiers. Describing the piles of mangled bodies, General Sherman wrote home, "The scenes on this field would have cured anybody of war." There would be more such scenes—and worse—before the war was over.

> "**The** scenes on this field would have cured anybody of war."
>
> —*General Sherman on the Battle of Shiloh, 1862*

THE FALL OF NEW ORLEANS

The South was just hearing the news of Shiloh when more bad news arrived. On April 25, 1862, a Union fleet led by David Farragut took New Orleans. Farragut's ships had to run through cannon fire and then dodge burning rafts in order to reach land. City folk stood on the docks and cursed the Yankee invaders, but were powerless to stop them.

In despair, Mary Chesnut wrote in her diary, "New Orleans gone—and with it the Confederacy. Are we not cut in two?" Indeed, after the victories of Grant and Farragut, only a 150-mile stretch of the Mississippi was left in southern hands. Guarding that section

1861 Daniel Hough, a Confederate gunner, becomes first casualty of Civil War when killed by an explosion during celebration ceremonies following the surrender of Fort Sumter.

   First income tax enacted (Aug. 5).

1862 The *Cairo* is first warship sunk by an underwater torpedo mine, near Vicksburg, Mississippi (Dec. 12).

1863 First monument to commemorate the Civil War dedicated, Kensington, Conn. (July 25).

   Abraham Lincoln proclaims Thanksgiving a regular national holiday.

1864 First coin to use "In God We Trust" authorized (April 22).

was the heavily armed fort at Vicksburg, Mississippi. Vicksburg would hold out for another year.

THE WAR IN TEXAS AND THE SOUTHWEST

Not all of the fighting took place east of the Mississippi. North and South also fought for control of Texas, the westernmost state in the Confederacy.

Even before the Confederates fired on Fort Sumter in April 1861, Texans had taken over Union military outposts in that state. In the summer of 1861, a force of Texans headed west into New Mexico Territory. They captured the cities of Albuquerque and Santa Fe but later had to withdraw into Texas.

In 1862 the Union, looking to shut down all Confederate ports, took aim at the Texan port of Galveston on the Gulf of Mexico. Northern troops seized the city in October. A few months later Texan forces recaptured it.

The Union also tried to block access to the Rio Grande, which divided Texas and Mexico. In November 1863, northern troops took the city of Brownsville, on the Rio Grande. Still, Texan ships continued to slip past the northern patrols and into the Gulf of Mexico. Tex-

ans also traded with Mexico, selling such goods as cotton and wool. Ships then carried these goods to Europe.

Texas had to defend itself against American Indians as well as Union soldiers. While some Indian peoples did join the South, others remained loyal to the Union. They made attacks on Texas settlements. Because the Confederate government in Richmond was busy with other matters, Texas could not rely upon outside help. Yet Texas was able not only to guard its own frontier but to send troops to other fronts.

THE VICTORIOUS MEN IN GRAY

After Bull Run the eastern front had been fairly quiet. McClellan built up the new Army of the Potomac, preparing for the day when the North would try once again to capture Richmond. McClellan had more men than the Confederates, but he was slow to move. He was afraid, some said, of failure. Even Lincoln grew weary of McClellan's cautious approach. "If McClellan is not using the army, I should like to borrow it," he snapped.

In the spring of 1862 McClellan finally made his move. He planned to attack Richmond by way of the York Peninsula, a stretch of land between the York and James rivers.

Robert E. Lee was now in charge of the Army of Northern Virginia. Lee sent Jeb

BIOGRAPHY

ROBERT E. LEE (1807–1870) was the son of "Light-Horse Harry" Lee, a Revolutionary War hero. Lee married Martha Washington's great-granddaughter. He fought in the Mexican War and in 1859 led the capture of John Brown at Harpers Ferry. Lee's bold strategies in the Civil War rank him among history's greatest generals. After the war he became president of Washington College, later renamed Washington and Lee University.

Stuart and his cavalry—soldiers on horse-back—to spy on McClellan. With 1,200 men, the dashing Stuart rode around the whole Union army in four days and reported its size back to Lee. Lee then attacked McClellan. The two armies clashed for a week in what became known as the Seven Days' Battle. The Virginians suffered heavier losses, but McClellan's army was forced to retreat.

In late August the Confederates won a second victory at Bull Run. With Washington now in danger, Union troops withdrew from much of Virginia to protect the capital. By the end of the summer of 1862, southern troops once again stood on the banks of the Potomac.

SECTION REVIEW

1. KEY TERMS First Battle of Bull Run

2. PEOPLE AND PLACES Manassas Junction, Stonewall Jackson, George B. McClellan, Ulysses S. Grant, Nashville, Shiloh, David Farragut, Texas

3. COMPREHENSION What was the effect of the First Battle of Bull Run on the North?

4. COMPREHENSION Why were Union victories in the West important?

5. CRITICAL THINKING Explain why the naval war between North and South was as much an economic contest as a military one.

3 Turning the Tide

Section Focus

Key Terms Emancipation Proclamation ■ draft ■ Copperhead ■ Battle of Gettysburg ■ Battle of Vicksburg

Main Idea Union forces stopped Lee's invasions of the North and then invaded the South.

Objectives As you read, look for answers to these questions:
1. Why did Lee invade the North in 1862? In 1863?
2. Why did Lincoln issue an order freeing the slaves?

Riding a wave of Confederate victories, General Lee decided to invade the Union in the fall of 1862. It was a crucial time, for the fate of the Confederacy was at stake.

Lee had several reasons for taking the war north. A victory in the North would, he hoped, force Lincoln to talk peace. The invasion, too, would give northern Virginia a rest from war during the harvest season and let the hungry Confederates fill their stomachs with northern food. Finally, Lee hoped the invasion would show that the Confederacy could indeed win the war. This might convince Europe to side with the South.

By now, both Britain and France were leaning toward recognizing the Confederacy.

They were impressed by Lee's military successes, and their textile mills were closing down for lack of cotton. The Confederates knew that European backing would help them. At the most, it would bring them money and guns. At the very least, it would pressure Lincoln to leave the South alone.

ANTIETAM: A TURNING POINT
However, luck was not on Lee's side. A Confederate officer lost a copy of Lee's battle plans, and it fell into Union hands. McClellan saw his chance to stop Lee. "Here is a paper with which, if I cannot whip Bobbie Lee, I will be willing to go home," he said. Union forces went on the attack.

SOJOURNER TRUTH (1797?–1883) was born into slavery in New York and freed in 1828. She became a preacher who spoke out for women's rights and the abolition of slavery. In 1864 she visited President Lincoln at the White House and stayed on in Washington, D.C., working to improve conditions for African Americans there. Born Isabella Baumfree, she took the name Sojourner Truth to reflect her life's work: to travel (or sojourn) and preach the truth.

The clash came on September 17, 1862, at Antietam Creek near Sharpsburg, Maryland. The Battle of Antietam (an–TEE–tuhm) was the bloodiest of the war. The two armies fought all day, and at nightfall they held the same ground that they had held in the morning. The only difference was that 23,000 men were dead or wounded. Lee, who had lost one-third of his army, withdrew to Virginia. The ever-cautious McClellan did not follow, missing a chance to finish off the crippled southern army.

Although a military draw, Antietam was a political victory for the Union. It caused the British and French to delay any plans to recognize the Confederacy. Antietam also gave Lincoln the chance to tell the nation about one of his most fateful decisions: to free the slaves.

THE EMANCIPATION PROCLAMATION

From the war's outset, Lincoln believed that the basic aim of the North was to preserve the Union, not to free the slaves. As he put it:

> If I could save the Union without freeing any slave, I would do it; if I could save it by freeing all the slaves, I would do it; and if I could save it by freeing some and leaving others alone, I would also do that.

Yet when Lincoln wrote these words, he had already decided to move against slavery. He saw that freeing the slaves would hurt the South. While some northerners would oppose it, others would rally to the northern cause.

After the Battle of Antietam, Lincoln announced that he would emancipate, or free, all slaves in the rebelling states as of January 1, 1863. On New Year's Day he issued the **Emancipation Proclamation**. To an aide Lincoln said, "If my name ever goes into history, it will be for this act, and my whole soul is in it."

The call for emancipation changed the character of the war. The old South was to be destroyed and, in Lincoln's words, "replaced by new propositions and ideas." Abolitionists were overjoyed. "We shout for joy that we live to record this righteous decree," wrote Frederick Douglass.

> "**W**e shout for joy that we live to record this righteous decree."
>
> —*Frederick Douglass on the Emancipation Proclamation, 1863*

The Emancipation Proclamation (1863)

On January 1, 1863, President Lincoln proclaimed the freedom of all slaves in states in rebellion against the United States.

Whereas, on the twenty-second day of September, in the year of our Lord one thousand eight hundred and sixty-two, a proclamation was issued by the President of the United States containing among other things the following, to wit:

"That on the first day of January, in the year of our Lord one thousand eight hundred sixty-three, all persons held as slaves within any State, or designated part of a State, the people whereof shall then be in rebellion against the United States, shall be then, thenceforth and forever free; and the Executive Government of the United States, including the military and naval authorities thereof will recognize and maintain the freedom of such persons, and will do no act or acts to repress such persons, or any of them, in any efforts they may make for their actual freedom.

That the Executive will, on the first day, designate the States and parts of States, if any, in which the people therein respectively shall then be in rebellion against the United States, and the fact that any State . . . shall on that day be in good faith represented in the Congress of the United States by members chosen thereto . . . shall, in the absence of strong countervailing testimony, be deemed conclusive evidence that such State and the people thereof are not then in rebellion against the United States."

Now, therefore, I, Abraham Lincoln, President of the United States, by virtue of the power in me vested as Commander-in-Chief of the Army and Navy of the United States in time of actual armed rebellion against the authority and Government of the United States, and as a fit and necessary war measure for suppressing said rebellion, do . . . designate, as the States and parts of States wherein the people there-of . . . are this day in rebellion against the United States, the following, to wit: Arkansas, Texas, Louisiana (except [certain] parishes . . . including the City of New Orleans), Alabama, Florida, Georgia, South Carolina, North Carolina, and Virginia (except the forty-eight counties designated as West Virginia and also [seven] counties) . . .

And, by virtue of the power and for the purpose aforesaid, I do order and declare that all persons held as slaves within these said designated States and parts of States are, and henceforward shall be free . . .

And I hereby enjoin upon [urge] the people so declared to be free, to abstain from all violence, unless in necessary self-defense, and I recommend to them, that in all cases, when allowed, they labor faithfully for reasonable wages.

And I further declare and make known that such persons of suitable condition will be received into the armed service of the United States to garrison forts, positions, stations, and other places, and to man vessels of all sorts in said service.

And, upon this, sincerely believed to be an act of justice, warranted by the Constitution, upon military necessity, I invoke the considerate judgment of mankind and the gracious favor of Almighty God.

From *United States Statutes at Large,* Vol. XII, p. 1268.

ANALYZING HISTORICAL DOCUMENTS

1. By what authority did President Lincoln claim to be freeing the slaves?

2. Why did the Emancipation Proclamation specify freedom for slaves in areas "in rebellion against the United States"?

3. What was the immediate effect of the Emancipation Proclamation on slaves? Explain your answer.

After the Emancipation Proclamation, Frederick Douglass encouraged the recruitment of African American soldiers. About 38,000 black troops died for the Union cause during the war. African Americans suffered especially harsh treatment if captured. **CIVIC VALUES** Why might African Americans have been particularly motivated to fight in the Civil War?

Why, critics charged, did Lincoln free slaves in the South and not in the loyal border states? The reason lay in the Constitution. Freeing Confederate slaves weakened the South and thus was seen as a military action. As commander-in-chief of Union forces, Lincoln had the authority to do this. Yet the Constitution did not give the President the power to free slaves within the Union. Lincoln did recommend, however, that Congress gradually abolish slavery throughout the land.

AFRICAN AMERICANS JOIN THE STRUGGLE

The Emancipation Proclamation also declared that African American men willing to fight "will be received into the armed service of the United States." From the start of the war, African Americans had served in the navy, but the army had rejected black volunteers. As of 1863, however, free blacks in Louisiana, Kansas, and the South Carolina Sea Islands formed their own units. Massachusetts later raised two African American regiments. One of these, the 54th Regiment, gained fame for its heroic attempt to capture a South Carolina fort, Fort Wagner, in the summer of 1863.

African American regiments were led by white officers, and for most of the war were paid less than white regiments. Despite such unequal treatment, black leaders urged African Americans to enlist. Once the black man had fought for his country, Douglass said, "there is no power on earth which can deny that he has earned the right to citizenship." By war's end about 200,000 African Americans had served in the Union army and navy. African American women, too, formed aid societies and worked behind the lines. Harriet Tubman, the famous conductor of the Underground Railroad (page 417), traveled with Union gunboats bringing slaves to freedom.

THE ROAD TO GETTYSBURG

President Lincoln's great frustration was finding a general who would attack Lee. Lincoln tried one general after another. General

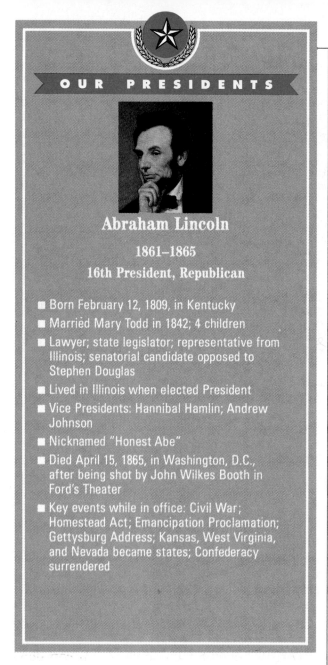

Abraham Lincoln

1861–1865
16th President, Republican

- Born February 12, 1809, in Kentucky
- Married Mary Todd in 1842; 4 children
- Lawyer; state legislator; representative from Illinois; senatorial candidate opposed to Stephen Douglas
- Lived in Illinois when elected President
- Vice Presidents: Hannibal Hamlin; Andrew Johnson
- Nicknamed "Honest Abe"
- Died April 15, 1865, in Washington, D.C., after being shot by John Wilkes Booth in Ford's Theater
- Key events while in office: Civil War; Homestead Act; Emancipation Proclamation; Gettysburg Address; Kansas, West Virginia, and Nevada became states; Confederacy surrendered

McClellan was put to pasture after he failed to pursue Lee at Antietam. The next general, Ambrose Burnside, fared no better. He lost his job as commander of the Army of the Potomac after Lee defeated him in December 1862 at Fredericksburg, Virginia.

When General "Fighting Joe" Hooker took on Lee the next spring at Chancellorsville, Virginia, the result was a Union disaster. With fewer than half as many men as Hooker, Lee still managed to cut the Union force to pieces and send it retreating north.

By the summer of 1863 the Confederate army seemed invincible. Lee decided to head north once again, this time from the Shenandoah Valley into Pennsylvania.

Lee had two goals in heading north. First, he needed food and supplies for his army. His men were as thin and ragged as scarecrows, and horses were dying of starvation. Second, Lee hoped to force a peace settlement.

Time was running out for the Confederacy. The northern blockade was strangling the South. What had cost one dollar in 1861 now cost seven dollars. With the men gone, farm output dropped. Many of the men in gray deserted to help their families survive. "We are poor men and are willing to defend our country, but our families [come] first," a Mississippi soldier wrote the governor. Things were no better in the cities. Just a few months earlier a mob in Richmond had rioted, shouting for bread and breaking into stores.

Lee knew that northerners were also growing tired of the war. Lacking volunteers for the army, Congress had recently imposed a draft. (A draft, also called conscription, is a system of choosing people for required military service.) In July 1863, protesters against the draft battled police and soldiers in the streets of New York City.

In the North, more and more people were listening to the Copperheads—northern Democrats who called for peace and a compromise with the South. A successful invasion of the North, Lee figured, would encourage the "peace party" and thereby divide the enemy. Lee also hoped that an invasion would revive European interest in the South.

THE BATTLE OF GETTYSBURG

In late June 1863, Lee's army crossed into the fertile farmlands of southern Pennsylvania. "You never saw such a land of plenty," a Confederate soldier wrote home. "We could live here mighty well for the next twelve months. . . . Of course we will have to fight here, and when it comes it will be the biggest on record." The soldier was right.

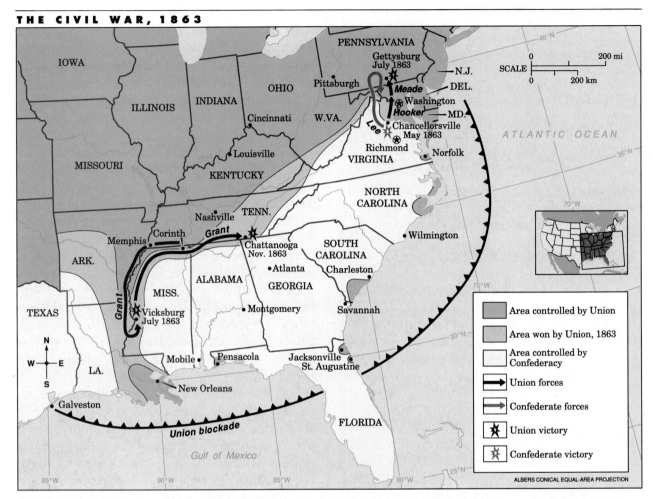

MAP SKILLS By mid-1863, Union forces had beaten back an attempted Confederate invasion of the North and extended Union control of the West. What important battle was fought in Pennsylvania? Which southern states were almost entirely in Union hands by the end of 1863? Which side controlled the Mississippi River in 1863? **CRITICAL THINKING** Why was control of the Mississippi River important?

In a line parallel to Lee's, the Army of the Potomac marched north along the east side of the Blue Ridge Mountains. "We cannot help beating them, if we have the man," Lincoln said. Still, Lincoln was not sure that he had the right general. Lee's army was already in Pennsylvania when Lincoln replaced General Hooker with General George Meade.

Meanwhile, morale had risen in the Army of the Potomac. The men knew that they would be fighting on their own soil to protect their country. "They are more determined than I have ever before seen them," a Union doctor wrote.

Neither Meade nor Lee planned to fight at Gettysburg. It just happened. On July 1, 1863, Lee sent soldiers into the town of Gettysburg to get a supply of shoes. There they stumbled upon some Union cavalry, and the Battle of Gettysburg was on.

The fighting lasted for three days in what would be the greatest single battle of the Civil War. The most famous, and most crucial, moment of the battle was Pickett's Charge. For two days the armies had held their positions on opposite ridges. On the third day, Lee ordered General George Pickett to lead a charge of 13,000 men against the Union cen-

ULYSSES S. GRANT (1822–1885), a native of Ohio, graduated from West Point and served in the Mexican War. Later, he was posted to the Oregon Territory where, depressed and lonely, he became an alcoholic and resigned his commission. Grant rejoined the army at age 39. His courage in battle against Confederate forces in the West led Lincoln to appoint him commander of the Union armies.

ter on Cemetery Ridge. Pickett's troops had to cross a wide-open field in order to reach the Union army. Within half an hour, intense Union gunfire had leveled half the attackers. Though Pickett's men reached the top of the ridge, they could not hold their position.

Pickett's Charge ended the Battle of Gettysburg. Lee's hopes of victory were dashed. "It's all my fault," he said, and ordered a retreat. Meade was amazed at his own success. "I did not believe the enemy could be whipped," he said.

The Confederates lost the Battle of Gettysburg largely because new technology had made Lee's tactics outdated. By 1863, rifles had replaced the old, inaccurate muskets that soldiers on both sides had carried at the start of the war. Rifling—the cutting of spiral grooves in a gun's bore—made guns more accurate and gave them a longer range. Soldiers marching in close formation, as they did in Pickett's Charge, could be mowed down far from enemy lines.

General Meade was so pleased with the Union victory that he did not pursue and finish off Lee's army. Lincoln was furious. When would he find a general who was a match for Lee?

Then good news came from the Battle of Vicksburg. On July 3, 1863, the day of Pickett's Charge, General Grant had taken Vicks-

burg after a three-month siege. The victory was even more important than Gettysburg, for it gave the Union complete control of the Mississippi. The Confederacy had been cut in half. "Grant is my man," decided President Lincoln.

Though revered today as a great leader, President Lincoln was criticized by many northerners for his handling of the war. One of his most controversial acts was ordering people to be arrested without being formally charged. **CIVIC VALUES** Should the government be able to suspend civil rights during wartime?

The Gettysburg Address (1863)

President Lincoln presented his memorable Gettysburg Address on November 19, 1863, at the dedication of a national cemetery on the battlefield of Gettysburg. His eloquent words expressed his hopes for a war-torn nation.

Four score and seven years ago our fathers brought forth on this continent, a new nation, conceived in liberty, and dedicated to the proposition that all men are created equal.

Now we are engaged in a great civil war, testing whether that nation or any nation so conceived and so dedicated, can long endure. We are met on a great battlefield of that war. We have come to dedicate a portion of that field, as a final resting place for those who here gave their lives that that nation might live. It is altogether fitting and proper that we should do this.

But, in a larger sense, we cannot dedicate—we cannot consecrate—we cannot hallow—this ground. The brave men, living and dead, who struggled here, have consecrated it, far above our poor power to add or detract. The world will little note, nor long remember what we say here, but it can never forget what they did here. It is for us the living, rather, to be dedicated here to the unfinished work which they who fought here have thus far so nobly advanced. It is rather for us to be here dedicated to the great task remaining before us—that from these honored dead we take increased devotion to that cause for which they gave the last full measure of devotion—that we here highly resolve that these dead shall not have died in vain—that this nation, under God, shall have a new birth of freedom—and that government of the people, by the people, for the people, shall not perish from the earth.

From *The Writings of Abraham Lincoln,* Constitutional ed., Vol. VIII, p. 20.

ANALYZING HISTORICAL DOCUMENTS

1. Why did Abraham Lincoln begin the Gettysburg Address by recalling the founding of the United States?

2. Explain the phrase "We here highly resolve that these dead shall not have died in vain."

3. What, in your opinion, is the overall message of the Gettysburg Address?

THE GETTYSBURG ADDRESS

In November 1863, President Lincoln journeyed to Gettysburg to dedicate the cemetery in which about 6,000 battle dead lay buried. The speech he gave that day was short, but powerful. Lincoln used simple language to make it clear that the Union soldiers were fighting to save democracy. The nation, Lincoln said, was founded on "the proposition that all men are created equal." The "great task remaining" was "that this nation, under God, shall have a new birth of freedom—and that government of the people, by the people, for the people, shall not perish from the earth." No one has ever expressed better the spirit of democracy.

SECTION REVIEW

1. KEY TERMS Emancipation Proclamation, draft, Copperhead, Battle of Gettysburg, Battle of Vicksburg

2. PEOPLE AND PLACES Sharpsburg, Harriet Tubman, George Meade, Vicksburg

3. COMPREHENSION Why did the Emancipation Proclamation not apply in Union states?

4. COMPREHENSION What did Lee hope to gain when he invaded Pennsylvania?

5. CRITICAL THINKING What did Lincoln mean by the words "government of the people, by the people, for the people"?

Gaining Skill: Special-Purpose Maps

Maps that present specific types of information are called special-purpose maps. Special-purpose maps can be used to present many types of information. Some special-purpose maps present economic information, such as the kinds of industries found in a particular area. The map on page 119 is an example of an economic map. Other special-purpose maps provide political information, such as population figures or election results. Special-purpose maps may alter the shape of geographical features in order to make the information clearer. For example, on a population map of the United States, New York might appear as a very large state because it has a large population.

BATTLE MAPS

The special-purpose map on this page gives military information about the Battle of Gettysburg. Like other kinds of maps, this map shows important information in the form of symbols that are explained in the map key. The key explains the meaning of the different colored bars, arrows, and lines on the map. Study the map and key carefully. Then answer the following questions.

PRACTICING YOUR SKILL

1. What do the red arrows on this special-purpose map represent?
2. What do the black bars represent? The black arrows?
3. Did most of the fighting take place to the north or south of Gettysburg?
4. Which high points near Gettysburg did the Union forces hold?
5. From which ridge did Pickett lead his charge?
6. Using information found on the map and in this chapter, determine what advantages helped the Union troops overcome Pickett's Charge.

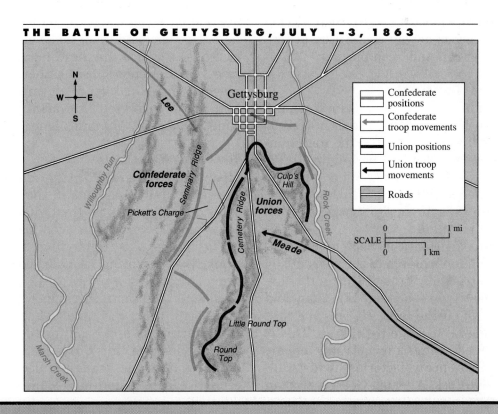

THE BATTLE OF GETTYSBURG, JULY 1–3, 1863

4 The Union Victorious

Section Focus

Key Term total war

Main Idea Led by Ulysses S. Grant, the Union armies bore down on Confederate forces in 1864 and 1865. The South was forced to surrender. The Civil War brought great changes to the nation.

Objectives As you read, look for answers to these questions:
1. How did the Union defeat the South?
2. What were the results of the war?

The battles of Gettysburg and Vicksburg marked the turning point of the war. From then on, it was all downhill for the Confederacy. Late in 1863 Grant seized the important railroad center of Chattanooga, Tennessee. He thereby opened up another invasion route into the lower South.

Impressed with Grant's ability to get things done, Lincoln gave him command of all the Union armies. Grant certainly did not look the part of a general. Unlike the formal and dignified Lee, Grant wore wrinkled uniforms. Yet like Lee, Grant knew how to lead an army. As Grant put it, "The art of war is simple enough. Find out where your enemy is. Get him as soon as you can. Strike at him as hard as you can and keep moving."

GRANT TAKES COMMAND

In the spring of 1864, Grant was in Washington. His plan was to attack the Confederacy on all fronts. He would go into the field himself to pursue Lee. Meanwhile, Admiral Farragut would go after Mobile, one of the few ports in Confederate hands. William Tecumseh Sherman was to move southeast from Chattanooga to Atlanta.

Sherman took Atlanta in September 1864. He then set out on a march to the sea, cutting a path of destruction through Georgia. Leaving his supply trains behind, Sherman told his men to live off the land. He was the first American general to wage total war. This is a war designed to destroy not only enemy troops but also enemy factories, fields, railroads, and livestock. A young Georgia woman described the scene after Sherman had passed through:

> There was hardly a fence left standing. . . . The fields were trampled down and the road was lined with carcasses of horses, hogs, and cattle that the invaders, unable either to consume or to carry away with them, had wantonly shot down, to starve out the people and prevent them from making their crops. The stench in some places was unbearable.

Sherman himself made no apologies. "We are not only fighting hostile armies, but a hostile people, and must make old and young, rich and poor, feel the hard hand of war," he said. In December 1864, Sherman's army reached the port city of Savannah. Behind him lay a corridor of devastation 60 miles wide and nearly 300 miles long.

THE WAR ENDS

Meanwhile, General Phil Sheridan was doing the same kind of damage in the Shenandoah Valley. Sheridan knew that without this fertile region, Lee could not feed his troops.

The noose was tightening around Lee's army. By the spring of 1865, Grant had an army twice the size of Lee's—120,000 to Lee's 55,000. In addition, Sherman was now moving north from Savannah. Lee decided to leave Richmond and head for the mountains. Then he learned that Sheridan was ahead of him. Trapped, Lee made the decision to surrender. "There is nothing for me to do but go

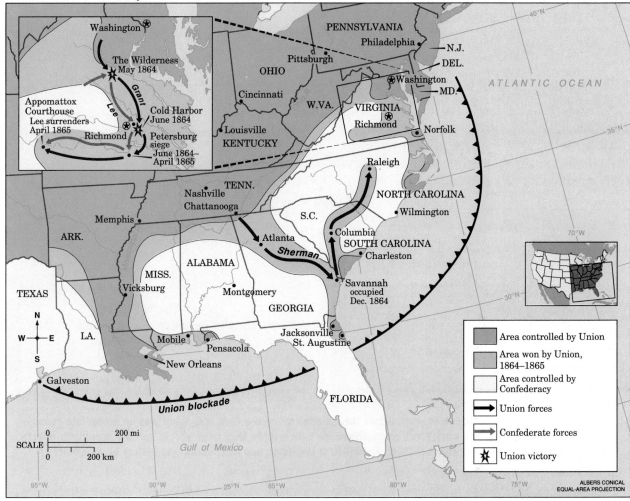

THE CIVIL WAR, 1864–1865

Washington ⊛

The Wilderness
May 1864

Appomattox
Courthouse
Lee surrenders
April 1865

Richmond

Cold Harbor
June 1864

Petersburg
siege
June 1864–
April 1865

PENNSYLVANIA
Philadelphia
N.J.
DEL.
Pittsburgh
OHIO
Cincinnati
⊛ Washington
MD.
W.VA.
VIRGINIA
Richmond ⊛
Norfolk
ATLANTIC OCEAN

40°N

35°N

70°W

Louisville
KENTUCKY

TENN.
Nashville
Chattanooga

Memphis

ARK.

Raleigh

NORTH CAROLINA
Wilmington

S.C.

Atlanta
Sherman

Columbia
SOUTH CAROLINA
Charleston

Savannah
occupied
Dec. 1864

30°N

TEXAS

N
W ✦ E
S

LA.

MISS.
Vicksburg

ALABAMA

Montgomery

GEORGIA

Mobile
Pensacola
New Orleans

Jacksonville
St. Augustine

Galveston

FLORIDA

Union blockade

Gulf of Mexico

0   200 mi
SCALE
0   200 km

70°W

Area controlled by Union

Area won by Union,
1864–1865

Area controlled by
Confederacy

Union forces

Confederate forces

✸ Union victory

ALBERS CONICAL
EQUAL-AREA PROJECTION

95°W   90°W   25°N   85°W   80°W   75°W

MAP SKILLS This map shows the final events of the war. Around which capital were the final battles fought (inset map)? In what year did Sherman's march across Georgia take place? **CRITICAL THINKING** How was Sherman's march to the sea an example of total war?

and see General Grant, and I would rather die a thousand deaths," Lee said sadly.

On April 9, 1865, in the small Virginia town of Appomattox Courthouse, Lee and Grant arranged the terms of surrender. As Lincoln had ordered, Grant was generous. The Confederate soldiers were to return to their homes, and those who owned horses or mules could keep them. When Lee left Appomattox, Grant ordered his men to supply food to the hungry Confederate soldiers.

THE PRESIDENT SLAIN

The final act of the Civil War tragedy was now played out. A few days after Appomat-

tox, President and Mrs. Lincoln went to the theater to see a popular comedy. During the third act John Wilkes Booth, a Confederate supporter, crept through the theater to the door of Lincoln's box. Suddenly he threw open the door. Booth stepped into the box and shot Lincoln in the back of the head. Then he leaped over the railing and half jumped, half fell, to the stage. As he fell, he shouted a Latin phrase that means, "Thus be it ever to tyrants!" The fall had broken his leg, and he limped across the stage to the back door, mounted his horse, and rode away. Booth was killed a few days later by soldiers who were sent to capture him.

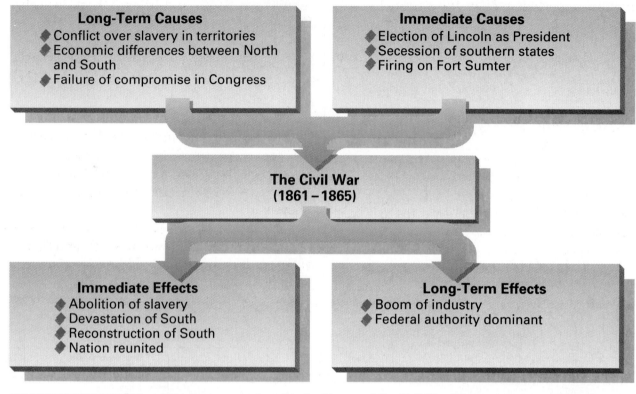

Long-Term Causes
- Conflict over slavery in territories
- Economic differences between North and South
- Failure of compromise in Congress

Immediate Causes
- Election of Lincoln as President
- Secession of southern states
- Firing on Fort Sumter

The Civil War (1861–1865)

Immediate Effects
- Abolition of slavery
- Devastation of South
- Reconstruction of South
- Nation reunited

Long-Term Effects
- Boom of industry
- Federal authority dominant

CHART SKILLS This chart summarizes the significance of the Civil War. What was an immediate cause of the war? What is the difference between the long-term effects and the immediate effects of the war? **CRITICAL THINKING** If the North had lost, how might history be different?

Lincoln was carried to a house across the street from the theater. The bullet in his brain was too deep to be extracted. Early the next morning, April 15, 1865, the President died. With Lincoln's last breath rose up a wail of grief from freedom-lovers the world over.

CONSEQUENCES OF THE WAR

The Civil War was the most wrenching experience in our nation's history. The Union was saved and slavery ended, but at a frightening cost. In four years 620,000 men died—360,000 for the Union, 260,000 for the Confederacy. No other war in our history caused such loss of life.

Throughout most of the war, the outcome was in doubt. Even today, historians cannot say exactly why the North won and why the South lost. They do agree, however, that final

Union victory reflected the leadership of Abraham Lincoln. During the nation's darkest hour, he held firm to the principles of freedom and democracy. As great leaders must, he bore the terrible burden of responsibility for the fate of his nation.

The consequences of the war were enormous:

(1) *The war changed the way Americans thought about their nation.* In fighting to defend the Union, people accepted that the nation itself was more important than the states that formed it. After 1865, people no longer said "the United States are," but instead, "the United States *is.*"

(2) *The war helped the federal government expand.* Before the Civil War, the federal government was a fairly small body with limited powers. By placing new demands on the government, the war made it necessary for gov-

ernment to grow. The government began to play an important role in the day-to-day life of its citizens.

To pay for the war, the government set up the first federal income tax in 1861. Congress also funded a transcontinental railroad, gave western land to settlers, and provided for state colleges. The growth in federal power would continue long after the guns of war had fallen silent.

(3) *The war spurred industry.* The war aided the early growth of several great post-war industries—petroleum, steel, food processing, manufacturing, and finance. This growth would continue for years after the end of the war.

For the South, of course, the war was a disaster. Defeated, occupied, many of its cities and farms destroyed, the South faced an un-certain future. The nation's next task was to rebuild the South and bring it back into the Union.

SECTION REVIEW

1. KEY TERM total war

2. PEOPLE AND PLACES William Tecumseh Sherman, Atlanta, Appomattox Courthouse

3. COMPREHENSION What Union victories in 1864–1865 led to the South's surrender?

4. COMPREHENSION List three consequences of the war.

5. CRITICAL THINKING Explain the following statement: "The war aims of North and South ensured that the war would have to continue until one side won total victory."

CHAPTER 20 SUMMARY AND TIMELINE

1. Early in 1861, North and South prepared for war. The North had more people and industry, greater wealth, and the inspired leadership of Abraham Lincoln. The South had better generals and was fighting on its own soil.

2. In the early years of the war, the South held its own in the East but lost ground in the West. The Union's naval blockade of the South hurt the Confederacy. Union victories in the West, including the Battle of Shiloh and the capture of Nashville and New Orleans, weakened the South.

3. The turning point of the war came in July 1863, when Union forces blocked a Confederate offensive in the North at Gettysburg. A victory at Vicksburg gave the Union control of the Mississippi River. By 1865 the Union held the upper hand.

4. Led by General Ulysses S. Grant, Union forces invaded the Confederacy. The last southern army surrendered by the end of May 1865. The war changed Americans' attitude toward their country, strengthened the authority of the federal government, and encouraged industrial growth.

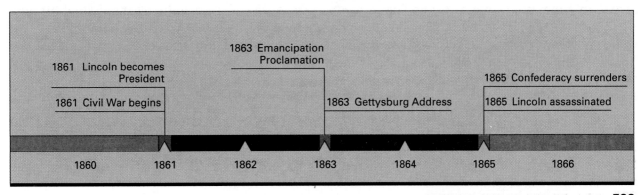

1863 Emancipation Proclamation

1861 Lincoln becomes President

1865 Confederacy surrenders

1861 Civil War begins

1863 Gettysburg Address

1865 Lincoln assassinated

1860   1861   1862   1863   1864   1865   1866

Chapter 20 REVIEW

PLACES TO LOCATE

Match each of the letters on the map with the places that are listed below. Then explain the importance of each place.

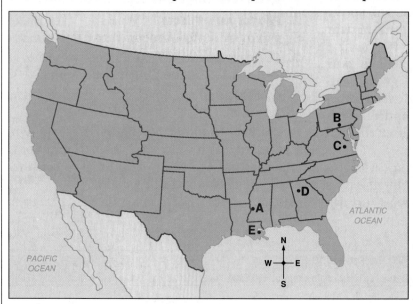

1. Atlanta
2. Gettysburg
3. New Orleans
4. Richmond
5. Vicksburg

KEY TERMS

Use the following terms to complete the sentences.

Battle of Vicksburg
border state
cavalry
Copperhead
First Battle of Bull Run
total war

1. Against Georgia, Sherman practiced ____, destroying factories and crops as well as armies.
2. The ____, the first battle of the war, was a Confederate victory.
3. A ____ was a northerner who sympathized with the South during the Civil War.
4. Both sides used ____, or soldiers mounted on horseback.
5. Maryland was a ____ that Lincoln worked to keep in the Union.
6. The Union victory at the ____ meant that the North controlled the Mississippi River.

PEOPLE TO IDENTIFY

Identify the following people and tell why each one was important.

1. Elizabeth Blackwell
2. Jefferson Davis
3. Ulysses S. Grant
4. Stonewall Jackson
5. Robert E. Lee
6. William Tecumseh Sherman

REVIEWING THE FACTS

1. Where did Confederate leaders decide to establish their capital? Why was this a risky decision?
2. What were the strengths of the North and the South?
3. What were the war aims of the North and the South?
4. What factors led both sides to begin focusing more on winning decisive victories on the battlefield?
5. Why did the North blockade southern ports? How effective was the blockade by the end of the war?
6. Where was the western front in the war? Why was it important?
7. What battles marked the turning point in the war? Why were they significant?
8. When, where, and why did Lee finally surrender?
9. When was President Lincoln killed? Who killed him?
10. What were the consequences of the war?

PRACTICING YOUR SKILL

The special-purpose map below shows General Grant's moves along the Mississippi and Tennessee rivers in 1862 and 1863. Study the map. Then answer these questions.

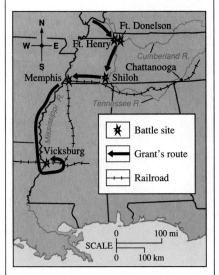

1. In what direction did Grant head when he left Fort Henry?
2. Which battle did Grant fight first, the Battle of Vicksburg or the Battle of Shiloh?
3. Where did Grant cross the Mississippi?
4. How far is it from Vicksburg to Memphis by rail?

CITIZENSHIP

1. How would the emotions of a soldier involved in a civil war differ from those of a soldier involved in a war between two different nations?
2. Frederick Douglass said that once the African American soldier had fought for the Union, "there is no power on earth which can deny that he has earned the right to citizenship." Explain what Douglass meant.
3. First defend, and then criticize, the idea that government should be given more power in wartime than in peacetime.

CRITICAL THINKING SKILLS

1. **STATING BOTH SIDES OF AN ISSUE** Make the strongest possible case for each side in the debate over whether states had the right to secede.
2. **ANALYZING A QUOTATION** Reread Lincoln's statement about slavery on page 512. Explain what it says about Lincoln's views on the war and slavery.
3. **IDENTIFYING CAUSE AND EFFECT** Choose one of the battles discussed in this chapter and describe its effects on the South's chances for survival.
4. **FORMING A HYPOTHESIS** Why did Lincoln order Grant to treat the surrendering Confederates generously?

PROJECTS AND ACTIVITIES

1. **GIVING AN ORAL REPORT** Find out about one of the following topics: the ironclad warships, African American soldiers in the war, Sherman's march through the South, medical care during the war. Present an oral report to the class.
2. **WRITING A DIARY** Imagine that you are a soldier at one of the major battles of the war. Write down your experiences in the form of a diary entry.
3. **WRITING A REPORT** Find out about persons from your community who fought in the Civil War. Write a report on who they were, what units they joined, and what battles they fought.
4. **ANALYZING LITERATURE** Though he had little formal education, President Lincoln was known for his eloquence. Study one of his speeches or other writings and write an essay analyzing his use of language.

WRITING ABOUT TOPICS IN AMERICAN HISTORY

1. **CONNECTING WITH LITERATURE** A selection from *The Slopes of War* by Nora A. Perez appears on pages 659–660. Read it and answer the questions. Then answer the following question: Why is the Battle of Gettysburg sometimes seen as the beginning of the end for the Confederacy?
2. **APPLYING THEMES: CONSTITUTIONAL GOVERNMENT** The Civil War increased the power of the federal government at the expense of the states. Do wars in general increase the power of the central government? Explain.

*R*ebuilding a South devastated by war was a pressing task for the United States after 1865. Southern farms, towns and cities, roads and bridges, mills and factories—all had to be rebuilt or repaired.

KEY EVENTS

1865	Slavery ended
1866	Civil Rights Bill passed
1867	Reconstruction Act of 1867
1868	President Johnson impeached
1870	African American men gain voting rights
1896	*Plessy v. Ferguson* decision

1 The Challenge of Freedom

★ Section Focus

Key Terms   Reconstruction ■ amnesty ■ Thirteenth Amendment ■ black codes

Main Idea   After the Civil War, Americans had to work out a plan to rebuild the South.

Objectives   As you read, look for answers to these questions:
1. What was the African American response to the ending of slavery?
2. What was the President's plan for rebuilding the South?
3. How did southern states seek to restore the old order?

When the Civil War ended in 1865, the nation had been changed forever. The North was about to enter the modern industrial age. Business was booming in all the industries involved with the war effort. These included railroads, meat-packing plants, woolen mills, shoe-and-boot factories, and agriculture.

The South, on the other hand, was in ruins. Its railroads had been torn up, its barns and houses burned, its livestock killed. The South also faced another challenge: to build a new society, one not based on slavery. The federal government played an active role in both tasks. Its plan to rebuild the South is known as Reconstruction. Reconstruction took place during the years 1865–1877.

THE AFRICAN AMERICAN RESPONSE TO FREEDOM

The day freedom came was an event former slaves remembered for the rest of their lives.

Years later one freedman (freed slave) described the feeling:

> The end of the war, it come just like that—like you snap your fingers. . . . Soldiers, all of a sudden, was everywhere—coming in bunches, crossing and walking and riding. Everyone was a-singing. We was all walking on golden clouds. Hallelujah! . . . Everybody went wild. We all felt like heroes, and nobody had made us that way but ourselves. We was free. Just like that, we was free.

African Americans' first reaction to freedom was to escape white control over their lives. Some returned to where they had been born. Others began looking for family members, or just traveled for fun. "Right off colored folks started on the move," recalled one freedman. "They seemed to want to get closer

Winslow Homer's oil painting *Sunday Morning* depicts an African American family reading from the Bible. Homer traveled to Petersburg, Virginia, to make the portrait in 1877. CULTURAL PLURALISM Which members of the family were probably born into slavery?

to freedom, so they'd know what it was—like it was a place or a city."

Freedom allowed families to reunite and strengthened family ties. Under slavery, marriage had been an informal affair. With freedom, many couples went through marriage ceremonies.

African Americans also took steps to free their religion from white control. Throughout the South, they created their own churches. The church then became the center of the African American community. It was a place for social events and political meetings. Often it was also a school.

Schools for African Americans sprouted up throughout the South. Both adults and children flocked to these schools. Reading and writing was, as many saw, the road to a new economic freedom. Within five years after the end of the war, African Americans had raised over $1 million toward their own education. However, even this was not enough to meet the need. In the long run, government and private groups in the North would pay most of the cost of education for freedmen.

The teachers in these schools were both black and white. Ten percent of the South's

African American adults could read, and a number of them chose to become teachers. Other teachers included African Americans from the North, such as Charlotte Forten of Philadelphia. "My heart sings a song of thanksgiving," she wrote, "that even I am permitted to do something for a long-abused race." Racist whites harassed teachers in African American schools. In some parts of the South, schools were burned and teachers beaten or killed.

ISSUES OF LAND AND LABOR

More than anything else, freed slaves hoped to own land. General Sherman had ordered that coastal South Carolina be split into 40-acre parcels of land and given to freedmen. The rumor then spread through the South that all freedmen would be given "40 acres and a mule." That was, most believed, no more than their right. As one Virginian explained:

> Didn't we clear the land, and raise the crops of corn, of cotton, of tobacco, of rice, of sugar, of everything? And then didn't them large cities in the North grow up on the cotton and the sugars and the rice that we made?

In fact, most freedmen never received land. Those who did often had to return it.

In the early years of Reconstruction, many African Americans had no way to earn a living. It was clear that the South needed a new system of labor. There were landowners with little cash and no laborers, and laborers without land.

Planters and freedmen alike had trouble getting used to their new working relationship. Planters were not used to bargaining with workers over hours and wages. Many freedmen assumed that the wage was an extra—that the landowner still had to clothe, house, and feed them.

PRESIDENT JOHNSON AND RECONSTRUCTION

The federal government played a key role in rebuilding the South. In the last year of the war, Lincoln had begun to consider how the South should be treated when peace came. In his Second Inaugural Address in March 1865, Lincoln declared:

> With malice toward none, with charity for all, with firmness in the right as God gives us to see the right, let us strive on to finish the work we are in, to bind up the nation's wounds . . . to do all which may achieve and cherish a just and a lasting peace among ourselves and with all nations.

> "**W**ith malice toward none, with charity for all, with firmness in the right as God gives us to see the right, let us strive on to finish the work we are in. . . ."
>
> —*Abraham Lincoln, 1865*

In a speech given during the last week of his life, Lincoln further explained his ideas for dealing with the South. From his point of view, the Confederate states had never left the Union. The task at hand was not to punish them. Rather, it was "to restore the proper practical relations between these states and the Union." What this meant exactly, Lincoln did not say.

Upon Lincoln's death, Vice President Andrew Johnson became President. Johnson, a former Democrat but now a member of the newly formed Union Party, had been put on the Republican ticket in 1864 to broaden its appeal to the border states. A self-made man from Tennessee, Johnson was a former slaveholder. As a backcountry politician, Johnson did not trust the wealthy planters. He also had little sympathy for African Americans. Unlike Lincoln, who knew how to compromise, Johnson was stubborn to a fault.

Johnson held that Reconstruction was the job of the President, not Congress. Johnson's policies were based on what he thought were Lincoln's goals. They included charity toward

This illustration shows a class at the Zion School for Colored Children, a freedmen's school in Charleston, South Carolina. A federal agency, the Freedmen's Bureau, established schools for African Americans during Reconstruction. Some of these schools developed into leading black colleges, such as Howard University and Hampton Institute. **HISTORY** Why was education so important for African Americans during Reconstruction?

Abraham Lincoln's Second Inaugural Address (1865)

Lincoln delivered his Second Inaugural Address just before the end of the Civil War. In it he recalled the circumstances that led the nation to war and his hope for the restoration of peace and unity.

Fellow Countrymen: At this second appearing to take the oath of the presidential office there is less occasion for an extended address than there was at the first. Then a statement of a course to be pursued seemed fitting and proper. Now, at the expiration of four years, during which public declarations have been constantly called forth on every point and phase of the great contest which still absorbs the attention and engrosses the energies of the nation, little that is new could be presented. The progress of our arms, upon which all else chiefly depends, is as well known to the public as to myself, and it is, I trust, reasonably satisfactory and encouraging to all. With high hope for the future, no prediction in regard to it is ventured.

On the occasion corresponding to this four years ago, all thoughts were anxiously directed to an impending civil war. All dreaded it, all sought to avert it. While the inaugural address was being delivered from this place, . . . insurgent agents were in the city seeking to destroy it without war—seeking to dissolve the Union. Both parties [disapproved of] war, but one of them would make war rather than let the nation survive, and the other would accept war rather than let it perish, and the war came.

One-eighth of the whole population was colored slaves, not distributed generally over the Union, but localized in the southern part of it. These slaves constituted a peculiar and powerful interest. All knew that this interest was somehow the cause of the war. To strengthen, perpetuate, and extend this interest was the object for which the rebels would tear the Union even by war, while the government claimed no right to do more than to restrict the territorial enlargement of it. Neither party expected for the war the magnitude or the duration which it has already attained. Neither anticipated that the cause of the conflict itself should cease. Each looked for an easier triumph, and a result less fundamental and astounding. . . . Fondly do we hope, fervently do we pray, that this mighty scourge of war may speedily pass away. Yet, if God wills that it continue until all the wealth piled by the slaves' two hundred and fifty years of unpaid toil shall be sunk . . . so still it must be said, "The judgments of the Lord are true and righteous altogether."

With malice toward none, with charity for all, with firmness in the right as God gives us to see the right, let us strive on to finish the work we are in, to bind up the nation's wounds, to care for him who shall have borne the battle and for his widow and his orphan—to do all which may achieve and cherish a just and a lasting peace among ourselves and with all nations.

From J. D. Richardson, ed., *A Compilation of the Messages and Papers of the Presidents,* Vol. VI, p. 276.

ANALYZING HISTORICAL DOCUMENTS

1. According to President Lincoln, what was the Civil War's main cause?

2. What does Lincoln say about each side's expectations as the war began?

3. What does the Inaugural Address suggest about the kind of policy Lincoln wanted to follow after the war?

the former Confederates and the creation of new state governments.

To most white southerners Johnson offered amnesty, or official pardon. He also promised to restore their property. In return, they had to pledge their loyalty to the United States. The great planters, top military officers, and ex-Confederate leaders were not included in this offer. Even they, however, were often able to win amnesty. Johnson was easily swayed when the once high-and-mighty asked him for pardon.

Johnson also took steps to set up temporary governments in the South that would write new constitutions for the states. These constitutions, he said, must forbid slavery. They must also reject the doctrine of nullification (page 389).

REVIVING THE OLD SOUTH

Congress was not in session when Johnson took over as President in April 1865. It did not meet until the following December. During these eight months the former Confederate states rebuilt their governments and societies. The problem was that the new states looked too much like the old ones.

For example, nothing was said about black suffrage. "This is a white man's government," said the governor of South Carolina, "and intended for white men only." After all, he pointed out, the Supreme Court's Dred Scott decision had said that African Americans could not be citizens.

President Johnson's "soft" and friendly attitude encouraged southern leaders to fight his policies. Mississippi and Texas refused to ratify the Thirteenth Amendment, which abolished slavery. Several states refused to reject the doctrine of nullification.

Southern states also began to pass laws limiting the freedom of African Americans. These laws, called black codes, aimed to return former slaves to plantation labor. In Mississippi, for instance, one law said that each person had to have written proof of employment. Anyone without such proof could be put on a plantation and forced to work

This photograph shows laborers on a South Carolina rice plantation. Rice output dropped sharply after the war because many freedmen refused to return to plantation work. **ECONOMICS** Why might the black codes be viewed as an attempt to save the plantation system?

there. In South Carolina, African Americans who chose a job other than farmer or servant had to pay a heavy tax. Other black codes said that African Americans could not meet in unsupervised groups or bear firearms. Those on plantations had to labor from sunup to sundown. They could not even leave the plantation without permission.

THE FREEDMEN'S BUREAU

Opposition to the black codes came from the Freedmen's Bureau. This federal agency had been set up during the war to distribute clothes, food, and fuel to the poor of the South. It was also put in charge of land abandoned by Confederates or taken from them. It divided this land into 40-acre plots. These were to be rented to freedmen until the land could be sold.

All too often, however, freedmen had to give up their new farms. With Johnson's help, pardoned Confederate landowners were able to regain their land. African Americans in the South, their land gone, had lost their best chance at economic freedom.

Some private citizens stepped in to help the freedmen. G. T. Ruby, a teacher from New Orleans, moved to Galveston, Texas, in 1866. There he opened schools for former slaves. However, not everyone was as charitable. As one Freedmen's Bureau agent wrote, former slaveowners "still have the ingrained feeling that the black people at large belong to the whites at large."

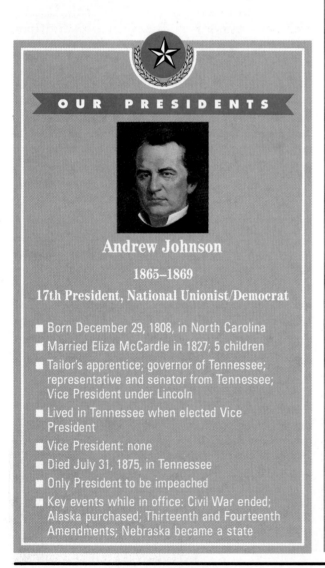

OUR PRESIDENTS

Andrew Johnson
1865–1869
17th President, National Unionist/Democrat

- Born December 29, 1808, in North Carolina
- Married Eliza McCardle in 1827; 5 children
- Tailor's apprentice; governor of Tennessee; representative and senator from Tennessee; Vice President under Lincoln
- Lived in Tennessee when elected Vice President
- Vice President: none
- Died July 31, 1875, in Tennessee
- Only President to be impeached
- Key events while in office: Civil War ended; Alaska purchased; Thirteenth and Fourteenth Amendments; Nebraska became a state

CONGRESS TAKES A STAND

When Congress met in December 1865, representatives from the South were there to take their seats. President Johnson was ready to welcome them. Yet the members of Congress were not willing to forget old differences quite so fast.

The problem was that many of the new southern representatives had been officials in the Confederate government only the year before. This list included 4 generals, 6 cabinet officers, and 58 congressmen. Even the former Confederate vice president was now about to enter Congress. Northern members of Congress were alarmed. They were also worried about conditions in the southern states. They asked: Had the Civil War been fought just to allow the South to return to its old ways?

Under the Constitution, Congress has the right to decide whether its members are qualified to hold office. Instead of admitting the southerners, therefore, Congress set up a committee. The committee would look into conditions in the South and decide whether the southern states should be represented in Congress. Congress thus let President Johnson know that it planned to play a role in Reconstruction.

SECTION REVIEW

1. KEY TERMS Reconstruction, amnesty, Thirteenth Amendment, black codes

2. PEOPLE Andrew Johnson

3. COMPREHENSION How did the lives of African Americans in the South change after they were freed?

4. COMPREHENSION How did the South respond to President Johnson's reconstruction policies?

5. CRITICAL THINKING President Johnson believed he was carrying out Lincoln's ideas on Reconstruction. Do you think Lincoln would have approved or disapproved of his policies? Explain your answer.

2 Radical Reconstruction

★ **Section Focus** ★

Key Terms   moderate ■ civil rights ■ override ■ Fourteenth Amendment ■ scalawag ■ carpetbagger ■ Fifteenth Amendment ■ Ku Klux Klan ■ lynch

Main Idea   Congress took over Reconstruction from the President and tried to give political equality to African Americans in the South.

Objectives   As you read, look for answers to these questions:
1.   How and why did Congress change its policy toward the South?
2.   How did the efforts of Congress affect politics in the South?
3.   Why did Congress try to limit the President's power?

As 1866 began, it was clear that the feelings that had led to war remained strong. A newspaper in Jackson, Mississippi, wrote, "We must keep the ex-slave in a position of inferiority. We must pass such laws as will make him *feel* his inferiority." The *Chicago Tribune* fired back. It wrote, "We tell the white men of Mississippi that the men of the North will convert the state of Mississippi into a frog pond before they will allow any such laws." The nation was in an angry mood as Congress began to consider the many problems of Reconstruction.

> "**W**e must keep the ex-slave in a position of inferiority. We must pass such laws as will make him *feel* his inferiority."
>
> —*Newspaper in Jackson, Mississippi*

THE REPUBLICANS IN CONGRESS

Republicans outnumbered Democrats in both houses of Congress. Most Republicans were moderates, or people who oppose extreme change. They wanted to work with the President on Reconstruction.

Moderate Republicans were bothered by the large number of ex-Confederates holding office. The abuses against African Americans in the South also concerned them. At the same time, they did not believe the federal government could solve all of the South's problems. Like most Americans of the time, they wanted government to stay out of the affairs of individuals and the states.

The Radical Republicans felt differently. They had long urged the ending of slavery. They now called for full and equal citizenship for the freedmen. They argued that a true republic should grant citizenship to all.

The Radical Republicans had two outspoken leaders. One of them was Representative Thaddeus Stevens of Pennsylvania. The other was Senator Charles Sumner of Massachusetts. Still, the Radicals were a minority in Congress.

BIOGRAPHY

CHARLES SUMNER (1811–1874), a senator and founder of the Republican Party, favored freeing the slaves and giving them the vote. After making an especially strong speech attacking slavery and its defenders, Sumner was beaten by an outraged congressman from South Carolina. It took Sumner more than three years to recover from his injuries.

The Radicals hoped that the federal government would remake southern politics and society. Their aim was to destroy the old planter class. They wanted to turn the South into a place of small farms, free schools, respect for labor, and political equality.

To reach this goal, Radicals called for four new policies:

(1) They wanted suffrage for all African Americans.

(2) They wanted to deny voting rights to ex-Confederates until African Americans could claim their rightful share of political power in the South.

(3) They demanded that the government seize land belonging to the large planters and give it to freedmen.

(4) They supported federally funded schools for African Americans.

In 1866 Congress was not ready for such ideas. As time went on, however, the Radicals would gain ground.

THE CIVIL RIGHTS ACT

Congress did pass two bills in 1866. The first bill gave new powers to the Freedmen's Bureau. Congress also passed a bill dealing with civil rights—the rights of all citizens. This bill declared that all persons born in the United States (except Indians) were citizens. It said that all citizens were entitled to equal rights regardless of their race.

Republicans were shocked when President Johnson vetoed both bills. Johnson tried to explain his opposition to the bills. He said that federal protection of black civil rights would lead "towards centralization" of the national government. He also argued that citizenship for black people would "operate against the white race."

Congress voted to override Johnson's veto of the Civil Rights Act. That is, two-thirds of the House and two-thirds of the Senate voted in favor of the bill even after the President's veto. The bill thus became law. It was the first time Congress had ever passed a major law over a presidential veto. Later, Congress also passed a new Freedmen's Bureau law

over the President's veto. Congress had taken over Reconstruction.

THE FOURTEENTH AMENDMENT

Republicans were not satisfied with laws protecting the equality of all citizens. They wanted that equality to be protected by the Constitution itself. To do this they proposed the Fourteenth Amendment. It said that all people born in the United States were citizens and had the same rights as citizens. It also prevented states from depriving "any person of life, liberty, and property" without due process of law. All citizens were to be granted the "equal protection of the laws."

The Fourteenth Amendment stopped just short of requiring black suffrage. Instead, it said that any state that kept African Americans from voting would lose representatives in Congress. This meant that the southern states would have less power in Congress if they did not grant black men the vote.

Support for black suffrage was still a radical position in 1866. Northerners wanted African Americans to be free from slavery. Equal voting rights, however, was another matter. Only five states in the North allowed African Americans to vote. Just the year before, three northern states had defeated constitutional amendments to give black men the vote. Racism was no stranger to the North.

Feminists attacked the Fourteenth Amendment too. Many women had long backed the abolitionist movement. Now, however, women began to ask why their own demands for voting rights were not being heard.

Elizabeth Cady Stanton, a leader of the women's suffrage movement, urged Congress to extend the vote to women. Yet even Senator Sumner found this proposal too radical. Women's suffrage, he said, was "the great question of the future." Embittered, many women withdrew from the movement for black rights.

The year 1866 was a congressional election year. President Johnson opposed the Fourteenth Amendment but wisely avoided it as a campaign issue. He argued that southerners were loyal Americans and that the real traitors were the Radical Republicans. The voters, however, disagreed. They returned a 3 to 1 Republican majority in both houses of Congress.

THE RECONSTRUCTION ACT OF 1867

Encouraged by Johnson's support, each of the ex-Confederate states except Tennessee voted to reject the Fourteenth Amendment. This move so angered moderate Republicans that they agreed to work with the Radicals. Together, the two groups passed the tough Reconstruction Act of 1867. Thus began a period known as Radical Reconstruction.

The Reconstruction Act of 1867 divided the South into five military districts, each run by an army commander. Members of the prewar planter class, about 10–15 percent of southern whites, lost their voting rights. The law also explained how the southern states could re-enter the Union. Voters in those states would have to do two things. (1) They would have to approve new constitutions that gave the vote to all adult men. (2) They would have to ratify the Fourteenth Amendment.

A NEW ORDER IN THE SOUTH

In 1867, Freedmen's Bureau agents began to register voters in the South. About 735,000 blacks and 635,000 whites were registered to vote. The voters then chose delegates to the new state conventions. Three-fourths of them were Republicans.

In this engraving, African Americans vote in an 1867 election in New Orleans. Beginning in 1867, the federal Freedmen's Bureau registered hundreds of thousands of African American voters in the South. These voters then elected delegates—most of them Republicans—to new state conventions. **POLITICS** Why might the great majority of African Americans have backed Republican candidates?

Almost half of these Republican delegates were whites who had supported the North. Living in the upcountry, they were poor people who produced just enough food to feed themselves. Many of them had lost faith in the Confederate cause long before the war's end. Angry at the destruction of their farms and livestock, they blamed the planter class for starting what they called "a rich man's war." Now that the war was over, they were eager to seize power from the old ruling class. The planters called them scalawags—meaning "scoundrels"—for going along with Radical Reconstruction.

Nearly one-fourth of the Republican delegates were white northerners who had moved south after the war. They liked the South and saw it as a place to get ahead in life. Many southerners thought that these northerners had come to exploit the South for their own gain. They called them carpetbaggers, after a cheap kind of suitcase. The idea was that these northerners had quickly stuffed their belongings in a suitcase and headed south to cash in on the South's distress. However, as one historian has pointed out:

> [They] brought not skimpy carpet-bags but rather considerable capital, which they invested in the South. They also invested human capital—themselves—in a drive to modernize the region's social structure, revive its crippled economy, and democratize its politics.

African Americans made up close to one-third of the Republican delegates. Of these, half had been free before the war. Most were ministers, teachers, or artisans. Eighty percent of them could read, and some had gone to college.

The delegates wrote new constitutions based on northern examples. They set up public school systems and gave the vote to all adult males. By 1869, voters had approved all these constitutions. The ex-Confederate states were let back into the Union, and thus back into Congress. Fourteen African American congressmen and two African American senators would serve in Congress during the era of Reconstruction.

THE IMPEACHMENT OF JOHNSON

Johnson obeyed the letter of the reconstruction laws, but he worked against them in spirit. For instance, he chose people friendly to the ex-Confederates to serve as military commanders in the South. Some in Congress would not stand for such actions. Finally there was a showdown between the President and Congress.

In 1867 Congress passed a law over Johnson's veto. It said that the President could not fire members of the Cabinet without the Senate's approval. This law broke with the tradition that a President controlled the Cabinet. It was meant to check Johnson's patronage power and to protect Radical politicians like Secretary of War Edwin Stanton.

Johnson opposed the law. To test it, he fired Stanton in February 1868. Three days later the House of Representatives voted to impeach the President. This means that the House formally accused him of improper conduct while in office.

The conflict between Congress and the President went far beyond the issue of the 1867 law. In the eyes of most members of Congress, Johnson's real offense was standing in the way of Congress's plans for Reconstruction. They hoped to convict Johnson. In this way they would strengthen Congress's hold over Reconstruction.

More generally, Congress wanted to make itself as powerful in the United States as Parliament was in Great Britain. A congressman made this point clear. "May we not anticipate a time," he asked, "when the President will no more think of vetoing a bill passed by Congress than the British Crown thinks of doing?"

In cases of impeachment, the Senate acts as the jury. A two-thirds vote is needed before a President can be removed from office. After a full trial, the Senate voted 35–19 for conviction. This was one vote short of the required two-thirds. Johnson was acquitted. By one vote, the tradition of a strong presidency and the separation of powers had remained intact.

THE FIFTEENTH AMENDMENT

One of the last trumpet calls of the Radicals was the Fifteenth Amendment, which became law in 1870. This amendment took the Fourteenth Amendment one step further. It declared that the right to vote should not be denied "on account of race, color, or previous condition of servitude."

The Fifteenth Amendment was not only aimed at the South. Its supporters were concerned about black suffrage throughout the country. African American men could not vote in sixteen states. "We have no moral right to impose an obligation on one part of the land which the rest will not accept," one Radical wrote. By approving the Fifteenth Amendment, the nation accepted the full consequences of ending slavery. It also committed itself once again to the principle of democracy.

THE RISE OF THE KU KLUX KLAN

In 1868 the nation elected Ulysses S. Grant as President. At the time, he was surely the most popular man in the North. In the South it was a different story. There, many people were violently opposed to the revolutionary changes forced on them. In response, they had already launched an outright assault on Reconstruction.

A revolution is likely to give rise to a counterrevolution—an attempt to undo the changes caused by the revolution. A counterrevolution started in the South with the election of 1868. Leading it were members of the old planter class and ex-Confederate soldiers. A number of these men joined the Ku Klux Klan, a secret group formed just after the war. The Klan's first goal was to control elections and destroy the Republican Party in the South.

Beyond that, the Klan aimed to keep African Americans powerless. It targeted blacks who owned their own land, any blacks who prospered, and teachers of black children. Such people were harassed by Klansmen.

This lithograph commemorates the passage in 1870 of the Fifteenth Amendment, which gave African American men the right to vote. The text of the amendment appears at the far right, above the picture of an African American soldier. **CONSTITUTIONAL HERITAGE** In what way was the Fifteenth Amendment a step beyond the Fourteenth Amendment?

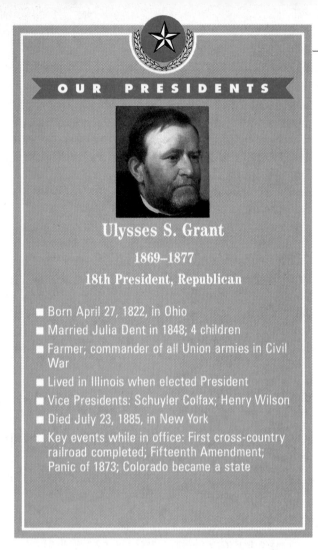

Ulysses S. Grant

1869–1877
18th President, Republican

- Born April 27, 1822, in Ohio
- Married Julia Dent in 1848; 4 children
- Farmer; commander of all Union armies in Civil War
- Lived in Illinois when elected President
- Vice Presidents: Schuyler Colfax; Henry Wilson
- Died July 23, 1885, in New York
- Key events while in office: First cross-country railroad completed; Fifteenth Amendment; Panic of 1873; Colorado became a state

GRANT VERSUS THE KU KLUX KLAN

At first, President Grant tried to avoid conflict with the Klan. After all, in the 1868 election he had campaigned on the slogan "Let us have peace." By 1871, however, it had become impossible to ignore the reign of terror that was sweeping the South. In that year Grant asked Congress to pass a tough law against the Klan. Joseph Rainey, an African American congressman from South Carolina who had received death threats from the Klan, spoke of the fear of Klan violence and of the need to combat it:

> When myself and [my] colleagues shall leave these Halls and turn our footsteps toward our southern home we know not but that the assassin may await our coming. Be it as it may we have resolved to be loyal and firm, and if we perish, we perish! I earnestly hope the bill will pass.

Congress did approve the anti-Klan bill. The federal government now moved against the Klan, as federal marshals arrested thousands of Klansmen. As a result, the 1872 election was both fair and peaceful in the South. Unfortunately, the same could not be said of later elections.

Some were even lynched—killed without a trial. The Klan was known to have murdered freedmen just because they could read and write.

The Klan became the terrorist arm of the Democratic Party. The Democratic platform in 1868 had called the reconstruction policies "unconstitutional, revolutionary, and void." It demanded that the Freedmen's Bureau be shut down. The white-robed, gun-toting, horse-riding Klansmen attacked Republican leaders and Republican voters. Across the South, Klan raids killed hundreds of African Americans—200 in Arkansas, for instance, and nearly 1,000 in Louisiana. The terror tactics worked. In every county where the Klan was active, Republican voters stayed away from the polls.

SECTION REVIEW

1. KEY TERMS moderate, civil rights, override, Fourteenth Amendment, scalawag, carpetbagger, Fifteenth Amendment, Ku Klux Klan, lynch

2. PEOPLE Thaddeus Stevens, Charles Sumner, Edwin Stanton, Ulysses S. Grant

3. COMPREHENSION In what ways did President Johnson try to interfere with the reconstruction policies of Congress?

4. COMPREHENSION How did Radical Reconstruction change the South?

5. CRITICAL THINKING Did Reconstruction increase or decrease states' power? Why did this happen?

Gaining Skill: Presenting an Argument

Speakers on both sides of an issue often state their ideas by presenting a formal argument. The purpose of an argument is to persuade other people to accept the speaker's position. History books may introduce an argument like this: "The President argued for the measure by saying . . ." or "The senator's argument against the policy was . . ." What usually follows is a summary of the reasons given to support or oppose an opinion or action.

THE PARTS OF AN ARGUMENT

A written argument is essentially a form of essay. Like other essays, it has an introduction, a body, and a conclusion. The introduction of an argument is called a **premise**. It expresses the main idea behind the argument. You should always state your premise strongly, simply, and clearly in order to gain your readers' attention.

The **body** of the argument consists of the evidence that backs up the premise. You may repeat the important ideas to advance your argument. You may also, if you wish, include some viewpoints that oppose your opinion. If you do, you should then offer arguments against those opposing viewpoints. Make sure that you do this in an open and fair way, avoiding sarcastic or insulting remarks.

Finally, you should close your argument with a short **conclusion** that restates your premise. Then briefly summarize the evidence you have to support it.

ANALYZING AN ARGUMENT

These guidelines will enable you not only to write your own arguments, but also to judge the arguments made by others. On this page is an argument by Representative Thaddeus Stevens. He is supporting a bill that would give the vote to African Americans living in the former Confederate states. Read Stevens' argument carefully. Then answer the questions that follow.

There are several good reasons for the passage of [the bill].

In the first place, it is just. I am now confining my argument to Negro suffrage in the rebel [Confederate] states. Have not loyal blacks as good a right to choose rulers and make laws as rebel whites?

In the second place, it is [necessary] in order to protect the loyal white [Union] men in the seceded states. The white Union men are in a great minority in each of those states. With them the blacks would act in a body, . . . the two united would form a majority, control the states, and protect themselves. Now they are the victims of daily murder. . . .

Another good reason is that it would insure the [rising power] of the Union [Republican] Party. "Do you admit to a party purpose?" exclaims some horror-stricken [hothead]. I do. For I believe, on my conscience, that on the continued rise of that party depends the safety of this great nation. . . .

For these, among other reasons, I am for Negro suffrage in every rebel state. If it be just, it should not be denied; if it be necessary, it should be adopted; if it be punishment to traitors, they deserve it.

PRACTICING YOUR SKILL

1. What is the premise of Thaddeus Stevens' argument?
2. What three reasons does Stevens offer for giving the vote to African Americans in the former Confederate states?
3. What opposing viewpoint does Stevens say might be raised?
4. What rebuttal does Stevens make to this opposing view?
5. On the basis of the guidelines given above, do you think this is a strong argument? Explain your answer.

3 The "New South"

In the 1870s most northerners grew tired of the issue of Reconstruction. The old abolitionist fire began to die out. Southern Republicans became cut off from northern support and from most white southerners.

RECONSTRUCTION LEGISLATURES

More than 600 African Americans served in the reconstruction legislatures. Still, the scalawags (white southerners) and carpetbaggers (white northerners) held most of the power. On some issues, African American lawmakers joined forces with carpetbaggers. Together the groups formed a loose coalition—combination of interests.

The two groups worked to give African Americans equal access to transportation and to such public places as restaurants and theaters. School integration, however, was another matter. (To integrate something is to open it up to people of all races and ethnic groups. Another word for integrate is *desegregate*.) Schools were segregated, meaning that blacks and whites went to different schools. African American leaders left the issue alone, though. They worried that if they stirred up the debate, more whites would oppose any kind of education for black children.

The reconstruction legislatures planned to create a new order in the South. They began rebuilding the South's roads, bridges, and railroads. They voted to build hospitals, orphanages, and schools. They also tried to at-

tract northern investment and raised funds for new railroads.

Schools, hospitals, and roads all cost money. To pay for them, the legislatures turned to property taxes (taxes based on the worth of a person's land). Thus plantation owners, who held the least political power in the new system, were paying the greatest

This print shows Frederick Douglass flanked by two of the first black senators, Blanche K. Bruce (left) and Hiram R. Revels (right), both of Mississippi. Reconstruction legislators hoped to transform the South economically and politically. HISTORY Why does John Brown appear at the bottom of the print?

In this cartoon, a "southern belle" stumbles barefoot on rough stones while President Grant lounges on a carpetbag full of guns. In the background are ruined southern homes and ships. **POLITICS** What emotions was the cartoonist trying to arouse?

share of the costs. Some Republicans hoped that the tax burden would force plantation owners to sell their land. Poor whites and blacks could then buy the land and set up farms.

Many landowners did indeed have to give up their plantations. One-fifth of the entire state of Mississippi went on the auction block. Yet little of this land went to the poor. Wealthy northern investors bought some of it. Other plantations were returned to their landowners after they repaid their debts.

Spending on public projects not only raised the South's tax burden. It also created openings for corruption. People bribed public officials to gain special favors, such as funding for a new bridge or railroad. Louisiana's governor, Henry C. Warmoth, retired a rich man from taking railroad bribes. Officeholders were not bashful about lining their own pockets while they were in the service of the public. Corruption was not limited to the former

Confederate states, however. In the North as well, lawmakers and business leaders were likewise making deals.

THE DEMOCRATS TAKE OVER

In Mississippi, white taxpayers overlooked the good things that their legislature had done. They were too distracted by a tax increase of 1,300 percent in five years. Determined to win back the government from the Republicans, Mississippi Democrats came up with a plan. Known as the Mississippi Plan, it called for forcing all whites into the Democratic Party. It also called for frightening African American voters. To do this, the Democrats used bullying, violence, and even murder. When they did, the federal government looked the other way.

Democrats in other states followed the Mississippi Plan. As a result, whites regained control of the state governments.

THE END OF RECONSTRUCTION

The presidential election of 1876 led to the end of Reconstruction. In that year the Democrats chose Samuel J. Tilden, governor of New York, to run for President. The Republicans nominated Rutherford B. Hayes, governor of Ohio. The race was so close that victory depended on the electoral votes in South Carolina, Louisiana, and Florida. Those results, however, were in dispute. It was up to Congress to settle the matter.

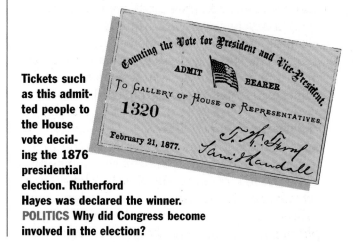

Tickets such as this admitted people to the House vote deciding the 1876 presidential election. Rutherford Hayes was declared the winner. **POLITICS** Why did Congress become involved in the election?

Rutherford B. Hayes

1877–1881

19th President, Republican

- Born October 4, 1822, in Ohio
- Married Lucy Webb in 1852; 8 children
- Lawyer; representative from Ohio; governor of Ohio
- Lived in Ohio when elected President
- Vice President: William Wheeler
- Died January 17, 1893, in Ohio
- Key events while in office: Reconstruction ended; Edison invented electric light

Congress appointed a special commission, which resolved the problem by an "understanding." Under the agreement, called the Compromise of 1877, Hayes was elected President. In return, Hayes agreed to remove the last federal troops from the South. As soon as he became President, Hayes did just that. The last few reconstruction governments then collapsed. With them went black southerners' best hope for political equality.

SHARECROPPING

One reason African Americans in the South could not hold on to political power was that they lacked economic power. Had they been given 40 acres of land and a mule, they would have been better able to defend their rights. However, most still worked for whites. They could be fired if they made use of their vote, and they knew it.

Many African Americans engaged in sharecropping. Under this system, a farmer and his family rented a plot of land to farm. The landowner provided the tools, seed, and housing. When harvest time came, the sharecropper gave the landowner a share of the crop. This system allowed landowners to keep their land and gave landless families a place to farm.

White farmers also became sharecroppers. Many had lost their land and livestock in the war. Others had lost their land to taxes. By 1880, one-third of the white farmers in the deep South worked someone else's land.

These farmers and landowners had opposite goals. The farmers wanted to grow food to feed themselves. Yet landowners forced them to grow cash crops such as cotton. Farmers therefore had to buy their food from the country store, which was often owned by the landlord. Most farmers got caught in a never-ending cycle of debt, in which this year's harvest went to pay last year's bills.

The South paid a heavy price for depending on cotton. Growing cotton exhausted the soil and reduced the amount of land available for food crops. As a result, the South had to import half its food. Sharecroppers could barely afford to feed their families. The deep South was doomed to years of rural poverty.

THE GROWTH OF INDUSTRY

The South's problems spurred calls for a shift away from farming. One of the best-known voices was that of Henry Grady, editor of the *Atlanta Constitution*. Grady urged the South to turn to business. He wanted a "New South"—one that was more like the North, with large cities and factories.

Aided by new leaders and by a nationwide boom in business, the South built new industries. It repaired its war-damaged railroads and laid new track. It also reduced the 5-foot gauge of its tracks to match that of the North, which was 4 feet, 8 1/2 inches. Trains could now run between North and South.

One Yankee who moved south after the Civil War was Harriet Beecher Stowe. Her book *Palmetto Leaves,* published in 1873, described the beauty of Florida. The state became a popular retreat from the North's blustery winters.

Tourism was one of the forces that made Florida part of the "New South." This was a South less dependent on cotton farming, a South with a more diverse economy.

THE CHANGE TO ORANGES

Most of Florida's prewar settlers had preferred the state's northern and central uplands to its coastal lowlands. The lowlands included vast areas of wetlands and sandy beaches.

After the war, Floridians went back to planting cotton on the uplands. Still, prices were low and times were hard. In the 1870s, the central part of the state caught "orange fever." (Florida's sweet oranges had first been developed in the 1830s and 1840s.) Orange groves began to replace cotton fields and grazing land. As the settlement line advanced south, so did the citrus groves.

NORTHERN CAPITAL

Northern capital and technology allowed the development of coastal Florida and its wetlands. In 1881 Hamilton Disston of Philadelphia bought from the state 4 million acres of wetlands north and west of Lake Okeechobee. Canals

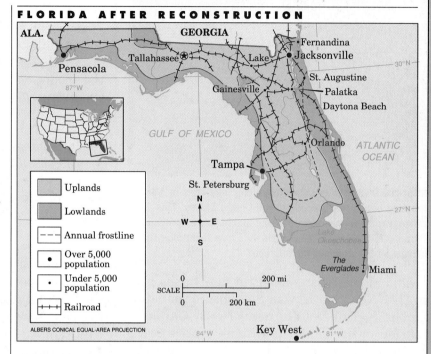

FLORIDA AFTER RECONSTRUCTION

were dug to drain the wetlands. Disston then sold the land to new settlers.

Two Yankee businessmen, Henry B. Plant and Henry M. Flagler, developed Florida's railroad system and changed Florida forever. A Connecticut native, Plant had settled in the South before the war. There he made a business of buying out bankrupt railway lines. In 1884 he extended an existing rail line to the fishing village of Tampa on Florida's west coast. Tampa grew into an important shipping center for lumber, phosphate, and cattle bound for Cuba.

Meanwhile, millionaire Henry M. Flagler was developing Florida's east coast. While vacationing in Florida in 1883, Flagler had been shocked by the narrow-gauge railway and

inadequate hotels on the east coast. He built a railroad down the east coast to link Florida with a rail route to New York. At the same time, Flagler built a string of elegant hotels to lure tourists. (Not to be outdone, Plant built a luxurious hotel in Tampa.)

Flagler's railroad opened new areas to farming, trade, and tourism. The railroad carried citrus fruit and vegetables north and brought tourists south. In 1896 the railroad reached the tiny settlement of Miami. It quickly became a boom town.

CRITICAL THINKING QUESTIONS

1. Why did most of the capital for Florida's expansion come from the North?

2. Why were railroads crucial to Florida's economic growth?

After the invention of cigarette-rolling machines in 1881, tobacco use spread rapidly in the United States. This photograph shows a worker using machinery to process tobacco. **ECONOMICS** Why might this new technology have increased the demand for tobacco?

One of the most successful new businesses in the "New South" was the tobacco industry. James B. Duke of Durham, North Carolina, started out with a small, family-run tobacco business. In 1881, however, he bought the rights to the first cigarette-making machine. Cigarette sales soared. By the 1890s his American Tobacco Company held a monopoly over the tobacco industry.

Southern textile mills also grew. "Bring the cotton mills to the cotton," southern boosters declared. Textile mills began sprouting up in the piedmont region. By 1900 the South was producing almost a quarter of the nation's cotton cloth. A visitor wrote:

> It is among the factory workers and the small farmers of Georgia that one finds the chief prosperity of the State. Here there is little or no debt; money circulates rapidly; improvements are seen.

The South had come a long way from the desperate poverty that followed the war. Life there still did not compare with conditions in the North, however. There white women and children earned double the wages of their counterparts in the South.

Steel was another important industry in the "New South." The workers in this Birmingham, Alabama, factory are casting iron into blocks. Birmingham's huge steel mills gave it the nickname "Pittsburgh of the South." **ECONOMICS** Why was it important for the South to become less dependent on cotton farming?

1866	Three national soldiers' homes opened.
1870	First pension to a President's widow (Mary Lincoln) authorized (July 14).
	Joseph Hayne Rainey from South Carolina sworn in as first African American representative in Congress (Dec. 12).
1872	Pinckney Pinchback, an African American, serves as acting governor of Louisiana, from Dec. 11, 1872 to Jan. 14, 1873.
1875	First African American senator to serve a full term, Blanche Bruce of Mississippi, begins service (March 4).

JIM CROW LAWS

After Reconstruction ended and African Americans lost political power, the South grew more segregated. The integrated streetcars, railroads, and theaters of the 1870s gave way in the 1890s to Jim Crow laws. (Jim Crow was a term commonly used to refer to African Americans.) Jim Crow laws made segregation official in a number of areas of southern life.

At the same time, some white Democrats revived efforts to keep black voters away from the polls. The old planter class had tried to maintain power by using the black vote or by controlling black officeholders. The next generation of southerners was even more racist. It tried to prevent African Americans from voting at all.

One way was to terrorize them. Jim Reeves, a black resident of Arkansas, remembered that in 1888 blacks and whites in Union County "had an insurrection [revolt] over the polls." White people went around the county ordering the blacks not to vote. One African American responded, "Well, I am going to the polls tomorrow if I have to crawl." On the day before the election, white gangs shot a number of blacks. "In that way,"

Reeves said, "quite a few of the Negroes disbanded their homes and went into different counties and . . . different states." Those who stayed quit voting.

> "**W**ell, I am going to the polls tomorrow if I have to crawl."
> —*African American voter, 1888*

New state laws also made it harder for African Americans to vote. In order to vote, people had to pay a fee (called a poll tax) and prove that they could read. Many African Americans could not meet these conditions. Neither could many whites, but for them the rules were often relaxed. By 1900 politics in the South had become so Democratic that the region became known as the solid South. It could be counted on to back solidly every Democratic candidate for office.

PLESSY V. FERGUSON

African Americans got little help from the Supreme Court. In the *Civil Rights Cases* (1883), the Court ruled that the Fourteenth Amendment did not bar a person or business from discriminating by race.

In 1896 the Court went even further in legalizing racism. In *Plessy v. Ferguson*, it ruled that segregation was lawful as long as blacks and whites had access to equal facilities. This became known as the "separate but equal" doctrine. The Court offered this explanation: "If one race be inferior to the other socially, the Constitution of the United States cannot put them upon the same plane."

One member of the Court disagreed with the decision in *Plessy*. Justice John Marshall Harlan wrote, "Our Constitution is color-blind, and neither knows nor tolerates classes among citizens. . . . The thin disguise of 'equal' accommodations . . . will not mislead anyone." Indeed, segregation had become a thin disguise for treating African Americans as second-class citizens.

BOOKER T. WASHINGTON (1856–1915), founder of Tuskegee Institute, was born into slavery. After the Civil War, Washington became an educator and social reformer. His concern for poor and illiterate African Americans led him to promote educational and economic advancement rather than political equality.

AFRICAN AMERICANS HELPING THEMSELVES

These were bitter days for African Americans in the South. The high hopes of the days of Reconstruction had been dashed. American society no longer seemed inspired by those words of the Declaration of Independence: "All men are created equal."

Frozen out of politics and white institutions, African Americans found hope in their own communities. Although short of funds, black schools and colleges continued to educate the new generation of free black persons. Black churches provided leadership and gave aid to the needy. Groups like the National Negro Business League enabled African Americans to help each other.

The founder of the National Negro Business League was a former slave named Booker T. Washington. Washington became one of the most noted African American leaders of his day. In 1881 he set up Tuskegee Institute, a vocational school for blacks in Tuskegee, Alabama. The school reflected Washington's view that African Americans needed to learn a useful trade instead of demanding social equality from the government. "It is at the bottom of life we must begin, and not at the top," he said. "The opportunity to earn a dollar in a factory just now is worth infinitely more than the opportunity to spend a dollar in an opera house."

Some African Americans doubted the wisdom of Washington's advice. Blacks could not make solid economic gains without political power, they argued. Winning this power would take years of struggle. Nevertheless, the Fourteenth and Fifteenth Amendments were important steps toward political equality. They showed that democracy had indeed advanced during Reconstruction. Perhaps this is why the black historian W.E.B. Du Bois (DOO BOYS) called Reconstruction "a glorious failure."

Tuskegee Institute, today a university with more than 3,000 students, was founded by Booker T. Washington in 1881. Tuskegee students constructed the school buildings and farmed the surrounding fields. Tuskegee's faculty included George Washington Carver, an internationally known agricultural researcher. This photograph shows a chemistry class at Tuskegee around 1900. **HISTORY** What was the aim of Tuskegee?

Writing in the 1930s, Du Bois was one of the first historians to take a new look at Reconstruction. At that time, most historians saw Reconstruction as a dismal chapter in American history. They described it as a time when an angry Congress, uneducated African Americans, crooked carpetbaggers, and greedy scalawags nearly ruined the South.

In the 1960s historians began to follow Du Bois's lead. They started to look at Reconstruction from the point of view of African Americans. Historians today are focusing more on the social and economic gains made by blacks during Reconstruction. As a result, they tend to view Reconstruction as a time in which the United States made one more advance toward its vision of liberty and justice for all.

SECTION REVIEW

1. KEY TERMS coalition, integration, Compromise of 1877, sharecropping, Jim Crow laws, solid South, *Plessy v. Ferguson*

2. PEOPLE Samuel J. Tilden, Rutherford B. Hayes, Henry Grady, Booker T. Washington, W.E.B. Du Bois

3. COMPREHENSION Why was corruption a problem for the reconstruction legislatures?

4. COMPREHENSION What led to the Democratic backlash in the South during the 1870s?

5. CRITICAL THINKING Why might the "New South" have offered African Americans new opportunities for advancement?

CHAPTER 21 SUMMARY AND TIMELINE

1. After the Civil War, the South's society and economy had to be rebuilt. This task was known as Reconstruction. The Thirteenth Amendment ended slavery, but most former slaves were still uneducated and landless. President Johnson followed a cautious policy toward the ex-Confederate states. When southerners resisted even minimal reform, many northerners took a harder line.

2. In 1867, Radical Republicans in Congress took over Reconstruction from the President. Congress imposed strict military rule on the South, thereby beginning a period known as Radical Reconstruction. Two constitutional amendments, the Fourteenth and the Fifteenth, protected the rights of African Americans. Still, some white southerners used violence in an attempt to prevent blacks from exercising their rights.

3. During the 1870s, white Democrats regained control of the South. The South's reconstruction governments collapsed. Rural southerners, lacking their own land, became trapped in a vicious cycle of poverty. On the other hand, the growth of southern industry led to the birth of a "New South."

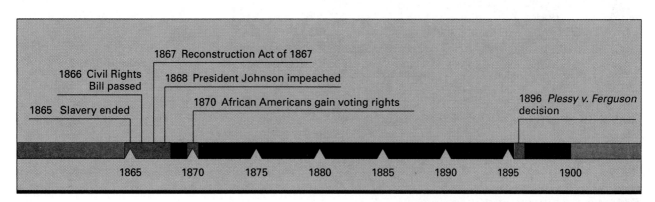

1865 Slavery ended

1866 Civil Rights Bill passed

1867 Reconstruction Act of 1867

1868 President Johnson impeached

1870 African Americans gain voting rights

1896 *Plessy v. Ferguson* decision

1865 1870 1875 1880 1885 1890 1895 1900

PLACES TO LOCATE

Match each of the letters on the map with the places that are listed below.

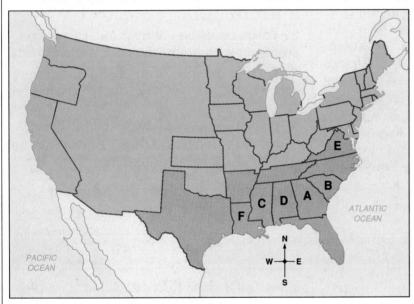

1. Alabama
2. Georgia
3. Louisiana
4. Mississippi
5. South Carolina
6. Virginia

KEY TERMS

Use the following terms to complete the sentences.

amnesty
black codes
carpetbagger
scalawag
sharecropping

1. A northerner who came to the South to live during Reconstruction was known as a ____.
2. Under ____, farm families were given land to work in return for part of the crop.
3. A ____ was a southerner who supported Radical Reconstruction.
4. President Johnson offered ____, or official pardon, to many former Confederate leaders.
5. Southern states passed laws known as ____ to return African Americans to plantation labor.

PEOPLE TO IDENTIFY

Identify the following people and tell why each one was important.

1. W.E.B. Du Bois
2. Henry Grady
3. Edwin Stanton
4. Charles Sumner
5. Samuel Tilden
6. Booker T. Washington

REVIEWING THE FACTS

1. What was the attitude of President Johnson toward Reconstruction?
2. How did white southerners try to restore the prewar order?
3. What was the Freedmen's Bureau? How did President Johnson undermine its efforts to help freedmen?
4. Why did moderate Republicans at first oppose the goals of the Radicals? Why did they change their minds?
5. How did the Thirteenth, Fourteenth, and Fifteenth Amendments affect African Americans?
6. Why was President Johnson impeached? What was the outcome of the trial?
7. How did the Ku Klux Klan harass African Americans? What were the group's aims?
8. What groups held office in the reconstruction legislatures? Why did many white southerners resent them?
9. What economic changes took place in the postwar South?
10. How did Supreme Court decisions in the late 1800s affect African Americans?

PRACTICING YOUR SKILL

Francis Cardoza, an African American member of South Carolina's constitutional convention, made the statement below in 1868. Read the statement. Then answer the questions that follow.

What is the main cause of the prosperity of the North? It is because every man has his own farm and is free and independent. Let the lands of the South be similarly divided. . . . We will never have true freedom until we abolish the system of [farming] which existed in the southern states. . . . If [the lands] are sold, . . . the chances are that the colored man and the poor [white] man would be the purchasers. I will prove this . . . by facts. About 100 poor colored men of Charleston met together and formed themselves into a Charleston Land Company. . . . They have been meeting for a year. Yesterday they purchased some 600 acres of land. . . . This is only one instance of thousands of others that have occurred in this city and state.

1. What is Cardoza proposing?
2. What sentence expresses the premise, or main idea, behind his argument?
3. How does Cardoza support his argument that small farms will bring prosperity?
4. How does he support his argument that African Americans would buy small farms?

CITIZENSHIP

1. Do research on the military governments in the South during Reconstruction. How did their laws differ from those of the civilian governments before the war?
2. During Radical Reconstruction, could white southern landowners justly object to property taxes on the grounds that there should be "no taxation without representation"? Why or why not?
3. Do you agree or disagree with Congress's decision in 1865 not to admit representatives with ties to the Confederacy? Explain.
4. Consider the Supreme Court's ruling in *Plessy v. Ferguson.* Is it possible for a society to be both segregated and free? Explain.

CRITICAL THINKING SKILLS

1. **PARAPHRASING** Reread the paragraphs under the heading "The African American Response to Freedom" (pages 527–528). In your own words, state the main idea of these paragraphs.

2. **PREDICTING CONSEQUENCES** How would the situation of black southerners have been different in the late 1800s if Radical Reconstruction had never happened?

3. **COMPARING** Industry began to take hold in the South during Reconstruction. What industries does the southern economy depend on today?

PROJECTS AND ACTIVITIES

1. **MAKING A CHART** Create a chart showing legislation passed during Reconstruction. Fill in information under these headings: "Law," "Year Passed," and "Effects."

2. **GIVING A SPEECH** Imagine that you are an African American legislator in the South during Reconstruction. Write a speech to give on your first day in office, telling how you feel about your position and what you hope to accomplish. Present your speech to the class.

3. **WRITING A LETTER** Imagine that you are a member of the old planter class during Reconstruction. Write a letter to a relative outside the South explaining your views on Reconstruction.

WRITING ABOUT TOPICS IN AMERICAN HISTORY

1. **CONNECTING WITH LITERATURE** A selection from *The Deliverance* by Ellen Glasgow appears on pages 660–662. Read it and answer the questions. Then answer the following question: Why did the South's defeat in the Civil War mark the end of a way of life?

2. **APPLYING THEMES: PLURALISTIC SOCIETY** Why was ending slavery only one step toward dealing with the nation's racial divisions?

Breathtaking technological changes have marked American history during the past century. This computer-generated map gives one view of an ever-changing world.

22 The United States Since 1877

1 The Nation Transformed

Section Focus

Key Terms corporation ■ Gilded Age ■ progressivism ■ prohibition ■ Great Depression ■ New Deal

Main Idea Economic development, urbanization, and the settlement of the West led to deep-reaching changes in the United States.

Objectives As you read, look for answers to these questions:
1. What three important trends took place in the United States in the late 1800s?
2. What factors spurred widespread reforms in the early 1900s?
3. How did American attitudes toward the role of government shift throughout this period?

The United States changed rapidly in the years after the Civil War. By the late 1800s an economic and social revolution had begun to have important effects on American life. These changes in turn triggered reforms, which further reshaped the nation. By the 1930s the United States was a far different country than it had been decades before.

CHANGES IN DAILY LIFE

To understand the changes in American society, let us compare daily life in 1860 and 1900. In 1860 most Americans lived on farms or in small towns, in houses with no electricity or running water. Running the household was thought to be "women's work." It was a full-time job, and even included sewing most of the family's clothes. There were no modern conveniences either—no refrigerators, vacuum cleaners, or washing machines. Children walked to and from school, even if it was far away. In the evenings they spent most of their time doing schoolwork or such chores as chopping wood.

By 1900, however, the small town had become a city, with factories and new neighborhoods where immigrants and ex-farmers lived. Streets were paved and lit at night by electric lights, and the houses had lights and plumbing. Most women still worked at home, but many had begun to buy labor-saving appliances and to shop for ready-made clothes. Young people still had chores and schoolwork to do, but they also had free time

George Bellows, a leading American artist of the early 1900s, painted many scenes of poorer city neighborhoods and their inhabitants. He belonged to a group of painters that critics labeled the "Ash Can School" for their gritty, down-to-earth subject matter. CULTURE Why might Bellows have titled this painting *Cliff Dwellers*?

to ride bicycles or listen to phonograph records. These and other new products, such as telephones, helped change American life.

EXPANDING CITIES AND INDUSTRY

The changes just described were part of deeper movements in the United States in the late 1800s. These movements were:

(1) *The growth of American industry.* Between the Civil War and the end of the century, industries grew at a tremendous rate.

(2) *The settling of the West.* Farmers, miners, and ranchers successfully challenged the Indians for control of the western interior.

(3) *The growth of cities.* Towns grew in area and population. New cities were born and old ones expanded. Some had more than one million residents.

These patterns were all linked. Industry drew on western resources such as iron ore.

By trading these resources the West grew richer, sparking further development. Cities and industry grew together. Cities meant workers for new factories, and factories formed an economic base for growing cities. Cities such as Chicago that lay on railroad routes to the West grew especially fast.

INDUSTRIAL GROWTH

Over a 50-year period beginning in the late 1800s, the amount of goods produced in the United States increased twelve-fold. Industrial growth was fueled by new resources and labor, as well as by hundreds of new inventions. The discovery of a way to make cheaper steel, for example, made it possible to build long-distance railroads, skyscrapers, and large bridges. The invention of the electric light bulb and the telephone opened up whole new industries.

New ways of raising money also helped businesses grow. Corporations—businesses chartered by states and owned by shareholding investors—were formed. They sold stock in order to raise capital to run the business. Large corporations often bought up smaller ones and by the 1890s played a major role in the economy. In general, government policies helped big business and did little to control unfair business activities.

URBANIZATION AND IMMIGRATION

As industry grew, so did cities. In 1875 around one-quarter of all Americans lived in cities; by 1920 more than half did. Boston, New York, Philadelphia, and other older cities grew rapidly, but so did newer ones such as Pittsburgh and Minneapolis. These newer cities lay on trade routes and were often near sources of raw materials—iron and coal, for example.

As cities grew, so did problems of overcrowding and disease. To cope with these problems, new types of buildings and advances in health care appeared. In fact, many things people in cities now take for granted—skyscrapers, subways, street lights, sewer systems, and large police and fire departments—first appeared in the late 1800s in response to specific needs.

Immigration was a major cause of city growth. In the years before 1880, most immigrants were Protestants from northern and western Europe who settled down as farmers in the Midwest. After 1880, however, millions of Catholics and Jews from southern and eastern Europe began arriving in American cities. There they found factory jobs and formed neighborhoods with the look and feel of "the old world."

The new immigrants changed life in America. They gave their labor and inventions to the nation's economy. Immigrant customs enriched America's culture. Many native-born Americans, however, were hostile to the immigrants. They feared the immigrants would change American society and take away jobs from those already here.

SOCIETY AND POLITICS IN THE GILDED AGE

By the late 1800s the nation's economic expansion had created great wealth. Yet poverty and corruption lay beneath the shining surface of prosperity. For that reason, the last years of the 1800s were known as the Gilded Age (gilded means "gold-covered"). While Americans at the top enjoyed lives of luxury, many others suffered from hunger and sickness. Political leaders of the time, many of whom accepted bribes, did little to change this situation. In general, government chose not to face the nation's difficulties: the growing gap between rich and poor, unsafe living and working conditions, and political corruption.

GRAPH SKILLS

This graph shows immigration to the United States in the 1800s. Which decade had the highest immigrant total? How many people arrived in that decade? CRITICAL THINKING What conclusions can you draw about the availability of jobs for immigrants in the late 1800s?

IMMIGRATION, 1821–1900

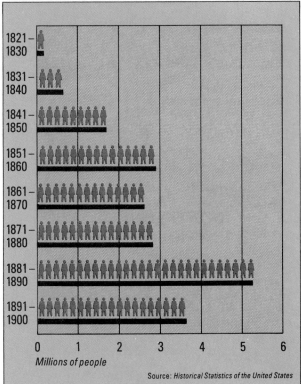

Millions of people

Source: *Historical Statistics of the United States*

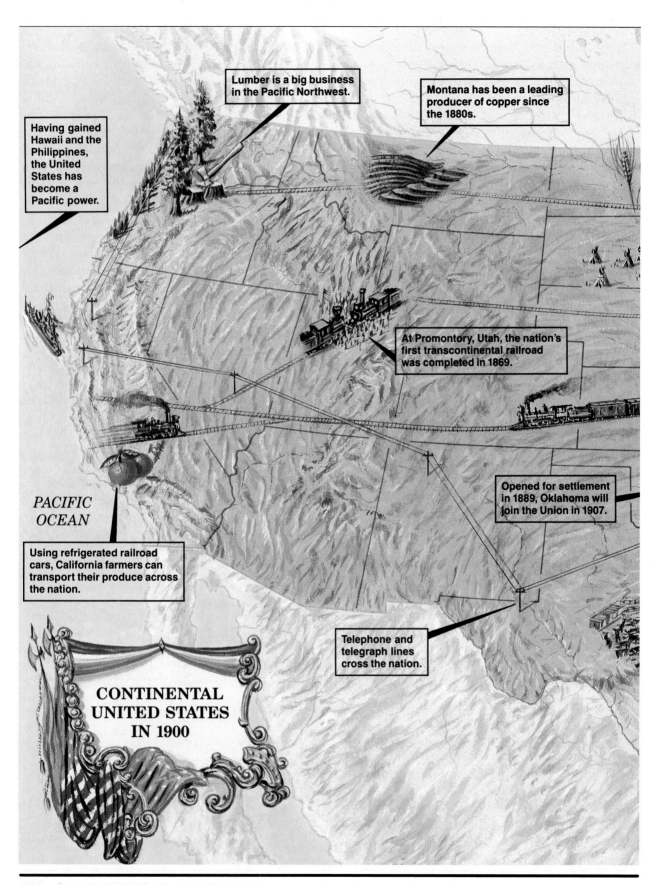

Having gained Hawaii and the Philippines, the United States has become a Pacific power.

Lumber is a big business in the Pacific Northwest.

Montana has been a leading producer of copper since the 1880s.

At Promontory, Utah, the nation's first transcontinental railroad was completed in 1869.

Opened for settlement in 1889, Oklahoma will join the Union in 1907.

PACIFIC OCEAN

Using refrigerated railroad cars, California farmers can transport their produce across the nation.

Telephone and telegraph lines cross the nation.

CONTINENTAL UNITED STATES IN 1900

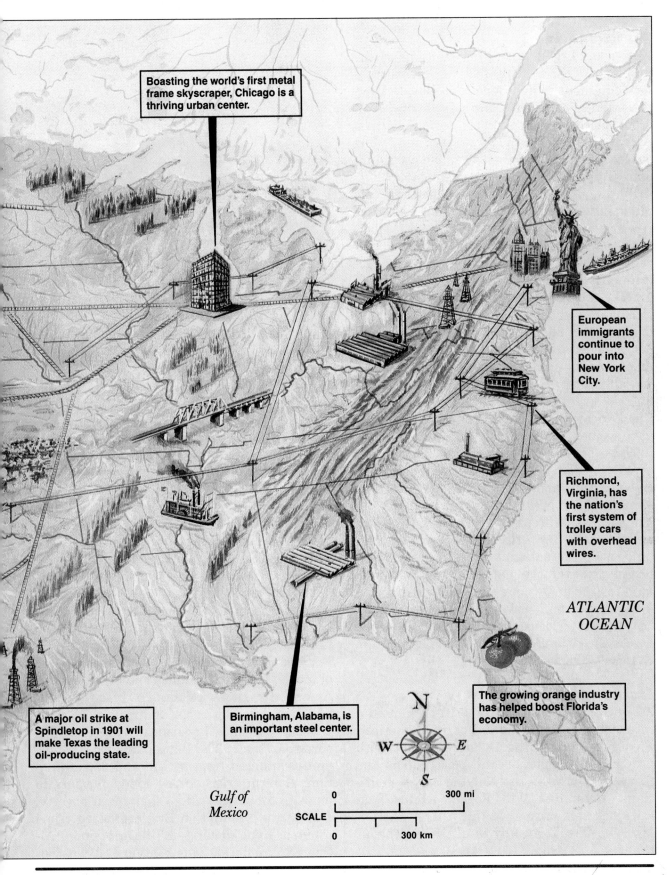

Boasting the world's first metal frame skyscraper, Chicago is a thriving urban center.

European immigrants continue to pour into New York City.

Richmond, Virginia, has the nation's first system of trolley cars with overhead wires.

A major oil strike at Spindletop in 1901 will make Texas the leading oil-producing state.

Birmingham, Alabama, is an important steel center.

The growing orange industry has helped boost Florida's economy.

ATLANTIC OCEAN

Gulf of Mexico

N
W   E
S

SCALE

0   300 mi

0   300 km

THE REFORM ERA

Americans began to call for solutions to the problems of the Gilded Age. Workers in cities formed unions to fight for higher pay and better working conditions. Farmers hurt by low crop prices formed their own political party—the Populist Party. Neither effort succeeded. However, their example helped inspire a broader reform movement.

By the early 1900s many middle-class people in cities supported a movement known as progressivism. Progressives hoped to pass laws to protect the well-being of average citizens. They therefore voted for new city governments and forced states to give citizens a greater voice in government. Progressive politicians passed laws to control unfair business dealings and unsafe working conditions. They also pushed through several constitutional amendments. One of these amendments, known as prohibition, banned the making and selling of alcoholic beverages. Another, the Nineteenth Amendment (1920), finally gave women the vote after a long fight.

Three Presidents served during the Progressive Era: Theodore Roosevelt, William Howard Taft, and Woodrow Wilson. All three supported progressive reforms. These included laws to break up business monopolies and promote competition. Roosevelt also set land aside for national parks. He thus protected some of the nation's most beautiful land for the enjoyment of its citizens. During Wilson's term, however, World War I (1914–1918) focused America's attention across the Atlantic to Europe and away from changes at home.

THE ROARING TWENTIES

After World War I most Americans wanted a return to security and prosperity. American Presidents during the 1920s responded with pro-business policies. Prosperity took the place of reform as the rallying cry of politicians. Columnist Will Rogers wrote, "You can't lick this prosperity thing. Even the fellow who hasn't got any is all excited about the idea."

This magazine cover shows a "flapper," the 1920s term for a fashionably wild young woman. Her short skirt, short hair, use of makeup, and love of unrestrained dancing upset traditionalists. **HISTORY** What image of the 1920s does this picture convey?

This was the decade known as the Roaring Twenties. During this time, the radio, the movies, and sports grew very popular. People filled nightclubs to dance to a swinging new form of music called jazz, which also gave the 1920s the name "the Jazz Age." Many young women cut their hair and shortened their skirts, shocking their elders. At the same time, writers such as Ernest Hemingway and F. Scott Fitzgerald described America's loss of ideals. Langston Hughes and other African American writers celebrated black culture and also called for social change.

Many problems lay beneath the fun-filled surface of the 1920s. Blacks and other ethnic groups suffered from racism and discrimination. A farm crisis forced many farmers to move to the cities, where they faced poverty. During the Prohibition Era, organized crime profited from dealing in illegal liquor. Although prohibition was a failure, it was not repeated until 1933. By that time, the United States was fighting for economic survival.

THE DEPRESSION YEARS

During the 1920s Americans invested heavily in the stock market. Most people believed that corporations would always grow bigger and richer. Then, in October 1929, the stock market crashed. Soon the country was caught in the Great Depression, a time of economic hardship that lasted until 1941.

The stock market crash sent the economy into a nose dive, but it was only one of many causes of the Great Depression. The farm crisis, large debts, bad management by businesses, banks, and government, all contributed to the economy's collapse.

Never before had the country faced such hard times. Many people lost their life's savings. Millions more lost their jobs as whole industries ground to a halt. By 1932 nearly one-fourth of the nation's workers were jobless. Tens of thousands were homeless, living in shelters or shantytowns, doing what they could to get by.

President Herbert Hoover believed in hands-off government. He did little to help those out of work. As a result, he was soundly defeated in the 1932 election by a man with a very different approach to government, Franklin D. Roosevelt.

THE NEW DEAL

Roosevelt, known to many as "FDR," brought back a reformist style of government not seen since the Progressive Era. Roosevelt tried to end the Depression through the New Deal, begun in 1933. This plan provided money and jobs for the needy. It took steps to revive the economy and to avoid future crises. Not all of FDR's policies worked, and many were unpopular with business. Still, he remained popular with most Americans and was re-elected in 1936.

Many artists and writers were employed by the government during the New Deal. This policy not only helped artists through the Great Depression, it enriched the nation culturally. This scene from a 1931 mural by Thomas Hart Benton uses strongly sculptured shapes and bright colors to show workers building a city. **ECONOMICS** Why might a painting of people working have been particularly powerful in the 1930s?

The New Deal brought a number of lasting changes to American society and government. These include the following:

(1) The power of the federal government and the President was increased.

(2) The practice of deficit spending—spending more money than the government raises in taxes—was encouraged.

(3) The notion of the welfare state—a system of federal programs to care for the needy—was born.

(4) A greater concern for working people was promoted.

Most importantly, the New Deal gave Americans back their faith in democracy. This faith had been weakened by the Depression. The New Deal did not fully revive the economy, though. That only came about as the result of another world war.

2 Becoming a World Power

★ Section Focus

Key Terms imperialism ■ Fourteen Points ■ League of Nations ■ isolationism ■ Holocaust ■ United Nations ■ superpower

Main Idea By 1900 the United States had begun to extend its power and influence around the world. Over the next few decades, the United States would emerge as the world's leading power.

Objectives As you read, look for answers to these questions:
1. Why did the United States become more involved in world affairs?
2. What goals did the United States pursue in Asia and Latin America?
3. How did the two world wars affect the United States' position in the world?

In the years following the Civil War, few Americans cared much about events outside the United States. Americans gave their energy and attention to economic growth and the settlement of the West. In foreign policy, Americans followed George Washington's advice to have few ties. (See page 312.)

Then, in the 1890s, Americans began to look outward. As a news report in 1898 put it, "A new consciousness seems to have come upon us—the consciousness of strength—and with it a new appetite, the yearning to show our strength."

AMERICAN EXPANSION

A number of factors made the United States more interested in world affairs. One of these was rivalry with European nations, which were setting up colonies in Asia and Africa. Another was a continued belief in manifest

destiny. This was the idea that the United States was destined to grow in size and influence. A third factor was America's booming economy. The nation's factories made more goods than Americans needed. Businesses therefore looked for markets for their goods outside the United States.

America emerged as a world power after the Spanish-American War of 1898. The war began when America took sides in a fight between Spain and Spain's colony, Cuba. The United States easily won the war and took over the Spanish colonies of Puerto Rico and the Philippines. The United States allowed Cuba to become independent. However, the island remained under American influence. Around the same time, the United States annexed Hawaii, Samoa, and several other island groups in the Pacific.

Some Americans saw nothing wrong with these actions. American rule, they said, would bring progress to the people of these islands. Others, however, accused the government of imperialism—the policy of gaining political and economic control over other nations against their will. In spite of these protests the United States kept its new possessions.

POLICIES TOWARD ASIA AND LATIN AMERICA

As the United States gained territory in the Pacific, it grew more interested in Asia. Most of all, it wanted to trade with China, which was then controlled by European powers. It also worked to form ties with Japan. By the early 1900s, the United States, with a large new navy, had become a force in the Pacific.

Closer to home, the United States was even more ready to flex its new muscles. In the early 1900s President Theodore Roosevelt announced his "big stick" policy toward Latin America. This was an extension of the Monroe Doctrine. It meant that the United States would use its military to protect American interests. In the years that followed, the United States often sent troops to take control of Central American and Caribbean nations. For example, United States Marines occupied Nicaragua from 1912 to 1933. The "big stick" policy often resulted in support for dictators who promised to stay pro-American.

During this time, the United States also built the Panama Canal. For years both the United States and European countries had dreamed of a canal across Central America that would connect the Atlantic and Pacific oceans. President Roosevelt wanted to make

Chicago Historical Society

Some of the fiercest fighting of the Spanish-American War took place in Cuba, near the port city of Santiago. This painting shows American forces charging San Juan Hill, a fortified position outside the city. HISTORY Why did Americans consider the war a great success?

Gassed is the title of this painting by American artist John Singer Sargent. It shows British soldiers blinded by poison gas clinging together as they retreat from a battlefield in World War I. **CULTURE** What attitudes towards war does the picture convey?

sure that such a canal would be controlled by the United States. In 1903 he backed a revolt in Panama, then a part of Colombia. When Panama declared itself independent, Roosevelt quickly signed a canal treaty with the new government. The canal opened in 1914. It was praised as a triumph of engineering. Many Latin Americans, however, saw the canal as a symbol of their powerful northern neighbor's meddling in the region.

WORLD WAR I

In the same year that the Panama Canal was finished, an event took place across the globe in a country that few Americans knew much about. In June 1914 Austria's Archduke Franz Ferdinand was shot and killed. Austria was soon at war with Serbia, the nation it blamed for the killing. At the time, most European nations belonged to alliances in which they promised to fight if their allies did. Because of these alliances the war soon drew in most of Europe. World War I lasted from 1914 to 1918 and proved to be the bloodiest war known up to that time.

On one side were the Central Powers—Germany and Austria-Hungary; on the other were the Allies—France, Russia, and Great Britain. More countries later joined the fighting. Everyone expected a quick war, but they were mistaken. After several fast German victories, the two sides dug into trenches. The Western Front stretched 450 miles from the North Sea to Switzerland. The war became a bloody stalemate, made worse by new and deadly weapons such as tanks, machine guns, airplanes, and poison gas. In 1917 Russia made peace with Germany and left the war.

For several years President Woodrow Wilson tried to keep America neutral in the war. However, Wilson did send Britain arms to use against Germany. Finally, in April of 1917, after repeated German attacks on merchant ships in the Atlantic, the United States declared war on the Central Powers. Americans would fight a war, said Wilson, to make the world "safe for democracy."

By 1918 the United States had a million soldiers in Europe. Soon, these troops helped turn the tide of the war. In November 1918 Germany surrendered.

THE WAR'S AFTERMATH

Ten million young men died on battlefields during World War I. Twenty million people died of war-related hunger and sickness. To try to address the causes of war and keep it from happening again, President Wilson proposed a peace plan that became known as the Fourteen Points. This plan called for a ban on the kind of secret treaties that had helped a war between Austria and Serbia become a "world war." Wilson's plan limited the amount of weapons a nation could have. Wilson also called for a League of Nations, an international organization where leaders could meet to solve conflicts.

Wilson's European allies, however, cared more about revenge against the Central Powers. The Treaty of Versailles, which set the terms for peace, carved up Germany, Austria, and Turkey. It also stripped Germany of its colonies and made it pay the victors a huge amount of money.

President Wilson was not happy with the treaty. He agreed to it anyway because it included his plans for a League of Nations. Wilson, however, had not counted on the power of isolationism—the policy of staying out of world affairs. His hopes were dashed after the Senate rejected the Treaty of Versailles. Senators did not like the idea of the League of Nations. They worried it would take power over foreign policy away from Congress

Still, many recognized that the United States had become a world leader. Unlike Europe, the United States had not suffered greatly from the war. In fact, war had helped the economy grow and had left the United States the world's richest nation.

BETWEEN THE WARS
Isolationism after World War I changed policy toward Latin America. In the 1930s, under Franklin Roosevelt, the United States moved away from its "big stick" policy. FDR's Good Neighbor Policy avoided sending troops to Latin America. It aimed instead to improve economic and cultural ties between that region and the United States.

Across the ocean in Europe, World War I had left Germany and Italy with broken economies. Germany's was made worse by its war debts to the Allies under the Treaty of Versailles. In addition, near the end of World War I Russian Communists led by Vladimir

Lenin had overthrown the country's monarchy and established the Soviet Union. Communists also formed strong political movements in other European countries. Among those opposing the Communists were groups known as Fascists. Fascists called for military rule and spouted racist slogans.

Taking advantage of the division and fear in their countries, two dictators came to power—Benito Mussolini in Italy and Adolf Hitler in Germany. Hitler's Nazi Party blamed Jews and other minorities for Germany's troubles. Meanwhile, military leaders had taken power in Japan. In 1931 Japan invaded the Chinese province of Manchuria.

THE SECOND WORLD WAR
In the mid-1930s the Nazis began to build up Germany's military might. Germany formed an alliance with Italy and took over Austria and part of Czechoslovakia. Other European nations watched nervously, hoping to avoid war. After the Nazis invaded Poland in 1939, the British and French finally declared war on Germany. World War II had begun.

At first, the German military machine was unstoppable. By June 1940 the Nazis had swept through most of Western Europe. Of the European allies, only Britain held out. In 1941 German forces smashed through Eastern Europe and invaded the Soviet Union.

Meanwhile, Japan was invading territories in Asia and the Pacific. On December 7, 1941, it attacked the United States' largest naval base, at Pearl Harbor, Hawaii. Many Americans had been unsure about entering the war. The attack on Pearl Harbor united them behind the declaration of war passed by Congress the next day. Japan's allies—Italy and Germany—in turn declared war on the United States. Once again, the United States was part of a world war.

During 1942, it seemed as if the Axis Powers—Germany, Italy, and Japan—might crush the Allies—the United States, Britain, and the Soviet Union. The Allies fought back fiercely. Millions of Soviets died in a desperate fight to turn back the German invaders.

Early in 1943 Soviet victories turned the tide on the Eastern Front, and the Germans began to retreat. By mid-1943 British and American troops had taken the offensive by invading Italy.

On the home front, Americans pitched in just as they had during World War I. The economy boomed, bringing an end to the Great Depression. As before, women and minorities·filled some of the jobs vacated by soldiers. However, discrimination against African Americans and other ethnic groups was still common in American society. How, blacks asked, could the United States fight abroad in the name of democracy, when at home it allowed prejudice and injustice? Another injustice was suffered by Japanese Americans, many of whom were forced into detention camps. Only in 1988 did Congress apologize for this policy.

THE WAR IS WON

On June 6, 1944, known as D-Day, the Allies launched the largest sea invasion in history, crossing the English Channel to northern France. By winter, the Allied forces were closing in on Germany from both sides—the British and Americans from the west, the Soviets from the east. Germany finally surrendered in May 1945.

In the Pacific, the Allies were taking island after island against tough Japanese resistance. How long could Japan hold out? America's new President, Harry S. Truman, made

Adolf Hitler, Nazi leader of Germany during World War II, gives the Nazi salute at a parade of brown-shirted members of his "security police," known as the SS. Under Hitler, the government had almost complete control over people's lives. **CULTURAL PLURALISM** How did Hitler use prejudice against Jews and other minorities to help himself politically?

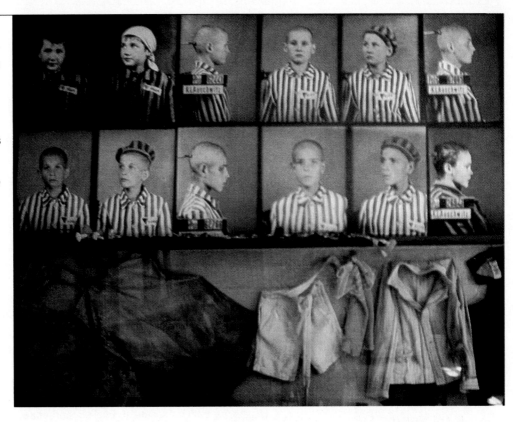

These photographs of Holocaust victims and their clothing are on display at a memorial in Auschwitz, Poland, site of a Nazi concentration camp. Nazi leaders were put on trial after the war for their roles in the Holocaust and accused of committing "crimes against humanity." **ETHICS** How would you define "crimes against humanity"?

a decision: He would use a new and secret weapon, the atomic bomb, on Japan's cities. In August 1945, American bombers dropped two A-bombs on Hiroshima and Nagasaki, killing or wounding hundreds of thousands of Japanese civilians. On September 2, 1945, Japan surrendered. The war was over.

World War II had been the costliest and most destructive war ever. Whole cities were destroyed, and between 40 and 60 million people died. Among these were some 6 million Jews—a third of the world's entire Jewish population—who were killed in Nazi concentration camps. This mass murder became known as the Holocaust.

With much of the world in ruins, leaders met as they had after World War I. Again, they pondered how to prevent another such war in the future. They decided to replace the League of Nations with a stronger international organization, the United Nations. More important, though, was that the United States and the Soviet Union had become the world's two superpowers—nations that

have great military power and international influence. Tensions between the superpowers would dominate world news for the next 45 years.

SECTION REVIEW

1. KEY TERMS imperialism, Fourteen Points, League of Nations, isolationism, Holocaust, United Nations, superpower

2. PEOPLE AND PLACES Panama Canal, Adolf Hitler, Harry S. Truman, Hiroshima

3. COMPREHENSION What contrasting approaches did the United States take toward Latin America during the years 1900–1935?

4. COMPREHENSION What factors caused the United States to become more involved in world affairs?

5. CRITICAL THINKING How might American attitudes toward war differ today if one or both of the world wars had been fought on American soil? Explain your answer.

An International Menu

From the time of Columbus's arrival, people in the Americas have encountered foods from several different cultures. As each new group arrived, its people brought different foods and words to describe them. By 1900, Americans were eating an "international" menu without realizing it.

North America had so many unfamiliar food plants that English and French settlers used—and mispronounced—the Indians' names for them. **Squash, succotash,** and **pecan** all come from Algonkian languages.

The English not only took over the Dutch colonies around New York, they also eagerly borrowed ideas from Dutch cooks and bakers. **Waffle** and **cookie** were originally words for Dutch treats.

In the Caribbean islands, the Carib Indians built frames of green wood and sticks for smoking fish and grilling meat. Spanish explorers called these *barbacoa,* which became, in English, **barbecue.**

The first settlers from Germany, usually called "Pennsylvania Dutch," introduced country dishes like **sauerkraut, pretzels,** and **noodles.** They also brought the custom of—and the word—**dunking** doughnuts.

In California and throughout the Southwest, early Spanish-speaking settlers brought with them a spicy cuisine from Mexico that included **tortillas, frijoles, tamales,** and **chili con carne.**

Some foods that were favorites of the Aztecs of Mexico were taken first to Spain, then brought back to America by European settlers. Along the way, their names changed only a little from the original Nahuatl language: *tomatl* to **tomato**, *chocolatl* to **chocolate**, *ahuacatl* to **avocado**.

Visitors to the 1893 World's Fair in Chicago could sample another Latin American custom—the **cafeteria**, or coffee-seller's shop. The word quickly came to mean a self-service eating place.

People from the German city of Hamburg are "Hamburgers." When immigrants from northern Germany first served a plate of raw or cooked chopped beef, it was called "Hamburger steak"—and then **hamburger**. During World War I, when German names were thought unpatriotic, restaurants renamed it "Salisbury steak."

No cook in China ever made **chop suey**, and no one can be sure what Chinese cook in the United States invented this dish to appeal to American tastes. In any case, he or she used the Mandarin Chinese term *tsa-sui* [zasui], which means "odds and ends."

The corner deli, or **delicatessen**, got its start in the United States among Jewish and German immigrants to large eastern cities. The word means "fine food."

What do you call a long sandwich of French bread filled with meat, cheese, and salad? It depends on where you live. In the South it's a **poor boy**, from the New Orleans French word *pourboire*, which means "a tip"—the price of a sandwich. In other cities you might ask for a **hero, submarine, grinder, Garibaldi,** or **hoagie.**

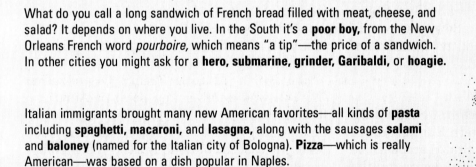

Italian immigrants brought many new American favorites—all kinds of **pasta** including **spaghetti, macaroni,** and **lasagna,** along with the sausages **salami** and **baloney** (named for the Italian city of Bologna). **Pizza**—which is really American—was based on a dish popular in Naples.

3 The Cold War

★ **Section Focus** ★

Key Terms cold war ■ containment
■ Third World ■ domino theory ■ détente
■ realpolitik

Main Idea After World War II, the United
States and the Soviet Union entered into a
deadly struggle for world power. This rivalry between the superpowers dominated
postwar world politics.

Objectives As you read, look for answers
to these questions:
1. How did the United States and the
Soviet Union respond to the situation in
Europe after World War II?
2. How did the United States become involved in the Vietnam War?
3. How did the cold war come to an end?

In February 1945, with victory over the Axis in sight, the Allied leaders—Joseph Stalin, Franklin Roosevelt, and Britain's prime minister Winston Churchill—met at the Soviet city of Yalta, on the Black Sea. There the three made decisions that helped shape the postwar world. One important point remained unclear, though: the fate of Eastern Europe. Stalin wanted to keep control over the region so that it could not again be used as an invasion route into the Soviet Union. For his part, Roosevelt hoped that the region would be governed democratically. Stalin made a vague promise to allow elections in Eastern Europe, but he had no intention of doing so.

THE START OF THE COLD WAR

Instead of holding free elections, Stalin built up Communist rule in Eastern Europe during the late 1940s. The United States accused the Soviet Union of wanting to dominate the world. Truman and his advisers began to seek ways to limit Soviet power. This was the start of the cold war between the superpowers. The cold war was not a direct confrontation but rather a war of spying and sabotage, of propaganda, and of nerves.

Truman called his policy against the Soviets containment. This meant that the United States would try to contain, or stop, the Soviet Union from gaining influence outside its borders, by force if necessary. Containment became the cornerstone of postwar

American foreign policy. Over the years, it led the United States to oppose many revolutionary movements around the world on the grounds that they were Soviet-inspired or supported.

In 1947 the idea of containment led to the Marshall Plan. The plan, presented by Secretary of State George Marshall, gave money to Western Europe to help it rebuild after World War II. American leaders understood that Communism's appeal was greatest for those who lived in poverty. They therefore hoped that a stable, economically healthy Europe would be less sympathetic to communism. In addition, after Europe recovered it would buy American goods.

The North Atlantic Treaty Organization (NATO) was another key point of American foreign policy. NATO was an agreement among the Western allies to defend each other in case of outside attack. Its member nations formed a standing army in Western Europe. They faced an army of Soviet and East European troops. Each side believed it was defending itself against a possible invasion by the other side.

In the United States, fear of communism led to an anti-Communist crusade. In 1950 Senator Joseph McCarthy questioned the loyalty of many Americans and even accused government officials of secretly being Communists. McCarthy's anti-Communist smears ruined the lives of many loyal Americans before he was stripped of power.

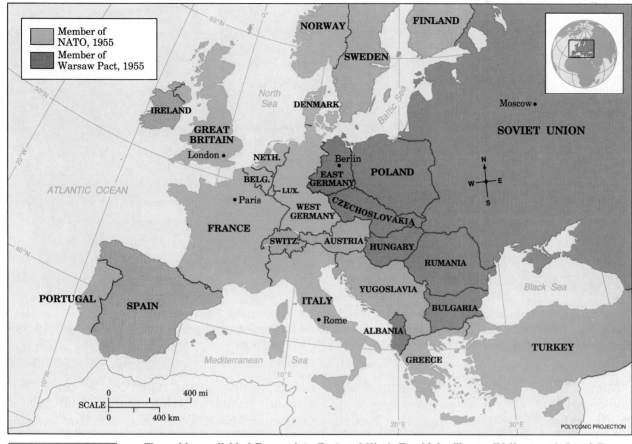

MAP SKILLS The cold war divided Europe into East and West. To which alliance did Hungary belong? To which alliance did France belong? **CRITICAL THINKING** Most of the nations (indicated in brown) which joined neither NATO nor the Warsaw Pact were neutral during World War II. Why might that be true?

THE COLD WAR HEATS UP

In 1949 Communist revolutionaries led by Mao Zedong took power in China, the world's most populous nation. The following year, North Korea, also a Communist state, attacked American-backed South Korea. President Truman sent American troops to fight as part of a United Nations force. They drove the North Korean forces out of the South. Then they pushed onward into North Korea, near the border with China, North Korea's ally. China entered the war and drove the UN troops back. The war became a stalemate.

In 1953 General Dwight D. Eisenhower, the Allied leader in World War II, became the new American President. He soon negotiated a truce that ended the Korean War. No national boundaries had been changed, but the Americans had delivered a powerful message: the free world would fight Communist aggression wherever and whenever it occurred. The Korean War had caused over 160,000 American casualties and cost $67 billion.

THE NUCLEAR AGE

Meanwhile, the nuclear age had begun. In 1945 American leaders believed that their monopoly on nuclear weapons would last many years. They were thus taken by surprise when in 1949 the Soviets built their own atomic bomb. American scientists (many of them European refugees) then built a weapon many times more destructive: the hydrogen bomb, or H-bomb. Soviet scientists worked hard and soon built one too. The nuclear arms race moved into high gear.

Media coverage of Vietnam brought the distant war into American living rooms. These magazine covers show (from left) a Vietnamese prisoner, American draftees, and an American prisoner in North Vietnam. **HISTORY** Describe how such images might have affected Americans at home.

More potent nuclear weapons meant death and destruction on a level never before seen. Neither the Soviet Union nor the United States wanted to risk all-out war. The superpowers therefore fought each other indirectly. They sent arms and advisers to opposite sides of conflicts in the Third World, the poorer, agricultural nations of Latin America, Asia, and Africa.

One of the cold war's most frightening moments came in Cuba. In 1959 Fidel Castro successfully led a Communist revolution there. Two years later the United States tried, but failed, to overthrow Castro by invading Cuba's Bay of Pigs. Then, in 1962, President John F. Kennedy learned that the Soviets were shipping missiles to Cuba. He demanded their removal. For several tense days the world waited to see whether nuclear war would break out between the superpowers. Finally the Soviets gave in and the crisis ended.

In 1961, competition with the Soviet Union led to a space race. The Soviets had carried out the first manned space flight, and Kennedy did not want the United States to be left behind. The American space program aimed to put a man on the moon by the end of the decade. It reached that goal in 1969, when astronaut Neil Armstrong set foot on the moon.

In 1963 Kennedy was shot and killed in Dallas, Texas. Experts still disagree on the motives behind the killing. Kennedy's Vice President, Lyndon B. Johnson, continued the cold war. In 1965, Johnson sent troops to the Dominican Republic to crush a leftist rebellion. At the same time, he steered the United States into a far greater war in Vietnam.

THE VIETNAM WAR

Like Korea, Vietnam in the early 1960s was divided into two parts: the Communist North and the non-Communist South. President Johnson, like Presidents Eisenhower and Kennedy before him, believed that the United States could not let South Vietnam fall to the Communists. If it did, he said, the other countries of Southeast Asia would fall like a line of dominoes. This belief was known as the domino theory.

Johnson sent thousands of combat troops to South Vietnam and ordered thousands of tons of bombs dropped on the North. By 1968 there were over 500,000 American soldiers in Vietnam. In spite of its large, well-equipped military, the United States was not able to defeat the North Vietnamese. American soldiers won most of the battles, but they were unable to win the war.

In 1968 Johnson announced that he would seek a negotiated peace in Vietnam. The next President, Richard Nixon, also pledged to end the war, but still the war continued. Over the next four years, Nixon ordered American planes to bomb North Vietnam heavily. At the same time, he slowly removed American troops from the South.

Finally, in 1973, a cease-fire was signed and the last American troops came home. Two years later, North Vietnam broke the ceasefire and invaded the South. Without American aid, the South Vietnamese army fell apart. In 1975 Communists brought the two Vietnams together under their rule.

THE NIXON YEARS

In the early 1970s, President Nixon tried to better relations with the Communist world. He called this new foreign policy détente, a French term meaning "relaxation of tensions." In 1972, Nixon also made a historic visit to China in an effort to improve U.S.-Chinese relations.

At home, Nixon's presidency was hurt by the Watergate scandal. People who worked for Nixon had carried out illegal "dirty tricks," such as burglary and spying, against political opponents. Nixon had ordered his staff to cover up those crimes. The Senate charged Nixon with hiding evidence, blocking justice, and using the government to violate citizens' rights. Congress was ready to impeach the President. In August 1974, Nixon resigned to keep from being impeached. It was the first time an American President had resigned.

President Nixon's misuse of power shocked the American people. Still, many viewed the way Watergate had been handled as a victory for the rule of law.

CHANGES IN FOREIGN POLICY

Under Nixon and his successor, Gerald Ford, American foreign policy was based on a concept known as realpolitik. This German word means "practical politics." In realpolitik, international relations are guided by questions of power, not by law or ideals. Whether you liked them or not, the enemies of your enemies were your friends.

This policy changed under President Jimmy Carter, who believed that moral principles had a place in foreign policy. Carter spoke out against governments that tortured

Nixon reviews Chinese troops at Beijing airport during his 1972 visit. To Nixon's right is Chinese premier Zhou Enlai, and behind them is First Lady Pat Nixon. POLITICS How was this trip an example of the policy of détente?

or mistreated their citizens. He also spoke in favor of the rights of less powerful nations. Carter signed the Panama Canal Treaty, which promised to return the canal to Panamanian control. Carter also negotiated the Camp David Accords, which made peace between Egypt and Israel.

President Carter's hopes of improving ties between the superpowers were dashed when the Soviet Union invaded Afghanistan in 1979. That same year, revolutionaries in Iran held 52 Americans hostage. Carter failed to end the hostage crisis, and to many Americans he appeared weak and indecisive.

THE END OF THE COLD WAR

In 1981 a new President took office. Ronald Reagan, calling the Soviet Union an "evil empire," began to beef up the armed forces. He also pledged to fight Soviet-backed communism in Central America.

In his speeches, President Reagan took a hard line against terrorism. Yet the public learned in 1986 that Reagan officials had sold arms to the government of Iran, hoping to gain the release of American hostages in Lebanon. They had then broken the law by sending the money to the contras who were fighting to reverse the Sandinista revolution in Nicaragua. Several officials resigned and were later found guilty of crimes.

During Reagan's second term, there was a dramatic improvement in superpower relations. A new Soviet leader, Mikhail Gorbachev, introduced new freedoms to the Soviet Union. Gorbachev tried to revive the economy through reforms. Reagan and Gorbachev held four summit meetings, agreeing to destroy some of their nations' nuclear weapons.

Reagan was followed as President by George Bush, who continued many of Reagan's policies. Soon after Bush took office, most of the nations of Eastern Europe got rid of their Communist rulers and formed democratic governments. The Soviet Union showed its new approach by refusing to interfere. At the same time, the superpowers kept up their cooperation. A treaty, the Charter of Paris, officially ended the cold war in 1990.

The new cooperation among the major powers was made quite clear during the Persian Gulf crisis. In the summer of 1990, Iraq in-

Germans celebrate atop the Berlin Wall after East Germany's announcement of free travel between East and West Germany in 1989. A year later, the wall was torn down and Germany was unified under a non-Communist government. HISTORY What role did the Soviet Union play in the decision by many Eastern European countries to end Communist rule?

Women soldiers were among the hundreds of thousands of Americans sent to Saudi Arabia in response to Iraq's 1990 invasion of Kuwait. The presence of women in the American military created some tensions in Saudi Arabia's traditional society. Troops from other countries such as Great Britain and Egypt joined the Americans. **GLOBAL AWARENESS** How did the end of the cold war affect the international response to the Persian Gulf crisis?

vaded its neighbor Kuwait. Fearing that Iraq might next invade oil-rich Saudi Arabia, President Bush sent a huge armed force to the Middle East. The Soviet Union backed Bush's move, as did the United Nations. In January 1991 the United States and its allies drove Iraq out of Kuwait.

During the summer of 1991, hard-line Communists in Russia tried to overthrow Gorbachev. The coup failed when Boris Yeltsin, the first popularly elected president of Russia, rallied supporters of reform. Under increasing pressure to speed up the pace of reforms, Gorbachev soon resigned, and the Soviet Union split into eleven republics, of which Russia was the largest.

Both Bush and his successor, Bill Clinton, supported Yeltsin's efforts to move Russia toward a market economy. In 1993, President Clinton and Yeltsin met in Vancouver, Canada, and concluded the START II treaty. The treaty would reduce the number of nuclear warheads in both nations by 75 percent.

Foreign policy dilemmas also arose elsewhere. In the former Yugoslavia, the collapse of communism led to civil war. Although concerned by reports of "ethnic cleansing," the United States was hesitant to commit troops without the agreement of their allies. In Somalia, troops sent to ensure the safe distribution of the food and aid needed to ease the famine there soon became involved militarily. When U.S. soldiers were killed in action, Clinton began to withdraw the troops.

SECTION REVIEW

1. KEY TERMS cold war, containment, Third World, domino theory, détente, realpolitik

2. PEOPLE Dwight Eisenhower, John F. Kennedy, Lyndon Johnson, Richard Nixon, Gerald Ford, Jimmy Carter, Ronald Reagan, George Bush, Bill Clinton

3. COMPREHENSION How did the goals of the Soviet Union and the United States in Eastern Europe differ after World War II? How did these differences lead to the cold war?

4. COMPREHENSION What was the outcome of the Vietnam War?

5. CRITICAL THINKING What effects do you think the collapse of communism has had on world affairs?

4 Social and Economic Change Since 1945

After World War II and the Korean War, Americans turned their attention toward issues at home. Over the past 40 years movements for social change have helped make the United States one of the most dynamic societies in the world.

SOCIAL CHANGE IN THE 1950S

At the end of World War II, with Europe, Japan, and the Soviet Union in ruins, the United States was the world's richest and most powerful nation. Home to just 6 percent of the world's people, the United States produced fully half of the world's goods and consumed about one-third of them.

American prosperity during the 1950s made possible the growth of a large and educated middle class. The demand for homes caused the rapid growth of suburbs across the United States. As a result, Americans bought more cars and built more highways. They also began having more children, a trend known as the baby boom. The nation's population shifted southward. The sunbelt states, those in the warmer southern half of the nation, grew particularly fast.

America's wealth also brought changes in its culture. Televisions appeared in almost every home. Young people bought millions of rock 'n' roll records. People read slick new magazines filled with advertisements for cars, gadgets, cosmetics, drugs, and processed foods.

In general, the 1950s were a conservative time. Fears caused by the cold war, along with memories of the Depression and World War II, made people want security rather than change. Many Americans turned to organized religion to satisfy this need and to confirm their faith.

Not all Americans were prosperous or content during the 1950s, however. Many minorities suffered discrimination, as did working women. Levels of poverty remained high in America's countryside and inner cities. Calls sounded for social and political reforms to fight poverty and discrimination.

Martin Luther King, Jr., a leader of the civil rights movement of the 1950s and 1960s, preached the policy of nonviolence. CIVIC VALUES Explain King's belief that "injustice anywhere is a threat to justice everywhere."

THE CIVIL RIGHTS MOVEMENT

The Civil War had ended slavery nearly a century before. By 1960, however, African Americans still did not enjoy the same rights as white Americans. In the segregated South, laws discriminated against blacks. In the North and West as well, blacks were generally treated as second-class citizens.

African Americans had been fighting for change for many years, but it was in the 1950s and 1960s that they finally began to win important victories. In 1954 the Supreme Court ruled that segregation in public schools was against the law. Two years later, after a black-led boycott of the bus system in Montgomery, Alabama, the Court ruled that segregation on buses was also illegal.

By 1960 the civil rights movement was in full swing. Its leader was a young Baptist minister named Martin Luther King, Jr. Although violently attacked by white racists and harassed by the Federal Bureau of Investigation (FBI), King and other civil rights workers kept the movement nonviolent. They led peaceful protests throughout the South. Their struggle slowly won national support. Under President Johnson, Congress passed the Civil Rights Act of 1964. The act banned discrimination and gave the government greater power to enforce civil rights laws.

Despite such gains many African Americans were dissatisfied with the slow pace of change. Malcolm X called on blacks to form a separate all-black society. In the mid-1960s, anger over life in the slums of northern cities led to riots by African Americans. Militant black leaders began a movement for black power—greater political influence for African Americans.

King's work for peaceful change was cut short in 1968 when he was shot by a white assassin. His death stunned the nation and further divided the civil rights movement.

The civil rights movement fell short of its goals. Discrimination and racism can still be found in American society. On the other hand, African Americans now have equality under the law and a greater influence in the

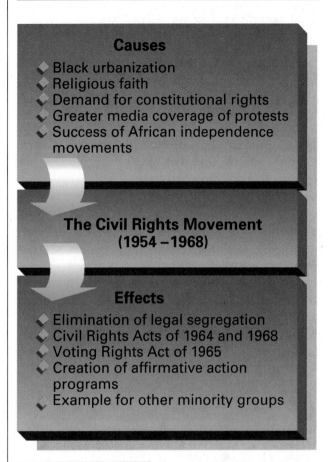

CAUSE AND EFFECT: THE CIVIL RIGHTS MOVEMENT

Causes
- Black urbanization
- Religious faith
- Demand for constitutional rights
- Greater media coverage of protests
- Success of African independence movements

The Civil Rights Movement (1954–1968)

Effects
- Elimination of legal segregation
- Civil Rights Acts of 1964 and 1968
- Voting Rights Act of 1965
- Creation of affirmative action programs
- Example for other minority groups

CHART SKILLS

This chart presents some major factors that fueled the civil rights movement. What was the Civil Rights Act of 1964? **CRITICAL THINKING** Which of the effects of the movement do you consider most important? Why?

nation. Growing numbers of black leaders have won election to public office. Others have achieved distinction in appointed positions. They include Supreme Court Justice Thurgood Marshall and Colin Powell, former Chairman of the Joint Chiefs of Staff.

OTHER SOCIAL AND POLITICAL MOVEMENTS

Other groups used the example of the civil rights struggle to work for change. Like African Americans, Native Americans had long been denied their rights. In 1968 a group of young, urban Indians formed the American

Indian Movement (AIM) to fight for "red power." AIM demanded a voice in federal Indian policy. Also in the 1960s, Mexican Americans formed their own political party, *La Raza Unida*. One of their goals was to improve life for farmworkers.

Women also used lessons learned in the civil rights movement to fight for women's rights. In 1966 Betty Friedan and other activists founded the National Organization for Women (NOW). NOW tried to advance women's rights and to eliminate sexism, the idea that one sex is naturally superior to the other. The women's movement has supported abortion rights and the Equal Rights Amendment (ERA), which would guarantee women equality under the Constitution.

Not all Americans support the women's movement, but few would deny that men's and women's social roles have changed in recent decades. Women now make up a large share of the work force. Many have jobs once held only by men. Men have also taken on

family tasks once thought of as "women's work." As a group, however, women continue both to receive lower pay than men and to do a larger share of housework.

The civil rights and women's movements sparked heated debates in American society. No issue, however, was more controversial than the Vietnam War. Not since the Civil War had a question so divided American society. Critics of the war called it immoral and illegal. The war's supporters called its critics unpatriotic. Antiwar demonstrations involved millions of Americans and frequent clashes with police. At Kent State University in 1970, National Guardsmen fired on protesters, killing four students.

Vietnam helped widen the "gap" between younger and older Americans. The generation gap gave rise to a counterculture—a culture with values different from those of the established culture. Young people stressed the importance of love and personal freedom. They celebrated these values at music festivals, such as the one at Woodstock, New York, in 1969. Critics, such as President Nixon, charged the counterculture with trying to tear the nation apart. They denounced the way young people were questioning long-held American values and experimenting with dangerous drugs. Still, in 1971 the 26th Amendment to the Constitution lowered the voting age to 18.

Rock music helped spread the message of the counter-culture. Here, audience members watch the 1969 Woodstock festival. HISTORY How did the Vietnam War help lead to the rise of the counterculture?

REAGAN AND THE 1980s

For much of the 1960s and 1970s, many Americans seemed to favor "big government" policies that had their origins in the New Deal. These included regulation of big business, support for organized labor, and public spending on the needy.

In 1980, however, the nation entered a new period with the election of Ronald Reagan. "Government," Reagan declared, "is not the solution to our problem. Government is the problem." Reagan's solution was to cut taxes and government spending in order to spur economic growth. He also increased military spending. In addition, Reagan wanted to outlaw abortion and to allow prayer in schools. His policies won the support of the many television evangelists who enjoyed large followings during the 1980s.

Reagan pushed pro-business economic policies. Like Presidents during the Gilded Age and the 1920s, he lifted government regulations on business. Spending by consumers rose sharply, most notably among a new, wealthy class of young professionals, known as **yuppies**.

While the incomes of the wealthiest Americans rose greatly during the Reagan years, so did the numbers of poor and homeless. In addition, the loosening of government regulations allowed fraud and bad investments by savings and loan banks (S&L's) to go unchecked. As a result, many S&L's failed and even regular banks were in shaky condition. According to estimates, restoring stability to the savings and loan banks will cost taxpayers billions of dollars.

Because the government borrowed money to pay for spending, the national debt of the United States soared during the 1980s. The United States became the world's greatest borrower of money.

THE BUSH PRESIDENCY

The next president, George Bush, shared Reagan's conservative outlook. In the first years of his term, the country headed into recession. The causes of the weak economy included a growing national debt, a rise in oil prices as a result of the Persian Gulf crisis, and shrinking factory production.

Another problem President Bush faced was drug trafficking and use in the United States, and the violence and suffering it caused. He called for a war on drugs. In 1989 he sent troops to Panama to capture that country's leader, Manuel Noriega, a suspected drug trafficker. Such moves made little dent in the drug problem. Critics pointed out that it was not enough to restrict the inflow of drugs. They urged national leaders to address the social and economic problems that led many Americans to take or sell drugs.

Former Presidents Jimmy Carter (left) and George Bush (right) watch President Bill Clinton sign side agreements to NAFTA. ECONOMICS What are the advantages to lower trade barriers? The disadvantages?

THE CLINTON PRESIDENCY

Entering office in 1993, Bill Clinton was determined to concentrate on domestic policy. Although he became bogged down in an angry debate over lifting the ban on homosexuals in the military, he succeeded in pushing his budget plan through Congress. The plan called for new taxes, including an energy tax, to reduce the federal deficit.

Clinton also formed a task force to design a health-care reform plan. The task force called for a system of managed care that would give basic coverage to all Americans.

Violent crime became a growing concern of Americans in the 1990s. In 1993, after a seven-year delay, Congress passed the Brady bill. The law required a five-day waiting period after the purchase of a handgun. Congress also proposed a ban on the manufacture and sale of some semiautomatic weapons.

Two free trade agreements, the North American Free Trade Agreement (NAFTA) and the General Agreement on Trade and Tariffs (GATT), also caused debate. Congress passed NAFTA in the fall of 1993.

Technology and Everyday Language

The late twentieth century has been called the Atomic Age and the Space Age. More recently, it has been the Computer Age. All these important themes have something in common—technology. Today even small children know technical terms that would have meant nothing to their parents at the same age. Much scientific "jargon," in fact, has moved into everyday language.

The Atomic Age began in 1945. Two years later, a daring new style in swimsuits was popular on the beaches of France. It had such a stunning effect on fashion that it was named after the tiny Pacific island where atomic bombs were being tested—**bikini.**

Once the Atomic Age began, terms from nuclear physics moved into everyday speech. There can be **fallout** (though not the radioactive kind) from any important decision. Many things can cause a **chain reaction,** a series of happenings one after another. When things really get out of hand, they can reach **critical mass** or **meltdown.**

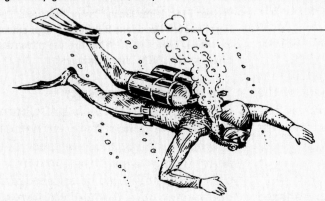

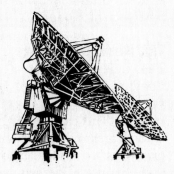

Some familiar words are actually short forms of complicated technical descriptions. **Radar,** for instance, is "*r*adio *d*etecting *a*nd *r*anging." Scuba divers are using "*s*elf-*c*ontained *u*nderwater *b*reathing *a*pparatus."

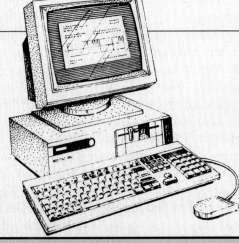

From the language of computers come a number of handy terms, particularly **glitch,** an error somewhere in the system—or any small mistake—and **user-friendly,** meaning "easy to operate or get along with."

Some old words have gained new meanings in "computerese." When your grandparents bought **hardware,** they got hammers, nails, and similar tools—not computer equipment. And to most people, **digital** referred to fingers, not watches.

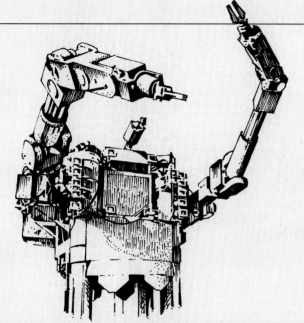

In 1920 a playwright in Czechoslovakia first used the word **robot** for a machine that did the work of humans (the Czech word meant "forced labor"). From science fiction, we now know many other types of **bionic** beings, who combine human and electronic characteristics. R2D2 and Commander Data, for example, are **androids.** This word sounds new but was first used in 1727 for a "machine that looks or acts like a human."

Aeronautics and the space program have given us many new words, including a variety of ways to start something: **blast-off, lift-off, take-off,** and **launch** (which was borrowed from sailing). And almost any event can be preceded by a **countdown.**

Astronaut comes from two ancient Greek roots, as old as mythology. Together they mean "sailor among the stars."

Politicians also borrowed from scientists. A person's stand on a single crucial issue was termed a **litmus test**—the chemical test that tells, in one reaction, acids and bases.

A group of scientific prefixes found their way out of the laboratory and quickly gave us new ways of saying "big" and "little": **mega-, maxi-, mini-, micro-.** Starting with megaton, maxiskirt, macrobiotic, miniseries, and microdot, what other combinations can you think of for each of these prefixes?

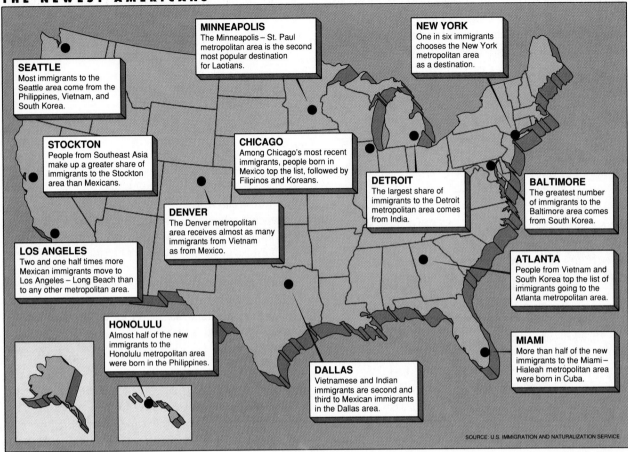

SEATTLE
Most immigrants to the Seattle area come from the Philippines, Vietnam, and South Korea.

MINNEAPOLIS
The Minneapolis – St. Paul metropolitan area is the second most popular destination for Laotians.

NEW YORK
One in six immigrants chooses the New York metropolitan area as a destination.

STOCKTON
People from Southeast Asia make up a greater share of immigrants to the Stockton area than Mexicans.

CHICAGO
Among Chicago's most recent immigrants, people born in Mexico top the list, followed by Filipinos and Koreans.

DETROIT
The largest share of immigrants to the Detroit metropolitan area comes from India.

BALTIMORE
The greatest number of immigrants to the Baltimore area comes from South Korea.

DENVER
The Denver metropolitan area receives almost as many immigrants from Vietnam as from Mexico.

LOS ANGELES
Two and one half times more Mexican immigrants move to Los Angeles – Long Beach than to any other metropolitan area.

ATLANTA
People from Vietnam and South Korea top the list of immigrants going to the Atlanta metropolitan area.

HONOLULU
Almost half of the new immigrants to the Honolulu metropolitan area were born in the Philippines.

DALLAS
Vietnamese and Indian immigrants are second and third to Mexican immigrants in the Dallas area.

MIAMI
More than half of the new immigrants to the Miami – Hialeah metropolitan area were born in Cuba.

SOURCE: U.S. IMMIGRATION AND NATURALIZATION SERVICE

MAP SKILLS This map shows how recent immigrants are changing American cities. From what countries are the largest immigrant groups in Dallas? To which city do most Cuban immigrants move? **CRITICAL THINKING** What kinds of factors influence in which area of the United States an immigrant will choose to settle?

FACING THE FUTURE

American society in the 1990s was more diverse than ever. A new wave of immigrants, mostly from Asia and Latin America, brought their traditions to the United States. Migration has made Hispanics the fastest-growing minority group in the country. Now that the borders of formerly Communist countries are open, more immigrants may arrive to add their traditions to American society.

Breakthroughs continue in science and technology. Gene mapping has opened the door to new medical discoveries. New technologies, such as genetic engineering, will greatly affect the future. America's space program goes on despite setbacks such as the explosion of the space shuttle *Challenger* in 1986.

For all its benefits, technology can also have harmful effects. For example, the burning of fossil fuels in cars and factories has polluted the air, which in turn may lead to global warming. This is a rise in the earth's temperature, caused by carbon dioxide gas in the atmosphere. Such warming could cause big changes in the way people live on much of the planet. A shift in the world's resources and food growing patterns could cause strife, and even war.

The country has responded to the challenge of environmental hazards. In the 1960s concerned Americans began to push the government into action to protect the environment. As a result, both local and national governments have passed laws to restrict harmful pesticides, prevent oil spills, and protect endangered wildlife. In 1970 Congress took an important step forward and created the Environmental Protection Agency (EPA).

The air and waters of the world do not stay within national boundaries—nor does technology. It has become increasingly clear, therefore, that environmental challenges need global cooperation. As a result, international commissions have begun to set standards that protect the earth and its resources. Once technology and the movement to protect the environment were considered to be on opposite sides of the fence. Now we know that technology is but a tool—and a tool that can be used to make the world a safe and healthy place in the 21st century.

SECTION REVIEW

1. KEY TERMS baby boom, black power, sexism, counterculture, yuppie, global warming

2. PEOPLE AND PLACES Montgomery, Martin Luther King, Jr., Malcolm X, Woodstock, Betty Friedan

3. COMPREHENSION Describe the effects of the civil rights movement.

4. COMPREHENSION Describe some of the major concerns of the American people during the late 1980s and the 1990s.

5. CRITICAL THINKING Is it right to spend money on space exploration when so many problems remain on earth? Why or why not?

CHAPTER 22 SUMMARY AND TIMELINE

1. Major changes after the Civil War included the growth of cities, the settling of the West, and the expansion of industry. In response to the corruption of the Gilded Age, progressives passed laws to regulate business. Further regulation came after 1932 with Franklin D. Roosevelt's New Deal.

2. The United States began to assert its influence overseas in the late 1800s. It took over several island groups from Spain after the Spanish-American War. Following victories in two world wars, the United States emerged in 1945 as the world's leading power.

3. The United States and the Soviet Union entered into a period of tension in the years after 1945. Two conflicts, the Korean War and the Vietnam War, ended in frustration for the United States. By 1990, however, the cold war seemed to be over.

4. The 1950s saw many middle-class Americans move to the suburbs. Meanwhile, the civil rights movement fought to win basic rights for African Americans. In the 1960s and 1970s the women's movement sought equality for women. A conservative period followed in the 1980s. However, concerned about increases in the national debt and corruption in the banking industry, Americans focused on domestic policy in the 1990s. Many also recognized that advancing technology has created problems such as pollution and global warming.

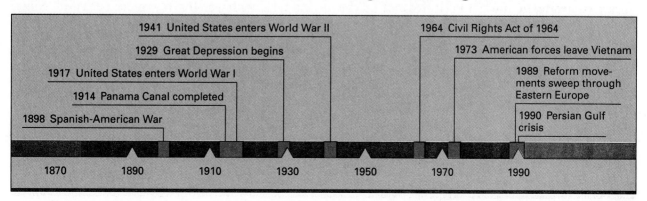

1941 United States enters World War II

1929 Great Depression begins

1917 United States enters World War I

1914 Panama Canal completed

1898 Spanish-American War

1964 Civil Rights Act of 1964

1973 American forces leave Vietnam

1989 Reform movements sweep through Eastern Europe

1990 Persian Gulf crisis

1870   1890   1910   1930   1950   1970   1990

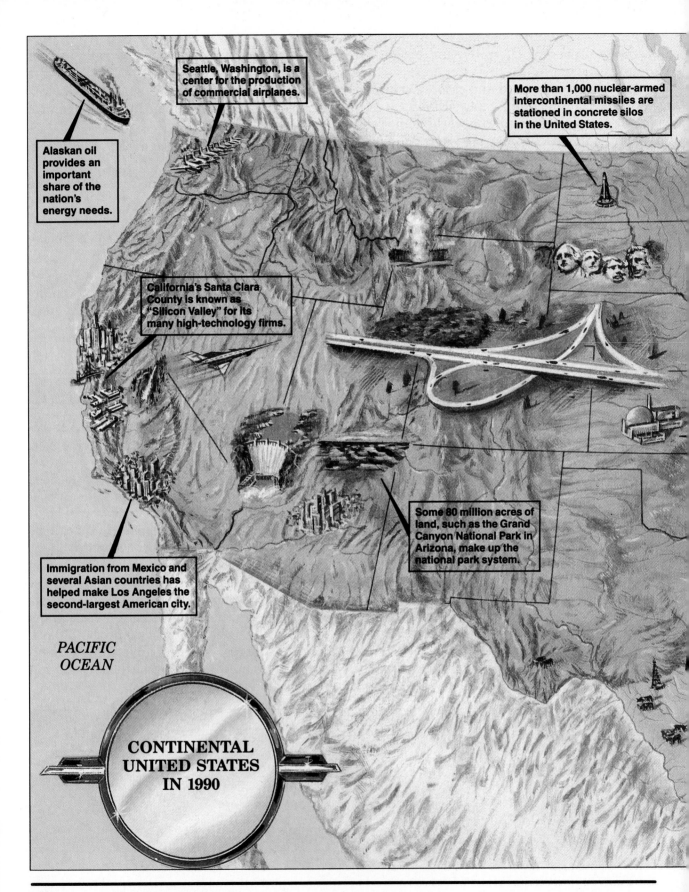

Seattle, Washington, is a center for the production of commercial airplanes.

More than 1,000 nuclear-armed intercontinental missiles are stationed in concrete silos in the United States.

Alaskan oil provides an important share of the nation's energy needs.

California's Santa Clara County is known as "Silicon Valley" for its many high-technology firms.

Immigration from Mexico and several Asian countries has helped make Los Angeles the second-largest American city.

Some 80 million acres of land, such as the Grand Canyon National Park in Arizona, make up the national park system.

PACIFIC OCEAN

CONTINENTAL UNITED STATES IN 1990

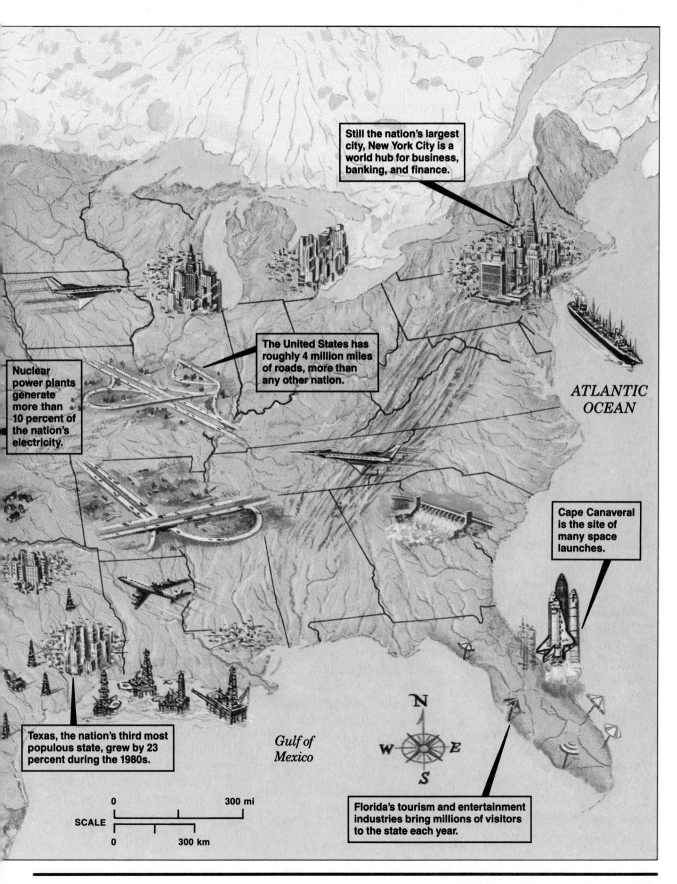

Still the nation's largest city, New York City is a world hub for business, banking, and finance.

The United States has roughly 4 million miles of roads, more than any other nation.

Nuclear power plants generate more than 10 percent of the nation's electricity.

ATLANTIC OCEAN

Cape Canaveral is the site of many space launches.

Texas, the nation's third most populous state, grew by 23 percent during the 1980s.

Gulf of Mexico

N
W   E
S

Florida's tourism and entertainment industries bring millions of visitors to the state each year.

0   300 mi
SCALE
0   300 km

PLACES TO LOCATE

Match each of the letters on the map with the countries listed below.

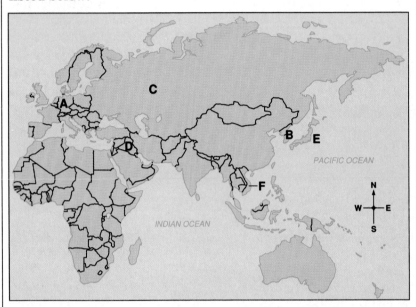

1. Germany
2. Iraq
3. Japan
4. Korea
5. Soviet Union
6. Vietnam

KEY TERMS

Use the following terms to complete the sentences.

cold war
Gilded Age
global warming
Holocaust
isolationism
Prohibition
superpower

1. During the ____ of the 1890s, the gap between rich and poor widened.
2. ____, a ban on alcoholic beverages, was called for by progressive reformers.
3. The Soviet Union and the United States each became a ____ after World War II.
4. The ____ resulted from Hitler's policy of persecuting Jews.
5. The revolutions in Eastern Europe suggested that the ____ had ended.
6. The United States failed to join the League of Nations because of support for ____ among the country's people and leaders.
7. ____ is one of the most dangerous threats to the environment today.

PEOPLE TO IDENTIFY

Choose the name in parentheses that best completes each sentence.

1. (*Harry S. Truman, Joseph McCarthy*) made the decision to use nuclear weapons against Japan.
2. (*Franklin D. Roosevelt, Theodore Roosevelt*) promoted construction of the Panama Canal.
3. The President who launched the Bay of Pigs invasion was (*Richard Nixon, John F. Kennedy*).
4. The United States entered World War I under the administration of (*Woodrow Wilson, Herbert Hoover*).
5. (*F. Scott Fitzgerald, Martin Luther King, Jr.*) led the civil rights movement in the United States.

REVIEWING THE FACTS

1. What were some of the developments during the late 1800s that contributed to the growth of industry?
2. What kinds of conditions inspired political reforms in the early 1900s?
3. During which war did the United States gain possession of Hawaii, the Philippines, and Puerto Rico?
4. Describe how the United States came to build and control the Panama Canal.

5. In what year did a constitutional amendment give women the right to vote?

6. What was the idea behind the League of Nations?

7. What factors helped Hitler and Mussolini rise to power?

8. Which were the major Allied and Axis nations during World War II?

9. What were the results of the Watergate scandal?

10. What are some of the goals of the environmental movement?

CITIZENSHIP

1. What methods did progressives use to achieve political and social reforms? What methods can be used to pass reforms in the United States today?

2. Under what circumstances, if any, do you believe a President should be forced to resign? Should his or her behavior be judged by the same standards as those applied to ordinary citizens? Explain your answer.

3. What, in your opinion, are the three most important issues that need to be addressed in today's world? Explain your answers.

CRITICAL THINKING SKILLS

1. IDENTIFYING CAUSE AND EFFECT What was the relationship between the Treaty of Versailles and the rise of Hitler?

2. PREDICTING OUTCOMES AND CONSEQUENCES Improved relations between superpowers brought the cold war to an end in 1990. How has this development affected the United States?

3. FORMING A HYPOTHESIS What conclusions might be drawn from the fact that the conservative 1950s were followed by movements for change in the 1960s and 1970s, which were in turn followed by the conservative 1980s?

PROJECTS AND ACTIVITIES

1. CULTURAL HISTORY Find out about popular music during each decade since the 1920s. Listen to recordings from the different eras and find ones that seem typical of each time period. Play them in class and explain why they are representative of their time.

2. LEARNING THROUGH PHOTOGRAPHS Find a book or magazine showing photographs of important events during the 1960s. Study the images and then make a presentation or write an essay saying what you found interesting about them.

3. MAKING A PRESENTATION Find out more about one of the movements for social change mentioned in this chapter (Populist, farmers, progressive, civil rights, American Indian, Mexican American, women's). Present your findings to the class.

WRITING ABOUT TOPICS IN AMERICAN HISTORY

1. CONNECTING WITH LITERATURE A selection from *Through the Eye of the Needle* by William Dean Howells appears on pages 663–664. Read it and answer the questions. Then answer the following question: What difficulties might Howells have overlooked in creating a society such as Altruria's?

2. APPLYING THEMES: RELIGION Do research and write a report on one of the following aspects of the religious revivals of the 1950s or the 1980s: the use of television by evangelical preachers; controversy over prayer in public schools; religion as a factor in the election of public officials.

3. GLOBAL AWARENESS Find out more about the history of a Third World nation that gained independence after World War II. Write a report telling how that nation was affected by the cold war.

UNIT 6: American Mosaic

★ *A Multicultural Perspective* ★

The Civil War and Reconstruction Era was a period of enormous change for the United States. All Americans were involved in the epic events that swept across the nation.

Thousands of African American women aided the Union cause, serving as nurses, spies, teachers, and cooks. One was **Susie King Taylor** (left), who published her diary after the war, recounting her four years as an army nurse. A high point of her war years was the time she accompanied a black regiment that captured Jacksonville, Florida. News of the city's capture thrilled the North. Lincoln himself, who had earlier opposed the use of black troops in the war, admitted that he had underestimated their bravery and wrote a letter of praise to their commander.

Santos Benavides (shown above on the right, leading his men), a descendant of the founder of Laredo, Texas, was active during the war years on the Confederate side. A member of the 33rd Texas Cavalry, he recruited Mexican Americans for the South and, most important, secured the vital cotton trade with Mexico from the attacks of border bandits. He was promoted to colonel, the highest military rank of any Mexican American in the Civil War.

The first governor of the Territory of Alaska after its purchase by the United States was Brigadier General Wlodzimierz Krzyzanowski, a Polish immigrant who had served with distinction during the Civil War.

During the Civil War thousands of American Indians fought on both the Union and Confederate sides. In fact, the last Confederate leader to surrender was said to be General **Stand Watie** (left), a Cherokee chief who did not lay down his arms until a month after Appomattox. General **Ely Samuel Parker,** or Hasanoanda, (right) was a notable figure on the Union side. A famous Seneca chief, Parker was also a friend of Ulysses S. Grant and joined the Union commander during the campaign at Vicksburg. Grant named Parker his military secretary. At Appomattox, when a top general was too nervous to write clearly, Parker wrote out the final copy of the surrender agreement.

At her wedding in 1855 Dr. **Mary Edwards Walker** (right), an early reformer, appeared in trousers, scorning women's clothes as impractical. She also refused to take her husband's name or, in her marriage vows, to promise to honor or obey him. Later, during the Civil War, doctors were badly needed, and Dr. Walker volunteered her services. She angered many soldiers by boldly wearing a United States uniform complete with gold-striped trousers. Her devotion and bravery as a surgeon were unquestioned, however, and she caught the attention of General Sherman, who recommended her for the Congressional Medal of Honor. President Johnson presented it to her in 1865.

Despite the gains made by African Americans during Reconstruction, hostility to blacks remained strong, in the North as well as in the South. When **J. W. Smith** became the first African American to enter the United States Military Academy at West Point in 1870, he encountered unceasing antagonism. In a letter, Smith reported that "not a moment has passed . . . but some one of [the cadets] has been cursing and abusing me." Smith was finally forced out of West Point. In 1877, however, another cadet, **Henry O. Flipper** (left) became the first black graduate of West Point.

"I am a Negro and proud of my race," declared the first African American to serve a full term in the Senate, **Blanche Kelso Bruce** (right). Born into slavery, Bruce escaped to freedom during the Civil War. He started several schools to educate African American children before moving to Mississippi during Reconstruction, where he became a landowner and politician. Elected to the Senate in 1874, Bruce fought to protect the civil rights of Native Americans and Chinese immigrants, as well as African Americans. The end of Reconstruction brought an end to Bruce's congressional career. He later served twice as register of the Treasury, and his signature appeared on all U.S. bills issued from 1881 to 1885 and 1897 to 1898.

HISTORIANS' CORNER

Reconstruction—Radicals and Revisionists

For many years, traditional historians described the Republican plan for the post-Civil War South as a disastrous experiment. Reflecting widespread social prejudices, they focused more on southern politics than on black civil rights. By the 1960s, however, new social attitudes and an awareness of black history changed how history was written. Compare the attitudes in these accounts from 1927 and 1965.

Samuel Eliot Morison

In every reconstructed state government there was a Radical-Republican majority, composed of Negroes and their white leaders. These last were composed of two classes: the 'carpet-baggers'—Northerners who went South after the war, largely for the purposes of political profit—and the 'scalawags' or Southern white renegades. . . .

The resulting state administrations offered the most grotesque travesty of representative government that has ever existed in an English-speaking country. For a period varying from two to nine years the Southern States were governed by majorities composed of lately emancipated slaves, led by carpet-baggers and scalawags. A certain amount of good legislation was passed, especially in the field of education, but corruption was the outstanding feature. . . .

Something might be said for these governments if they had really done anything for the Negro; but the money voted for his schools and land was largely stolen by scalawags, his social and economic status was in no way improved, and his political equality ended with the restoration of white rule.

From Samuel Eliot Morison, *The Oxford History of the United States 1783-1917* (1927). Reprinted by permission of Oxford University Press.

Kenneth M. Stampp

In the nineteenth century most white Americans, North and South, had reservations about the Negro's potentialities. . . . But some of the radical Republicans refused to believe that the Negroes were innately inferior and hoped passionately that they would confound their critics. The radicals then had little empirical evidence and no scientific evidence to support their belief—nothing, in fact, but faith. Their faith was derived mostly from their religion: all men, they said, are the sons of Adam and equal in the sight of God. . . . Here, surely, was a projection into the reconstruction era of the idealism of the abolitionist crusade and of the Civil War.

Radical idealism was in part responsible for two of the momentous enactments of the reconstruction years: the Fourteenth Amendment to the Federal Constitution which gave Negroes citizenship and promised them equal protection of the laws, and the Fifteenth Amendment which gave them the right to vote. The fact that these amendments could not have been adopted under any circumstances, or at any other time, before or since, may suggest the crucial importance of the reconstruction era in American history.

From Kenneth M. Stampp, *The Era of Reconstruction , 1865-1877.* Copyright © 1965 by Kenneth M. Stampp. Reprinted by permission of Alfred A. Knopf, Inc.

Critical Thinking

1. How are the motives of the Radical Republicans explained by Morison? By Stampp?

2. What does Morison's account reveal about general attitudes toward black Americans in the early 1900s?

3. How does Stampp's description support the idea that Reconstruction was a "glorious failure"?

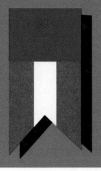

History of the United States in Perspective

At the beginning of *History of the United States (Volume 1),* the authors introduced you to the book's themes—seven key stories that have unfolded over the course of American history. Throughout your study of American history, you have encountered these themes time and again. Now it is time to review the themes. The following pages contain timelines and brief essays charting the progression of each theme. They will help you review some of the material you covered during the course of the year. They can also serve as starting points for you to consider the United States' future. For one of the chief values of studying history is to understand how the past shapes the future—*your* future.

CONTENTS

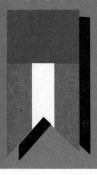

Global Interactions

The United States has always been influenced by events beyond its borders. The American people themselves are the best proof of this. Americans of every ethnic and racial group can point to ancestors who came from other lands. The nation they built reflects this diversity—not merely in its culture, but in the values and political ideas on which it is based.

Still, the American people have been ambivalent about the outside world. George Washington, fearful for the survival of the young republic, urged Americans to pursue economic relations with other nations but to limit political ties. This advice set the tone for American foreign policy for 150 years. Yet even during those years of what some called "isolation," American economic expansion led to political entanglements. (Latin America is one example.) And in the 1900s the United States has twice entered world wars as part of an alliance.

The United States of the 1990s is a global power, with countless ties to other nations. Current world trends suggest that these ties will only increase. But will the United States continue its role of world leadership and promote the spread of its values around the world? Or will it concentrate on narrower issues of self-interest? These questions, as old as this nation, must be faced by every new generation of Americans.

1492	Christopher Columbus reaches the Americas
1521	Cortés conquers Aztecs
1588	Spanish Armada defeated
1763	Britain wins French and Indian War
1775	American Revolution begins
1778	France joins Patriots against Britain
1783	Treaty of Paris
1812	War with Britain
1819	Spain cedes Florida
1823	Monroe Doctrine issued
1836	Texas Republic founded
1845	Texas annexed
1846	War with Mexico begins
1898	Spanish-American War
1917	United States enters World War I
1941	United States enters World War II
1950	Korean War begins
1968	American troops in Vietnam at highest level
1973	American withdrawal from Vietnam
1989	Reform movements sweep through Eastern Europe; end of cold war
1990	Persian Gulf crisis

Constitutional Government

The American system of government, a blend of political theory and the lessons of experience, combines stability and flexibility. The ideas underlying American democracy were born in Europe. They gained strength in the American colonies, eventually producing a revolution in the name of self-government. The Articles of Confederation proved unable to cope with the nation's problems. In 1787 the Constitutional Convention was called in Philadelphia to set forth the form of government the United States enjoys today.

Over the past two centuries the size and power of the federal government have grown tremendously. This growth reflects the expansion of the nation itself, as well as a broadened concept of the role of government. Crises such as the Civil War, both world wars, and the Great Depression required increases in federal power.

While new times have produced new changes, the nation's stability depends on a balance among the parts of government. Power remains divided between the federal and state governments. Power within the federal government is shared among its three branches. Maintaining this balance in the midst of rapid change is difficult. How do we keep the President from gaining a monopoly over foreign policy, or the courts from becoming lawmakers instead of judges? How do we prevent conflicts among the branches of government from preventing decisive action when necessary? Such questions have no easy answers—not in Philadelphia in 1787, and not today.

1215	Magna Carta
1619	House of Burgesses assembles
1774	First Continental Congress meets
1776	Declaration of Independence
1781	Articles of Confederation
1787	Constitutional Convention meets
1788	Constitution ratified
1791	Bill of Rights amends Constitution
1798	Kentucky and Virginia Resolutions assert states' rights
1803	*Marbury v. Madison* establishes judicial review
1820	Missouri Compromise
1832	South Carolina nullifies tariffs
1865	Union victory in Civil War asserts power of federal government
1868	President Johnson impeached
1933	New Deal expands role of federal government
1974	Watergate scandal leads to Nixon resignation
1986	Iran-contra affair

Expanding Democracy

Throughout American history—and world history, to some extent—the definition of liberty has steadily broadened. In England, a historic step toward liberty was taken with the signing of the Magna Carta in 1215. Parliament solidified its power over the monarchy in the Glorious Revolution of 1688.

American colonists shared this tradition of limits on government power. Conditions in America, such as the abundance of land on the frontier, encouraged the ideas of equality and self-government. The Great Awakening of the 1740s reinforced the notion of religious liberty.

The Bill of Rights laid out the fundamental rights of American citizens. But many Americans were denied such rights. Slaves, for example, had no rights at all. The struggle for equal rights for African Americans began with the abolitionist movement. It continued through the Civil War and Reconstruction, and reached a partial triumph with the civil rights movement of the 1960s. Women too had long been denied political rights. They won the vote in 1920 and, following World War II, gained new economic power and independence.

The United States has also witnessed an enduring conflict between the rights of the individual and limits placed on those rights by society and government. Freedom of speech in particular has sparked controversies throughout American history, in peacetime as well as during war. This basic conflict is bound to continue.

1619	Virginia House of Burgesses created
1620	Mayflower Compact
1691	Massachusetts extends voting rights to Baptists and Quakers
1791	Bill of Rights amends Constitution
1798	Alien and Sedition Acts passed
1821	First public high school opens
1848	Women's rights convention at Seneca Falls
1863	Emancipation Proclamation
1865	Thirteenth Amendment abolishes slavery
1867	Reconstruction Act of 1867
1868	Fourteenth Amendment defines citizenship
1870	Fifteenth Amendment grants voting rights to blacks
1920	Nineteenth Amendment gives women the vote
1964	Civil Rights Act of 1964
1971	26th Amendment lowers voting age to 18

Economic Development

Economic success has played a critical role in American history. The promise of land and trade drew many early settlers to the American colonies. The robust economic health of those colonies strengthened American assertiveness, leading to disagreement with Great Britain over tax policy. These factors helped spark the American Revolution.

During the 1800s, the search for wealth motivated the United States' westward expansion. The 1800s was also a time of dramatic economic change. The Industrial Revolution, begun in Britain, spread through the United States during the nineteenth century. Federal and state governments aided the growth of industry. Later they began to regulate industry to protect small businesses and consumers.

Following World War II the United States was by far the world's greatest economic power. Inventions, vast natural resources, and economic competition had all played a role. Problems, however, lay ahead. The Vietnam War was followed by stagflation in the 1970s and skyrocketing budget and trade deficits in the 1980s. Millions of Americans lived trapped in poverty, seemingly without hope of escape. Can the United States survive as a democratic nation if the promise of economic success dies? That question, asked seriously during the Great Depression, may return to haunt American leaders.

1606	English joint-stock company receives charter to build settlement at Jamestown
1612	First tobacco planted in Virginia
1776	Adam Smith publishes *Wealth of Nations*
1790	First American factory built in Rhode Island
1791	Bank of the United States established
1793	Eli Whitney invents cotton gin
1807	Fulton's *Clermont* steams up the Hudson River
1817	Erie Canal begun
1837	Financial panic
1849	Gold Rush begins in California
c. 1850	Railways expand rapidly
1929	Great Depression begins
1933	Roosevelt's New Deal passed by Congress
1981	Congress passes Reagan's economic policies
1990	Nation faces economic recession

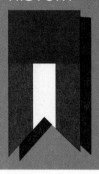

Pluralistic Society

The United States is, in John F. Kennedy's words, a "nation of immigrants." From the nation's beginnings, people have come to its shores from distant lands. The result has been a nation distinguished by its diverse population.

Diversity requires tolerance, however, and Americans have not always been a tolerant people. Slavery was not ended until 1865, and many decades passed before African Americans were guaranteed political equality. Social equality remains elusive. Anti-immigrant feeling—a result of racism and fear of competition from immigrant labor—has also surfaced in the United States.

Nevertheless, the United States is still a haven for people from all corners of the world. The Statue of Liberty remains a powerful symbol, of economic opportunity as well as liberty. Preserving the promise of economic opportunity will be a challenge for American society. The United States is no longer an undeveloped land with an open frontier, but a mature society where success depends more and more on advanced skills and training. Therefore, making a pluralistic society work requires a common effort by government and citizens. All Americans must receive equal protection under the laws and have an equal chance of sharing in the nation's prosperity.

1517	Reformation begins
1619	Dutch bring first Africans to Jamestown
1654	First Jews settle in New York
1783	Massachusetts outlaws slavery
1831	Nat Turner's Rebellion
1831	First issue of *The Liberator* printed
1838	Eastern Indians forced to resettle
1845	Irish potato crop famine begins
1852	*Uncle Tom's Cabin* published
1857	Dred Scott case
1859	John Brown's raid
1863	Emancipation Proclamation
1954	Supreme Court outlaws public school segregation
1955–1968	Martin Luther King, Jr., leads civil rights movement
1962	Migrant farm workers begin organizing
1966	National Organization for Women founded
1968	American Indian Movement formed
1989	Colin Powell named Chairman of Joint Chiefs of Staff

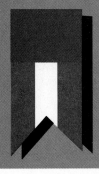

American Culture

The culture of the United States mirrors its society and politics. American culture reflects both the pluralism of its society and the democratic values of its system of government.

An important feature of American pluralism is the many different religious beliefs that have coexisted in this nation. Religion has aided the development of the United States in countless ways. It provided a structure and purpose for Puritan society. It energized reform movements, from abolitionism to temperance to civil rights. It was for immigrants both a source of security and a family value that could be transplanted to America.

Another sign of this nation's pluralistic culture is the variety of its artistic achievement. Such variety reflects not only ethnic diversity but also the individual liberty that is essential to artistic expression.

The American commitment to individual liberty has influenced American culture in other ways. One is this nation's rich tradition of statements on liberty. Another is the importance Americans have placed on education, the foundation of a lasting democracy. Education strengthens pluralism by transmitting shared ideals; it strengthens democracy by helping young Americans understand their rights and duties as citizens of a free society.

1636	Harvard College founded
1692	Salem Witchcraft Trials
c. 1740	Great Awakening
1777	American flag formally adopted
c. 1800	Second Great Awakening
1814	Francis Scott Key writes "The Star-Spangled Banner"
1821	First public high school opens
1825	Robert Owen founds New Harmony
1831	*The Liberator* begins publication
c. 1840	Transcendentalist writers make New England a center for American literature
1841	Oberlin College confers degrees on women
1851	Melville's *Moby-Dick* published
1854	Thoreau's *Walden* published
1855	Whitman's *Leaves of Grass* published
1863	Lincoln proclaims Thanksgiving a national holiday
1969	Woodstock Festival
c. 1980	Television evangelism achieves new prominence

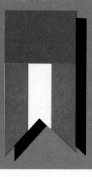

Geography

The land and its resources lie at the center of American history. They not only drew immigrants to the United States, but also provided a focus for American energies. The 1800s saw the acquisition, exploration, and settlement of the western frontier. Westward expansion meant the West could supply food to the nation's cities and raw materials to its factories.

Before the 1800s were over, concern had already begun to grow over the need to preserve the land from overdevelopment. In 1872 Congress made Yellowstone the first national park. Theodore Roosevelt used the presidency to make conservation a national issue. Later, federally funded programs, such as the Tennessee Valley Authority, also became involved in conservation efforts.

Pollution is the dominant environmental issue currently facing the United States. Automobiles and factories have fouled the air, particularly in cities with little mass transit. Some industries have dumped toxic wastes into land and water, thereby poisoning people and animals and necessitating costly cleanups. The creation of the Environmental Protection Agency in 1970 marked the federal government's commitment to dealing with pollution. But that commitment was weakened during the 1980s. Meanwhile, global problems like the greenhouse effect and ozone depletion pose a threat to our health and economic security.

c. 1420	Portugal begins exploration of Africa
1492	Columbus reaches the Americas
1519–1522	Magellan voyage circles the globe
1630	Great Migration begins
1682	La Salle reaches Gulf of Mexico
1787	Northwest Ordinance passed
1803	Louisiana Purchase
1804	Lewis and Clark expedition
1824	Jedediah Smith discovers passage through Rockies
1843	First major migration to Oregon
1848	Mexico cedes territories to United States
1849	California Gold Rush
c. 1852	National Road completed
1898	Hawaii annexed
1970	Environmental Protection Agency created

Civics Handbook

"**P**roclaim liberty throughout the land unto all the inhabitants thereof." This inscription on the Liberty Bell in Philadelphia is an enduring reminder of the American belief in the right of free people to govern themselves. The Constitution of the United States expresses this belief in the language of government—in its powers, in its laws, and in the rights it guarantees. The following pages will help you learn more about the American system of government, and about the rights and responsibilities of citizens of our nation.

Learning how their government operates is a critical task for young Americans— tomorrow's voters and leaders. CONSTITUTIONAL HERITAGE Why is it especially important for citizens of a free society to understand the workings of their government?

Who Is an American Citizen?

The richness of American life is due in large part to the different peoples who make up this nation's citizenry. Since the arrival of Europeans and Africans in the sixteenth century, millions more have come from all over the world to help America grow and prosper. All citizens enjoy the special privileges of living in a nation whose government and society is based on democratic principles. In return, citizens must take responsibility for preserving these principles through such means as paying taxes, serving on juries, and voting.

Defining Citizenship

The Fourteenth Amendment, ratified in 1868, gave America its first definition of citizenship: "All persons born or naturalized in the United States, and subject to the jurisdiction thereof, are citizens of the United States and of the State wherein they reside." This means that anyone born or naturalized in the United States is an American citizen. In other words, if you were born in any of the 50 states or in any United States territory, you are a citizen. You are also a citizen if you were born in a foreign country but both your parents were American citizens.

Naturalization

Those who do not become citizens by birth may gain citizenship through a process called **naturalization**. The requirements are five years of residence in the United States (three years if married to an American citizen), the ability to read, write, and speak English, and an understanding of American government and history.

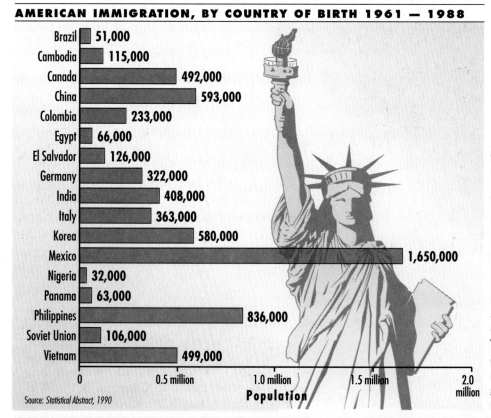

AMERICAN IMMIGRATION, BY COUNTRY OF BIRTH 1961 — 1988

Brazil	51,000
Cambodia	115,000
Canada	492,000
China	593,000
Colombia	233,000
Egypt	66,000
El Salvador	126,000
Germany	322,000
India	408,000
Italy	363,000
Korea	580,000
Mexico	1,650,000
Nigeria	32,000
Panama	63,000
Philippines	836,000
Soviet Union	106,000
Vietnam	499,000

0   0.5 million   1.0 million   1.5 million   2.0 million

Population

Source: *Statistical Abstract, 1990*

CHART SKILLS

This chart shows, for the years 1961–1988, the number of immigrants to the United States from various nations. From which nation did the greatest number of immigrants come? Once they have arrived in the United States, immigrants gain citizenship through the process of naturalization. CRITICAL THINKING Why are noncitizens required to have an understanding of American government and history before gaining citizenship?

Rights and Responsibilities of Citizens

The American government guarantees its citizens fundamental rights. These guarantees are found in the Constitution, the Bill of Rights, and other amendments to the Constitution. Along with these rights, however, come responsibilities. When Americans carry out their responsibilities, they help to preserve their freedom and the American system of government.

The Rights of Citizens

Every member of society is entitled to **civil rights**—the rights of a citizen. The Constitution and laws passed by Congress spell out many of these rights. They include freedom of speech, freedom of assembly (the right to meet with others peacefully for political or other purposes), freedom of the press, and freedom of religion. Others include the right to a fair trial and protection against illegal searches.

Civil rights also means that citizens are equal under the law. That is, each person's vote counts equally, and the government does not discriminate against certain individuals or groups. In a broader sense, citizens are also entitled to equal opportunity. That is, each citizen has an equal chance to develop his or her capabilities without discrimination.

Responsibilities of a Good Citizen

In addition to rights, citizens also have responsibilities. There are certain responsibilities that the government requires from each citizen. These include paying taxes, defending the country, and obeying the laws.

A good citizen has many other duties. One of these is participating in government. There are many ways to participate. One of the most important ways is by voting. When you turn eighteen, you will be given that right. Until then, there are many other ways you can effectively participate in government. Working for a political party, or writing your member of Congress are good examples.

The rights and responsibilities of citizenship unite Americans of all ages and backgrounds. Citizens' basic rights include freedom of speech, freedom of assembly, and freedom of religion. CITIZENSHIP What are some of Americans' basic responsibilities?

Voting is the most obvious way for citizens to participate in the process of government. Americans over the age of eighteen are entitled to vote. HISTORY How have the rules regarding voter eligibility changed over the course of American history?

What are some other characteristics of a good citizen? One is to be well-informed on important issues. This can be accomplished by regularly reading a newspaper or watching the news on television. Another is to respect people who may have a different way of life than you. Our nation is filled with citizens who have grown up in different cultures and who speak different languages. Understanding that there is no one "correct" cultural background is the mark of a good citizen. A third characteristic is helping your community. Examples include recycling paper and other products or volunteering at a local hospital. There are many other qualities of citizenship that may come to your mind. By training to be an effective citizen, you will help to maintain the democratic values that this country is based upon.

Good citizens make an effort to keep up with the fast pace of events in their community and around the world. Newspapers and television are popular means of getting the news. GLOBAL AWARENESS What have been some of the biggest headlines in world events during the past year?

Volunteering For a Cause

Suppose for a moment that you played basketball for your junior high school. A month before school was to begin, the school superintendent announced that the only way the school could afford to keep its sports programs would be if the people of the community donated a total of $10,000. Can you picture *yourself* volunteering, that is, working for no pay, to help raise the money? Would you sign a petition supporting the cause? Would you write letters to other citizens asking for their help? Would you go door-to-door to raise funds?

These are questions that may not be easy to answer without actually being in that type of situation. They may, however, help you to understand how and why many citizens become involved with community issues.

Small Volunteer Groups

There are thousands of small volunteer groups in the United States. Sometimes they have been in existence for years; other times they are formed for a specific purpose, such as in the example above. Examples of small groups include volunteer firefighters, hospital volunteers, and crossing-guard volunteers. Newspapers or your city hall are good sources of information about such local groups.

Large Volunteer Groups

Large national volunteer organizations are plentiful as well. They include groups ranging from the American Red Cross to the Little League. Other well-known groups include the League of Women Voters, the National Society for the Prevention of Cruelty to Animals, and the Girl Scouts. Your school or local library has information on those groups.

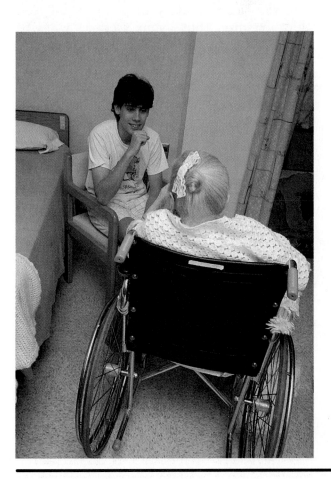

Hospitals benefit greatly from the dedication of volunteer workers. At left, a volunteer chats with a patient. Above, volunteers known as candy stripers (because of their colorful uniforms) help with office tasks. **PARTICIPATION** How do volunteers benefit from their efforts?

Expressing Your Political Opinions

One morning while listening to the news on the radio, you hear your member of Congress speaking in support of a bill that would cut one half of the summer jobs in your community. After a minute you realize that the job you had lined up for the summer could be included in those cuts! You decide at that moment to let your representative know that you oppose the bill. How should you go about voicing your opposition?

Writing an Opinion Letter

The right to express your opinion about local, state, or national issues is one of the important rights you have as a citizen of a democracy. One of the ways to do this is by writing an opinion letter to a public official. The official may be the mayor of your town or your member of Congress. These officials welcome opinion letters, for it allows them to remain in touch with those they represent.

Some Writing Guidelines

There are a few things to keep in mind when writing to a public official:

- **Be sure of what you want to say.** Look into the issue thoroughly and state your opinion thoughtfully.

- **Write your opinions briefly and clearly.** Three or four well-written paragraphs are more effective than several long pages that make the same point.

- **Write your letter in the correct format.** It should follow the format of a proper business letter. Guidelines for business letters can be found in your school or local library.

A letter following these guidelines will help you clearly state your point. It will also help ensure that your letter will be read—and that your opinion will be heard.

Kika de la Garza, a member of the House of Representatives, reads through his mail in his Washington, D.C., office. Elected officials pay careful attention to letters written by the people they represent. POLITICS Why might letters to public officials not always give an accurate picture of public attitudes?

Voter's Handbook

When you turn 18 you become entitled to one of the great privileges and responsibilities of American citizenship—the right to vote.

Voting allows you to participate in American government. It gives you a voice in determining the kind of city, county, state, and nation you live in.

This *Voter's Handbook* gives you the information you need to be ready to vote on the next election day.

Who Can Vote?

To vote in the United States, you must be:

1. an American citizen

2. at least 18 years old

If you meet these two requirements (and are not a convicted felon or legally insane), your right to vote cannot be taken away, regardless of your race, sex, religion, national origin, or income. The 26th Amendment, ratified in 1971, lowered the voting age to 18 in both federal and state elections.

Are you eligible to vote now?

When will you be?

GRAPH SKILLS This graph shows that younger American voters have a lower turnout at the polls than all eligible voters. **CRITICAL THINKING** What factors might explain this?

VOTER TURNOUT FOR AMERICANS BETWEEN 18 AND 21

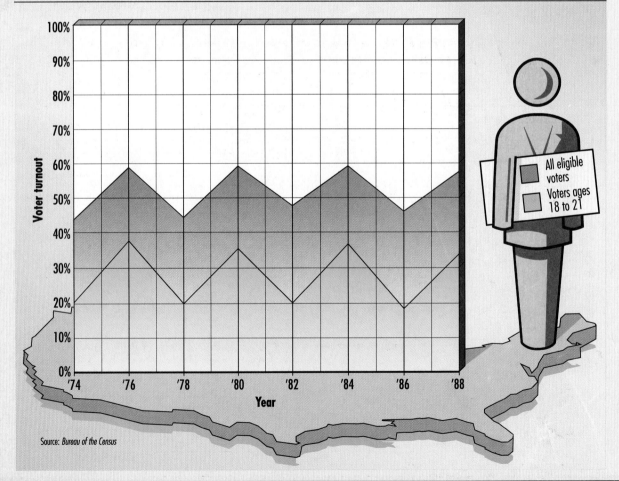

Source: *Bureau of the Census*

How Do You Register to Vote?

In every state except North Dakota you must register to vote. Registration is a simple procedure intended to ensure honest elections. Registration forms are easy to fill out. You usually need to provide little more than your name and address. Some states ask you to declare which political party you belong to.

In most states you can register at a nearby government office, such as a town or municipal hall. Sometimes registration booths are set up in public places such as shopping centers and supermarkets. Some states allow you to register by mail. Be prepared to show proof of your age (such as a birth certificate) and your address.

The detailed requirements for registering to vote vary considerably from state to state. In most states you must register a certain number of days before the election is held. To ensure that voters are knowledgeable about local issues, many states have a minimum residency requirement, usually around 30 days. (The details for registering to vote in each state are shown in the table on the next page.)

Where can you register to vote?

A SAMPLE VOTER REGISTRATION FORM In areas where more than 10 percent of voters speak a language other than English, election materials are printed in several languages.

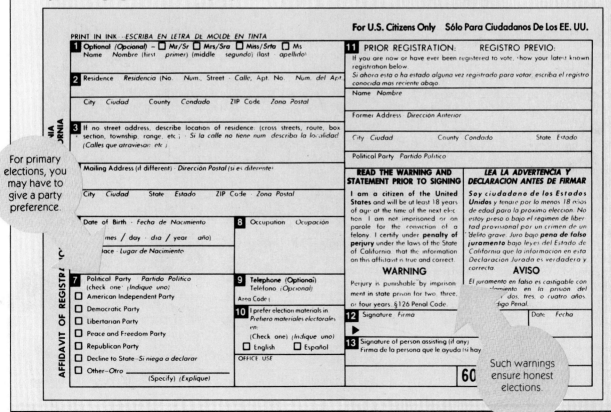

For primary elections, you may have to give a party preference.

Such warnings ensure honest elections.

What Are the Requirements for Registration?

STATE	How long before the election must I register?	What is the residency requirement?	Must I declare party preference for the primaries?[1]	Is there registration by mail?
Alabama	10 days	none	yes; at the polls	no
Alaska	30 days	30 days	no; blanket primary	yes
Arizona	50 days	50 days	yes; at registration	no
Arkansas	20 days	none	yes; at the polls	no
California	29 days	none	yes; at registration	yes
Colorado	25 days	32 days	yes; at registration	no
Connecticut	21 days/14 days[2]	none	yes; at registration	yes
Delaware	21 days[3]	none	yes; at registration	no
Florida	30 days	none	yes; at registration	no
Georgia	30 days	none	yes; at the polls	no
Hawaii	30 days	none	yes; at the polls	yes
Idaho	10 days[4]	30 days	yes; at the polls	no
Illinois	28 days	30 days	yes; at the polls	no
Indiana	29 days	30 days	yes; at the polls	no
Iowa	10 days	none	yes; at the polls	yes
Kansas	20 days	20 days	yes; at the polls	yes
Kentucky	30 days	30 days	yes; at registration	yes
Louisiana	24 days/30 days[2]	none	no; blanket primary	no
Maine	election day	none	yes; at the polls	yes
Maryland	29 days	none	yes; at registration	yes
Massachusetts	28 days	none	yes; at the polls	no
Michigan	30 days	30 days	yes; at the polls	no
Minnesota	election day	20 days	yes; at the polls	yes
Mississippi	30 days	30 days	yes; at the polls	no
Missouri	28 days	none	yes; at the polls	yes
Montana	30 days	30 days	yes; at the polls	yes
Nebraska	10 days	none	yes; at registration	no
Nevada	30 days	30 days	yes; at registration	no
New Hampshire	10 days	10 days	yes; at registration	no
New Jersey	30 days	30 days	yes; at the polls	yes
New Mexico	28 days	none	yes; at registration	no
New York	30 days	30 days	yes; at registration	yes
North Carolina	21 business days	30 days	yes; at registration	no
North Dakota	no registration	none	yes; at the polls	—
Ohio	30 days	30 days	yes; at the polls	yes
Oklahoma	10 days	none	yes; at registration	no
Oregon	20 days	20 days	yes; at registration	yes
Pennsylvania	30 days	30 days	yes; at registration	yes
Rhode Island	30 days	30 days	yes; at the polls	no
South Carolina	30 days	none	yes; at the polls	yes
South Dakota	15 days	none	yes; at registration	yes
Tennessee	30 days	20 days	yes; at the polls	yes
Texas	30 days	none	yes; at the polls	yes
Utah	20 days	30 days	yes; at the polls	yes
Vermont	17 days	none	yes; at the polls	no
Virginia	31 days	none	yes; at the polls	no
Washington	30 days	30 days	no; blanket primary	no
West Virginia	30 days	30 days	yes; at registration	yes
Wisconsin	election day	10 days	yes; at the polls	yes
Wyoming	30 days	none	yes; at the polls	no
District of Columbia	30 days	none	yes; at registration	yes
Puerto Rico	50 days	none	yes; at the polls	yes
Virgin Islands	45 days	45 days	yes; 30 days in advance	no

1. for first-time voters   2. general election/primary election   3. for primary election, before 3rd Saturday in October for general election
4. with country clerk; 17 days with precinct registrar.

When and Where Are Elections Held?

When Do You Vote?

National elections are held on the Tuesday following the first Monday in November of even-numbered years. Elections for House of Representatives and one-third of the Senate seats are held every two years. Presidential elections are held every four years. Election day in 1992 is November 3; in 1994, November 8.

Elections for state and local offices are often held on the same day as the national elections. However, states may call their own elections at any time they wish. Voters may also be asked to vote "Yes" or "No" on ballot measures such as bond issues and referendums.

A preliminary round of elections, called primary elections, usually precedes the general elections. The primaries decide which candidates' names will go on the ballot in November. The dates of primary elections differ from state to state.

Election judges are allowed to assist voters with disabilities, helping to ensure that everyone will have the chance to vote.

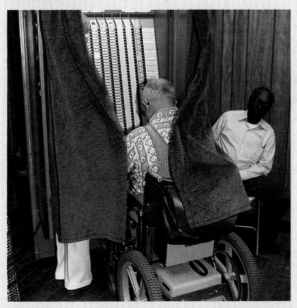

Where Do You Vote?

Based on your home address, you will be assigned to the polling place in your precinct. Although voting hours vary from place to place, polls are generally open from 7 A.M. to 7 P.M.

Before the day of the election, find where your polling place is located and how to get there. If your polling place is not within walking distance of your home, make travel arrangments in advance. Make sure to plan on getting to the polls during voting hours.

At the poll, the names of all registered voters appear on a list. (A few states allow you to register at the polling place on election day.) When you arrive, tell the election officials your name. A judge will check your name off the list, hand you a ballot or punch card (if you need one), and direct you to a voting booth. If you have questions about voting procedures, don't hesitate to ask one of the officials.

You cast your vote in secret, in a private booth behind a closed curtain. Take your ballot or card with you into the voting booth and close the curtain behind you. Now you are free to vote as you choose, without fear or intimidation or pressure. Take your time, read the ballot carefully, and then cast your vote.

> Do you know the date of the next election in your state? How can you find out?

How Do You Read the Ballot?

Two kinds of ballots are most common in the United States. They are illustrated and explained on this page.

The Office-Group Ballot

The office-group (or "Massachusetts") ballot lists candidates together by the office they are seeking. Their party affiliation is listed beside their name.

Select one pair of candidates

The Commonwealth of Massachusetts
STATE ELECTION
SPECIMEN BALLOT

GOVERNOR - LIEUTENANT GOVERNOR

☐ DUKAKIS and MURPHY • • • • • • • • • • • • • • • Democratic 3

☐ KARIOTIS and NIKITAS • • • • • • • • • • • • • • • Republican 4

ATTORNEY GENERAL   Vote for ONE

☐ EDWARD F. HARRINGTON - 732 Great Plain Ave., Needham Republican 7

☐ JAMES M. SHANNON - 401 Prospect St., Lawrence • • • • • Democratic 8

SECRETARY OF STATE
Vote for ONE

☐ MICHAEL JOSEPH CONNOLLY - 42 Corden Ave., Boston • Democratic 11
Candidate for Re-election

☐ DEBORAH R. COCHRAN - 982 High St., Dedham • • • • • Republican 12

TREASURER

☐ ROBERT Q. CRANE - 7 ...

☐ L. JOYCE HAMPERS - 82 ...

Select one candidate for treasurer.

The Party-Column Ballot

The party-column (or "Indiana") ballot lists all the candidates from each party in a single row or column. The parties are identified by symbols at the top of the column. You may vote for one party's entire slate of candidates or office by office, selecting candidates from any party.

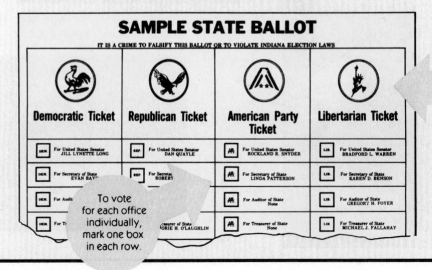

SAMPLE STATE BALLOT

IT IS A CRIME TO FALSIFY THIS BALLOT OR TO VIOLATE INDIANA ELECTION LAWS

Democratic Ticket | **Republican Ticket** | **American Party Ticket** | **Libertarian Ticket**

DEM. For United States Senator JILL LYNETTE LONG	REP. For United States Senator DAN QUAYLE	AM. For United States Senator ROCKLAND R. SNYDER	LIB. For United States Senator BRADFORD L. WARREN
DEM. For Secretary of State EVAN BAY...	REP. For Secreta... ROBERT...	AM. For Secretary of State LINDA PATTERSON	LIB. For Secretary of State KAREN D. BENSON
DEM. For Audit...		AM. For Auditor of State None	LIB. For Auditor of State GREGORY H. FOYER
DEM. For Tr...	...reasurer of State ...ORIE H. O'LAUGHLIN	AM. For Treasurer of State None	LIB. For Treasurer of State MICHAEL J. FALLAHAY

To vote for all the candidates of one party, mark one circle.

To vote for each office individually, mark one box in each row.

How Do You Use a Voting Machine?

If your polling place uses paper ballots, simply mark your choices directly on the ballot with a pencil in the secrecy of the voting booth. Follow the ballot instructions for marking inside the squares. When you are through, fold your ballot and deposit it in the locked ballot box.

Many polling places now use voting machines to count ballots more quickly and accurately. The most common are the lever and punch-card machines, illustrated on this page.

The Lever Machine

The lever machine is both the ballot and the voting booth. Enter the booth and pull the large lever to one side, which closes a curtain around you. Next, turn down the small levers by the names of candidates you prefer. On a lever machine, you can reset the levers and change your vote up to the last moment. Once you are sure you have turned all the levers you want, a second pull on the large lever records your vote, opens the curtain, and resets the machine for the next voter.

The Punch-Card Machine

In some states, you will be handed a punch-card to use as your ballot. Once you are inside the private booth, insert your card in the voting machine. This lines up the card with the names of the candidates. To vote, use the stylus provided to punch holes at the appropriate places on the ballot. Once you have punched the card, your vote is final. Place your completed card in its envelope and give it to the election judge, who puts it in the ballot box. Your votes will later be counted electronically.

The United States was the first country to use voting machines in elections. The lever machine (below) and punch-card machine (bottom) both have improved the accuracy and lowered the cost of administering elections.

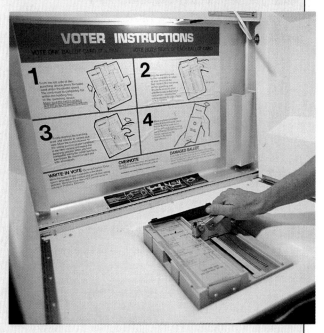

How Do You Decide How to Vote?

Your first important voting decision should be *deciding to vote*. Then, to vote intelligently, you must keep informed. This means reading the newspaper, learning about the candidates and the issues, and discussing the election with friends, family, and others. You can get information from the media, from candidates' headquarters, and nonpartisan organizations like the League of Women Voters. The ultimate decision on how you vote, however, is your own.

Most states provide sample ballots well before the elections are held. These give you a chance to become familiar with the candidates and the issues. (Usually you can take your sample ballot into the voting booth.) Before you enter the voting booth, you should know what your choices are. And you should have the information that will help you choose wisely when you finally cast your vote.

> Make sure you know the answer to all of these questions before election day.

★ Voter's Checklist

- Do you know the date of the next primary election in your state?
- The date of the next general election?
- Do you know the requirements for registering in your state?
- Do you know where you can register?
- Are you registered to vote?
- Do you know where your polling place is?
- Do you know when the polls are open?

- Do you know what kind of voting method is used at your polling place?
- Do you know who the candidates are and where they stand on issues you care about?
- Are there any other questions (such as a referendum) on the ballot?
- Do you know where to get more information if you need it?
- Have you carefully read and understood the sample ballot?

Great Words in American History

Americans are proud of their great nation and of the freedom for which it stands. Throughout the nation's history, that pride has been expressed in solemn pledges, memorable speeches, and rousing anthems, all of which celebrate freedom and express love of country.

The Pledge of Allegiance

I pledge allegiance to the flag of the United States of America and to the republic for which it stands; one nation under God, indivisible, with liberty and justice for all.

"America the Beautiful"

Oh beautiful for spacious skies, for amber
  waves of grain
For purple mountains majesties above the
  fruited plain
America! America! God shed his grace on
  thee
And crown thy good with brotherhood from
  sea to shining sea

"My Country 'Tis of Thee"

My country 'tis of thee, sweet land of liberty,
  of thee I sing.
Land where my fathers died, land of the
  pilgrims pride,
From every mountainside, let freedom ring.

"God Bless America"

God bless America, land that I love,
Stand beside her and guide her through the
  night with a light from above;
From the mountains, to the prairies to the
  oceans white with foam,
God bless America, my home sweet home.

Great Americans on Patriotism

God grants liberty only to those who live it, and are always ready to guard and defend it.
Daniel Webster
1782–1852

Our country, right or wrong. When right, to be kept right; when wrong, to be put right.
Carl Schurz
1829–1906

There are no days of special patriotism. There are no days when you should be more patriotic than on other days, and I ask you to wear every day in your heart our flag of the Union.
Woodrow Wilson
1856–1924

Ask not what your country can do for you—ask what you can do for your country.
John F. Kennedy
1917–1963

A nation is formed by the willingness of each of us to share in the responsibility for upholding the common good.
Barbara Jordan
1936–

In this two-hundredth anniversary year of our Constitution, you and I stand on the shoulders of giants—men whose words and deeds put wind in the sails of freedom . . . We will be guided tonight by their acts, and we will be guided forever by their words.
Ronald Reagan
1911–

Symbols of Our Nation

The Liberty Bell

The Liberty Bell is one of America's most enduring symbols of freedom. It was rung on July 8, 1776, to celebrate Congress's adoption of the Declaration of Independence. It is inscribed with the words from the Bible, "Proclaim Liberty throughout all the land unto all the inhabitants thereof."

The Liberty Bell, first cast in England and weighing over 2,000 pounds, was shipped to Pennsylvania in 1752. Following 1776, the Liberty Bell rang on each anniversary of the adoption of the Declaration until 1835. In that year, the bell received its famous crack while being rung during the funeral of John Marshall, the first Chief Justice of the United States.

The Liberty Bell is now rung only on special occasions. On display in Philadelphia, it attracts thousands of visitors every year.

The Great Seal of the United States

Throughout history, governments have used official seals to signify that documents are authentic. The United States, wanting to show its equal rank with the governments of Europe, adopted the Great Seal in 1782. Both sides of the seal can be found on the back of a one dollar bill.

The face of the seal shows an American bald eagle with a shield on its breast. There are thirteen stripes to represent the thirteen original states. The thirteen leaves and olives in one claw and the thirteen arrows in the other symbolize the nation's desire for peace but its ability to wage war. The words *E pluribus unum* are Latin for "One [nation] out of many [states]."

The reverse side of the seal shows a pyramid with thirteen layers, representing the Union. The Eye of Providence guards the pyramid. The Latin motto *Annuit coeptis* means "He [God] has favored our undertakings." The motto *Novus ordo seclorum* means "New order of the ages."

The Bald Eagle

The bald eagle is one of America's best-known symbols. It became the national bird of the United States in 1782, and appears on the face of the Great Seal. The eagle has been used as a symbol of strength and bravery dating back to Roman times.

The bald eagle is found only in North America. The eagle is not really bald, but has that appearance because white feathers cover its head. Bald eagles are protected by federal law.

Statue of Liberty

The Statue of Liberty has become a symbol of the United States and a symbol of freedom to people all over the world. It stands on Liberty Island at the entrance of New York Harbor. The statue, one of the largest ever built, shows a proud woman in flowing robes holding a torch in her uplifted right hand. Her left hand holds a tablet with the date of the Declaration of Independence in Roman

numerals. At her feet lies the broken chain of tyranny, or unjust rule. On her head rests a crown.

The Statue of Liberty was given to the United States by the people of France in 1884 as a symbol of the friendship between the two nations. The statue, which stands on a large concrete pedestal, rises over 150 feet high and is made of 300 copper sheets fastened together. A spiral staircase brings visitors up from the base of the statue to the crown. Windows in the crown give people an unforgettable view of the harbor.

Millions of immigrants passed the statue upon entering the United States. A poem by American poet Emma Lazarus is inscribed on a plaque on the pedestal. Its well-known lines, "Give me your tired, your poor, Your huddled masses yearning to breathe free," symbolize the nation's dedication to freedom.

Mount Rushmore

The Black Hills of South Dakota are home to a spectacular memorial. Carved into a granite cliff are the heads of George Washington, Thomas Jefferson, Theodore Roosevelt, and Abraham Lincoln, four of America's greatest Presidents. They were chosen to represent, respectively, the nation's founding, philosophy, expansion, and unity.

The sculptures are approximately 60 feet high, and are situated 5,725 feet above sea level. On a clear day, they can be seen from over 60 miles away.

Gutzon Borglum designed and supervised construction of the Mount Rushmore memorial, which was completed in 1941. The figures were cut from the stone by using drills and dynamite.

Uncle Sam

The figure of Uncle Sam is a well-known patriotic symbol in the United States. He is generally shown as a tall figure with long white hair and a white beard. His costume is red, white, and blue, and decorated with stars and stripes.

Although the exact origin is unclear, the name "Uncle Sam" is thought to have originated with Samuel "Uncle Sam" Wilson, a resident of Troy, New York, who supplied the army with barrels of food stamped with the initials "U.S." Workers joked that the initials stood for Wilson's nickname, "Uncle Sam."

Following the Civil War, the cartoonist Thomas Nast began to draw Uncle Sam as he is pictured today. The symbol soon became widely known, and was heavily used on recruiting posters during World Wars I and II. In 1961 Congress officially recognized Samuel "Uncle Sam" Wilson as being the source of this patriotic symbol.

The United States Capitol

House of Representatives

1 Speaker's Office
2 Committee on Ways and Means
3 Cloakrooms
4 Members' Retiring Room and Lobby
5 House Chamber
6 Committee on Appropriations
7 Minority Whip
8 House Reception Room
9 House Conference Room
10 Committee Meeting Room
11 Representatives' Offices
12 Minority Leader

Central Area

13 Statuary Hall
14 Rotunda
15 Senate Rotunda
16 Old Senate Chamber

Senate

17 Senators' Offices
18 Senate Conference Room
19 Minority Leader
20 Majority Leader
21 Office of the Vice President
22 Senators' Reception Room
23 Cloakrooms
24 Senate Chamber
25 President's Room

National Government: The Congress

The framers of the Constitution divided the national government into three separate branches. The **legislative branch** is the lawmaking branch of government. The framers believed that Congress, the lawmaking body, should play the leading role because its members are closer to the people.

The Two Houses of Congress

Congress is the lawmaking body of the national government. It is a bicameral, or two house, legislature. Each house acts as a check on the other, so that laws are not passed without the consent of the people.

The lower house is called the **House of Representatives**. Its 435 members are known as representatives, or, more commonly, as congressmen or congresswomen. The number of seats each state has is based on the size of its population. Representatives are elected from congressional districts that are roughly equal in population. Representatives serve two-year terms.

The upper house is called the **Senate**. Its members are known as senators. Membership in the Senate is not based on population; rather, there are two senators from each of the 50 states, for a total of 100. Senators serve six-year terms. Each senator represents his or her whole state.

Who Are Members of Congress?

The Constitution does set up a few qualifications for representatives and senators. Representatives must have been United States citizens for seven years and must be at least 25 years old when taking office; senators must be 30 years old and citizens for nine years.

How Is Congress Organized?

With rare exception, members of Congress today belong to either the Democratic or Republican party. In each house of Congress, the party with more members is known as the **majority party**. The one with fewer members is known as the **minority party**.

The majority party in the House chooses one of its members to be the Speaker, the most powerful member of the House. The House Majority Leader is the second most powerful officer. In the Senate, the Majority Leader is most powerful. Other floor leaders in the House and Senate include the Minority Leader and assistant floor leaders known as whips. They help to push through legislation that is favored by their party.

Committees help Congress deal with the thousands of bills that are introduced every year. They are small groups of members, each group with a specific area of expertise, that gather and study information about proposed legislation.

Congress Has Many Powers

The Constitution gives Congress the lawmaking power of the national government. Those powers specifically granted to Congress are known as the **delegated powers**. These include maintaining an armed force, raising money through taxation, and regulating trade. The **implied powers**, on the other hand, are not listed in the Constitution. However, Congress has the power to make all laws that are "necessary and proper" for carrying out the delegated powers. This clause, known as the **elastic clause**, has allowed the national government to stretch its powers into other areas.

The Capitol (at left) is where Congress meets to debate the issues of the day. **CONSTITUTIONAL HERITAGE** Why did the framers want Congress to play the leading role in government?

The White House

Third Floor

Second Floor

Main Floor

First Floor

Ground Floor

West Wing

Mansion

West Wing

1   Oval Office
2   Cabinet Room
3   West Lobby
4   Roosevelt Room (conference room)
5   Presidential Press Secretary
6   Press Room
7   Vice President's Office
8   Chief of Staff
9   National Security Advisor
10 Director of Communications
11 Assistants to the President

12 State Dining Room
13 Red Room
14 Blue Room
15 Green Room
16 Private Dining Room
17 Main Lobby
18 Cross Hall
19 East Room

National Government: The Presidency

The President of the United States heads the executive branch of the federal government, which carries out the laws. The framers of the Constitution wanted a strong leader as Chief Executive, but they did not want a monarchy. Therefore, the President is given enormous powers by the Constitution, but is checked by the other two branches.

Qualifications and Term of Office

There are three qualifications that the Constitution establishes for a President. First, the President must be a natural-born citizen, that is, born on United States territory. Second, the President must be at least 35 years old. Third, the President must have lived in the United States for 14 years.

The President is elected to a four-year term. In 1951, the 22nd Amendment was ratified, which limited the number of terms a President could serve to two. The Constitution does allow a President to be impeached—charged with wrongdoing—and removed from office. Only one President, Andrew Johnson, has ever been impeached. He was found not guilty, however.

Electing the President

The political parties nominate a candidate for President every four years at a national convention. The candidate then selects a vice-presidential candidate, and the two begin a long and expensive campaign that takes them to every part of the nation. The election takes place in November.

The President is not directly elected by popular vote but by an **Electoral College** made up of 538 electors. The winning candidate begins a four-year term in January.

The Office of the President

The President heads the executive branch of government. The branch consists of the presidential staff, independent agencies, and fourteen executive departments. The heads of these fourteen departments make up the Cabinet, which assists the President in making decisions.

The Powers of the President

The President is the Chief Executive of the nation. In this role, the President (1) develops federal policies; (2) enforces the law; (3) appoints federal officials; and (4) prepares the national budget. The President influences legislation by suggesting or recommending laws to Congress. The President delivers a more formal message to Congress through the **State of the Union Address,** which is given yearly at the beginning of each session of Congress. The President can also **veto,** or reject, any bill passed by Congress.

As Chief Executive, the President is responsible for the nation's foreign policy. The Constitution gives the President the power to make treaties, appoint ambassadors, and receive foreign diplomats. The President is also commander-in-chief, which gives the President additional power in foreign affairs. In this role, the President has supreme power over the armed forces. The President defends the country during wartime and keeps it strong during peacetime.

The President is also Chief of State, that is, the symbolic leader of the nation. In that role, the President awards medals to military heroes, dedicates monuments and parks, and performs other ceremonial duties that show pride in American achievements.

The White House (at left) is the official residence of the President of the United States. The President both lives and works in the stately mansion. NATIONAL IDENTITY Why might the White House symbolize world leadership?

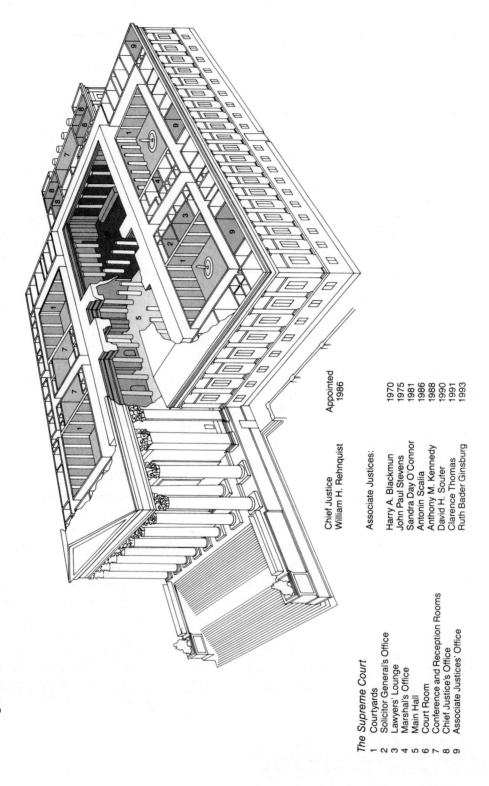

The Supreme Court

The Supreme Court

1 Courtyards
2 Solicitor General's Office
3 Lawyers' Lounge
4 Marshal's Office
5 Main Hall
6 Court Room
7 Conference and Reception Rooms
8 Chief Justice's Office
9 Associate Justices' Office

	Appointed
Chief Justice	
William H. Rehnquist	1986

Associate Justices:	
Harry A. Blackmun	1970
John Paul Stevens	1975
Sandra Day O'Connor	1981
Antonin Scalia	1986
Anthony M. Kennedy	1988
David H. Souter	1990
Clarence Thomas	1991
Ruth Bader Ginsburg	1993

National Government: The Supreme Court

The **judicial branch** of the federal government interprets the nation's laws. The Supreme Court heads the judicial branch and is the highest court in the land.

Membership of the Supreme Court

The Supreme Court has nine members—a Chief Justice and eight associate justices. The justices are appointed by the President, but those nominated must be approved by a simple majority of the Senate. Although there are no constitutional qualifications, most have been well-known lawyers, judges, law professors, or government officials.

Justices are appointed for life, which ensures that they will not be politically controlled by another branch of government. They may be removed for wrongdoing but this has never happened.

Selecting Supreme Court Cases

The Constitution gives the Court authority to hear cases arising from the Constitution, federal laws, treaties, or disputes between states. Its most important power is known as **judicial review**. This allows the Court to decide if a federal or state law, or an action by the President, is constitutional. If it is declared unconstitutional, the law is no longer in force.

Most cases heard by the Court come from its power to review decisions made by lower courts. The Supreme Court itself decides what cases it wants to hear. Certain guidelines apply; in general, the Court will only hear cases involving important national or constitutional questions. Although the Court reviews only a small percentage of the applications it receives, the amount of work it deals with is large.

The Supreme Court building, completed in 1935, has been home to some of the greatest judicial decisions in American history. CONSTITUTIONAL HERITAGE What cases does the Court generally hear?

The Supreme Court in Action

After a case is accepted, lawyers for each side file **briefs**, written arguments that support their case. After studying the briefs, the justices hear each side present its case during oral arguments. The justices then meet in private to discuss and vote on the case. Cases are decided by majority vote.

One justice is then selected to write the majority opinion of the case, which becomes the "law of the land." This opinion explains the reasons behind the majority decision in the case and must be followed by all lower courts. A justice has the option to write a concurring opinion, agreeing with the majority decision, but for different reasons. A dissenting opinion is written when a justice disagrees with a majority decision. All opinions are made public.

Influences on Supreme Court Decisions

One of the most important legal principles affecting judicial decisions is *stare decisis,* a Latin term meaning "to let the decision stand." According to this principle, previous Court rulings are used as precedents, or models, for future decisions. However, justices will sometimes depart from *stare decisis* if they feel that the precedent is no longer correct.

Two major philosophies play a role in how a justice will rule. Those who follow **judicial restraint** believe that justices should not contradict the wishes of elected members of government unless the Constitution has clearly been violated. Supporters of **judicial activism** have a different view. They believe that justices should play an active role in policymaking, not simply follow the desires of elected officials.

Facts About the States

State	Admitted to Union	Population	State Capital	Nickname
Alabama	Dec. 14, 1819	3,984,000	Montgomery	Yellowhammer State
Alaska	Jan. 3, 1959	546,000	Juneau	Land of the Midnight Sun
Arizona	Feb. 14, 1912	3,619,000	Phoenix	Grand Canyon State
Arkansas	June 15, 1836	2,337,000	Little Rock	Land of Opportunity
California	Sept. 9, 1850	29,279,000	Sacramento	Golden State
Colorado	Aug. 1, 1876	3,272,000	Denver	Centennial State
Connecticut	Jan. 9, 1788	3,227,000	Hartford	Nutmeg State
Delaware	Dec. 7, 1787	658,000	Dover	Diamond State
Florida	March 3, 1845	12,775,000	Tallahassee	Sunshine State
Georgia	Jan. 2, 1788	6,387,000	Atlanta	Peach State
Hawaii	Aug. 21, 1959	1,095,000	Honolulu	Aloha State
Idaho	July 3, 1890	1,004,000	Boise	Gem State
Illinois	Dec. 3, 1818	11,325,000	Springfield	Prairie State
Indiana	Dec. 11, 1816	5,499,000	Indianapolis	Hoosier State
Iowa	Dec. 28, 1846	2,767,000	Des Moines	Hawkeye State
Kansas	Jan. 29, 1861	2,468,000	Topeka	Sunflower State
Kentucky	June 1, 1792	3,665,000	Frankfort	Bluegrass State
Louisiana	April 30, 1812	4,181,000	Baton Rouge	Pelican State
Maine	March 15, 1820	1,218,000	Augusta	Pine Tree State
Maryland	April 28, 1788	4,733,000	Annapolis	Free State
Massachusetts	Feb. 6, 1788	5,928,000	Boston	Bay State
Michigan	Jan. 26, 1837	9,180,000	Lansing	Wolverine State
Minnesota	May 11, 1858	4,359,000	St. Paul	North Star State
Mississippi	Dec. 10, 1817	2,535,000	Jackson	Magnolia State
Missouri	Aug. 10, 1821	5,079,000	Jefferson City	Show-Me State

State	Admitted to Union	Population	State Capital	Nickname
Montana	Nov. 8, 1889	794,000	Helena	Treasure State
Nebraska	March 1, 1867	1,573,000	Lincoln	Cornhusker State
Nevada	Oct. 31, 1864	1,193,000	Carson City	Silver State
New Hampshire	June 21, 1788	1,103,000	Concord	Granite State
New Jersey	Dec. 18, 1787	7,617,000	Trenton	Garden State
New Mexico	Jan. 6, 1912	1,490,000	Santa Fe	Land of Enchantment
New York	July 26, 1788	17,627,000	Albany	Empire State
North Carolina	Nov. 21, 1789	6,553,000	Raleigh	Tar Heel State
North Dakota	Nov. 2, 1889	634,000	Bismarck	Sioux State
Ohio	March 1, 1803	10,778,000	Columbus	Buckeye State
Oklahoma	Nov. 16, 1907	3,124,000	Oklahoma City	Sooner State
Oregon	Feb. 14, 1859	2,828,000	Salem	Beaver State
Pennsylvania	Dec. 12, 1787	11,764,000	Harrisburg	Keystone State
Rhode Island	May 29, 1790	989,000	Providence	Ocean State
South Carolina	May 23, 1788	3,407,000	Columbia	Palmetto State
South Dakota	Nov. 2, 1889	693,000	Pierre	Coyote State
Tennessee	June 1, 1796	4,822,000	Nashville	Volunteer State
Texas	Dec. 29, 1845	16,825,000	Austin	Lone Star State
Utah	Jan. 4, 1896	1,711,000	Salt Lake City	Beehive State
Vermont	March 4, 1791	560,000	Montpelier	Green Mountain State
Virginia	June 25, 1788	6,128,000	Richmond	The Old Dominion
Washington	Nov. 11, 1889	4,827,000	Olympia	Evergreen State
West Virginia	June 20, 1863	1,783,000	Charleston	Mountain State
Wisconsin	May 29, 1848	4,870,000	Madison	Badger State
Wyoming	July 10, 1890	450,000	Cheyenne	Equality State

Flags of Our Nation

Flags that have flown over the United States are shown to the left and below. Patriot forces fought under the Grand Union flag during the first days of the Revolution. In 1777 Congress approved a new flag, with 13 stripes and 13 stars. After independence was won, an additional stripe and star were added each time a state entered the Union. In 1818 Congress decided to set the number of stripes at 13 and to add a star for each new state. That practice has been followed ever since.

The American Flag

The Grand Union Flag

The First Stars and Stripes

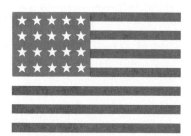

The Flag of 1818

Alabama

Alaska

Arizona

Arkansas

California

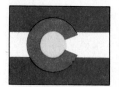

Colorado

Connecticut

Delaware

Florida

Georgia

Hawaii

Idaho

Illinois

Indiana

Iowa

Kansas

Kentucky

Louisiana

Maine

Maryland

Massachusetts

Michigan

Minnesota

Mississippi

Missouri

Montana

Nebraska

Nevada

New Hampshire

New Jersey

New Mexico

New York

North Carolina

North Dakota

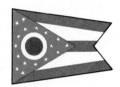

Ohio

Oklahoma

Oregon

Pennsylvania

Rhode Island

South Carolina

South Dakota

Tennessee

Texas

Utah

Vermont

Virginia

Washington

West Virginia

Wisconsin

Wyoming

Local Government

Think about one of your typical mornings. Do you wake up and take a shower? How did that water get to your house? Did you put out the trash in the morning? Who picked up the garbage? The answer to both of the above is your local government. Good local governments protect citizens and improve the quality of life in a community.

Local Governments Provide Needed Services

Protecting citizens is an important role for all local governments. One way this is accomplished is through a local police force. Police provide three basic services: preventing crime, enforcing the laws, and controlling traffic. Fire protection is another important service provided by local governments. Firefighters may be full-time or volunteer. Finally, local governments protect the public health. This is achieved by such means as providing clean drinking water and maintaining hospitals.

Improving citizens' lives is the other main goal of local governments. Many governments help the needy through cash assistance, free medical clinics, homeless shelters, and volunteer programs. Some communities provide public housing developments for low-income families. Improving transportation and offering cultural and recreation activities also help to improve the quality of life in a community.

County Governments

Most states are divided into sections called **counties**, which are the basic unit of local government. They vary widely in size and number. For example, Los Angeles County in California has about 8.6 million people while Loving County in Texas has only about 100.

County governments are responsible for carrying out state government policies. At the head of the county sits an elected board or committee, which oversees the operation of the county. Officials, such as a sheriff and

Here Kathryn Whitmire, the mayor of Houston, Texas, helps assemble a podium for a political rally. Mayors, like other local officials, deal with many different issues that affect the day-to-day lives of people in their communities. POLITICS What are some of the qualities that make a local politician successful?

THREE LAYERS OF GOVERNMENT

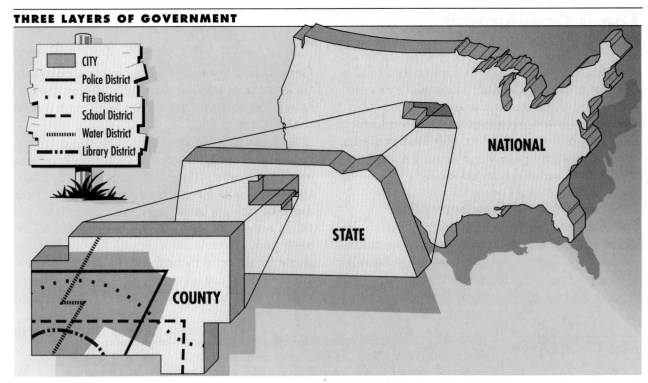

CITY
Police District
Fire District
School District
Water District
Library District

NATIONAL

STATE

COUNTY

CHART SKILLS This chart shows the different levels of government in the United States. Most public services are handled at the local level. **CRITICAL THINKING** Name one advantage and one disadvantage of local control over public services.

treasurer, carry out the county's functions. Some of the services that counties provide are supervising elections, keeping records, and maintaining jails.

Towns, Townships, and Districts

The town is the most important form of government in some states. This form of government began in New England and still plays an important role there. One significant feature of towns is the **town meeting**. Once a year, and sometimes more frequently, the citizens of a town meet to decide the town's policies. Because each citizen has a direct vote, it is the best example of direct democracy in the United States today.

Townships are still common in the Middle Atlantic and Midwestern states. Some are nothing more than lines on a map, while others function much as county governments. Districts serve a more specialized function. School districts are a common example. Most

school districts are governed by an elected school board that determines school policies, such as hiring teachers.

City Government

Because about three-fourths of Americans now live in urban areas, city governments are an important local unit of government. Cities provide many of the necessary services, such as sewage treatment and police protection, that keep the lives of its citizens safe and enjoyable.

There are three main types of city government. The **mayor-council form** has a mayor as the chief executive and an elected council to perform legislative duties. The **council-manager form** of government runs a city more like a business might. An appointed city manager oversees the city's operations. Under the **commission form** of government, a commission of five to nine members is elected to run the city.

The American Economy

Americans are fortunate to live in one of the world's most successful economic systems. An economic system includes the production, distribution, and exchange of goods and services. The home you live in, the food you eat, and the clothing you wear are all a product of the American economic system.

Capitalism Means Free Enterprise

Capitalism describes an economic system in which anything that can be used to produce goods and services—capital—is privately owned by individuals or businesses. Capital is also known as the means of production.

Capital is a broad category that includes factories, machinery, and money. Money is capital because it can be saved and invested to make other goods.

A capitalist economic system is often called a **free enterprise system**. In other words, owners of capital are free to do as they like without government interference. For example, a business owner can decide to build a new factory, or you can decide to invest your money in a small business. The same is not true in **command** economic systems. These are systems where the government controls the four factors of production:

CHART SKILLS   Three different economic systems are compared in the chart below. Under capitalism, what determines the kind and quantity of goods sold? CRITICAL THINKING Which is more consistent with democracy, capitalism or communism? Explain.

COMPARATIVE ECONOMIC SYSTEMS

	Capitalism (market economy)	Socialism (mixed market economy)	Communism (command economy)
Ownership and Control	▶ Means of production owned by individuals and businesses ▶ Market determines what goods will be sold and in what quantity	▶ Basic means of production owned and managed by government ▶ Private ownership, with regulation, of many businesses	▶ Government owns means of production ▶ Government determines what goods will be sold and in what quantity
Competition and Efficiency	▶ Freedom to compete helps to keep prices low and quality high ▶ Desire for profits encourages efficiency	▶ Cooperation stressed over competition ▶ Central planning by government can hinder efficiency of market	▶ Government control over economic decisions hinders efficiency; market not allowed to work ▶ Lack of competition hurts quality of goods
Standard of Living	▶ Goals are high standard of living and economic security ▶ Individuals free to earn profits, but may risk losses	▶ Goals are high standard of living and economic security ▶ High taxes provide free health care and free education	▶ Goals are full employment and income equality ▶ Individual efforts are not rewarded; workers work for nation ▶ Low standard of living with few luxuries

A free enterprise system, such as that in the United States, is powered by the work and imagination of individuals. In recent years, barriers to women and minority groups have been lowered. This trend should bring new prosperity to these groups and new energy to the American economy. **ECONOMICS** In what ways besides preventing discrimination does the government influence the economy?

land, labor, capital, and management. Individuals are not allowed the freedom to make their own economic decisions.

Capitalism is based on the following four principles:

1. Freedom to own—every person has the right to own things, such as land or personal belongings, for themselves.

2. Freedom of choice—individuals are free to choose where they live and work, while business owners can produce the product of their choice.

3. Freedom to compete—businesses compete with one another for customers and for profits, the income left after expenses are paid.

4. Freedom to earn a living—people have the right to better themselves, whether through school, changing their job, or starting their own business.

Government Policy

Government policy influences the nation's economy in a number of ways. For example, it acts to ensure the safety of workers, prevent discrimination in hiring, and reduce pollution from factories. American citizens also expect their government to provide them with an education, defense against attack, care for the needy, and many other goods and services. The government annually spends more than $1.2 billion providing such services.

To pay for the benefits that government brings, citizens must pay taxes. A tax is a payment from an individual or a business to the government. Paying taxes is a duty required by law. There are many types of taxes—income, property, and sales, to name a few. The largest source of income for the government is income taxes. This is a tax based on how much money a person earns.

The amount of money the government takes in ideally should match the amount of money it spends. When this happens, the government's budget, or plan for raising and spending money, is said to be balanced. However, in recent decades, the government has spent more that it has earned. This results in a deficit, which can lead to problems in the economy.

Managing Your Money

You may have heard the expression, "Money makes the world go 'round." In fact, there's some truth to this statement. Money is the means of exchange between buyers and sellers. Without money, the economy would screech to a halt. The kind of money you are most familiar with, bills and coins, is called **currency**. The federal government issues currency and guarantees its value.

Money and Credit

Most Americans make greater use of other kinds of money, especially for larger purchases. They write checks—a written order telling a bank to withdraw money from a checking account and give it to someone else. Credit is another popular means of exchange between buyers and sellers. Credit allows a person to buy something now in return for the promise to pay later. One example is credit cards. If you purchase something with a credit card, you promise to pay back at least part of the purchase every month. Loans are yet another form of credit. A car loan, for example, would allow you to buy a new car by paying a monthly installment with interest until the loan is paid off.

Saving and Investing

Saving money helps both the American economy and you. It helps the economy by making more money available for businesses; it helps you by allowing you to save for long-term spending goals. Your savings should be invested to earn interest, such as in a bank, and not be set aside in a jar at home.

People save their money in a number of ways. Some of the more popular ways include contributing to bank savings accounts, buying bonds from the government, and buying stock in corporations.

HOW SAVING HELPS THE AMERICAN ECONOMY

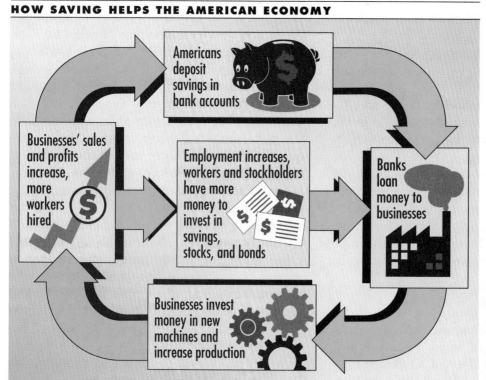

Americans deposit savings in bank accounts

Businesses' sales and profits increase, more workers hired

Employment increases, workers and stockholders have more money to invest in savings, stocks, and bonds

Banks loan money to businesses

Businesses invest money in new machines and increase production

CHART SKILLS

Money that individuals and businesses deposit in banks does not gather dust. It circulates through the economy, spurring economic growth. **CRITICAL THINKING** Using each of the steps outlined in the chart, explain the effects of a drop in savings.

Thinking About Careers

American citizens are fortunate to live in a society with thousands of different career paths. Although many people think of a career as a specific job, it actually involves all the jobs you may hold until your retirement. By making thoughtful decisions as to what career path you choose, you can help yourself build the life you desire.

Learning About Yourself

Before you begin your career exploration, there are some basic things you should think about. Most people will be happiest in jobs that fit their (1) values, (2) interests, and (3) abilities. By addressing these areas, you will learn more about the careers that fit you best.

Values are those things that people believe to be most important in their life. They are thus the goals one usually seeks in a career. Do you want to be famous? Is helping others most important? Do you want to be wealthy? Answering questions such as these will help you learn about your values.

Interests are a reflection of your values. Are you happier working alone or in groups? Are you an artistic person? Athletic? Scientific? Pursuing your main interests will help you to narrow down your career choices.

Abilities, or aptitudes, is another area to examine. For example, if you have artistic ability you might look at careers in the arts. People with mechanical ability, who can construct or repair machines with great skill, might be happy in a training program for automobile or computer repair.

The Importance of Education

Getting the best education you can will help you to reach your career goals. Graduating from high school is an important step in the process. By getting your high school diploma,

The skyrocketing popularity of computers in recent years has created many new jobs for computer programmers and operators. Like most careers, those dealing with computers require education. EDUCATION How does a college degree help a person in the search for a job?

PROJECTED JOB GROWTH, 1988 — 2000 (Numbers in thousands)

Occupation	1988	Projected, 2000	Percent change
▶ Accountants and auditors	963	1,174	22.0
▶ Clergy	185	199	7.2
▶ Computer programmers	519	769	48.1
▶ General managers and top executives	3,030	3,509	15.8
▶ Mail clerks	136	137	1.2
▶ Lawyers	582	763	31.0
▶ Registered nurses	1,577	2,190	38.8
▶ Salespersons, retail	3,834	4,564	19.0
▶ Secretaries	3,373	3,944	16.9
▶ Teachers, secondary school	1,164	1,388	19.3
▶ Truckdrivers	2,641	3,024	14.5
▶ Waiters and Waitresses	1,786	2,337	30.9

Source: U.S. Department of Labor

CHART SKILLS This chart projects the number of new positions that will be created in various occupations in the near future. What two occupations are expected to grow the most? **CRITICAL THINKING** What other factors should people consider when choosing an occupation?

you will be qualified for a number of occupations. However, more opportunities will be available to you with a college degree. Studies show that persons with a college degree also earn close to 50 percent more than those who have only finished high school.

The World of Work

Occupations can be classified into four major groups, based on the activities of each group. These are (1) white collar, (2) blue collar, (3) farm, and (4) service.

White collar work mainly involves dealing with people and ideas. Managers, salespeople, and clerical workers are examples. Most blue collar occupations, on the other hand, involve working with things. Examples include construction, assembly-line work, and truck driving. Farm workers include anyone who owns, manages, or works on a farm. Service jobs involve providing the public with protective, health, personal, and educational assistance.

Information About Careers

There is a plentiful amount of source material to help you on your career search. Your library and guidance office are two good places to start your search. Both have books, magazines, and other literature describing different careers and giving answers to commonly asked questions. The Department of Labor publishes the popular *Dictionary of Occupational Titles*, which describes over 20,000 jobs. Interviewing people about their jobs and working or volunteering part-time are two other excellent ways to find out more about the world of work.

American Literature

CHAPTER 1
Great River

PAUL HORGAN

Great River, by Paul Horgan, tells the history of the Rio Grande and the many peoples who have made that area their home. In the following passage, Horgan describes life among the Pueblo Indians, descendants of the Anasazi who lived along the Rio Grande in New Mexico.

All winter the river ran shallow and lazy from the faraway north, and deep against the sky of the whole valley the snow was locked on the peaks by cold air. The fields by the pueblo were dry and the irrigation ditches which ran to them from the river were overgrown with the dry golden stalks, the pink brush, of the past year's weeds. In March it was time to clean the ditches and then with prayer, dancing and prayer sticks, open the ditches to bring the river water in upon the spring plantings. The masked gods came from the otherworld to attend. They were seen right there in their masks among the dancers.

In April with four days of preparations the assembled kiva groups of the pueblo held a dance for the blessing of corn, which would come to summer harvest. Water, rain, were the greatest of blessings, and all was asked in their name, and in their image, gesture, and sound. The curing societies [groups of people who tried to cure illnesses] during this month went into retreat for purification and for prayer, again invoking rain, upon whose coming the lives of plant and person and animal alike depended. . . .

In early summer the ceremony was held by the curing societies to pull the sun to the south, where his hot light would make long days and help things to grow.

In full summer they danced again for corn. Sometimes they started out in clear day, with all the kiva groups in fullest magnificence under a spotless blue sky which gave back heat like stone near fire. Rain could never come from such a sky. But all day they pounded the prayer into the ground and showered the sound of falling drops of rain from the air to the earth while the heat grew and grew and the shadows of the houses stood like triangles painted on pottery in black paint; and presently they might see without giving any sign what loomed in the north and the west against the ringing blue—dazzling white thunderheads marching slowly and powerfully over the sky toward this town, these fields and seeds. . . . Sometimes it rained so hard and long that the earth ran and the gullies deepened, and new cracks appeared leading to them, and rocks rolled scouring new ways to the river, and the river rose and flowed fast carrying unaccustomed things sideways in the queer sailing current of flood.

In September as the border of summer and winter was reached the Summer People and the Winter People both held dances. Autumn brought hunting dances too, and some of them were given later in wintertime. In November came the feast of the dead, when all the ancestors came back to the pueblo to visit for a day and a night. It was a blessed occasion and a happy one. And before long it was time to urge the four curing societies to watch the sun, and call it back to the north before it went too far southward.

In midwinter the kiva groups chose their officers for the next year, and held dances to honor them, to bless them and to make them know the right ways. The curing societies now frequently in the winter held general cures for everyone. People could come to the curing ceremonies with their ailments and have them included with the other ills against which the doctors gave battle. They purged everyone, the whole town, of evil spirits. Again they cried out and struck blows against the witches, while all heard the encounters, and were reassured.

In February the koshare danced, the clowns, the critics, who hazed the people, sometimes to laughter, sometimes to shame, the spirits of irony and perversity thus accounted for and made useful.

And it was by then observed that the sun was safely on his way north again, and there was a ceremony to confirm this and give thanks.

Then the winter's weeds stood thick again in the ditches, and the path of life from the river to the fields had to be readied. Once again it was time to burn the weeds away, clean the ditches, let the river in, and set the plantings of another year.

From *Great River: The Rio Grande in North American History* by Paul Horgan (Farrar Straus Giroux Inc.). Copyright © 1984 by Paul Horgan. Reprinted by permission of Benjamin Keen.

Critical Thinking

1. Why did the Pueblo open the irrigation ditches in the spring?
2. What were the kiva groups asking for when they assembled in spring and summer?
3. What were the curing societies? Why were they important to the Pueblo community?
4. What was the feast of the dead? Why does Horgan term it a "blessed" and "happy" occasion?

★

CHAPTER 2

History of the Indies
BARTOLOMÉ DE LAS CASAS

Before Columbus could win support for his project to cross the Atlantic Ocean, he had to convince the advisers to Spain's king and queen that his idea would work. In his History of the Indies, *Bartolomé de Las Casas writes of the objections these advisers made to Columbus's plans.*

Some said that it was impossible that after so many thousands of years these Indies should be unknown, if there were such places in the world, for surely Ptolemy and the many other astronomers, geographers, and sages that had lived would have known something of them in writing, since they had written of many other matters; hence, they said, to affirm what Columbus affirmed was to claim to know or divine more than anyone else. Others argued this way: The world is infinitely large, and therefore in many years of navigation it would be impossible to reach the end of Asia, as Christopher Columbus proposed to do by sailing westward. . . .

Still others, who vaunted their mathematical learning, talked about astronomy and geography, saying that only a very small part of this inferior sphere is land, all the rest being entirely covered with water, and therefore it could only be navigated by sailing along the shores or coasts, as the Portuguese did along the coasts of Guinea; the proponents of this view had read precious few books on navigation, and had done even less sailing themselves. They added that whoever sailed directly west, as Christopher Columbus proposed to do, could never return, for supposing that the world was round, and that going westward you went downhill, then once you had left the hemisphere described by Ptolemy, on your return you must go uphill, which ships could not do—truly a subtle and profound reason, and proof that the matter was well understood! Others cited Saint Augustine, who . . . denied the existence of antipodes . . . and their refrain was: "Saint Augustine doubts." Then someone had to bring up the business of the five zones, of which three, according to many are totally uninhabitable; this was a commonly held opinion among the ancients, who, after all, did not know very much. Others adduced still other reasons, not worth mentioning here since they came from the kind of people who disagree with everybody—who find any statement illogical, no matter how sound and clear it is, and never lack for reasons to contradict it. . . .

And so Christopher Columbus could give little satisfaction to those gentlemen who the monarchs had convened, and therefore they pronounced his offers and promises impossible and vain and worthy of rejection. Having formed their opinion, they went to the monarchs and stated their views, persuading them that it did not become their royal authority to favor a project that was based on such weak foundations and that must appear vague and unfeasible to any sensible person, even an uneducated one, for if they sponsored it, they would lose the money that they spent on it and would weaken their own standing, with no benefit to anyone. Finally the monarchs sent a reply to Columbus, dismissing him for the time being, though not entirely depriving him of the hope of a return to the subject when their Highnesses should be less occupied with important business, as they were at that time by the War of Granada.

From *Historia de Las Indias* by Bartolomé de Las Casas, as reprinted in *Readings in Latin American Civilization: 1492 to the Present,* edited by Benjamin Keen. Copyright 1955, © 1967 by Benjamin Keen. Reprinted by permission of Benjamin Keen.

Critical Thinking

1. What was the advisers' attitude toward the ancient scholars?

2. What tone did Las Casas take when he wrote, "truly a subtle and profound reason, and proof that the matter was well understood"?

3. How did Las Casas view the opinions given by the advisers to the king and queen?

4. What was Las Casas's probable opinion of Columbus?

■■■■ ★ ■■■■

CHAPTER 3
Estebanico
HELEN RAND PARISH

While researching the period of Spanish exploration and colonization of the Western Hemisphere, the historian Helen Rand Parish became interested in the life of Estebanico (also spelled Estevanico). She decided to write a book about Estebanico, whom she called "the first great black man in America." In her novel Estebanico, *Parish imagined how Estebanico might have told the story of his many adventures. In the following passage, Estebanico and three companions, having escaped from Indians who had enslaved them, begin their long journey through Texas and toward Spanish-held territory.*

We were four—three Castilian [Spanish] gentlemen and one African Negro. All four of us grew taller in that flight.

We had all been slaves, and now we were free. So we were equals and we helped each other. Captain Castillo kept up our spirits with his reckless courage; my master Dorantes taught us to remain nobly aloof with the Indians; Cabeza de Vaca meticulously memorized our distances and dates; and I had a special assignment, as I shall detail. We went in the guise of peddlers; each of us bore on his back a bundle of trade goods and simples, only thus could we move freely along the trails. Your Royal Treasurer [Cabeza de Vaca] we chose as our leader, he was the oldest and most prudent, and my master and Castillo were Captains who had served under his command. Wherefore in our councils we deferred to his decisions on our course and strategy, but on the road it was I who led. . . .

I was the one the natives admired and feared, for my imposing height and my beautiful black color. And I was the one who first entered the villages as ambassador, and prepared the Indians for our coming, and searched out the ways we were to travel. For we went inland from the coast, over rugged country and up onto a great High Plain—an endless sea of green and grayish grasses . . . crossed by many hidden trails. And I alone could inquire *which trail should be ours.* For I knew the Indian speech, while my three Spanish companions still used mostly the sign language; they were not ignorant of the native tongues but there are six languages along that coast, and they had only a smattering of each, whereas I spoke all six fluently. As I have told, I had always a great facility with languages; I spoke Arabic at home in Azamur, and I learned the tongue of the Portuguese when they took our town, and Spanish in the Duke's household in Seville, and now I had been talking with the Indians by word and sign nearly seven years.

So I went ever in advance, bringing and seeking news of the region in constant conversation with the natives. They advised us to travel north and east—to the vast prairies where they hunted the thundering herds of woolly humpbacked cows [buffalo]! I could not take those trails, Your Majesty, they led away from New Spain, and I continued northwest instead.

And in the very first tribe we reached on that high grassland, I made the decision that determined the success of our journey. For I overheard the Indians saying that we must surely be shamans (or medicine men) because of my black complexion, which they considered magical, and because of our beards, they being beardless. For this people had a tale or legend—afterward they repeated it to us, though we could never understand it well—about a wandering medicine man named Bad Demon. He was small and dark and bearded, and he would suddenly appear at their doors in dazzling torchlight and show his sinister magical skill as a surgeon: whoever he seized and cut, whether on the arm or the entrails, would be healed in three days, and he could also dislocate and set bones. They feared him greatly, for there were no physicians among them.

Accordingly they received us with eagerness, and a delegation came to us at night—some men suffering great pains in the head; and they besought us, as we were shamans, to cure them.

From *Estebanico* by Helen Rand Parish. Copyright © 1974 by Helen Rand Parish. Reprinted by permission of Penguin USA.

Critical Thinking

1. At first, what disguise did the four men use when they were traveling among the Indians?

2. What special skill did Estebanico have? How did he put it to use?

3. Who did the Indians on the high grassland think the four travelers were? How was this misunderstanding an advantage for the travelers?

CHAPTER 4

Roanoke: A Novel of the Lost Colony

SONIA LEVITIN

Roanoke: A Novel of the Lost Colony, *by Sonia Levitin, is a story of the second attempt to build a settlement on Roanoke Island. To narrate the story, Levitin created the character of William Wythers, a sixteen-year-old colonist at Roanoke in 1587. In the passage below, Wythers describes a discussion among the colonists about rebuilding a wall that earlier colonists had constructed around the settlement.*

The dispute raged all morning. Work was at a standstill. The question had all the marks of one of those riddles that amuse men endlessly as they sit over their evening wine. But this was in earnest.

"It's unthinkable to build a settlement without a wall!" cried John Spendlove. "What's to protect our possessions? These flimsy houses?"

"But you see how quickly a fort can crumble," argued John Sampson. "What use is a wall, really?"

"Gentlemen," said Richard Berry stiffly, obviously restraining himself, "never in all history has any land been won and held without a certain show of force. There's absolutely no question. We must rebuild the walls of the fort."

"The women need a roof over their heads first," put in Dyonis Harvie solemnly. His wife, too, was with child. As usual, nobody listened to him.

Contemptuously Maurice Allen put in, "If you've just bought a valuable horse, what shall you build first? The fence to keep him in, or his winter stall?"

Of all of them, only Ananais leaned first toward one side of the argument, then to the other. "We must keep an open mind," he said. "The Governor feels that if we build a wall it might offend the savages."

"Offend the savages!" cried Chris Cooper, bent over with laughter. "How does one offend a savage?"

"By behaving in a way that seems rude and hostile," Ananais said gravely, and Cooper burst out laughing again.

Thoughtfully Roger Prat spoke up, rising as he did so. "If we wish to reach them," he said, "it seems wrong to first build a wall."

"We must consider our objectives," said the lawyer, Stevens, puffing out his chest for a long-winded lecture. "We must define our purpose in coming here. Is it to bring religion to the savages? Are we willing to sacrifice ourselves for this lofty, though impractical goal? Or did we come to claim and hold this land, to establish rule over it? If *that* is the case, then our actions are prescribed by *this* goal, and our physical survival is the only valid concern. Next, we must ask ourselves, is power better won by persuasion, or by superior strength, including all the signs and symbols of such strength? . . ."

I could picture the very process of decay taking place before my eyes, while Stevens droned on eternally, each point leading to another.

"Go and fetch the Governor," Ananais whispered to me, and with relief I went to find him.

I found him near the beach, speaking to Captain Spicer. . . . When the Governor turned to me, I gave the message. "The Assistants ask that you decide, sir," I concluded, "whether we ought to build a wall first or finish mending the huts. And some," I added, "think we ought not to build a wall at all."

He turned to me, smiling in a half-serious, half-jesting way and asked, "What do you think, William?"

The question brought me up short, as if it were an obstacle in my path. Never before had anyone asked me what I thought.

"In truth," I stammered, "I'm not sure." His silence forced me to think about it, and [as] we walked, all the arguments I'd heard tumbled together in my mind.

"Well, William?" he prompted, waiting for my reply.

"A wall," I began, "might make us feel safer at night. And yet, I hear the natives build no walls, and George Howe has told me how it feels to be out—out in the open spaces with only a sky for cover and no walls at all. I think," I said slowly, "if it were possible to build a town without a wall, and to live there without being afraid—it would be a fine thing. John Sampson said that the wall we build to keep them out will also keep us in. And I—I don't think I want to be kept in, sir."

He walked beside me silently, and at last I asked, with a sudden touch of fear, "Have you already made your decision, sir?"

He flashed at me a stern, astonished look, then he laughed heartily. "What you mean, my young friend, is, am I asking you to make the decision?" Again he chuckled, then said, "Yes, I have made the decision, based on a different reason from yours. Though your arguments," he added quickly, "are good ones. We will not build a wall. A wall won't make us stronger than we are. We are stronger than the savages, in many ways, but . . . it's all in the way you look at it. If we could see ourselves not as conquerors, but as guests. . . ." His voice faded, then resumed its strength. "After all, Roanoke is not to be our home. We're moving to Chesapeake next year, and until then we need the friendship of these natives. We have to move into their lives gradually, make ourselves blend into the countryside, so to speak. A wall would only teach them to fear us, and fear always turns into violence in the end."

Critical Thinking

1. What arguments did John Spendlove and Richard Berry use in favor of rebuilding the wall?

2. According to Stevens, what were two possible goals for the Roanoke colony? How would the choice of a goal affect the decision of whether or not to rebuild the wall?

3. What was William's reason for opposing the wall?

4. What did the Governor mean by the statement, "If we could see ourselves not as conquerors, but as guests"?

★

CHAPTER 5
The Serpent Never Sleeps
SCOTT O'DELL

Scott O'Dell's novel The Serpent Never Sleeps *describes a young woman named Serena Lynn who sails in 1609 from England to the struggling settlement at Jamestown, Virginia. In the passage below, Serena and her fellow passengers finally arrive, after a long and difficult journey, at Jamestown. There they learn first-hand of the conditions within Jamestown's walls.*

Tides and shifting winds held us for a day. Then a gentle breeze carried us up the James to a point of land and Jamestown. Below the settlement, tall trees overhung the riverbank. Sailors tied the two ships to the trees, quietly, as if they were tying a pair of horses. Sir Thomas Gates shouted for everyone to line up in an orderly fashion and not to move until he gave the order.

Deliverance fired her cannon. Muskets roared. Bugles sounded. Everyone cheered. Sir Thomas shouted for quiet.

Signaling us to follow, he strode ashore and took a path that led upward to a huddled settlement atop a hillock [small hill]. He held his sword aloft. His scarlet cloak fluttered in the wind and showed a glint of gold braid. Beside him, right and left, drummers beat upon their drums. We followed, singing a sprightly tune. It was a fine display, meant to hearten all the citizens of Jamestown.

But tramping along behind Sir Thomas, I thought it curious that the path we followed was overgrown with weeds and doubly curious that no one from the settlement had come to greet us.

Above me, at the end of the weed-grown path, I caught a glimpse of a stockade with most of the stakes missing, the sagging roof of what was once a fort, a row of ruined huts. Had the settlers left? Had Jamestown been abandoned? If so, Sir Thomas surely would have been told when he talked to those at Fort Comfort.

He came to a halt in front of the stockade. Through the gate, which hung loose on its hinges, stumbled a grizzled old woman, leading a child. Behind her stood a cluster of silent figures. The woman wanted to know if the ships had brought food.

Sir Thomas, though shocked by the desolation that lay around him, by the starving woman and the silent figures, said in a hearty voice, "Two shiploads, good lady. Fish, eggs, turtle meat, strings of smoked birds. We'll spread a grand feast for you ere the sun goes down."

"Now would be the better," the old woman said. "A little now. Some of us will not be here when the sun goes down."

"So now it is," said Sir Thomas in the same hearty voice, and sent a bevy of guards headlong to the ships.

The child wandered over and grasped the hem of my skirt. She had blue eyes and corn-colored hair that needed combing.

"What name do you have?" I asked her.

"Humility," she said. "And my mother's name is Humility, too."

"It's a pretty name. How nice. Where is your mother?"

"In heaven," the child said. "My father is in heaven, too. I will see them soon. . . ."

Our people gazed at the ruined fort and the tumbled barricade and the starving. They must have wished, all of them except our leaders and the Reverend Bucke, that they were back in the soft airs of Bermuda, among the palm trees and the blue water and bounteous shoals of food, just for the taking. Their groans were tight-lipped and silent, but I heard them nonetheless.

Barrels of smoked pork were trundled up the hill. Governor Gates had them opened for all to see, but the starving people hung back.

"Step up, my friends," he said in his stentorian voice. "There are more barrels of pork, barrels of fish, and birds laid down in fat awaiting you."

A man standing beside the governor said, "It's been a terrible time. We've had scarce a handful of corn each day. This, for weeks now. The smell of food, the mere sight of it, must make them ill as it does me. Bear with us, I pray you. We'll soon get our stomachs back."

The man, I learned, was Sir George Percy. He had been president of the colony since the day Captain Smith was badly burned in a fire and forced to return to England.

The colony had fared well under Smith's guidance. . . . He had frowned on laziness. Those who did not work did not eat. Those who disobeyed orders were punished. He went boldly among the Indians, often alone, threatening them if himself threatened, carrying out his threats if need be.

But no more than sixty of some five hundred settlers had survived the past six months. "A deathly winter," Sir George Percy said as he stood gazing at the food spread out upon the grass, still unable to touch it.

"We called it 'the Starving Time.' We ventured outside the fort only to bury our dead, but only at night in shallow graves, for the earth was frozen and we feared death from savage arrows. Inside the fort stalked famine and pestilence. Huts of the dead and pickets from the stockade were burned for firewood. So great was the famine that an Indian we managed to slay was consumed. One amongst our starving slew his wife and was secretly eating her when discovered. Truly, a Starving Time. My friends, if you had not come at this fateful hour, we all would have been dead within the week."

From *The Serpent Never Sleeps* by Scott O'Dell. Copyright © 1987 by Scott O'Dell. Jacket painting © 1987 by Ted Lewin. Reprinted by permission of Houghton Mifflin Co.

Critical Thinking

1. Contrast the appearance of the new arrivals with that of the Jamestown settlers.
2. What did the old woman mean when she told Sir Thomas that "some of us will not be here when the sun goes down"?
3. Why did the Jamestown settlers not want to eat the food brought to them right away?
4. Why were the settlers in such poor health?
5. Explain why the success of England's North American colonies depended on a strong English navy.

CHAPTER 6

The Interesting Narrative of the Life of Olaudah Equiano

OLAUDAH EQUIANO

An important source of labor in the American colonies was African slavery. A few Africans, such as Olaudah Equiano, wrote about their enslavement. Equiano, who was taken from his home in present-day Nigeria and sold into slavery in the mid-1750s, was later able to buy his freedom. He wrote a book in which he told of the horrors of the journey to America from Africa.

I loved my family, I loved my village, and I especially loved my mother because I was the youngest son and I was her favorite. She made great efforts to develop my mind. She trained me from my earliest years to be skilled in agriculture and war. She rewarded me whenever I did well on the lessons she gave me. I was very happy. But my happiness ended suddenly when I was eleven [and was captured by enemies and sold into slavery].

The first object which saluted my eyes when I arrived on the coast was the sea, and a slave ship, which was then riding at anchor and waiting for its cargo. The sight filled me with astonishment, then with a feeling of terror which I am still not able to describe.

I was soon put down under the decks, and then I received a salutation in the nostrils as I had never experienced in my life; so that with the loathsomeness of the stench, and crying, I became so sick and low that I was not able to eat. I now wished for the last friend, death, to relieve me. But soon, to my grief, two of the

★ AMERICAN LITERATURE ★

white men offered me eatables. On my refusing to eat, one of them held me fast by the hands and laid me across, I think, the windlass, and tied my feet, while the other flogged me severely. I had never experienced anything of this kind before, and, although not being used to the water, I naturally feared that element the first time I saw it; nevertheless, could I have got over the nettings, I would have jumped over the side. But I could not. Besides, the crew used to watch very closely those of us who were not chained down to the decks, lest we should leap into the water. I have seen some of these poor African prisoners most severely cut for attempting to do so and hourly whipped for not eating. This indeed was often the case with myself.

At last, when the ship we were in had got in all its cargo, they made ready with many fearful noises. We were all put under deck, so that we could not see how they managed the vessel. But this disappointment was the least of my sorrow. The closeness of the place and the heat of the climate, added to the number of people in the ship, which was so crowded that each had scarcely room to turn himself, almost suffocated us. This . . . brought on sickness amongst the slaves, of which many died. This wretched situation was aggravated by the rubbing of the chains, the shrieks of the women, and the groans of the dying, all of which rendered the whole a scene of horror almost inconceivable. Often did I think many of the inhabitants of the deep much more happy than myself.

One day, when we had a smooth sea and moderate wind, two of my countrymen who were chained together (I was near them at the time), preferring death to such a life of misery, somehow made through the nettings and jumped into the sea. Immediately, another dejected fellow, who on account of his illness had been allowed out of irons, also followed their ex-

ample. I believe many more would very soon have done the same if they had not been prevented by the ship's crew, who were instantly called.

At last we came in sight of the island of Barbados, at which the whites on board gave a great shout and made many signs of joy to us. We did not know what to think of this; but as the vessel drew nearer, we plainly saw the harbor and other ships of different kinds and sizes; and we soon anchored amongst them off Bridge-Town. Many merchants and planters now came on board, though it was in the evening. They put us in separate parcels and examined us attentively. They also made us jump and pointed to the land, signifying we were to go there. We thought by this we should be eaten by these ugly men, as they appeared to us. And, when soon after we were all put down under the deck again, there was so much dread and trembling among us and bitter cries to be heard all the night from these apprehensions that at last the white people got some old slaves from the land to pacify us. They told us we were not to be eaten, but to work, and were soon to go on land, where we should see many of our countrypeople. This report eased us much; and sure enough, soon after we landed there came to us Africans of all languages.

We were not many days in the merchant's custody before we were sold after their usual manner, which is this:—On a signal given (as the beat of a drum) the buyers rush at once into the yard where the slaves are confined, and make choice of that parcel they like best. The noise and clamor and the eagerness of the buyers serve not a little to increase the apprehension of the terrified Africans. In this manner, without scruple, are relations and friends separated, most of them never to see each other again.

Adapted from *The Interesting Narrative of the Life of Olaudah Equiano, or Gustavus Vassa, the African* by Olaudah Equiano (W. Durell, 1791).

Critical Thinking

1. What kind of impression did the sight of the slave ship make on Equiano?

2. Describe the conditions on the slave ship.

3. What evidence is there that some African slaves preferred death to slavery? Why might some people prefer death to slavery?

■■■■ ★ ■■■■

CHAPTER 7

Northwest Passage

KENNETH ROBERTS

Kenneth Roberts' exciting historical novels of colonial life gained him a wide readership. In Northwest Passage, *set mainly in New York State, Roberts uses the French and Indian War as a backdrop. A high-spirited young artist named Langdon Towne has been thrown out of Harvard College. He signs on with the forces of Robert Rogers, who has vowed to wipe out the Indian village of St. Francis in French Canada. In the following passage, "Rogers' Rangers" approach the village.*

When we had carried the boats a hundred yards to dry earth and packed their lockers with provisions we'd use after our return, we hid them beneath screens of pine. I had expected Canada to be cold, but the marshy forest steamed with a breathless sultry heat. Clouds of mosquitoes rose from the swamp whining and singing about our heads. With every breath, we drew them into our throats, and coughed and spat mosquitoes. . . .

No sooner were the boats hidden than he [Rogers] paraded us. Possessed of a de-mon of impatience, he was up and down our lines and everywhere, urging us to move faster, and the same time strapping on his knapsack and blanket, hanging his belt with hatchet and corn-meal bag. He hovered around us like a persistent bee, tweaking knapsack straps, shaking powder-horns, looking at moccasins.

To me he said, to be noted in my orderly book, "I'm leaving two Indians on the high land to watch the boats—Lieutenant Solomon and Konkapot. They'll stay here till we come back, unless the French find the boats. In that case Solomon and Konkapot'll come after us to bring the report."

As the men jostled into position, fastening the last of their equipment to their belts, Sergeant Bradley hustled me into place behind Ogden and beside Jesse Beacham. Captain Jacobs and eight of his Stockbridge Indians, stripped to the waist and covered with grease and paint, ran ahead to act as advance scouts and stopped at the end of the high land to look back at us.

"Follow the lake shore to the northeastern tip of Missisquoi Bay," Rogers called up and down the lines. "That's our meeting place in case we have to scatter. We'll strike inland there. Until we're out of the swamps, we'll march abreast."

He looked from one end of his tiny army to the other, and I saw a hint of a dubious smile appear upon his heavy lips, as if we were only partly to his liking. From neck to thigh we were hung with clumsy equipment. Our labors in the heat and dampness had given us a sweaty and raffish look, and splashed us with mud and water; and some had even rubbed themselves with mud to protect themselves from mosquitoes. No wonder Rogers wore that dubious smile.

The advance guard of Indians ranged forward, vanished, and then the long advance of the rest of us began. We struck wet ground at once, of course, and plodded into it. I hoped that we might pass it soon, and that my breeches, unlike poor Bradley's, might remain upon me. Through the dense trees, to our left, we caught glimpses of blue Missisquoi Bay, as cool and tranquil as we were hot and uncomfortable. . . .

When, at dusk, we reached a dry ridge, he gave the word to camp for the night. The straps of my blanket and knapsack had cut me like iron bands, and to sit down was torture, but to get up was worse.

I stood there watching Rogers; wondering how he did it. He had Bradley and Lieutenant Farrington, and with their help had hoisted himself to the lower branches of a tall spruce.

He went up it like a big squirrel, almost to the top, and clung there, peering back along our route. There was nothing, no exertion or hardship, he couldn't bear and be fresh at the end of it.

Through the dull fatigue that numbed me, his thick voice, mumbling to Ogden, was the last thing I heard at night, and it was that same thick voice that, in the morning, awakened me to a wet blanket and aching joints.

I can hear him now, shouting to the officers: "Get 'em up! They got ten minutes to get started! Get 'em up! Get 'em up!"

From *Northwest Passage* by Kenneth Roberts. Copyright 1936, 1937 by Kenneth Roberts. Reprinted by permission of Doubleday, Inc., a division of Bantam Doubleday Dell Publishing Co.

Critical Thinking

1. What difficulties did the men encounter as they approach the enemy village?
2. Why did Rogers wear a "dubious smile"?
3. Although Rogers' force was on its way to attack an Indian village, he was accompanied by Indians as well. Explain why this was so.
4. How did the narrator regard Rogers?

CHAPTER 8
Johnny Tremain
ESTHER FORBES

Johnny Tremain, by Esther Forbes, tells the story of a fourteen-year-old apprentice silversmith in Boston during the early years of the American Revolution. Johnny becomes a spy for the Committee of Public Safety, a Patriot group preparing to fight the British. In the excerpt below, Johnny pumps a stablehand for information about a British plan to stop the Patriots.

This very night—come darkness—the men would move, but in what direction? And who would be in charge of the expedition? Surely not more than one of the colonels would be sent.

Johnny, who had his own colonel to watch, Colonel Smith, hardly left the Afric Queen all day and helped the pot-boy serve drinks to the officers in the dining room. A young officer sitting with Stranger did say, as he stirred his brandy-and-water with his thumb, that he hoped before long thus to stir Yankee blood—and what of that? Colonel Smith did have an army chaplain to dine with him that day. Did that mean he was suddenly getting religious, as people are said to before they go into danger?

Of one thing Johnny was sure. Dove knew much less than he did. Dove was so thick-witted he had no idea anything unusual was afoot. He honestly believed that the grenadiers and light infantry were merely going to be taught "new evolutions." As usual, Dove was too wrapped in his own woes to think much of what was happening about him.

By five Johnny thought he would leave the Queen and report to Paul Revere that he had discovered nothing new. First one more glance at Dove.

For once he found him hard at work, his lower lip stuck out, his whitish pig-lashes wet. He was polishing a saddle.

"That guy," he complained, "hit me for nothing. He said I was to get to work on his campaign saddle."

"Who's he?"

"Colonel Smith, of course."

"Did you do as he told you?"

"I tried. I didn't know he had two saddles. So I went to work on the usual one. I shined it until you can see your face in it. And he takes it out of my hands and hit me on the head with it. Says I'm a stupid lout not to know the difference between a parade saddle and a campaign saddle. How'd I know? Why, he's been over here about a year and that campaign saddle hasn't ever been unpacked. I had to get it from Lieutenant Stranger. How'd I know?"

Johnny said nothing. He realized he had heard something which conceivably might be important. Careful . . . careful . . . don't you say anything to scare him.

"Where's your polish? I'll help with the stirrups."

The instant Johnny went to work, Dove as usual lay back on the hay.

"One of the stirrups wrapped 'round my head. Cut my ear. It bled something fierce."

Johnny was studying the saddle on his knees. It was of heavy black leather, brass (not silver) mountings. Three girths instead of two. All sorts of hooks and straps for attaching map cases, spy-glasses, flasks, kits of all sorts.

Colonel Smith is going on a campaign. But perhaps not. He might merely be riding down to New York.

He leaned back on his heels. "Say, what if you and I took time out to eat supper? The Queen's cook has promised me a good dinner because I helped them at table this afternoon. Roast goose. I'll fix it so you can get in on it, too."

"Oh for goodness' sake—no."

"It's past five o'clock. Colonel can't be going anywhere tonight."

"Oh for land's sake, Johnny, he says I'm to show him that saddle by six sharp, and if he don't like its looks he's going to cut me to mincemeat. He's always saying things like that. He's the . . ."

Johnny did not listen to what Colonel Smith was. He was thinking.

"Well after that—when Colonel Smith has settled down to play whist. Can you get off?"

"Tonight isn't like any other night. He told me to bring Sandy around for him, fed and clean and saddled with this old campaign saddle by eight o'clock tonight . . ."

Colonel Smith is going on a long journey. Starting tonight at eight. It might be a campaign. He had an idea.

"I should think if the Colonel was making a long trip he'd take Nan, she's so light and easy to ride . . . if he has far to go."

"He does like her better—she don't jounce his fat so. He always rides her 'round Boston. But only yesterday he had Lieutenant Stranger take her over to the Common when the men were drilling. Stranger says she still is squirmy when she hears drums and shooting. I heard him say so."

"Oh." Drums and shooting. This was not to be a peaceful ride to, say, New York. His cloth whipped over the black saddle leather. He spat on it and rubbed even harder. The one thing he must not say was the wrong thing. Nothing was better than the wrong thing. So for a while he said nothing.

"Sandy's good as gold, but he's an old horse and a little stiff. His front left leg won't last forever."

"Colonel Smith didn't say he was going off on him forever."

This did not help much. But Dove went on:

"He and the horse doctor and Lieutenant

Stranger were all looking at him just this morning. The horse doctor said, old Sandy could do thirty miles easy. And Stranger said no, he wouldn't swear you could get Nan on and off a boat without her fussing."

So . . . the campaign would start around eight that night. The Colonel's horse would be put on and off a boat. There would be a risk at least of drums and shooting. They were not going farther than thirty miles. Those men who thought the target of the expedition was going to be Lexington and Concord were right. And it would be Colonel Smith who would go in command.

All Johnny's hidden excitement went into his polishing. The brass mountings turned to gold. The black leather to satin.

"There! You take that in and show your Colonel!"

But he would wait one moment more, Dove might have something more to say when he came back after he had seen the Colonel. . . .

Dove came back in a jubilee.

"Colonel says I've done a fine job and so quick he's going to give me tomorrow as a holiday. He don't expect to get back before night." Certainly this campaign was going to be a short one—if everything went as the British expected.

From *Johnny Tremain* by Esther Forbes. Copyright 1943 by Esther Forbes Hoskins. Copyright © renewed 1971 by Linwood M. Erskine, Jr., Executor of the Estate. Reprinted by permission of Houghton Mifflin Co.

Critical Thinking

1. What was the significance of the colonel's choice of saddles?
2. Did Johnny get Dove to talk by asking direct questions? Explain.
3. What was the destination of the British march?
4. What was Johnny going to do with the information he obtained from Dove?

CHAPTER 9
Sarah Bishop
SCOTT O'DELL

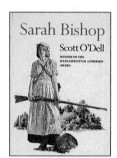

Sarah Bishop describes the experiences of a young girl named Sarah Bishop during the Revolutionary War. Sarah lives on a farm on Long Island, New York with her father, a Loyalist, and her brother, Chad. In the passage below, Sarah and her father stand by their house as shots come from a nearby mill.

"Why is Quarme shooting at us?" I asked.

"He's not shooting at us," my father said. "He's shooting in our direction. Just to remind us."

"Of what?"

"That he owns a new firelock. That he's for the revolution. That he's hot to run King George and all his men out of the country. And that he knows we are against the revolution and for King George."

Another bullet went over, no closer than the others, but it seemed closer. I thought it would be a good idea if we got ourselves in the house until Quarme was through shooting, but my father didn't move. He was a tall man with a gaunt face and a long, stubborn chin, which he rubbed when he was thinking hard.

He stood there rubbing his chin until the shooting stopped. Then he went off to the house without saying a word. . . .

The day was streaming hot, even for August; even the breeze from the sea was hot. So I started the fire in the firebox outside, where it was cooler than inside the house, and mixed up some cakes, using the fish Chad had caught, red-eared corn we had raised and the fresh milk.

Father came in when he couldn't see to work any longer; Chad was late from the tavern.

Father was worried. "He's been coming late the last week."

"The tavern is full, Chad says, running over with travelers from everywhere."

"Mostly from Boston," Father said. "They ran Admiral Howe out of the city, clean up to Halifax, but some of the wiser ones figure that he'll return one of these days soon, this time with the whole British navy in back of him, and make mincemeat out of all the so-called patriots."

Father was bitter about the rebellion. He talked a lot about it and brooded over it when he wasn't talking. We had a drawing of King George with his crown on and a long jeweled robe. It hung on the wall above my father's bed, and every morning and evening he would stand stiff in front of the picture and raise his hand and salute like a soldier, although he had never been one in his life nor ever planned to be.

That was up to three weeks ago, before the picture disappeared. Father blamed Chad for taking it down. When Chad said he hadn't and swore on the Bible, Father still didn't believe him. They didn't speak to each other for a whole day. Then my brother finally admitted that he had put the picture of King George in the fire.

"I've been learning things up at the tavern," Chad said. "For one thing, it's a good idea to keep your mouth shut about the feelings you have."

"A man should do what he wants in his own home," Father said. "Hang a picture of the devil on the wall, if he wants to."

"If one of the patriots happened to walk in here and see a picture of King George sitting up there on the wall, it would be all over the countryside by next day noon."

"Also a man should stand up for what he thinks, not mince around."

"That's what old man Somers over in Hempstead tried to do. He called John Adams a windbag. The patriot boys heard about it and went over and burned his pigsty. They told him that unless he minded his ways, they'd come back and burn his barn."

Father gave Chad a sharp look. "You're not getting scared? You're not changing over, are you? I'm not going to wake up one morning to find you've joined the Skinners."

The Skinners were gangs of young men who went around burning people's property and wanted to hang King George from the nearest tree. I knew that Chad had several friends who belonged to the Skinners. Likewise, that he was not so strong against the rebellion as Father was. In fact, he had told me once that he didn't believe in being taxed by a king who lived thousands of miles away.

I put the fishcakes on the trestle with a bowl of tomato sauce and lit the lamp.

Father sat down and said grace. Then he said to Chad, "You're sure you are just being cautious, not changing your mind about the war?"

Chad put a whole fishcake in his mouth and was silent. . . .

"No, just being sensible," Chad said, talking around the fishcake. "I'm trying to keep out of trouble with the Skinners and the rest of the patriots."

It was quiet for a while. Then from the direction of Purdy's mill came a bang, and after a moment a whistling sound, like a long sigh, passed over the house.

Chad got up and turned out the lamp and we sat in the dark.

From *Sarah Bishop* by Scott O'Dell. Copyright © 1980 by Scott O'Dell. Reprinted by permission of Houghton Mifflin Co.

Critical Thinking

1. Why did Chad burn the king's portrait?
2. What was his father's reaction?
3. How are the Patriots presented?
4. How did the conflict between Patriots and Loyalists affect Sarah's family?

CHAPTER 10
The Trees
CONRAD RICHTER

*After the Northwest Ordinance of 1787 answered the question of how the land west of the Appalachians was to be governed, hardy settlers crossed the mountains and traveled down the Ohio River. In the 1940s, Conrad Richter wrote three historical novels—*The Trees, The Fields, *and* The Town—*telling the story of a pioneer family in Ohio in the early 1800s. In this scene from the first book,* The Trees, *we meet the Lucketts: Worth and Jary (who is ill), with their children Sayward, Genny, Achsa, Wyitt, and Sulie. A shortage of wild game has forced them to leave their Pennsylvania home.*

Now they had crossed the Ohio on a pole ferry and the mud on their feet was no longer the familiar red and brown earth of Pennsylvania. It was black like dung. The young ones were wild over tramping the same trace [trail] their father had tramped as a boy with Colonel Boquet. Here was where the army sheep had to be shut in for the night and here where the soldiers had axed the trace wider to let the army train through. It was a country of hills and Jary had said she could breathe again like on those mortal sweet hills of Pennsylvania. Now that those hills were so far behind her, it was easier to give them up. Perhaps it wouldn't be so bad out here like she thought. What was the use of living in the same state as your folks if you never saw them anyhow?

They rounded a high ridge. A devil's race-course cleared the air of limbs below. Here was something Worth had not told them about.

For a moment Sayward reckoned that her father had fetched them unbeknownst to the Western ocean and what lay beneath was the late sun glittering on green-black water. Then she saw that what they looked down on was a dark, illimitable expanse of wilderness. It was a sea of solid treetops broken only by some gash where deep beneath the foliage an unknown stream made its way. As far as the eye could reach, this lonely forest sea rolled on and on till its faint blue billows broke against an incredibly distant horizon.

They had all stopped with a common notion and stood looking out. Sayward saw her mother's eyes search with the hope of finding some settlement or leastwise a settler's clearing. But over that vast solitude no wisp of smoke arose. Though they waited here till night, the girl knew that no light of human habitation would appear except the solitary red spark of some Delaware or Shawnee campfire. Already the lowering sun slanted melancholy rays over the scene, and as it sank, the shadows of those far hills reached out with long fingers.

It was a picture Sayward was to carry to her grave, although she didn't know it then. In later years when it was all to go so that her own father wouldn't know the place if he rose from his bury hole, she was to call the scene to mind. This is the way it was, she would say to herself. Nowhere else but in the American wilderness could it have been.

The sun was gone now. Far out they heard the yelping of a wolf and nearer the caterwauling of a panther. Worth stood leaning on his long Lancaster rifle, his nose wrinkling like a hound's.

"You kin smell the game!" he said hungrily.

Sayward sniffed. All she could wind was the scent of wild herbs and leaves mingled with the faint strange fetor [stench] of ranker, blacker earth than she knew in

Pennsylvania. She looked at her brother and sisters. They stood with young eyes drinking in this place, and it was plain as if drawn on shellbark that what they saw were otters coasting down muddy slides and gray moose crashing through the woods and fat beaver cracking down their broad tails on gat water [a narrow channel] like pistol shots. They could see skins drying on the log walls of a cabin yet unbuilt and skins in a heavy pack on their father's shoulders and skins handed over the counter of a trader's post along the Scioto or Ohio where the shelves hung heavy with black and white English blankets, Turkey red calico, bolts of Merrimac blue, shawls with fringes, brass bound muskets and buckets of white beads.

"We might even git rich and have shoes!" Sulie spoke out.

That broke the tension. They all looked down on her and smiled. Little Ursula, the baby of the family, the one they gave in to the most. . . .

It seemed strange the next few days when Sayward recollected the vision and realized that now they were down under that ocean of leaves. A red-tailed hawk screeching high over the tree-tops would hardly reckon there was a road down here. You had to be a porcupine rooting under the branches to find it or the black cat of the forest that could see in the dark and that some called the fisher fox.

This place, Jary quavered to Sayward, must be the granddaddy of all the forests. Here the trees had been old men with beards when the woods in Pennsylvania were still whips [saplings]. Sayward watched her mother puttering along between the great shaggy butts [stumps] that dipped with moss and moisture. All day she could see Jary's sunken eyes keep watching dully ahead for some sign that they might be coming out under a bit of sky.

Down in Pennsylvania you could tell by the light. When a faint white drifted through the dark forest wall ahead, you knew you were getting to the top of a hill or an open place. You might come out in a meadow or clearing, perhaps even in an open field with the corn making tassels and smelling sweet in the sun. But away back here across the Ohio, it had no fields. You tramped day long and when you looked ahead, the woods were dark as an hour or a day ago.

Sayward could feel the woods most when the time came to step a few feet into the brush. Sometimes Sulie or Genny ran in after her. Sometimes she went alone. The family bobbed on in single file and in a lick or two the forest had swallowed them up. While she waited here with the green leaves brushing her skin, with the monster brown trunks close enough to touch and all around her those wild unkept graves of ancient windfalls, she minded what her father had once told her.

He had been tramping in the black forest when he felt it. He was a grown man and had followed the woods since he was a boy, and yet something came over him in those dark pines and hemlocks where the sun never came so that he wanted to run. He had hardly seen even a piney squirrel all day, and he saw nothing afterwards.

"I was so afeared I broke out into a sweat," he said.

Two hunters from the West Branch told him they knew what he meant. What made it they didn't know. It came over them no place but the deep woods. When pressed, Worth reckoned it might be a panther following his scent, for panthers were curious about humans. . . .

But Sayward had a feeling her father hadn't said what lay deepest in his mind. Alone here in these woods sometimes she could feel it. The trace was gone as if it had never been. The only roads were the deer paths. . . . They coaxed you to come on. . . . But well she knew that once she followed, they would twist and turn and circle on themselves and peter out in the middle of some swamp. Nothing moved in here. Even the green daylight stood still. The moss was thick and soft as a pallet. It invited you to lay down, and yet Sayward's feet wanted to run.

"It's nothin' but the woods fever," she would tell herself. . . .

From *The Trees* by Conrad Richter. Copyright 1940 and renewed 1968 by Conrad Richter. Reprinted by permission of Alfred A. Knopf, Inc.

Critical Thinking

1. In what way did the deep woods make Ohio seem very different from the Lucketts' home in Pennsylvania?

2. Do you think, from this selection, that the Lucketts are among the earliest pioneers or are going to a settlement? Why?

3. What resources of the new country seem most important to the children?

CHAPTER 11
Miracle at Philadelphia
CATHERINE DRINKER BOWEN

In Miracle at Philadelphia, *written in 1966, historian Catherine Drinker Bowen retells the events surrounding the writing and ratification of the Constitution. The following selection describes the battle between Federalists and Antifederalists at the Virginia ratifying convention, attended by such famous names as James Madison, James Monroe, Patrick Henry, John Marshall, and Edmund Randolph.*

While New Hampshire met and adjourned and delayed, Virginia was holding her convention at Richmond, in the new Academy on Shockoe Hill. The country looked to the Old Dominion, wondering which way she would go. Virginia's territory reached to the Mississippi; it included the District of Kentucky and West Virginia. Her population was a fifth of the population of the entire Union. Should Virginia ratify, she would be the ninth state, or so she thought; New Hampshire's final vote was still three weeks away. If Virginia refused, New York, North Carolina and Rhode Island would doubtless follow her lead. This was to be the ablest of all the ratification conventions and the best prepared, a gathering studded with stars, with names and faces known throughout the state and beyond—well-speaking gentlemen on both sides, well-dressed, wellborn. More than a fourth were military men. . . . They had fought the British, they had fought the Indians, and in political conviction they were ranged on both sides. . . .

Chief among Antifederalists was Patrick Henry, tall, thin, stooped, and at fifty-two looking on himself as aged and broken in health. He wore spectacles, concealed his reddish-brown hair by a brown wig, not too well-fitting. His blue eye was still keen, his long face alive with feeling; the old magic waited to be called up at will. "I fear that overwhelming torrent, Patrick Henry," wrote General Knox to Rufus King when the convention was well under way.

From the first day, Henry was the nerve center of the room. "The Henryites," they called his followers. Every Federalist came girded against them. And the Federalist ranks were impressive. . . .

Among the stars and the patriot orators, it was Edmund Randolph who supplied the prime shock and surprise of the convention. The handsome young Governor was much beloved in his state. The great part he had played in Philadelphia was known to many; his refusal to sign the Constitution had become common knowledge; the *Virginia Gazette* in January,

1788, carried a letter with his reasons. But since then, Randolph had begun to waver; already he had been attacked in a newspaper for inconsistency. Yet no one knew for certain what the Governor's final decision would be. . . .

On June fourth, the first day of full debate, the Governor rose and made his declaration. It took him some time to reach his point. Plainly on the defensive, Randolph said he had not come hither to apologize. . . . He was not a candidate for popularity. . . . If the Constitution were put before him as in Philadelphia—wholly to adopt or wholly to reject—he would again refuse his signature. But Massachusetts had urged amendments to be enacted by Congress *after* full ratification. For himself, he had originally been for *previous* amendments, to be approved by the several states before they ratified. But the postponement of this convention to so late a date made this impossible, "without inevitable ruin to the Union." Eight states had adopted the Constitution; they could not recede. He stood, then, to express his earnest endeavors for a firm, energetic government, and to concur in any practical scheme of amendments. Randolph, in short, was for the Constitution.

From this day on, no matter how it was argued, the base of difference between Federalists and Antifederalists in the Virginia convention would be "previous amendments" or "subsequent amendments"—whether the Constitution should be ratified as it stood, with amendments to be enacted later; or whether new state conventions should be called to alter the document before ratification.

From *Miracle at Philadelphia: The Story of the Constitutional Convention, May to September 1787* by Catherine Drinker Bowen. Copyright © 1966 by Catherine Drinker Bowen. Reprinted by permission of Little, Brown & Co.

Critical Thinking

1. Why was Virginia's vote for ratification so important?

2. Why was Randolph's behavior a surprise to the other Virginians?
3. What was the argument between Federalists and Antifederalists regarding the question of amendments to the Constitution?
4. What were the historical results of this debate regarding adding amendments to the Constitution?

──── ★ ────

CHAPTER 12
The Glorious Conspiracy
JOANNE S. WILLIAMSON

In The Glorious Conspiracy, *Joanne S. Williamson tells the story of an orphaned British immigrant, Benjamin Brown, who makes his way in New York City in the 1790s. Brown works for a printer, Thomas Greenleaf, owner of the newspaper* Argus. *In the selection below, Brown finds himself threatened by the Alien and Sedition Acts because the* Argus *opposes the policies of the Federalists in power.*

The bells rang in the new year of 1798. It drew on into spring and another summer, and one morning I came into the office of the *Argus* to find Mr. Greenleaf reading over something he had written. He looked up as I entered and said: "Ben, what would you say if I told you it was time for us to part company?"

I stared at him, aghast.

"Why do you ask me, sir? Don't I give satisfaction?"

"No, no, Ben, it's nothing like that. Here's your answer." He slapped the paper he held. "I wrote it up just now. The

Alien Act has been signed into law. You know what that means?"

"Yes, sir," I said. "It means that no one can become a citizen now for fourteen years. And that anyone not a citizen can be arrested and deported from the country without a hearing."

"So you see?" said Mr. Greenleaf. "You're a Britisher, Ben. And the *Argus* is a journal that don't support Federalists. Don't you see? Hamilton's been saying that all British journalists that supported Jefferson ought to be deported, that they're dangerous revolutionaries. It matters none to him that most of them are refugees, that they'll wind up in Botany Bay if they're sent home."

"But I'm a printer's apprentice," I said. "I never wrote any political articles."

"'Without a hearing,' the law says. And they're setting their sights now on the opposition journals. Have you read their new Sedition Act? How it's a criminal offense to print or publish criticism of the President and Congress or to foster opposition to their acts?"

He banged his fist on the desk.

"These Federalists! These tyrants! They have us now for sure. Their bully boys at the polls and their property laws against the voters weren't enough for them. Now it's a crime to speak against them. Was this why we fought the lobsterbacks?" He sighed and brushed his hand across his forehead. "Well, that's neither here nor there. My point is, it'd be safer for a lad like you, and an alien, to break off with us. You're learning to be a gentleman. It's all ahead of you. Don't spoil it."

I stared at him. I felt as if I were seeing him for the first time.

"Mr. Greenleaf," I said. "I need the money. And I'm not ashamed of the *Argus*. If it's all the same to you, we'll say no more about it."

From *The Glorious Conspiracy* by Joanne S. Williamson. Copyright © 1961, renewed © 1989 by Joanne S. Williamson. Reprinted by permission of the author.

Critical Thinking

1. Explain why the Federalists supported the Alien and Sedition Acts.
2. How was Ben threatened by the Alien and Sedition Acts? How was Mr. Greenleaf threatened by those laws?
3. What did Greenleaf mean by "property laws against the voters"?
4. Do you agree with Ben's decision? Explain your answer.

━━━━ ★ ━━━━

CHAPTER 13
Great River

PAUL HORGAN

The selection below, like the literature excerpt for Chapter 1, comes from Great River, *by Paul Horgan. This selection deals with the many tasks of a woman on the American frontier.*

When she wasn't cooking she was working toward cloth at her spinning wheel or loom; or making new garments; or mending old ones. It was said on the frontier that the first thing a young man did was to get him a wife so's to have her make him some clothes. When she wasn't sewing she was teaching the children their ABC's, and how to read, and how to cipher [add and subtract], and who the Lord Jesus was, and where their grandparents were, and what America was, and how a living was made. She had very little money and needed no more, for her husband obtained goods by trade; and what money they had was enough to pay the government, "as there were no unreasonable taxes." The mother told her young ones of what was dangerous in the surrounding country—wolves, snakes, big cats, bears. She made it plain that not all Indians were to be feared, for many went by on camping and hunting trips, and though queer and with outlandish notions, and a shock to see with all the cranky nakedness they showed, many of them were almost friends. She spoke of other kinds, of whom all had heard, who came with brand and scream and arrow and stolen rifle, to kill all who lived in a cabin like hers. Thinking of it, she raised her head, and put her hand under her children's chins and made them raise theirs, and said that fear was no excuse not to stay where you wanted to stay if you did no harm there, and bore your share of work. There were days when she even found time to surprise the children with a cornhusk doll, dressed and painted, or a rag doll that she had made for the girls; for the boys, perhaps a little horse made of twigs and a spool, or a toy bear stuffed with pine needles, or a beanbag, or a buckskin ball worked and worked until its seams met just right to create the sphere.

She kept her girls by her till late; her boys she lost early. The boys had hardly a cubhood. They went from boy to man; for as soon as their bodies were lengthening and filling to meet physical toil, they were ready to do a man's work; and were granted leave to do it. None could read the prickling thoughts of a youth or guess where they would turn him. The father watched his sons come to independence; and he saw this with pride, as an extension of the national ideal of equality and democratic opportunity. If the son wanted to stay at home to work, he was welcome; he was equally at liberty to do what many did at fourteen or fifteen—make a bundle of what he owned, take a rifle from the family's armory, and with a sweet bloom of ignorance on his confident face, go out on his own to a still farther West than the one he grew up in. He went with trading trains, or trapping parties, or with exploring expeditions of the Army, or joined a wild and dissolute crew of rivermen; and what he learned he measured by the gaunt, strong image of life to which he was born in the forest clearing, where in little he saw the community of work that in the large held America together. Everyone worked, and no job for man or woman was high or low, but all were respectable if honest. No one was embarrassed to work for pay. The President himself was paid.

From *Great River: The Rio Grande in North American History* by Paul Horgan (Farrar Straus Giroux Inc.). Copyright © 1984 by Paul Horgan. Reprinted by permission of Benjamin Keen.

Critical Thinking

1. Why did frontier women not need much money? What was money needed for?
2. What potential dangers were there on the frontier?
3. What kinds of work away from home might young men do?
4. Explain what Horgan meant by "the community of work that . . . held America together."

━━━ ★ ━━━

CHAPTER 14

Jubilee
MARGARET WALKER

Jubilee, *a novel by Margaret Walker, was written in 1966. It tells the story of the author's own ancestors, including Vyry, a slave on a Georgia plantation belonging to "Marse John" and his wife, "Big Missy."*

Early in the spring of 1851 a fairly well-developed plot for an uprising among the slaves of Lee County, with the assistance of free Negroes and white abolitionists, became known to the High Sheriff of the county. How the news began to leak

649

out and through what sources could not be determined by most Negroes. In the first place, the slaves on Marse John's plantation were not fully informed as to what nature the plot took nor how an uprising could take place. Brother Zeke was so troubled that he confided to his flock at their regular meeting place at the Rising Glory Church that it must be a false rumor since no definite plans had ever come to his knowledge. It was first suspected, however, by the guards . . . and the drivers, who claimed that the Negroes were unusually hard to manage. And the neighboring whites claimed there were unusual movements in town among strange whites and in the county among free Negroes. At first the planters were not suspicious and hardly dared believe the piece-meal information they received. Why would their slaves want to do such a thing?

As Big Missy said to Marse John, "They are all well treated, and we love them and take good care of them just like a part of our family. When they are sick we nurse them back to health. We feed and clothe them and teach them the Christian religion. Our nigras are good and wouldn't try such a thing unless some criminal minds aided and abetted them. . . ." Such monstrous activities were beyond the wildest imaginations of their good and happy childlike slaves!

Nevertheless, if there was such ingratitude lurking among them, after all the money that had been spent on food and clothes and doctor bills, the owners must be realistic and resort to drastic methods to counteract such activity. They must not wait too long to listen to reason. Hastily and secretly, Marse John and his planter friends gathered with this purpose. There they decided, as their drivers had suggested, that the first thing was to seek out the culprits and see that they were punished to the full extent of the law, chiefly by hanging. Thus they would make an example of them and put the

fear of God in the rest of the slaves. Second, they must clamp down harder on the movements of all blacks, enforce the curfew laws and all of the Black Code, thereby rigorously maintaining control over their property, both land and chattel slaves. Finally, but not least, they must seek out all abolitionists guilty of giving aid and comfort to the black enemies of the Georgia people, and either force them out of the state or deal with them so harshly that they would willingly leave. As for the free Negroes, all of them should be called in for questioning and under threat of revoking their papers, forcing them back into slavery, they should be made to leave the state. Meanwhile, the planters should continue to question trusted slaves for any information and should keep watch for any signs of development of the plot or for any unusual movements of the slaves. The guards and patter-rollers were ordered to search the slave cabins to make sure no weapons or firearms of any kind came into the possession of any black person, slave or free.

May Liza and Caline told Vyry and Lucy and Aunt Sally, "Marster and Big Missy done taking to whisper and shush all the time."

"We act like we don't see nothing and don't hear nothing neither."

If any Negroes were caught in the woods or in the swamps they always said, "We's looking for greens and herbs for medicine and teas."

Many slaves, like Aunt Sally, had gardens around their cabins with collards growing almost into the door. These they cultivated when they did not go to the fields. But the tension was growing so they were forbidden any free activity. Marse John like his other planter friends redoubled his guards and patter-rollers and changed the curfew from nine o'clock to first dark or about one hour after sundown.

The growing tension exploded when the two Negro women accused of having killed their master and his mother by poisoning his food were convicted of murder and sentenced to be hanged. Like Aunt Sally and Vyry and Lucy, they worked in the kitchen of their Marster's Big House. When they were brought to county jail for trial one afternoon it was quickly decided that they were guilty and had confessed the crime so that nothing was left but to hang them as soon as a judge could set the time and a hangman nearby could be summoned to do the deed.

This episode created a great disturbance among both planters and slaves. Among the planters' families there was unmistakable panic, and among the slaves there was great fear. Mutual distrust hung in the air between blacks and whites. In addition to the recent increase of guards on his place, Marse John, at the request of Grimes, purchased three additional bloodhounds for his plantation.

One of the murders had been committed several months before the second crime and the women were not at first suspected but when the master died, a doctor confirmed suspicions expressed earlier when the man's mother died. The news traveled fast, and long before the date of the hanging had been set, the crime was common knowledge in every household.

The darkest day in Vyry's young life came without warning. Big Missy and Marse John had arranged to sell Aunt Sally. She would go first to Savannah and then by boat to New Orleans, where she would go on the auction block and be sold to the highest bidder. The morning she was ordered to go, she and Vyry went as usual to the kitchen. Big Missy came out in the kitchen after breakfast and told Aunt Sally to get her things together; there was a wagon in the backyard waiting to take her to Savannah. Now Aunt Sally was ready. She had her head-rag on and she had tied in a bundle the few things she had in the world including the few rags of clothes she wore. She had spread out one of her big aprons and tied them in it. Now she carried it in her arms. Tears were running down her fat black cheeks and she could not control her trembling lips. Vyry stood dazed and numb. Even when Aunt Sally hugged and kissed her, Vyry did not cry. She could not believe this was real, that she would be forced apart from Aunt Sally, that Aunt Sally was leaving and going somewhere. She heard Aunt Sally saying, "Goodbye, honey, don't yall forget to pray. Pray to God to send his chilluns a Moses; pray to Jesus to have mercy on us poor suffering chilluns. Goodbye, honey, don't you forget Aunt Sally and don't forget to pray. Aunt Sally know she ain't never gwine see yall no more in this here sinful world, but I'm gwine be waiting for you on the other side where there ain't gwine be no more auction block. Goodbye, honey-child, goodbye."

Even then Vyry's eyes were dry. But then she saw poor old Aunt Sally clinging to Sam and Big Boy. She heard her sobbing pitifully, "Oh Lord, when is you gwine send us that Moses? When you gwine set us peoples free? Jesus, how long? Marster, how long? They is taking all I got in the world from me, they is sending me way down yonder to that cruel auction block! Oh, Lord, how long is we gotta pray?" They were pulling her away but stumbling along crying and muttering she kept saying, "Oh, Lord, have mercy!"

Then Vyry found herself shaking like a leaf in a whirlwind. Salt tears were running in her mouth, and her short, sharp finger nails were digging in the palms of her hands. Suddenly she decided she would go with Aunt Sally, and just then Big Missy slapped her so hard she saw stars and when she saw straight again Aunt Sally was gone.

Critical Thinking

1. Why did Big Missy say her slaves would never want to rebel? Do you think she was right? Why or why not?

2. How did the slaveowners respond to rumors of an uprising?

3. How did Vyry react when Aunt was sold away? How did Aunt Sally react? Why, in your opinion, would slaveowners break up friendships and families in this way?

■■■■ ★ ■■■■

CHAPTER 15

Indian Legends of the Trail of Tears and Other Creek Stories

ELIZABETH SULLIVAN

Elizabeth Sullivan, a Creek Indian, collected the stories told to her by her great-grandmother and other older Creeks in the book Indian Legends of the Trail of Tears and Other Creek Stories. *The following passage is a story of a seven-year-old girl's experiences on the Trail of Tears.*

When the removal began Annakee could not understand all the changes taking place. She only knew her grandmother's eyes were bloodshot, her cheeks sunken, her lips cracked. Annakee held closely to her grandmother's hand as they walked on with so many Indians. Some she did not know. Everyone appeared fearful and sad. She saw many crying. Annakee began to suffer from irritating mosquito bites. She would scratch mercilessly until she bled. Her little legs were so tired and her feet ached.

At night she saw the stars in the sky that used to twinkle and shine like dew drops in the rainbow as her grandmother's tales had told about the mystery of the heavenly bodies. But tonight the stars appeared dim and seemed to be hiding from her as she looked up in the sky.

Annakee remembered her home. The corn crib was full of corn. They had plenty of dried fruit and meat. Her father and mother saw to that. Her two older brothers were hunting all of the time. They even knew how to shoot with bow and arrow to kill fish when they came up for air after shoe string roots had been pounded and put into the river up stream and a dam was made. . . .

"God lives, Creator of all things, be fearful and pray." They sang songs in whispers not audible to the soldiers who would camp nearby. The aroma of the soldiers' food reached them and hunger became almost unbearable.

Her grandmother was very stern and told her—"Learn never to cry, even if you are hurt or hungry. Never look back to see what is going on in the back." This she learned very quickly. . . .

In the dense forest Annakee saw strange birds, different-shaped leaves than she had ever seen. She asked her grandmother about it. Her grandmother held her very close by the campfire and told her that they had come far far away from home and they would never see their homeland and advised her to be brave and never cry.

From "Legend of the Trail of Tears" in *Indian Legends of the Trail of Tears and Other Creek Stories* as retold by Elizabeth Sullivan. Copyright © 1974 by Elizabeth Sullivan.

Critical Thinking

1. How did Annakee figure out that something was wrong?

2. What were the hardships of the Trail of Tears?

3. Why did Annakee's grandmother tell Annakee never to cry?

4. What did Annakee remember about her home? Why did she have that particular memory?

■■■■ ★ ■■■■

CHAPTER 16

The Narrative of the Life of Frederick Douglass

FREDERICK DOUGLASS

Frederick Douglass, born into slavery in 1818, eventually escaped. In the North, Douglass became a dedicated human rights activist. The following excerpts are taken from Douglass's autobiography. In the first passage, Douglass describes a scene from his childhood as a slave. The second selection details Douglass's first experiences as a free man in Massachusetts and his involvement with the antislavery movement.

My new mistress [Mrs. Auld] proved to be all she appeared when I first met her at the door,—a woman of the kindest heart and finest feelings. She had never had a slave under her control previously to myself, and prior to her marriage she had been dependent upon her own industry for a living. She was by trade a weaver; and by constant application to her business, she had been in a good degree preserved from the blighting and dehumanizing effects of slavery. I was utterly astonished at her goodness. I scarcely knew how to behave towards her. . . .

But, alas! this kind heart had but a short time to remain such. The fatal poison of irresponsible power was already in her hands, and soon commenced its infernal work. The cheerful eye, under the influence of slavery, soon became red with rage; that voice, made all of sweet accord, changed to one of harsh and horrid discord; and that angelic face gave place to that of a demon.

Very soon after I went to live with Mr. and Mrs. Auld, she very kindly commenced to teach me the A, B, C. After I had learned this, she assisted me in learning to spell words of three or four letters. Just at this point of my progress, Mr. Auld found out what was going on, and at once forbade Mrs. Auld to instruct me further, telling her, among other things, that it was unlawful, as well as unsafe, to teach a slave to read. To use his own words, further, he said, "If you give a [slave] an inch, he will take an ell. A . . . [slave] should know nothing but to obey his master—to do as he is told to do. . . . Now," said he, "if you teach . . . (speaking of myself) how to read, there would be no keeping him. It would forever unfit him to be a slave. He would at once become unmanageable, and of no value to his master. As to himself, it could do him no good, but a great deal of harm. It would make him discontented and unhappy." These words sank deep into my heart, stirred up sentiments within that lay slumbering, and called into an existence an entirely new train of thought. It was a new and special revelation, explaining dark and mysterious things, with which my youthful understanding had struggled, but struggled in vain. I now understood what had been to me a most perplexing difficulty—to wit, the white man's power to enslave the black man. It was a grand achievement, and I prized it highly. From that moment, I understood the pathway from slavery to freedom. It was just what I wanted, and I got it at a time when I least expected it. Whilst I was saddened by the thought of losing the aid of my kind mistress, I was gladdened by the invaluable instruction which, by the merest accident, I had gained from my master. Though conscious of the difficulty of learning without a teacher, I set out with high hope, and a fixed purpose, at whatever cost of trouble, to learn how to read.

* * *

I found employment, the third day after my arrival, in stowing a sloop with a load of oil. It was new, dirty, and hard work for me; but I went at it with a glad heart and a willing hand. I was now my own master. It was a happy moment, the rapture of which can be understood only by those who have been slaves. It was the first work, the reward of which was to be entirely my own. There was no Master Hugh standing ready, the moment I earned the money, to rob me of it. I worked that day with a pleasure I had never before experienced. I was at work for myself and newly-married wife. It was to me the starting-point of a new existence. When I got through with that job, I went in pursuit of a job of calking; but such was the strength of prejudice against color, among the white calkers, that they refused to work with me, and of course I could get no employment. Finding my trade of no immediate benefit, I threw off my calking habiliments [clothing], and prepared myself to do any kind of work I could get to do. . . .

In about four months after I went to New Bedford, there came a young man to me, and inquired if I did not wish to take the "Liberator." I told him I did; but, just having made my escape from slavery, I remarked that I was unable to pay for it then. I, however, finally became a subscriber to it. The paper came, and I read it from week to week with such feelings as it would be quite idle for me to attempt to describe. The paper became my meat and my drink. My soul was set all on fire. Its sympathy for my brethren in bonds—its scathing denunciations of slaveholders—its faithful exposures of slavery—and its powerful attacks upon the upholders of the institution—sent a thrill of joy through my soul, such as I had never felt before!

I had not long been a reader of the "Liberator," before I got a pretty correct idea of the principles, measures and spirit of the anti-slavery reform. I took right hold of the cause. I could do but little; but what I could, I did with a joyful heart, and never felt happier than when in an anti-slavery meeting. I seldom had much to say at the meetings, because what I wanted to say was said so much better by others. But, while attending an anti-slavery convention at Nantucket, on the 11th of August, 1841, I felt strongly moved to speak, and was at the same time much urged to do so by Mr. William C. Coffin, a gentleman who had heard me speak in the colored people's meeting at New Bedford. It was a severe cross, and I took it up reluctantly. The truth was, I felt myself a slave, and the idea of speaking to white people weighed me down. I spoke but a few moments, when I felt a degree of freedom, and said what I desired with considerable ease. From that time until now, I have been engaged in pleading the cause of my brethren—with what success, and with what devotion, I leave those acquainted with my labors to decide.

From *The Narrative of the Life of Frederick Douglass, an American Slave* by Frederick Douglass (Anti-Slavery Office, 1845).

Critical Thinking

1. How did Douglass explain Mrs. Auld's kind treatment of him at first? How did becoming a slaveholder affect Mrs. Auld?
2. Why did Douglass attach so much importance to learning to read?
3. Describe the positive and negative experiences Douglass had while working in the North.
4. How did his experience as a slave continue to enslave Douglass even after he gained his freedom?

★ AMERICAN LITERATURE ★

CHAPTER 17
Texas

JAMES MICHENER

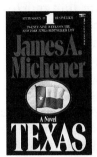

One of the most widely read novelists of the twentieth century, James Michener uses his lucid narrative style to present vast amounts of detailed information on various cultures. Among his best-known works is Texas *(1985). In the following passage, Michener explains some of the changes to place names that came about in the early days of the Republic of Texas.*

In the social life of the republic there were subtle changes. People began dropping the name Texican; they became Texians. Spanish accents on some words were eliminated and names simplified so that the old Béjar became Bexar; Bexar became San Antonio. The Río Grande lost its accent, and all other ríos lost not only their accent but also their Spanish designation; henceforth they would be rivers. The lovely word *arroyo* became *creek*. As if to symbolize the transition from Spanish lyricism to Kentucky realism, poetic family names like Treviño became Trevino for the anglos and the music was lost.

To facilitate administration, counties had to be established, and in time almost all the heroes participating in the battles were honored by having counties named after them: Austin, Bonham, Bowie, Crockett, Fannin, Houston, Lamar, Rush, Travis; and all but Travis also had towns named in their honor. To the delight of future schoolchildren, Deaf Smith's county would retain his full name.

The names of certain famous places also became enshrined as counties: Bexar, Goliad, Gonzales and Victoria, with San Jacinto following later. The first-named was awarded an area much larger than many European nations; from Bexar County, in decades to come, well over a hundred normal-sized counties would be carved.

By this lavish display of honors Texas served notice that it took its history seriously and sought to enshrine its nobler moments. Massachusetts and Virginia produced many national leaders, but they did not become the warp and woof of existence as did the heroes of Texas; Pennsylvania had its Valley Forge and New York its Saratoga, but they never became a living part of their region's religion the way the Alamo did in Texas. From the start new Texians proclaimed, and in a rather loud voice: 'Look at us. We're different.'

Among the counties formed in the first flush of victory was one named after Zave Campbell, whose exploits atop the wall were recited by both Señora Mordecai Marr and Joe, the Negro slave belonging to Colonel Travis, both of whom were spared by Santa Anna. Both told of Zave's Ajax-like defense, but the most telling testimony came from a Mexican captain, who said: 'There was this tall old man whose name was called out as I bore down upon him. "Xavier! Watch out!" someone shouted as I ran him through, and when we counted the dead bodies of our soldiers around his feet, there were nine.'

It was agreed that Xavier County should be established west of the Brazos River, but how the name should be pronounced was not so quickly settled. Older settlers who spoke Spanish wanted to call it Hah-vee-ehr, with accent on the last syllable, but newcomers promptly changed that to Ecks-ah-ver, with accent on the second. Within a few months it was agreed that the county was Za-veer, with a heavy accent on the second syllable, and so it became. Like many of the early counties, and like more than half of those that were to follow, Xavier County had no principal town; there was a miserable crossroads settlement of nine houses called Campbell, and it was designated the county seat, but it would never dominate thinking or become as important as the county it served. A settler rarely said: 'I live in Campbell.' He almost invariably said: 'I live in Xavier County.'

From *Texas* by James Michener. Copyright © 1985 by James Michener. Reprinted by permission of Random House, Inc.

Critical Thinking

1. How did Texas demonstrate that it took its history seriously?

2. In what subtle ways did Texas make a break from its Spanish past?

3. What is Michener's opinion about these changes? Explain.

4. Michener writes, "From the start new Texians proclaimed, and in a rather loud voice: 'Look at us. We're different.'" Does that attitude still hold true today? Explain.

■■■ ★ ■■■

CHAPTER 18

Two Years Before the Mast

RICHARD HENRY DANA, JR.

During the nation's westward expansion, American writers produced a literature of the frontier. Aristocratic New Englander Richard Henry Dana, Jr., wrote Two Years Before the Mast, *a classic account of American seafaring in the early 1800s. In this excerpt, Dana describes his ship's stopover in Monterey.*

It was a fine Saturday afternoon that we came to anchor, the sun about an hour high, and everything looking pleasantly. The Mexican flag was flying from the little square presidio, and the drums and trumpets of the soldiers, who were out on parade, sounded over the water, and gave great life to the scene. Everyone was delighted with the appearance of things. We felt as though we had got into a Christian (which in the sailor's vocabulary means civilized) country. . . .

The next day . . . we began trading. . . . For a week or ten days all was life on board. The people came off to look and to buy. . . . Our cargo was an assorted one; that is, it consisted of everything under the sun. We had spirits of all kinds (sold by the cask), teas, coffee, sugars, spices, raisins, molasses, hardware, crockery-ware, tin-ware, cutlery . . . shawls, scarfs, necklaces, jewelry, and combs for the women; furniture; and, in fact, everything that can be imagined, from Chinese fireworks to English cartwheels—of which we had a dozen pairs with their iron tires on.

The Californians are an idle, thriftless people, and can make nothing for themselves. The country abounds in grapes, yet they buy, at a great price, bad wine made in Boston and brought round by us. . . . Their hides, too, which they value at two dollars in money, they barter for something which costs seventy-five cents in Boston; and buy shoes (as like as not made of their own hides, which have been carried twice round Cape Horn) at three and four dollars. . . .

Every town has a presidio in its centre; or rather every presidio has a town built around it; for the forts were first built by the Mexican government, and then the people built near them, for protection. The presidio here was entirely open and unfortified. . . . Each town has a commandant . . . while two or three alcaldes and corregidores, elected by the inhabitants, are the civil officers. . . . No Protestant has any political rights, nor can he hold property, or, indeed, remain more than a few weeks on shore, unless he belong to a foreign vessel. Consequently, Americans and

English who intend to reside here, become Papists—the current phrase among them being, "A man must leave his conscience at Cape Horn."

But, to return to Monterey. The houses here, as everywhere else in California, are of one story, built of *adobes*. . . . The Indians . . . do all the hard work, two or three being attached to the better house[s]; and the poorest persons are able to keep one, at least, for they have only to feed them, and give them a small piece of coarse cloth. . . .

In Monterey there are a number of English and Americans . . . who have married Californians, become united to the Roman Church, and acquired considerable property. Having more industry, frugality, and enterprise than the natives, they soon get nearly all the trade into their hands. They usually keep shops, in which they retail the goods purchased in the larger quantities from our vessels, and also send a good deal into the interior, taking hides in pay, which they again barter with our ships. In every town on the coast there are foreigners engaged in this kind of trade, while I recollect but two shops kept by natives. The people are naturally suspicious of foreigners, and they would not be allowed to remain, were it not that they conform to the Church, and by marrying natives, and bringing up their children as Roman Catholics and Mexicans, and not teaching them the English language, that they quiet suspicion, and even become popular and leading men. The chief alcaldes in Monterey and Santa Barbara were Yankees by birth.

From *Two Years Before the Mast, A Personal Narrative of Life at Sea* by Richard Henry Dana, Jr. (Harper, 1840).

Critical Thinking

1. What prejudices are evident in Dana's observations of the Hispanic people of California?

2. What prejudices and class distinctions existed among the Californians?

3. Do Dana's attitudes reflect the idea of "manifest destiny"? Do you think he supported making California and Texas part of the United States? Explain.

━━━ ★ ━━━

CHAPTER 19

Incidents in the Life of a Slave Girl

HARRIET JACOBS

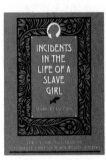

Fiery speeches, impassioned essays, and moving books such as Uncle Tom's Cabin *helped build antislavery sentiment before the Civil War. Abolitionist literature also included narratives by former slaves. With help from editor Lydia Maria Child, Harriet Jacobs published* Incidents in the Life of a Slave Girl *in 1861, disguising the names of people and places, and using the pseudonym of Linda Brent. It describes her life in the South, her seven years spent in hiding from her master, and her escape to the North and eventual freedom. The following scene describes her life in New York after passage of the Fugitive Slave Law.*

On my return from Rochester [to New York City], I called at the house of Mr. Bruce. . . . Mr. Bruce had married again, and it was proposed that I should become nurse to a new infant. I had but one hesitation, and that was my feeling of insecurity in New York, now greatly increased by the passage of the Fugitive Slave Law. However, I resolved to try the experiment. I was again fortunate in my employer. The new Mrs. Bruce was an American, brought up under aristocratic influences, . . . but if she had any prejudice against color, I was never made aware of it; and as for the system of slavery, she had a most hearty dislike of it. . . .

About the time that I reentered the Bruce family, an event occurred of disastrous import to the colored people. The slave Hamlin, the first fugitive that came under the new law, was given up by the bloodhounds of the North to the bloodhounds of the South. It was the beginning of a reign of terror to the colored population.

Many a poor washerwoman who, by hard labor, had made herself a comfortable home, was obliged to sacrifice her furniture, bid a hurried farewell to friends, and seek her fortune among strangers in Canada. Many a wife discovered a secret she had never known before—that her husband was a fugitive, and must leave her to insure his own safety. Worse still, many a husband discovered that his wife had fled from slavery years ago, and as "the child follows the condition of its mother," the children of his love were liable to be seized and carried into slavery.

All that winter I lived in a state of anxiety. When I took the children out to breathe the air, I closely observed the countenances of all I met. I dreaded the approach of summer, when snakes and slaveholders make their appearance. I was, in fact, a slave in New York, as subject to slave laws as I had been in a Slave State. Strange incongruity in a State called free!

Spring returned, and I received warning from the South that Dr. Flint [her owner] knew of my return to my old place, and was making preparations to have me caught. . . .

I immediately informed Mrs. Bruce of my danger, and she took prompt measures for my safety. . . .

I was sent into New England, where I was sheltered by the wife of a senator, whom I shall always hold in grateful remembrance. . . .

Some months after I returned from my flight to New England, I received a letter from [my grandmother], in which she wrote, "Dr. Flint is dead. He has left a distressed family. Poor old man! I hope he made his peace with God." . . .

. . . I thought to myself that she was a better Christian than I was, if she could entirely forgive him. . . . There are wrongs which even the grave does not bury. . . .

His departure from this world did not diminish my danger. He had threatened my grandmother that his heirs should hold me in slavery after he was gone; that I never should be free so long as a child of his survived. . . .

I kept close watch of the newspapers for arrivals. . . . Reader, if you have never been a slave, you cannot imagine the acute sensation of suffering at my heart, when I read the names of Mr. and Mrs. Dodge [Flint's daughter], at a hotel in Courtland Street. It was a third-rate hotel, and that circumstance convinced me of the truth of what I had heard, that they were short of funds and had need of my value, as *they* valued me; and that was by dollars and cents. . . . It was impossible to tell how near the enemy was. He might have passed and repassed the house while we were sleeping. He might at that moment be waiting to pounce upon me if I ventured out of doors. . . .

From *Incidents in the Life of a Slave Girl (Written by Herself)* by Harriet Jacobs (Linda Brent), edited by L. Maria Child (1861). Reproduced from the original, with an introduction by Valerie Smith (Oxford University Press, 1988).

Critical Thinking

1. What effect did the Fugitive Slave Law have even on slaves who had escaped safely to free states in the North?

2. Why would Jacobs have changed the names of real people and places when her book was published in 1861?

3. According to this account, what kind of treatment could southern slaves expect from northerners?

4. What explanation do you suppose the members of the Flint family would have given for their efforts to recapture Harriet Jacobs?

━━━━ ★ ━━━━

CHAPTER 20
The Slopes of War

NORAH A. PEREZ

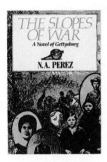

Norah Perez is the author of several historical novels. After visiting the national military park at Gettysburg, Pennsylvania, with her family, Perez decided to write a book about the Battle of Gettysburg. The result was The Slopes of War, *which describes the epic battle and its effect on the people of Gettysburg. Below is a passage from the novel, told from the viewpoint of the Confederate commander, Robert E. Lee.*

At Chambersburg General Lee tried to make sense out of the reports coming in to him. On Tuesday Pettigrew's men had headed into Gettysburg to find some desperately needed shoes; they had seen a few enemy uniforms and had reported back to General Heth. Convinced that what they had seen was probably the local militia, Heth had agreed to let Pettigrew return for the shoes the next morning. That was how it had started. Now a little skirmish had developed into something bigger.

As he pressed Traveller to reach Gettysburg quickly, Lee hoped that the Old Soldier's Disease, which was draining his energy, wouldn't be a nuisance to him much longer. He was feeling his age these days. It was as if his body, once fit and healthy and uncomplaining, nagged him for attention. First the heart and the troubling shortness of breath, and then this annoying dysentery. It worried him not to be in peak condition. A victory here and it was possible the war might end.

A. P. Hill, the commander of the Third Corps, was waiting, his bearded face blotched with red, twitching nervously above the collar of the crimson shirt he liked to wear into battle. He admitted that the brigades had met some surprising resistance on their shopping trip to town that morning. "But I have another division ready to go in and back up Heth. Dorsey Pender's men . . . good fellows." Hill was usually unsettled during military operations, but on this bright July morning Lee thought the man really looked quite ill as he repeated that he had men ready to go in. "With your permission, sir."

"Wait. Wait. . . ." Lee would not be rushed into this. He moved to and fro on his horse, listening to the familiar crack of muskets and the steady rumble of artillery, straining to understand what lay behind it. Heavy casualty reports were coming in now, and word had arrived that General Archer had been taken prisoner. In spite of his composure a hot cone of anger against his cavalry burned in his chest. No, he was not angry with them, but with his favorite, Jeb Stuart, the officer who had let him down. He had known that the marvelous man had flaws, that he was sometimes too buoyant and reckless, but this time he was unforgivably late, and Lee felt like a blinded man. He did not know what the danger was or where it was located. For all he knew, the soldiers scrambling through the woods and fields northwest of town might be involved with the whole Army of the Potomac. A spy had reported columns of the enemy in the area, but he knew he wasn't ready yet for a major encounter, not until all of his troops had arrived.

Hill said, "Just give me the word, sir. Pender will clear the road for us in no time."

"Not yet." The general never minded taking risks when he had to, but he refused to be stupid. "Let's wait and see just what it is we're up against."

And so a lull occurred, a little yawn in time, even as the snap of musketry went on and shells continued to burst and blossom white against the innocent blue sky. Time for parched soldiers to swallow tepid water and exhausted gun crews to reposition batteries and replenish ammunition, as a long slow scarf of yellow smoke drifted across the damaged ground.

Then, abruptly, things began to happen again. The murky puzzle that was baffling Lee came together sharply with a sudden shape and clear design. Five brigades of Rodes's division appeared north of the pike on Oak Hill in exactly the right position to swoop down on the tired blue troops that faced the west. If Pender drove in now with his fresh supports, and Rodes's men slammed down hard from the hill, the Union line would have to give. Integral parts clicked smoothly into place as if they had been planned. General Lee, his instincts for opportunity humming, gave the orders.

Yet Federal gears were whirring, too. The Eleventh Corps had just arrived, men fresh for battle hurrying double-quick along the pike and fanning out north of town. It was a hard luck unit, the scapegoat of the army because of its large number of immigrant recruits, but this time it was fortunate. The Confederates rushing down from Oak Hill came too fast, too eagerly, and the Eleventh hurled them back and forced them to regroup. Now the war machine boomed heavily across the landscape, knocking down fence rails, blasting wildflowers, smashing thousands of men under as it rumbled through the sultry summer afternoon.

From *The Slopes of War* by N. A. Perez. Copyright © 1984 by N. A. Perez. Reprinted by permission of Houghton Mifflin Co.

Critical Thinking

1. Why had Confederate troops gone into Gettysburg in the first place?
2. Why was Lee upset with Jeb Stuart? What did he need Stuart to do for him?
3. When did Lee finally give the orders for his troops to attack?

★

CHAPTER 21

The Deliverance

ELLEN GLASGOW

Novelist Ellen Glasgow grew up in Virginia during Reconstruction. Her realistic novels made her the first writer of the modern South. Her books described changes she had seen taking place: new styles in politics, the loss of family lands and fortunes, rivalry among social classes. The Deliverance shows some ironies of Reconstruction. For example, the former overseer now owns the Blake family mansion, while Christopher Blake works in the tobacco fields his family once owned. In this scene, Guy Carraway, a lawyer, visits Blake's shabby cottage and discovers that his elderly mother, now blind, is unaware of these changes.

From a rear chimney a dark streak of smoke was rising, but the front of the house gave no outward sign of life, and as there came no answer to his insistent knocks he [Carraway] at last ventured to open the door and pass into the narrow hall. From the first room on the right a voice spoke at his entrance, and following the sound he found himself face to face with Mrs. Blake in her massive Elizabethan chair.

"There is a stranger in the room," she said rigidly, turning her sightless eyes; "speak at once."

"I beg pardon most humbly for my intrusion," replied Carraway, conscious of stammering like an offending schoolboy, "but as no one answered my knock, I committed the indiscretion of opening a closed door."

Awed as much by the stricken pallor of her appearance as by the inappropriate grandeur of her black brocade and her thread lace cap, he advanced slowly and stood awaiting his dismissal.

"What door?" she demanded sharply, much to his surprise.

"Yours, madam."

"Not answer your knock?" she pursued, with indignation. "So that was the noise I heard, and no wonder that you entered. Why, what is the matter with the place? Where are the servants?"

He humbly replied that he had seen none, to be taken up with her accustomed quickness of touch.

"Seen none! Why, there are three hundred of them, sir. . . .

I don't think I ever had the pleasure of meeting a Carraway before."

"That is more than than probable, ma'am, but I have the advantage of you, since, as a child, I was once taken out upon the street corner merely to see you go by on your way to a fancy ball, where you appeared as Diana." . . .

"It was more than fifty years ago," murmured the old lady. . . . "The present is a very little part of life, sir; it's the past in which we store our treasures."

"You're right, you're right," replied Carraway, drawing his chair nearer the embroidered ottoman and leaning over to stroke the yellow cat; "and I'm glad to hear so cheerful a philosophy from your lips."

"It is based on a cheerful experience— I've been as you see me now only twenty years."

Only twenty years! He looked mutely round the soiled whitewashed walls, where hung a noble gathering of Blake portraits in massive old gilt frames. . . .

"Life has its trials, of course," pursued Mrs. Blake, as if speaking to herself. "I can't look out upon the June flowers, you know, and though the pink crape-myrtle at my window is in full bloom I cannot see it."

Following her gesture, Carraway glanced out into the little yard; no myrtle was there, but he remembered vaguely that he had seen one in blossom at the Hall.

"You keep flowers about you, though," he said, alluding to the scattered vases of June roses.

"Not my crape-myrtle. I planted it myself when I first came home with Mr. Blake, and I have never allowed so much as a spray of it to be plucked."

. . . Recalling herself suddenly, her tone took on a sprightliness like that of youth.

"It's not often that we have the pleasure of entertaining a stranger in our out-of-the-way house, sir—so may I ask where you are staying—or perhaps you will do us the honour to sleep beneath our roof. It has had the privilege of sheltering General Washington."

"You are very kind," replied Carraway. . . "but to tell the truth, I feel that I am sailing under false colours. The real object of my visit is to ask a business interview with your son. I bring what seems to me a very fair offer for the place."

Grasping the carved arms of her chair, Mrs. Blake turned the wonder in her blind eyes upon him.

"An offer for the place! Why, you must be dreaming, sir! A Blake owned it more than a hundred years before the Revolution."

At the instant, understanding broke upon Carraway like a thundercloud, and as he rose from his seat it seemed to him that he had missed by a single step the yawning gulf before him. . . . He looked up to meet, from the threshold of the adjoining room, the enraged flash of Christopher's eyes. So tempestuous was the glance that Carraway . . . squared himself to receive a physical blow; but the young man . . . came in quietly and took his stand behind the Elizabethan chair.

"Why, what a joke, mother," he said, laughing; "he means the old Weatherby farm, of course. The one I wanted to sell last year, you know."

"I thought you'd sold it to the Weatherbys, Christopher."

"Not a bit of it—they backed out at the last; but don't begin to bother your head about such things; they aren't worth it. And now, sir," he turned upon Carraway, "since your business is with me, perhaps you will have the goodness to step outside."

With the feeling that he was asked out for a beating, Carraway turned for a farewell with Mrs. Blake. . . .

"Business may come later, my son," she said, detaining them by a gesture of her heavily ringed hand. "After dinner you may take Mr. Carraway with you into the library . . .; meanwhile, he and I will resume our very pleasant talk which you interrupted. He remembers seeing me in the old days when we were all in the United States, my dear."

Christopher's brow grew black, and he threw a sharp and malignant glance of sullen suspicion at Carraway, who summoned to meet it his most frank and open look. . . .

"You may assure yourself," he [said] softly, "that I have her welfare very decidedly at heart."

At this Christopher smiled back at him. . . .

"Well, take care, sir," he answered and went out . . . while Carraway applied himself to a determined entertaining of Mrs. Blake.

To accomplish this he found that he had only to leave her free, guiding her thoughts with his lightest touch into newer channels. . . . Everywhere he felt her wonderful keenness of perception—that intuitive understanding of men and manners which had kept her for so long the reigning belle among her younger rivals.

As she went on he found that her world was as different from his own as if she dwelt upon some undiscovered planet. . . . She lived upon lies, he saw, and thrived upon the sweetness she extracted from them. For her the Confederacy had never fallen, the quiet of her dreamland had been disturbed by no invading army, and the three hundred slaves, who had in reality scattered like chaff before the wind, she still saw in her cheerful visions tilling her familiar fields. It was as if she had fallen asleep with the great blow that had wrecked her body, and had dreamed on steadily throughout the years. . . . In her memory there was no Appomattox, news of the death of Lincoln had never reached her ears, and president had peacefully succeeded president in the secure Confederacy in which she lived. Wonderful as it all was, to Carraway the most wonderful thing was the intricate tissue of lies woven around her chair. Lies—lies—there had been nothing but lies spoken within her hearing for twenty years.

From *The Deliverance,* by Ellen Glasgow (Doubleday, Page & Co., 1904).

Critical Thinking

1. What clues are given to the Blake family's former wealth?

2. What did Mrs. Blake mean when she referred to "the old days when we were all in the United States"?

3. What did Mrs. Blake believe was the outcome of the Civil War?

4. Would a northerner after the Civil War have behaved toward Mrs. Blake in the same way that Carraway, a southern lawyer, did? Why or why not?

CHAPTER 22

Through the Eye of the Needle

WILLIAM DEAN HOWELLS

The novelist William Dean Howells wrote around the beginning of the twentieth century in the midst of rapid social change. Howells was deeply concerned with questions of civil rights and economic equality. In two novels, Howells created the imaginary country of "Altruria" to reflect his vision of what America could be. In this excerpt from Through the Eye of the Needle, *Eveleth Strange, an American who has married an Altrurian named Aristides, describes her new country in a letter to a friend.*

It is no use my explaining again and again that in a country like this, where everybody works, nobody *over* works, and that when the few hours of obligatory labor [the "Obligatories"] are passed in the morning, people need not do anything unless they choose. . . .

I should say the Altrurians had artists' manners, free, friendly, and easy, with a dash of humor in everything, and a wonderful willingness to laugh and make laugh. Aristides is always explaining that the artist is their ideal type; that is, some one who works gladly, and plays as gladly as he works; no one here is asked to do work that he hates, unless he seems to hate every kind of work. When this happens, the authorities find out something for him that he had *better* like, by letting him starve till he works. . . .

As I have kept saying, I am a great curiosity everywhere, and I could flatter myself that people were more eager to see me than to hear Aristides. Sometimes I couldn't help thinking that they expected to find me an awful warning, a dreadful example of whatever a woman ought not to be, and a woman from capitalistic conditions *must* be logically. . . . They generally asked if I would like to go back to America, and when I said No, they were delighted beyond anything. They said I must become a citizen and vote and take part in the government, for that was every woman's duty as well as right; it was wrong to leave the whole responsibility to the men. They asked if American women took no interest in the government, and when I told them there was a very small number who wished to influence politics socially . . . but without voting or taking any responsibility, they were shocked. . . .

I suppose you are anxious, if these letters which are piling up and piling up should ever reach you, or even start to do so, to know something about the Altrurian cities, and what they are like. . . . There are no private houses here, in our sense—that is, houses which people have built with their own money on their own land, and made as ugly outside and as molestive to their neighbors and the passers-by as they chose. As the buildings belong to the whole people, the first requirement is that they shall be beautiful inside and out. There are a few grand edifices looking like Greek temples, which are used for the government offices, and these are, of course, the most dignified, but the dwellings are quite as attractive and comfortable. They are built round courts, with gardens and flowers in the courts, and wide grassy spaces round them. They are rather tall, but never so tall as our great hotels or apartment-houses, and floors are brought to one level by elevators, which are used only in the capitals; and generally speaking, I should say the villages were pleasanter than the cities. In fact, the village is the Altrurian ideal. . . .

Meanwhile, I must say the capitals are delightful: clean, airy, quiet, with the most beautiful architecture, mostly classic and mostly marble, with rivers running through them and round them, and every real convenience. . . . In the streets there are noiseless trolleys (where they have not been replaced by public automobiles) which the long distances of the ample ground-plan make rather necessary, and the rivers are shot over with swift motor-boats; for the short distances you always expect to walk, or if you don't expect it, you walk anyway. The car-lines and boat-lines are public, and they are free, for the Altrurians think that the community owes transportation to everyone who lives beyond easy reach of the points which their work calls them to.

Of course the great government stores are in the capitals, and practically there are no stores in the villages, except for what you might call emergency supplies. But you must not imagine, Dolly, that shopping, here, is like shopping at home. . . . That is, you don't fill your purse with bank-notes, or have things charged. You get everything you want, within reason, and certainly everything you need, for nothing. You have only to provide yourself with a card . . . which certifies that you belong to this or that working-phalanx, and that you have not failed in the Obligatories for such and such a length of time. If you are not entitled to this card, you had better not go shopping, for there is no possible equivalent for it which will enable you to carry anything away or have it sent to your house. At first I could not help feeling rather indignant when I was asked to show my work-card in the stores; I had usually forgotten to bring it, or sometimes I had brought my husband's card, which would not do at all, unless I could say that I had been ill or disabled, for a woman is expected to work quite the same as a man. Of course her housework counts, and as

we are on a sort of public mission, they count our hours of travel as working-hours, especially as Aristides has made it a point of good citizenship for us to stop every now and then and join in the Obligatories when the villagers were getting in the farm crops or quarrying stone or putting up a house. I am never much use in quarrying or building, but I come in strong in the hay-fields or the apple orchards or the orange groves. . . .

You must worry into the idea somehow that in Altruria you cannot buy anything except by *working,* and that work is the current coin of the republic: you pay for everything by drops of sweat, and off your own brow, not somebody else's brow. The people built these monuments and colonnades, and aqueducts and highways and byways, and sweet villages and palatial cities with their own hands, after the designs of artists, who also took part in the labor. But it was a labor that they delighted in so much that they chose to perform it during the Voluntaries, when they might have been resting, and not during the Obligatories, when they were required to work. So it was all joy and all glory. They say there never was such happiness in any country since the world began.

From *Through the Eye of the Needle,* by W. D. Howells (Harper & Brothers, 1907)

Critical Thinking

1. What were the Obligatories in Altrurian life?

2. What was shopping like for the people of Altruria?

3. How were Altrurian cities different from American cities?

4. On the basis of this excerpt, what things in his own society do you think Howells wanted to change?

Atlas, Gazetteer, and Reference

The United States

CITIES AND STATES

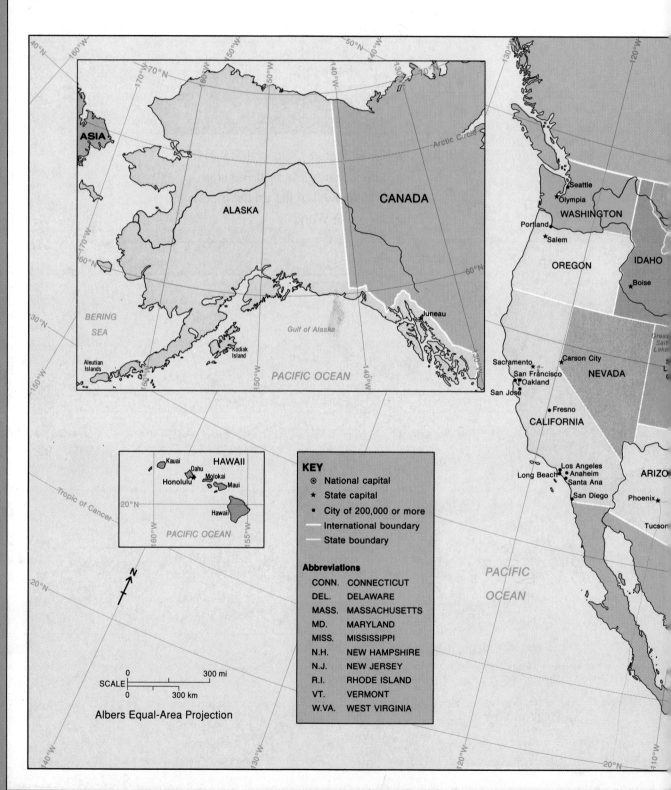

ASIA

ALASKA

CANADA

BERING
SEA

Gulf of Alaska

Juneau

Aleutian
Islands

Kodiak
Island

PACIFIC OCEAN

Arctic Circle

Seattle
★Olympia
WASHINGTON
Portland
★Salem

OREGON

IDAHO
★Boise

Great
Salt
Lake

Sacramento
San Francisco   ★Carson City
Oakland
San Jose   NEVADA

• Fresno

CALIFORNIA

Los Angeles
Long Beach   • Anaheim   ARIZO
Santa Ana
San Diego   Phoenix★

Tucson

PACIFIC

OCEAN

HAWAII
Kauai
Oahu
Honolulu   Molokai
Maui
Hawaii

Tropic of Cancer

PACIFIC OCEAN

KEY
⊙ National capital
★ State capital
• City of 200,000 or more
— International boundary
— State boundary

Abbreviations

CONN.	CONNECTICUT
DEL.	DELAWARE
MASS.	MASSACHUSETTS
MD.	MARYLAND
MISS.	MISSISSIPPI
N.H.	NEW HAMPSHIRE
N.J.	NEW JERSEY
R.I.	RHODE ISLAND
VT.	VERMONT
W.VA.	WEST VIRGINIA

N

0   300 mi
SCALE
0   300 km

Albers Equal-Area Projection

The United States

PHYSICAL FEATURES

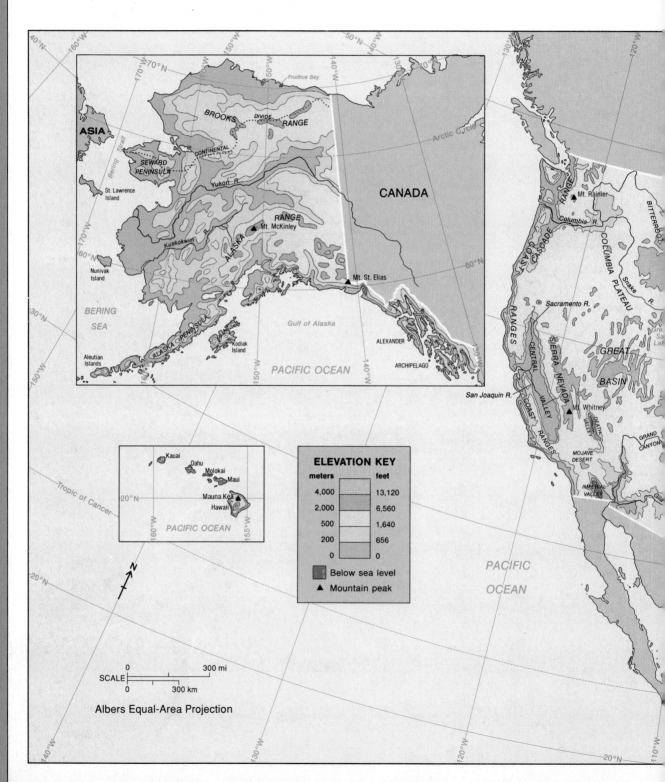

ASIA

BROOKS _DIVIDE_ RANGE

Prudhoe Bay

Arctic Circle

CANADA

CONTINENTAL

SEWARD
PENINSULA

Yukon R.

St. Lawrence
Island

RANGE
Mt. McKinley

Kuskokwim

ALASKA

60°N

60°N

Nunivak
Island

Mt. St. Elias

BERING
SEA

Gulf of Alaska

ALASKA PENINSULA

Kodiak
Island

ALEXANDER

ARCHIPELAGO

Aleutian
Islands

PACIFIC OCEAN

Mt. Rainier

Columbia R.

COAST RANGE

CASCADE

BITTERROOT

COLUMBIA PLATEAU

Snake R.

Sacramento R.

Gre
Sal
Lak

GREAT

BASIN

San Joaquin R.

COAST RANGES

CENTRAL VALLEY

SIERRA NEVADA

DEATH VALLEY

Mt. Whitney

GRAND
CANYON

MOJAVE
DESERT

IMPERIAL
VALLEY

Gila

Kauai

Oahu

Molokai
Maui

Mauna Kea
Hawaii

20°N

PACIFIC OCEAN

Tropic of Cancer

ELEVATION KEY

meters		feet
4,000		13,120
2,000		6,560
500		1,640
200		656
0		0

Below sea level

▲ Mountain peak

PACIFIC

OCEAN

N

SCALE

0   300 mi

0   300 km

Albers Equal-Area Projection

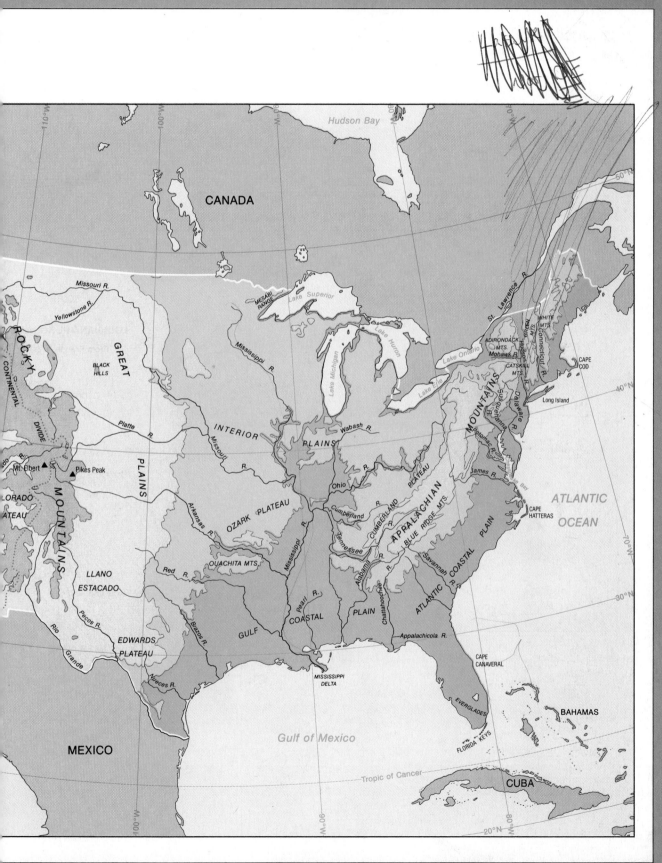

CANADA

Hudson Bay

Missouri R.

Yellowstone R.

R O C K Y

GREAT

BLACK
HILLS

CONTINENTAL

DIVIDE

Platte

Mt. Elbert

Pikes Peak

PLAINS

COLORADO

PLATEAU

M O U N T A I N S

LLANO

ESTACADO

Pecos R.

Rio

Grande

EDWARDS

PLATEAU

Nueces R.

Brazos R.

Red R.

Arkansas R.

OUACHITA MTS.

OZARK PLATEAU

Mississippi R.

Missouri R.

INTERIOR

PLAINS

Wabash R.

Ohio

Cumberland

Tennessee

MESABI
RANGE

Lake Superior

Lake Michigan

Lake Huron

Lake Ontario

Lake Erie

Mississippi R.

St. Lawrence

ADIRONDACK
MTS.

Mohawk R.

CATSKILL
MTS.

WHITE
MTS.

Connecticut R.

Hudson R.

Susquehanna R.

Delaware R.

Potomac R.

James R.

CUMBERLAND
PLATEAU

BLUE RIDGE MTS.

A P P A L A C H I A N

M O U N T A I N S

Long Island

CAPE
COD

CAPE
HATTERAS

ATLANTIC

OCEAN

Alabama R.

Pearl R.

Chattahoochee

GULF

COASTAL

PLAIN

Savannah R.

ATLANTIC COASTAL PLAIN

Appalachicola R.

MISSISSIPPI
DELTA

CAPE
CANAVERAL

EVERGLADES

FLORIDA KEYS

MEXICO

Gulf of Mexico

BAHAMAS

Tropic of Cancer

CUBA

50°N

40°N

30°N

20°N

110°W

100°W

90°W

80°W

70°W

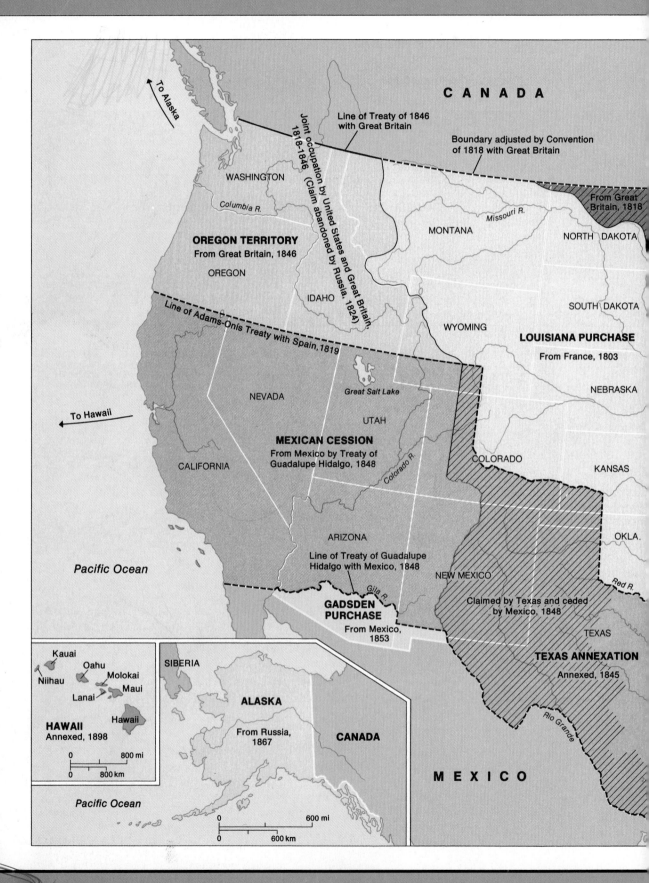

CANADA

Line of Treaty of 1846
with Great Britain

Boundary adjusted by Convention
of 1818 with Great Britain

To Alaska

Joint occupation by United States and Great Britain,
1818-1846 (Claim abandoned by Russia, 1824)

WASHINGTON

Columbia R.

From Great
Britain, 1818

MONTANA

Missouri R.

NORTH DAKOTA

OREGON TERRITORY
From Great Britain, 1846

OREGON

IDAHO

SOUTH DAKOTA

WYOMING

LOUISIANA PURCHASE
From France, 1803

Line of Adams-Onís Treaty with Spain, 1819

Great Salt Lake

NEBRASKA

To Hawaii

NEVADA

UTAH

MEXICAN CESSION
From Mexico by Treaty of
Guadalupe Hidalgo, 1848

COLORADO

KANSAS

CALIFORNIA

Colorado R.

OKLA.

ARIZONA

Line of Treaty of Guadalupe
Hidalgo with Mexico, 1848

NEW MEXICO

Red R.

Pacific Ocean

Gila R.

GADSDEN
PURCHASE
From Mexico,
1853

Claimed by Texas and ceded
by Mexico, 1848

TEXAS

TEXAS ANNEXATION
Annexed, 1845

Kauai

Oahu

SIBERIA

Rio Grande

Niihau

Molokai

Lanai

Maui

ALASKA

HAWAII
Annexed, 1898

Hawaii

From Russia,
1867

CANADA

0   800 mi

0   800 km

MEXICO

Pacific Ocean

0   600 mi

0   600 km

★ ATLAS ★

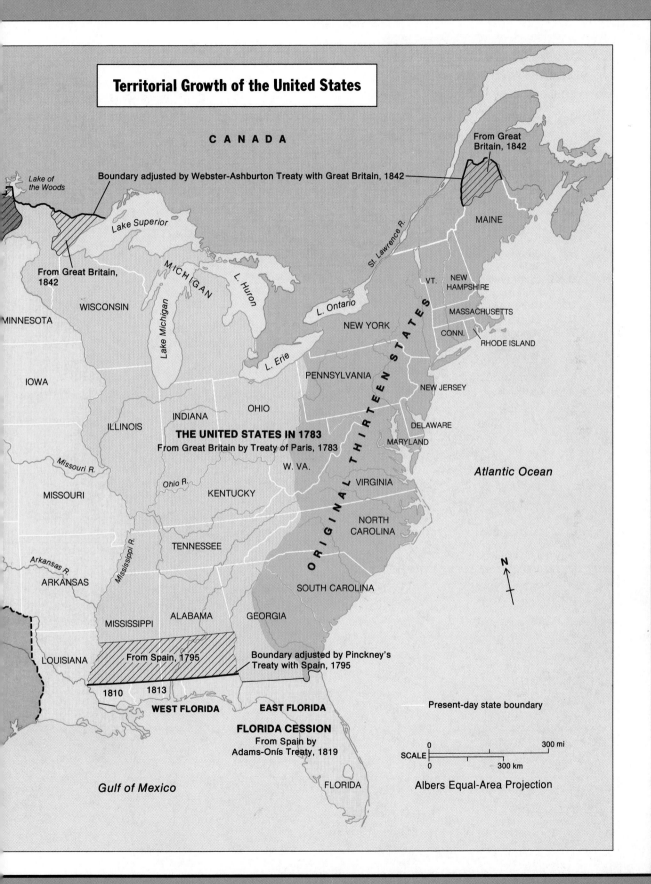

Territorial Growth of the United States

C A N A D A

From Great
Britain, 1842

Boundary adjusted by Webster-Ashburton Treaty with Great Britain, 1842

Lake of
the Woods

Lake Superior

MAINE

From Great Britain,
1842

MICHIGAN

L. Huron

St. Lawrence R.

VT.

NEW
HAMPSHIRE

WISCONSIN

Lake Michigan

MINNESOTA

L. Ontario

NEW YORK

MASSACHUSETTS

CONN.

RHODE ISLAND

IOWA

L. Erie

PENNSYLVANIA

NEW JERSEY

ILLINOIS

INDIANA

OHIO

DELAWARE

THE UNITED STATES IN 1783
From Great Britain by Treaty of Paris, 1783

MARYLAND

W. VA.

Atlantic Ocean

Missouri R.

MISSOURI

Ohio R.

KENTUCKY

VIRGINIA

O R I G I N A L   T H I R T E E N   S T A T E S

NORTH
CAROLINA

Arkansas R.

TENNESSEE

ARKANSAS

Mississippi R.

SOUTH CAROLINA

N

MISSISSIPPI

ALABAMA

GEORGIA

LOUISIANA

From Spain, 1795

Boundary adjusted by Pinckney's
Treaty with Spain, 1795

1810   1813

WEST FLORIDA   **EAST FLORIDA**

Present-day state boundary

FLORIDA CESSION
From Spain by
Adams-Onís Treaty, 1819

SCALE

0   300 mi

0   300 km

Gulf of Mexico

FLORIDA

Albers Equal-Area Projection

★ A T L A S ★

NATIONS OF THE WORLD

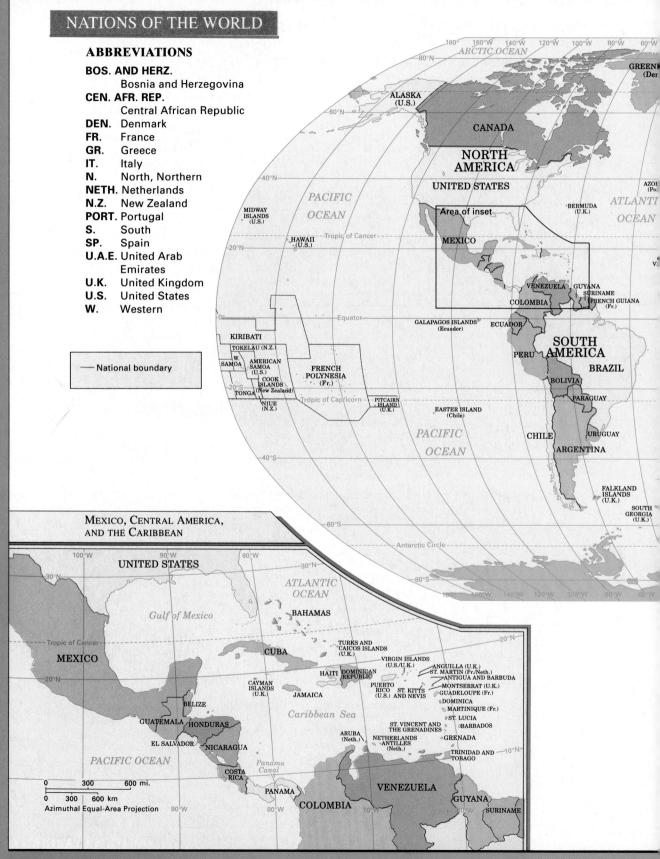

ABBREVIATIONS

BOS. AND HERZ.
    Bosnia and Herzegovina
CEN. AFR. REP.
    Central African Republic
DEN. Denmark
FR. France
GR. Greece
IT. Italy
N. North, Northern
NETH. Netherlands
N.Z. New Zealand
PORT. Portugal
S. South
SP. Spain
U.A.E. United Arab
    Emirates
U.K. United Kingdom
U.S. United States
W. Western

—— National boundary

ARCTIC OCEAN
80°N
GREENL
(Der
ALASKA
(U.S.)
60°N
CANADA
NORTH
AMERICA
UNITED STATES
40°N
PACIFIC
OCEAN
Area of inset
BERMUDA
(U.K.)
ATLANTI
OCEAN
MIDWAY
ISLANDS
(U.S.)
AZOI
(Po.
Tropic of Cancer
20°N
HAWAII
(U.S.)
MEXICO
VENEZUELA
GUYANA
SURINAME
COLOMBIA
FRENCH GUIANA
(Fr.)
0°
Equator
GALAPAGOS ISLANDS
(Ecuador)
ECUADOR
V
KIRIBATI
TOKELAU (N.Z.)
W.
SAMOA
AMERICAN
SAMOA
(U.S.)
FRENCH
POLYNESIA
(Fr.)
PERU
SOUTH
AMERICA
BRAZIL
20°S
COOK
ISLANDS
(New Zealand)
BOLIVIA
TONGA
NIUE
(N.Z.)
PITCAIRN
ISLAND
(U.K.)
PARAGUAY
Tropic of Capricorn
EASTER ISLAND
(Chile)
URUGUAY
CHILE
40°S
PACIFIC
OCEAN
ARGENTINA
FALKLAND
ISLANDS
(U.K.)
SOUTH
GEORGIA
(U.K.)
60°S
Antarctic Circle
80°S
160°W 140°W 120°W 100°W 80°W 60°W

MEXICO, CENTRAL AMERICA, AND THE CARIBBEAN

100°W
UNITED STATES
90°W
80°W
30°N
ATLANTIC
OCEAN
Gulf of Mexico
BAHAMAS
Tropic of Cancer
MEXICO
CUBA
TURKS AND
CAICOS ISLANDS
(U.K.)
20°N
VIRGIN ISLANDS
(U.S./U.K.)
ANGUILLA (U.K.)
ST. MARTIN (Fr./Neth.)
ANTIGUA AND BARBUDA
HAITI
DOMINICAN
REPUBLIC
CAYMAN
ISLANDS
(U.K.)
PUERTO
RICO
(U.S.)
ST. KITTS
AND NEVIS
MONTSERRAT (U.K.)
GUADELOUPE (Fr.)
BELIZE
JAMAICA
DOMINICA
MARTINIQUE (Fr.)
GUATEMALA
HONDURAS
Caribbean Sea
ST. LUCIA
ST. VINCENT AND
THE GRENADINES
BARBADOS
EL SALVADOR
ARUBA
(Neth.)
NETHERLANDS
ANTILLES
(Neth.)
GRENADA
NICARAGUA
PACIFIC OCEAN
Panama
Canal
TRINIDAD AND
TOBAGO
10°N
COSTA
RICA
0 300 600 mi.
0 300 600 km
PANAMA
VENEZUELA
GUYANA
Azimuthal Equal-Area Projection
90°W
COLOMBIA
80°W
70°W
SURINAME

★ A T L A S ★

672

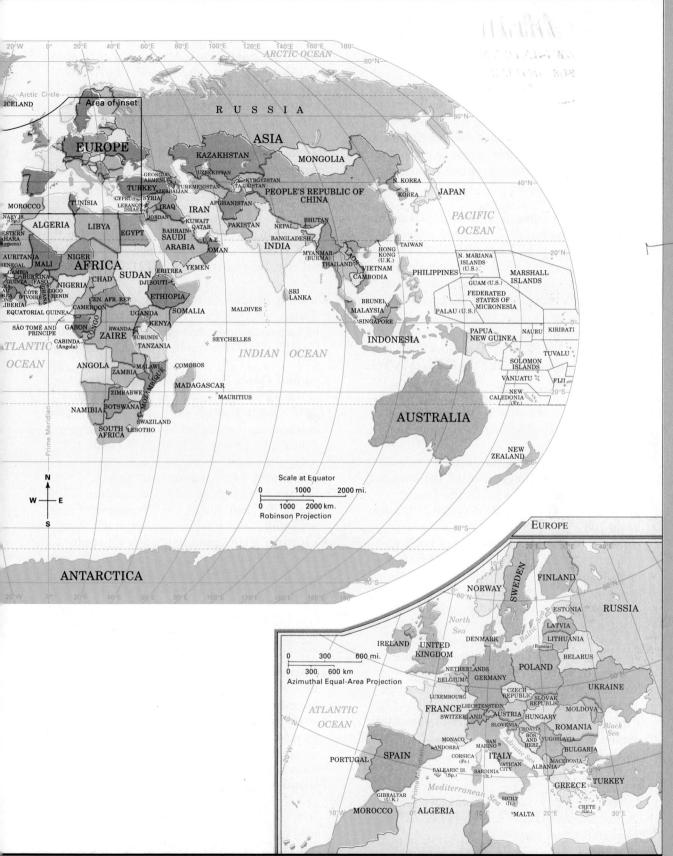

Gazetteer

The gazetteer provides information about important places and geographical features in this book. Entries include a short description, a reference to the text page on which the entry is discussed, and a reference to the map on which the place appears. Latitudes and longitudes are approximate, and for large areas (e.g. countries) they are generally a central point.

A

Alabama 22nd state, known as the Heart of Dixie, from Indian tribe *Alibamu* meaning "I open (I clear) the thicket." Capital city: Montgomery (32°N 86°W) *map, page 667*

Alamo Texan-held mission captured by the Mexicans in 1836. (29°N 93°W) *page 441; map, page 446*

Alaska largest state in United States, bought from Russia for $7,200,000 or about two cents per acre. Capital city: Juneau (58°N 134°W) *map, page 666*

Albany city on the Hudson River connected to Buffalo and the west by the Erie Canal in 1825. (42°N 73°W) *page 353; map, page 352*

Appalachian Mountains eastern United States mountain range, marked the boundary of white settlement as set in the Proclamation of 1763. (36°N 82°W) *page 171; map, page 108*

Appomattox Courthouse site of Lee's surrender to Grant. (37°N 79°W) *page 521; map, page 521*

Arizona 48th state, from Indian word *arizonac* probably meaning "little spring"; nicknamed the Grand Canyon State. Capital city: Phoenix (33°N 112°W) *map, page 666*

Arkansas part of territory acquired from France in 1803 in Louisiana Purchase. Capital city: Little Rock (34°N 92°W) *map, page 667*

Atlanta city in Georgia captured by northern forces in 1864. (33°N 84°W) *page 520; map, page 521*

B

Baltimore city where William Lloyd Garrison began his abolitionist career. (39°N 76°W) *page 416; map, page 407*

Barbary Coast North African states of Morocco, Algeria, Tunis, and Tripoli. (35°N 0°W) *page 324; map, page 324*

Bering Strait body of water separating Asia and North America. (66°N 170°W) *page 3; map, page 15*

Brazos River river near which the first Anglo-American settlement in Texas was built. (30°N 96°W) *page 434; map, page 446*

C

California territory colonized by Spain in the late 1700s, it gained statehood in 1850. Capital city: Sacramento (38°N 121°W) *map, page 666*

Canada country to the north of the United States, with which it has had a relationship of cooperation and friendship since the 1800s. Capital city: Ottawa (42°N 75°W) *map, page 672*

Cape of Good Hope name given to southern tip of Africa by the king of Portugal. (35°S 20°E) *page 32; map, page 32*

Charleston South Carolina port and important trading center. (32°N 80°W) *page 126; map, page 119*

Chihuahua Mexican city that was the final destination for most American traders on the Santa Fe Trail. (28°N 106°W) *page 430; map, page 456*

Colorado the Centennial State, Colorado was admitted to the Union in 1876, the centennial of the Declaration of Independence. Capital city: Denver (39°N 105°W) *map, page 667*

Columbia River great river that divides the states of Washington and Oregon. (46°N 120°W) *page 327; map, page 332*

Concord town near Boston where Patriot and British forces fought in 1775. (42°N 71°W) *page 181; map, page 180*

Confederate States of America new nation formed in 1861 when eleven southern states seceded from the Union. Capital city: Richmond (37°N 77°W) *page 492; map, page 500*

Connecticut colonial Connecticut was governed under the Fundamental Orders, the first written constitution. Capital city: Hartford (41°N 72°W) *map, page 667*

D

Delaware first state to approve the United States Constitution, on December 7, 1787. Capital city: Dover (39°N 75°W) *map, page 667*

Detroit city where William Henry Harrison landed in pursuit of the retreating British in 1813. (42°N 83°W) *page 340; map, page 344*

E

El Paso city in West Texas first founded as trading outpost between Santa Fe and Chihuahua. (31°N 106°W) *page 437; map, page 456*

Erie Canal important trade route between the Atlantic seaboard and the West, it created an all-water route from New York City to the Great Lakes. (43°N 75°W) *page 352; map, page 352*

F

Florida obtained from Spain by the Adams-Onís Treaty, it became the 27th state in 1845. Capital city: Tallahassee (30°N 84°W) *map, page 667*

Fort Duquesne name given to the fort at the Forks of the Ohio built by the French in 1754. (40°N 80°W) *page 158; map, page 152*

Fort Sumter United States fort in Charleston harbor attacked by Confederates, beginning the Civil War. (32°N 80°W) *page 494; map, page 508*

Fort Vancouver trading town in the Oregon Country. (45°N 123°W) *page 453; map, page 456*

G

Genoa Italian city-state where Columbus was born. (44°N 9°E) *page 33; map, page 30*

Georgia last of the thirteen colonies, it was named for England's King George II. Capital city: Atlanta (33°N 84°W) *map, page 667*

Gettysburg site of battle at which Union forces halted Confederate invasion of North; also where Lincoln delivered the Gettysburg Address. (40°N 77°W) *page 515; map, page 519*

Goliad location of a Mexican victory over Texan forces in 1836. (28°N 97°W) *page 443; map, page 446*

H

Haiti wealthy French colony in the Caribbean that imported African slaves to produce sugar and coffee. (18°N 73°W) *page 154; map, page 672*

Harpers Ferry site of United States arsenal in western Virginia attacked by John Brown in 1859. (39°N 77°W) *page 489; map, page 508*

Hawaii the 50th state, it is the only state not on mainland North America. Capital city: Honolulu (21°N 157°W) *map, page 666*

Hispaniola Caribbean island where Columbus found gold; colonized by Spain and France. (19°N 71°W) *page 36; map, page 40*

Hudson River discovered in 1609 by Henry Hudson. (41°N 73°W) *page 75; map, page 74*

I

Idaho famous for its potatoes, Idaho became the 43rd state in 1890. Capital city: Boise (43°N 116°W) *map, pages 666-667*

Illinois the Land of Lincoln, the 16th President lived most of his life here. Capital city: Springfield (39°N 89°W) *map, page 667*

Indiana the Crossroads of America, it lay on the path of westward movement in the 1800s. Capital city: Indianapolis (39°N 86°W) *map, page 667*

Indian Territory land west of the Mississippi, in what is now Oklahoma, to which Indians were forced to relocate under the Indian Removal Act of 1830. (36°N 97°W) *page 386; map, page 386*

Iowa farms make up about 93 percent of the state's area; its chief crops are corn and soybeans. Capital city: Des Moines (41°N 93°W) *map, page 667*

Isthmus of Panama site of Spanish colony of Darien and of Balboa's expedition. (9°N 80°W) *page 48; map, page 50*

J

Jamestown English colony established in Virginia in 1607. (37°N 77°W) *page 96; map, page 108*

K

Kansas Midway, U.S.A., it lies midway between the Atlantic and Pacific oceans. Capital city: Topeka (39°N 95°W) *map, page 667*

Kansas Territory a battleground over slavery in the mid-1850s. (38°N 98°W) *page 485; map, page 485*

Kentucky birthplace of Abraham Lincoln and Jefferson Davis, opposing Presidents in the Civil War. Capital city: Frankfort (38°N 85°W) *map, page 667*

L

Lake Erie site of British defeat by Oliver Perry in 1813. (42°N 82°W) *page 340; map, page 344*

Lexington town near Boston where Patriot and British forces fought in 1775. (42°N 71°W) *page 181; map, page 180*

Lisbon capital of Portugal. (38°N 9°W) *page 33; map, page 32*

Louisiana state in which there is a mixture of many cultures, representative of early French and Spanish influence. Capital city: Baton Rouge (30°N 91°W) *map, page 667*

Lowell center in Massachusetts of early industrial growth. (42°N 71°W) *page 359; map, page 352*

M

Maine the easternmost state, an important farming and fishing state. Capital city: Augusta (44°N 70°W) *map, page 667*

Manassas Junction site of the Battle of Bull Run, the first great battle of the Civil War and a Union defeat. (39°N 78°W) *page 504; map, page 508*

Maryland site of Fort McHenry, where a War of 1812 battle inspired Francis Scott Key to write "The Star-Spangled Banner." Capital city: Annapolis (39°N 76°W) *map, page 667*

Massachusetts the Bay State, it is the birthplace of four American Presidents. Capital city: Boston (42°N 71°W) *map, page 667*

Mexico ruled by the Aztecs and conquered by the Spanish, it lost almost half its territory in the Texas Revolution and Mexican War. Capital city: Mexico City (19°N 99°W) *map, page 461*

Michigan the Wolverine State, it is a leader in the production of automobiles and steel. Capital city: Lansing (42°N 85°W) *map, page 667*

Minnesota the largest of the midwestern states, it entered the Union in 1858. Capital city: St. Paul (45°N 93°W) *map, page 667*

Mississippi state named for the river that forms most of its western border. Capital city: Jackson (32°N 90°W) *map, page 667*

Mississippi River 2,350 miles long, it flows southward from Minnesota to the Gulf of Mexico. (40°N 92°W) *page 150; map, page 152*

Missouri state through which flow the nation's two longest rivers, the Missouri and the Mississippi. Capital city: Jefferson City (38°N 92°W) *map, page 667*

Missouri River important waterway explored by Lewis and Clark. (40°N 95°W) *page 331; map, page 332*

Montana site of an 1862 gold rush, the Treasure State has a great wealth of gold and silver mines. Capital city: Helena (46°N 112°W) *map, pages 666-667*

N

Nashville first Confederate city to fall to the North. (36°N 86°W) *page 509; map, page 516*

Nebraska devoting 95 percent of its area to agriculture, the Cornhusker State is a leading corn producer. Capital city: Lincoln (40°N 96°W) *map, page 667*

Neuces River river that Mexico regarded as its border with Texas. (28°N 98°W) *page 459; map, page 461*

Nevada a mining state rich in gold, silver, and petroleum. Capital city: Carson City (39°N 119°W) *map, page 666*

New Hampshire first of the original thirteen colonies to adopt its own constitution, on January 5, 1776. Capital city: Concord (43°N 71°W) *map, page 667*

New Jersey the most densely populated state, it gained statehood in 1787 as the third state. Capital city: Trenton (40°N 74°W) *map, page 667*

New Mexico the first atomic bomb was built and exploded in this state in 1945. Capital city: Santa Fe (35°N 106°W) *map, page 667*

New Orleans port city near the mouth of the Mississippi River. (30°N 90°W) *page 509; map, page 508*

New York 11th state, it ranks second only to California in population. Capital city: Albany (43°N 74°W) *map, page 667*

New York City early capital of the United States. (41°N 74°W) *page 295; map, page 407*

North Carolina 12th state, it is a leading producer of tobacco products. Capital city: Raleigh (35°N 78°W) *map, page 667*

North Dakota the geographic center of North America is near this state's city of Rugby. Capital city: Bismarck (47°N 100°W) *map, page 667*

Northwest Territory the land north of the Ohio River to the Great Lakes and west to the Mississippi. (42°N 85°W) *page 225; map, page 227*

O

Ohio first state formed out of the Northwest Territory in 1803. Capital city: Columbus (40°N 83°W) *map, page 667*

Ohio River originating in Pittsburgh, it was a main trade route for settlers heading west; boundary between free and slave states west of the Appalachians. (38°N 85°W) *page 149; map, page 152*

Oklahoma obtained in the Louisiana Purchase from France, and the destination for many Native Americans removed from the East, it became a state in 1907. Capital city: Oklahoma City (35°N 97°W) *map, page 667*

Oregon this northwestern state leads the United States in the production of lumber. Capital city: Salem (45°N 123°W) *map, page 666*

Oregon Country the area between Alaska and California, now known as the Pacific Northwest, which is drained by the Columbia, Snake, and Fraser rivers. (45°N 120°W) *page 453; map, page 456*

Oregon Trail trail pathway to the Pacific Northwest, beginning in Missouri and ending 2,000 miles away in Oregon. (39°N 94°W) *page 454; map, page 456*

P

Palos Spanish port from which Columbus launched his first voyage of exploration. (37°N 7°W) *page 35; map, page 40*

Pennsylvania known as the Keystone State because of its central position in the "arch" of the original thirteen states. Capital city: Harrisburg (40°N 77°W) *map, page 667*

Peru area ruled by the Incas and later conquered by the Spanish. (10°S 75°W) *page 55; map, page 66*

Philadelphia trading center and leading colonial city near the mouth of the Delaware River. (40°N 75°W) *page 133; map, page 119*

Plymouth colony established by Separatists in 1620. (42°N 70°W) *page 99; map, page 108*

Portugal European nation that led the search in the 1400s for new routes to Asia. (39°N 8°W) *page 30; map, page 32*

Potomac River its banks became the location for the new capital after Philadelphia. (39°N 77°W) *page 299; map, page 228*

Proclamation Line of 1763 line drawn by Britain forbidding colonists to settle west of the Appalachian Mountains. (39°N 79°W) *page 171; map, page 172*

Q

Quebec fur trading post on St. Lawrence River, first permanent French settlement in North America. (47°N 71°W) *page 75; map, page 74*

R

Red River river that formed part of the border between the United States and Texas according to the treaty of 1819. (32°N 95°W) *page 435; map, page 456*

Rhode Island the smallest state, it covers only 1,214 square miles. Capital city: Providence (42°N 71°W) *map, page 667*

Richmond capital of Virginia built along the fall line of the James River, also capital of Confederacy. (37°N 77°W) *page 500; map, page 508*

Rio Grande river that became the southern border of Texas. (30°N 105°W) *page 459; map, page 456*

Roanoke Island island off the coast of North Carolina where the first English colony in the Americas was started in 1585. (36°N 75°W) *page 83; map, page 74*

S

Saint Augustine city in Florida, oldest permanent European settlement in the United States. (30°N 81°W) *page 78; map, page 74*

★ G A Z E T T E E R ★

Saint Lawrence River in Canada, empties into the Atlantic Ocean. (45°N 74°W) *page 75; map, page 74*

Saint Louis city at the junction of the Missouri and Mississippi rivers, on the edge of the frontier in the 1820s. (38°N 90°W) *page 451; map, page 456*

Salt Lake City city in Utah built by the Mormons. (40°N 112°W) *page 456; map, page 456*

San Antonio city where the fight for the Alamo took place in 1836. (29°N 98°W) *page 441; map, page 446*

San Francisco cultural and financial center of the Far West; also site of devastating 1906 earthquake. (38°N 122°W) *page 465; map, page 456*

San Jacinto site of a victory for Texas that led to its establishment as an independent nation. (29°N 95°W) *page 444; map, page 446*

Santa Fe trading outpost to which William Becknell headed in 1822, thus opening up the Santa Fe Trail. (35°N 106°W) *page 437; map, page 456*

Santa Fe Trail wagon route from Independence, Missouri, to Santa Fe, New Mexico, along which a large trade developed during the 1800s. (35°N 106°W) *page 437; map, page 456*

Saratoga site of American victory over General Burgoyne's troops in 1777 which led France to join the American side. (43°N 73°W) *page 201; map, page 207*

Sharpsburg site in Maryland of the Battle of Antietam. (39°N 77°W) *page 512; map, page 508*

Shiloh name of a church, site of Union victory in Tennessee during Civil War. (35°N 88°W) *page 509; map, page 508*

Sierra Nevada California mountain range crossed by Jedediah Smith in 1827. (38°N 120°W) *page 452; map, page 668*

South Carolina eighth state, it was the first to secede from the Union before the Civil War. Capital city: Columbia (34°N 81°W) *map, page 667*

South Dakota primarily a farming state, the geographic center of the United States is near the city of Castle Rock. Capital city: Pierre (44°N 100°W) *map, page 667*

South Pass pass in Wyoming through the Rocky Mountains. (42°N 110°W) *page 453; map, page 456*

Strait of Magellan narrow waterway at southern tip of South America connecting the Atlantic and Pacific oceans. (53°S 70°W) *page 49; map, page 50*

T

Tennessee last Confederate state to leave the Union and first to return. Capital city: Nashville (36°N 87°W) *map, page 667*

Tenochtitlán Aztec capital city, modern-day Mexico City. (19°N 99°W) *page 53; map, page 56*

Texas the second largest state, originally part of Mexico, it was admitted to the Union in 1845. Capital city: Austin (30°N 97°W) *map, page 667*

Trenton George Washington's victory here on the day after Christmas, 1776 gave the Patriot army new hope. (40°N 74°W) *page 200; map, page 201*

U

Utah the first white settlers in the state were Mormon pioneers led by Brigham Young; Utah became the 45th state in 1896. Capital city: Salt Lake City (40°N 112°W) *map, pages 666-667*

V

Valley Forge site near Philadelphia where Washington and his army spent the winter of 1777-1778. (40°N 75°W) *page 202; map, page 201*

Venice wealthy city-state on eastern border of Italy. (45°N 12°E) *page 29; map, page 30*

Vermont the first state admitted to the Union after the original thirteen colonies, in March 1791. Capital city: Montpelier (44°N 72°W) *map, page 667*

Vicksburg site of a Civil War battle in Mississippi that gave the Union complete control of the Mississippi River. (32°N 91°W) *page 517; map, page 508*

Virginia birthplace of eight American Presidents, including four of the first five; also site of first permanent English settlement at Jamestown. Capital city: Richmond (37°N 77°W) *map, page 667*

W

Washington 42nd state, it is the only one named in honor of a United States President. Capital city: Olympia (47°N 123°W) *map, page 666*

Washington, D.C. capital city on the banks of the Potomac. (39°N 77°W) *page 340; map, page 344*

West Indies islands lying between North America and South America controlled largely by Britain, Spain, and France. (19°N 70°W) *page 154; map, page 66*

West Virginia part of Virginia until the Civil War, it broke away and remained loyal to the Union, becoming a state in 1863. Capital city: Charleston (38°N 81°W) *map, page 667*

Wilderness Road route crossing the Appalachian Mountains, connecting Virginia with Kentucky. (38°N 84°W) *page 224; map, page 228*

Wisconsin the nation's leading milk producer, also birthplace of progressivism in the early 1900s. Capital city: Madison (43°N 89°W) *map, page 667*

Wyoming the Equality State, Wyoming was the first state to allow women to vote, hold public office, and serve on juries. Capital city: Cheyenne (41°N 105°W) *map, page 667*

Y

Yorktown site of the last battle of the Revolutionary War. (37°N 76°W) *page 209; map, page 207*

Yucatán peninsula of Mexico and home of Maya Indians. (18°N 90°W) *page 52*

★ G A Z E T T E E R ★

Critical Thinking Skills Review

History of the United States (Volume 1) takes you on a journey through American history, from the arrival of the first people on the continent to the Civil War, Reconstruction, and the present day. Along the way you encounter many people, events, and issues that may be new to you. At times the people and events may seem so remote and the issues so distant that it is hard for you to grasp their importance.

To help you understand American history and remember it clearly, there are certain skills that you can use. Some of these skills are *study skills,* skills which help you locate, gather, and organize information. You have had opportunities to learn and practice these skills throughout this book. Every chapter but the last one in-

cludes a page entitled "Gaining Skill," which introduces and discusses different study skills and includes opportunities for practicing the skill.

Study skills make it possible for you to learn more effectively and efficiently. To be able to *understand* history, however, you must also be able to *think* effectively. If you can look critically at the people and events of other times, you will be better able to make sense of the way the world is today.

Critical thinking skills will help you look below the surface of American history, as well as other subjects. Critical thinking makes the study of history more interesting, because it enables *you* to become the historian.

CRITICAL THINKING SKILL 1

Interpretation

Interpretation is the attempt to identify a relationship between one fact, idea, or value and another fact, idea, or value. In the study of history, it often means offering an opinion as to why something happened or explaining what a group of seemingly unrelated events had in common. You may be asked to use the skill of interpretation in any of the ways described below.

Determining cause-and-effect relationships. Identifying **cause-and-effect relationships** is essential to understanding both life and history. An action that produces an event is a *cause.* The event or development produced by an action is an *effect.* Why some things happened and others did not can be traced to causes. In other words, what made certain things happen and what kept other things from happening?

For example, in 1763 after Britain defeated France in the French and Indian War, the British gained control of most of the land east of the Mississippi River. This caused the Shawnee, Chippewa, Delaware, and Ottawa Indians who lived there to fear that American colonists would move into the area and take the land. The Indians rebelled in a bloody uprising, which the British put down. The effect of the uprising was to convince Britain to close the West to settlement. Colonists were angered by that ruling. The proclamation closing the West was one of the early causes of the Revolutionary War.

In that example, the Indian uprising was an effect of the French and Indian War. Yet it was also a cause of the Revolution, because it led to the closing of the West. It is important to note that the uprising was only one of several effects of the French and Indian War and that there were other causes of the American Revolution.

Make it a habit to note the various effects of certain causes. Determine which of those effects in turn became new causes, and whether multiple causes or multiple effects were involved.

Making and supporting generalizations. Generalizations are brief summaries or conclusions based on facts. You may often recognize them as topic sentences. A topic sentence expresses the main idea of a paragraph.

In Chapter 9, page 213, for example, you will note the topic sentence, "The effects of the American Revolution spread around the world like ripples in a pond." The paragraph gives facts that support this generalization. It tells you that the French Revolution was inspired by the Declaration of Independence. The paragraph goes on to explain how Thaddeus Kosciusko, a Polish general who aided the American forces, went on to lead Poland's independence movement.

Keep in mind that generalizations are general. They are used to make broad statements such as the example given above, that the American Revolution had world-wide significance. Do not assume that every nation was equally affected by the Revolution or that every single country in the world was affected.

Inferring and drawing conclusions. The skills of inferring and drawing conclusions require you to make up your mind about something you read. **Inferring** is getting more information from reading than is actually and specifically stated. It might be described as reading between the lines.

In Chapter 10 on page 220, for instance, you read about the many faces of republicanism. Examples included a lawyer complaining about the wig a judge wore. Knowing that the republican virtues included equality and simplicity, you can in-

fer that a great wig was a showy sign of rank. When you infer, you make an assumption based on what you read.

When you draw **conclusions,** you make a judgment about what you have read. This judgment is based on careful thought and available information.

Read this paragraph about slavery in the American colonies from page 128:

African American men and women resisted slavery in a number of ways. From time to time they rose in open revolt, even at the risk of severe punishment. Slaves more often resisted by slowing down work, damaging goods, or carrying out orders incorrectly. Some ran away and tried to pass as free blacks in other colonies. Because other colonies did not ban slavery until after the American Revolution, runaway slaves had nowhere to turn. They were usually caught and returned to their owners.

From this you can draw the conclusion that the African American community was caught in a no-win situation in colonial days, with all means of escaping slavery closed to them. Their means of resistance against slaveowners was severely limited, and running away to freedom was almost impossible.

Recognizing points of view. A point of view reflects an opinion, attitude, belief, or feeling. A useful skill in studying history is the ability to recognize a point of view for what it is.

Favorable points of view are written in positive language, such as "This will benefit all people." Negative points of view will take an opposite approach, such as "The election of this candidate will lead to mass unemployment."

Detecting bias. Look carefully for **bias**—personal preference—on the part of the person whose views are being presented. If a writer or politician wants to persuade people to act in a certain way, he or she will usually try to appeal to people's emotions. Many famous historical figures had strong opinions that show up in their writings and speeches. These views should be examined critically. Just because a person is famous or highly regarded does not mean that you must agree with his or her opinions. A good student will detect bias and opinion when examining documents of the past or reading newspapers and magazine articles today.

Practicing Skills

1. Read the material on pages 459–463 of Chapter 18. What were the causes of the Mexican War? How did the effects of the Mexican War in turn become new causes of other events?
2. Why do generalizations make good topic sentences?
3. What is the difference between drawing a conclusion and offering an opinion?

CRITICAL THINKING SKILL 2

Analysis

The purpose of **analyzing** is to show that you understand what you read. When you analyze information, you do three things:

1. Break the information down into its different parts.
2. Recognize the relationship of one part to another.
3. Understand why the material has been organized as it has.

Analysis can be applied to large reading selections, such as chapters, or to single paragraphs or even sentences.

Look at Chapter 11, pages 240–241. Read the paragraphs under the subheadings "Views on Government" and "The Virginia Plan." What is the relationship between these two parts of the section? Why has the author chosen this method for organizing the material on the opening of the Constitutional Convention?

If you look closely at "Views on Government," you will see that it gives background information on the delegates' attitudes toward the role of government. It also explains how those attitudes had changed since independence. "The Virginia Plan" describes the initial plan for a new government introduced by James Madison. You can conclude that the authors wanted to de-scribe how delegates were prepared to consider an entirely new plan for the national government of the United States before they told you about that plan.

Distinguishing facts, opinions, and values. Facts are those things that are known to be true or to have happened. Facts are based on information that can be checked for accuracy. **Opinions** express how people feel about something, what their beliefs are, and what attitudes they take. **Values** are opinions that often involve the standards of right and wrong. Values are the most basic opinions people hold, their way of judging the world.

All values are opinions, but not all opinions are values. You may express an opinion on a subject you know little about. You may also express an opinion about what you think will happen in a certain situation. In either example, your opinion may prove to be a fact. Values are never facts. They may be so much a part of the creed you live by that they seem like facts. If they cannot be proven to be true, however, they are not facts.

It is important that you distinguish among facts, opinions, and values. Even though opinions are not always based on fact, and values cannot be proven to be true, you can still learn from them. You can learn how people felt at a certain time, what they considered important, and what they thought about. Understanding what people valued and what their opinions were will help you understand why they acted in certain ways.

Certain words give clues that opinions are being presented—"It is my belief" or "in my view" are lead-ins to what somebody thinks. Not all opinions are easily recognized. You need to read carefully to identify what you read as fact or opinion. When people write facts, they use little emotional language. When people express opinions and values, however, they may become emotional in their choice of words.

Practicing Skills

1. Read the paragraphs under the headings "Concerns of the Antifederalists" and "The Federalists Respond" in Chapter 11, pages 245–246. What is the relationship between these two parts? Why might the authors have put the arguments of the Antifederalists first and then the response of the Federalists instead of the other way round?

2. Read the primary source document, *The Crisis,* in Chapter 9 on page 199. What can you identify as a fact? What can you identify as an opinion? Do you recognize any value statements?

CRITICAL THINKING SKILL 3

Translating and Synthesizing

Translating and synthesizing are skills that require you to play an active role in the process of studying history. With these skills you can bring a fresh approach to an old subject.

Translating. Translating is presenting information in a form that is different from the way you receive it. If you tell a classmate about something you read, you are translating from the written to the oral form. You might make a chart or draw a picture of something you have read, instead of giving the information orally. That too would be translating.

Historians must translate in order to write histories. They gather as much information as they can about a historical period, including sources such as paintings, photographs, and oral histories. They must then find a way of conveying in their writing what impression these things give about the time period they describe. Look at the photograph of a New Orleans marketplace in the early 1800s on page 304. What does it tell you about the different ethnic groups that lived in the city?

Synthesizing. Synthesizing allows you to use your imagination to explain events of history and to speculate about what might have happened. When you synthesize, you create a new or different approach to looking at a subject. In order to do this effectively, you need to employ whatever knowledge you already have of a historical event.

Take the Civil War as an example. You could synthesize by writing a diary of a northern soldier in a Confederate prison, based on research about what prisoners-of-war actually experienced in the South. You might also write a one-act play detailing the conversation between General Grant and General Lee at Appomattox.

In this type of synthesis, you should not alter known events. You should merely add to the information, using what you know about the geography of the area, the personalities involved, and the customs of the period.

Predicting events. Another aspect of synthesizing is **predicting.** Predicting can be separated into two categories.

The first of these asks you to speculate about what might have happened if something else had not. Suppose, for example, that Britain had not supported the Monroe Doctrine (page 358). How would the United States have reacted if Britain tried to take over a Latin American country? How might the course of history have been changed?

The other form of predicting asks you to suggest the outcome of an event that is not yet resolved. Again, your prediction should be based on solid evidence and should not be guesswork. News commentators often use this skill when they examine recent events. For example, they may report a minor controversy in a political campaign and then predict its effect on the election.

Practicing Skills

1. Why is the ability to translate information important to a historian?
2. Choose an important event, such as a battle, an inauguration, a debate in Congress, or a political rally, in a section of this book. Write an account of the event as it would be given by a first-hand observer.
3. Consider the present justices of the Supreme Court. Predict how vacancies and new appointments might change the character of the Court. What important laws might change if the Court changes?

CRITICAL THINKING SKILL 4

Problem Solving

When you try to solve a problem, you draw on previous experiences and on knowledge you already have. The solution you offer might be an idea, a suggestion, or an action. It is your creation, and it may or may not solve the problem. When you participate in problem solving, you are expected to come up with an answer to a problem for which no answer yet exists.

Problem solving involves making choices or **making decisions.** It can be something as simple as what to choose to eat in a restaurant or something as complex as deciding on what to pursue as a career.

With difficult problems, you can take steps to help you make the right decision:

1. Clearly identify the problem.
2. Consider the various alternatives.
3. Consider the consequences and merits of each of the alternatives.
4. Make a decision.

Throughout history people have been faced with solving problems, some of which have affected not only their own lives, but the lives of thousands or even millions of people. For instance, Andrew Johnson became President of the United States after Abraham Lincoln was assassinated. He served from 1865 to 1868 and faced the task of reconstructing the South after the Civil War. To achieve this goal, Johnson had to solve several serious problems. The first step was to identify and list the problems. Here are some of them:

1. How to treat newly freed African Americans.
2. How to treat former Confederate soldiers and supporters.
3. How to create new state governments in the South.
4. How to rebuild the southern economy.

After Johnson identified the problems, he had to consider various ways of solving them. When he had decided on what course to take, he put a plan of action into effect.

When the problems are of the size and scope of those facing Johnson, the results of a plan of action may not be known for many years. Johnson was not able to follow through on many of his solutions because of congressional opposition. Members of Congress considered the problems in reconstructing the South and came up with different solutions (pages 533–534).

Practicing Skills

1. What is the first step in the process of making a decision?
2. Read the description of Radical Reconstruction on pages 533–537 of Chapter 21. What problems were Radical Republicans trying to solve? How did they hope to solve them?

CRITICAL THINKING SKILL 5

Forming Hypotheses

Many people think that history consists of the dates and descriptions of important events, such as political rallies, financial panics, elections, revolutions, and assassinations. They assume that a history book can tell them all there is to know about events like these. That is partly true. Clear records do exist of many important events, particularly in American history. The recorded history of the Americas is a few hundred years old, but these written records do not tell the whole story. How can you know, for instance, how a nation was affected by a political assassination? How can a historian explain what suddenly caused a country to go into an economic decline or how prosperity was restored? Is it possible to understand how national values affected the outcome of a presidential election?

These are matters that can never be known for sure. Many historical events are too complicated to have precise explanations and descriptions. Still, that does not mean they are not of interest to the historian. Like archeologists and scientists, historians piece together the scattered bits of information they acquire in order to answer puzzling questions. When they feel they may know what caused something or what occurred in a given situation, they form a **hypothesis**—a theory based on evidence.

Hypotheses are not proven facts. It might be more accurate to call them "educated guesses."

After doing research on the Compromise of 1850, for example, a historian might form this hypothesis: though the aim of the compromise was to strengthen and enlarge the Union, the Fugitive Slave Law increased the tensions between northerners and southerners. To support his or her hypothesis, the historian would explain why the Fugitive Slave Law was part of the compromise and offer evidence to link the law with increased sectionalism.

Historians often use each other's hypotheses as the basis for further discussion. They may put forward new evidence that proves an old hypothesis correct. Or, if new evidence seems to prove the hypothesis incorrect, they may propose a new hypothesis to replace it.

Practicing Skills

1. What kinds of questions are historians unable to solve with certainty? How do historians address these "unknowns"?
2. Turn to a chapter you have recently read and form a hypothesis about an event in that chapter. List evidence to back up your hypothesis.

Evaluation

When you **evaluate** you are making a judgment. It may be a judgment about an action, an event, or something you have read. You should not make a judgment without first thinking it through. You need to provide reasons that explain why you have judged something as you have.

Developing criteria for making judgments. When you evaluate for the purpose of making a judgment, you need to do two things:

1. Set standards. That is, determine the purpose of the evaluation.
2. Decide how well your standards are met. In judging material, you might question how accurate, adequate, or biased it is.

Suppose you were asked to identify which American Presidents were good leaders and which were poor leaders. When you are faced with making that judgment, you need first to establish what makes a good leader. You might list such considerations as:

1. Brought prosperity to the country.
2. Suggested just and useful laws.
3. Managed foreign affairs successfully.
4. Gained the confidence of the people.

Once you have decided what qualities a good President should have, you can judge how well various Presidents measure up to your standards.

Evaluating historical sources. Different historical sources often provide varying accounts of the same event. When this happens, you need to evaluate the accuracy and fairness of these differing views.

When you evaluate historical documents, consider the following questions:

1. *Is the information from primary or secondary sources?* It is important to know whether the material is a **primary source,** written at the time the event happened, or a **secondary source,** written long after the event occurred. Primary sources are records from the past such as letters and government documents. Secondary sources are written by people who were not witnesses to or participants in the events they write about. Sometimes secondary sources may be more useful than primary sources. Secondary sources may be more accurate, more objective, and more complete. This textbook, for example, is a secondary source.

2. *Is the material fact or opinion?* As you know, most historical evidence includes statements of both fact and opinion.

3. *Is the information accurate?* A good way to check accuracy is to see how the information is presented in other sources. If you find that different sources give different data, you may wonder where your source got the information. You may also begin to question its accuracy. On the other hand, if you find that different sources give the same basic information, you may be fairly certain the material is accurate. Determining a writer's credentials is another way to check accuracy. What makes this person qualified to write about this subject?

The skills described in this Skill Review will benefit you not only in history courses but in other subjects that you study. Many of them are also known as life skills because you will use them throughout your life.

Practicing Skills

1. What is a primary source? What is a secondary source?

2. What methods can you use to determine whether information is accurate?

3. Choose a President and consider the goals that he outlined at the beginning of his administration. Set standards for judging those goals and decide how close he came to meeting them.

The Presidents

President	Dates	Years in Office	Party	Elected From
1 George Washington	1732–1799	1789–1797	None	Virginia
2 John Adams	1735–1826	1797–1801	Federalist	Massachusetts
3 Thomas Jefferson	1743–1826	1801–1809	Democratic-Republican	Virginia
4 James Madison	1751–1836	1809–1817	Democratic-Republican	Virginia
5 James Monroe	1758–1831	1817–1825	Democratic-Republican	Virginia
6 John Quincy Adams	1767–1848	1825–1829	National Republican	Massachusetts
7 Andrew Jackson	1767–1845	1829–1837	Democratic	Tennessee
8 Martin Van Buren	1782–1862	1837–1841	Democratic	New York
9 William H. Harrison	1773–1841	1841	Whig	Ohio
10 John Tyler	1790–1862	1841–1845	Whig	Virginia
11 James K. Polk	1795–1849	1845–1849	Democratic	Tennessee
12 Zachary Taylor	1784–1850	1849–1850	Whig	Louisiana
13 Millard Fillmore	1800–1874	1850–1853	Whig	New York
14 Franklin Pierce	1804–1869	1853–1857	Democratic	New Hampshire
15 James Buchanan	1791–1868	1857–1861	Democratic	Pennsylvania
16 Abraham Lincoln	1809–1865	1861–1865	Republican	Illinois
17 Andrew Johnson	1808–1875	1865–1869	Nat.Union/Dem.	Tennessee
18 Ulysses S. Grant	1822–1885	1869–1877	Republican	Illinois
19 Rutherford B. Hayes	1822–1893	1877–1881	Republican	Ohio
20 James A. Garfield	1831–1881	1881	Republican	Ohio
21 Chester A. Arthur	1830–1886	1881–1885	Republican	New York
22 Grover Cleveland	1837–1908	1885–1889	Democratic	New York
23 Benjamin Harrison	1833–1901	1889–1893	Republican	Indiana
24 Grover Cleveland	1837–1908	1893–1897	Democratic	New York
25 William McKinley	1843–1901	1897–1901	Republican	Ohio
26 Theodore Roosevelt	1858–1919	1901–1909	Republican	New York
27 William H. Taft	1857–1930	1909–1913	Republican	Ohio
28 Woodrow Wilson	1856–1924	1913–1921	Democratic	New Jersey
29 Warren G. Harding	1865–1923	1921–1923	Republican	Ohio
30 Calvin Coolidge	1872–1933	1923–1929	Republican	Massachusetts
31 Herbert Hoover	1874–1964	1929–1933	Republican	California
32 Franklin D. Roosevelt	1882–1945	1933–1945	Democratic	New York
33 Harry S. Truman	1884–1972	1945–1953	Democratic	Missouri
34 Dwight D. Eisenhower	1890–1969	1953–1961	Republican	New York
35 John F. Kennedy	1917–1963	1961–1963	Democratic	Massachusetts
36 Lyndon B. Johnson	1908–1973	1963–1969	Democratic	Texas
37 Richard M. Nixon	1913–	1969–1974	Republican	New York
38 Gerald R. Ford	1913–	1974–1977	Republican	Michigan
39 Jimmy Carter	1924–	1977–1981	Democratic	Georgia
40 Ronald Reagan	1911–	1981–1989	Republican	California
41 George Bush	1924–	1989–1993	Republican	Texas
42 Bill Clinton	1946–	1993–	Democratic	Arkansas

The States

	State Name	Date of Admission	Population	Number of Representatives	Capital
1	Delaware	1787	658,000	1	Dover
2	Pennsylvania	1787	11,764,000	21	Harrisburg
3	New Jersey	1787	7,617,000	13	Trenton
4	Georgia	1788	6,387,000	11	Atlanta
5	Connecticut	1788	3,227,000	6	Hartford
6	Massachusetts	1788	5,928,000	10	Boston
7	Maryland	1788	4,733,000	8	Annapolis
8	South Carolina	1788	3,407,000	6	Columbia
9	New Hampshire	1788	1,103,000	2	Concord
10	Virginia	1788	6,128,000	11	Richmond
11	New York	1788	17,627,000	31	Albany
12	North Carolina	1789	6,553,000	12	Raleigh
13	Rhode Island	1790	989,000	2	Providence
14	Vermont	1791	560,000	1	Montpelier
15	Kentucky	1792	3,665,000	6	Frankfort
16	Tennessee	1796	4,822,000	9	Nashville
17	Ohio	1803	10,778,000	19	Columbus
18	Louisiana	1812	4,181,000	7	Baton Rouge
19	Indiana	1816	5,499,000	10	Indianapolis
20	Mississippi	1817	2,535,000	5	Jackson
21	Illinois	1818	11,325,000	20	Springfield
22	Alabama	1819	3,984,000	7	Montgomery
23	Maine	1820	1,218,000	2	Augusta
24	Missouri	1821	5,079,000	9	Jefferson City
25	Arkansas	1836	2,337,000	4	Little Rock
26	Michigan	1837	9,180,000	16	Lansing
27	Florida	1845	12,775,000	23	Tallahassee
28	Texas	1845	16,825,000	30	Austin
29	Iowa	1846	2,767,000	5	Des Moines
30	Wisconsin	1848	4,870,000	9	Madison
31	California	1850	29,279,000	52	Sacramento
32	Minnesota	1858	4,359,000	8	St. Paul
33	Oregon	1859	2,828,000	5	Salem
34	Kansas	1861	2,468,000	4	Topeka
35	West Virginia	1863	1,783,000	3	Charleston
36	Nevada	1864	1,193,000	2	Carson City
37	Nebraska	1867	1,573,000	3	Lincoln
38	Colorado	1876	3,272,000	6	Denver
39	North Dakota	1889	634,000	1	Bismarck
40	South Dakota	1889	693,000	1	Pierre
41	Montana	1889	794,000	1	Helena
42	Washington	1889	4,827,000	9	Olympia
43	Idaho	1890	1,004,000	2	Boise
44	Wyoming	1890	450,000	1	Cheyenne
45	Utah	1896	1,711,000	3	Salt Lake City
46	Oklahoma	1907	3,124,000	6	Oklahoma City
47	New Mexico	1912	1,490,000	3	Santa Fe
48	Arizona	1912	3,619,000	6	Phoenix
49	Alaska	1959	546,000	1	Juneau
50	Hawaii	1959	1,095,000	2	Honolulu
	District of Columbia		638,000	1 (non-voting)	

THE STATES

435

Important Dates in American History

Here is a list of benchmark dates in American history. All of these events had consequences that remain with us today. Study the list. Think about the effects each event has had and how it still affects our lives.

1492	Columbus reaches Americas
1607	Jamestown settled
1620	Pilgrims settle Plymouth
1775–1783	American Revolution
1788	Constitution ratified
1861–1865	Civil War
1877	Reconstruction ends
1890	Indian wars end Census declares end of frontier; all areas settled
1898	Spanish–American War
1914–1918	World War I
1929	Great Depression begins
1939–1945	World War II
1964	Civil Rights Act
1969	American astronauts land on the moon
1973	Last American troops leave Vietnam
1989–1990	Collapse of communism in Eastern Europe; cold war ends

Glossary

The glossary defines important words and terms in this book. Remember that many words have more than one meaning. The definitions given here are the ones that will be most helpful in your reading of this book. The page number in parentheses after each definition refers to the page on which each word or term is first used in the textbook.

A

abolitionist a person who worked in the movement to do away with slavery. *(page 415)*

administration a President's term in office. *(page 324)*

adobe a sun-dried clay brick. *(page 61)*

Albany Plan of Union a plan proposed by Benjamin Franklin at the Albany Congress of 1754, under which the American colonies would form a loose confederation to promote mutual defense. *(page 157)*

alien an unnaturalized foreign resident of a country. *(page 316)*

Alien and Sedition Acts laws passed in 1798 to curb immigration and limit criticism of the government. *(page 316)*

alliance an agreement by two or more nations to act together in a cause. *(page 201)*

ally a partner in a common cause. *(page 54)*

amendment an addition. *(page 252)*

American System Henry Clay's program to spur national economic growth and national self-sufficiency. *(page 351)*

amnesty official pardon. *(page 531)*

Anasazi an ancient Indian farming culture centered on the Colorado Plateau. *(page 10)*

anesthetic a pain-killer. *(page 503)*

annex to add to an existing country or area. *(page 444)*

anthropologist someone who studies human culture and development. *(page 3)*

Antifederalist one who opposed ratification of the Constitution. *(page 245)*

antiseptic a germ-killing drug. *(page 503)*

apprentice a person learning a trade from a master worker. *(page 120)*

archeologist someone who studies remains to learn about the past. *(page 3)*

armada a giant fleet of warships. *(page 81)*

arsenal a storehouse for weapons. *(page 236)*

Articles of Confederation the plan, ratified by the states in 1781, that established a national congress with limited powers. *(page 218)*

artifact an item made by humans. *(page 3)*

Aztec an Indian people who built an empire in the Valley of Mexico during the 1300s. *(page 7)*

B

baby boom the rapid population increase during the 1950s. *(page 572)*

backcountry the hilly frontier region between the fall line and the Appalachian Mountains. *(page 130)*

balance of power an equal distribution of strength among nations. *(page 156)*

Battle of Bunker Hill the battle in June 1775 between colonists and the British army near Boston. *(page 183)*

Battle of Gettysburg the greatest single battle of the Civil War, won by the Union in 1863. *(page 516)*

Battle of Quebec the decisive battle of the French and Indian War in 1759, won by Britain. *(page 161)*

Battle of San Jacinto the 1836 battle in which Texas won independence from Mexico. *(page 444)*

Battle of Saratoga the American victory over the British in 1777, which led to French entry into the war on the American side. *(page 201)*

Battle of Vicksburg the Union capture of Vicksburg, Mississippi, in the Civil War, which gave the Union control of the Mississippi. *(page 517)*

Battle of Yorktown the last major battle of the Revolutionary War, won by combined American and French troops. *(page 209)*

Bear Flag Revolt the uprising in 1846 in which Americans living in California rebelled against Mexican rule and formed an independent republic. *(page 460)*

Bill of Rights the first ten amendments to the Constitution, guaranteeing the basic rights of American citizens. *(page 252)*

black codes laws passed by

southern states after the Civil War to stop the movement of freedmen and to return them to plantation labor. *(page 531)*

black power the 1960s movement by African Americans for greater political influence. *(page 573)*

blockade the blocking off of a city or port by enemy ships or other forces. *(page 339)*

bond a certificate promising to repay a loan at a certain time. *(page 297)*

boomtown a town that grew rapidly in population as a result of sudden prosperity. *(page 466)*

border state a state lying on the border between North and South. *(page 491)*

Boston Massacre the clash in 1770 between British troops and a group of Bostonians in which five colonists were killed. *(page 176)*

Boston Tea Party the 1773 protest against British trade policies in which Patriots boarded vessels of the East India Company and threw the tea cargo into Boston Harbor. *(page 177)*

boycott to refuse to buy. *(page 174)*

C

Cabinet the group of presidential advisers made up of the heads of the executive branch departments. *(page 254)*

capital money for investment. *(page 29)*

capitalism an economic system based on private enterprise and free competition. *(page 298)*

caravel a double-rigged ship, used by Portuguese sailors in the 1400s, that could sail with the wind or against it. *(page 31)*

carpetbagger a term of insult applied to northerners who moved to the South during Reconstruction. *(page 536)*

cash crop a crop grown to be sold. *(page 133)*

casualty a wounded or dead person. *(page 160)*

caucus a meeting of important party members. *(page 415)*

cede to give up. *(page 462)*

charter a written grant, issued by a government or other authority, giving the holder the right to establish a colony, corporation or other organization. *(page 95)*

checks and balances a system that allows each branch of government to limit the powers of the other branches. *(page 250)*

circumnavigate to sail completely around. *(page 51)*

civil rights the rights of all citizens. *(page 534)*

civilization a distinct and highly developed culture. *(page 6)*

clergy religious officials. *(page 67)*

coalition a combination of interests. *(page 540)*

cold war a competition, falling short of open warfare, between nations, especially the United States and the Soviet Union in the post-World War II period. *(page 566)*

colonist one who leaves his own land to settle and govern in another. *(page 40)*

Columbian exchange the transfer of plants, animals, and diseases between the continents that took place after Columbus reached the Americas. *(page 38)*

commerce the buying and selling of goods. *(page 120)*

Committee of Correspondence a citizens' group in the American colonies that formed part of a network designed to transmit information. *(page 177)*

commonwealth a community in which people work together for the good of the whole. *(page 103)*

compromise the resolution of a disagreement by granting each side some of its demands. *(page 242)*

Compromise of 1850 the deal between proslavery and antislavery forces over the extension of slavery. *(page 482)*

Compromise of 1877 the deal that gave Rutherford B. Hayes the presidency in return for the ending of Reconstruction. *(page 542)*

Confederate States of America the nation formed by the southern states in 1861. *(page 492)*

confederation a loose union. *(page 218)*

conquistador a Spanish adventurer or conqueror. *(page 51)*

Constitutional Convention the meeting of state delegates in 1787 that resulted in the writing of the Constitution. *(page 237)*

containment the post-World War II American policy of preventing the Soviet Union from expanding its influence. *(page 566)*

convention a meeting of delegates. *(page 236)*

convert to change someone's beliefs. *(page 50)*

Copperhead a northerner who called for peace with the South during the Civil War. *(page 515)*

corporation a business chartered by a state and owned by shareholding investors. *(page 553)*

cotton gin a machine designed to separate cotton seeds from cotton fiber, invented in 1793 by Eli Whitney. *(page 367)*

counterculture a group whose values are opposed to those of the established culture. *(page 574)*

covenant a promise or agreement. *(page 103)*

credit money on loan, as from a bank. *(page 393)*

creditor a person who loans money. *(page 230)*

Creole a person of Spanish ancestry born in New Spain. *(page 66)*

Crusades wars between Christians and Muslims over the Holy Land during the Middle Ages. *(page 25)*

currency paper money. *(page 172)*

D

debtor a person who borrows money. *(page 229)*

Declaration of Independence the document adopted by the Continental Congress on July 4, 1776, establishing the United States as a nation independent from Great Britain. *(page 187)*

deism the view that reason and the understanding of nature could lead to a knowledge of God. *(page 121)*

democracy a system of government by the people. *(page 217)*

depression a period of deep economic hardship. *(page 396)*

détente a relaxation of tensions between nations. *(page 569)*

dissenter a person who challenges the dominant view of church or society. *(page 106)*

doctrine of nullification the theory that a state could declare a federal law null and void within its borders if the law favored one sectional interest over another. *(page 389)*

domestication the breeding of plants or animals designed to meet specific human needs. *(page 5)*

domino theory the idea that a Communist victory in one nation would lead to similar victories in neighboring nations. *(page 568)*

draft a system of choosing people for required military service. *(page 515)*

Dred Scott case the 1857 Supreme Court case in which the Court ruled that African Americans were not citizens and that Congress could not forbid slavery in the territories. *(page 487)*

due process the right of the accused to be treated fairly and according to the law. *(page 253)*

E

ecology the relationship between living things and their environment. *(page 16)*

elastic clause a clause in the Constitution that permits Congress to pass laws that are necessary for Congress to carry out its existing powers. *(page 254)*

El Camino Real "The King's Highway," the name for major roads in Spain's American empire. *(page 66)*

Electoral College the group of delegates from each state who cast the official votes that elect the President. *(page 243)*

Emancipation Proclamation the announcement on January 1, 1863, by President Lincoln that all slaves in Confederate territory would be considered free. *(page 512)*

embargo a government order to stop foreign trade. *(page 179)*

emigrant a person migrating from one place to another. *(page 453)*

empire a group of peoples or lands controlled by one nation or ruler. *(page 8)*

empresario a person awarded a grant of land in return for bringing settlers into a Mexican province. *(page 435)*

encomienda system the system in which the Spanish Crown gave Indian laborers to loyal colonists for a specific number of days each year. *(page 40)*

English Bill of Rights the document signed in 1689 that guaranteed English citizens certain rights and stated that elections for Parliament were to be held often. *(page 137)*

executive concerning the branch of government that enforces laws. *(page 218)*

expansionist a person who wanted to enlarge the territory of the United States. *(page 459)*

export to send goods to another country for trade or sale. *(page 69)*

F

fall line the point at which a river passes from high land to a low, coastal plain. *(page 127)*

famine a shortage of food. *(page 406)*

federalism the sharing of power between a central government and its political subdivisions. *(page 245)*

Federalist a person who favored the plan of government created by the Constitution. *(page 245)* Also, a political party during the late 1700s and early 1800s. *(page 310)*

Federalist, The the series of essays written by Madison, Hamilton, and Jay in support of the Constitution. *(page 246)*

feudalism a system in which people exchanged loyalty to a lord in exchange for land and protection. *(page 23)*

Fifteenth Amendment the 1870 constitutional amendment declaring that the right to vote should not be denied "on account of race, color, or previous condition of servitude." *(page 537)*

First Battle of Bull Run the first major battle of the Civil War, resulting in a Confederate victory. *(page 505)*

First Continental Congress the group of colonial delegates who met in 1774 to discuss opposition to British policies. *(page 179)*

forty-niner a person who took part in the California Gold Rush. *(page 466)*

Founding Fathers the delegates to the Constitutional Convention, as well as other American leaders of the time. *(page 237)*

Fourteen Points Woodrow Wilson's 1918 plan for world peace after World War I. *(page 561)*

Fourteenth Amendment the 1868 constitutional amendment declaring that all native-born or naturalized persons were citizens and had the same rights as citizens. *(page 534)*

French and Indian War the conflict between France and Britain in North America fought from 1754 to 1763. *(page 159)*

French Revolution the rebellion, beginning in 1789, in which the French people overthrew the monarchy. *(page 307)*

Fugitive Slave Law the law against runaway slaves, passed as part of the Compromise of 1850. *(page 482)*

G

Gilded Age the late 1800s, a period characterized by great wealth, corruption, and inequality. *(page 553)*

global warming an increase in the earth's temperature as a result of the burning of fossil fuels. *(page 578)*

glyphic writing the use of symbols and images to express words and ideas. *(page 7)*

Gold Rush of 1849 the mass migration to California following the discovery of gold there in 1848. *(page 466)*

Grand Banks the rich fishing area in the Atlantic Ocean near Newfoundland. *(page 73)*

Great Awakening the religious movement in the colonies around 1740 that emphasized personal religious experience. *(page 122)*

Great Compromise the plan, approved by the Constitutional Convention, providing for a two-house Congress in which the people would be represented in a House of Representatives and the states would be represented in a Senate. *(page 242)*

Great Depression the time of severe economic hardship from 1929 to World War II. *(page 557)*

Great Migration the emigration to America by English Puritans during the 1630s. *(page 103)*

Grito de Dolores "Cry of Dolores," the call for revolt against Spanish rule of Mexico. *(page 431)*

H

hacienda a large agricultural community in Spanish America that replaced the encomienda system and made Indians tenants rather than slaves. *(page 66)*

Hartford Convention the 1814 meeting at which delegates from New England states met to discuss their opposition to government policies. *(page 343)*

headright a land grant offered by the Virginia Company in the early 1600s to attract new English settlers to Virginia. *(page 97)*

hidalgo a member of the lower order of the Spanish nobility. *(page 41)*

Hohokam an Indian people who migrated from Mexico to the Southwest, living there until the 1400s. *(page 9)*

Holocaust Nazi Germany's systematic murder of European Jews. *(page 563)*

Holy Land the area of the Middle East where Jesus Christ lived. *(page 25)*

homestead land on which to build and settle houses. *(page 481)*

Hopewell culture an Indian culture that emerged in the Ohio Valley about 500 B.C. and lasted about 1,200 years. *(page 11)*

House of Burgesses the Virginia legislature, founded in 1619, that served as an early step toward the establishment of representative government in America. *(page 97)*

hunter-gatherer a person who depends on wild plants and animals for food. *(page 5)*

I

impeach to bring an official to trial for misconduct in office. *(page 243)*

imperialism the policy of gaining political and economic control over other nations against their will. *(page 559)*

import a good brought from one country for trade or sale in another. *(page 69)*

impressment the practice of drafting sailors by force. *(page 173)*

inaugurate to swear into office. *(page 295)*

Inca a powerful empire on the western coast of South America during the 1400s and 1500s. *(page 8)*

indentured servant an individual who worked without wages for a specified number of years in exchange for transportation to the American colonies. *(page 97)*

Indian Removal Act the 1830 law that authorized the President to move Indians to new homelands west of the Mississippi. *(page 385)*

Industrial Revolution the period of rapid industrial growth that began in Britain in the 1700s and then spread to other nations. *(page 360)*

inflation steadily rising prices. *(page 229)*

integration the opening of something to people of all races and ethnic groups. *(page 540)*

interchangeable parts identical parts that can be substituted for one another in the manufacture or repair of products. *(page 362)*

interest an extra payment in return for the use of money loaned. *(page 297)*

Intolerable Acts laws enacted by Parliament in 1774 severely restricting the rights of Massachusetts colonists. *(page 179)*

investor a person who puts money into a project in order to earn profits. *(page 95)*

isolationism the policy of avoiding involvement in world affairs. *(page 561)*

J

Jacksonian democracy the emerging democratic spirit in the United States after Andrew Jackson's election as President in 1828. *(page 382)*

Jay's Treaty the 1794 agreement between Britain and the United States in which Britain promised to evacuate the Ohio Valley and to allow American vessels to trade in the West Indies. *(page 308)*

Jim Crow laws laws introduced in southern states following Reconstruction that segregated schools, railway cars, and eventually all public facilities. *(page 545)*

joint-stock company a form of business arrangement whereby investors pool their funds, thereby creating greater amounts of capital for investment. *(page 29)*

judicial concerning the branch of government that interprets laws. *(page 218)*

judicial review the power of the Supreme Court to declare laws unconstitutional. *(page 350)*

jury a group of citizens who listen to the facts of a certain case and then give judgment. *(page 137)*

K

Kansas-Nebraska Act the 1854 law creating the territories of Kansas and Nebraska and allowing settlers there to decide the issue of slavery. *(page 485)*

Ku Klux Klan a secret group formed after the Civil War to control elections, to destroy the Republican Party in the South, and to keep African Americans powerless. *(page 537)*

L

land speculator a person who buys land in order to sell it later at a profit. *(page 157)*

League of the Iroquois an American Indian federation established around 1570 to ease tensions among the Iroquois tribes of the Northeast. *(page 155)*

League of Nations an international organization established after World War I to prevent future conflicts. *(page 561)*

legislative concerning the branch of government that makes laws. *(page 218)*

Lewis and Clark expedition an expedition by Meriwether Lewis and William Clark in 1804–1806 that explored the Louisiana Territory from St. Louis to the Pacific coast. *(page 331)*

libel printing statements that harm a person's reputation. *(page 142)*

limited monarchy a monarchy in which the ruler does not have complete power. *(page 138)*

Line of Demarcation an imaginary line around the earth's poles established by the Pope in 1493, giving Portugal the right to claim all non-Christian lands on one side of the line, and Spain all such lands on the other. *(page 47)*

literacy the ability to read and write. *(page 384)*

loose construction the interpretation of the Constitution claiming that the government can do anything the Constitution does not plainly forbid it to do. *(page 300)*

Louisiana Purchase the United States' purchase from France in 1803 of 828,000 square miles of land west of the Mississippi River. *(page 330)*

Loyalist a colonist who remained loyal to Britain during the Revolutionary War. *(page 180)*

lyceum a private organization sponsoring public programs and lectures. *(page 412)*

lynch to kill without a trial. *(page 538)*

M

Magna Carta the charter of English liberties granted by King John in 1215. *(page 137)*

manifest destiny the idea that it was the nation's destiny to expand across the continent to the Pacific Ocean. *(page 459)*

Marbury v. Madison the 1803 case in which the Supreme Court asserted its right to declare laws passed by Congress unconstitutional. *(page 350)*

Mason-Dixon Line the boundary between slave and free states east of the Appalachians. *(page 477)*

Maya a Mesoamerican people whose culture flourished during the period A.D. 300–700. *(page 7)*

Mayflower Compact an agreement signed by the male passengers aboard the *Mayflower* in which they vowed to respect laws agreed upon for the general good of the colony. *(page 99)*

medieval relating to the Middle Ages. *(page 23)*

mercantilism an economic policy based on a state monopoly over trade and an attempt to transfer wealth, especially precious metals, from colonies to the parent country. *(page 68)*

mercenary a soldier who serves in a foreign army for pay. *(page 93)*

Mesoamerica the middle region of the Western Hemisphere, extending from central Mexico to Panama. *(page 6)*

mestizo a person of mixed Spanish and Indian ancestry. *(page 66)*

Mexican Cession the land that Mexico ceded to the United States in 1848 under the terms of the Treaty of Guadalupe Hidalgo. *(page 462)*

Mexican War the 1846–1848 war between Mexico and the United States ending in a United States victory. *(page 460)*

Middle Ages the period between A.D. 500 and 1500. *(page 23)*

migration the movement of people from one region to another. *(page 4)*

Minuteman a member of a colonial militia who needed to be ready to fight given only a minute's notice. *(page 180)*

missionary a person sent abroad to do religious work. *(page 51)*

Mississippian culture an Indian culture that emerged in the Southeast and the Mississippi Valley about 900. *(page 11)*

Missouri Compromise a congressional agreement in 1820 whereby Missouri was admitted as a slave state, Maine was admitted as a free state, and slavery was forbidden north of the parallel 36°30′. *(page 380)*

moderate a person who opposes extreme change. *(page 533)*

monopoly complete control over a product or service. *(page 30)*

Monroe Doctrine President Monroe's 1823 warning against new European colonization in the Americas. *(page 359)*

Moor a Muslim from North Africa or the Iberian Peninsula. *(page 25)*

N

National Road a road, financed by the federal government and built in the early 1800s, that connected Cumberland, Maryland, to Wheeling, Virginia, and Vandalia, Illinois. *(page 352)*

nationalism love for and loyalty to one's country. *(page 27)*

nativist a person hostile to immigrants. *(page 407)*

Navigation Acts laws, beginning 1651, enacted to tax and regulate trade in the colonies. *(page 118)*

navigator a person who knows the science of sailing ships. *(page 31)*

neutral taking no side in a disagreement. *(page 308)*

New Deal Franklin Roosevelt's program to end the Great Depression. *(page 557)*

New England Way the beliefs and way of life of the Puritans in colonial New England. *(page 105)*

Non-Intercourse Act the 1809 act that repealed the Embargo Act of 1807 and reopened trade with all nations except Britain and France. *(page 337)*

Northwest Ordinance the 1787 law that set forth a plan of government for the Northwest Territory and provided for freedom of worship, protection of civil liberties, and free public education. *(page 226)*

Northwest Passage a water route around the Americas to Asia sought by European explorers. *(page 74)*

Northwest Territory the land north of the Ohio River to the Great Lakes and west to the Mississippi River. *(page 225)*

O

Olive Branch Petition an unsuccessful 1775 appeal by the Continental Congress to King George III to avoid war. *(page 184)*

Olmec a Mesoamerican people whose civilization developed about 1000 B.C. *(page 7)*

ordinance a government regulation. *(page 225)*

Oregon Country the area between Alaska and California, now known as the Pacific Northwest, which is drained by the Columbia, Snake, and Fraser rivers. *(page 453)*

Oregon Trail the pathway to the Pacific Northwest, beginning in Missouri and ending in Oregon. *(page 454)*

override to pass a bill over a President's veto by having two-thirds of both houses of Congress support the bill. *(page 534)*

overseer a supervisor of slaves. *(page 128)*

P

Paleo-Indian a member of the first group of humans in the Americas. *(page 4)*

pamphlet an unbound, printed essay. *(page 179)*

panic a sudden fear among investors. *(page 396)*

Panic of 1837 the period of bank closings and rising unemployment beginning in 1837. *(page 396)*

partisan a member of an unofficial or guerrilla military unit. *(page 208)*

passive resistance peacefully refusing to obey a given law. *(page 423)*

Patriot a person who supported American independence at the time of the Revolutionary War. *(page 180)*

Petition of Right the 1628 document stating that people could not be taxed without the consent of Parliament. *(page 137)*

Pinckney's Treaty the 1795 agreement in which Spain granted the United States free navigation on the Mississippi and the right to deposit goods at New Orleans for three years. *(page 308)*

plantation a large farm. *(page 126)*

Plessy v. Ferguson the 1896 Supreme Court decision upholding segregation. *(page 545)*

political party a group that works for certain goals and candidates. *(page 310)*

portage the carrying of boats overland. *(page 150)*

precedent an example that becomes standard practice. *(page 295)*

pre-Columbian occurring before Columbus's arrival in the Americas. *(page 3)*

prime minister in a parliamentary system, the chief executive. *(page 160)*

privateer an armed, privately owned ship enlisted by a government to attack enemy vessels. *(page 82)*

Proclamation of 1763 the British decree prohibiting colonial settlement in any lands west of the Appalachians. *(page 171)*

progressivism the early 1900s movement for political, economic, and social reform. *(page 556)*

profits money left over after costs are paid. *(page 30)*

prohibition a ban on the manufacture and sale of

alcoholic beverages. *(page 556)*

propaganda the spreading of one's political views and beliefs. *(page 176)*

proprietor an owner. *(page 110)*

Protestant someone who rebelled against the Catholic Church in the 1500s, or a member of one of the Christian groups founded after that rebellion. *(page 76)*

public debt money owed by a government. *(page 297)*

Puritan a member of an English religious group that believed the Anglican Church should purify itself by abandoning much of its ritual and ceremony. *(page 102)*

Q

Quartering Act legislation requiring colonists to house and supply the soldiers that King George III sent to America to enforce the Proclamation of 1763. *(page 171)*

R

radical one who takes an extreme position. *(page 321)*

ratify to approve. *(page 218)*

raw materials natural resources used to make other goods. *(page 118)*

realpolitik "practical politics," in which power matters more than law or morality. *(page 569)*

Reconquista the movement, which succeeded by 1492, by the Christian kingdoms of Spain to drive the Moors from Spain. *(page 35)*

Reconstruction the federal government's plan to rebuild and re-establish the states of the former Confederacy. *(page 527)*

redcoat a British soldier. *(page 176)*

Reformation the revolt against the Catholic Church begun by Martin Luther in 1517. *(page 76)*

refuge a place of protection. *(page 106)*

rehabilitate to help to return to normal. *(page 413)*

relocate to move. *(page 386)*

Renaissance the cultural and intellectual "rebirth" of Europe that began in the 1300s. *(page 28)*

repeal to overturn or withdraw. *(page 174)*

republic a form of government controlled by the people through elected representatives. *(page 217)*

republicanism a belief among Americans after the Revolution that a virtuous life embracing simplicity, sacrifice, and freedom of conscience was necessary for the nation to thrive. *(page 220)*

resolution a proposal placed before the members of Congress that requires a vote. *(page 187)*

revenue government income. *(page 171)*

right of deposit the right to deposit goods in a given place for later shipment. *(page 309)*

Roanoke Island the island off the coast of North Carolina and the site of the first English colony in the Americas, started in 1585. *(page 83)*

S

Salem Witchcraft Trials trials in Massachusetts in 1692 that resulted in the execution of twenty persons for witchcraft. *(page 121)*

Santa Fe Trail the wagon route from Independence, Missouri to Santa Fe, New Mexico, along which a large trade developed during the 1800s. *(page 437)*

scalawag a southern white who supported Radical Reconstruction and who joined with African Americans in reconstruction legislatures. *(page 536)*

sea dog the captain of an English pirate ship. *(page 80)*

search warrant a document giving officials the right to search a person's property for a particular object. *(page 136)*

secede to withdraw from the Union. *(page 391)*

secession the withdrawal of a state from the Union. *(page 343)*

Second Continental Congress the assembly of colonial delegates organized in 1775. *(page 182)*

Second Great Awakening the evangelical religious movement that spread through parts of the West and South in the early 1800s. *(page 408)*

sectionalism loyalty to local interests. *(page 380)*

sedition saying or doing anything to bring down a government. *(page 307)*

self-sufficient able to make most of the things one needs for survival. *(page 66)*

serf a common person who, under the feudal system, was bound to the lord's manor. *(page 24)*

separation of powers the division of governmental power into executive, legislative, and judicial branches. *(page 250)*

Separatist an individual in England who called for a total break with the Anglican Church. *(page 98)*

sexism the idea that one sex is superior to the other. *(page 574)*

shaman an Indian religious leader. *(page 17)*

sharecropping a system in which a farmer rented land, tools, seed, and housing from a landowner in return for a share of the crop. *(page 542)*

shares of stock shares of ownership in a company. *(page 95)*

Shays' Rebellion the attempt by Massachusetts farmers in 1786–1787 to stop local courts from imprisoning debtors. *(page 235)*

slash-and-burn farming a way of clearing land for farming by cutting strips of bark from trees to kill them and then burning the undergrowth. *(page 16)*

smuggling illegal trade. *(page 118)*

social class a group of people who share the same status or degree of wealth in a society. *(page 14)*

solid South an expression coined around 1900 to denote the Democratic Party's control of southern politics. *(page 545)*

Sons of Liberty a secret citizens' group organized in the American colonies during the 1760s to protest the Stamp Act. *(page 173)*

South Pass an open pass through the Rocky Mountains. *(page 453)*

spoils system the practice of giving government jobs to political backers. *(page 383)*

Stamp Act the 1765 British decree taxing all legal papers issued in the colonies. *(page 172)*

Stamp Act Congress the group assembled in October 1765, consisting of delegates from nine colonies, that sent a protest to Great Britain declaring that the right to tax belonged to colonial assemblies rather than to Parliament. *(page 173)*

states' rights the theory that states had the right to judge whether a law passed by Congress was constitutional. *(page 316)*

steerage the lowest deck on a ship. *(page 404)*

strait a narrow passage of water. *(page 49)*

strict construction the interpretation of the Constitution claiming that the government has only the powers that the Constitution specifically gives it. *(page 300)*

suffrage the right to vote. *(page 418)*

superpower a nation possessing both military and economic might to an outstanding degree. *(page 563)*

surplus an extra amount. *(page 119)*

survey to measure land in order to determine its exact boundaries. *(page 226)*

T

tariff a tax on imported goods. *(page 300)*

technology the use of science to make and invent things. *(page 18)*

Tejano a Spanish-speaking Texan. *(page 430)*

temperance the giving up of drinking alcoholic beverages. *(page 413)*

tenant a person who works another person's land in exchange for part of the produce. *(page 66)*

tenement an apartment building designed to house large numbers of people as cheaply as possible. *(page 406)*

textile industry the large-scale production of woven fabric. *(page 360)*

Third World the poorer agricultural nations of Latin America, Asia, and Africa. *(page 568)*

Thirteenth Amendment the 1865 constitutional amendment that abolished slavery in the United States. *(page 531)*

tidewater a region of low coastal land whose rivers are affected by ocean tides. *(page 107)*

total war a war aiming at the total destruction of the enemy. *(page 520)*

Townshend Acts British decrees of 1767 levying duties on imported items in the colonies, such as tea, paper, and glass. *(page 175)*

Trail of Tears the forced journey of Cherokee Indians from their homes in Georgia to lands in the West in 1838–1839. *(page 387)*

transcendentalism an American philosophy, inspired by Ralph Waldo Emerson, that stressed individualism. *(page 422)*

Treaty of Ghent the treaty between Britain and the United States that ended the War of 1812. *(page 343)*

Treaty of Guadalupe Hidalgo the treaty that ended the Mexican War in which Mexico ceded New Mexico,

California, and the land between them to the United States. *(page 462)*

Treaty of Paris (1763) the treaty in which France gave up its North American empire to Britain, thereby ending the French and Indian War. *(page 161)*

Treaty of Paris (1783) Britain's official recognition of the independence of the United States. *(page 211)*

triangular trade the trade routes connecting the colonies, England, and Africa. *(page 118)*

tribute the payment of goods and produce by conquered peoples to their conquerors. *(page 8)*

U

unconstitutional violating the Constitution. *(page 251)*

Underground Railroad an informal system that moved runaway slaves north. *(page 417)*

United Nations the international organization founded in 1945 to replace the League of Nations. *(page 563)*

utopia an ideal community. *(page 413)*

V

vaquero a Mexican cowhand. (page 434)

vassal a knight or lord who promised to be loyal to a higher lord or a king or queen. *(page 23)*

veto to reject. *(page 250)*

viceroyalty a subdivision of Spain's American empire ruled by a viceroy. *(page 65)*

Virginia Plan the plan proposed at the Constitutional Convention to establish a new type of national government with three branches: executive, judicial and legislative. *(page 240)*

W

War Hawk in the early 1800s, the name given a southern or western leader who favored war with Great Britain. *(page 339)*

War of 1812 the war between Britain and the United States from 1812–1815. *(page 337)*

Whiskey Rebellion the 1794 refusal by western farmers to pay the federal tax on whiskey. *(page 307)*

writs of assistance warrants that gave British officers unrestricted rights to search for illegal goods. *(page 175)*

X

XYZ Affair a failed attempt by French ministers to seek a bribe from American representatives who had been sent to negotiate peace in 1798. *(page 315)*

Y

yuppie a young urban professional. *(page 575)*

★ GLOSSARY ★

Index

The purpose of the index is to help you quickly locate information on any topic in this book. The index includes references not only to the text but to maps, pictures, and charts as well. A page number with *m* before it, such as *m143,* refers to a map. Page numbers with *p* and *c* before them refer to pictures and charts.

★ INDEX ★

★ **I N D E X** ★

★ I N D E X ★

★ I N D E X ★

★ I N D E X ★

Acknowledgments

Text Credits

Grateful acknowledgment is made to authors, publishers, and other copyright holders for permission to reprint (and in some cases to adapt slightly) copyright material listed below.

16 From *American Indian Mythology* by Alice Marriott and Carol K. Rachlin. Copyright © 1968 by Alice Marriott and Carol K. Rachlin. Published by Harper & Row, Publishers, Inc. **248** From "A Child's Faith" by Roger Wilkins, as reprinted in *The Washington Post Magazine*, June 28, 1987. Reprinted by permission of the author. **353** From *The Erie Canal* (An American Heritage Junior Book) by Ralph K. Andrist and the Editors of *American Heritage*. Copyright © 1964 by American Heritage Publishing Co. **369** From quotes by Phoebe Henderson and Sarah Ford as reprinted in *The Slave Narratives of Texas*, edited by Ronnie C. Tyler and Lawrence R. Murphy. Copyright © 1974 by The Encino Press, Austin, Texas. **387** From *Indian Removal: The Emigration of the Five Civilized Tribes of Indians* by Grant Foreman. Copyright © 1932, 1953, 1972 by the University of Oklahoma Press. Reprinted by permission of the University of Oklahoma Press. **442** Excerpt A from *History of Texas* by Henderson Yoakum (New York, 1856). Excerpt B From *Texas* by James Michener. Copyright © 1985 by James Michener. Reprinted by permission of Random House, Inc. **455** From "Diary, 1862" by Jane A. Gould Tourtillott, as reprinted in *Women's Diaries of the Westward Journey* by Lillian Schlissel. Reprinted by permission of the family of Jane A. Gould Tourtillott. **458** From "Notes by the Wayside En Route to Oregon, 1852" by Lydia Allen Rudd. Reprinted by permission of the Huntington Library. **467** From *Eldorado or Adventures in the Path of Empire* by Bayard Taylor with an introduction by Robert Glass Cleland. Published by Alfred A. Knopf, Inc. **468** From *The World Rushed In: The California Gold Rush Experience* by J. S. Holliday. Copyright © 1981 by J. S. Holliday. Published by Simon & Schuster Inc. **471** From "Diary of an Oregon Pioneer of 1853" by Amelia Stewart Knight, as reprinted in *Transactions of the Oregon Pioneer Association*, 1928. Reprinted by permission of the Oregon Historical Society. **477** From *Democracy in America* by Alexis de Tocqueville, edited by J. P. Mayer; translated by George Lawrence. Copyright © 1969 by J. P. Mayer. Copyright © 1966 in the English translation by Harper & Row, Publishers.

Art Credits

Cover design: Conrad Warre
Cover image: © Rick Berkowitz/The Picture Cube
Text design: James Stockton and Associates
Text maps: Richard Sanderson; map p. G1, Precision Graphics; maps pp. G3, 666–673, RR Donnelley and Sons, Cartographic Services; maps pp. 302–303, 554–555, 580–581, Howard S. Friedman.
Charts and Graphs: pp. 181, 225, 243, 250, 251, 338, 367, 501, 553, Dave Fischer; pp. 45, 79, 87, 140, 141, 145, 203, 230, 245, 301, 319, 420, 596, 602, 623, 624, 626, 628, Neil Pinchin Design; p. 28, Tim Jones.
Cause and Effect Charts: Precision Graphics
Illustrations: pp. 124, 125, 564, 565, 576, 577, Chris Costello; p. 463, Ruth Brunner-Strosser
Photo Research: Linda L Rill

Positions are shown in abbreviated form as follows: T—top; **B**—bottom; **C**—center; **L**—left; **R**—right
Key: BA—Bettmann Archive. **GC**—Granger Collection. **LC**—Library of Congress. **PR**—Photo Researchers.

v From manuscript 264, fol. 220 in Bodleian Library. Bridgeman/Art Resource, New York; **vi** GC; **vii** Colonial Williamsburg Foundation; **viii** "Surrender of Lord Cornwallis at Yorktown," by John Trumbull. Copyright Yale University Gallery of Art; **ix** "Abigail Adams and Grand-Daughter Susanna Supervise as a Servant Hangs the Wash in the East Room," by Gordon Phillips, 1966. White House Historical Association, Photo: National Geographic Society; **xi** "Patron" (detail), by James Walker. Bancroft Library, University of California, Berkeley; **xii** New York Public Library, Print Collection, Art, Prints and Photographs Division, Astor, Lenox and Tilden Foundation; **xiii** Culver Pictures; **xxiv** Laurie Platt Winfrey; **1T** © Michael D. Coe; **1C** National Maritime Museum. Photo by Michael Holford, London; **1B** GC; **2** Courtesy, Ohio Historical Society, Photo by Dirk Bakker, Detroit Institute of Art; **4L** © Kenneth Garrett. All rights reserved; **4R** © Frankie Wright; **5** © Jerry Jacka Photography, Phoenix; **7** © Michael D. Coe; **8** GC; **9T** © Richard Bergmann 1988/Photo Researchers, Inc.; **9B** © H.W. Silvester/Photo Researchers, Inc; **10** David Muench Photography; **11TL** Catalogue No. 240915, Anthropology Department, Smithsonian Institution. Photo by Dirk Bakker, Detroit Institute of Art; **11TR** Courtesy of National Park Service. Photo by Dirk Bakker, Detroit Institute of Art; **11C** Ohio Historical Society. Photo by Dirk Bakker, Detroit Institute of Art; **12** The Saint Louis Art Museum, purchase: Eliza McMillen Fund; **12** "A Philadelphia Anabaptist Immersion During a Storm" by Pavel Petrovich Svinin. Watercolor on paper. H.7. in. W. 9 3/4 in. The Metropolitan Museum of Art, Rogers Fund, 1942 (42.95.20); **13** Peabody Museum, Harvard University. Photo by Hillel Burger; **15** Arizona State Museum, University of Arizona, Tucson. © Jerry Jacka Photography, Phoenix; **16** GC; **17** After Karl Bodmer "Mih-Tutta-Hang-Kusch, A Mandan Village." Josyln Art Museum, Omaha, Nebraska; **18TL** National Museum of American Art, Smithsonian Institution, Gift of Mrs. Joseph Harrison, Jr.; **18BR** Evans/Shostal Associates; **22** Courtesy, Trustees of the British Museum; **24** Seal of the City of Bergen, circa 1280. Riksarkivet, National Archives of Norway; **25** Spencer Collection, New York Public Library, Astor Lenox and Tilden Foundations; **26** GC; **27** From manuscript 264, fol. 220 in Bodleian Library. Bridgeman/Art Resource, New York; **28** "The School of Athens" (detail) by Raphael. Vatican. Photo Scala/Art Resource; **29R** From "Nurenburg Chronicles;" **29L** Courtesy of the Trustees of the British Library; **31** The British Museum. Photo by Michael Holford, London; **34** Museo Navale/Scala/Art Resource; **35** GC; **36** United States Naval Academy Museum; **40CR** National Maritime Museum. Photo by Michael Holford, London; **41** GC; **42** Jean-Loup Charmet, Paris; **46** Photo by Kirk Gittings. Exhibit © The Albuquerque Museum. All rights reserved; **48** Firenze, Uffizi. Scala/Art Resource, New York; **491/4** Private Collection. Photo © Michael Holford; **52** "The Arrival of Cortes at Veracruz" anonymous. In the Ownership of Mis M. L.A. Strickland, York, England. On Loan to the Government Art Collection, London; **53B** Archivo Fotographico/Ampliaciones Reproducciones MAS; **53C** Courtesy of the Trustees of the British Museum; **54** GC; **59** GC; **60** "Coronado" by Frederick Remington. Courtesy of Remington Art Museum, Ogdensburg, New York; **67** Laurie Platt Winfrey, Inc; **72** National Maritime Museum, Greenwich; **75** "Henry Hudson and Son Adrift in Hudson's Bay," (detail) anonymous. Tate Gallery, London; **77TL** "Martin Luther" by Lucas Cranach, The Elder, 1526. Nationalmuseum, Stockholm; **77BR** Museum Service Historique de la Marine/Giraudon/Art Resource; **78R** © 1987 Maryilyn Davids/Folio, Inc; **78L** Odyssey/Frerck/Chicago/© Robert Frerek; **80** "Henry VIII" by Hans Holbein. Scala/Art Resource, New York; **81** "Elizabeth I and Sir Francis Drake on Board the 'Golden Hind'," by Gustave A. Laux. Mansell Collection; **82** National Maritime Museum, Greenwich; **84** GC; **88C** "Catalan Atlas of 1375." Courtesy of The Trustees of the British Library; **88B** From "Cortez and Montezuma, # 1412" Library Services Department, © American Museum of Natural History; **88CL** University Museum of National Antiquities, Oslo, Norway; **89CL** New York State Museum; **89T** "The Last of the Aztecs" (detail), by George Ottinger. © Church of Jesus Christ of Latter-Day Saints. Used by permission; **89B** GC; **91T** "Hooker and Company Journeying through the Wilderness from Plymouth to Hartford in 1636" (detail) by Frederick Edwin Church. Wadsworth Atheneum; **91C** Plate V from "Ten Views of Antigua 1786." By courtesy of the Trustees of the British Library; **91B** "Tee Yee Neen Ho Ga Row, 1710 'King Hendrick'," by John Verelst. National Archives of Canada, Neg #C–92414; **92** Paul Rocheleau; **93** The Virginia State Library; **94** GC; **95** Colonial Williamsburg Foundation; **97** GC; **98** "Mayflower" (detail) by Halsall. Courtesy of the Pilgrim Society, Plymouth, MA.; **103** British Museum. Photo © Michael Holford; **105** Frederick Edwin Church, "Hooker and Company Journeying Through the Wilderness from Plymouth to Hartford in 1636." 1846 c/o 40 1/4 x 60 3/16 in. Wadsworth Atheneum; **106** Courtesy, American Antiquarian Society; **110** The J. Clarence Davies Collection, Museum of the City of New York; **111** Anonymous, "Quaker Meeting." Bequest of Maxim Karolik. Courtesy, Museum of Fine Arts, Boston; **112** New York Public Library, Print Collection, Art, Prints and Photographs Division; **116** "Mrs. Christian Bannister and Son" by Gilbert Stuart. Courtesy The Redwood Library and Athenaeum, Newport, RI; **120** GC; **121** GC; **122L** GC; **122R** "George Whitefield" by J. Wollaston. By Courtesy of the National Portrait Gallery, London; **126** Print Collection, Miriam and Ira D. Wallach Division of Art, Prints and Photographs. New York Public Library, Astor, Lenox and Tilden Foundations; **127** National Maritime Museum, London; **128** American Antiquarian Society; **129** "The Rice Hope Association," by Charles Fraser. Carolina Art Association, Gibbes Art Gallery; **132** New York Public Library, Print Collection, Art, Prints and Photographs Division, Astor,

Lenox and Tilden Foundations; **133** New York State Historical Associations, Cooperstown; **134** Harvard University Portrait Collection, Bequest, Dr. John C. Warren in 1856; **137** "First Legislature in the New World," by Jack Clifton. Virginia State Library; **139** © 1983 Greg Pease/Folio, Inc; **142** BA; **146** "Broken Silence," by George de Forest Brush. Manoogian Collection; **148** "White Mud Portage, Winnipeg River" by Paul Kane. National Gallery of Canada, Ottawa; **149** "Father Marquette and the Indians," (detail), by William Lamprecht, oil, 1869. Marquette University Art Collection; **151** "Chief of the Taensa Indians Receiving La-Salle,March 1682," (detail), by George Catlin. National Gallery of Art, Washington, Paul Mellon Collection; **154** Plate V from "Ten Views of Antigua 1786." By courtesy of the Trustees of the British Library; **155** "The Deerfield Massacre, February 29, 1704," by Henry H. Brooks and Theodore B. Pitman. Oil on canvas. Fruitlands Museums, Harvard, MA; **156** "Tee Yee Neen Ho Ga Row, 1710 'King Hendrick'," by John Verelst. National Archives of Canada, Neg #C–92414; **157** New York Public Library, Astor, Lenox and Tilden Foundations; **161** "View of the Taking of Quebec, 1759," (detail), by Laurie and Whitt. Documentary Art Division, National Archives of Canada, Ottawa, #C–1078; **166B** Courtesy of Chicago Historical Society; **166R** Culver Pictures, Inc; **166CL** "Anne Arundel, Lady Baltimore" by Lewis P. Dietrich. Maryland Historical Society, Baltimore; **167B** San Jacinto Museum of History Association, Houston,TX.; **167C** Courtesy, Redwood Library and Athenaeum, Newport. Photo by John Hopf; **169T** Library of Congress; **169**; **169B** Architect of the Capitol; **170** "Battle of Bunker's Hill" (detail) by John Trumbull. Copyright Yale University Art Gallery; **173** Historical Pictures Service; **175** GC; **176** "The Bloody Massacre," by Paul Revere. 1770. Mezzotint. H. 10 3/8 in. W. 9 in. Metropolitan Museum of Art, Gift of Mrs. Russell Sage, 1909; **177** GC; **179** Courtesy of the John Carter Brown Library at Brown University; **183** "Attack on Bunker's Hill, With the Burning of Charles Town," (detail), anonymous. National Gallery of Art, Gift of Edgar William and Bernice Chrysler Garbisch; **184** "Portrait Traditionally Said That to be of Abigail Adams," by unknown artist. Copyright New York State Historical Association, Cooperstown, New York; **185** National Portrait Gallery, Smithsonian Institution; On loan from the National Gallery of Art; **187** "Signing of the Declaration of Independence," by John Trumbull. Copyright Yale University Art Gallery; **188** GC; **196** The Henry Francis du Pont Winterthur Museum; **198** LOC; **200** "Washington Crossing the Delaware," by Emanuel Gottlieb Leutze. Oil on canvas. H. 149 in. W. 255 in. Signed and dated (lower right): E. Leutze/Dusseldorf 1851. The Metropolitan Museum of Art, Gift of John Stewart Kennedy, 1897; **202** "Washington Reviewing His Troops," by William Trego. The Valley Forge Historical Society; **204** Culver Pictures, Inc; **205R** Museo Nacional de Historia, Mexico City; **209** "Surrender of Lord Cornwallis at Yorktown," by John Trumbull. Copyright Yale University Art Gallery; **210** Diplomatic Reception Rooms, U.S. Department of State; **216** "Daniel Boone Escorting Settlers Through the Cumberland Gap," (detail), by George Caleb Bingham. Washington University Gallery of Art, St. Louis, Gift of Nathaniel Phillips, Boston 1890; **220R** © 1984 Steve Wilcoxson/Folio, Inc; **220L** © John Hopf; **221** Massachusetts Historical Society; **222** "Reverend Lemuel Haynes in the Pulpit," anonymous, on painted tray. Museum of Art, Rhode Island School of Design; **224** "Squire Boone Crossing the Mountains," by William Ranney. Collection of Miss Amelia Peabody, Courtesy of Time-Life Books, Inc; **229** National Archives; **234** Keller and Peet Associates; **236** Historical Pictures Services; **237** Architect of the Capitol; **238** "Gouverneur Morris" by James Sharples. National Portrait Gallery, Smithsonian Institution, Gift of Miss Ethel Turnbull in Memory of Her Brothers John and Gouverneur Morris Wilkins; **240** LOC; **241** Copyright 1983 Richard J. Quataert/Folio, Inc; **243** "An Overseer Doing His Duty," by Benjamin Henry Latrobe. Maryland Historical Society, Baltimore; **247** "Alexander Hamilton" (detail), by John Trumbull. Copyright Yale University Art Gallery. Photo by Joseph Szaszfai; **248** © 1987 Ben Boblett, all rights reserved; **249** © 1983 Mark Segal/Folio, Inc; **253ins** © 1988 Ken Heinen; **253** © 1986 Ken Heinen; **254** © 1987 Blair Seitz/PR, Inc; **263** GC; **264T** GC, **B** Robert Llewellyn; **265T** GC, **B** Culver Pictures; **266** Dennis Brak/Black Star; **267** GC; **268T** GC; **B** BA; **269** GC; **270** LC; **271T** BA, **B** GC; **272T** BA, **B** Frank Scherschel, Life Magazine © Time Inc.; **274T** GC, **B** Randy Duchain/Stock Market; **275** Historical Picture Services; **277** Historical Picture Services; **279** GC; **280** GC; **281** GC; **282** LC; **283** GC; **284** BA; **286** UPI/Bettmann Newsphotos; **287** Robert Llewellyn; **290CL** GC; **290CR** "Joseph Brandt" by George Rommey, 1775. National Gallery of Canada, Ottawa. Transfer from the Canadian War Memorial, 1921; **290B** GC; **291T** GC; **291C** "Kamehameha I" (#XC 76905), courtesy Bishop Museum; **293T** "First Bank of the United States," by William Birch. Courtesy of the John Carter Brown Library at Brown University; **293C** GC; **293B** "Dolly Madison" by unknown artist (has been attributed to James Peale and Anna Claypoe Peale). Watercolor on ivory. Yale University Art Gallery, Gift of Mrs. John Hill Morgan; **294** Copyright, New York State Historical Association, Cooperstown; **296** LOC; **297** "President Washington and His First Cabinet," anonymous. Historical Art Collection — Continental Insurance Companies; **298** © White House Historical Association, photograph by National Geographic Society; **299R** Maryland Historical Society, Baltimore; **299B** LOC; **300** "First Bank of the United States," by William Birch. Courtesy of the John Carter Brown Library at Brown University; **304** "Market Folks," by Benjamin Henry Latrobe. Maryland Historical Society; **305** "The Treaty of Greenville," 1795. Chicago Historical Society, Neg. #1914; **306** "Washington Reviewing the Western Army at Fort Cumberland, Maryland," by Frederick Kemmelmeyer. Oil on canvas. H.22 3/4 in. W. 37 1/4 in. The Metropolitan Museum of Art, Gift of Edgar William and Bernice Chrysler Garbisch, 1963 (63.201.2); **307** Giraudon/Art Resource; **309** "Shipbuilding," by William Birch. New York Public Library, I.N. Phelps Stokes Collection, Art, Prints and Photographs Division, Astor, Lenox and Tilden Foundations; **311** "He That Tilleth the Land Shall be Satisified," (detail), anonymous. Philadelphia Museum of Art; **313** "Abigail Adams and Grand-Daughter Susanna Supervise as a Servant Hangs the Wash in the East Room," by Gordon Phillips, 1966. White House Historical Association. Photo: National Geographic Society; **314** BA; **315** "U.S. Merchant Ship 'Planter' July 10, 1799." Franklin D. Roosevelt Library; **316** © White House Historical Association, photograph by National Geographic Society; **320** United States Naval Academy Museum; **322** "Monticello Home of Thomas Jefferson 1743–1826," by Vail. Musee de la Cooperation Franco-Americaine, Chateau de Blerancourt. Photo: Edimedia; **323** © White House Historical Association, photograph by National Geographic Society; **325** "Burning of the Frigate Philadelphia," anonymous. Courtesy of the Mariner's Museum of Newport News, VA; **326** David Muench; **328** "Buffalo Hunt," by George Catlin. American Museum of Natural History, Smithsonian Institution; **329** "Fur Trappers," by Karl Bodmer. Rare Book Division, New York Public Library, Astor, Lenox and Tilden Foundations; **330** GC; **333R** Missouri Historical Society, Neg. CT LA 109; **333L** The Thomas Gilcrease Institute of American History and Art, Tulsa, Oklahoma; **334** GC; **339** "Boarding the Chesapeake," by Thomas Hemy, 1985. Private Collection.; **340** The Anne S.K. Brown Military Collection, Brown University Library; **342R** "Dolly Madison" by unknown artist (has been attributed to James Peale and Anna Claypoe Peale). Watercolor on ivory. Yale University Art Gallery, Gift of Mrs. John Hill Morgan; **342L** © White House Historical Association, photograph by National Geographic Society; **344B** Environment Canada-Canadian Parks Service: Fort Malden National Historic Site, Amherstburg, Ontario; **348** "Kindred Spirits," by Asher B. Durand. New York Public Library; **350** James Monroe Museum, Fredericksburg, VA.; **351** "John Marshall," (detail), by William Hubard. National Portrait Gallery, Smithsonian Institution; **356** © Robert Frerck/Odyssey Productions; **360** Courtesy of the Museum of American Textile History; **361** "Old Slater's Mill," (detail), by J. Reuben Smith, Smithsonian Institution; **362** Yale University Art Gallery, The Mabel Brady Garvan Collection; **363** "Robert Fulton" (detail), by Benjamin West. Copyright New York State Historical Association, Cooperstown, New York; **364** Museum of the City of New York, Harry T. Peters Collection; **366** "Julius Meyenberg's Farm, Bluff, Williams Creek Settlement, by LaGrange, Fayette County, State of Texas," by Louis Hoppe, watercolor. San Antonio Museum Association, San Antonio, TX; **369** GC; **374TC** GC; **374CR** Courtesy, Vassar College Library; **374L** St. Joseph's Provincial House Archives, Daughters of Charity; **375TR** BA; **375TL** Culver Pictures, Inc; **375CL** State Historical Society of Wisconsin; **375B** Courtesy, The New-York Historical Society, New York; **377T** "View of San Antonio, East Side, Main Plaza" by William G.M. Samuel. San Antonio Museum Association, San Antonio, Texas; **377C** "Sam Houston," attributed to George Catlin, c. 1838. R.W. Norton Art Gallery; **377B** GC; **378** "The County Election" (detail) by George Caleb Bingham. Saint Louis County Museum, Purchase; **379** "View of the Capitol, Washington, D.C. 1824," (detail), by Charles Burton. The Metropolitan Museum of Art, purchase, 1942 Joseph Pulitzer Bequest; **381** "The Old House of Representatives" (detail), by Samuel F.B. Morse. © Corcoran Gallery of Art; **382** © White House Historical Association, photograph by the National Geographic Society; **383** "Rachel Jackson" (detail), by Ralph E.W. Earl. The Hermitage—Home of Andrew Jackson; **384** "Se-Quo-Ya" by Lehman & Duval, Philadelphia Museum of Art: Given by Miss Willian Adger; **385** "Osceola by Robert J. Curtis. Courtesy of The Charleston Museum, Charleston, South Carolina; **387** "Endless Trail" (detail), by Jerome Tiger. Philbrook Art Center, Tulsa; **389** Rare Books and Manuscripts Division, The New York Public Library, Astor, Lenox and Tilden Foundations; **390** "Webster's Reply to Hayne" (detail), by G.P.A. Healy. City of Boston Art Commission. Photo by Richard Creek; **391** Art, Print and Photographs Division, The New York Public Library, Astor, Lenox and Tilden Foundations; **392** "General Andrew Jackson" (detail) by John Wesley Jarvis. Metropolitan Museum of Art, Harris Brisbane Dick Fund; **393** Courtesy, The New-York Historical Society, New York City; **394** Courtesy, The New-York Historical Society, New York City; **395** © White House Historical Association, photograph by National Geographic Society; **396** "The Long Bill," by James Henry Beard. Cincinnati Art Museum; **397L** "William Henry Harrison" (detail) by Albert Gallatin Hoit. National Portrait Gallery, Smithsonian Institution, Washington, D.C.; **397R** "John Tyler" (detail) by George Peter Alexander Healy. National Portrait Gallery, Smithsonian Institution, Washington D.C.; **398** Culver Pictures, Inc; **401** Print once owned by the Old Print Shop, New York; **402** "Interior of Park Theatre" by John Searles, 1822. Courtesy The New-York Historical Society, New York City; **404** GC; **405** Rare Books